Gabriele D'Annunzio and World Literature

Gabriele D'Annunzio and World Literature

Multilingualism, Translation, Reception

Edited by
Elisa Segnini and Michael Subialka

EDINBURGH
University Press

Edinburgh University Press is one of the leading university presses in the UK. We publish academic books and journals in our selected subject areas across the humanities and social sciences, combining cutting-edge scholarship with high editorial and production values to produce academic works of lasting importance. For more information visit our website: edinburghuniversitypress.com

Edinburgh University Press Ltd
13 Infirmary Street, Edinburgh, EH1 1LT

Typeset in Sabon and Futura
by Manila Typesetting Company
A CIP record for this book is available from the British Library

ISBN 978 1 3995 0685 4 (hardback)
ISBN 978 1 3995 0686 1 (paperback)
ISBN 978 1 3995 0687 8 (webready PDF)
ISBN 978 1 3995 0688 5 (epub)

Contents

Acknowledgements

This book is the product of many forms of collaboration stretching across languages and geographical boundaries. The editors are greatly indebted to a host of individuals and institutions who have helped to make this collection a reality. We would like to thank Donatella Cannova, Director of the Italian Cultural Institute in Buenos Aires, and Davide Scalmani, Director of the Italian Cultural Institute of Cairo, for facilitating contacts with local researchers. Thanks also to Chenxin Jiang for mediating with D'Annunzio's Chinese translator, Emei Shen, who unfortunately passed away in 2022 – and who we commemorate here. Stuart Oglethorpe, Alessia Zinnari, Sophie Maddison and Peter Bruckner's skills have been indispensable to make chapters written in languages other than English available to Anglophone readers. We also want to acknowledge the financial assistance that helped pay for these translations, by Edinburgh University Press, the University of California, Davis and the University of Glasgow. We are most grateful to Sandro Abate, Susan Bassnett, Assumpta Camps, Muriel Gallot, Mariko Muramatsu, Lara Raffaelli, Natalia Stavrovskaja and Naagla Waly for their kind willingness to converse with us about their experiences translating D'Annunzio. While we have not been able to include the entire correspondence we had with each, the concluding chapter in this book offers an overview of their ideas and experiences. Michelle Houston, brilliant editor at Edinburgh University Press, saw the merit of this project and helped to make it a reality; to Susannah Butler's editorial work we owe much. Finally, we'd like to acknowledge the hard work and flexibility of all contributors, who patiently worked with us during the Covid crisis, often under difficult conditions. Likewise, we'd like to thank those who expressed an interest in participating in the project but, for different reasons, were not able to: we look forward to future collaborations.

Notes on Contributors

Sandro Abate is Professor of Modern European Literature at the Universidad Nacional del Sur (Bahía Blanca, Argentina), researcher with the Consejo Nacional de Investigaciones Científicas y Técnicas (CONICET) and advisor to various research centres and periodicals. He has published widely on Italian literature and comparative European literatures, including his books *El Modernismo, Rubén Darío y su influencia en el Realismo Mágico* (1998), *Mediterráneas: Notas de literatura italiana y comparada* (2001) and *El tríptico esquivo: Manuel Mujica Lainez en su laberinto* (2004). He directs the research project 'Atributos y representaciones del Humanismo (Siglos XVI–XIX)' and has been a visiting researcher at the Universidad Complutense de Madrid (Spain), the Foundation Il Vittoriale degli Italiani (Gardone, Italy) and the Centro Studi Dannunziani (Pescara, Italy). His studies and translations of D'Annunzio's poetry into Spanish are published in two volumes: *El último humanista. Antología bilingüe 1882–1893* (2008) and *Los jardines del Vate. Antología bilingüe 1903–1933* (2011).

Ikuho Amano is Associate Professor of Japanese at the University of Nebraska-Lincoln, where she teaches literature, film, popular culture and language. Her research, including her book *Decadent Literature in Twentieth-Century Japan* (2013), has explored various themes salient in modern and contemporary Japanese literature, in particular the idea of Decadence, the reception of European culture and literature, post-war body politics and issues of economy. In recent years, her research has expanded its parameters to other areas such as popular cultural production (anime, manga and photography) and economic as well as industrial memory of the nation. She is currently working on a book project that commemorates Japan's economic bubble in the 1980s, consumer culture of the time and its continuing legacy.

Assumpta Camps is Chair of Italian Philology and Full Professor of Literary Translation and Italian Literature at the University of Barcelona (Spain). Her many publications include books focused on D'Annunzio, translation and the reception of Italian Decadence: *Recepción de Gabriele D'Annunzio en Cataluña*, 2 vols. (1996–1999); *Estudios literarios I: La traducción* (1998); *Estudios literarios II. La recepción literaria* (2002); *Italia-España en la época contemporánea. Estudios críticos sobre la traducción y recepción literarias* (2009), *El Decadentismo italiano en la literatura catalana* (2010); *Italia en la prensa periódica durante el franquismo* (2014); *Traducción y recepción de la literatura italiana* (2014) and *La traducción en la creación del canon poético. Recepción de la poesía italiana en el ámbito hispánico en la primera mitad del siglo XX* (2015). She is also the chief editor of '*TRANSFER, e-journal on Translation and Intercultural Studies*' (Barcelona) and lead researcher for several national and international research projects.

Annalisa Ciano has recently graduated from La Sapienza Università di Roma and Sorbonne Université with a thesis on D'Annunzio's *Phaedre*. She received a bachelor's degree in Lettere Moderne, a master's degree in Filologia Moderna from La Sapienza Università di Roma, and a master recherche's degree in LLCE Études Italiennes from Sorbonne Université. She is interested in comparative literature, reception studies and theatre and in the reception of the classics in twentieth-century literature.

Stefano Evangelista is Professor of English and Comparative Literature at Oxford University and Fellow of Trinity College and of the Centre for British Studies of the Humboldt University (Berlin). His main interests include nineteenth-century English and comparative literature, the reception of the classics and the relationship between literary and visual cultures. He is the author of *British Aestheticism and Ancient Greece: Hellenism, Reception, Gods in Exile* (2009) and the editor of *The Reception of Oscar Wilde in Europe* (2010), *A. C. Swinburne: Unofficial Laureate* (2013, with Catherine Maxwell), *Pater the Classicist: Classical Scholarship, Reception, and Aestheticism* (with Charles Martindale and Elizabeth Prettejohn, 2017) and *Arthur Symons: Poet, Critic, Vagabond* (with Elisa Bizzotto, 2018). His most recent book is *Literary Cosmopolitanism in the English Fin de Siècle: Citizens of Nowhere* (2021).

Filippo Fonio received his PhD from the University of Pisa and is Associate Professor at Université Grenoble Alpes (France). His research on D'Annunzio focuses mainly on his French writings, especially the *Martyre de saint Sébastien*, including both its literary and historico-linguistic aspects, as well as on D'Annunzio's translations into French and the traductological reflections of the writer. He is currently completing a monograph on Italian writers and world literature, which focuses in particular on their imaginary of the French language and their francophone writings.

Elda Garetto is Associate Professor Emerita of Slavic Studies at the University of Milan. Her major research interests include twentieth-century Russian literature, Russian cultural emigration and the spread of Russian culture in Italy in the first half of the twentieth century. She has particularly focused on developing new studies of archival materials on Russian emigration in Italy. She has been coordinating a project on Russian artists working in Milan and Northern Italy, in partnership with the Teatro alla Scala, the Mondadori Foundation and the Vittoriale degli Italiani (www.arterussamilano.it).

Pietro Gibellini, a native of Brescia and Professor of Italian Literature Emeritus, has taught at the universities of Pavia, Geneva, L'Aquila, Trieste and Venice. He chairs the scientific committee of the National Edition of D'Annunzio's works, is editor of the journal *Archivio D'Annunzio* and is an advisor to the Vittoriale and member of the board of the D'Annunzio Studies Center in Pescara. He conceived and directed two major collected volumes published by Morcelliana: *Il mito nella letteratura italiana* (5 vols, 2005–2009) and *La Bibbia nella letteratura italiana* (6 vols, 2009–2017). In 2020 he was awarded the Natalino Sapegno Lifetime Achievement Award. He has edited editions of D'Annunzio's texts for important publishers (Mondadori, Garzanti, Einaudi, Rizzoli, Electa), including the critical edition of *Alcyone* (Mondadori, 1988; Marsilio, 2018). He has also published on D'Annunzio in academic journals and miscellaneous volumes, and in two non-fiction volumes: *Logos e mythos* (1985) and *D'Annunzio dal gesto al testo* (1995).

Noriko Hiraishi received her PhD from the University of Tokyo and is Professor of Comparative Literature at the University of Tsukuba

(Japan) and author of *Angst-Ridden Youths and Girl Students in Modern Japan: Literary Reinterpretation of the West* (2012) in Japanese, which was awarded the 18th Japan Comparative Literature Association Prize and the 12th Kinji Shimada Academic Prize. Her major research interest has been aspects of modernisation and exoticism from the perspective of female representations. In addition to her ongoing interest in European *fin-de-siècle* literature and modern Japanese literature, her current research includes studies on contemporary Japanese literature and culture, focusing on its reception and transformation in the world.

Arturo Larcati is Director of the Stefan Zweig Zentrum at the University of Salzburg, and Associate Professor of German Literature at the University of Verona. His scholarly work includes monographs and edited volumes focusing on Austrian literature, particularly on Ingeborg Bachmann and Stefan Zweig, as well as on the cultural transfers among Austria, Germany and Italy. He also publishes on the historical avant-gardes, focusing in particular on Expressionism and Futurism.

Sofia Lurie is an independent translator, researcher and journalist. She graduated in Italian Studies from St Petersburg State University, where she also worked as a lecturer of Italian language and literature. Her research at the Vittoriale archives, where she studied D'Annunzio's reception in Russia, was supported by a scholarship from the Swiss Confederation. As a research fellow at the State University of Milan, she collaborated on the project 'Russians in Italy' (http://www.russinitalia.it), with a study of archival material held in St Petersburg. Her work as a journalist focuses on the history of St Petersburg and the presence and role of Italians in the Russian Empire.

Hussein Mahmoud is Dean and Professor of Italian Language and Literature at Badr University in Cairo (BUC), where he has been involved in research in the areas of comparative literature and translation. Prior to joining BUC, Mahmoud worked at Helwan University and Misr for Science and Technology. He is the author of numerous books and articles covering a wide range of topics in literature, philosophy, politics and translation studies. He has also translated several books from Arabic to Italian and vice versa. Throughout his career, he has organised conferences and courses in Egypt and beyond, especially in Italy, where he was a visiting professor at the

University of Rome and taught at the universities of Naples, Milan and Bologna. He has been recognised with prestigious awards such as the Flaiano and the Pagliarani prizes in Italy, as well as the 'best research' award at Helwan University.

Mariko Muramatsu received doctoral degrees from both the University of Tokyo and the University of Bologna. She has taught Italian language and culture in the Department of Area Studies of the Graduate School of Arts and Sciences in the University of Tokyo since 2002. Her main publications are *Il suddito di Mikado. D'Annunzio japonisant* (1997) and *Segni e voci dalla letteratura italiana. Da Dante a D'Annunzio* (2012). She has translated into Japanese contemporary Italian novels including Antonio Tabucchi's *La piazza d'Italia* (2009) and Italo Calvino's *Il visconte dimezzato* (2020). She has also translated into Italian Japanese poets including Miyazawa Kenji (*Il violoncellista Gosh e altri scritti*, 1996) and Matsuo Basho (*Poesie. Haiku e scritti poetici*, 1996).

Guylian Nemegeer is a postdoctoral researcher at Ghent University and the Academia Belgica. His PhD dissertation examined the Renaissance in D'Annunzio's cultural nationalism. He previously studied French and Italian Linguistics and Literature, writing his Bachelor's dissertation on D'Annunzio's war rhetoric. He received his Masters in Comparative Modern Literature with a dissertation on short story collection theory. His research interests lie primarily in literary history, reception studies and intellectual history, with particular focus on the interaction between tradition and modernity. His articles have appeared in *Forum Italicum*, *Romance Quarterly*, *The Italianist*, *Quaderni d'Italianistica*, *Aevum* and *Language and Literature*.

Christine Samir is Lecturer of Italian Literature at Badr University Linguistics School, where she is coordinator of the Italian curriculum. Her research has focused on Italian literature, literary criticism and comparative literature since joining the University of Milan in 2009 and the University of Helwan in 2017. Christine's publications on literary criticism focus on modern and contemporary Italian literature, aiming to explore new philosophical approaches to literary texts. She has also worked with Italian and foreign students in humanistic subjects through Italian NGOs including Caritas, in Milan (2010–2014). In 2004, Christine received the award of 'Il migliore giovane scrittore' (Best Young Writer) in Lombardy, Italy.

Mara Santi is Associate Professor of Italian Literature and Head of the Department of Literary Studies at Ghent University, where she was appointed in 2008 after having worked at Basel University and at Zurich University. She graduated in Italian philology at the University of Pavia, where she wrote her PhD thesis on Gabriele D'Annunzio. Her main research interests lie in modern and contemporary Italian narrative, narratology, philology and literary theory. She is particularly interested in authors who greatly influenced Italian culture between the nineteenth and twentieth centuries, above all Gabriele D'Annunzio, Italo Svevo and Carlo Emilio Gadda. She has published several articles on Gabriele D'Annunzio alongside a book, *Commento al 'Notturno' di Gabriele d'Annunzio* (2008–2009).

Russell Scott Valentino has authored two scholarly monographs, co-edited three literary and scholarly collections and translated eight books of fiction and literary nonfiction from Italian, Russian and Bosnian-Croatian-Serbian into English, including Fulvio Tomizza's *Materada*, Carlo Michelstaedter's *Persuasion and Rhetoric* and Predrag Matvejević's *The Other Venice*. His essays and short translations have appeared in *The New York Times*, *Modern Fiction Studies*, *Defunct*, *The Buenos Aires Review*, *Slavic Review*, *91st Meridian* and elsewhere. He is the recipient of two Fulbright research awards and three National Endowment for the Arts translation grants. He served as Editor-in-Chief at *The Iowa Review* from 2009 to 2013 and as President of the American Literary Translators Association from 2013 to 2016. He is professor of Slavic and East European languages and cultures and adjunct professor of comparative literature at Indiana University Bloomington. His most recent translation is the Bosnian author Miljenko Jergović's historical saga *Kin* (2021).

Elisa Segnini received her PhD from the University of Toronto and teaches Italian and Comparative Literature at the University of Glasgow. Her research focuses on Italian literature in a world literature perspective, with a focus on fin-de-siècle and contemporary fiction. She has written on the relationship between literature, visual arts and thought, on theatre translation and on translingual writing. She is the author of *Fragments, Genius and Madness: Masks and Mask Making in the* fin-de-siècle *Imagination* (2021) and of several articles on multilingualism in fiction. Her current monograph explores the different meanings that fiction featuring more than one language acquires as it travels across languages and media, reaching new and diverse audiences. She is a co-editor of *Comparative Critical Studies*.

Michael Subialka received his PhD from the University of Chicago and is Associate Professor of Comparative Literature and Italian at the University of California, Davis. His research focuses on the intersection of literature and philosophy in the long Modernist period, examining Europe from a global perspective. Publications in this field include his recent monograph, *Modernist Idealism: Ambivalent Legacies of German Philosophy in Italian Literature* (2021), and a co-authored book with Carlo Di Lieto and Lisa Sarti, *Scrittura d'immagini: Pirandello e la visualità tra arte, filosofia e psicoanalisi* (2021), as well as various articles, edited volumes and edited journal issues. He is the Co-President of the Pirandello Society of America and Co-editor of the society's scholarly journal, *PSA*. He previously co-edited, with Lara Raffaelli, a special issue of the journal *Forum Italicum* on 'Reawakening Beauty: Gabriele d'Annunzio's Seduction of the Senses' (51: 2, 2017).

Clive Thomson is Professor Emeritus, School of Languages and Literatures, University of Guelph (Canada) and faculty member of the Toronto Institute for Contemporary Psychoanalysis. Books and edited collections include: *Dialogues with Bakhtinian Theory* (2012, co-ed.); *Georges Hérelle, archéologue de l'inversion sexuelle 'fin de siècle'* (2014); *Mikhaïl Bakhtin: His World and Ours* (*Bakhtiniana: Journal of Discourse Studies*, 2016, ed.); *Autobiographie et homosexualité en France au XIXe siècle de Philippe Lejeune* (2017); *Fières archives: documents d'homosexuels fin de siècle* (2017, in collab.); *On croit comprendre le monde avec ça: Entretiens mémoriels avec Henri Mitterand* (2021). He has published chapters in edited collections and articles in journals (*Les Cahiers naturalistes*, *Bakhtiniana*, *Figura*, *Heterity: Psychoanalytic Review*, *Semiotic Inquiry*, etc.). His current research project is *Correspondance croisée 1869–1873: Georges Hérelle, Adrien Juvigny, Paul et Félix Bourget, Maurice Bouchor* (co-ed. with Michael Rosenfeld, Daniel Ridge).

Adriana Vignazia graduated in aesthetic philosophy with a thesis on 'Karl Kraus and Linguistic Satire' at the University of Turin, and she completed her doctorate in comparative literature in Vienna with a dissertation on 'The German Translations of Gabriele D'Annunzio's Prose Works. Editorial History and Translation Analysis'. She worked as a tenured lecturer in Italian language and culture at the Institute of Roman Studies of the Karl Franzens Universität in Graz and at the Institute of Comparative Literature of the University of Vienna, where she also collaborated on the Fackel Wörterbuch der

Redensarten project at the Vienna Academy of Sciences. She is currently affiliated with the National Library of Vienna, working in the manuscripts department on a project reading and cataloguing Italian letters (from Italians and to Italians). Her fields of research include Italian culture of the nineteenth and twentieth centuries, textual semantics, translation and imagology.

Enzo Zappulla co-founded and is president of the Istituto di Storia dello Spettacolo Siciliano, based in Catania, which exists to recover, preserve and promote the rich documentary heritage of Sicilian literature and theatre. He has curated numerous exhibitions on writers and actors in Italy and abroad. He also helped to create the 'Sicilian Chair' at the University of Salamanaca, together with Vicente González Martín (its director), Sarah Zappulla Muscarà, the Ambassador of Italy, the Director of the Italian Cultural Institute in Madrid, the Association of Spanish Italianists and the Banco di Sicilia Foundation. Among numerous publications, he has collaborated with Sarah Zappulla Muscarà on: *Angelo Musco: Il gesto, la mimica, l'arte* (1987); *Martoglio cineasta* (1995); *Giovanni Grasso: "Il più grande attore tragico del mondo"* (1995); *Brancati-Patti per immagini* (2004); *"La figlia di Iorio" di d'Annunzio fra lingua e dialetti* (1997); *Bonaviri inedito* (2001) and *Turi Ferro: Il magistero dell'arte* (2006). He directs the 'Il Copione' series of theatrical texts.

Sarah Zappulla Muscarà, Professor of Italian Literature at the University of Catania (where she has also taught History of Theatre and Cinema), is the author of numerous contributions on literature, dramaturgy and cinema in the nineteenth and twentieth centuries. She has edited editions of texts and unpublished correspondences, including the volume *Tutto il teatro in dialetto di Luigi Pirandello* (1993). In collaboration with Enzo Zappulla, she has edited: Stefano Pirandello's *Tutto il Teatro* (2004) and the novel *Timor Sacro* (2011); the unpublished epistolary of Luigi and Stefano Pirandello, *Nel tempo della lontananza* (2008); Federico De Roberto and Ernesta Valle's *Si dubita sempre delle cose più belle: Parole d'amore e di letteratura* (2014); *I Pirandello: La famiglia e l'epoca per immagini, riccamente illustrato* (with 626 largely unpublished photos, 2017) and the monumental volume *Ercole Patti, Tutte le opere* (2019). Her works have been translated into numerous other languages.

Introduction

Elisa Segnini and Michael Subialka

> Er eroberte Fiume, die Duse und das Besitztum am Gardasee [. . .] Er was ein Scharlatan, aber Scharlatan schrieb Hirtengedichte, die kaum untergehen werden, und die Charta der Seeleutegewerkschaft wird längere Zeit ein interessantes Dokument bleiben. Auch seine Provokationen könnte man, mit Opusnummern versehen, herausgeben. Seine Eitelkeit ist der Selbstgefälligkeit Hollywoods turmhoch überlegen, so ist sein Geschmack, wenn er auch etwas disparat ist, und sein ganzer Lebensstil, der immerhin nicht nur der Arbeit, sondern auch der Ausschweifung etwas Produktive verleiht.[1]
>
> (He conquered Fiume, Duse and the possessions on Lake Garda [. . .] He was a charlatan, but this charlatan wrote pastoral poems that will hardly be forgotten, and the Maritime Workers Union Charter will remain an interesting document for a long time. His provocations could be published with opus numbers. His vanity is far superior to the complacency of Hollywood, so is his taste, even if a bit disparate, and his whole lifestyle, which after all gives something productive not only to work, but also to debauchery).[2]

These lines, which so cleverly and concisely summarise D'Annunzio's varying and ambiguous achievements, were written in July 1942 by the poet, theatre practitioner and convinced Communist Bertolt Brecht – an author one would struggle to identify as a D'Annunzio admirer. Indeed, Brecht himself was the literary hero and friend of none other than Walter Benjamin, who in his essay on 'The Work of Art in the Age of Its Technological Reproducibility' (1935/6), named D'Annunzio as one of the primary instances of the 'aestheticizing

[1] Bertolt Brecht, 'Journale 2', *Werke: große kommentierte Berliner und Frankfurter Ausgabe*, 27 (Berlin: Aufbau Verlag, 1995), 115.

[2] Throughout this Introduction, translations are our own unless otherwise noted.

of politics' practised by Fascism, grouping him with Marinetti and Hitler.[3] Despite their evident ideological differences, Brecht showed surprising respect for D'Annunzio's work, defining his 1923 Maritime Workers Union Charter, the *Patto marinaro* that regulated the rights of seafarers following the libertarian principles of Fiume's 'Carta del Carnaro', as an 'interesting document'. He also extended D'Annunzio a certain 'feudal dignity'.[4] And while there is no evidence that he even knew Italian, Brecht's fascination with D'Annunzio's poetry was such that he went as far as translating into German, probably using another German version or a French intermediary translation, one of D'Annunzio's most iconic poems, 'La pioggia nel pineto' – a work that can certainly be grouped amongst the aestheticising literary feats of the Italian *fin-de-siècle*.[5] D'Annunzio's 'vanity', 'taste' and 'lifestyle' all align, in Brecht's reading, with the unforgettable verse that makes this 'charlatan' a figure of interest and importance.

This brief anecdote underlines D'Annunzio's transnational and transtemporal influence and the extent to which his texts crossed linguistic, cultural and political borders, at least for a few decades, before he fell into international disrepute, if not oblivion – though that is a complex story that needs yet to be told, and which this volume will endeavour to illuminate. D'Annunzio's provocative works and controversial actions left hardly anybody indifferent. Larger than life, he was not only, as Giuliana Pieri underlines, 'one of the most charismatic and influential public figures in Italy in the late nineteenth century and the first decades of the twentieth century',[6] but also the most internationally known and widely translated Italian writer. His legacy spread out quickly to span from Europe all across the

[3] Walter Benjamin, 'The Work of Art in the Age of Its Technological Reproducibility. Second Version', in *The Work of Art in the Age of Its Technological Reproducibility, and Other Writings on Media*, ed. by Michael W. Jennings, Brigid Doherty and Thomas Y. Levin, trans. by Edmund Jephcott, Rodney Livingstone and Howard Eiland (Cambridge, MA: Harvard UP, 2008), pp. 19–55 (p. 41). In 1924, it must be noted, Benjamin had also translated a poem from the *Laudi*; two years later, he translated the ode to Eleonora Duse in the volume *Francesca da Rimini.* See Paola Sorge, 'D'Annunzio e il mondo germanico', *Rassegna dannunziana*, 72 (2018), 75–82 (p. 81).

[4] Brecht, entry from December 1945, 'Journale 2', p. 235.

[5] Bertolt Brecht, 'Regen im Pinienhain', in Bertolt Brecht, *Gesammelte Werke in 20 Bänden, Gedichte aus den Nachlaß 2, Supplementband IV* (Frankfurt am Main: Suhrkamp, 1982), pp. 449–50.

[6] Giuliana Pieri, 'Gabriele d'Annunzio and the Self-fashioning of a National Icon', *Modern Italy*, 21: 4 (2016), 329–43 (p. 329).

globe: prominent figures such as Henry James, G. B. Shaw, James Joyce, D. H. Lawrence, Ezra Pound, Ernest Hemingway in the UK and the US, Stefan George, Hugo von Hofmannsthal, Karl Kraus, Heinrich and Thomas Mann in Austro-Hungary and Prussia, Nikolay Gumilev in Russia and J. L. Borges in Argentina, not to mention a whole host of French intellectuals,[7] all attentively studied his work and were inspired by it – even though, in many cases, they later turned against him. D'Annunzio thus remains a fascinating case today, just as he was for Brecht some hundred years ago. Complicated by his outsized persona and overtly nationalist politics, his works are a paradigmatic instance of the complex networks of inspiration, translation and adaptation that characterised Decadence and Symbolism as transnational phenomena.

Adopting a transnational lens, the contributions gathered in this volume examine the global dynamics of D'Annunzio, from his appropriation of the foreign and engagement with multilingual and translingual writing to the different, often controversial meanings that his texts acquired as they were received in translation. In this volume, world literature is both, as Jane Hiddleston puts it, 'a particular form of reading and writing that at once seeks, reveals, and engenders encounter with other cultures'[8] and, as in David Damrosch's famous definition, a 'mode of circulation and reading' of texts that travel beyond their context of origin.[9] This framework allows a global account not only of D'Annunzio's writing but also of the place that Dannunzian Decadence holds in a larger, conflicted artistic tendency – one that is profoundly cosmopolitan and yet also problematically nationalistic, bridging aesthetic and political modernity in provocative but challenging ways.

Rethinking D'Annunzio through World Literature Today

In September of 2019, a statue of Gabriele D'Annunzio, marking the 100-year anniversary of his military expedition to seize and govern

7 See Maurizio Serra, *L'Imaginifico: Vita Di Gabriele D'annunzio*, trans. by Alberto Folin (Vicenza: Neri Pozza, 2018), p. 11.

8 Jane Hiddleston, '"Un Nouvel Internationalisme Littéraire"? Dreams and Delusions of "World Literature" in Khatibi, Djaout, and Adimi', *PMLA*, 137: 2 (2022), 389–95 (p. 391).

9 David Damrosch, *What is World Literature* (Princeton: Princeton University Press, 2003), p. 5.

the Dalmatian city of Fiume, now Rijeka (Croatia), was inaugurated in Trieste's *Piazza della Borsa* to a mix of fanfare and anger.[10] The debate over the statue was motivated not by D'Annunzio's literary production but by his political persona, a small proxy battle in the conflict between renascent Italian right-wing militarism and the values of liberal cosmopolitanism that might seem to resonate more with Trieste's past identity as the multicultural, multilingual port city of the Austro-Hungarian Empire. As with the controversies over other statues depicting figures of an imperialist, nationalist past, the conflict in Trieste speaks to a broader moment in which contemporary efforts to take distance from problematic historical figures come up against a resurgent impulse toward nationalism and right-wing politics. It also signals an uncomfortable legacy that still associates with D'Annunzio, of extreme right-wing individuals sustaining a kind of cult of this author honouring the poet as a hero to their nationalist causes.[11] With these considerations in mind, we might wonder if now is the time to revisit D'Annunzio. As scholarship and syllabi both shift to embrace a decolonised vision of Italian literature, and as there continue to be battles over his persona, what role can rethinking a figure like D'Annunzio and his place in configurations of world literature play?

Our volume proposes two ways of responding to this question, each important for rethinking both D'Annunzio and Italian literature in the context of Decadence as a global movement. In the first place, by examining D'Annunzio's engagement with foreign literature, as well as the global reception of his texts, we aim to shift the focus from his self-aggrandising gestures and Nietzschean outlook (his notion of the '*superuomo*', developed from Nietzsche's *Übermensch*, for instance), opening the door to a transnational view of his multifaceted production. What we propose, drawing on frameworks from global Decadence studies and the new Modernist studies, is a denationalised, de-centred approach to D'Annunzio's oeuvre that does

[10] See, for instance, Jason Horowitz, 'New Statue Unsettles Italian City: Is It Celebrating a Poet or a Nationalist?', *The New York Times*, 16 November 2019: <https://www.nytimes.com/2019/11/16/world/europe/trieste-statue-dannunzio-fascism.html?smid=url-share> [accessed 3 November 2022].

[11] As Susan Bassnett has remarked in a recent publication, D'Annunzio's figure sometimes functions as a rallying point for neo-Fascist or right-wing communities in Italy. 'Translating Gabriele D'Annunzio for the Twenty-first Century Reader', 6 March 2020, on *Decadence and Translation Network*, <https://dandtnetwork.glasgow.ac.uk/translating-gabriele-dannunzio-for-the-twenty-first-century-reader/> [accessed 3 November 2022].

not ignore the role of the political but rather sees it as one element in a complex system of imitation, circulation, reception and multilingual transfer.

A second aspect of our volume's response to the push for a more open, global and decolonised canon emerges in how we seek to reconfigure the imaginary map of Decadence as a global movement, putting a new emphasis on how Italian literature participated in this literary exchange. In the last decade, scholars such as Matthew Potolsky, Regenia Gagnier and David Weir have placed new emphasis on the extent to which writers affiliated with the Decadent movement and based in different countries borrowed from one another, and the role of translation in constructing a shared Decadent aesthetics.[12] That growing tendency in the field is confirmed by the proliferation of new scholarly networks, conferences and journals, from the founding of *Volupté*, an interdisciplinary journal of Decadence studies engaging translational and comparative dimensions, to the AHRC Network 'Decadence and Translation', led by Matthew Creasy and Stefano Evangelista, to the conference 'Fin du Globe: Decadence, Catastrophe, Late Style', hosted at Cornell University (10–13 September 2020). The forging of a transnational paradigm of Decadence as a global exchange dovetails with the shift that has been underway in Modernist studies more generally, expanding the field to conceive of its boundaries in a fashion that turns toward the world, emphasising globality or planetarity to increase the scope of the Modernist canon.[13]

[12] Matthew Potolsky, *The Decadent Republic of Letters: Taste, Politics, and Cosmopolitan Community from Baudelaire to Beardsley* (Philadelphia: University of Pennsylvania Press, 2013); Regenia Gagnier, *Individualism, Decadence and Globalization: On the Relationship of Part to Whole, 1859–1920* (London: Palgrave, 2010) and 'The Global Circulation of the Literatures of Decadence', *Literature Compass*, 10: 1 (January 2013), 70–81; Stefano Evangelista, 'Transnational Decadence', in *Decadence and Literature* (Cambridge University Press, 2019), pp. 316–31; David Weir, *Decadence: A Very Short Introduction* (Oxford: Oxford University Press, 2018). A related comparative view of global Decadence emerges in Michael Saler, *The Fin-De-Siecle World* (London and New York: Routledge, 2015).

[13] On this paradigm shift expanding the temporal and geographical scope of Modernist studies, see Douglas Mao and Rebecca L. Walkowitz, 'The New Modernist Studies', *PMLA*, 123: 3 (2008), 737–48; and Peter Kalliney, *Modernism in a Global Context* (London: Bloomsbury, 2016). Contributions to this expansive move are many and varied, but see especially: Susan Stanford Friedman, *Planetary Modernisms: Provocations on Modernity across Time* (New York: Columbia UP, 2018); Lise Jaillant and Alison E. Martin, eds, 'Global Modernism', special issue of *Modernist Cultures*, 13: 1 (2018); Eric Hayot and Rebecca L. Walkowitz,

D'Annunzio has long been recognised as the 'most encyclopaedic representative' of *Decadentismo*.[14] In the third edition of his seminal study on *fin-de-siècle* literature, Mario Praz had already signalled his role in shaping Decadence as an international movement.[15] Despite this, recent English-language scholarship examining the transnational dynamics of Decadence have seldom seen Italy as a central site.[16] Potolsky's outstanding study of global Decadence, for instance, makes virtually no mention of Italian authors, examining the transnational formation of a 'community of taste' that is nevertheless largely bound to French and anglophone writing.[17] The same can be said of Weir's excellent introduction to Decadence, where Italy's role is as the site of Classical Decadence (the fall of the Roman Empire) and its subsequent influence on modern writers in France, Britain, Austria/Hungary and Germany.[18] Italian authors, indeed, have remained a 'peripheral' presence in anglophone scholarly visions of this period. Welcome moves that expand the map by applying a postcolonial, or decolonial lens,[19] while maintaining a focus on francophone and anglophone Decadence, need to be supplemented by work that shows how the European context itself is more multifaceted and complex than a French-Anglo model might suggest, and how that complex European map in turn relates in even more nuanced ways to the unfolding dynamics of globalisation in the colonial era.

Until a few years ago, it was very challenging to teach D'Annunzio in an anglophone setting, as the translations available in English were not only dated but also heavily censored. This also impacted

eds, *A New Vocabulary for Global Modernism* (New York: Columbia UP, 2016); Stephen Ross and Allana C. Lindgren, eds, *The Modernist World* (New York: Routledge, 2015); Mark Wollaeger and Matt Eatough, eds, *The Oxford Handbook to Global Modernisms* (Oxford: Oxford University Press, 2012).

14 Guy Tosi, 'D'annunzio parnassiano, "bizantino" e simbolista: alle fonti di una poetica complessa (1886–1894)', in *D'Annunzio e la cultura francese*, vol. 2 (Lanciano: Rocco Carabba, 2013), p. 848.

15 Mario Praz, *La carne, la morte e il diavolo nella letteratura romantica* (Florence: Sansoni, 1948).

16 An important exception here is the work of Stefano Evangelista, which has made a strong case for the need to include Italy in this broader conversation. See for example his 'Aestheticism in Italy: A New Sense of Place', in *The Edinburgh Companion to Fin de Siècle Literature, Culture and the Arts*, ed. by Josephine M. Guy (Edinburgh: Edinburgh University Press, 2018), pp. 263–80.

17 Potolsky, *The Decadent Republic*, p. 11.

18 Weir, *Decadence*.

19 Julia Hartley, Wanrug Suwanwattana and Jennifer Yee, eds, *French Decadence in a Global Context: Colonialism and Exoticism* (Liverpool: Liverpool UP, 2022).

scholarship and interest in D'Annunzio's work beyond the circuits of Italian studies: his texts was read mostly by specialists, and in Italian.[20] A new translation of *Il fuoco* (1900), by Susan Bassnett, was published in 1991.[21] But D'Annunzio's first and most famous novel *Il Piacere* (1889) was, until very recently, only accessible in the bowdlerised 1898 translation by Georgina Harding.[22] Only in 2013 did Lara Gochin Raffaelli's translation finally open the way for students and scholars who do not read Italian to engage with this seminal Decadent text.[23] Curiously, 2013 also saw the publication of Lucy Hughes-Hallett's highly acclaimed biography *The Pike: Gabriele D'Annunzio, Poet, Seducer and Preacher of War*[24] – issued in Italian with the de-militarised subtitle *L'uomo, il poeta, il sogno di una vita come opera d'arte* [The Man, the Poet, the Dream of Life as an Artwork].[25] In addition to Hughes-Hallet's book, it is worth mentioning the first biography in Russian, by Elena Shvarts, published posthumously in 2010;[26] two biographies in Swedish by Göran Hägg (2015) and Magnus Bärtås and Fredrik Ekman (2017)[27] and Maurizio Serra's 2018 biography in French.[28] Moreover, the 100-year anniversary of the Fiume escapade (12 September 1919) led to scholarly

[20] Barbara Spackman's works can be considered an exception, as her important contributions consider D'Annunzio alongside other major figures of Decadence. See especially Barbara Spackman, *Decadent Genealogies: The Rhetoric of Sickness from Baudelaire to D'Annunzio* (Ithaca: Cornell UP, 1989). See also Mary Ann Frese Witt, *The Search for Modern Tragedy: Aesthetic Fascism in Italy and France* (Ithaca: Cornell UP, 2001).

[21] Gabriele D'Annunzio, *The Flame*, trans. by Susan Basnett (London: Quartet, 1991). Prior to this, the novel was only available in the 1900 translation by Vivaria Kassadra (pseudonym of Magda Sindaci), which was simultaneously released in both the UK and US under the title *The Flame of Life* (London: Heinemann; Boston: H. Fertig; New York: L. C. Page & Co., 1900).

[22] Gabriele D'Annunzio, *Child of Pleasure*, trans. by Georgina Harding (London: Heinemann, 1898).

[23] D'Annunzio, Gabriele, *Pleasure*, trans. by Lara Gochin Raffaelli (New York: Penguin, 2013).

[24] Lucy Hughes-Hallett, *The Pike: Gabriele D'Annunzio, Poet, Seducer and Preacher of War* (London: 4th Estate, 2013).

[25] Lucy Hughes-Hallett, *Gabriele D'Annunzio: L'uomo, Il Poeta, Il Sogno Di Una Vita Come Opera D'arte*, trans. by Roberta Zuppet (Milano: Rizzoli, 2021).

[26] Elena Shvarts, *Krylatyi tziklop* (St Petersburg: Vita Nova, 2010).

[27] Göran Hägg, *D'Annunzio: dekadent diktare, krigare och diktator* (Norstedts 2015); Magnus Bärtås and Fredrik Ekman, *Bebådaren: Gabriele D'Annunzio och fascismens födelse* (Stockholm: Albert Bonniers, 2017).

[28] Maurizio Serra, *D'annunzio Le Magnifique* (Paris: Grasset, 2018), trans. by Alberto Folin as *L'imaginifico*.

reassessments of this episode in both English and Italian studies, reconsidering D'Annunzio's ideology in the post-war period, and his collaboration with workers' movements.[29] As new editions on or by D'Annunzio become available, the urgency to reposition this author on the map of *fin-de-siècle* studies emerges with renewed force.[30]

D'Annunzio and/in Translation

A 'peripheral' author in the context of the European *fin-de-siècle*, writing in the language of a young nation, D'Annunzio was keen to internationalise Italian literature. In a sense, his work participated in world literature from the start, shaped, as it was, by encounters with other languages and cultures. Pietro Gibellini's chapter in our volume underlines his roots in classical culture and his reworking of Greek mythology. Guy Tosi's writing has documented the extensive influence of French and Russian literature on D'Annunzio's works, as well as his readiness to embrace transnational trends, including Decadence and Symbolism.[31] Despite his limited knowledge of English, D'Annunzio was also inspired by English Aestheticism, especially in the vein of Walter Pater, whom he re-writes extensively in *Il fuoco* (1900). He knew little or no German, but he cited extensively from Goethe, to whom, with characteristic modesty, he compared himself, and whose collected works and conversations with Eckermann can be found in his library.[32] His interest in Nietzsche, Schopenhauer and Wagner is well documented. Usually described as a poet anchored to the Classical and European tradition, he also looked beyond Europe:

[29] See, for instance, the treatment of D'Annunzio's Adriatic military expedition in the recent history by Charles Emmerson, *Crucible: The Long End of the Great War and the Birth of a New World, 1917–1924* (London: The Bodley Head, 2019), or the chapter dedicated to D'Annunzio in Claudio Fogu, *The Fishing Net and the Spider Web: Mediterranean Imaginaries and the Making of Italians* (London: Palgrave, 2021). Of course, there is an expansive literature on the topic in Italian, as well. See, for example, Federico Lorenzo Ramaioli, *Quis Contra Nos? Storia della reggenza del Carnaro da D'Annunzio alla costituzione di Fiume* (Rome: Historia edizioni, 2018), and the special issue of *Rassegna dannunziana* (2018).

[30] This renewed academic interest is also attested by the special issue of *Forum Italicum* devoted to D'Annunzio: 'Reawakening Beauty: Gabriele D'Annunzio's Seduction of the Senses', ed. by Lara Raffaelli and Michael Subialka, *Forum Italicum*, 51: 2 (August 2017).

[31] Tosi's articles and book chapters have been recently gathered in *D'Annunzio e la cultura francese*, ed. by Maddalena Rasera (Lanciano: Carabba, 2013).

[32] See Paola Sorge, p. 75.

he was fascinated by Arabic culture and Chinese art, wrote about Japanese poetry, established contacts with Argentina, Brazil and Japan – even though, as emerges from the essays gathered in this volume, the persona he projected was far more well-travelled and polyglot than his actual self. Pietro Gibellini and Mariko Muramatsu demonstrate that the incorporation of temporally and geographically distant elements, exemplified by his reworking of Greek mythology and experiments with Japanese meter, was fundamental to his poetics. D'Annunzio's outward look and open attitude even manifests itself in his endeavour to renovate the Italian language, going back to its Latin roots but also incorporating foreign words from modern languages (especially French and English). Moreover, his writing involved a continuous practice of translation. In borrowing from foreign authors, whether this occurred in the form of citations or in the rewriting of entire passages, he was incorporating the foreign into the local, practising transculturation and syncretism. In his recent biography, Maurizio Serra goes so far as to compare his collage-technique, his continuous experimentation with and integration of the 'other', to the practice of Picasso.[33] Frequently accused of plagiarism, and unquestionably influenced by the cosmopolitan circulation of European (especially French and British, but also Russian) Decadent texts and tastes himself, D'Annunzio in turn became a source for the imitation of both Italian and foreign writers, demonstrating how Italian writers contributed not only as a site of reception but also as a source in turn amongst the cosmopolitan networks of the period.[34] Indeed, the dialogues D'Annunzio had with his translators, along with the impact that his writing had on other authors, foreground the dynamics of international circulation at play in what Potolsky has called the 'Decadent Republic of Letters'.[35] And these features remained crucial even when, as a more mature writer, D'Annunzio ventured into his own efforts at translingual writing and started composing in French.

For those engaged with his work, D'Annunzio's persona also functioned as a text that was admired and emulated. The fact that he

[33] Serra, *L'Imaginifico*, p. 18.

[34] For instance, David Weir, among others, has shown the close affinity of D'Annunzio to the cult and legacy of Huysmans: *Decadence and the Making of Modernism* (Amherst: University of Massachusetts Press, 1995), Chapter 5. He likewise establishes how D'Annunzio's response to Huysmans is itself situated in an exchange with other figures (Wilde, Gide) as a source for James Joyce (Chapter 6), tracing out the complex circulations of this transnational paradigm.

[35] Potolsky, p. 8.

attracted the most disparate personalities, from the extravagant Arthur Symons to the 'Timidum animae' André Doderet to the avant-garde practitioner Gustav Vollmoeller, is a testament to his polyhedric personality. Indeed, as one recent volume has shown, D'Annunzio can be thought of as a 'character' in European culture, which can be emulated and admired, or caricatured and denigrated, depending on who is interested in playing with that character and in what medium.[36] As contributions in our volume demonstrate, this phenomenon was in fact not limited to the European scene but rather global: from Japan to the United States, his contemporaries were often more interested in the legend of D'Annunzio (encouraged, of course, by his own, often overtly theatrical actions) than the literary works he produced.

D'Annunzio's afterlife in translation began through the fortuitous, and much-documented encounter with Georges Hérelle, the translator who, in the words of Matilde Serao, contributed to 'more than half' of D'Annunzio's success in France.[37] D'Annunzio and Hérelle's correspondence, published in 1946 by Tosi and in a more recent, comprehensive edition by Mario Cimini, is an important document to assess how Italian *Decadentismo*, a peripheral movement influenced by French literature, travelled back to Paris, which, as Pascale Casanova has argued, at the time was the 'centre' of the European artistic scene, its '"denationalized" universal capital'.[38] It also offers an insight into D'Annunzio's view and theories of translation. Moreover, as Muriel Gallot has shown,[39] it foregrounds the inextricable link of erotism and translation, for Hérelle, an early anthropologist of homosexuality, was, as Clive Thomson's essay in our volume shows, seduced by D'Annunzio's writing as much as by his persona – a phenomenon that, as Ikuho Amano demonstrates in her chapter here, would repeat itself with the Japanese author Yukio Mishima. On the other hand, Hérelle's fascination with D'Annunzio's hybrid language clashed with his commitment to defend French from foreign influences, his attraction to D'Annunzio's sensual imagery and his

[36] Luciano Curreri, ed., *D'Annunzio come personaggio nell'immaginario italiano ed europeo (1938–2008): una mappa* (Peter Lang, 2008).

[37] Matilde Serao to Georges Hérelle, 1 November 1895, in Raffaele Giglio, *Per la storia di un'amicizia* (Naples: Loffredo, 1977), p. 146.

[38] Pascale Casanova, *The World Republic of Letters*, trans. by M. B. DeBevoise (Cambridge, MA: Harvard University Press, 2004), p. 108.

[39] Muriel Gallot, 'Gabriele D'Annunzio et Georges Hérelle: érotisme et traduction', in *Traduire avec l'auteur*, ed. by Patrick Hersant (Paris: Sorbonne Université, 2020), pp. 129–146.

preoccupation with the respectability of the prestigious journals in which D'Annunzio's novels were published. In a famous letter from 4 January 1905, discussing the translation of *La figlia di Iorio* (1903), D'Annunzio accuses Hérelle of flattening his prose in fear of violating the conventions of the French language and reminds him that 'un'opera tradotta non deve entrare a far parte della letteratura nazionale ma deve conservare la sua impronta d'origine, magari contro il genio della nazione che la ospita' (a translated work must not become part of national literature but must retain its original mark, perhaps against the genius of the host nation). In line with the notion of translation dear to the German romantics, he adds that 'una buona traduzione moderna non deve avvicinare l'opera al lettore ma sí bene il lettore all'opera, magari *malgré lui*' (a good modern translation should not bring the work closer to the reader but the reader closer to the work, even *malgré lui*').[40]

With such statements, D'Annunzio comes close to the notion of translation articulated by Friedrich Schleiermacher and later adopted by Lawrence Venuti in the concept of foreignising translation: translation that allows the features of the source language to influence the language of the target text.[41] On the other hand, D'Annunzio took an essentialist conservative stance as, frustrated with Hérelle's translation of his play *Francesca da Rimini* (1901), he argued that 'questa Francesca è opera così profondamente italiana che non è possibile trasportarla in altra lingua né farla sentire a uomini d'altra razza' (this Francesca is a work so profoundly Italian that it is not possible to translate it into another language or make men of another race feel it).[42] Here, D'Annunzio's position is underwritten by a cultural determinism that excludes the possibility of cross-cultural exchange. Such contradictions are not uncommon, as D'Annunzio's cosmopolitan ethos often coexists with nationalistic views, even before the First World War and his debut as poet-soldier.

Determined to shape the 'worlding' of his works, and to facilitate his reception in Paris, in 1892 D'Annunzio prepared for Hérelle, and his French readership, a fictional biography that romanticised his youth and underlined the transgressive features of his writing.

[40] D'Annunzio to Hérelle, 4 January 1905, in Mario Cimini, ed., *Carteggio D'Annunzio – Hérelle (1891–1931)*; Clive Thomson, *Georges Hérelle: archéologue de l'inversion sexuelle 'fin de siècle'* (Paris: Éditions du Félin, 2014), p. 589.

[41] Lawrence Venuti, *The Translator's Invisibility: A History of Translation* (London: Routledge, 1995).

[42] D'Annunzio to Hérelle, February 1903, in Cimini, p. 556.

After being hailed by French critic Melchior de Vogüé as a champion of the Latin Renaissance in an article published in the *Revue des deux mondes* in 1895,[43] despite personal reservations, he publicly embraced his new role. In the same vein, he asked Hérelle for permission to publish the French version of the play *La cittá morta* (1896) omitting any reference to translation, as if had been written directly in French, thus fostering his image as a cosmopolitan, avant-garde writer, born in Italy almost by accident, who naturally composed in French and then 'translated' his own words into Italian. This was then followed by other works, those actually written in French, in which he dared to defy the norms and structures of the French language.

In other instances, D'Annunzio used the opposite strategy, modifying international sources to shape his Italian reception. This was the case with an article by Hugo von Hofmannsthal in the *Frankfurter Zeitung* (9 August 1893), later published in Italian in the Neapolitan journal *La tavola rotunda* on 17 December 1893. Hofmannsthal's essay was flattering, but D'Annunzio did not hesitate to 'correct' it by amplifying words of praise, substituting citations and rewriting passages. For example, he underlined the modernity of his writing and modified the comparison Hofmannsthal had drawn between *L'Innocente* and the novels by Paul Bourget and Maupassant, defining the latter as 'superficial' and thus using the authority of 'Hofmannsthal' to mark his own superiority to French models in the eyes of his co-citizens.[44]

As these episodes show, D'Annunzio's objective was twofold: facilitating his reception in France, and increasing his cultural capital in Italy by demonstrating his consecration abroad. In the end, the poems and dramas purportedly or actually written in French had limited success. It was instead mainly through the novels translated by Hérelle that D'Annunzio reached a global audience. Moreover, his translations ended up being the intermediary for D'Annunzio's works not only in France but also beyond, as translations into other languages were heavily influenced by the French versions. Despite the density and opacity of his musical prose and the complexity of his poetry, D'Annunzio was one of the few Italian authors to be read by

[43] Eugène-Melchior de Vogüé, 'La Renaissance Latine. G. d'A : Poèmes et romans', *Revue des deux mondes* (1895): 187–206.

[44] See Roberta Ascarelli, 'Hugo von Hofmannsthals "Gabriele d'Annunzio" in der Übersetzung von Gabriele d'Annunzio', *Hofmansthals Jahrbuch zur Europäischen Moderne*, 3 (1995): 169–213; and Paola Sorge, D'Annunzio e il mondo germanico', *Rassegna dannunziana* 72 (2018): 75–82 (p. 80).

intellectuals from France to Austria-Hungary, Russia, Egypt, Israel, Japan, the US and Argentina. He became an inspiration for artists fascinated by his polyphonous writing, charismatic persona and *vivere inimitabile*. As Assumpta Camps and Noriko Hiraishi show in their contributions here, his writing also functioned as a catalyst for the introduction of new gender identities in key international contexts. And in the context of young nations in which nation-building was of utmost importance – from *fin-de-siècle* Catalonia to Israel to post-war Japan – he provided a template for a national rhetoric and a model for the poet-soldier.

Aesthetics, Politics and a Changing Reception

The relation between D'Annunzio's poetics and politics has always been complicated and fraught, just as D'Annunzio's public persona itself can be situated between the Decadent dandy and the militant patriot. Biographers have often divided D'Annunzio's life into two phases, that of the Aesthete-poet before the First World War, and the poet-soldier after 1914; however, it is worth noting that the collection of essays on the Italian navy published in *Tribuna* and later gathered in *L'armata d'Italia* (1888) – thus almost contemporary with the Decadent-Aesthetic novel *Il Piacere* (1889) – already includes an anti-Aesthetic statement:

> '. . . Io non sono e non voglio essere un poeta mero. Al perfetto rimatore Théodore de Banville piacque confessare [. . .] "Je ne m'entends que'a la métrique!". A me, invece, codesta perpetua professione di prosodismo non va. Tutte le manifestazioni della vita e tutte le manifestazioni dell'intelligenza mi attraggono ugualmente'.[45]
>
> (I am not and I do not want to be a mere poet. The perfect rhymer Théodore de Banville took pleasure in confessing [. . .] : 'Je ne m'entends que a la métrique!'. For me, instead, this perpetual profession of prosody is no good. All the manifestations of life and all the manifestations of intelligence attract me equally).

Shortly after the battle of Dogali, in present-day Eritrea (26 January 1887), D'Annunzio published in *Capitan Fracassa* a poem ('Per gli Italiani morti in Africa') celebrating the fallen Italian soldiers,

[45] *L'armata d'Italia* (Venezia: Zanetti, 1915), p. 66. On the connections between *L'armata d'Italia* and *Il Piacere*, see Giansiro Ferrata, 'Introduzione', *Il Piacere* (Milano: Mondadori, 1951), pp. 33–5.

which he was subsequently accused of having plagiarised from Niccolò Tommaseo's 'Gli italiani morti in Ispagna' (1837). However, in *Il Piacere* (1889), masked behind his protagonist, D'Annunzio dedicates a few lines to the massacre and calls the same soldiers 'bruti, morti brutalmente' (brutes, brutally killed) – a comment that led to accusations that the author lacked patriotism. Igiaba Scego has recently called attention to the fact that D'Annunzio was in good company among artists who, like Matilde Serao, Giovanni Pascoli and Emilio Salgari, enthusiastically supported Italy's colonial enterprise, and that his 'dual reaction' to the massacre underlined the absurdity of this sacrifice.[46] Today, the lack of patriotism of Sperelli's comment – which D'Annunzio justified by taking distance from his character, whom he defined as a 'monster' – appears far less problematic than the fervent colonialism of *Più che l'amore* (1906), a drama about a tragic love set against the background of an expedition to Africa, or of the tragedy *La nave* (1907), an allegory of Italy's colonial ambition in the Adriatic, and, interestingly, one of his most multilingual texts.

D'Annunzio's military enterprises, just like his writing, gathered support and admiration from the most unexpected sides. An emblematic example is the occupation of the Dalmatian city of Fiume (September 1919–December 1920), a former Habsburg city-state disputed between Italy and the Kingdom of Serbs, Croats and Slovenes. The enterprise was supported by Mussolini and war veterans, but also attracted anarchists, syndicalists and left-wing activists, and was hailed by the Dadaists, the Italian Futurists and even by Lenin. Moreover, while the Fiume escapade was grounded in nationalist-colonialist ideology – and many of its rituals would later be incorporated by the Fascist party – it also involved an anti-imperialist aspect, represented by the *Carta del Carnaro*, its new constitution, and by the broader project to create an anti-league of nations, the *Lega di Fiume*. This project was designed to bring together small nations or ethnic groups – including the Irish *Sinn Fein* and the Egyptian nationalist movement – to oppose the British and the Ottomans. In politics, too, D'Annunzio's nationalist ideas coexisted with a cosmopolitan and liberal outlook, for, as Claudio Fogu has noted, in Fiume 'D'Annunzio began to see Italians as a people who needed to be liberated not only from an oppressive and treacherous government, but also from the tyranny of imperialist-capitalist relations'.[47]

[46] Igiaba Scego, *Roma negata* (Roma: Ediesse, 2020), p. 58.

[47] Fogu, p. 148.

Just as new research thus complicates the ambivalent picture of D'Annunzio's militarism, patriotism and nationalism, so too has the extent to which D'Annunzio's actions influenced Fascism, and to which Fascist ideology is represented in his writing, been much debated by historians and literary critics alike. In this book, we aim to explore the discomfort that the figure of D'Annunzio still stirs in the anglophone world, as well as in other contexts – not to eliminate it, but to understand its roots. The compromise with Fascism naturally played a crucial role in D'Annunzio's transition from internationally acclaimed author to a marginal, almost forgotten figure beyond Italy's borders. Despite his ambivalent relationship to Mussolini – who referred to D'Annunzio as a rotten tooth that needs to be covered in gold[48] – this association has affected D'Annunzio's afterlife far more than that of other writers who enthusiastically embraced the movement, such as Luigi Pirandello, who publicly declared his adhesion to the party in 1924 in the midst of the polemics following Giacomo Matteotti's murder, or like Massimo Bontempelli, who headed the National Fascist Writers Union in the 1920s. We must also take into account that D'Annunzio's writing, despite his outward gaze and intellectual curiosity, remains a showcase of what Potolsky has identified as the 'less savory' aspects of Decadence: 'misogyny, orientalism, and antidemocratic elitism'.[49] At the same time, there are also practical reasons for D'Annunzio's works being eclipsed or forgotten in the post-war context, such as their intricate webs of intertextual references and allusions. In fact, precisely the intertextuality that in the late nineteenth century contributed to D'Annunzio's modernity has today become an obstacle for the lay reader. During the *fin-de-siècle*, his texts were widely read beyond their culture of origin, either in the original or in translation. After the Second World War, his deeds and life continued to sell books, but his literary works largely disappeared from anglophone, francophone as well as German and Japanese maps of world literature for many decades.

D'Annunzio and World Literature – A Note on Methodology

Scholarship on D'Annunzio has always been attentive to the international dimension of his work, and the pathway for future comparative

[48] Serra, p. 13.
[49] Potolsky, p. 15.

readings of D'Annunzio's oeuvre in an international context was set by post-war studies. Tosi's articles documented D'Annunzio's relationship to French culture, as well as the reception of his work in France.[50] Two volumes, *D'Annunzio e il simbolismo europeo* (1973) and *D'Annunzio europeo* (1989), gathered conference proceedings discussing his engagement with Symbolism and his European reception.[51] These studies, however, are limited to the European context, and, while still solid and helpful, the way in which they are framed is mostly of their time. Other important contributions, mostly published in Italian, are focused on single area studies, such as D'Annunzio's relationship to German,[52] Russian[53] and British culture,[54] to name a few key instances. Some recent studies, also written in Italian, have likewise explored or addressed D'Annunzio's influence beyond Europe.[55] Indeed, listing all the works that consider connections between D'Annunzio and other countries and cultures would result in a very large list and go beyond the scope of this Introduction.[56]

50 Tosi, D'Annunzio e la cultura francese.

51 Emilio Mariano, ed., *D'Annunzio e il simbolismo europeo. Atti del convegno di studio, Gardone Riviera, 14–15–16 settembre, 1973* (Milano: Il Saggiatore, 1976); Pietro Gibellini, ed., *D'Annunzio europeo: atti del convegno internazionale: Gardone Riviera-Perugia 8-13 maggio 1989* (Roma: Lucarini, 1991).

52 *D'Annunzio e la cultura germanica: atti del vi convegno internazionale di studi dannunziani, Pescara, 3–5 maggio 1984* (Pescara: Centro studi dannunziani: 1985).

53 *Percorsi russi al Vittoriale: archivi, testimonianze, prospettive di studio. Atti del convegno internazionale di studi, Gardone Riviera-Gargano sul Garda, 14–15 ottobre 2011*, ed. by Maria Pia Pagani (Milan: Silvana Editoriale, 2012).

54 See especially John Woodhouse, *D'Annunzio tra Italia e Inghilterra* (Pescara: Ediars, 2003).

55 See Mariko Muramatsu, *Segni e voci dalla letteratura italiana. Da Dante a D'Annunzio* (Tokyo: UTCP, 2012); Luca Scarlini, *D'Annunzio a Little Italy* (Roma: Donzelli editore, 2008); see also the special issue of *Rassegna dannunziana, D'Annunzio in Italia e nel mondo a ottant'anni dalla morte, 45esimo convegno internazionale di studi*, 72 (2018).

56 Already in 1935, two scholars working to compile a bibliography of D'Annunzio's reception abroad (primarily in English, French and German), found it necessary to foreground the enormity of the task, saying that 'D'Annunzio's world-wide celebrity has naturally given rise to a vast amount of bibliographical material on the man and his writings, so vast and so scattered that the task of assembling it would call for the work of a lifetime and travel into different portions of the globe': Joseph G. Fucilla and Joseph M. Carrière, *D'Annunzio Abroad: A Bibliographical Essay* (New York: Columbia University, 1935–1937), Part I, p. viii. Their own two-part bibliography of materials spans more than 2,500 entries and does not even include translations of novels that had already been listed in an earlier bibliography by Giulio de' Medici (pseudonym of Vincenzo Moretti), *Bibliografia di Gabriele d'Annunzio* (Rome: Edizioni del centauro, 1928).

What motivated us to create the present collection is that, despite the numerous publications, no volume on D'Annunzio with a global scope exists in English. Moreover, the present volume significantly departs from previous studies in methodological terms. Using translation and the transnational as conceptual frames, we believe, offers new ways to reconsider D'Annunzio's legacy outside of Italy; it likewise contributes to our critical understanding of the world literature scene before the label and methodological framework of world literature as we now know it became current.

The contributions to this volume engage a broad number of case studies across languages, nations and cultures, including Japan and the Middle East, as well as pan-European and transatlantic perspectives spanning both North and South America. While the volume thus offers extensive coverage of D'Annunzio's engagement with the foreign, and of how his texts and persona were refracted across national and linguistic boundaries, it cannot aim for comprehensiveness; in the chapters that follow, we have instead sought to privilege areas and connections that have not received as much attention, or to look at established connections through new theoretical frameworks. For instance, the volume emphasises locations where the reception of D'Annunzio's political persona dovetailed with burgeoning nationalist sentiments or where his innovations were integral to rethinking modernity, as in the connection between D'Annunzio and Japan, which occupies several chapters here. Likewise, the section on translators shifts the focus from D'Annunzio's persona to the way this persona was imitated/challenged/mediated by his international interlocutors. This is paired with our interest in moving from examining Italy in relation to central European languages (French, English, German) to a more expansive map of other so-called 'peripheries'. Instead of focusing on Spain, we thus decided to study the Argentinian reception; and by including chapters on Catalan and on dialect translation, we have made a point of exploring how D'Annunzio's many afterlives challenge the centrifugal paradigm generally associated with world literature, as his reception was just as much centripetal; 'inwardly' directed.

The essays bring together chapters written by scholars from twelve countries (Italy, France, Belgium, Austria, Spain, the UK, the US, Canada, Russia, Egypt, Argentina, Japan), ensuring a variety of perspectives as well as a global outlook. The target audience we had in mind – not only Italianists but also scholars of comparative literature, translation studies and Decadence studies – determined our choice of English as a medium, despite the non-negligible ethical and practical implications of this choice. Some contributors wrote in their native languages and then had the chapter translated for the volume, while others wrote directly in English. In both cases there was of course substantial translation and editorial work. We have encouraged authors to adopt writing conventions that would give the volume a sense of overall consistency, but readers will likely notice differences as well, underpinned by the authors' different approach to formulating research questions and structuring an essay's argument. We think of this complex intercultural compromise as both a challenge and a strength. Likewise, the volume is framed by the conjunction of two scholars themselves working in different but overlapping areas: the place of Italian literature in transnational circuits of Decadence (Elisa Segnini), and Italian literature and philosophy in relation to transnational Modernism (Michael Subialka).[57] Bringing together our expertise, language skills and backgrounds has been crucial for the development of the volume.

We have provided English translations for all citations, but we have left it up to authors to determine when it was important to cite in the original. It is interesting to note that contributors writing in global languages such as French or Spanish, or European languages such as German, tended to think this of utmost importance, whereas authors tackling reception in languages such as Russian and Japanese decided to cite in English translation only, and contributors addressing reception in dialects ended up not citing at all. Like many other details, this reminds us that any conception of world literature is conditioned by the context of production and envisioned readership:[58] in this case, a volume edited by two Italian and comparative literature scholars, one originally from Italy, trained in Canada and based in Scotland, the other raised and based in the US, working toward a publication for a UK publisher with contributors based across the world. World literature, as Djelal Kadir has noted, is 'invariably a product of our optic and our grasp'.[59] We are aware that

[57] See Elisa Segnini, *Fragments, Genius and Madness: Masks and Mask-Making in the Fin-de-siècle Imagination* (Cambridge: Legenda, 2021) and the forthcoming 'Decadence, Ethnicity and Gender: Georges Hérelle's translations of Matilde Serao and Grazia Deledda', *Modern Philology* (2023); Michael Subialka, *Modernist Idealism: Ambivalent Legacies of German Philosophy in Italian Literature* (Toronto: University of Toronto Press, 2021).

[58] David Damrosch, 'Frames for World Literature', in *Tensions in World Literature: Between the Local and the Universal*, ed. by Weigui Fang (Singapore: Springer, 2018), pp. 93–102 (p. 100).

[59] Djelal Kadir, 'To World, to Globalize: World Literature's Crossroads', *Comparative Literature Studies* 41: 1 (2004), 1–9 (p. 7).

our stance as editors is far from neutral, and that the map of world literature we are constructing is influenced by our backgrounds and position in the academic world, by the cultural frameworks in which we work, as well as by new trends in our disciplines.

In addition to this situation for the scholarship, we also want to address the cover image of the volume here. Guido Reni's *Saint Sebastian*, painted around 1615 and now held at the Palazzo Rosso in Genoa, speaks to the transnational circulation of D'Annunzio's Decadence: D'Annunzio himself obsessively collected icons of Sebastian's martyrdom, and the Japanese writer Yukio Mishima shared his passion, even to the point of co-translating D'Annunzio's *Le Martyre de Saint Sébastien*. Mishima was particularly drawn to Reni's painting, which triggered the erotic discovery of his own sexuality. As a queer image of Decadent interest, it thus represents the global exchanges that place D'Annunzio in a world-literature context.

Volume Structure and Chapter Synopsis

The case studies proposed in the individual chapters of this book are grouped into four sections based on conceptual similarities in approach rather than geographical or linguistic categories: first, looking at what we term D'Annunzio's 'poetics of fusion' and how he engages the Other, drawing on world literature to form his outlook and style; second, turning to his interactions with translators and their role in placing him on the European scene via foreign canons; third, considering his global reception in the *fin-de-siècle* period and how his work and persona circulated; and fourth, examining what we call his 'complex legacies', the multifaceted and changing afterlives that can be traced either over time in specific national or linguistic contexts or else in concentrated instances that play out the tug-of-war between interest and imitation on the one hand and rejection or disapproval on the other.

The first section, 'A Poetics of Fusion: Cultural Appropriation, Multilingualism, Translingual Writing', focuses on D'Annunzio's 'outward' gaze, how his engagement with world literature shaped his own poetics. It explores how D'Annunzio borrowed from the classics, experimented with Japanese poetic forms, rewrote European authors and practiced multilingual and translingual writing. As these chapters demonstrate, the coupling between multilingualism and cosmopolitanism does not preclude, and in fact introduces, a link between multilingualism and nationalist ambitions. D'Annunzio's writing can thus be seen as engaging world literature in a way characterised by both literary and linguistic appropriation.

Pietro Gibellini considers D'Annunzio's debt to ancient models and thus the temporal as well as geographical dimensions of his place in world literature in his opening chapter, 'D'Annunzio and the Greek and Latin Classics'. Hellenic and Latin sources – from Sappho, Pindar, Homer and the Greek tragedians to Ovid, Virgil, Horace and Seneca – combine alongside D'Annunzio's interest in modern French literature, speaking to his view of the modernity of the classics and their ability to play a role in revitalising Italian literature through translation and adaptation. D'Annunzio's self-shaping as the new poet of Italy was thus situated at the threshold of both ancient and modern world literary intertexts. Mariko Muramatsu's chapter on 'D'Annunzio and Japonism' highlights how this intertextual formation of D'Annunzio's poetics encompassed more than the European milieu, including a multimedia focus on not only Japanese literary sources but also painting, as well as the broader aesthetic sensibility of European *Japonisme* characteristic of nineteenth-century art. What Muramatsu uncovers is an evolving Orientalism spanning from D'Annunzio's experiments with Japanese verse forms to the aesthetics of his house-museum, the Vittoriale degli Italiani, later in his life. The incorporation of the foreign and the exotic is thus a central element of innovation in his poetics.

The next three chapters of this section trace the development of D'Annunzio's linguistic experimentation chronologically, moving from foreign borrowings and rewriting as a form of cosmopolitanism in his first novels to an increased engagement with language mixing, including dialect, in later works. In '*Il Piacere* as a Multilingual Text and its Afterlife in Translation', Elisa Segnini demonstrates how the tension between cosmopolitanism and nationalism that pervades the novel is reflected in the multilingual fabric of the text, and explores how such dynamics were renegotiated in translation as the book travelled back to France, the centre of the Decadent movement that had inspired it. In their chapter '"The Essence of the Race": *La figlia di Iorio* and Italian Dialects', Sarah Zappulla Muscarà and Enzo Zappulla similarly focus on translation and circulation, contending that *La figlia di Iorio* was inspired by dialect plays and owes its status as a 'masterpiece' precisely to its translation into dialects. Tracing how this drama was translated and transformed by Giuseppe Antonio Borgese in Sicilian and then Cesare de Titta in the Abruzzo dialect, and how it recirculated in a Neapolitan dialect parody by Eduardo Scarpetta, the authors argue that translation into dialect, rather than being a peripheral phenomenon, played a crucial role in facilitating the play's popularity beyond the national context, and thus its access to world literature. Filippo Fonio's chapter on 'The "Latin sister": D'Annunzio's Relationship to the French Language' considers the multilingual dimension of D'Annunzio's francophone writing. While critics have tended to downplay or marginalise these works, Fonio shows how the Italian writer developed a sophisticated strategy to integrate himself into a transnational francophone canon through linguistic experimentation. Ultimately, these chapters draw attention to the engagement with languages and dialect beyond a mimetic function, as Modernist poetic devices, and uncover how the complex linguistic structure of D'Annunzio's works constitutes a challenge for translators across contexts and continues to condition the reception of D'Annunzio's texts today.

The second section of the book, 'Translators as Transcultural Negotiators', highlights the bi-directional relationships at play in D'Annunzio's relationships with his translators, who influenced him and were influenced by his works and persona. D'Annunzio took an active role in shaping the international networks responsible for disseminating his works and helping to craft his reception, but the collaboration of translators as cultural managers should not be underestimated. His close involvement in the translation process is marked by his conception of translation as an inter-cultural practice that should retain the 'foreignness' of the original, and as a collaborative endeavour that requires intense empathy between author and translator.

The first chapter in this section, Clive Thomson's 'Gabriele D'Annunzio and Georges Hérelle: Virility, Machismo, and the Homoerotic', offers a new perspective on D'Annunzio's relationship with Georges Hérelle, who, by presenting the Italian poet as a 'world author' in the French context, jumpstarted his global reception. Drawing on D'Annunzio and Hérelle's correspondence, as well as on other documents preserved at Hérelle's archive, Thomson unearths how complicated dynamics of homoerotic desire and simultaneous distaste for D'Annunzio's hyper-masculine virility shaped their interactions as well as Hérelle's own retelling of them. In 'After Hérelle: André Doderet, the (In)visible Translator', Annalisa Ciano sheds light on another French translator with whom D'Annunzio collaborated after his relationship with Hérelle deteriorated. She argues that Doderet was particularly influential in facilitating a resurgence of interest in D'Annunzio after the Fiume episode, acting not only as a translator but also a kind of spokesperson and manager helping to ensure the author's continued place on the French cultural landscape. Aligning himself with D'Annunzio's desire for a literal translation that respected the foreign, Doderet advocated for him as a representative of the new 'Latin Renaissance' in France. A similar focus on literal translation strategies – used, however, to different ends – is central to Stefano Evangelista's chapter, '"An Artist in Translation": D'Annunzio, Arthur Symons, and Symbolist Drama', which uncovers how Symons advocated for unexpurgated translations of the Italian author's 'scandalous' plays, which circulated in written form for an elite readership thanks to his interventions. Symons's double-role as both translator and critic had a major impact on D'Annunzio's English reception, one that Evangelista measures in part through a comparison with the role that the famous Italian actress, Eleonora Duse, played in rendering D'Annunzio's art accessible to a morally scandalised audience. The office of the translator as cultural agent is also a point traced in Adriana Vignazia's chapter on 'Gabriele D'Annunzio and Karl Gustav Vollmoeller: From Classical Culture to the Attractions of Motor Power'. Vollmoeller shared D'Annunzio's interest in ancient Greek culture, modern technology and new mass media. He followed the footsteps of the author in real life and in his own writings, but demonstrated autonomy and initiative as he successfully adapted several of D'Annunzio's plays and came close to succeeding in involving in their staging the famous director, Max Reinhardt. Together, then, these chapters emphasise the intimate, sometimes conflictual relationship D'Annunzio had with his translators, the deep significance that the identification with D'Annunzio's persona played in both stimulating and directing the translation of his works, and the role played by translators as cultural mangers in the first phase of dissemination of the Italian author's work into European languages.

The third section of the book, 'D'Annunzio's Global *Fin-de-siècle* Reception', illustrates how the circulation of D'Annunzio's texts and the impact of his persona contributed to the shaping of artistic and political milieux across the globe. In some cases, this dissemination provided an aesthetic model that was integrated into and reformed local literary production, as we see in the appropriation of D'Annunzio's writings by Catalan Modernists or the Japanese interest in his Decadent novels. In these settings, D'Annunzio's writings triggered a debate about modernity's transformation of gender norms and resultant anxieties about the new man/woman. In other cases, political factions in foreign locales responded against D'Annunzio's persona and association with Italy's entry into the Great War, as in the Viennese debates over his artistic merits.

This section opens with Noriko Hiraishi's chapter on 'Fin-de-Meiji as *Fin-de-siècle*: D'Annunzio and Japanese Literature'. Here, Hiraishi shows how D'Annunzio's writings, particularly *Trionfo della morte* (1894), played a major role in both the Japanese reception of European Decadence and in the reshaping of modern gender roles. The sensualisation that made D'Annunzio scandalous in European contexts led to reconfiguring models of masculinity in modern Japanese culture, while the Dannunzian *femme fatale* challenged female gender norms. Similarly, the *femme fatale* archetype emerges as a key element of D'Annunzio's reception in Catalan literature, as argued by Assumpta Camps in her chapter on 'D'Annunzio's Feminine Archetypes, Nationalist Ideology and Catalan Modernism'. Offering an overview of the major figures integral to transforming the Catalan literary scene in the Modernist period, this chapter shows how D'Annunzio's texts inspired new gender archetypes, linguistic innovations, and contributed to the burgeoning sense of nationalism. Such political dynamics are also central to Arturo Larcati's chapter on 'Gabriele D'Annunzio and the Austrian Reception after Italy's Entry into the War', which demonstrates how D'Annunzio's German-language reception was impacted by fierce debates around his highly politicised persona. The Austrian literary establishment saw D'Annunzio as responsible for pushing Italy into war; however, the figure of Stefan Zweig stands out, Larcati argues, for his effort to separate the poetic merits of D'Annunzio as a writer from the politicised persona that critics like Hugo von Hofmannsthal railed against.

The fourth section of the book, 'Complex Legacies', expands this focus on reception to include a wider selection of case studies, attesting to the ways in which D'Annunzio's many afterlives are both shaped by and in turn contribute to shaping political and social dynamics informing twentieth-century literature. The first four chapters examine different geographical and linguistic contexts – the United States, Argentina, Russia and the Arab-speaking world – to trace the varied trajectories of his fortune, starting with the reception of D'Annunzio's works during and immediately after his lifetime and moving forward to illustrate shifts in his popularity and impact. The final two chapters focus on how D'Annunzio interfaces with specific figures in ways that reshape his legacy: in Yugoslavia-Croatia, looking at the Luxardo brand of brandy; and in Japan, examining the infamous author Yukio Mishima.

The section begins with the case of his shifting status in Argentina. In his chapter on 'D'Annunzio and Argentina: From Elitism to Mass Nationalism', Sandro Abate shows how important Argentinian literary culture was for the Spanish-language reception of D'Annunzio due to the sizeable Italian diaspora there and its connections to D'Annunzio during his lifetime. Abate delineates three phases in the Argentine reception from the 1890s through the Second World War, starting with his close connection to key figures including the anthropologist Guido Boggiani and Giovanni del Guzzo, and transforming with changing political dynamics in the country. Likewise, shifting political winds play a large role in the assessment that Guylian Nemegeer and Mara Santi offer in their chapter on 'Gabriele D'Annunzio in the United States: Politics and Stereotypes'. They argue that D'Annunzio's political notoriety helped his status in the US before the 1930s, as he featured as a political opinionist in American newspapers; however, a growing tendency to associate D'Annunzio with Fascism and to link his persona to negative stereotypes about Italians led to critical focus on the moral scandal attributed to him as a person rather than serious evaluation of the poetic qualities of his work. In 'D'Annunzio's Legacy in Post-Revolutionary Russia', the chapter by Elda Garetto and Sofia Lurie, another picture of shifting historical moments of reception and rejection emerges. They distinguish three periods in D'Annunzio's reception in Russia. While between 1900 and 1914 he was among the most translated European authors and a major influence on Russian Modernists as an Aesthete and poet-solider, by the 1930s he was much less prominent and his image had been reconceived to make him a spokesperson for the common people. After a long period of obscurity, the first decade of the new millennium gave rise to an unexpected revival of interest in D'Annunzio, depicting him as a 'winged cyclops' and reintroducing him in a new social and political context. Shifts in global geopolitics and critical trends likewise played a prominent role in the transforming view of D'Annunzio that characterises his reception in the Arab-speaking world, the topic of Hussein Mahmoud and Christine Samir Girgis's chapter 'From "Great Italian Poet" to "Fascist Writer": D'Annunzio and Arabic Culture'. This chapter examines how, despite D'Annunzio's endorsement of the wars in Libya and Ethiopia and a narrative style that Arabic journalists considered 'obscene', he was known in Egypt as 'the Great Italian Poet' until the late 1930s. That image was reshaped in the post-war years, when D'Annunzio was labelled a Fascist collaborator. However, a recent series of cultural events held in Egypt on the occasion of D'Annunzio's 150th anniversary suggest the possibility of another shift in this reception.

The final two chapters continue to address the political dimensions of D'Annunzio's complex legacy, turning to more localised cases. In his chapter on 'Morlach's Blood in Fiume's *Mensa*: D'Annunzio and the Intimate Adriatic', Russell Scott Valentino reconsiders Italy's long and troubled relationship with the independent territories that would become Yugoslavia by examining how the Luxardo brand crossed from Zara (present-day Zadar, Croatia) to Italy. Luxardo brandy, which labels itself with the loaded description 'Sangue Morlacco', features D'Annunzio's flowing signature on its bottles, tying their brand to the long afterlife of D'Annunzio's Fiume adventure and thus serving as a window onto D'Annunzio's perceived cultural authority, especially for Italians displaced from Istria and Dalmatia following the Second World War, as well as the stereotypes and cultural assumptions of Italians vis-a-vis their eastern neighbours. A similarly multifaceted story of authority and reception is visible in a very different case – that of the Japanese writer Yukio Mishima. In her chapter, 'Infatuated with *Il Vate*: Mishima's Transnational Mimesis of D'Annunzio', Ikuho Amano draws on Beebe's notion of 'transmesis' to consider Mishima's fascination with the writings and persona of D'Annunzio as a 'belated' instance of the Japanese response to D'Annunzio's Decadence. In this lens, she re-reads Mishima's attraction to the aesthetics of sensuality and violence in *Trionfo della morte* and his desire to transform the pacifist post-war politics of Japan, which led him to occupy the Ministry of Defence with a private army in a symbolic restaging of D'Annunzio's occupation of Fiume before then committing ritual suicide. Throughout these chapters, D'Annunzio emerges not only as a literary intertext but also as a political model, whose status shifted according to the historical context of reception while also influencing actors and objects within those contexts.

The volume concludes with a chapter that considers new developments in contemporary translations of D'Annunzio's work. The volume editors, Elisa Segnini and Michael Subialka, conducted a wide-ranging set of interviews with translators from across the globe, which provide the basis for the conversation in 'D'Annunzio in the Twenty-First Century'. Informed by the conceptual questions that emerge throughout the chapters in this volume – especially the political dynamics of D'Annunzio's work, questions of gender and questions of multilingual and intertextual complexity – this concluding conversation on translation shows that while D'Annunzio's legacy may indeed be complex and even in many moments troubled, it nevertheless continues to unfold in new directions and open new conversations about the place of Italian literature in global Decadence.

Part I

A Poetics of Fusion: Cultural Appropriation, Multilingualism, Translingual Writing

Chapter 1

D'Annunzio and the Greek and Latin Classics

Pietro Gibellini, translated by Stuart Oglethorpe

The three most celebrated poets of post-unification Italy – Giosuè Carducci, Giovanni Pascoli and Gabriele D'Annunzio – shared an openness towards new directions in European literature. Carducci was attracted to French and, especially, German writers, including Béranger and Heine; Pascoli had quickly recognised and often anticipated the innovations of Symbolist poetry, in particular its French strand; and D'Annunzio absorbed and gave fresh creative impetus to the thematic and linguistic ideas of the Decadent movement, using France as the launching pad for his international fame. For all three, this cosmopolitan vein coexisted with a sense of the modernity of the ancient world and a desire to return to Greek and Latin classics. All three engaged in translations or, as D'Annunzio called them, 'betrayals' (*tradimenti*); indeed his first book, *Primo vere* (1879), its Latinate title a reference to Carducci's poem 'Vere novo', included an appendix with versions of classical poems (fourteen from Horace, two from Catullus, one from Tibullus and four from the *Homeric Hymns*). Of the three, Pascoli was the most diligent and philologically skilled; he not only compiled classical anthologies (*Lyra* and *Epos*), but also composed poetry in Latin. For Carducci, the return to antiquity involved experimentation with classical metre in his '*metrica barbara*', something the young D'Annunzio also tried. First and foremost, however, it involved a view of the world: the Risorgimento nostalgia for the glories of Rome and a forceful, heroic neopaganism. In this regard, D'Annunzio situated himself as Carducci's heir, declaring himself to be the '*vate*' (bard) of the new Italy.

This chapter focuses on D'Annunzio's role as a *fin-de-siècle* classicist. It first investigates his library at the Vittoriale and then discusses classical echoes in *La città morta* (1898), *Fedra* (1909) and *Alcyone* (1903). This allows for an exploration of D'Annunzio's approach to translations from Latin and Greek, his use of Latin sources to revitalise Italian, classical references in his writing and the inspiration he found in Greek theatre to reconceive tragedy. While D'Annunzio's celebration of the ancient world was selective and based on his own political perspective, his interpretation of ancient Greece and Rome profoundly influenced his creative vision. This chapter illustrates how a rich dialogue with the classics shaped his concept of *Weltliteratur*.

Classics in the Vittoriale Library

Having completed his secondary education at the renowned Cicognini College in Prato, D'Annunzio enrolled in the Faculty of Literature at Rome's La Sapienza University. However, he barely attended lectures and quickly abandoned the pursuit of a degree; the few university teachers whom he later recalled with respect included the Romance philologist Ernesto Monaci and the Latin scholar Onorato Occioni. Yet his familiarity with Latin and Greek was never to fade. The library at the Vittoriale, the residence to which he withdrew in 1921, contained an abundance of works by classical authors. Some came from the collection of Henry Thode, a German art historian of the Renaissance and previous owner of the villa; meanwhile only parts of D'Annunzio's previous libraries, from the Capponcina and his house in Arcachon, made it to the Vittoriale.

D'Annunzio described himself in *Il libro segreto* (1935) as a '*bibliomante*', a neologism from the term '*rabdomante*' (diviner). He moved deftly through the thousands of pages in his library, aided by valuable reference works: Tommaseo's *Vocabolario* guided him on the Italian language and literature, while for Latin he turned to the *Totius Latinitatis Lexicon* in the 1839–1841 edition compiled by Egidio Forcellini. D'Annunzio's knowledge of classical literature was extensive and went beyond the better-known authors. His library is more illustrative of his re-readings than first readings, which occurred during his youth and early adulthood. The major works are often present in various editions, including the most respected European series. For Greek texts, he made use of convincing translations, like Vincenzo Monti's rendering of the *Iliad* or Felice Bellotti and Leconte de Lisle's versions of Greek tragedies, when he had them (as Ilvano Caliaro has shown in regard to *Fedra*).[1] In editions with

[1] Ilvano Caliaro, *D'Annunzio lettore-scrittore* (Florence: Olschki, 1991), pp. 11–31.

the original text and facing translation, page markings show that D'Annunzio, at least after the age of fifty-eight, preferred reading the translation, shifting his gaze and pencil to the original only at the points that most interested him. For problematic interpretations or passages that were noteworthy, he was able to check the original.

Details regarding the volumes of Ovid, D'Annunzio's best-loved Latin poet, illustrate the quantity, quality and use made of the classical texts in his library. Of the thirty-five editions on the villa's shelves, fourteen bear D'Annunzio's 'ex libris' bookplate, one that of Thode and three that of Leo Olschki. These rare books might have arrived as purchases or gifts, or as thanks for the rescue of part of the Capponcina library, which had been put up for auction to clear the poet's debts. A good number were valuable editions, including six from the sixteenth century; amongst these was the illustrated edition printed in Lyon in 1557, bearing a dedication to D'Annunzio from the *marchesa* Luisa Casati Stampa, his eccentric lover whom he described in *Contemplazione della morte* (1912) and *Il libro segreto* (1935).

Many of these books bear signs typical of D'Annunzio's reading: notes, underlining, vertical lines in the margin, annotated bits of paper, turned-down corners and dried flowers placed between the pages. Many such traces mark the large volumes of *Metamorphoses* translated into Italian by Arrigo Simintendi (Prato, 1846–1850) and the edition of Ovid's works published by Teubner, including *Tristia*, *Ibis*, *Epistulae ex Ponto* and *Fasti* (Leipzig, 1889). Simintendi's translation had a place on the writing desk in his meditation room, the 'Stanza del Lebbroso' (Room of the Leper), while the Teubner volume was in the 'Officina', his workroom. The placing of these books suggests that rereading Ovid continued to stimulate him in his old age, a supposition supported in at least two ways: first, D'Annunzio had written that cinema, of which he was an avid enthusiast, might employ its special effects to present the *Metamorphoses*; second, two enduring themes for the Vittoriale's ageing hermit, who was all but an exile there, were his celebration of the fatherland and diaristic reflections of sadness.[2]

Amongst the editions of Greek classics was the two-volume *Anthologie grècque*, edited by Friedrich Jacobs (Paris: Hachette, 1863), with works by the lyric poets, its pages marked by D'Annunzio's reading. Of sixteen volumes presenting the plays of

[2] On cinema: Gabriele D'Annunzio, 'Del cinematografo considerato come strumento di liberazione e come arte di trasfigurazione' [1914], in D'Annunzio, *Scritti giornalistici, II: 1889–1938*, ed. by Annamaria Andreoli and Giorgio Zanetti (Milan: Mondadori, 2003), pp. 668–74.

Euripides, four are German editions (three with Thode's bookplate, the fourth with a dedication to him by its editor); D'Annunzio had little or no knowledge of German and acquired few if any volumes in that language other than those coming from Thode. Surprisingly, two editions dedicated to D'Annunzio by Ettore Romagnoli – the 'Hellenist, contrapuntalist and poet' mentioned in *Il libro segreto*[3] – are partially uncut; however, these were published in 1911 and 1912, thus after D'Annunzio's study of Euripides' *Hippolytus the Wreath-Bearer* as he wrote *Fedra* (1909). The edition of Euripides' plays with the most marks is actually the version by Leconte de Lisle (Paris: Lemerre, 1884), while there are none in the version by Felice Bellotti (the Florentine edition of 1875).

Classical Echoes in D'Annunzio's Works

D'Annunzio's full command of Latin and Greek impacted the features of his own language. I am not referring to his syntax: the construction of long sentences rich in subordinate clauses, characteristic of centuries of Italian prose since Boccaccio and Bembo followed Cicero, was alien to D'Annunzio, whose sentence structure is usually more straightforward. His vocabulary, however, frequently employs Latinisms, both semantic and orthographic. The reader thus encounters the noun '*numero*' used in reference to the rhythm of prose, and spellings such as '*imagine*', '*ebro*' and '*transposizione*' (rather than '*immagine*', '*ebbro*' and '*trasposizione*'); there are countless similar examples. D'Annunzio's use of Graecisms was more limited and generally restricted to passages evoking ancient Greek civilisation and associated technical terms (for example, '*peltasti*', '*lebete*', '*porfirogenito*') or names he gave his lovers ('Corè', a young woman of statuesque beauty; 'Mélitta', fair as a bee and sweet as honey; 'Lachne', having delightfully downy cheeks, etc.). The corrections he made to Georges Hérelle's French translation of *La città morta* included replacing 'Achéron', the translator's rendering of 'Acheronte', with the Greek-like spelling 'Akheron'.[4] D'Annunzio's use of Graecisms such as these is in need of further exploration.[5]

3 Gabriele D'Annunzio, *Il libro segreto*, ed. by Pietro Gibellini (Milan: Rizzoli, 2010), p. 163. All Italian quotations in this chapter translated by Stuart Oglethorpe.

4 I have previously termed this 'linguistic archaeology': Pietro Gibellini, 'L'archeologia linguistica della "Città morta"', *Italianistica*, 5: 1 (1976), 88–92.

5 On D'Annunzio's classical culture, see Emilio Mariano, ed., *D'Annunzio e il classicismo (Quaderni del Vittoriale, 23)* (Gardone Riviera: Fondazione del Vittoriale degli Italiani, 1980).

D'Annunzio's writings, especially in prose, abound with Latin quotations and sayings, particularly in his patriotic oratory. While the books of verse dedicated to the conquest of Libya (*Merope. Canzoni della guerra d'oltremare*, 1912) and the Great War (*Asterope. Canti della guerra latina*, 1915–1918) evoked Carolingian epic and anti-German brotherhood, his writings for the Abyssinian campaign (*Teneo te Africa*, 1936) took Julius Caesar's Latin motto for their title. This presented the *Duce* and the King, celebrated in the hugely popular song 'Faccetta nera' by Renato Micheli and Mario Ruccione, as a reincarnation of the Roman leader.[6] Likewise references and quotations in Italian from the Greek poets abound; *La città morta*, for example, opens with a translated passage from Sophocles' *Antigone*, while its title page features an epigraph in Greek lettering from the same play: ''Ερως ἀνίκατε μάχαν' ('Eros, unconquered in strife').[7] There are also many quotations in Greek, as in the erotic poem 'Carmen votivum' (1927, and included in *Il libro segreto*), scattered with fragments from the Greek poets initially written in Latin script and then replaced, in handwriting, by Greek lettering. Notable among these are the words 'ἀλλὰ πᾶν τόλματον' from the final line of 'Φαίνεταί μοι', the famous poem fragment by Sappho that Pseudo-Longinus cited as an example of stylistic excellence.[8] In his Latin version of Sappho's poem, Catullus translated the phrase as 'sed omnia, perferendum' (but everything must be endured), rendering it as a final exhortation, primarily to himself, to withstand the sufferings of love. In contrast, D'Annunzio's short poem interprets the phrase as encouragement of erotic boldness (but everything must be dared), revealing the difference between the Latin poet's moral vision of love and the modern poet's athletic one.[9]

D'Annunzio's 'Greek mind', a term he uses to describe his erotic stance before a lover in the 'Carmen votivum', as well as his Latin one, is especially apparent in *Il libro segreto*, where for instance he describes having known the 'true Greece' before ever travelling there

[6] See Lorenzo Braccesi, *L'antichità aggredita. Memoria del passato e poesia del nazionalismo* (Rome: L'Erma di Bretschneider, 1989).

[7] Gabriele D'Annunzio, *La città morta* (Milan: Treves, 1898), title page.

[8] The poem is also known as 'Fragment 31' (from the Voigt numbering system) and is widely available in translation. Saffo, *Frammenti*, ed. by Antonio Aloni (Florence: Giunti, 1997), fr. 22; Sappho, *Stung with Love: Poems and Fragments*, ed. and trans. by Aaron Poochigian (London: Penguin, 2009), p. 23.

[9] Catullo, *Le poesie*, ed. by Guido Ceronetti (Turin: Einaudi, 1969), poem number 51.

in his trip of 1895.[10] That trip led to his plan to reinvigorate tragedy, articulated later in *Il fuoco* (1900) by its protagonist Stelio Effrena, and launched with the writing of *La città morta* (1898) and substantial parts of *Maia* (1903), the first volume of D'Annunzio's *Laudi*. Meanwhile, another passage in *Il libro segreto* connects his interest in Greek to a broader *Weltliteratur*:

> If humanism is but the art of becoming man beyond the human [. . .], if humanism is but the art of constructing one's own self by becoming the creator of one's own spirit, one's own mental creator, then I am the supreme humanist, because I had the patience and the perseverance to live in communion of spirit with the entire sum of human experience, with the intellectual and moral accumulation preserved for us by Greek, Latin, Italian, and French literature.[11]

This humanism involves a desire for the total fulfilment of human existence, nurtured and realised by contact with four branches of literature, two ancient (Greek and Latin) and two modern (Italian and French). D'Annunzio's *Weltliteratur* involved reading, aided by translations, spanning English and Anglo-American, German and Russian literature; good knowledge of the Bible, including the apocrypha; and sporadic expeditions to the ancient regions of India and Persia, and as far as Japan; however, the essential terrain remained the four areas specified in this passage on humanism.[12]

We therefore need to address the issue of D'Annunzio's *Weltanschauung*, his vision of civilisation going beyond language and sources. In regard to ancient Rome, he especially celebrated its conquering and civilising energy, sentiments prominent in the mainstream of Italy's Risorgimento as well as the nationalism, irredentism and – unfortunately – imperialism of the nineteenth and twentieth centuries. In *Il Piacere* (1889), D'Annunzio already challenged the

[10] D'Annunzio, *Il libro segreto*, p. 341.

[11] Ibid., p. 343.

[12] D'Annunzio's interest in foreign literature has been widely studied in various edited collections: *D'Annunzio e il simbolismo europeo*, ed. by Emilio Mariano (Milan: Il Saggiatore, 1976); *Gabriele d'Annunzio nelle culture dei paesi slavi* (*Quaderni del Vittoriale*, 7) (Gardone Riviera: Fondazione del Vittoriale degli Italiani, 1978); *D'Annunzio e la cultura germanica* (Pescara: Centro nazionale di studi dannunziani, 1985); *D'Annunzio europeo*, ed. by Pietro Gibellini (Rome: Lucarini, 1991); *D'Annunzio a cinquant'anni dalla morte* (Pescara: Centro nazionale di studi dannunziani, 1989); Guy Tosi, *D'Annunzio e la cultura francese. Saggi e studi (1942–1987)*, 2 vols, ed. by Maddalena Rasera (Lanciano: Carabba, 2013).

stunted Italietta (little Italy) of the bourgeoisie and 'Byzantine', Aestheticist Rome; the delusional protagonist of *Le vergini delle rocce* (1895) cherishes the dream of siring a new 'King of Rome' to renew the heroic deeds of the *caput mundi*; and in *Elettra* (1903) he celebrated the heroes doing their utmost to restore their country's ancient glory. Increasingly, he exalted not the Baroque Rome of *Il Piacere* but rather the imperial city built by Julius Caesar, while republican Rome remained in the background; D'Annunzio extolled only the martial aspects of the ancient traditions, which were prerequisites of the will to power connected to his vision of the superman. In regard to ancient Greece, he primarily celebrated the absolute worship of beauty; the democratic ideals of the city-state were of little interest to him, and the figure he most admired, apart from the poets, was the conquering ruler Alexander. Carlo Diano has used the figures most loved by D'Annunzio to encapsulate his vision of Greek civilisation: among men, the daring and unconventional Alcibiades; among heroes, Odysseus, the explorer and warrior; and among gods, Hermes, the mercurial champion of dynamism and seizing the fleeting moment of opportunity.[13]

Space only permits me to single out the writers who had the most impact on D'Annunzio here. Amongst his Greek influences, we must mention Homer and the so-called *Homeric Hymns* and *Orphic Hymns*, which played an important part in the genesis of the *Laudi* cycle. Hesiod was also significant: a passage sparked the idea of titling each of the *Laudi* volumes based on the constellation of the Pleiades, which both guides sailors and regulates the agricultural calendar.[14] Greek historians, essayists and biographers including Herodotus, Xenophon, Pausanias and Plutarch, were also important; but poets such as Theocritus and Callimachus seem to have exerted less influence. In addition, D'Annunzio consulted the Septuagint (Greek Old Testament) for his quasi-blasphemous rewriting of the Gospel in

[13] Carlo Diano, 'D'Annunzio e l'Ellade', in *L'arte di Gabriele d'Annunzio*, ed. by Emilio Mariano (Milan: Mondadori, 1968), pp. 51–67. See also Emilio Mariano, 'D'Annunzio e la Grecia', *Il Verri*, 7–8 (1985), 48–76; Pietro Gibellini, *Logos e mythos. Studi su Gabriele d'Annunzio* (Florence: Olschki, 1985); Sabino Caronia, 'Gabriele d'Annunzio. "Torna con me nell'Ellade scolpita"', in *Il mito nella letteratura italiana, III: Dal neoclassicismo al decadentismo*, ed. by Raffaella Bertazzoli (Brescia: Morcelliana, 2003), pp. 293–332; Guerri, Giordano Bruno, ed., *Da Ovidio a D'Annunzio. Miti di metamorfosi e metamorfosi dei miti* (Cinisello Balsamo: Silvana, 2019).

[14] Gabriele D'Annunzio, *Alcyone*, ed. by Pietro Gibellini, with commentary by Giulia Belletti, Sara Campardo and Enrica Gambin (Venice: Marsilio, 2018).

'Il Vangelo secondo l'Avversario' (in the second volume of *Le Faville del maglio*, 1928).

From Latin literature, Ovid particularly stands out; he is the most obvious influence in D'Annunzio's *Alcyone*. Ovid was favoured not only because of their shared origins in the Abruzzo but also because of their alignment in content and form: both share the contrast between eroticism and melancholy, intense mythological imagination, celebration of the glories of the fatherland, richness of vocabulary and musical style. Ovid was followed by Virgil. While Ovid's *Metamorphoses* generated the subjects and titles of three poems in *Alcyone* ('Terra, vale!', 'Stabat nuda Aestas' and 'Altius egit iter'), Virgil's *Aeneid* was the source for a fourth ('Furit aestus'). D'Annunzio was less attracted to Horace, whose moderateness did not suit him, drawn as he was to pushing beyond customary limits; Horace's gentle satire was a far cry from his bombastic propensities. The elegiac poets Propertius and Catullus were of some importance, while the part played by prose writers was less significant, with the exception of Saint Augustine: the 'neopagan' D'Annunzio was an attentive and responsive reader, and not just of the *Confessions*, which he valued highly as a memoirist in his more introspective late period.

Space in this chapter does not allow for a full account of the classical themes and echoes within D'Annunzio's vast output; in any case, we already have a substantial range of analyses that offer an excellent review of his classical references as a writer and, especially, as a poet. In this regard, we should acknowledge the annotation of D'Annunzio's poetry undertaken by Enzo Palmieri in the 1940s and 1950s; the commentary in the 'Meridiani' series drew on this pioneering work, though without sufficient recognition.[15] I will focus here on the cases that best illustrate the theme of this chapter: *La città morta*, *Fedra* and *Alcyone*.

La città morta *and Classical Renewal*

D'Annunzio's trip to Greece in 1895 marked a turning point in his intellectual and artistic career. This journey is well documented, both

[15] The collections of poetry by D'Annunzio edited by Enzo Palmieri and published by Zanichelli (Bologna) are: *Primo vere, Canto novo, Intermezzo* (1953); *L'Isottèo, La Chimera* (1955); *Elegie romane, Poema paradisiaco, Odi navali* (1959); and the five volumes in the *Laudi* cyle, *Maia* (1941), *Elettra* (1943), *Alcyone* (1944), *Merope* (1945) and *Asterope* (1964). For the 'Meridiani' series, see Gabriele D'Annunzio, *Versi d'amore e di gloria*, 2 vols, ed. by Annamaria Andreoli and Niva Lorenzini (Milan: Mondadori, 1982–1984).

in D'Annunzio's own notebooks and in the diaries of two friends who accompanied him on Edoardo Scarfoglio's yacht: Guido Boggiani, an anthropologist, and Georges Hérelle, his French translator. The poet loaded the craft with so many volumes of Greek classics – epics, tragedies, poetry and history, but no philosophy – that it sat dangerously low in the water.[16]

Episodes from this trip were reworked in the poetry of *Maia* under a classical lens: the encounter with a solitary yachtsman made D'Annunzio imagine that he had met Ulysses, and the prostitute at the brothel he rushed to straight after arriving in Piraeus was reinvented as a faded Helen, returned to Greece after the burning of Troy. D'Annunzio also brought Charles Diehl's *Excursions archéologiques en Grèce*, and his experience of the so-called 'tombs of the Atreides', discovered amongst the ruins of Mycenae by Heinrich Schliemann, inspired the composition of his first tragedy, *La città morta*. However, during this period D'Annunzio's most crucial reading was of Friedrich Nietzsche, who he first discovered through texts in French.[17]

Nietzsche's vision of the dialectic between Apollo and Dionysus as a fundamental opposition within Hellenic culture led D'Annunzio to reinvigorate his classicism, which had previously been aligned with neoclassical, Carduccian and Parnassian perspectives.[18] His discovery of the instinctual drives transformed a Greek classicism that had been stuck in the mould of harmony, moderation and rationality. Although D'Annunzio described himself as 'Nietzschean' in a letter to his friend Vincenzo Morello before he had really read him, Nietzsche's work was to later exert an important influence on him.

D'Annunzio was now enthused by the idea of restoring tragedy, which had been largely sidelined in favour of romanticist and naturalist theatre during the nineteenth century: he envisaged a theatre with the spirit of a sacred festival, presented in the open air to the whole populace, with spoken verse as the basis of its expression of beauty. As a result, D'Annunzio's plays had limited success on the stage but were well suited to being read. At the turn of the century, he dreamed of restoring and relaunching the Roman amphitheatre of Albano; he returned to this idea at the Vittoriale, where he planned

16 Guy Tosi, *D'Annunzio en Grèce. Laus Vitae et la croisière de 1895* (Paris: Calmann-Lévy, 1947).

17 Guy Tosi, 'D'Annunzio découvre Nietzsche (1892–1894)', *Italianistica*, 2: 3 (1973), 481–513.

18 See Friedrich Nietzsche, *The Birth of Tragedy*, trans. and ed. by Douglas Smith (Oxford: Oxford University Press, 2000). First published in German in 1872, it appeared in French translation by 1886.

an open-air theatre in the classical tradition – though that plan only came to fruition after his death. His essential notion, consonant with Nietzsche's antihistoricism, was that beneath the semblance of historical progress persist the powerful and unchanging instincts of our forebears, which have always stirred the human heart and influenced behaviour: competition for power and sex, jealousy and hate both within and between families, and incestuous passion. Sigmund Freud was moving in substantially the same direction, looking for the archetypes of his 'complexes' in Greek myth (notably in *Oedipus* and *Electra*).

In *La città morta*, D'Annunzio imagined an archaeologist like Schliemann, but more learned and aristocratic, who discovers the royal tombs of Mycenae and the golden masks of the Atreides dynasty; however, in addition to disturbing the dust of millennia, the excavation removes the boundary between past and present, and as a result the ancient curses that had afflicted the Atreides, a family tainted with murder and incest, resurface. The archaeologist falls in love with his poet friend's young sister; the archaeologist's wife, who is blind but clairvoyant, becomes aware of this cruel and unavoidable fate; the poet, however, stands in its way and in order to spare his friend the dishonour of adultery (but also driven by jealousy), kills his sister, for whom he harbours an incestuous passion. This deed distinguishes the modern hero from his classical counterparts: the former is at least in part able to challenge destiny. However, D'Annunzio's protagonists, as he wrote in a letter to the actress Sarah Bernhardt, have the titanic power of Aeschylus' and Sophocles' creations, but also the lightness of renderings by travelling actors; like the characters in Greek theatre, they are spectral figures and more symbols than real people.[19]

Fedra *and World Literature*

D'Annunzio took on Greek mythology once again in his verse tragedy *Fedra* (1909), rewriting and altering the story of Theseus's wife. Traditionally, the protagonist is languishing with love for her stepson Hippolytus, who pushes her away in horror when he learns of this illicit passion. Phaedra decides to kill herself, but not without leaving a message in which she accuses Hippolytus of having tried to seduce her.

[19] Fondazione Il Vittoriale degli Italiani, Archivio, ms. n. 685, letter from Gabriele D'Annunzio to Sarah Bernhardt. For excerpts, see Gibellini, *Logos e Mythos*, p. 243.

In consequence, Theseus curses Hippolytus, the curse is heard by Poseidon–Neptune, and the final outcome is the death of Theseus's innocent son. D'Annunzio's version, however, envisions significant changes that reveal his fusion of different times and traditions.[20]

This story inspired works by great writers of both the remote and recent past: the Greek tragedy by Euripides (though his title, *Hippolytus the Wreath-Bearer*, showcased the male protagonist); one of Ovid's *Heroides*, featuring a letter from Phaedra to Hippolytus; a tragedy by Seneca; another by Racine; and a dramatic poem by Algernon Swinburne, which D'Annunzio read in French translation. All these texts were taken into consideration by the poet, whose vision of *Weltliteratur* was bounded by neither time nor language. In his customary fusion of material from different sources, D'Annunzio used not just the thematic and linguistic suggestions of these five rewritings of the myth of Phaedra, but added further classical elements. He drew on a range of episodes from Aeschylus's *Seven Against Thebes*, Euripides' *The Suppliants* and *The Phoenician Women*, and Sophocles' *Oedipus* plays; he also consulted scholarly sources for descriptions of the ancient Mediterranean (Pausanias) and precise equestrian terminology (Xenophon). For D'Annunzio's account of Capaneus being struck by a thunderbolt from Zeus while scaling the walls of Thebes, he even drew liberally on another version, Dante's *Inferno*.

The transcultural character of D'Annunzio's practice involved drawing from a range of sources that also varied in type. When interviewed in 1909 by the *Corriere della Sera*, he located the origins of his tragedy in the excavations conducted by Arthur Evans on Crete: in 1903, they inspired him to compose the fourth 'Ditirambo' (a sort of rhetorical address) in *Alcyone*, dedicated to the myth of Icarus; and they prompted his interest in the labyrinth, which featured both on the cover and in the text of his novel *Forse che sì forse che no* (1910), written at much the same time as *Fedra*.[21] Another type of source was the aria 'Divinités du Styx' from Gluck's opera *Alceste*; this gave D'Annunzio the idea of making his heroine a devotee of the gods of the underworld revered on Crete, in contrast to the gods of Olympus

[20] Gabriele D'Annunzio, *Fedra*, ed. by Pietro Gibellini with notes by Tiziana Piras (Milan: Mondadori, 2001). See also: *Fedra da Euripide a D'Annunzio*, *Quaderni Dannunziani*, n.s., 5–6 (1989) and *Verso l'Ellade. Dalla 'Città morta' a 'Maia'* (Pescara: Centro nazionale di studi dannunziani, 1995).

[21] Renato Simoni, [Interview with Gabriele D'Annunzio], *Corriere della Sera*, 9 April 1909.

associated with the Athenian Theseus. Likewise, D'Annunzio declared his admiration for Racine and quoted his famous line 'C'est Venus tout entière à sa proie attachèe' (It's Venus entire latched onto her prey).[22] However, he wanted to restore the pagan flesh and blood of Euripides' heroine; he felt that Racine's version was dressed in the style of Louis XIV's court and cloaked in Christian values.

D'Annunzio made radical changes to the character that had featured in previous versions, including that of Euripides. In the myth, Phaedra is the innocent victim of Aphrodite–Venus, who is enraged because the young Hippolytus devotes himself exclusively to hunting, revering the chaste Artemis–Diana and spurning love; Aphrodite–Venus gets her revenge by making Hippolytus's stepmother fall in love with him. In the Greek, Latin and French tragedies Phaedra endures her unmentionable passion and would let herself die but for the intervention of her nurse, who takes pity and encourages Phaedra to reveal her feelings to the young man; despairing over his rejection, but also offended by the scorn he shows toward her and the entire female sex, she decides to kill herself, and redirects the accusation of incestuous passion back at Hippolytus. D'Annunzio instead makes his Phaedra (Fedra) a sort of female superman: she brazenly reveals her desire to Hippolytus; she justifies it with moral and practical reasons drawn from Ovid, namely that she is his stepmother not his mother and that their belonging to the same household will allow the affair to proceed unsuspected; she displays a sensuality in the spirit of Swinburne; she openly declares that she has been assaulted by Hippolytus and after the latter's death reproaches Theseus for having betrayed her sister Ariadne; and she proudly lays claim to her royal Cretan dynasty, despised by the Greeks, boldly worshipping the underworld gods and not those of Olympus. The tragedy concludes with Phaedra, having taken poison, picking up the dead body of Hippolytus to cross over into the next world; there, she may be able to unite with him in an ambiguous embrace, resurrecting the example of the wife of Capaneus, who had climbed onto the pyre where his body was burning as if onto their marital bed. Phaedra is proud of having held to her goddess and her fate, a feature that distinguishes the classical tragedy from the modern; this distinction was the subject of Paul de Saint-Victor's *Les deux masques*, a weighty study whose Paris edition of 1889–1894 was read and annotated by D'Annunzio prior to drafting *Fedra*.

[22] Jean Racine, *Phèdre*, ed. by Boris Donné (Paris: Flammarion, 2019), Act I, v. 306.

It has been rightly argued that D'Annunzio's Phaedra embodies a female elaboration of the 'superman'.[23] Alongside the strong correspondence with Nietzsche, however, the influence of the philologist Ulrich von Wilamowitz-Moellendorff, a critic of Nietzsche's, can also be detected. One indication of D'Annunzio's philological sensibilities is visible in a significant detail. Prior to his tragedy *Hippolytus the Wreath-Bearer*, Euripides had used the same myth in his *Hippolytus Veiled*. This earlier play provoked a scandal, presumably for moralistic reasons – perhaps because of an explicit confession by Phaedra or a kiss on stage. For this reason, Euripides wrote the *Wreath-Bearer* (which survives), while the *Veiled* was lost. The two titles refer, respectively, to the laurels placed on the statue of Hippolytus in the small temple dedicated to him, and the veil the young man drew across his face to conceal his agitation over his stepmother's proposed affair. The earlier tradition of the veil is restored in D'Annunzio's rewriting, as seen in Phaedra's lines in the final scene:

> Sola
> io porterò su le mie braccia d'ombra
> Ippolito *velato* all'Invisibile.[24]
> (I, alone, / will carry in my protective arms / the *veiled* Hippolytus into the Hereafter.)

She subsequently addresses Aphrodite:

> O dea,
> tu non hai più potenza.
> Spenti sono i tuoi fuochi. Un fuoco bianco
> io porto all'Ade. Ippolito
> io l'ho *velato* perché l'amo.[25]
> (O goddess / You no longer have strength. / Your fires are extinguished. A white fire / I bring to Hades. I have *veiled* / Hippolytus because I love him.)

The veil over Hippolytus is mentioned one further time:

> *Velato* all'Invisibile
> lo porterò su le mie braccia azzurre,
> perché l'amo.[26]

23 Eurialo De Michelis, *Guida a D'Annunzio* (Turin: Meynier, 1988), pp. 313–16.
24 D'Annunzio, *Fedra*, lines 3147–9 (emphasis added).
25 Ibid., lines 3165–9 (emphasis added).
26 Ibid., lines 3209–11 (emphasis added).

(I will bear him *veiled* / in my blue-veined arms into the Hereafter, / because I love him.)

What this suggests is that D'Annunzio probably wanted to reinvigorate the original lost tragedy and scandalise the audience once again.

Alcyone

My final example, *Alcyone*, has been seen as the high point of D'Annunzio's verse production and a cardinal work of twentieth-century Italian poetry. This collection, which includes some of his most well-known poems (for example 'La sera fiesolana', 'La pioggia nel pineto', 'I pastori'), was dated 1904 but actually appeared in December 1903 together with *Elettra*, only a few months after publication of the first book in the *Laudi* cycle, *Maia*. Much of *Alcyone* was dedicated to the re-examination of classical Greece inspired by D'Annunzio's trip of 1895. A substantial part was composed in the summer of 1902, and it was described by Sergio Solmi as 'the poetical diary of a summer on the sea'.[27] In reality, as I have shown elsewhere, the volume pulled together texts that had gradually accumulated between 1899 and 1903.[28] However, they were now organised within a structure that transformed D'Annunzio's personal experiences into phases of an archetypal trajectory. This was not only a fictionalised version of his stays in Tuscany and Rome with Eleonora Duse, but also a voyage into mythology, following a temporal arc running from the end of spring to the beginning of autumn, passing through the explosion of summer, within the notional year to which the poems refer. The approach, experience and loss of the embodiment of Summer, and with this the atmosphere of myth, are the three essential phases of the book. Justifiably, D'Annunzio preferred to use the word 'poema' (a long or epic poem) for this collection, whose shorter poems can be appreciated on their own but are located within a strongly structured ensemble. The voyage into mythology also signifies a voyage into classicism, to the extent that the work has been

[27] Sergio Solmi, 'L'"Alcyone" e noi', *Letteratura*, 3 (1939), 3–12 (pp. 6–7), reprinted in *Scrittori negli anni. Saggi e note sulla letteratura italiana del '900* (Milan: Il Saggiatore, 1963), pp. 179–91.

[28] Pietro Gibellini, 'Per la cronologia di "Alcione"', *Studi di filologia italiana*, 33 (1975), 393–424; 'La storia di "Alcyone"', in Gibellini, *Logos e mythos*, pp. 31–84.

appropriately described by Diego Valeri as a 'new *Metamorphoses*', not least because the classical author most referenced is Ovid.[29]

We can pick out some significant passages among the many references to classical culture to summarise the broader collection. The opening text, 'La tregua' ('The Truce'), represents a departure from the previous book, *Elettra*, which addressed the celebration of heroes, and announces the idyllic and pastoral register of the new volume. The real introduction to *Alcyone* is the second poem, 'Il fanciullo' ('The Youth'), where D'Annunzio presents his *ars poetica*. While Pascoli, in a prose piece just a few years earlier, had presented the *fanciullino* as the child within the poet's soul who retains the capacity to be amazed by the simplest of things, D'Annunzio's *fanciullo*, a 'nudo fanciul pagano' (naked pagan youth), is a flautist combining features of Hermes and Orpheus.[30] This youth can bewitch animals with the sound of his flute, made from two reeds, with which he plays two types of melody, one of light and one of shadow, reflecting the poet's contrasting propensities: radiant and dark, dynamic and melancholic. He has taken the reeds from the garden of a faun, or perhaps from the Orti Oricellari, the garden at the heart of the Florentine Renaissance, in a form of cultural encroachment:

> quando di Grecia le Sirene eterne
> venner con Plato alla Città dei Fiori.[31]
> (when the eternal Sirens of Greece / came with Plato to the City of Flowers.)

Later on, the poet begs the youth to return with him to Greece:

> nell'Ellade scolpita
> ove la pietra è figlia della luce
> e sostanza dell'aere è il pensiere.[32]
> (to sculpturesque Hellas / where the stone is a daughter of the light / and thought is the essence of the air.)

[29] See Diego Valeri, 'L'"Alcyone" o le nuove metamorfosi', in *L'arte di Gabriele d'Annunzio*, ed. by Emilio Mariano (Milan: Mondadori, 1968), pp. 173–9. For a critical interpretation of *Alcyone* see Pietro Gibellini, 'Introduzione', in D'Annunzio, *Alcyone*, pp. 17–42, and the conference proceedings *Da Foscarina a Ermione. 'Alcyone': prodromi, officina, poesia, fortuna* (Pescara: Centro nazionale di studi dannunziani, 2000).

[30] 'Il fanciullo', line 32, in D'Annunzio, *Alcyone*, p. 104.

[31] Ibid., lines 23–4.

[32] Ibid., lines 178–80.

To hold back the youth, who is on the point of leaving, he promises to rebuild the ruined pagan temple, taking up the image and words of Nietzsche to announce the death of Pan and the ancient world. However, the youth disappears over the horizon, either merging into the stars or turning into some other life form. The seven ballads in which the figure of the *fanciullo* is laid out clearly trace the arc of the whole collection: the aspiration to rebuild the pagan temple and to revive the mythological dimension, which is fulfilled in the manifestation of Summer as a gigantic naked goddess, and the loss of this dimension with the autumn, when the poet visits the ruins of ancient Rome. The city's modern residents, and the modern world in general, have only this archaeological legacy of the classical world, having lost the imagination and beliefs of their forebearers; however, poetic imagination can give it new life.

As the seasons progress, the connection with mythology develops. The Tuscan landscape is compared to the Greek in 'A Gorgo', part of the poem 'Corona di Glauco', whose title references the anthology compiled by Meleager, known in Italian as 'La corona' ('The Garland'). Myth also, and especially, means metamorphosis: adapting Ovid's model for his own purposes, D'Annunzio converts the fisherman Glauco into a sea god in the second 'Ditirambo'; he transforms Daphne into a laurel tree in 'Oleandro' (although this Daphne, unlike the classical model, begs Apollo to stop her transmutation so that he can take carnal advantage of her); and he and Ermione themselves become like trees when they enter the enchanted space of the pine forest, whose denizens have become a magical orchestra in the rain.[33] In the fourth 'Ditirambo' D'Annunzio reworks the story of Daedalus and Icarus from Ovid's poem, peppering it with references to the original text. For example, in Ovid the father warns his son to avoid damaging his feathered wings, held together with wax, by flying at mid-level:

> 'Medio' que 'ut limite curras,
> Icare,' ait 'moneo, ne, si demissior ibis,
> unda gravet pennas, si celsior, ignis adurat'.

[33] Glauco appears in *Alcyone* again, in the eclogue 'Bocca di Serchio', where D'Annunzio takes this name for himself and calls his son 'Ardi' (a name used in Greek and Latin pastoral poetry).

In D'Annunzio's elegant transposition, the Latin ablative 'medio limite' is taken as it is and reused in a somewhat affected but formally correct Italian phrase:

> Giova nel medio limite volare;
> ché, se tu voli basso, l'acqua aggreva
> le penne, se alto voli, te le incende
> il fuoco.[34]
>
> (Best to fly within the middle range; / because if you fly low, the water will weigh down / your feathers, and if you fly high, the fire / will set them aflame.)

The major deities of Olympus do not appear in *Alcyone*; instead, we see the lesser gods, who were also the protagonists in Henri de Régnier's earlier collection *Les Jeux rustiques et divins* (1897). We encounter characters who reflect D'Annunzio's nature worship and scholarship on the relationship between botany and mythology: the dryad whom the poet hoists onto his horse in 'La corona di Glauco', the scaly triton prostrate on the sand ('Il tritone'), the centaur thirsting for wine ('Il Tessalo'), the little satyr swimming in the river ('L'otre') and the faun from whom the poet learns of the death of his beloved Summer ('Gli indizii').

Some compelling and freshly invented fables stand out. There is the dramatic fight between the deer and the centaur ('La morte del cervo'), a sensual encounter with the wood nymph whose fleshly body breaks through her bark to seduce the poet ('Versilia') and the naiad, for whom the ripples of the waves are like musical notes ('Undulna'). Then, the end of summer marks leaving not only the Tuscan coast, but also the mythical and classical world that landscape evoked. The focus of D'Annunzio's classicism shifts from nature to culture, and in this shift the goddess of modernity, 'Melancolìa', emerges. Heralded toward the end of 'Il fanciullo' and in 'L'oleandro', this takes the form of nostalgia in 'Sogni di terre lontane' ('Dreams of Faraway Lands') and is at the same time a yearning for the distant past. D'Annunzio, with Eleonora Duse transmuted into Ermione, has flattered himself that he can recreate the miracle of the perfect halcyon summer in a timeless dimension; in September, however, an archaeological tour leaves this dream in ruins, so to speak. D'Annunzio's vision of the unrestrained pleasures of the Tuscan coast at the end of summer went much further than the inventive reworking of a seaside holiday;

[34] 'Ditirambo IV', in D'Annunzio, *Alycone*, lines 496–499.

it marked the passage from the imaginative vitality of the writers of antiquity to the melancholy and erudition of their modern counterparts. This break had been expressed, in other ways, by Schiller in his essay *On Naïve and Sentimental Poetry*, in Leopardi's poem 'Alla primavera' and in Baudelaire's 'Voyage to Cythera'.

D'Annunzio initially considered dedicating the book to Carducci but decided instead on Pascoli, describing his friend and rival in the poem 'Il commiato' as the last son of Virgil. In 'La vittoria navale', the sonnet that introduces poems relating to the arrival of September, the harvest, and the Dionysian revelry that goes with it, the poet offers this contrasting description of himself:

> Io son l'ultimo figlio degli Elleni:
> m'abbeverai alla mammella antica;
> ma d'un igneo dèmone son ebro.[35]
> (I am the last child of the Hellenes: / I drank from the ancient breast; / but I am inflamed by the fiery demon within.)

The decision to dedicate the book to Pascoli rather than Carducci must have been influenced by D'Annunzio's awareness of the more modern manner in which both he and Pascoli were reinterpreting classicism. These disciples of Carducci had both found their own voice, although D'Annunzio emphasised the differences in their approach to antiquity: Pascoli was Virgilian and more receptive to the Romans, while he was Dionysian and more in tune with the Greeks.

After the poetry of *Maia* and *Alcyone* and the tragedies *La città morta* and *Fedra*, D'Annunzio wrote no further works in which classical culture played such an important part. Other than in the patriotic compositions dedicated to the conquest of Libya and the Great War, his voice as a poet was largely stilled, with some fragments of verse collected in *Il libro segreto*, allowing us to use the term 'prosimetrum', derived from post-classical Latin, to describe this work. During the first two decades of the new century, D'Annunzio shifted away from the 'prosa di romanzo' (prose of the novel) – stories in which the author hides behind the protagonist's mask – and toward the 'prosa di ricerca' (prose of enquiry), in which he expressed himself directly. The latter was essentially split between introspective writing of an autobiographical or imaginative nature and celebratory, patriotic oratory. In the first category, references to Greek and Latin literature are somewhat limited, while in the second Latin is primarily

[35] 'La vittoria navale', in D'Annunzio, *Alcyone*, lines 12–14.

used to offer sayings (such as *Quis cintra nos?*, *Semper adamas* and *Memento audere semper*). The case that stands on its own is *Il libro segreto*, D'Annunzio's last important piece of writing, long ignored or underrated by critics. In this work, which consists of a selection of notes and fragments penned over the previous fifteen years – many of them including reflections on aesthetics – he renewed his earlier relationship with the ancient world. Among D'Annunzio's numerous classical references, often linked either to personal memories or his erudite spirit of curiosity, frequent mentions of the beauty of form were now prominent, especially in regard to metrics: the naked body of his lover is as perfect as a Greek ode, for example. In its rhythm and prosody, his writing in this twilight period surpasses the best examples from antiquity. The classical legacy that the elderly and melancholic gentleman of the Vittoriale most acknowledged and admired seems to have been that of a purely aesthetic nature.

Conclusion

This chapter has provided an overview of Gabriele D'Annunzio's classical learning, recognising that his knowledge of Greek and Latin literature, alongside that of Italy and France, was fundamental to his conception of humanism. I hope to have given some sense of D'Annunzio's linguistic competences: his thorough knowledge of classical languages and his familiarity with French. Although the poet was able to consult the original texts, translations into the latter language meant that it became a 'mediator' of the classical world. The preference that D'Annunzio gave these two classical literatures and two of their neo-Latin counterparts clarifies his geo-literary vision: the centre of gravity of his Europe was Mediterranean and Latin. Greek and Latin culture provided his neopagan ideology and worship of beauty. In the thinking of both D'Annunzio the artist and the soldier-poet, convinced of the enduring modernity of the ancient world, the sister nations of glorious Italy and gentle France had taken on this classical heritage and were now responsible for transmitting it to his contemporaries.

Chapter 2

D'Annunzio and Japonism

Mariko Muramatsu

> The words *lontano*, *antico*, and the like are very poetic and pleasurable because they evoke vast, indefinite, indeterminable, and indistinct ideas.
> (Giacomo Leopardi, *Zibaldone*)[1]

This chapter studies references to Japanese culture and literature in Gabriele D'Annunzio's poetry. It explores how Japonism, a cultural phenomenon that swept through Europe at the end of the nineteenth century, was absorbed by D'Annunzio and reflected in his lyrics. To this end, I begin by tracking traces of Japan at D'Annunzio's villa-museum, the Vittoriale. I then turn to D'Annunzio's early writings and examine how they portray and interpret the fascination with Japan. The main focus of my analysis is 'Outa occidentale', a poem by D'Annunzio written in Italian with adapted Japanese metrics. This poem was first published on 14 June 1885 in *Fanfulla della domenica*, on the same day as D'Annunzio's review of an anthology of Japanese poems by Judith Gautier, *Poémes de la libellule*. 'Outa occidentale' was later included in *Chimera*, the collection of D'Annunzio's poetry released by the editor Treves in 1890. As I will argue, this is a case of absorbing Japanese poetics into the Italian language, which is rooted in a very different linguistic structure. While embedded in Orientalism and exoticism, it can be considered a remarkable transcultural operation, which involved blending methods, metrics and subjects from Italian and Japanese traditions. In what follows, I show that this exercise was not an episodic experiment but an integral part of D'Annunzio's program to renew modern poetic language, in which the absorption of new, 'distant' elements was of primary importance. Studying D'Annunzio's fascination with Japan

[1] Giacomo Leopardi, *Zibaldone*, ed. by Michel Caesar and Franco D'Intino (New York: Farrar Straus Giroux, 2013), p. 809.

and Japanese poetry also contributes to our understanding of his view of translation as cross-cultural adaptation.

Testimonies of *Japonaiserie* in the D'Annunzio's Late Years

The Vittoriale degli Italiani in Gardone, a villa-museum surrounded by a vast park with a breathtaking view of Lake Garda, testifies to D'Annunzio's taste for exotic 'kitsch' and to his penchant for the Oriental. Among the so-called 'chinoiseries', things of Chinese taste found in the *Bagno blu* (blue bathroom), and in the dining room featuring an enormous tortoise named Cheli, there are also several Japanese pieces. Of note is a prestigious historical sword from Bicchu Osafune, a renowned place producing traditional samurai swords; this was brought by the Japanese mission for the Project of Translating the *Decameron*. Another example is a set of small porcelain dishes from Kutani with designs of erotic scenes, stored and hidden in a lacquered box with a dragon drawn on the top.

Over many years, D'Annunzio maintained a personal and institutional relationship with Japan, cultivating various personal ties.[2] The country was for him a culturally different universe. Today, a Japanese person who is well-read in European literature may never have heard of D'Annunzio. Still, in the last years of the poet's life, between 1920 and 1930, even young boys and girls were familiar with his name. His notoriety is attested by the number of Japanese visitors who came to meet him at the Vittoriale in these years, as well as the contacts he maintained among the Japanese. D'Annunzio was appreciated as a writer and admired as a daring statesman.[3] He was also known for envisioning the first flight to Japan from Europe: after his famous flight over Vienna during the First World War, he planned to carry out the first Rome-Tokyo-Rome journey in the history of world aviation. The problematic situation in Fiume, occupied by D'Annunzio and his fellow soldiers, prevented him from carrying out the project himself, but it was completed by the Italian Air Force in 1920.

[2] See Mariko Muramatsu, 'La fortuna dannunziana nel Giappone del primo Novecento. Studi dei documenti giapponesi nell'Archivio del Vittoriale degli Italiani', in *Segni e voci dalla letteratura italiana. Da Dante a D'Annunzio* (Tokyo: UTCP, 2012), pp. 95–120.

[3] See Mariko Muramatsu, 'D'Annunzio in Giappone', in *Gabriele d'Annunzio 150 'Vivo, scrivo'. Atti del convengno internazionale di studi. Pescara, Aurum, 12-13 marzo 2013* (Milano: Silvana Editoriale, 2014), p. 183–91.

The Japanese did not give up on having D'Annunzio come to Japan; and in 1924, they invited him to make the journey by more ordinary means, namely, by ship. The library of the Vittoriale preserves letters signed by the Naval Attaché of the Italian Embassy in Japan, which reported the official invitation to the poet from two leading Japanese newspapers of that period, *Hochi Shinbun* and *Asahi Shinbun*; it also contains some books with travel information and ship operation guides, which bear signs of having been read by D'Annunzio. But after Fiume, the poet was no longer attracted by the idea of travelling to the Far East, probably because of the complex political dynamics he shared with the person promoting his invitation – a relationship that was simultaneously compromising and conflicting: that is, his relationship with Mussolini himself. The Duce in fact urged him to at least respond to the Japanese newspapers, but D'Annunzio disregarded this recommendation.[4]

Thus, despite his fascination with the country, D'Annunzio never travelled to Japan. As a consequence, he never witnessed in person any of the Oriental landscapes and images – cherry blossoms, infantilised women in kimonos, full autumn moons, gorgeous sunsets – described in his writing.

D'Annunzio's *Japonaiseries*: The Young Journalist and Rising Poet

Toward the end of his literary and political career, D'Annunzio became familiar with Japan as an emerging Asian nation with military and political ambitions. In his youth, however, Japan was for him, as for many European artists and intellectuals, a symbol of all that is distant, different and new. Images related to Japan were poetic or juvenile, as in the description of Japanese artifacts, paintings and women by the Goncourt brothers.

In the early 1880s, the young D'Annunzio settled in Rome, the capital of the newly reunited Italy, with the desire to live a glamorous social life and the ambition to become a successful poet. By then, he had already published a collection of poems, *Primo Vere* (1879), and was beginning his activity as a journalist. The essays he published for *Capitan Fracassa* (starting in 1880), *Fanfulla della domenica* (starting in 1879), and *Cronaca bizantina* (starting in 1884) – the new cultural magazines issued in Rome – ranged from play reviews, art and literary

4 Muramatsu, *La fortuna dannunziana*, pp. 110–12.

criticism, and book reviews to social bulletins known as '*cronaca mondana*'. The young journalist followed the latest trends of the vibrant capital with his exceptional curiosity and sensibility, reporting the latest rumours from Roman high society, new fashion trends, as well as cultural and artistic news. These short essays, which are written in a witty tone and display a strong sense of irony, enable us to follow D'Annunzio's cultural development and provide evidence of how he skillfully combined and exploited the same sources to create texts of various genres. He signed his publications with a variety of pen names, such as Duca Minimo, Vere de Vere, Musidoro and Micaele d'Avviso.

Let's look at the pages published on 1 December 1884, which marked D'Annunzio's debut in *Tribuna*, the prestigious magazine launched by Prince Mario Sciarra with the collaboration of already acclaimed authors such as Giosuè Carducci and Matilde Serao. The heading of the column written by D'Annunzio is 'Giornate romane' (Roman Days), and the article of the day is titled 'Tsoung-Hoa-Lou, Ossia Cronica del Fiore dell'Oriente' (Tsoung-Hoa-Lou, or Chronicle of the Flower of the Orient). The pseudonym used for this short sketch of Roman social life is Shun-Sui-Katsu-Kava, probably modelled after a Japanese painter of *ukiyo-e* from the middle of the 18th century, considered a master of Hokusai. The mysterious *incipit* reads: 'Salute a O Tsouri Sama, a Sua signoria la Gru!' (Hail to O Tsouri Sama, to His Lordship the Crane!).[5] This strange beginning is followed by a description of Fujimaru Tanaka, the Japanese Ambassador in Rome, who was recently nominated to be received by the King of Italy:

> Il buon suddito del Mikado, lucido e gialliccio come un avorio di tre secoli, dai mansueti occhi lungamente obliqui, non portava alla cintola le due sciabole, segno di nobilità nell'Impero del Sole Levante. . . Egli era tutto umiliato nel nero abito europeo, pur sorridendo d'un infaticabile sorriso che gli faceva battere rapidamente le palpebre e tremolare i pomelli delle gote.[6]

> (The good vassal of the Mikado, shiny and yellowish like three-century-old ivory, with tame long-slanted eyes, did not wear on his belt the two sabers, the sign of nobility in the Empire of the Rising Sun . . . He was utterly humiliated in a black European suit while smiling a tireless smile that made his eyelids blink rapidly and the knobs of his cheeks quiver.)

[5] D'Annunzio's spelling/transcription of Japanese words is mediated by the French translation and often presents mistakes. '*O Tsouri sama*' should be written 'o tsuru sama'.

[6] Gabriele D'Annunzio, *Scritti giornalistici, 1882–1888*, ed. by Annamaria Andreoli (Milan: Mondadori, 1996), p. 197.

After the presentation of this official event, the chronicler is in front of Mrs Beretta's Oriental art and crafts shop:

> Intanto pioveva; e una turpe caligine occidentale contaminava le cose di una egual tinta di fango. La vita cittadina andavasi trascinando con fatica e dolore pe'l lastrico sdrucciolevole.
>
> Ed io, ch'ero nella via dei Condotti, d'innanzi alle vetrine giapponesi dove una gigantesca gru di bronzo drizzava il collo di fra i vasi multicolori, dissi con un intenso ardore d'idolatria:
>
> «Salute a O Tsuouri Sama!»
>
> Ed entrai a ristorami nel tepore delle stoffe di seta e nell'odor prezioso dei legni esotici e del thé.[7]
>
> (Meanwhile, it was raining, and a foul western caliginous gloom defiled things with an equal tint of mud. The city life was dragging with fatigue and pain on the slippery pavement.
>
> And I, who had arrived at Via Dei Condotti, was in front of the Japanese shop windows where a gigantic bronze crane stretched its neck forward among the colorful vases and said with an intense ardor of idolatry:
>
> 'Salute to O Tsouri Sama!'
>
> And I entered to sit in the warmth of silk fabrics and the sweet odor of exotic woods and tea.)

Following this ironic *incipit*, the author makes a list of the aristocratic ladies who were good clients of Mrs Beretta's shop and describes the objects they buy and put in their elegant salons. This article testifies to the aura of exoticism that Japanese art craft and culture had for Roman society of the period. According to one of the 'Favole mondane', entitled 'Mani fredde, cuore caldo' (Cold Hands, Warm Heart), published in *Tribuna – Cronaca bizantina* on 5 October 1886, this trend lasted until the summer of two years later, when new fashions came about.

We can find traces of this Japanese vogue in D'Annunzio's publications during this time, here listed in chronological order:

1. Short stories ('Favole mondane'): 'Mandarina' (in *Capitan Fracassa*, 22 June 1884), Donna Claribel (in *Tribuna*, a column with the title 'Giornate romane', 21 December 1884);
2. 'Cronaca mondana', a news column on Roman society which reports about the popularity of Japanese taste, with descriptions of

[7] Ibid.

Mrs Beretta's shop of Oriental arts and crafts (in *Tribuna*, a column with the title 'Giornate romane', 1 and 28 December 1884);
3. Articles on Japanese literature and art, mainly reviews of Judith Gautier's *Poéms de la libellule* (*Dragonfly Collection*) illustrated by the Japanese painter Hōsui Yamamoto, and poems inspired by this book, entitled 'Outa occidentale' and 'Il Ventaglio' (in *Tribuna*, *Fanfulla della domenica*, *Domenica letteraria – Cronaca bizantina* and *Capitan Fracassa*, published on 19 May, 1, 11, 14, 15 and 22 June and 15 August 1885);
4. An article on a party entitled 'Casa Primoli', decorated with many refined objects including Japanese fabrics, small fans from *Jokohama, foukousa* and a Japanese saber (in *Tribuna*, 25 March 1886);
5. Another short story ('Favole mondane'), entitled 'Mani fredde, cuore caldo', which describes the end of the fashion of Japanese objects (in *Tribuna – Cronaca bizantina*, 5 October 1886);
6. And finally, D'Annunzio's novel, *Il Piacere* (*Pleasure*, 1889).

In D'Annunzio's early works, his fascination with all things Japanese was closely related to the influence of foreign sources – in this case, the exoticism that pervaded French *fin-de-siècle* literature. Both contributed to the creation of a new, original style.[8] The *Japoneseries* of D'Annunzio's early prose works – the 'favole mondane' 'Mandarina' and 'Donna Claribel', as well as his first novel, *Il Piacere* – capture the atmosphere and the mood of the period. Descriptions of Japanese objects and characters are linked to or directly taken from journalistic articles he had written on the costumes of contemporary Roman society. D'Annunzio drew on various sources and incorporated them into his works in terms of style and motifs with a sort of collage technique. His early works in prose and verse, influenced by the exoticism of French authors like the Goncourt Brothers, are thus connected to each other in a complex network of references.

Duca Minimo on Judith Gautier's *Poémes de la libellule*

It is not surprising that D'Annunzio, who frequented Rome's aristocratic circles with privileged channels to Parisian literary society,

[8] Mariko Muramatsu, *Il buon suddito del Mikado* (Milan: Archinto Editore, 1997).

should read and review *Poémes de la libellule* (1885),[9] an anthology of traditional Japanese poetry edited in Paris by Judith Gautier in collaboration with Saionji Kinmochi (1849–1940), would-be Prime Minister of Japan. Giuseppe Primoli, who had spent his youth in Paris and was well connected to French salons and to Judith's father, Théophile Gautier, may have been a crucial intermediator. At any case, the anthology was first mentioned by D'Annunzio in *Tribuna*, on 1 June 1885, and then in an article on 'Japanese Literature' in *Domenica letteraria – Cronaca bizantina*.

Judith Gautier had become known across Europe for her works on Oriental cultures. In 1867, she had published an anthology of Chinese poetry, entitled *Libre de jade*, under the pseudonym of Judith Walter. Her collaborator, Saionji, was a young Japanese nobleman who studied in the 1870s in France as a government-financed student and frequented Paris's literary milieu. In *Poémes de la libellule*, Gautier, with Saionji, introduced French readers to the world of Japanese traditional poetry, *uta* – 'outa' in French transliteration – or *waka*, composed in a straightforward metrics of 5-7-5-7 syllables, for a total of thirty-one syllables basically without rhymes.

Whereas in the articles published previously in *Tribuna*, D'Annunzio was concerned with the objects and fashion of Roman social life, his reviews of this Japanese anthology shift the focus from objects to Oriental art, and then from Oriental art to poetry. With these articles, he transitions from witty descriptions of high Roman society to a more serious and pedantic artistic and literary style.

Let's take a closer look at the 'rare and sophisticated book' that drew D'Annunzio's attention; indeed an elegant book with precious binding and delicately coloured pages that exists in only a limited number of copies. The anthology features eighty-eight short Japanese poems, *waka*, translated into French by Gautier on the basis of Saionji's literal translation. In her versions, Gautier applied a traditional French rhyme scheme, which did not excessively modify the meaning of Saionji's literal translations.[10] The poems, in Gautier's French translation, are printed one by one on each page, and all pages are illustrated in colour (seven types of illustrations are repeatedly used). All eighty-eight lyrics in the literal version by Saionji are

[9] *Poémes de la libellule,* trans. by Judith Gautier and M. Saionzi (Paris: Gillot, 1885).

[10] See William Leonard Schwartz, *The Imaginative Interpretation of the Far East in Modern French Literature 1860–1925* (Paris: Librairie Ancienne Honoré Champion, 1927), p. 52.

listed on the last seven pages of the volume. The book opens with a preface, a translation of the well-known historical introduction ('*Kanajo*') by Ki-no-Tsurayuki (872–945) to the ancient Japanese Imperial Anthology of poems, *Kokin Waka Shū* (905). The Japanese poets most represented in the French anthology are Ki-no-Tsurayuki, Ki-no-Tomonori (970–904), Murasaki Shikibu (970[?]–1019[?]) and Fujiwara Teika (1162–1241). The poems selected come mainly from ancient imperial anthologies, *Manyō Shū* (late 8th century), *Kokin Waka Shū* and *Shin Kokin Waka Shū* (1216). But Saionji also added several modern poets.

The illustrations in Gautier's anthology are by the Japanese painter Yamamoto Hōsui, who was living and studying in Paris in those years, an artist who today is emerging from oblivion and being re-evaluated for his pioneering and rare attempt, among the artists of his time, to fuse Japanese subjects with Western painting techniques.[11] This probably made it difficult for him to be appreciated after returning to his home country because, at that time, Japanese artists of westernised paintings tended to introduce in their work imported methods combined with European subjects.

The review published by D'Annunzio in *Tribuna* is collocated in the column 'La vita ovunque – Piccolo corriere' and signed with one of D'Annunzio's favourite pseudonyms, Duca Minimo, with the *incipit* 'Libri nuovi e commedie nuove' (New Books and Recent Performances).[12] In this short essay, the young journalist explicitly addresses female readers. After reviewing several illustrated books published in the same period, he presents 'another illustrated book', by Judith Gautier, which he calls 'un libro unico, singolarissimo, un libro d'artista, di amante, di poeta e d'imperatrice' (a unique, utterly singular book, a book of an artist, a lover, a poet and an empress). D'Annunzio draws attention especially to the illustrations and artistic aspects of the book and writes about the painter who illustrated it. His name, he says, was Yamamoto, and four or five years ago, he left the country of the Rising Sun to go to Paris. He further notes that 'Egli cerca di riuscire alla difficilissima fusione delle due arti; ma l'arte nativa lo trascina quasi sempre alla rappresentazione dei fiori, dei paesaggi, delli animali, delle leggende buddhistiche e delle scene familirari così care al grande Hokusai' (He tries to succeed in

[11] See Erika Takashina, *Ikai no umi: Hōsui Seiki Tenshin ni okeru seiyō* (Chiba: Miyoshi Kikaku, 2000).

[12] Gabriele D'Annunzio, *Scritti giornalistici, 1881–1888*, ed. by Annamaria Andreoli (Milan: Mondadori, 1996), vol. 1, p. 388.

the challenging fusion of the two arts; but his native art almost always drags him to represent flowers, animals, landscapes, Buddhist legends and family scenes so dear to the great Hokusai).[13] He also adds information on the exhibition of his works held in Paris, and reports positive comments on his watercolours. For the reviewer, Yamamoto's illustrations are masterpieces:

> Basta a Yamamoto un ramo di pesco di prugno o di mandorlo su un lembo di cielo per fare un capolavoro. I rami fioriti contornano e abbracciano i versi; e non si sa più se il pittore abbia scritto i versi fioriti o se il poeta abbia dipinto.
>
> (All Yamamoto needs is a branch of peach, plum or almond on a piece of the sky to make a masterpiece. The branches in blossom surround and frame the verses, and it is no longer clear whether the painter wrote the poems in bloom or whether the poet painted them.)[14]

In the conclusion, the reviewer quotes two examples from Gautier's version in French. The first is of Ki-no-Tomonori, and describes snow on the branches of a prune tree in bloom, fusing the images of flowers and snow into one:

> Tout semble fleurir
> sous la neige qui voltige.
> Comment découvrir
> le prunier dans ce prestige,
> pour en cueillir une tige.
>
> (Everything seems to bloom
> under the swirling snow.
> How can we discover
> the plum tree in the snow,
> to pick a stem?)[15]

The second poem quoted is by Kiyohara-no-Fukayabu (D'Annunzio's transcription is incorrectly 'Gouka-Jabau', whereas in the French book it features as 'Fouka-Yabou'). This *waka* develops the comparison

[13] Ibid., pp. 390–1 (translation my own).

[14] Ibid., p. 391 (translation my own).

[15] Ibid., p. 391 (translation my own). The literal meaning of the original Japanese text is: 'After snowfall, / every tree is in bloom. / How can I distinguish / the blossom from the snow / to take a branch of plum?'

in the opposite sense, as the snowflakes falling from the sky are compared to flowers:

Puisque c'est du ciel
qu'en hiver nous sont venues,
ces fleurs inconnues,
c'est qu'un printemps éternel
réside au de là des nues.

(Since it's from the sky
that in winter came to us,
these unknown flowers,
it means that an eternal spring
lies beyond the clouds.)[16]

Among the poems in Gautier's anthology, D'Annunzio chose two examples focused on a rhetorical topos of Japanese poetry in the Heian era (around the tenth century): 'flower-like snow' (especially cherry or prune blossom) or 'snow-like flowers'. In the Japanese poetic tradition, the topos had become a manneristic cliché as an expression of sorrow for lost beauty, or for the fragility of beauty, detected from the very moment of its highest blooming. The two poems above, in their original version in Japanese, conjure the fleetingness of time and the evanescence of seasons. In the French version quoted by Duca Minimo, the effect of the comparison is converted into a curious visualisation of white colour, in contrast to the sky framing it, where the petals are fused in snow, creating a queer sense of reversed seasons and time. The word 'éternel' that Gautier inserts in her version to describe the spring is far from the allusion to the fleeting passage of time and fragile beauty in the original Japanese *waka*.

The Duca Minimo ends his review by announcing further developments on the topic: 'Torneremo sul libro con più serietà, qui o altrove. Per oggi basta' (We will return to this book more seriously, here or elsewhere. That's enough for today).[17]

Two weeks later, on 14 June, D'Annunzio, in fact, came back to this topic and reviewed Judith Gautier's book in *Cronaca bizantina*. The article, this time, was signed with his own name and entitled

[16] Ibid., p. 391 (translation my own). The literal meaning of the original Japanese text is: 'Although it is wintertime, the snowflakes are falling from the sky. There should already be the spring over the clouds.'

[17] D'Annunzio, *Scritti giornalistici*, p. 391.

'Japanese Literature'. D'Annunzio begins by citing his favourite French authors, Edmond and Jules De Goncourt, to whom he attributes the merit of promoting in France the taste of Japonisme.[18] He adds that Philippe Burty, Louis Gonse and Judith Gautier contributed to making known the delicate art of Hokusai and Kokkei. After the short introduction to Japonism, D'Annunzio presents the *Poémes de la libellule,* a 'curious book of Japanese poems' that 'is in truth nothing more than a kind of illustrated and coloured album by Yamamoto.'[19] He introduces the Japanese painter, and describes the landscapes in his illustrations. After mentioning his exposition in Paris, he claims that the influence of Western art is obvious, and argues that Yamamoto's intention is to 'fondere le due arti in una o almeno prendere dall'arte occidentale ed assimilarsi quel che all'arte giapponese manca' (fuse the two arts into one, or at least to borrow from Western art and adopt that which Japanese art lacks).[20] This time he is more critical of the contamination of the two ways of painting than in his presentation of the same book that had come out two weeks earlier. He appreciates the exotic character of the images, but criticises the imitation of Western techniques, which in his view brings about a loss of authenticity:

> Nell'insieme però, come le poesie nella traduzione francese perdono alquanto del loro profumo natale, così anche le illustrazioni paiono, diremmo quasi, tradotte.[21]
>
> (On the whole, however, just as the poems in the French translation lose some of their native scents, so do the illustrations seem, we might almost say, translated.)

This consideration of the westernised influence as a decline of the 'exotic' element finds a parallel in his critique of the poetic translations, where, in D'Annunzio's view, something genuine is lost.

After commenting on the illustrations, the reviewer presents a compact history of Japanese literature, which begins with an introduction to Japanese phonetics and includes examples from the third century CE to the tenth century. The central part of the review is dedicated to Gautier's anthology. In the review published two weeks earlier, he had, as mentioned above, quoted two poems in French as expressions

[18] Ibid., p. 160.
[19] Ibid., p. 160.
[20] Ibid., p. 161.
[21] Ibid., p. 161.

of the topos of 'snow-like flowers' and 'flower-like snow'. This time, D'Annunzio quotes in Japanese, using the same alphabetical transcription of Gautier's edition, the poem of Princess Ise:

> Harou goto ni
> Nagarourou Kawa o
> Hanato mité
> Orarénou mizou ni
> Sodé ya Norénamou.[22]

The poem represents the beauty of the plum blossoms and their reflections on the floating water. The summarised meaning of the text is: every spring the images on the floating water are so attractive as to make the lady poet try to break off a reflected branch, soaking her sleeves of kimono in vain. The reflection of the branch in bloom on the floating water can be interpreted as a symbol of unobtainable and swaying beauty and the impression of wet sleeves evokes the physical feeling of emptiness.

In D'Annunzio's article the alphabetised text of Ise is followed by an Italian translation, which seems to have been produced after Saionji's literal version:

> Per cogliere i fiori di prugno, i cui colori agita l'acqua, io mi sono chinato verso l'acqua; ma, ahimè!, io non ho colto i fiori e la mia manica è tutta bagnata.[23]

> (To pluck the plum blossoms, whose colours shake the water, I have stooped toward the water, but alas, I have not plucked the flowers, and my sleeve is completely wet.)

D'Annunzio was struck by the poetic world of *waka* or *outa*, previously unknown to him. In his survey of Japanese literature, he presents categories of Japanese short poems. In his view, Japanese poets 'very often achieve a spontaneous grace that we would in vain seek in our petrarchists'. His judgment on Gautier's translation is favourable, but his conclusion is not devoid of criticism. Just like Yamamoto's illustrations, these translations 'domesticate' Japanese subjects through Western techniques. Gautier has, in D'Annunzio's opinion, 'francified' the poems by adopting French metrics, and in

[22] Ibid., p. 165. The literal meaning of the original Japanese text is as follows: 'Every spring / I mistake the reflections on a floating stream / for real plum blossoms / and with unbreakable water / soak my sleeves in vain.'

[23] Ibid., p. 165.

doing so, has deprived them of their 'primitive' character and made Japanese poetry resemble 'the madrigals of the shepherds of France'.

'Outa occidentale': The First *Waka* in a Western Language

Shortly after the review and the article on the history of Japanese literature, D'Annunzio composed two poems filled with Japanese imagery, titled 'Il ventaglio' (The Fan) and 'Outa occidentale' (Western *Outa*). The second one is of particular interest for us, because in it, D'Annunzio applied Japanese metrics. A precious source offers us insight into D'Annunzio's creative process: it is a copy, owned by D'Annunzio, of Gautier's book, discovered by Yukiko Ozaki in Tokyo in 2000.[24] This copy preserves what is (presumably) D'Annunzio's handwriting on the margin of the front page. According to Ozaki's hypothesis, the poem and the book were a gift from D'Annunzio to his wife. From the explanatory notes found within the book and left behind by the antiquarian, it looks like D'Annunzio, after some years, gave it to a close friend and poet, Augusto Sindici. It is unclear whether it was later sold separately in Tokyo or if it travelled to Tokyo as a part of some private collection. The book can now be consulted in Tokyo, in the Toyama collection of the library of Waseda University.

According to Ozaki's analysis of this unique copy of the *Libre de la libellule*, the handwriting on the title page represents the first draft of a series of poetic creations which would be finalised in 'Outa occidentale' and published in *Fanfulla della domenica* on 14 June 1885. This poetic 'prototype' can be considered a preliminary sketch or 'studio' and consists of twelve short poems to be reorganised and assembled in final form.

In the blank space on the front page, which follows the opening illustration of the title page, D'Annunzio wrote several short poems, distributing them in the shape of a fan. These twelve *outa* were later modified by the poet to be published in *Fanfulla della domenica*. While originally each *waka* was composed as a short poem, here the twelve poems were arranged as twelve strophes of a single poem.[25]

[24] Yukiko Ozaki, 'Poèmes de la libellule e d'Annunzio: nuovi documenti di *Outa occidentale*', in *Rassegna Dannunziana* 59:60 (2011): III–X.

[25] Ibid., pp. V–VI.

In the version published in *Fanfulla della domenica*, the poem features a quotation from Ki-no-Tomonori as an epigraph, like a riddle. It is the text of the *outa* that closes the volume of *Poèmes de la libellule*; D'Annunzio translates it into Italian from Saionji's literal French translation:

> A chi manderò questi fiori, se non a voi? Sol chi ama colore e profumo merita di riceverli.
>
> (To whom shall I send these flowers, if not to you? Only those who love colour and perfume deserve to receive them.)

When the definitive version was published in 1890 in *Chimera*, D'Annunzio removed both these lines of the epigraph and the final lines of the 'farewell'. The farewell, quoted here, is in response to the riddle of the epigraph; with the name of the poet, Tomonori, with whom the poet (the 'I' of these lines), identifies:

> Dò questi versi,
> Fragili come fiori
> da l'acqua emersi,
> a te che i fiori adori
> io novo Tomonori.
>
> (I give these verses,
> fragile as flowers
> from the water emerged,
> to you who adore flowers
> I, the new Tomonori.)

It is indeed remarkable that, even though D'Annunzio did not know Japanese, he experimented with Japanese metrics by imitating the rhyme scheme of *waka* or *uta*, and the rhythms of Japanese poetry, to conjure an atmosphere of Oriental taste. In the version published in *Fanfulla della domenica*, the poem has twelve stanzas, including the farewell, each composed according to Japanese metrics, i.e., thirty-one syllables in five lines, but with rhyme, which is not the rule in Japanese poetry. In each stanza, two end rhymes alternate with variations according to the scheme abba, cDcDC, eFeFF, etc.

> Guarda la Luna
> tra gli alberi fioriti;
> e par che inviti
> ad amare sotto i miti
> incanti ch'ella aduna.

Veggo da i lidi
selvagge gru passare
con lunghi gridi
in vol triangolare
su 'l grand occhio lunare.

Veggo per 'l lume
le donne entro i burchielli:
vanno su 'l fiume,
dati all'acqua i capelli,
tra i gridi delli uccelli.[26]

(Look at the Moon
among the flowering trees;
and it seems to invite
to love under the mythical
enchantments that she adorns.

I see from the shores
wild cranes pass by
with long cries
in triangular flight
upon the great lunar eye.

I see by the light
the women within the *burchielli*
they go upon the river,
gave to the water their hair,
amid the cries of the birds.)

The images described are nocturnal and dreamlike; the lovers on the boats float on the river under the branches of the trees in blossom, illuminated by the moon's light; high in the sky, cranes fly. Various Oriental or Japanese images can be recognised among the motifs of this poem, juxtaposed with others of different derivation: for example, the women's hair glides on the water in a mysterious way reminiscent of Pre-Raphaelite painting; the flowers are from a rose garden, rather than a cherry or peach tree garden; the beautiful hands picking the flowers are compared to butterflies. In the final version in *Chimera*, which deletes both the epigraph and the farewell, which had the function of a specific marker of the vogue of Japanism in the

[26] Gabriele D'Annunzio, 'Outa occidentale', in *Versi di amore e di gloria*, I, ed. by Annamaria Andreoli and Niva Lorenzoni (Milan: Mondadori, 2006), p. 530.

version of *Fanfulla della domenica*, the datable Orientalism is less notable and more dissolved into other poetic influences.

Niva Lorenzini, who edited the 1989 Meridiani volume published by Mondadori, noted that, in this poem, there is a strong influence of Verlaine, whose musicality exerted a particular fascination on the young D'Annunzio. Verlaine's lines:

> O ces mains, ces mains vénérées,
> Faites le geste qui pardonne!

Indeed find an echo in the 'beautiful hands' in the eleventh stanza:

> e dolcemente
> stan su i fiori adagiati
> le mani. - Oh fate,
> belle mani adorate,
> il gesto che consente!
>
> (and sweetly
> lie on the flowers
> your hands. "Oh make,
> beautiful adored hands,
> the gesture that permits!)[27]

In the version published in *Chimera*, D'Annunzio writes about how, after reading Gautier's translations of Japanese poems, he attempted to reproduce in Italian the structure of an *outa*, but with rhymes. D'Annunzio's curiosity about Japanese poetry led him to adopt a method of composition that went further than Gautier and Yamamoto's in terms of the appropriation of sources and methods, and also in the fusion of influences: a poem in Italian with Japanese metrics, featuring rhymes as in the Western tradition, filled with Oriental images as well as with motifs derived from the French Symbolists. The juxtaposition of Orientalist topoi with Verlainian symbolism signals D'Annunzio's tendency to absorb and fuse different elements in his aesthetic, poetic world. The poet concludes the explanation of his *outa* with a note of self-criticism:

> Nella mia occidentale la frequenza della rima e il ritmo troppo accentuato tolgono alla strofa gran parte del suo carattere primitivo.
>
> (In my *outa occidentale*, the frequency of the rhyme and the over-emphasized rhythm take away much of the primitive character from the strophe.)

[27] Ibid., p. 531 (translation my own).

This is a familiar comment, which reproduces the exact phrase he had used to criticise Gautier's French versions in *Poèmes de la libellule*. Cross-cultural translation and syncretism, he seems to imply, inevitably result in an attenuation of the 'native' or 'primitive'. Despite this self-criticism, D'Annunzio's attempt to shape his poetics on Japanese metrics is an interesting case of cultural syncretism. It is also testament to his eclecticism, which marked his poetic language, prose and taste for interior design. Most importantly, it demonstrates how the poet innovated his poetic language by borrowing from culturally or historically distant sources. Classical poetry and ancient French poetry also featured among his poetic models. In his verses, neologisms coined from Latin terms and the metrics of *lai* often merge in poetic experimentalism. *Intermezzo melico*, the section in which 'Outa occidentale' is inserted in the *Chimera* collection, features several examples of these cross-cultural experiments, and it is not by coincidence that the *outa* is placed between a *romanza* and a *lai*.

Mocking Japonism

The fascination with all things Japanese in Europe at the end of the 1880s was so pervasive that D'Annunzio did not hesitate to make fun of it. We have mentioned the description of the Japanese ambassador in the journalistic piece in *Tribuna*, the male character Sakumi in the short story 'Mandarina' and the description of Japanese people and objects in *Il Piacere*. This ironic, critical gaze also underpins D'Annunzio's parody following 'Outa occidentale'. On the day after the publication of 'Outa', the poet wrote a short, grotesque poem, with the title 'Yuta Federale', under the name Micaele D'Avviso, in the newspaper *Capitan Fracassa*. It featured black bats flying in the sky under the moon, and the syllabic metrics were 7-7-5-7-7, a reversal of 5-7-5-7-7. The epigraph reads:

> Quando un sigaro non tira, vuol dire che ha un buco: così con tutte le cose mortali. Pomodoro[28]
>
> (When a cigar doesn't pull, it has a hole: so too with all mortal things. – Pomodoro [Tomato].)

A week later, in the same newspaper, D'Annunzio published another short poem structured with 5-7-5-7-7 syllables under the name

[28] *Capitan Fracassa*, 16 June 1884.

'Nunzio Gabriele'. The epigraph is an allusion to tomato; in Italian, *Pomodoro:*

> Quale cosa amerò io? Sol quella / che ha colore e sapore. – Tenemori[29]
>
> (Which thing will I love? Only the one / that has colour and flavour. – Tenemori)

Needless to say, this strange composition was a parody of the epigraph of 'Outa occidentale' in the original version in *Fanfulla della domenica*. What is distant could be ambiguous, poetic and fascinating but at the same time strange, odd, indefinite and only superficially comprehensible. In these parodies, which seem ironic and mocking toward both the general vogue of exoticism and the poet's own enthusiasms, what matters is primarily what one can see on the surface.

Conclusion: Did the Fascination with Japanese Things Leave Any Trace in D'Annunzio's Poetry?

D'Annunzio's case shows how, in the nineteenth century, Western culture came into contact with the poetry transmitted from Japan and remade it by adapting the same metrics in Western languages. The so-called Japonism in the arts was a similar phenomenon. Among the paintings produced in that historical period, we can find copies and partial imitations of Japanese paintings, especially woodcut print art (*Ukiyo-e*). The influence of Japanese art on the techniques and styles of the European arts after Impressionism was particularly present in artistic currents which set out to break with classical perspective and the traditional use of colours. Could we recognise in D'Annunzio an approach to Japanese poetry comparable to the influence of *Ukiyo-e* in Van Gogh's works? Or should we speak of an affinity with Japanese aesthetics, evoked by the encounter with the other, defined as what is 'distant' and 'different'?

I would like to address for a moment D'Annunzio's depictions of nature. The 'moon' and the swallows, for example, are recurrent topoi in his poems, and as Ezio Raimondi has noted, there must be a reason behind this insistence.[30] In 'Lungo l'Africo', in *Alcyone*, we have the rising moon in the predawn sky with flying swallows. At the

[29] *Capitan Fracassa*, 23 June 1884.

[30] Ezio Raimondi, '*Gabriele D'Annunzio*', in *Storia della letteratura italiana. Il Novecento*, ed. by Nataliano Sapegno (Milan: Garzanti, 1987), p. 435.

beginning of the poem, the moon, an anthropomorphised figure, is in contact with the water of the small river and the grass, in a world without human words:

> O nere e bianche rondini, tra notte
> E alba, tra vespro e notte, o bianche e nere,
> ospiti lungo l'Africo notturno!
> Volan elle sì basso che la molle
> erba sfiora coi petti, e dal piacere
> il loro volo sembra fatto azzurro.
> Sopra non ha susurro
> l'arbore grande, se ben trema sempre.
> Non tesse il volo intorno alle mie tempie
> fresche ghirlande?[31]
>
> (O black and white swallows, between night
> and dawn, between eventide and night, O black and white,
> hosts along the nocturnal Africo!
> They fly so low that the soft
> grass grazes with their breasts, and from pleasure
> their flight seems made azure.
> Above has no susurrus
> the great arbore, if well it ever trembles.
> Does not the flight weave around my temples
> fresh garlands?)

In the quoted verses, we have a sort of picture with colour contrasts of black, white and blue: the white and black swallows take on bluish shades, flying low against the dark sky of the night. We are in a harmonious world of *Alcyone*, in strict contact with nature and, at the same time, it is possible to notice the affinity with the Orientalist and pictorial image of the moon and the flying cranes in 'Outa occidentale'. In these descriptions of nature, we find proof that D'Annunzio's tendency to combine and merge, in his poems and novels, the ancient and the modern, the far and the near, was underpinned by a remarkable openness to various elements, borrowed from distant and diverse worlds, such as Japanese art and poetry.

[31] Gabriele D'Annunzio, 'Lungo l'Africo. Nella sera di giugno dopo la pioggia', in *Versi d'amore e di gloria*, II, ed. by Annamaria Andreoli and Niva Lorenzoni (Milan: Mondadori, 2006), p. 427 (translation my own).

Chapter 3

Il Piacere as a Multilingual Text and its Afterlife in Translation

Elisa Segnini

Set in *fin-de-siècle* Rome, *Il Piacere* (1889) combines psychological analysis and Decadent atmospheres with stunning descriptions of the recent Italian capital. It is a text rooted in an Italian city and written for Italian readerships, but it also displays a transnational dimension, testified by references to European literature, music and the arts, as well as by words and sentences in English, French, German, Japanese, Latin, Greek and even Sanskrit. On the one hand, literary cosmopolitanism signals engagement with the other: the novel stages an intimate dialogue with foreign literary traditions, including Decadence and Aestheticism. On the other hand, this very dialogue is used for nationalistic ends, as it aims to challenge Italy's peripheral role in modern Europe and to demonstrate the superiority of the highly educated Italian upper class.

This chapter explores the tension between cosmopolitanism and nationalism inherent to the multilingual fabric of the text, focusing on how this dynamic was renegotiated as *Il Piacere* crossed cultural and linguistic boundaries. To this end, I will first foreground the role of foreign borrowings, translation and intertextual references, paying particular attention to the function that languages other than Italian assume within and beyond the text, and to how they relate to gender and class constructs. Drawing on D'Annunzio's correspondence with his French translator, Georges Hérelle, and on Hérelle's memoires, I will then explore how this 'romanzo di pura forma' (novel of pure form)[1] that, as D'Annunzio noted, had 'qualche parentela con *À Rebours* di J. K. Huysmans' (something to do with *À Rebours* by

[1] D'Annunzio to Hèrelle, 12 November 1894, in Mario Cimini, ed., *Carteggio D'Annunzio-Hérelle (1891–1931)* (Lanciano: Rocco Carabba, 2004), p. 251.

J. K. Huysmans),[2] travelled back to France, the 'centre' of the Symbolist and Decadent movement in the nineteenth century, and how the multilingual fabric of the text was affected in this transition. The worlding of the novel, as I shall show, involved a series of compromises and negotiations, and D'Annunzio had to fight hard for the coexistence of cosmopolitanism and international fame.

Multilingualism in *Il Piacere*

D'Annunzio's correspondence with his Italian publisher, Emilio Treves, indicates that the multilingual aspect of the novel was for him of primary importance. Worried that most readers would not be able to understand citations in foreign languages, Treves advised D'Annunzio to translate them in footnotes. D'Annunzio wrote back: 'Per le citazioni da poeti stranieri credo inutile la traduzione in nota. Le note danno un'aria di pretenzione odiosa. Se i lettori e le lettrici non capiranno, non sarà poi un gran male!' (Concerning the quotations from foreign poets, I believe translations in footnotes are useless. Footnotes convey an unpleasant impression of presumption. If male and female readers don't understand, it won't be such a bad thing!).[3] With a similar argument, he rejected Treves's suggestion to eliminate the words in Greek, or at least to render them in Roman letters: 'Bisogna che le tre parole greche rimangano. Se i lettori e le lettrici non capiranno, non sarà poi un gran male! Quelle tre parole non hanno nessuna importanza: ne hanno una di stile. Il romanzo non soffrirà alcun danno dalla dolce ignoranza della lettrice' (The three Greek words must stay. If male and female readers don't understand, it won't be such a bad thing! Those three words are of no importance: their importance lies in style. The novel will suffer no harm from the sweet ignorance of the female reader).[4] Leaving aside the patronising tone, and the unflattering portrayal of female readers, D'Annunzio is here making an important point: multilingualism, in *Il Piacere*, functions as a rhetorical device and is more connotative than denotative; that is, its significance goes beyond the meaning of

2 D'Annunzio to Hérelle, 14 November 1892, in Cimini, p. 101.

3 Gabriele D'Annunzio to Emilio Treves, 30 March 1889, in Gabriele D'Annunzio, *Lettere ai Treves*, ed. by Gianni Oliva, Katia Berardi and Barbara Di Serio (Milan: Garzanti, 1999), p. 70. All translations into English, unless otherwise stated, are my own.

4 D'Annunzio to Treves, 21 April 1889, in D'Annunzio, *Lettere ai Treves*, p. 71.

foreign words. Anticipating the theories of contemporary translation theorists,[5] D'Annunzio thus challenged the assumption that multilingual texts require multilingual readers, or that multilingualism necessarily has a mimetic function. The reasons behind the inclusion of foreign words and citations, as I shall show, are far more complex.

Firstly, words and sentences in foreign languages signal the status of Rome – which became Italy's capital only in 1871, and was considered backward and peripheral compared to other European cities – as a centre and epitome of European culture, as well as the superiority of the Roman upper-class protagonists, their international education and familiarity with European languages and literatures.[6] The protagonist, Count Andrea Sperelli, is not only an Aesthete but also a polyglot, as Giorgio Barberi Squarotti puts it, an 'absolute master of words'.[7] Educated across Europe, he is proficient in English, French and Spanish, reads Greek and Sanskrit, and is especially well versed in Latin. His lovers are just as cosmopolitan. When Andrea meets Elena Muti, she has just travelled back from Switzerland and Paris, and she is about to marry an Englishman. Andrea's other flame, Maria Ferres, studied in Brussels, is married to the ambassador of Guatemala, and possesses 'la parlata colorita di chi ha vissuto in molti paesi, ha vissuto in diversi climi, ha conosciuto genti diverse' (the colourful speech of those who have lived in many countries, in many climates, and have known different peoples).[8] Secondly, as Stefano Evangelista has noted, the incorporation of passages, in the

[5] See Rainier Grutman, 'Le bilinguisme littéraire comme relation intersystémique', *Canadian Review of Comparative Literature/Revue Canadienne de Littérature Comparée*, 17: 3–4 (1990), 198–212 and '« Besos para golpes »: l'ambiguïté d'un titre hugolien', in *Les langues du roman. Du plurilinguisme comme stratégie textuelle*, ed. by Lise Gauvin (Montreal: Presses de l'Université de Montréal), pp. 37–51 (p. 40).

[6] Annamaria Andreoli, 'Il Piacere', in *Prose di Romanzi*, by Gabriele D'Annunzio, ed. by Ezio Raimondi and Annamaria Andreoli (Milano: Mondadori, 1988), pp. 1105–49 (p. 1125). See also Adriana Vignazia, *Die deutschen D'Annunzio-Übersetzungen* (Frankfurt am Main: Peter Lang, 1995), p. 11, and Stefano Evangelista, 'The Remaking of Rome: Cosmopolitanism and Literary Modernity in Gabriele D'Annunzio's *The Child of Pleasure*', *Forum for Modern Language Studies*, 53: 3 (2017), 314–24 (318).

[7] Giorgio Barberi Squarotti, 'Il Parato di Carta', in *Il Piacere: atti del XII Convegno: Pescara-Francavilla al Mare, 4–5 maggio 1989*, ed. by Edoardo Tiboni and Umberto Russo (Pescara: Centro nazionale di studi dannunziani, 1989), 15–36 (p. 36).

[8] D'Annunzio, *Il Piacere*, ed. by Giansiro Ferrata (Milan: Mondadori: 1989), p. 167. All references *to Il Piacere* refer to this edition.

original language, from Shelley and Goethe – not by chance, the favourite writers of the much admired French novelist Paul Bourget – implicitly inscribes the narrative into a larger, prestigious European tradition of writings about Rome of which Italian literature, through this very novel, becomes part.[9] Thirdly, given the conflation that D'Annunzio encouraged between himself and his polyglot protagonist, citations in foreign languages contribute to the image of a multilingual, cosmopolitan persona that D'Annunzio was shaping these years, for example through his articles in *Tribuna*, in which, in addition to using foreign words, he signed with French or English aliases. In reality, D'Annunzio's mastery of foreign languages was not as extensive as that of Andrea Sperelli. He had excellent knowledge of Greek and Latin, but Hérelle notes that, at the time in which he met D'Annunzio in person (in 1894, after he had published *Il Piacere*), he could read French well but would refrain from speaking for fear of making mistakes.[10] His knowledge of English was limited, and there is no proof that he could read German.[11]

D'Annunzio's xenophilia seems at odds with his insistence that Italian, as he would argue a few years later in the preface to *Trionfo della morte* (1894), had 'nulla da invidiare e nulla da chiedere in prestito ad alcun'altra lingua europea' (nothing to envy and no need to borrow from any other European language) and with his self-branding as a language purist, inspired by the classics.[12] His project to reinvigorate the Italian language by recuperating words of Latin or Greek origin, or using such words in their original, rather than contemporary meaning, rested on his conviction that the uniqueness of Italian derived from its closeness to classical languages. However, this strategy also resulted in newly coined words, and like his practice of inserting foreign expressions, aimed to innovate the native idiom through cross-cultural exchange and to turn Italian into a suitable language for modern literature.

French and English expressions, in the text, reflect Italy's Francophilia and Anglophilia in the 1880s. Andrea and his acquaintances drink *view cognac*, cultivate a passion for the *bibelot* and the

[9] Evangelista, 'The Remaking of Rome', p. 317.

[10] Georges Hérelle, *Pétit memoire d'un traducteur* (Bruxelles: Auspert & Cie, 2005), p. 43.

[11] Mario Praz, 'D'Annunzio nella cultura europea', *Lettere Italiane* 15: 4 (1963), 434–45 (p. 435); John Woodhouse, 'Curioser and Spurioser: Two English Influences on Gabriele D'Annunzio', *Italian Studies*, 42 (1987), 69–80 (p. 70).

[12] Gabriele D'Annunzio, 'Prefazione', in *Trionfo della morte* (Milan: Mondadori, 1894), VIII.

bric-à brac, spy into ladies' *corsage*, wish one another *bonne chance*, and take leave from one another with a *comprends et prends*. Andrea, the narrator stresses, speaks French 'naturally.'[13] But French is not portrayed as natural language, it is rather a 'linguaggio manierato' (mannered idiom) that Andrea, in his conversations with Elena, uses to control his feelings, 'quasi estenuando nell'artifizio delle parole la forza del suo sentimento' (almost exhausting the intensity of his feelings into the artifice of words).[14] As the language of Decadence, French thus comes across as an artificial idiom where the signifier is deliberately distanced from the signified. There is an implicit parallel with the self-conscious, artificial language, filled with precious details of 'form and colour',[15] that the author, inspired by French Decadents, uses to narrate his story.

English words dominate in quantitative terms. The narrator lets us know that Andrea made the palazzo Zuccari his 'home'; he rides a 'mail-coach', attends the 'jockey club', organizes 'luncheons' and, like other characters, is engaged in 'flirtation'. He also has close ties to Britain. In a chapter dedicated to the history of his family, closely reminiscent of Huysmans's *À Rebours*, his father is described as 'byroneggiante' (Byronic),[16] and we learn that Andrea, after his father's death, 'rimase quindici mesi in Inghilterra' (remained in England for fifteen months).[17] Elena also addresses him in English, while Maria is deeply familiar with English literature.

Since characters often weave citations of foreign literature into their conversations, multilingualism in *Il Piacere* is closely related to intertextuality. It is not, however, exhausted by it. Not all words and sentences in foreign languages are citations of literary texts, and not all literary texts are cited in the original. Intertextual references can be divided into two categories: unacknowledged borrowings and explicit citations. The first have been an object of debate in D'Annunzio's scholarship since 1896, when Enrico Thovez first accused D'Annunzio of plagiarism.[18] He would soon be followed by others. Mario Praz identified in D'Annunzio's incorporation and elaboration of foreign sources the continuation of a humanistic

[13] D'Annunzio, *Il Piacere*, p. 56.
[14] Ibid., p. 56.
[15] D'Annunzio to Hérelle, 14 November 1892, p. 101.
[16] D'Annunzio, *Il Piacere*, p. 114.
[17] Ibid., p. 37.
[18] Enrico Thovez 'L'arte del comporre del Signor Gabriele D'Annunzio', *Gazzetta letteraria,* 20: 1 (1896), reprinted in Enrico Thovez, *Il Pastore, il Gregge e la Zampogna* (Naples: Ricciardi, 1921), pp. 32–47.

tradition of erudite citations and allusions.[19] This was also, however, a practice familiar to European Decadent writers, who, as Matthew Potolsky has argued, extensively translated, cited and borrowed from one another to construct an international community of dissidents.[20] D'Annunzio cites Charles Baudelaire and Théophile Gautier, and he borrows from Paul Bourget's *Essais de psychologie contemporaine* and *Psychologie de l'amour*, Joséphin Péladan's *Initiation sentimentale*, Joris-Karl's Huysmans's *À Rebours*, and the Goncourts' *Maison d'un artiste* and *Idées et sensations* and Henri Amiel's *Journal intime* among others.[21] He also translates entire passages from authors such as Algernon Swinburne and Walter Pater, whom he read in French translations: in these cases, foreign texts underlie Italian sentences.[22] Explicit citations in French are left untranslated, but citations in English or German are repeated in Italian in the next clause. When quoting longer passages, D'Annunzio renders the first lines in English or German, then continues citing in Italian, translating from the French. Through these devices, he underlines characters' familiarity with multiple languages while at the same time translating for Italian readers, whom he could expect to understand French, but less English or German.

In most cases, foreign languages are associated with high culture, love and desire: Goethe mediates Andreas's relationship to Elena; Shelley and Shakespeare his affair with Maria. However, we also learn that in social gatherings, Andrea entertains himself by experimenting with code-switching and code-mixing in ways that involve vulgar jokes. In these instances, he develops a hybrid speech:

> Aveva, quando si trovava nel *demi-monde*, una sua maniera e un suo stile particolari. Per non annoiarsi, si metteva a compor frasi grottesche, a gittar paradossi enormi, atroci impertinenze dissimulate con l'ambiguità delle parole, sottigliezze incomprensibili, madrigali enigmatici, in una lingua originale, mista come un gergo, di mille sapori come un'*olla podrida* rabelesiana, carica di spezie forti e di polpe succulente.[23]

[19] Mario Praz, 'D'Annunzio nella cultura europea', p. 435.

[20] Matthew Potolsky, *The Decadent Republic of Letters: Taste, Politics, and Cosmopolitan Community from Baudelaire to Beardsley* (Philadelphia: University of Pennsylvania Press, 2013).

[21] Guy Tosi, 'Le fonti francesi dell'estetismo di Andrea Sperelli', in Tosi (2013), vol. 2, pp. 689–728.

[22] Woodhouse, 'Curioser and Spurioser', p. 71.

[23] D'Annunzio, *Il Piacere*, p. 254.

(When he was in the *demi-monde* he had his own particular manner and style. To fight boredom, he would compose grotesque phrases, throw enormous paradoxes, atrocious impertinences disguised by the ambiguity of words, incomprehensible subtleties, enigmatic madrigals, all in an original language, mixed like a jargon, of a thousand flavours like a Rabelaisian *olla podrida*, full of strong spices and succulent pulp.)

The narrator praises this Rabelaisian *olla podrida* (rotten pot) for its originality. In contrast, the secretary of the Japanese legation is mocked for his 'barbaric', 'hardly unintelligible language', which involves a mixture of English, French and Italian.[24] Barbarism (the import of foreign words), unintelligibility and multilingualism were all features associated with Decadent and Symbolist poetics, but they are represented as unrefined in the instance of westernised Japanese, where the attempt to imitate European nobility becomes a parody of it.

While Italian aristocrats exhibit their knowledge of foreign languages, English characters are portrayed as embarrassingly monolingual. Clara Green, the Pre-Raphaelite beauty who has an affair with Andrea, can only say three words in Italian, 'tre monosillabi che le donne straniere imparano subito; nei quali esse credono sia racchiusa tutta la malinconia dell'amore italiano. -*Chi lo sa*!' (three monosyllables that foreign women learn immediately, in which they believe all the melancholy of Italian love is contained. -*Chi lo sa*!).[25] Lord Heathfield, the English nobleman that Elena marries to pay off her debts, speaks very limited Italian and reverts to English as soon as he addresses complex subjects.

In addition to being a national prerogative and a class construct, multilingualism is also a gender construct. In the novel, men are more polyglot than women. Moreover, foreign languages, including Latin, are often used at the expense of women. In the scene when Andrea, together with other aristocrat friends, dines at a restaurant with English, Spanish and Italian women, lack of linguistic proficiency makes the latter vulnerable to jokes and allusions. Clara Green has very limited knowledge of Italian; Giulia Arici and Maria Fortuna have no knowledge of English. Even Mercedes Silva, who sports a cigarette box with a Latin motto, does not understand Andrea's jokes. She is described by the narrator as saying 'enormous things'; however, the only lines she is granted in the text echo the words used

[24] Ibid., p. 44.
[25] Ibid., p. 256.

by Andrea to define her, 'chica però guapa' (small but smart).[26] The mockery begins as soon as Sperelli makes his introductions:

> Andrea Sperelli salutò la compagnia e, portando per mano Clara Green, disse:
> -Ecce Miss Clara Green, ancilla Domini, Sibylla palmifera, candida puella.
> -Ora pro nobis - risposero in coro il Musèllaro, il Barbarisi e il Gremiti. Le donne risero, *ma senza capire*.[27]
>
> (Andrea Sperelli greeted the company and, leading Clara Green by the hand, said 'Here is Miss Clara Green, ancilla Domini, Sibylla palmifera, candida puella.'
> 'Ora pro nobis', Musèllaro, Barbarisi, and Gremiti answered in chorus. The women laughed, *but without understanding*.)

Andrea then amuses himself by crafting for the women Latin mottos, which are sophisticated, and at the same time obscene, sexual jokes: 'Semper parata' means 'always ready', 'diu saeper fortiter' 'for a long time, often and vigorously'. The last two proposed mottos are distorted quotations from the *Aeneaid*: Virgil's '*Timeo Danaos et dona ferentes*' (I fear Greeks bearing gifts) becomes '*Non timeo dona ferentes*' (I do not fear the bearers of gifts); '*rari nantes in gurgite vasto*' (only the few swim in the vast whirlpool/rough sea) turn into 'Rarae nates cum gurgite vasto' (buttocks with a vast whirlpool).[28] Andrea, we learn, is filled by delight at the 'dolce ignoranza di quelle oche' (sweet ignorance of those geese).[29] It's a familiar phrase, which reminds us of 'the sweet ignorance of the female reader' mentioned by D'Annunzio in his letters to Treves.[30] By leaving these passages untranslated, Andrea, the character, mocks Clara and her companions, and D'Annunzio, the author, teases the *dolce lettrice* and gratifies the 'educated', polyglot reader by making them feel special.

In some instances, the act of speaking a foreign language is incorporated in the novel at a thematic, rather than stylistic, level. When Ruggero Grimiti and Ludovico Barbarisi recall Gino Bommìnaco's sexual adventure with Giulia Moceto, they note that the humour involved in the episode is untranslatable, and can be captured only

[26] Ibid., p. 258.
[27] Ibid., p. 257. Emphasis mine.
[28] I am here drawing on the translations and explanation provided by Lara Gochin Raffaelli in her translation, *Pleasure* (London: Penguin, 2013).
[29] D'Annunzio, *Il Piacere*, p. 254.
[30] D'Annunzio to Treves, 21 April 1889, in D'Annunzio, *Lettere ai Treves*, p. 71.

in Neapolitan dialect. At Andrea's request, they resort to French to get to the story's climax.[31] Similarly, when Lord Heathfield illustrates to Andrea his collection of erotic books, D'Annunzio renders the dialogue in Italian, but lets the reader know that the words have been pronounced in English. Even though we do not have access to his speech in the original, we learn of Heathfield's exasperating interrogative intonation and of his monotonous, sickening cadence. In this scene, English words tear Andreas's ears 'come un suono aspro di ferri raschiati, come lo stridore d'una lama d'acciaio a contrasto d'una lama di cristallo' (like a harsh sound of scraped irons, like the screeching of a steel blade against a crystal blade).[32] The language of Byron and Shelley, of the lofty, romantic conversations with Elena and Maria, in this episode is associated with 'gli orrori del libertinaggio inglese' (the horrors of the English libertines)[33] – of which D'Annunzio had learned through the Goncourt's Journal. If the novel, as Barberi Squarotti has underlined, is characterised by dualities – as exemplified by the dyad Elena/Maria, but also by Andrea's sophistication/vulgarity[34] – the use of multiple languages offers a magnifying lens for this ambivalence.

Multilingualism in *L'Enfant de volupté*

As Blaise Wilfred-Portal has noted, the early 1890s in France were characterised by a return to nationalism. In these years, French intellectuals became increasingly concerned about contaminations by foreign influences and preoccupied with the purity of the national language, and translation assumed a conservative function, namely the construction of foreign national literatures for the French imagination.[35] As a response, translators enhanced national markers, thereby establishing strong boundaries between French texts and translations, or domesticated foreign writers for the use of French readers, implicitly prioritising the values of their culture over the source text.

31 D'Annunzio, *Il Piacere*, p. 248.
32 Ibid., p. 334.
33 Ibid., p. 335.
34 Barberi Squarotti, 'Il Parato di Carta', p. 26.
35 Blaise Wilfert-Portal, 'Cosmopolis et l'homme invisible', in *Actes de la recherche en sciences sociales*, 144 (2002): 33–46 (pp. 44–5).

It is in this setting that Hérelle started translating D'Annunzio. In *Pétit mémoire d'un traducteur*, an account of his activity as a translator written in the 1920s, written as a guide to would-be translators and as a memoir for posterity, Hérelle notes that he has always preferred narratives with a strong local flavour, which 'au lieu de se contenter d'un formule littéraire plus ou moins internationale, expriment vraiment quelque chose de leur propre pays' (instead of being satisfied with a more or less international literary formula, really express something of their own country).[36] He advises that 'il ne faut jamais traduire un roman, fût-il d'ailleurs intéressant et bien fait, lorsque ce roman est conçu et exécuté sur le types des romans français, et pourrait aussi bien avoir été écrit à Paris qu'à Rome ou qu'à Madrid' (one should never translate a novel, even if it is interesting and well written, when this novel is conceived and executed on the types of French novels, and could as well have been written in Paris as in Rome or in Madrid).[37] While the Roman setting was attractive to Hérelle, the cosmopolitan atmosphere of *Il Piacere* thus posed some problems. His attitude toward literary multilingualism can be summarised by the motto 'une traduction française doit être écrite en français' (A French translation must be written in French).[38] A translation into French, he stresses, should result in a fluent French text, honouring French style and syntax. His letters to D'Annunzio, and his reflections in *Pétit mémoire d'un traducteur*, show that he could not conceive of mimicking the style of the source language. His translations were praised for their fluency and elegance – he even won an award from the *Académie Française* in 1897. However, his academic French did little to render D'Annunzio's precious language, his complex linguistic research and the musicality of his prose: as Guy Ducrey has noted, he could hardly be characterised as a 'Decadent translator'.[39]

Il Piacere is Gabriele D'Annunzio's first novel, written at a time in which he did not yet imagine he would become an international celebrity. It was, however, the third novel to be translated by Hérelle. By the time in which Hérelle and D'Annunzio began discussing its translation, *L'Innocente* (1892) had been published as *L'intrus* (1893),

[36] Hérelle, *Pétit mémoire d'un traducteur* (Bruxelles: Les Éditions du Hazard, 2005), p. 33.

[37] Ibid., p. 34.

[38] Ibid., p. 59.

[39] Guy Ducrey, 'Is there such a thing as 'Decadent Translator?': The Case of Georges Hérelle (1848–1935)', *Volupté* 3: 2 (Winter 2020): 11–27 (p. 18).

and the translation of *Trionfo della morte* (1894) was underway. The 'beastly' cuts[40] to which *L'Innocente* had been subjected during its publication in *Le temps* had taught D'Annunzio a lesson: French editors would not hesitate to adapt his work to their needs. He had also begun to develop a sense of Hérelle's tendency to normalise his prose in translation. Aware that *Il Piacere* would have to be heavily edited to appear in the prestigious *Revue de Paris*, at the time directed by Louis Ganderax, he decided to take the matter into his own hands. On 30 May 1894, he answered Hérelle's invitation and declared himself willing to rework and shorten *Il Piacere*.[41] On 15 June, he shared this intention with Treves.[42] The next day, he asked Hérelle to reread the book and give him his opinion about possible modifications, to check if these corresponded to the ones he had already in mind.[43] This suggests that D'Annunzio was trying to second-guess Hérelle and Ganderax, and the taste of French readers. It also demonstrates that Hérelle's task went far beyond that of a translator and that he became a close collaborator: D'Annunzio consulted him about structural changes, cuts, even the choice of the French title.[44] On 14 November, D'Annunzio sent his translator the revised manuscript for translation. Unlike the 1889 version, which begins with a flashback, this document features a linear narrative in which the fabula coincides with the plot. It is divided into four books, consists of ten chapters (the Italian edition had fifteen) and is significantly shorter.[45]

Guy Tosi has argued that cuts in the French edition were motivated by three reasons: concerns about offending the sensibilities of the target readership, awareness that by 1895 naturalism and even certain references to Aestheticism were no longer cutting-edge, and fears that readers may be able to recognise passages transcribed from French books.[46] In Tosi's reading, episodes like that of the dinner party, where Andrea and his friends use Latin and Spanish to mock their female companions, were excised because D'Annunzio was

[40] D'Annunzio to Hérelle, 10 October 1892, in Mario Cimini, ed., *Carteggio D'Annunzio-Hérelle (1891–1931)* (Lanciano: Rocco Carabba, 2004), p. 92.

[41] D'Annunzio to Hérelle, 30 May 1894, in Cimini, p. 185.

[42] D'Annunzio to Treves, 15 June 1994, in Oliva, p. 134.

[43] D'Annunzio to Hérelle, 16 June 1894, in Cimini, p. 197.

[44] See D'Annunzio to Hérelle, 7 October 1894 in Cimini, pp. 237 and 241; and 5 November 1894, p. 257. See also the letter from 31 July 1894, pp. 213–14.

[45] This manuscript is held in Hérelle's archive at the Médiathèque of Troyes and was published in a critical edition by Ivanos Ciani (Milan: Il Saggiatore, 1976).

[46] Tosi, p. 90.

worried readers might identify borrowings from Péladan's *Éducation sentimentale*.[47] However, borrowings from Péladan were preserved elsewhere. In omitting this episode – as well as the episodes in which Andrea and his friends use French to address Gino Bomminaco's sexual adventure – D'Annunzio also eliminated passages in which Andrea used his talent for foreign languages to mock monolingual characters and D'Annunzio, by extension, monolingual readers. If this was acceptable at home, D'Annunzio knew it would not be tolerated in French translation, as it would involve a disrespectful view of the reputable (probably monolingual) readerships associated with prestigious journals. As a consequence of these cuts, in the French version, Andrea's multilingualism no longer reflects the sense of duplicity that characterises the novel. His language skills are applied to more decent ends, and a less complex – if still polyglot – Italian protagonist is presented to French readerships.

D'Annunzio thought these changes would be sufficient for the *Revue de Paris*. However, this was not the case, and the version that was published in this journal (15 September 1894 to 15 March 1895), titled *L'Enfant de volupté*, differs considerably from D'Annunzio's manuscript and was the result of a complex negotiation between D'Annunzio, Hérelle and Ganderax. Some of the modifications made by D'Annunzio were ignored, others – including cuts to some of the most daring erotic scenes – were carried out without the author's consent. D'Annunzio was outraged at Ganderax's cuts but was equally invested in preserving the novel's style. He had cut the passages in which multilingualism was potentially offensive, but he was otherwise keen to preserve the cosmopolitan flavour of the book, which underlined his status as a European author and the participation of the novel in a Decadent aesthetics. However, for Hérelle, Andrea's mastery of foreign languages and his cosmopolitanism were not as attractive as the picturesque views of Rome and the strong passions that characterised the text. In *L'Enfant de volupté*, his domesticating strategy is evident even at first glance. Rome features spaces such as 'Place d'Espagne', 'rue Quatre-Fontaines', 'palais Zuccari' etc. *Lire* are exchanged for 'francs'. The names of the protagonists are francified as André Sperelli, Hélène Muti, Jules Musellaro, et cetera. Rome is thus brought closer to the French reader, rendered simultaneously exotic and familiar. At the same time, Hérelle's adoption of standard vocabulary and syntax weakened the cosmopolitan vibe and shifted

[47] Ibid., p. 94.

the focus thematically onto Italy. Throughout his letters, D'Annunzio complains that Hérelle tends to replace uncommon and extraordinary terms with insipid, modern French equivalents. He encourages him to adopt a 'Dannunzian accent',[48] and goes as far as coining the verb '*dannunzieggiare*' to address the imitation of his own style.[49] With the call: 'Sperellizzatevi!', he invites Hérelle to identify, and therefore to express himself as the novel's protagonist.[50] All, needless to say, to no avail.

Besides Hérelle's preoccupation with defending the boundaries of French, translating linguistic multiplicity was problematic because one of the main languages embedded in the source – French – coincided with the target language. As Rainier Grutman notes, in such cases 'the linguistic elements that signalled Otherness in the original run the risk of having their indexical meaning reversed and being read as "familiar" signs of Sameness'.[51] D'Annunzio asked Hérelle to keep all sentences in French, to correct them if necessary, but 'senza trasformare il senso e neppure la giacitura delle parole' (without transforming the meaning or even the order of the words).[52] Hérelle, however, could not tolerate 'accented' French. French sentences in *L'Enfant de volupté* thus betray nothing of their translational origin and merge with the rest of the narrative. Moreover, the language of the narrative no longer mimics that of French Symbolists and Decadents. If, in the Italian version, Andrea addresses Elena in French as part of his seduction strategy, in *L'Enfant de volupté* French becomes the language of the entire novel, but it is far less 'artificial', or 'mannered'.

The 'literal' translation that D'Annunzio hoped to obtain from Hérelle involved preserving rare, archaic expressions, as well as foreign citations. It also required embracing newly coined words and Italianisms. Hérelle, who in his memoirs expresses his 'repugnance' for foreign words in a translation,[53] looked at all this with suspicion. In his letters, D'Annunzio corrects Hérelle, saying the primitive Italian form 'men rozze' is better suited to describe ancient Tuscan poetry than 'moins grossies';[54] 'tondi' refers to a shape of painting and should

[48] D'Annunzio to Hérelle, 16 March 1896, in Cimini, p. 372.

[49] D'Annunzio to Hérelle, 30 June 1894, in Cimini, pp. 205–6.

[50] D'Annunzio to Hérelle, 14 November 1894, in Cimini, p. 256.

[51] Rainier Grutman, 'Refraction and Recognition: Literary Multilingualism in Translation', *Target*, 18: 1 (2006): 17–47 (p. 22).

[52] D'Annunzio to Hérelle 12–13 March 1985, in Cimini, p. 293.

[53] Hérelle, *Pétit mémoire d'un traducteur*, p. 63.

[54] D'Annunzio to Hérelle, 1 December 1894, in Cimini, p. 262.

not be replaced by 'bas-reliefs';[55] 'toccata', a musical term, should not be rendered as 'prélude', et cetera.[56] He also encourages Hérelle to keep important quotes in Italian. The ballad by Lorenzo il Magnifico, he writes, should be cited in the original; something, he stresses, that is neither 'strange nor useless'.[57] Clara Green's words in Italian ('*Che pensi?*' '*chi lo sa?*') should absolutely not be translated into French.[58]

Faced with Hérelle and Ganderax's resistance, D'Annunzio insists on the right of a translation to be perceived as such, rather than as fluid French text, and complains about domestication: 'non mi sembra né buono né da me accettabile che si voglia *franciser* quanto è possibile l'opera mia originale. (The will to *franciser* my work as much as possible seems to me neither good nor acceptable).[59] Later, his strategy changes. He gives up the fight against Francisation, and makes his case by appealing to the very norms of the French language, quoting contemporary, fashionable French writers to demonstrate that the inclusion of Italian passages does not necessarily violate French literary norms:

> Non vi spaventate! Questi italianismi non faranno cattivo effetto, giacché vedo che molti scrittori francesi si sforzano di introdurre nei loro testi frasi identiche. L'ultimo libro di Anatole France – *Le puits de Sainte-Claire* – (l'avete veduto?) è scritto. . . . in italiano.
>
> (Don't be frightened! These Italianisms will not have a bad effect, in fact I see that many French writers try to introduce identical phrases into their texts. The latest book by Anatole France – *Le puits de Sainte-Claire* – (have you seen it?) is written . . . . in Italian.)[60]

He makes a similar argument as he instructs Hérelle to leave the epigraph by Leonardo Da Vinci – chosen specifically for the French volume – in Italian, and resorts again to citing France's *Le puits de Sainte-Claire*, which, he repeats, is filled with Italian epigraphs: 'questo è permesso agli scrittori francesi [. . .] sarà dunque permesso anche a me' (this is allowed for French writers [. . .] therefore it will also be allowed for me). D'Annunzio assumed that, by being translated into French, he would become part of the French literary

55 D'Annunzio to Hérelle, January 1895, in Cimini, p. 280.
56 D'Annunzio to Hérelle, 12–13 March 1895, in Cimini, pp. 293–4.
57 D'Annunzio to Hérelle, 16 December 1894, in Cimini, p. 269.
58 D'Annunzio to Hérelle, 4 February 1895, in Cimini, p. 283.
59 D'Annunzio to Hérelle, 23 December 1894, in Cimini 2004, p. 274.
60 D'Annunzio to Hérelle, 12–13 March 1895, in Cimini, p. 294.

system and have the same freedom as French authors. This assumption, however, turned out to be wrong: the corrections by Hérelle and Ganderax make clear that, in their vision, a translated book was subordinate, and it was unthinkable that it could challenge the grammar of a language of which the author was not himself a citizen.

Investing in preserving the elitist tone of the book, D'Annunzio also defended citations in Latin. 'Oliva speciosa', he notes in his letters to Hérelle, is a quotation from Jeremiah 11:16 and must be left in the Latin form.[61] The same applies to the adjective 'mascula' used to describe a lesbian character, an epithet that Horace uses to refer to Sappho.[62] The omission of the Latin words that describe the solemn gait of Maria Ferres ('*candida super nivem*' and '*incedit per liliam et super nivem*') triggers his fury.[63] He is astonished that the verses from Goethe's *Roman Elegies*, which, he clarifies, he quoted correctly, should be flagged by Ganderax, and he insists they should be retained.[64] English terms like 'home, comfort, luncheon, garden-party, keepsake, [. . .] babies, lady etc',[65] he writes, touching a sensitive point for Hérelle, should not be 'othered' by *italics*, because they have become part of the French language.

Just as he had rejected Treves's suggestion to translate foreign citations in footnotes, D'Annunzio requested that footnotes with translations of foreign words should be removed from the Calmann-Lévy edition: 'sopprimete naturalmente nel volume tutte le traduzioni delle frasi inglesi e tedesche messe a piè di pagina dal Ganderax. Quelle traduzioni, ad uso dei lettori ignoranti, sono una goffaggine' (in the volume delete, obviously, all translations from English and German placed in footnotes by Ganderax. Those translations, there for the use of ignorant readers, are awkward).[66] In the draft prepared for Hérelle's translation, D'Annunzio had removed the episode where Andrea explains to Elena that he prefers to be read by few, and to stay away from new readerships – another passage from Péladan, adapted to the Italian context.[67] However, he was not willing to give

61 D'Annunzio to Hérelle, 1 December 1894, in Cimini, p. 262.

62 D'Annunzio to Hérelle, 16 December 1894, in Cimini, p. 270.

63 D'Annunzio to Hérelle, 24 February and 7 March 1895, in Cimini, p. 289.

64 D'Annunzio to Hérelle, 23 December 1894, in Cimini 2004, p. 274.

65 D'Annunzio to Hérelle, 12–13 March 1895, in Cimini, p. 294.

66 D'Annunzio to Hérelle, 12–13 March 1895, in Cimini, p. 295.

67 'What does it matter to me to have, for example, to have one hundred readers on the island of the Sardinians and also ten in Empoli and five, let's say, in Orvieto? And what pleasure comes to me from being known as much as the confectioner Tizio or the perfumer Gaius': D'Annunzio, *Il Piacere*, p. 55.

up the elitist tone of the text – which had paradoxically contributed to its broad success among Italian readerships. His insistence on the multilingual character of the text was part of this intent.

Hérelle and Ganderax reluctantly accepted some, but not all, of D'Annunzio's requests. Hérelle's willingness to compromise can be explained by his fascination with the author, and by his conviction that, as a creator of masterpieces, D'Annunzio could be considered as an exception: he would be far stricter with other Italian writers.[68] Even so, citations in foreign languages and borrowings were considerably reduced in translation. As Robert Young writes, world literature may appear to celebrate 'global consciousness', but it instead 'reorganises each language and its literature in relation to nationality, region or cultural origin'.[69] D'Annunzio was pushing for a multilingual, experimental translation, one that would present him as a transnational author, insert him into contemporary literary French trends. Hérelle and Ganderax, in contrast, aimed to introduce him as a world author in the French context, and to do so, they needed to emphasise his Italianness. The success of *L'Enfant de volupté* proved them right, for even sympathetic critics like Melchior de Vogüé, who recognised Sperelli's cosmopolitan culture, conflated the author and his character, and inserted both in the discourse of the 'Latin Renaissance': Sperelli, for de Vogüé, was a 'Southerner', an example of 'ethnic immunity' in which strong passions coexisted with artistic sensibility, a case of atavism exhibiting features from the Italian Renaissance.[70] Stylistic similarities with French writing, in contrast, fed the narratives of D'Annunzio's detractors.[71] Those who, like the translator Edouard Rod, noted that French readers were exposed not so much to D'Annunzio, but to D'Annunzio 'revu, abrégé et atténué par M. Hérelle' (revised, abridged and toned down by M. Hérelle),[72] were

[68] See, for example, the systematic censuring of cosmopolitan references in the case of Matilde Serao and Grazia Deledda.

[69] Robert Young, 'That Which is Causally Called a Language', *PMLA* 131: 5 (2016), 1207–21 (p. 1209).

[70] Eugène-Melchior de Vogüé, 'La Renaissance Latine. G. d'A : Poèmes et romans', *Revue des deux mondes* (1895), 187–206.

[71] Jeanne-Marie Tosi, 'La fortune française de "L'Enfant de volupté"', *D'Annunzio Europeo*, ed. by Pietro Gibellini (Toma: Lucarini, 1991), pp. 61–78 (p. 70).

[72] Edouard Rod, *Journal des Débats*, 16 May 1889, cited in Guy Tosi, ed., *Gabriele d'Annunzio à Georges Hérelle. Correspondance, accompagnée de douze sonnets cisalpins* (Paris: Denoël 1946), p. 58.

rebuked by D'Annunzio himself, who defended Hérelle and assumed responsibility for all the modifications in the text.[73]

Conclusion

Scholars of literary multilingualism generally agree that by choosing to host more than one language in their texts, writers counter nationalism and promote inclusion.[74] These arguments, however, do not necessarily apply to *fin-de-siècle* fiction. In *Il Piacere*, multilingualism remains highly ambivalent. Citations from European literature display D'Annunzio's outward gaze, and the use of foreign words turns Italian into a hospitable language open to receiving the foreign. On the other hand, words and sentences in foreign languages underline the modernity of Italian literature, and mark the superiority of Italians over foreigners, men over women, educated over 'common' readerships. Multilingualism is thus closely bound to nationalism and elitism.

As *Il Piacere* travelled across linguistic and cultural contexts, it encountered another type of literary nationalism – that of domesticating translation, which, as Esperança Bielsa argues, 'by rendering the foreign falsely familiar and transparent [. . .] denies any true openness to the other and thus any genuine cosmopolitan commitment'.[75] In the French volume published by Calmann-Lévy, and even more so in the version published in the *Revue de deux mondes*, changes and cuts altered – among other things – the multilingual fabric of D'Annunzio's text. In Thomas Loué and Blaise Wilfert-Portal's view, D'Annunzio accepted these adjustments because of his limited investment in the French publication of his texts. They argue that he cared about being published in Paris because of the potential financial gain and because this enabled him to put pressure on Treves, who after the scandals that arose in Italy with the publication of *Il Piacere*, refrained from

[73] D'Annunzio to Hérelle, 21 May 1895, in Cimini, p. 311. See also Jeanne-Marie Tosi, 'La fortune française de 'L'Enfant de volupté', p. 68.

[74] Brian Lennon, *In Babel's Shadow: Multilingual Literatures, Monolingual States* (Minneapolis: University of Minnesota Press, 2010), p. 121; Juliette Taylor-Batty, *Multilingualism in Modernist Fiction* (London: Palgrave Macmillan, 2013), p. 27; Laura Lonsdale, *Multilingualism and Modernity: Barbarism in Spanish and American Literature* (London: Palgrave, 2018), p. 20.

[75] Esperança Bielsa, 'Cosmopolitanism as Translation', *Cultural Sociology*, 8: 4 (2014), 392–406 (397), p. 396.

publishing his books.[76] While it is doubtless true that the French publication involved considerable profit and that its symbolic value was transferable into the Italian context, D'Annunzio's letters show that he was all but detached from the afterlife of his text. In fact, he was determined to play an active role in the adaptation for French readerships. His pre-emptive strategy, however, was only partially successful. The price for entering world literature involved sacrificing the polyphony of the source text, reducing the number of intertextual references and foreign borrowings, and marking the remaining ones as 'different' through italics. Overall, Hérelle's translations opened the door to D'Annunzio in France, thereby also facilitating translations into other languages. D'Annunzio became a 'world author' – precisely what his own strategies of multilingualism and foreign borrowing had aimed to achieve in the Italian context, and was recognised by influential critics such as de Vogüé as an Italian exponent of Decadence, 'le plus latin des genies latins' (the most Latin of the Latin geniuses).[77] However, his attempts to turn French into a hospitable language, as he had done with Italian, were destined to fail, because this was not part of the vision of Hérelle and Ganderax, and because, in a context that was becoming increasingly nationalistic, D'Annunzio's transgressive writing was only acceptable insofar as it was marked as 'foreign' and 'different' from the French.

[76] Thomas Loué and Blaise Wilfert-Portal, 'D'Annunzio à l'usage des Français: la traduction comme censure informelle (fin du XIXe siècle)', *Ethnologie française*, 36:1 (2006), 101–10 (p. 106).

[77] de Vogüé, p. 187.

Chapter 4

'The essence of the race': *La figlia di Iorio* and Italian Dialects

Sarah Zappulla Muscarà and Enzo Zappulla, translated by Stuart Oglethorpe

On 6 November 1906, the philosopher and poet from Gorizia, Carlo Michelstaedter, an Austrian national of Jewish extraction with a central European education, attended the staging of *'A figghia di Joriu* by the Compagnia Drammatica Siciliana at Florence's Teatro Niccolini. That same night, 'completely drained due to the feelings experienced' and still prey to 'the anxiety that grows and makes one truly suffer, constricting one's throat', he conveyed his strong emotions to his family:

> Grasso is powerful in his every gesture and emphasis. He has one of those intense and fervent voices that make one's head spin. In particular, the story he tells to the saint in the second act, where in the Sicilian version there is nothing lyrical and all the poetic beauty has been removed, is a masterpiece. He seemed to be reliving the earlier scenes in all their intensity. I had experienced a similar feeling when I saw Tumiati perform, but to a lesser degree: Grasso is natural, and more absolute. Aguglia cannot always maintain the same high level; I did not like her final cry, 'you cannot, you must not', and 'the flame is beautiful'. But otherwise, she and the whole company are marvellous, and certainly better as an ensemble than any company not using dialect. They create the impression that the play, in Sicilian like this, is the original, and the Italian version the translation, and surely D'Annunzio conceived of it just as we hear it from Grasso.[1]

This assessment hit the mark, for *La figlia di Iorio* (*Iorio's Daughter*) was largely indebted to the attraction of dialect and the appeal of Giovanni Grasso, judged to be the world's greatest tragic actor by

[1] Carlo Michelstaedter, *Epistolario*, ed. by Sergio Campailla (Milan: Adelphi, 1983), p. 139. All quotations in this chapter have been translated from Italian by Stuart Oglethorpe.

Bjørnstjerne Bjørnson, Isaac Babel, Gordon Craig, Lee Strasberg and Vsevolod Meyerhold.[2]

This chapter documents the transformations of *La figlia di Iorio* during its 'second life' in dialect, including translations into Sicilian by Giuseppe Antonio Borgese and into the Abruzzo dialect by Cesare de Titta, and the parody in Neapolitan by Eduardo Scarpetta. Why was the play so well suited to dialect translations? What did dialect mean for Gabriele D'Annunzio, and how did he contribute to these translations and their staging? What was the relationship between the translations and individual interpretations by specific theatre companies? How were the translations and reworkings received? Press coverage, reviews, judicial depositions and other sources all help respond to these questions, generating a new perspective on one of the best-known and most important works of D'Annunzio's literary career. This highlights the fact that translation, for D'Annunzio, was a fundamental process going beyond the need to be known abroad. Pascale Casanova stresses that for writers from 'peripheral' countries, translation into dominant languages is necessary to make their presence felt internationally.[3] For *La figlia di Iorio*, however, it was translation into minority languages that contributed to its broadened popularity and ensured its status as a masterpiece.

Borgese's Sicilian Translation

On 16 April 1903, the Compagnia Drammatica Siciliana, directed by Nino Martoglio, put on Giuseppe Giusti Sinopoli's *La zolfara* (The Sulphur Mine) at the Teatro Manzoni in Milan, with Giovanni Grasso in the leading role. It was an unprecedented success. The Italian version of this naturalist play was already known in Milan: it received a lukewarm reception during the 1897–8 season of the Teatro Filodrammatici, where it was performed by Giovanni Emanuel and Achille Vitti's company. This time, its themes – property, passion, abject poverty and violence – won over the audience thanks to Grasso's powerful interpretation.

D'Annunzio was also in the Lombard capital at that time, for the publication of his cycle of poems, *Laudi*. His presence at a performance

[2] Sarah Zappulla Muscarà and Enzo Zappulla, *Giovanni Grasso. 'Il più grande attore tragico del mondo'* (Catania: La Cantinella, 1995).

[3] Pascale Casanova, *The World Republic of Letters*, trans. by M. B. DeBevoise (Cambridge, MA: Harvard University Press, 2004).

of *La zolfara* is confirmed by a letter dated 17 April 1903, responding to Martoglio's invitation to attend a tribute evening for Grasso:

> My dear sir, thank you for your kind offer. This ticket might make some other poet happy, and I therefore return it. I already have my seats, which I have booked in advance; and I eagerly look forward to the evening. In truth, joy over this unexpected discovery is, in me, mixed with melancholy; because I envy Sicilian writers a marvellous vehicle for their trade such as Giovanni Grasso, and I regret not being able to make use of him, and being forced to repress my longstanding desire to attempt rustic tragedy. Yesterday evening, in the profound emotion that assailed me, I was also afflicted by nostalgia for my old land of the Abruzzi. My thanks go to you, to the great and virtuous Giovanni Grasso and his theatrical companions, in whom the essence of the race is expressed with such power. I hope to be able to meet you and to reiterate, in person, my admiration and gratitude.[4]

La zolfara made a great impression on D'Annunzio. Grasso's acting was widely reported as revelling in strong gestural expressiveness, eschewing the allusive performance style that deliberately left aspects of a character ill-defined; he was accustomed to bending scripts to his animated style and dramatic force, injecting extra passion. It was his propitious combination of fierce emotion and innate theatricality that attracted D'Annunzio; the latter, although his response was mediated by his poetic sensibilities, felt both the remorseless intensity of passion and a yearning for the mythic rural past. In consequence, the poet promised to write a play for Grasso – that 'marvellous vehicle for art, honest and great' – which was to have a 'new spirit'.[5] On 18 July 1903, some months after seeing Grasso in *La zolfara*, he started to write *La figlia di Iorio*, a pastoral tragedy set in a timeless Abruzzo. Grasso thus played a part in the genesis of the play, together with a painting of the same title by D'Annunzio's friend Paolo Michetti, first shown in 1895, and the recollection of a mob scene he claimed to have witnessed with the painter, when a dishevelled crying woman was pursued by harvest workers driven wild by the sun and lust.[6]

[4] 'L'omaggio di Gabriele d'Annunzio alla Compagnia Siciliana', *La Perseveranza* (Milan), 30 April 1903.

[5] This description is quoted in Domenico Oliva, 'Intorno alla nuova "Figlia di Iorio"', *Il Giornale d'Italia*, 13 September 1904.

[6] Filippo Surico, *Ora luminosa. Le mie conversazioni letterarie con Gabriele d'Annunzio nell'ospitalità di Villa Cargnacco a Gardone Riviera* (Rome: Urbs, 1939), pp. 39–40.

The work was completed in August 1903, written quickly in just five weeks at the peaceful Villa Borghese in Nettuno (on the coast south of Rome), where D'Annunzio was staying with Eleonora Duse, his daughter Renata, and his friend Annibale Tenneroni. He immediately read it to Duse. 'What an amazing thing has been born there! What light of incomparable beauty! A divine work! Worthy of him!' she wrote to Benigno Palmerio two days after its completion. D'Annunzio also wrote to Palmerio: 'this last Saturday, at sunset, I finished *La figlia di Iorio*, which I think is the best thing that I have yet composed: a profound and simple work. While writing it, I felt my roots in my native earth.'[7] For this 'canto dell'antico sangue' (song of the ancient race), as it was described in the play's dedication to Abruzzo, D'Annunzio used the old form of Tuscan, a language with the 'flavour of dialect' that was nevertheless very Italian. He also made the most of the rich Abruzzo folklore he had previously collected, having already translated many songs from dialect with a view to capturing the popular spirit.

While writing the play, D'Annunzio was already considering its performance and worrying over finding suitable actors. On 31 August 1903, he wrote to Michetti that to stage this tragedy would require 'unspoilt actors, full of life's experiences, with simple and eloquent gestures, and voices governed by their poetic spirit. Because everything here is song and gesture. Where to find them?' His proposal was that 'shortly, I will come to the Abruzzo and read you the play. Would you like to help me with settling on the local actors, determining suitable locations, and identifying costumes?'[8]

The first formal read-through was at the end of September, attended by Adolfo de Carolis and a young Borgese, who was invited to translate *La figlia di Iorio* into Sicilian for Grasso's company. The memory of the staging of *La zolfara* in Milan must still have been vivid if D'Annunzio's first thought was the linguistic transposition of his pastoral tragedy into the styles and tones required by actors who spoke 'the language of primal passions', whose maieutic function is evident from another passage in his letter of 31 August to Michetti: 'this work had been living within me, unrecognised, for years'.[9]

[7] Benigno Palmerio, *Con d'Annunzio alla Capponcina (1898–1910)* (Florence: Vallecchi, 1938), pp. 148–9.

[8] Tomaso Sillani, *Francesco Paolo Michetti* (Milan–Rome: Treves–Treccani–Tumminelli, 1932), p. 113.

[9] Ibid., p. 113.

The first performance was given by the Compagnia Talli–Gramatica–Calabresi at the Teatro Lirico in Milan, on 2 March 1904. The part of Mila di Codro had initially been promised to Eleonora Duse, but in the meantime D'Annunzio's feelings for her had cooled; it was taken by Irma Gramatica, while Ruggero Ruggeri played Aligi. There was a gap of only six months between this and the staging by the Compagnia Drammatica Siciliana. The dialect performance was supposed to go ahead before the Italian one, but because of the elopement of lead actress Marinella Bragaglia with the company's manager, Vittorio Marazzi Diligenti, it had to be postponed. The work's 'second life' was actually intended to be its 'first'. In the new line-up, Bragaglia, who was now treading the boards in Italian, was replaced by Mimì Aguglia from Palermo: she too had been born into acting and was picked out by Martoglio from the Teatro Jovinelli, a variety theatre on Rome's Piazza Guglielmo Pepe. Borgese later recalled the impression D'Annunzio's reading of *La figlia di Iorio* made on him:

> It was something fresh and beautiful: a truly rustic *Aminta*, and a play entirely full of music without need of any musical instruments. To me, it seemed miraculous; and it seemed a marvellous gift from the poet to invite me to translate his poem into my native dialect for the Sicilian company, and give it its 'second life'. Too generously, he praised me for having done this by dedicating the book to me.[10]

Writing again many years later, Borgese described the first act as 'wonderful' and the whole play as 'extraordinary'. In consequence, when D'Annunzio asked him to translate it into Sicilian for Grasso's company, he accepted with alacrity:

> Really, a young man from Sicily at that time, rather than strengthening and deepening his roots, would have been working hard at shedding his dialect, by affecting the Florentine manner. That day, I was afraid that I had forgotten it, I would say. However, I energetically set to work, using dictionaries and books of the island's poetry both ancient and modern.[11]

Borgese was a twenty-one-year-old Sicilian from Polizzi Generosa, in the Madonie area, and as a young intellectual he had shown early promise: he was editor of the Florentine journal *Hermes* and author of

[10] Giuseppe Antonio Borgese, 'Grasso allo zenit', *Corriere della Sera*, 19 October 1930.

[11] Giuseppe Antonio Borgese, 'Con d'Annunzio a quei tempi', in Borgese, *Da Dante a Thomas Mann*, ed. by Giulio Vallese (Milan: Mondadori, 1958), pp. 282–9 (pp. 286–7).

'L'opera poetica di Gabriele d'Annunzio', a long essay that had been much appreciated by the poet himself. He set to work with enthusiasm:

> [I produced] a work in a high-flown and literary Sicilian, faithfully following the original even in the number of lines and the assonances, and setting it out on hand-made paper – then obligatory for poetry manuscripts just as for philosophical journals – in the handwriting of that era, with upright characters that looked like bayonets.[12]

The transposition into dialect was a reworking of primal passions, connected to the deepest and innermost emotions. It captured the characters and settings of the mythic country village with remarkable acuity and, while matching the beauty of D'Annunzio's Italian text and remaining largely faithful to it, heightened its primordial emotions. Around May of 1904, at the Teatro Adriano in Rome, Borgese read the Sicilian text to Martoglio's reconstituted Compagnia in the presence of de Carolis, the set designer, and D'Annunzio, who praised its 'beautiful verses'.[13] Borgese's translation was later described by the critic from *Tribuna* (11 September 1904) as 'human, very natural, effective and powerful', and 'a true and excellent work of art'. The difficulties the young man had to overcome were stressed, 'not least those concerning the meticulous conservation of the verse, retaining its nuances of meaning, and that of the harshness of the dialect', as was the care with which the text had been stripped of words that might have been hard to understand, thus making the dialect easily comprehensible to a wider Italian public. In *Il Giornale di Sicilia* on 14 September, Gioacchino Bartolone highlighted D'Annunzio's judgement of the translation as 'excellent' and his trust in the actors. Luigi Bellinzoni, in *L'Attualità Settimanale* on 11 September, found the translation 'masterly' and observed that 'the Sicilian lines are sometimes livelier and more effective than the marvellous lines of the [original] text itself, which, by offering a literal translation, it never betrayed'.

The play opened on 17 September 1904 at the Teatro Costanzi in Rome. This theatrical performance had been awaited with feverish interest not only by D'Annunzio but also many who did not wish

[12] Borgese, 'Grasso allo zenit'.

[13] The manuscript of Borgese's *'A figghia di Jorio* was lost in the bombing of Milan on 24 November 1942, but the script kept by Giovanni Grasso, now held by the Istituto di Storia dello Spettacolo Siciliano, allows us to reconstruct Borgese's text.

to miss out on a 'veritable artistic event'.[14] In *'A figghia di Joriu*, Martoglio, with D'Annunzio's agreement, shrewdly introduced Sicilian musical themes by the composer Alberto Favara, skilfully uniting dialect and music along the lines of classical Greek theatre. The harvesters' baying cries became a strong and threatening chant, while the laments in the third act were performed by professional mourners in the traditional manner, judged by the press to be 'still in force' in the provinces of Catania and Trapani.[15] The music thus contributed to reproducing the regional dimension, an 'exotic' feature for the Roman public, and helped give the tragedy an almost ethnographic aspect.

The opening performance by the Compagnia Drammatica Siciliana enjoyed a triumphal success. A few days later, at the suggestion of cabinet minister Vittorio Emanuele Orlando, the king made Giovanni Grasso an officer of the Order of the Crown of Italy. *'A figghia di Joriu* ran eight nights. However, alongside the enthusiastic press coverage, disapproval, in varying degrees, also made itself heard. The translation into Sicilian gave rise to very different reactions: the language used by Borgese, far from being a stable signifier, took on values varying with the reader. According to Martoglio, Borgese 'has used words from Sicily's various spoken forms that are closest to the common language', and he described the translation as 'excellent both in expressive intensity and in faithfulness'.[16] For Giustino Ferri, Borgese's dialect seemed 'select and Decadent'.[17] Domenico Oliva praised the translation as 'very faithful' and the lines as 'soft and musical', emphasising 'the theatrical realism of this well-constructed pastoral tragedy'.[18] Despite disagreements about the staging, there was universal emphasis on the 'double' translation, which involved linguistic transposition and also a different style of performance. Oliva's account, for example, seems not to refer to the play by the refined D'Annunzio but rather to a blood-curdling performance on the stage of Catania's cramped and vile-smelling Teatro Machiavelli. He praised the acting by Mimì Aguglia, a Mila di Codra

[14] Lucio D'Ambra, 'Le Théâtre. À propos de la nouvelle édition de "La figlia di Iorio"', *L'Italie* (Rome), 16 September 1904.

[15] 'Notizie teatrali', *Corriere della Sera*, 30 August 1904.

[16] Oliva, 'Intorno alla nuova "Figlia di Iorio"'.

[17] Leandro [Giustino Lorenzo Ferri], 'Sul carro di Tespi. Autunno teatrale', *Capitan Fracassa* (Rome), 12 September 1904.

[18] Domenico Oliva, '"La figlia di Iorio" tradotta in dialetto siciliano da G. A. Borgese al Teatro Costanzi', *Il Giornale d'Italia*, 18 September 1904.

who 'was more woman than actress: she wept, shook, begged and cried out as a woman should weep, shake, beg and cry out', and commended Grasso, who had been able to adapt the part to his temperament, transforming the protagonist into 'a hot-blooded Aligi', 'the central and dominant character of the whole piece'.[19] According to the deputising critic for *L'arte drammatica*, Grasso had put 'all the fire from the land of the sulphur mines' into his interpretation of Aligi, who 'has lost a little of the lyrical expressiveness that Gabriele D'Annunzio intended to give him, to take on the human passion of a man who feels the urges of the flesh, loves with his heart and his senses, weeps, grips tight, and kisses, all with furious intensity'.[20] Ugo Falena stressed the distance between linguistic and intersemiotic translation when he described Borgese's endeavour as 'literal, too faithful to the text and scarcely faithful to the dialect'; but he described the actors as 'spontaneous, full of energy and passion, rough-edged and wild'. He thought the actors were ill at ease precisely because they were 'held back by the bonds of a cadence that was new to them, and of an art hitherto unknown to them', while the costumes were 'simply hideous'.[21] The anonymous reviewer from *Il Corriere della Sera* emphasised the excessive theatrical violence, the antithesis of D'Annunzio's customary lyricism:

> *La figlia di Iorio*? No. A Sicilian drama. [. . .] The ascetic figure who in D'Annunzio's tragedy ennobles the violent and bloody episode, who contains the violence and brutality within strict boundaries, and who injects great tragic tension into what was merely an episode from the past, has completely disappeared . . . he is now long gone. Aligi is no longer the dreaming – and dreamy – soul of a shepherd: he is a violent man, who says that he has slept for seven hundred years but in reality is explosively alert and troubled.[22]

According to the pseudonymous critic 'Leporello', it was the 'coarse, brutal and violent' interpretation by the Sicilians that made the tragedy seem 'closer to its origin, like the jewel still imprisoned in its rough mineral shell'. The Sicilian company's interpretation, he

19 Ibid.

20 Vice Riccareo (pseudonym), '"La figlia di Iorio" al Costanzi', *L'arte drammatica* (Milan), 24 September 1904.

21 Ugo Folena, '"La figlia di Iorio" in siciliano', *Il Tirso* (Rome), 18 September 1904.

22 'Filodrammatici. "La figlia di Iorio" tradotta in siciliano da G. A. Borgese', *Corriere della Sera*, 21 December 1904.

suggested, gave the tragedy back its original purpose. He allowed that Grasso, whose Aligi seemed 'more a man possessed than a mystic', had overdone things, but Aguglia's interpretation, he argued, was worthy of praise.[23]

For the critic from *Il Marzocco*, the second staging in Florence, in January 1905, although more restrained and thus closer to the theatrical style of the Talli company than that of the production in Rome, did not seem a success, despite the dramatic quality of Aguglia's performance; this did not justify 'the enormous effort that the translation must have cost whoever brought it with such care to its conclusion'.[24] A few months earlier in the same publication, in the wake of the play's opening in Florence on 5 October 1904, Enrico Corradini had observed that 'the translation of Gabriele D'Annunzio's tragedy from Italian into Sicilian does not take place so much in the passage from the [national] language into dialect. More in the passage from the performance by Italian actors to that by Sicilian actors.' In Corradini's opinion, their execution transformed 'the simple harmony and classic line of the original picture into a canvas alight with colours and violent in its hues, and into a spectacle pulsing with action'.[25] The play's presentation in Genoa, as well as its translation, elicited the 'unparalleled' admiration of Alessandro Varaldo.[26] Filippo Mandalari, reviewing a performance in Catania for two different newspapers, maintained that Borgese's skill lay in not having despoiled 'the marvellous lines' by D'Annunzio 'of their incisive beauty and, especially, their singular character', and in having recreated in the Sicilian dialect 'in an admirable manner, the verse, rhythm and musicality of the original text, preserving all its heightened and poetic effectiveness'.[27] The actors drew enthusiastic comments almost everywhere: 'astonishingly effective'; 'marvellous'; 'not a single superfluity, nor any mournful delivery of the lines, but continuous action that could move and touch one in an extraordinary

[23] Leporello (pseudonym), 'Rivista teatrale. "La figlia di Iorio" in dialetto siciliano', *L'Illustrazione Italiana*, 25 December 1904.

[24] 'G.', '"La figlia di Iorio" in siciliano', *Il Marzocco* (Florence), 29 January 1905.

[25] E. C. [Enrico Corradini], 'Marginalia. "La figlia di Iorio" in siciliano', *Il Marzocco* (Florence), 9 October 1904.

[26] Alessandro Varaldo, '"La figlia di Iorio" al Politeama Regina Margherita', *Il Corriere di Genova*, 3 February 1905.

[27] Filippo Mandalari, 'D'Annunzio in siciliano', *La Sicilia* (Catania), 29–30 September 1904; and '"La figlia di Iorio" al Biondo', *L'Ora* (Palermo), 13 May 1905.

manner'; 'a true triumph'.[28] Mimì Aguglia was 'sublime and enchanting'.[29]

This 'pastoral tragedy' remained in Grasso's repertoire at length, although along the road it gradually lost the magic of its early performances; the original lively production by the Compagnia Drammatica Siciliana owed much to Martoglio, its skilled and sensitive artistic director, and to D'Annunzio, who restrained Grasso's excessively exuberant interpretation. How close was the relationship between the Italian and dialect texts, and why did *La figlia di Iorio*'s new guise suit it so well?

Dialect is the hallmark of linguistic improvisation, the popular sphere, passion, memory, nostalgia and myth. This can be contrasted with the world evoked by D'Annunzio, employing a constant flow of linguistic nuances drawing on both the wide span of Italian literary history and a sophisticated oral heritage: monastic prayer books, popular songs, ritual responses, chants and incantations. His language used ancient terms in the same way that dialect words can be employed, to give flesh to signs, concepts and sentiments. This was a sort of humanisation of the divine: its restitution to the earth, since the 'song of the ancient race' could not be intoned in a language remote from the people's way of speaking. It had to link back to the idioms of that world, to its geographical, biological and anthropological heritage, and to an indigenous Mediterranean tradition. By extracting the secret and sweet-smelling spirits of D'Annunzio's rich text and transforming them into the music of dialect, Borgese conjured the sense of a bygone time.

There were few differences between D'Annunzio's texts and Borgese's translation. Precisely because of their minimal nature, these were freighted with meaning. Displaying a more spontaneous emotional energy, the dialect version differed in the choice of vocabulary, figures of speech, tenses and punctuation; however, it always maintained a relationship with D'Annunzio's style, which dictated the metrical artistry, classical manner, lyrical high notes, musical cadences and the courtly and archaic vocabulary. The established literary tradition of Sicilian dialect, which ranged from the poetry of

[28] Il Capitan Spaventa (pseudonym), 'I teatri di Roma. "La figlia di Iorio" al Costanzi', *Il Tirso* (Rome), 25 September 1904; 'Notizie teatrali ed artistiche. Teatro Carignano', *Gazzetta del Popolo*, 16 March 1905; '"La figlia di Iorio" in siciliano', *L'arte drammatica* (Milan), 19 November 1904; 'Sul carro di Tespi. A Livorno', *Il Tirso* (Rome), 12 February 1905.

[29] 'Sul carro di Tespi. A Trieste', *Il Tirso* (Rome), 15 October 1905.

the thirteenth-century school of Frederick II to that produced by the followers of Giovanni Meli, meant that it was well suited to conveying D'Annunzio's sublime verse; its greater depth allowed the poet's images, which he weaves together in his portrayal of the human soul, to become yet more intimately bound together. Borgese's deft variations, minimal shifts in location and expressive repetitions were sometimes enough for the poetic nature of D'Annunzio's verse to be enhanced in the richness and musicality of Sicilian dialect, with its capacity to paint an impressionistic picture using the minimum of brushstrokes. Metaphorical nuances are more frequent; a character's actual name is sometimes replaced by that of their family, emphasising kinship; and exclamation marks are used much more, weakening the solemnity of D'Annunzio's verses but emphasising their passion.

Borgese employed all the seductive features of dialect: verb tenses, metathesis and the ample presence of modified nouns (with diminutive, augmentative and pejorative suffixes), which sometimes charge a sentence with affection or tenderness, by virtue of their intimate tone, and sometimes express belittlement or scorn. The dialect used was heterogeneous and without particularly marked features that would have linked it to a specific geographical area; instead, it brought together the spoken languages that would have been heard in the area around Palermo, in Catania, and in other parts of Sicily. It was thus a hybrid creation: a diverse and rich kind of unified Sicilian, which made *'A figghia di Joriu* a masterwork fashioned from the original masterwork.

De Titta's Translation in the Abruzzo Dialect

Translation into Sicilian had not been D'Annunzio's only immediate thought; naturally, he had also considered the Abruzzo dialect. He was therefore quick to read the pastoral tragedy to his friend Filippo de Titta, who later recalled his proposal: 'Do you hear? This is the song of our ancient blood. You and [your cousin] Cesare will translate it into *abruzzese*, bringing *La figlia di Iorio* back to its true maternal form of speech'.[30] In fact, Cesare de Titta saw this project through on his own, but out of respect for Filippo did not belie the

30 Filippo de Titta, 'Un capolavoro di G. d'Annunzio', *La Fiaccola* (Ortona), 25 December 1914.

myth of the translator cousins.[31] Just one instruction was given by D'Annunzio in his letter of 20 March 1910: 'keep the translation free of too many local forms'. The *abruzzese* version was staged many years later, on 24 August 1923, at an open-air theatre on the grounds of the Villa De Felice in Castellammare Adriatico. The performance enjoyed little success, not least because of the mediocre execution by the cast.

Whereas Borgese had used the Sicilian of the classics for his translation, de Titta employed the Abruzzo dialect of 'Monteclum' (its older name), a small town in the Chieti area. Despite the different approach, de Titta's translation was also acclaimed by the critics for its 'great faithfulness to the original text and technical skill'.[32] In *La figlia di Iorio*, D'Annunzio sought to recreate environments, traditions, customs and beliefs of his own Abruzzo, which by means of the insertion of dialect features still retained its presence in a language that recreated ancient Tuscan. In this return to the work's Nietzschean 'mythical maternal womb', *La fìjje di Iorie*, without betraying the original model, acquired an entirely local flavour that was strongly redolent of folklore. Once again, the guise in dialect 'proved to be not just a mechanical shift in vocabulary, but a "legitimate reincarnation" of an imaginative tale in a "more authentic form of speech"'.[33]

Scarpetta's Neapolitan Parody and Scandal

Despite their different approaches, the translations by Borgese and de Titta both elicited ancient or primitive experiences and emotions, using language to indicate a lost imaginary. D'Annunzio's work also gave rise to a different form of translation, whose objective was not to evoke the popular spirit but to generate laughter by transformation of the tragic form. Parody is the fate of every literary or

[31] The translation finally appeared in the 1980s: Gabriele D'Annunzio, *La figlia di Iorio, con a fronte la traduzione in dialetto abruzzese di Cesare de Titta*, ed. by Vittore Verratti (Pescara: Centro Nazionale di Studi Dannunziani, 1988).

[32] Umberto Russo, 'La traduzione in abruzzese della "Figlia di Iorio"', in *'La figlia di Iorio'. Atti del VII Convegno internazionale di studi dannunziani, Pescara, 24–6 October 1985*, ed. by Edoardo Tiboni (Pescara: Centro nazionale di studi dannunziani in Pescara, 1986), pp. 267–74 (pp. 272–3).

[33] Vittore Verratti, editorial introduction, in D'Annunzio, *'La figlia di Iorio' con a fronte la traduzione in dialetto abruzzese*, p. 7. Verratti quotes from reviews of the play.

theatrical masterpiece, and *La figlia di Iorio* was not exempt. The scandal surrounding it only increased the fame of D'Annunzio's tragedy, emphasising how dialect translation and adaptation necessarily involved a 'cultural translation'.

''A fava è bella! 'A fava è bella!': with this cry, 'beans are beautiful', mocking the original's 'la fiamma è bella' ('the flame is beautiful'), the Neapolitan comic actor and playwright Eduardo Scarpetta concluded *Il figlio di Iorio* (Iorio's Son), a 'commedia presepiana' (nativity-scene comedy) in two acts. As is evident from the title, it presented the comic inversion of D'Annunzio's celebrated pastoral drama. The Abruzzo mountains are replaced by the maritime surroundings of Pozzuoli, and each character switches gender: 'Candia della Leonessa' becomes 'il padre' (the father) and is called 'Nicola Paniello'; 'Mila di Codra' becomes 'Torillo'; 'Ornella' is 'Cornelio'; 'Lazaro di Rojo' is 'Zeza'; 'Aligi' becomes 'Alice'; and Torillo's pursuers are washerwomen rather than harvest workers, although they are no less unruly. The pastoral tragedy's fatal patricidal axe blow becomes a massive punch in Zeza's face by Torillo; he is then taken into custody amidst the curses of the crowd, which sends him to eat the tough beans of prison.

Scarpetta was present at the opening of *'A figghia di Joriu* in September 1904, when his own version of D'Annunzio's play was already in development. Later, he recalled its genesis:

> Every father may deliver a deformed child into this world. And it was just so with my *Figlio di Iorio*. [. . .] The first thought of parodying D'Annunzio's play came to me in Rome, hardly had I read the book; but what am I saying, 'read'? I devoured those three acts in a single night, and then could dream of nothing else but parodying that tragedy.[34]

In response to complaints from D'Annunzio, Scarpetta wittily hit back, saying that he did not believe 'that he has total control over Iorio's whole family'.[35] Nevertheless, partly in view of the heavy expenses he would be incurring over the staging, he was eager to obtain the poet's explicit consent; he therefore went to pay D'Annunzio a visit, accompanied by their mutual friend Gaetano Miranda. This meeting, marked by the reciprocal exchange of compliments and

[34] Eduardo Scarpetta, *Cinquant'anni di palcoscenico* (Naples: Gennarelli, 1922), pp. 357–8.

[35] Letter from Scarpetta to Ferdinando Russo, reproduced in articles by an unnamed reporter in *Il Mattino*, 18 July 1904, and 'Notizie teatrali. Drammatica', *Corriere della Sera*, 26 July 1904.

courtesies, was so cordial that Scarpetta was persuaded to leave without having received written permission; he was further heartened by assurances from Annibale Tenneroni of his friend D'Annunzio's complete goodwill.[36]

Il figlio di Iorio opened on 3 December 1904 in Naples, at the Real Teatro Mercadante. Soon after it was announced, protests and pressure were directed at the city's prefecture to prevent its staging; the play was still authorised, but it took place in an atmosphere of conflict and never reached the final curtain:

> An exceptionally elegant public filled the theatre and the parody's first quips met with laughter and applause. However, during the second act a hostile group spread discontent through the entire audience: there were whistles, countered by limited clapping; the whistles then continued. At one point, Scarpetta [in the role of Cornelio, the counterpart of D'Annunzio's Ornella, but in women's clothing] took the stage to ask the audience to wait for the performance to be concluded so that they could then give their opinion; but instead there were calls for an immediate end to the show, and the curtain had to be lowered. [Protesting] students then hailed D'Annunzio and Italian artistry.[37]

Aniello Falcone added to the story of this tempestuous evening:

> Last night, Eduardo Scarpetta felt the edifice that he had lovingly and enthusiastically constructed over several months, with every care and much sacrifice, come rapidly tumbling down. [. . .] To the lions! Scarpetta's opus has been devoured. The curtain comes down amidst the agitation of the ladies and the scornful laughter of the victors. From the same part of the same theatre, just a few years ago, a similar rumpus buried *La Gloria* by Gabriele D'Annunzio, whom last night's rioters judged offended by Scarpetta's parody.[38]

A few days later, on 10 December, Marco Praga, director of the Italian Society of Authors, initiated legal actions against Scarpetta on behalf of D'Annunzio and the society for copying the poet's tragedy and its illegal reproduction on the stage. The proceedings that followed elicited a high level of interest due to the hilarious and lively conduct

[36] Aniello Falcone, '"Il figlio di Iorio" di Eduardo Scarpetta. Scarpetta a . . . Canossa! – La pace con d'Annunzio', *Tribuna* (Rome), 15 September 1904.

[37] 'La parodia della "Figlia di Iorio" male accolta dal pubblico', *Corriere della Sera*, 4 December 1904.

[38] Aniello Falcone, 'La catastrofe del "Figlio di Iorio"', *L'Illustrazione Italiana*, 5 December 1904.

of the defendant and the calibre of the figures involved; the full hearings took place between 29 April and 14 May 1908.[39] Appearing for Scarpetta were his lawyers Francesco Spirito and Carlo Fioravanti and the expert witnesses Benedetto Croce and Giorgio Arcoleo, the latter a former pupil of Francesco De Sanctis and a lecturer in constitutional law.[40] Ranged on D'Annunzio's side were the parliamentary deputies Luigi Simeoni and Ferdinando Ferri as his lawyers, and then, as experts, Emiddio Martini, Francesco Colagrosso and Nicola Scarano, followed by Roberto Bracco, Salvatore Di Giacomo and the music critic Giulio Massimo Scalinger, who passed away as the case dragged on and was replaced, during the proceedings, by Enrico Cocchia.[41] Before entering into the substance of the issue, the expert testimony of Croce and Arcoleo offered a clarification:

> Copying – which because of the deceptive forms that it takes cannot always be punished by the law – consists in changing, when this serves a purpose, the language and details, preserving the spirit of the work. Parody, on the other hand, may preserve very many of the details and even keep the language of the work being parodied almost the same, but its driving spirit is always changed.[42]

Dissecting the submission from the experts on the opposing side, Croce and Arcoleo set out their case:

> In the case of *La figlia di Iorio*, Scarpetta had before him a work of exceptional and refined form and topic, which unfolds in an environment of remote or unfamiliar customs, sentiments, and traditions, employing difficult and novel words and names; he therefore felt obliged to reproduce its salient points so that his spectator, in amusement, could refer back to the drama, which by contrast had aroused terror and compassion. The second

39 Scarpetta, *Cinquant'anni di palcoscenico*, pp. 369–70. For a fuller account, see Emma Giammattei, '«Il figlio di Iorio», d'Annunzio, Scarpetta e Croce', in *'La figlia di Iorio'. Atti del VII Convegno internazionale di studi dannunziani, Pescara, 24–6 October 1985*, ed. by Edoardo Tiboni (Pescara: Centro nazionale di studi dannunziani in Pescara, 1986), pp. 255–62. See also Sergio Frau, 'D'Annunzio Scarpetta. Miseria e nobiltà', La Repubblica, 17 December 1996.

40 Scarpetta, *Cinquant'anni di palcoscenico*, pp. 368–9.

41 Luigi Simeoni, 'La figlia di Iorio'. *Per Gabriele d'Annunzio e la Società italiana degli Autori. Riduzione stampata. Recita abusiva. Parodia. Nel giudizio contro Eduardo Scarpetta per 'Il figlio di Iorio'* (Naples: Giannini, 1907).

42 'Appendice alla Memoria nella causa per "Il figlio di Iorio" contro Eduardo Scarpetta', submitted 24 April 1908, p. 5. Documents from the trial, held in Naples, are conserved in the Archivio di Stato di Napoli.

> piece of mistaken reasoning can be found in the switch from judgement of the nature of a work to judgement of its beauty or ugliness; or rather in having lost sight of the legal issue in favour of the literary issue.[43]

These arguments were repeated by Arcoleo during the public trial:

> The second error has been that of confusing the aesthetic issue with the legal one. Scarpetta will perhaps have insulted art by creating an unfortunate work, but he has not abused the rights of D'Annunzio by offering him unfair competition. Here, we are before a College that administers justice, not before a commission charged with awarding a prize for artistic endeavour.[44]

Scarpetta's expert witnesses concluded that the actor 'should be found guilty if he were to have committed a form of copying, which is not the case. But he cannot be found guilty for having executed a poor literary work.'[45]

This opinion was acknowledged by the verdict: 'non luogo a procedere per inesistenza di reato' (no reason to proceed due to the absence of a crime). The presiding magistrate, having established that 'D'Annunzio wishes to arouse sentiments of sorrow and terror, and Scarpetta those of enjoyment and laughter', added, in reference to the latter's comic talents, 'furthermore a tear, falling on his face, would be ridiculous'.[46] *Le Figaro* subsequently reproached D'Annunzio for a certain lack of *esprit*, given that 'masterpieces are in fact the only works of art that invite parody', and as a result 'more than one author would pay a large sum for the glory of being subjected to caricature!'; parody in fact 'always penetrates the places where there is an element of vitality'.[47]

Conclusion

The status of 'masterpiece' acquired by D'Annunzio's tragedy was reaffirmed by Mimì Aguglia in a letter to the poet dated 13 September

[43] Ibid., p. 9; the passage is also reproduced in Scarpetta, *Cinquant'anni di palcoscenico*, p. 371.

[44] Scarpetta, *Cinquant'anni di palcoscenico*, p. 373.

[45] 'Appendice alla Memoria nella causa per "Il figlio di Iorio"', p. 10.

[46] Scarpetta, *Cinquant'anni di palcoscenico*, p. 381.

[47] Quoted in: Il Capitan Spaventa (pseudonym), 'L'amante onorario. La famiglia di Iorio', *Il Tirso* (Rome), 3 December 1905.

1934, written in the United States, recalling the success she had enjoyed in the role of Mila di Codra:

> Many years have passed since this small Sicilian woman, dressed up as Mila di Codra, made all the audiences of Europe tremble. Do you remember this, divine maestro? When I was travelling between the two Americas, and switching between seasons, in Italian, English, and Spanish, I never neglected, even in different languages, to bring to the stage that *Figlia di Iorio* which had awarded me the supreme joy of meeting the greatest living poet in person, and interpreting his work. Now, in San Francisco, after performing *Salomè*, by Oscar Wilde, in the language of Shakespeare, at Berkeley's Greek Theatre, presented by the University of California, I have decided to put back on the dress of the 'daughter of the sorcerer of Codra, from the Farne' in order to give homage to the supreme poet of our time, in the largest theatre of that great metropolis. I would so appreciate a word from you, or one of your photographs, maestro, as the single decoration on the shelf of my little room for that evening; it would give me, and renew in me, the sweet illusion of your presence in the theatre, 'wishing for me' as in the beautiful past. May I hope? I will wait with the hope that throbs, lingers, and endures. Your supremely and splendidly devoted Mimì Aguglia.[48]

The 'Sicilian Duse' was by then an international actress capable of breathing life into the classics not only in Italian and Sicilian dialect but also, thanks to her multilingual talents, in English and Spanish. Her beautiful letter bears witness to the translatability in time and space of the classic *La figlia di Iorio*, not 'in spite of' but in fact by virtue of its dialect. The numerous translations of the play into different languages, idioms and styles of performance demonstrate that mobility and translatability were always inherent aspects of the work. Aguglia's notion of bringing it to the American public was thus in keeping with the model of the tragedy and the path it had originally taken.[49]

[48] The unpublished letter is conserved in the archive of the Istituto di Storia dello Spettacolo Siciliano. It was written in Italian apart from the fact that Aguglia herself added 'wishing for me' [*sic*] as a translation of '*bene augurando*'.

[49] The Italian script of *La figlia di Iorio* from 1904, the Sicilian version by Giuseppe Antonio Borgese, the Abruzzo dialect version by Cesare de Titta and the parody in Neapolitan by Eduardo Scarpetta can all be found together in one richly illustrated volume, which traces a century of stagings: Sarah Zappulla Muscarà and Enzo Zappulla, *Gabriele d'Annunzio. 'La figlia di Iorio' tra lingua e dialetti* (Catania: la Cantinella, 1998).

Chapter 5

The 'Latin sister': D'Annunzio's Relationship to the French Language

Filippo Fonio

All too often D'Annunzio has been labelled a monolingual Italian writer who also wrote in French. Quite a different destiny from, say, Nabokov, or Beckett, or others who are considered as plurilingual writers. Moreover, D'Annunzio's French writings have just as often been labelled second-rate works in comparison to his Italian ones. Giovanni Gullace, for example, describes them as 'of peripheral importance' as they 'reveal no new aspect of his artistic talent'.[1] Their adherence to a francophone literary system has constantly been neglected. At best, these works are considered as documents which show his connections to French literature – sometimes interesting because they are evidence of D'Annunzio's borrowings and plagiarism.

The idea that D'Annunzio's French writings cannot be as valuable as his Italian ones has even been theorised, and some critics have insisted that he is too rooted in the Italian tradition for his French writings to be of value. Gullace, for example, notes 'his artistic talent was too strongly established in his native tongue to be susceptible of radical metamorphoses, under whatever influence. His linguistic and cultural acquisitions remained, artistically, a foreign world superposed on his native world.'[2] However, a close reading of D'Annunzio's French writings shows that these judgements oversimplify the question; his relationship to the language of Italy's 'Latin sister' cannot be reduced to the bilingual and bicultural competence that, according to George Steiner,[3] characterises the artistic life of canonical bilingual writers.

1 Giovanni Gullace, 'The French Writings of Gabriele D'Annunzio', in *Comparative Literature*, 12: 3 (1960), pp. 207–28 (p. 207).

2 Ibid., p. 227.

3 George Steiner, *Extraterritorial: Papers on Literature and the Language Revolution* (London: Faber & Faber, 1972 and New York: Atheneum, 1976), p. 4.

D'Annunzio himself elaborated upon his relationship to the French language, adopting approaches that range from a pragmatism driven by dissatisfaction with his translators to love for the host language's expressiveness. The purpose of this chapter is to show how, through his writing in French, D'Annunzio was able to work toward his integration into a transnational francophone canon. I shall focus on elements of self-translation that can be spotted in D'Annunzio's writings: in his correspondence with Hérelle, in his *Sonnets cisalpins* (1896) – which constitute the first work written directly in French by D'Annunzio – and in *Le Dit du sourd et muet qui fur miraculé en l'an de grâce 1266 par Brunet Latin*. This last work provides fertile ground to discuss the plurilingual component of D'Annunzio's late writings, through the presence of instances of code-mixing and code-switching between modern French, *oc* and *oïl* languages, Italian and Latin. These works demonstrate that the interest D'Annunzio developed for the French language results in a case of 'extraterritoriality' that is unique for the time. Both D'Annunzio's French production, and his attitude toward writing in another language, point to a dimension of 'linguistic unhousedness',[4] as he is 'not thoroughly at home in the language of his production, but displaced or hesitant at the frontier',[5] as well as to the writer's ubiquitous sense of belonging, because, as Steiner notes, 'there is more than nationalist mystique to the notion of the writer *enraciné*'.[6] For a writer roots often present rhizomatic features, so that it is legitimate to explore the critical implications that emerge when examining D'Annunzio's French writings as 'D'Annunzio's multilingual recastings of D'Annunzio', as Steiner claims of Nabokov's multilingualism.[7] As such, my purpose in this chapter is to use the example of D'Annunzio to push beyond the linguistic or communicative aspects implied by the act of allophone writing in order to consider the writer's intellectual gesture as a form of 'metatranslation'.[8] If we accept, with Damrosch and, more recently, Mengozzi,[9] that world literature consists of works which travel outside of their countries of production, we can understand the way in which D'Annunzio's translingualism allows his works to

4 Ibid., p. 3.

5 Ibid., p. 4.

6 Ibid., p. 4.

7 Ibid., p. 7.

8 Ibid., p. 9.

9 Chiara Mengozzi, 'De l'utilité et de l'inconvénient du concept de *World Literature*', in *Revue de littérature comparée*, 359: 3 (2016), pp. 335–49 (p. 338).

circulate in a different way than through interlingual translation, thus connecting him to multiple patterns of reception, influence and imitation.

While focusing on D'Annunzio's imaginary of the French language, this chapter also questions the 'functional relation'[10] existing between French and Italian as artistic forms of expression mastered by the writer. More specifically, I suggest that Steiner's intuition regarding Nabokov, that is, 'the possible existence of a private mixed idiom "beneath", "coming before" the localization of different languages in the articulate brain',[11] can also be applied to D'Annunzio.

D'Annunzio and the Language of the 'Latin Sister'

Critics argue that D'Annunzio's French writings are of scarce value due to the quality of his style when writing in a language other than Italian, and to an insufficient mastery of French. Particularly harsh are the judgements contained in French conservative newspapers. Even if D'Annunzio, as Hérelle notes,[12] knew French well, critics have often labelled his French production as 'macaronic',[13] as a 'galimatias',[14] as 'bookish' (Tosi) and as 'invented'.[15] The judgement which has weighed heaviest on the reputation of D'Annunzio's French has

[10] Helmut Meter, 'D'Annunzio und die Dramatik des doppelten Registers. Die Tragödie *Le Chèvrefeuille* und ihre italienische Fassung *Il ferro*', in *Literarische Polyphonie: Übersetzung und Mehrsprachigkeit in der Literatur*, ed. by Johann Strutz and Peter V. Zima (Tübingen: Gunter Narr, 1996), pp. 175–91 (p. 177).

[11] Steiner, *Extraterritorial*, p. 10.

[12] In his memoirs on D'Annunzio, Hérelle recalls their first meeting in Venice in 1894. He underlines the 'bookish' character of D'Annunzio's French and states that: 'at the time he couldn't express himself correctly in French, he made many grammar mistakes and his pronunciation was bad'. Hérelle's judgement is partly mitigated by the following remark: 'he knew perfectly French literature, especially Flaubert, whom he admired without reserve'. Georges Hérelle, *Notolette dannunziane*, ed. and trans. by Ivanos Ciani (Pescara: Centro Nazionale di Studi Dannunziani, 1984), p. 16. Translations from French and Italian are my own.

[13] Gianfranco Contini, 'Vita macaronica del francese dannunziano' [1937], in *Esercizi di lettura* (Torino: Einaudi, 1974), pp. 274–85 (pp. 278–79).

[14] Schlumemberger on the *Pisanelle*, quoted by Pierre de Montera, 'L'accueil de D'Annunzio en France de 1910 à 1915', in *D'Annunzio in Francia*. Atti del Colloquio italo-francese (Roma, Accademia Nazionale dei Lincei, 9–10 maggio 1974) (Roma: Accademia Nazionale dei Lincei, 1975), pp. 23–58 (p. 45).

[15] Luisetta Elia Chomel, *D'Annunzio, un teatro al femminile* (Ravenna: Longo, 1997), p. 183.

undoubtedly been that of Contini. In his review of the 1936 novel *Le Dit du sourd et muet*, Contini asks himself, with alleged naivety, if 'D'Annunzio is writing in French, or not'.[16] And the answer is no.[17] In fact, Contini's judgement is that D'Annunzio's French is derivative, dependent on his – literary or documentary – sources, 'not autonomous' and 'translated from D'Annunzio's Italian'.[18] According to his view, D'Annunzio shows no interest in the 'spiritual reality' of the French language[19] because he does not comply with the – universal, according to Contini – tendency to imitate an abstract idea of the language when writing in a foreign language. Also, D'Annunzio 'pillages' illustrious elements of the French tradition, but without systematicity, and thus gives birth to a messy 'mosaic'.[20] Furthermore, his francophone writing is motivated only by 'narcissism'.[21] Contini sums up his argument even more peremptorily, by stating that D'Annunzio's French 'does not exist'. What seems somehow biased in Contini's position is that the critic was an admirer of Dante's, or Gadda's, expressionism, and unable to recognise D'Annunzio's attempt to reach the same expressive goal by resorting to the richness of the tradition of the languages of *oc* and *oïl* in his novel. In his judgement of D'Annunzio's French, Contini makes a distinction between writing in one's mother tongue or in a foreign language: in the first case, a writer – Dante or Gadda – has the right to make use of different registers, dialects and idiolects, in order to create a richly Babelic text, and this is appreciated by the critic; in the second, a writer should not dare to reach beyond the boundaries of using a standardised version of the foreign language.[22]

D'Annunzio's admirers had a very different appreciation of his *francophonie*, both as a speaker and a writer. Régnier in his diary states that: 'D'Annunzio speaks French well, with a perfect choice of words.'[23] Hardly any aspect of D'Annunzio's art leaves room for indifference, its appreciation or denigration being highly polarised. One exception to this, and a particularly accurate judgement, is that of Léon Blum, who, responding to the *Martyre de Saint Sébastien*,

[16] Contini, 'Vita macaronica', p. 276.
[17] Ibid., p. 283.
[18] Ibid., p. 277.
[19] Ibid., p. 278.
[20] Ibid., p. 278.
[21] Ibid., p. 284.
[22] We will see in the next paragraph that Hérelle's position was not different.
[23] Quoted by de Montera, 'L'accueil de D'Annunzio', p. 36.

wrote in *Comœdia* on 23 May 1911 that D'Annunzio's French has the primary characteristic of being 'synoptic'. Blum defines the language of the *Martyre* as 'a [. . .] condensation of all the resources and the charms of the French vocabulary considered in its different historical phases'.[24] D'Annunzio cherished that judgement, as emerges from a letter to Hérelle of around the same time,[25] in which he defended himself against those who claimed that the language of the *Martyre* was archaic. He reassures his translator – whom he asked to revise the manuscript for publication – by quoting Blum, and by stating that the language of the play has a modern 'core' to it.

This concise account of the criticisms of D'Annunzio's French should not be misleading, though. Close readings of D'Annunzio's texts show that his use of both Italian and French should not be seen as the simple mastery of two distinct linguistic codes, as in Contini's interpretation. Instead, the two languages interact harmoniously with one another without mutual interference. Considering D'Annunzio as a multilingual writer avoids neglecting the richness and the seemingly conflicting features of his linguistic mastery. One should dismiss, in his case, the assumption that multilingual writers tend to reproduce unconscious interferences between their different linguistic codes. The idea of D'Annunzio's French as an 'acquired monolingualism'[26] allows for a better understanding of the relationship between his two main languages of expression, which are constantly intertwined. Thus Muret[27] states in 1938 that 'D'Annunzio's sentences are shaped on French syntax' even when he writes in Italian. French and Italian are superimposed on the written page. Several years earlier, D'Annunzio himself displayed the same self-consciousness, writing to Hérelle (before 19 October 1896): 'Very often, while writing in Italian,

[24] Léon Blum, '*Le Martyre de Saint Sébastien*', in *Au théâtre, réflexions critiques*, vol. 4 (Paris: Ollendorff, 1911), pp. 247–57 (p. 253).

[25] Published in *Carteggio D'Annunzio-Hérelle (1891–1931)*, ed. by Mario Cimini (Lanciano: Carabba, 2004), p. 675. Cimini, as well as the first editor of D'Annunzio's correspondence with Hérelle, Tosi, mistakenly dated the letter to April – April 28, according to Cimini. This is probably due to the fact that both Tosi and Cimini dated Léon Blum's collected papers on theatre 1910, which is impossible because several papers contained in the collection are from 1911 (especially the one on the *Martyre de Saint Sébastien*, initially published after the *première* of the play, which took place on 22 May 1911).

[26] Claudio Galderisi, 'Faute contre nature? D'une langue à l'autre ou Gabriele D'Annunzio le collectionneur', in *Écrire dans la langue de l'autre*, ed. by Anna Maria Babbi (Verona: Fiorini, 2011), pp. 57–74 (p. 63).

[27] Quoted in *Georges Hérelle à Gabriele D'Annunzio. Correspondance accompagnée de douze Sonnets cisalpins*, ed. by Guy Tosi (Paris: Denoël, 1948), p. 48.

French sentences come under my pen, because French seems to me more effective and [. . .] a more spoken language.'[28] Some years later, in the French prose text 'Pour lealté maintenir – Aux bons chevaliers latins de France et d'Italie',[29] he refers to his writing through the evocative image of possessing 'two lungs'.

Why French? D'Annunzio and the 'Latin Renaissance'

Apart from the metalinguistic self-consciousness D'Annunzio displayed while still a young writer, there are other reasons which persuaded him to start writing in French. One of them is his dissatisfaction toward his translators. In particular, all through his relationship with Hérelle he complained, both to him and to others, about Hérelle's 'lack of stylistic aptitudes'.[30] For a writer such as D'Annunzio, whom his readers esteemed for his mastery of style, it was disturbing to find in Hérelle's translations a somehow standardised French version of himself. Moreover, one might question if the French public would have been less shocked by D'Annunzio's writings in French if they had read D'Annunzio's Italian in the original, because they would have experienced the continuity and homogeneity between the two 'lungs' that breathed life into his literary production. In fact, reading Hérelle's translations and the letters the writer and his translator exchanged shows that Hérelle was not the best translator for D'Annunzio, and especially for his novels. Ducrey speaks of Hérelle's 'incomprehension of decadent literature'.[31] This fact is even clearer when we compare Hérelle's standardised translations of D'Annunzio's complex style, and the way in which this incomprehension affected their relationship, to the attitude of his second main French translator, Doderet, who was a 'Dannunzian' enthusiast and prone to carry out D'Annunzio's will.[32]

A sort of estrangement with regard to D'Annunzio appeared amongst the French public once his works written directly in French

[28] *Carteggio D'Annunzio-Hérelle (1891–1931)*, ed. by Mario Cimini, p. 419.

[29] Gabriele D'Annunzio, *Prose di ricerca*, vol. 2, ed. by Annamaria Andreoli and Giorgio Zanetti (Milano: Mondadori, 2005), pp. 2454–99. This text has also partly been self-translated into Italian.

[30] Guy Ducrey, 'Is There Such a Thing as a "Decadent Translator"?: The Case of Georges Hérelle (1848–1935)', in *Volupté*, 3: 2 (Winter 2020), pp. 11–27 (p. 20).

[31] Ibid., p. 25.

[32] See Chapter 7 in this volume on Doderet.

were performed or published. This also contributed to tarnishing his previously successful appeal for the French readership, which was content to find just as much exoticism as was suitable for a foreign author, and nothing more. A statement such as that of Gullace,[33] who affirms that 'Gabriele D'Annunzio was perhaps the only modern Italian writer to find in France immediate and widespread acceptance', was undoubtedly true before his writings in French were known. At the same time, as Claudio Galderisi suggests, writing in French was, for D'Annunzio, a way to take distance from Italian (a sort of self-estrangement) and from his unique 'linguistic epidermis' by taking on a second one.[34] It was a way to access 'extraterritoriality' more than a method of conquering a broader public – which was already fond of him, as the success of Hérelle's translations shows. His '*passage à l'acte*' is also related to the mastery of a language he particularly revered.[35] Furthermore, D'Annunzio's aim was also to propose an alternative canon for French literature itself, through his own writings and through the many quotes he introduced in his French works. D'Annunzio's Franco-Italian canon encompasses Italians having written in French, with whom he engages in an emulative process, and French writers who lived in and wrote about Italy, including, for instance, Charles d'Orléans, Leonardo, the Franco-Italian medieval epic or Brunetto.

Dante Alighieri's teacher and a French exile from 1260 to 1266, Brunetto is the most important amongst D'Annunzio's Franco-Italian ancestors. He is one of the characters of D'Annunzio's last novel, the *Dit*, but his role is already crucial in a manifesto of his French poetics such as the *Prologue* to the *Martyre de Saint Sébastien*, in which he clearly identifies with Brunetto.[36] The gallery of Franco-Italian figures which composes D'Annunzio's canon is even more crowded in the other preliminary text to the published version of the *Martyre*, the dedication he wrote to Barrès. Here, D'Annunzio celebrates Barrès' love of Italy, and he offers his play to him by presenting it as the product of a craftmanship inherited from the skills of the Italian workers who came to France during the Middle Ages to build the cathedrals. Those Italian workers are wandering exiles with

[33] Giovanni Gullace, *Gabriele D'Annunzio in France: A Study in Cultural Relations* (Syracuse–New York: Syracuse University Press, 1966), p. IX.

[34] Claudio Galderisi, 'Faute contre nature?', p. 62.

[35] See Chapter 1 in this volume.

[36] Gabriele D'Annunzio, *Tragedie, sogni e misteri*, vol. 2, ed. by Annamaria Andreoli and Giorgio Zanetti (Milano: Mondadori, 2013), pp. 535–36.

whom he identifies, as he identifies also with those Italian artists who contributed to the richness of Medieval and Renaissance art and literature produced in France (Petrarch, Leonardo). This text aims to be a binational address, keen to satisfy both French and Italian readerships, that is why 'Italian' portraits are combined with the recollection of French artists who travelled, lived, or worked in Italy: Ronsard, Rabelais, Montaigne.

We should not leave out completely the idea that D'Annunzio's writing in French was also an attempt at conquering a broader readership, and the means to access, through France, European stardom. On the one hand, D'Annunzio's Italian readership would have been able to admire the virtuosity of his writing in French; and on the other, the French editorial world and newspapers and the Parisian stage would have given D'Annunzio access to the 'Greenwich literary meridian'[37] of the time. The literary *persona* which emerges from D'Annunzio's French texts, and the imaginary portraits he offered to French readerships demonstrate that this was not a naïve operation for the writer. Consider D'Annunzio's letter to Hérelle of 14 November 1892,[38] which was translated into French by Hérelle himself and published by Pigeon in *La Revue hebdomadaire* (57, 24 June 1893).[39] Here, D'Annunzio states that he was born in 1864 on open sea, on board the brigantine *Irene*. And he describes the course of his life from youth until the publication of the *Innocente* on the same tone. Several elements in the text are either invented or exaggerated, but the overall feeling is that D'Annunzio's aim was to rewrite his own life according to a hagiographical path which led him to the brink of damnation through multiple temptations. Thus, he describes himself as an *enfant prodige* in different fields: painting, music and literature, as well as a paragon of brilliant conversation and seduction. His remarkable achievements are not without risk:

[37] See Pascale Casanova, *La République mondiale des Lettres* (Paris: Le Seuil, 2008). Casanova's argument is that the attraction toward Paris was a common feature one may find in writers who were, or who considered themselves as being, somehow outside of the literary norm in their own country (see in particular p. 145).

[38] *Carteggio D'Annunzio-Hérelle (1891–1931)*, ed. by Mario Cimini, pp. 96–105.

[39] See de Montera, 'L'accueil de D'Annunzio', p. 24. This same text circulated in France for a long time after its first publication. In fact, it was included in the *Foreword* to the collection of D'Annunzio's short stories translated into French by Hérelle and published by Calmann-Lévy, *Episcopo et Cie*, from the first edition of 1895 up until the 1920s. It thus shaped part of D'Annunzio's image in the view of the French public.

he is able to mitigate his overwhelming pride and to prevent the risk of falling into a sort of jadedness through the exercise of his strength of will. And he's finally able to avoid perdition thanks to regaining spirituality. What is noticeable here is that this imaginary portrait has been written for the sole benefit of his French readership. Moreover, this epic autobiography hints at the ideal type of the French writer-adventurer modelled on Pierre Loti. Especially before the Fiume episode, D'Annunzio was considered in France as a sort of symbol, the incarnation of a certain intellectual and existential type. He was seen as the incarnation of the Latin Renaissance, according to the definition given by Eugène-Melchior de Vogüé on the occasion of the publication of *L'Enfant de volupté* (*Revue des deux mondes*, 1 January 1895).[40]

I am skeptical of interpretations suggesting D'Annunzio's 'unaware' attitude as regards his introduction to the French literary system.[41] Even more, I doubt that Hérelle might be considered, as critics have suggested, an older Amphitryon who, hiding behind the translator's preposterous invisibility, acted as D'Annunzio's literary agent in France. Hérelle's translations and the question of the translator's fidelity and authorship must be reconsidered as different attitudes toward the balance between linguistic norms and variation.[42] When writing in French, D'Annunzio sought to obtain an effect which is similar to that of his Italian writings, especially in terms of 'Dannunzianizing' the language, and he asked Hérelle to maintain this characteristic. The case of Hérelle shows that translators at the time hardly dared to force the limits of their own language in order to produce a 'source-oriented' translation (which is what D'Annunzio asked Hérelle to do in his letter of 4 January 1905).[43] In fact, in the midst of the universal praise of Hérelle's translations, another important translator of the time, Rod, remarked as early as 1895 that Hérelle 'revised, abridged and attenuated' D'Annunzio.[44]

40 See de Montera, 'L'accueil de D'Annunzio', pp. 26–7, and Giovanni Gullace, 'Les débuts de D'Annunzio en France et la question de la "renaissance latine"', in *Symposium*, 7: 2 (November 1953), pp. 232–49.

41 Thomas Loué and Blaise Wilfert-Portal, 'D'Annunzio à l'usage des Français. La traduction comme censure informelle (fin du XIXe siècle)', in *Ethnologie française*, 36: 1 (2006), pp. 101–10.

42 See Georges Hérelle, *Petit mémoire d'un traducteur*, ed. by Jean-Marie Van der Meerschen (Bruxelles: Les Éditions du Hazard, 2005).

43 *Carteggio D'Annunzio-Hérelle (1891–1931)*, ed. by Mario Cimini, pp. 587–90.

44 Quoted in *Georges Hérelle à Gabriele D'Annunzio*, ed. by Guy Tosi, p. 58.

Writing in French, Self-translation, and (Self-)inclusion in a Transnational Canon

In 1895, at a time in which D'Annunzio's works were becoming extremely popular in France through Hérelle's translations, the writer allegedly declared: 'I now write in particular for France. France is the only country which truly understands me.'[45] Apocryphal as it might be, this quote reflects the impression that he considered Hérelle's translations still of his own authorship.

There is hardly any evolution in D'Annunzio's attitude toward the French language during his French 'exile' (1910–15). I cannot agree with sociological approaches such as that of Helmut Meter, who claims that D'Annunzio's priority during his French years was to avoid losing his Italian readership while also acquiring a French one.[46] As we have seen, his French readership had been well established since 1892, and he was revered by the French intelligentsia during his first visit to Paris in 1898 for the staging of *La Ville morte*.[47] Eighteen years later, D'Annunzio left for France not only because it was the easiest way to flee his creditors and because he mastered the French language well, but also because of his reputation in France as a writer.[48] As regards Italy, the 'D'Annunzio-frenzy' was far from over.

D'Annunzio's French writings span over forty years (1896–1936).[49] They include two plays: *Le Martyre de Saint Sébastien* and *La Pisanelle*, written during his 'exile', the novel *Le Dit du sourd et muet*, as well as some poems,[50] essays and public speeches, written throughout his literary career. In order to illustrate the multilingual aspects of D'Annunzio's French writing, his *Sonnets cisalpins* are a good example. They consist of a series of twelve poems contained in a letter to Hérelle of 24 December 1896, of which only two were

45 The remark is from an interview with Diego Angeli, which was then disavowed by D'Annunzio. Quoted by Gullace, 'Les débuts de D'Annunzio en France', p. 234.

46 Meter, 'D'Annunzio und die Dramatik des doppelten Registers', p. 175.

47 See *Georges Hérelle à Gabriele D'Annunzio*, ed. by Guy Tosi, p. 42; Pierre de Nolhac's witness, quoted by Annamaria Andreoli, *D'Annunzio archivista. Le filologie di uno scrittore* (Firenze: Olschki, 1996), p. 121; de Montera, 'L'accueil de D'Annunzio', pp. 29–30.

48 De Montera, 'L'accueil de d'Annunzio'.

49 Fernando Coletti, 'Nascita del D'Annunzio francese. I *Sonnets cisalpins*', in *Annali di Ca' Foscari. Serie occidentale*, 1964, pp. 81–95 (p. 81).

50 In particular his farewell gift to France, 'Sur une image de la France croisée', published in *Le Figaro*, March 1915, and then in the collection *Canti della guerra latina*.

published in France during D'Annunzio's life. In presenting his sonnets to Hérelle as a sort of Christmas gift while asking for his help publishing them, D'Annunzio underlines that their value consists in their character of offerings to his love for French Medieval and Renaissance poetry. In the same letter, he preempts potential objections from Hérelle, explaining that the Italianisms, neologisms and seemingly mistaken sentence structures he might notice in the sonnets must be considered as part of an antiquarian operation which consists in looking back along the history of French to a time when its nature of Latin language was very apparent.[51] French and Italian were much closer then than they were in the nineteenth century, and as such D'Annunzio's poems, in his own words, should be considered 'Franco-Italian' texts. D'Annunzio's is also a claim of self-inclusion in the tradition of the 'Latin Renaissance'.

The topics of the sonnets are Franco-Italian as well: Leonardo in France, Valentina Visconti and Charles d'Orléans, Piccolomini ('the Italian pope'[52]) and his French translator, 'a word from Boccaccio' used by the duke de Valois.[53] Moreover, in the poems one can grasp a self-representation of D'Annunzio that is surprisingly modest and humble. Thus, the first sonnet is fictionally addressed by a 'modest page',[54] who is an autobiographical figure, to other French poets, announcing to them the recent discovery the page had made of a 'doux parler nouveau',[55] which is the 'doux parler de France'.[56] His choice of French for his poetry is aimed, on the one hand, at inscribing himself in the francophone poetical tradition, and on the other at innovating this tradition through his own contribution. The writer was well aware that his poems would be considered, especially by French fellow-poets, as strange, archaic, precious and, in his own words, 'Parnassian' (letter of 2 January 1897).[57] This reference to one of the most important poetical movements of the recent past allows D'Annunzio to position himself in an illustrious poetic lineage. A week earlier he also wrote to Hérelle that his sonnets should

[51] Letter quoted from *Carteggio D'Annunzio-Hérelle (1891–1931)*, ed. by Mario Cimini, p. 444.

[52] *Georges Hérelle à Gabriele D'Annunzio*, ed. by Guy Tosi, p. 310.

[53] Ibid., p. 311.

[54] Ibid., p. 308.

[55] Ibid., p. 308.

[56] Ibid., p. 309.

[57] *Carteggio D'Annunzio-Hérelle (1891–1931)*, p. 453.

be understood as '*cisalpine*, that is somehow Italianizing in some turns of phrase'.[58]

When reading the *Sonnets cisalpins*, one may think that some archaisms, for example 'Fleurance'[59] in 'L'Hôte du roi' for Florence, are out-of-place and pretentious, but this feature should rather be understood as an attempt at the creation of a personal style in French. The explanation for this choice (the Latin etymology of the city's name) gives birth to a polysemic chain of meanings which multiply the idea of 'flower' and of 'flowering'. Moreover, the lasting influence of the sonnets also emerges in their close relation to analogous motifs D'Annunzio develops in his Italian writings: the preference for 'Fiorenza' instead of 'Firenze' in Italian as well; the pomegranate, which is both the key symbol in one of these sonnets and in the novel *Il fuoco*;[60] the enigmatic deepness of Leonardo's painting *La Vergine delle rocce*, which is the core metaphor of his *Vergini delle rocce*.

The *Sonnets* are a fundamental text for understanding D'Annunzio's translingual poetics, as they establish his French canon and personal mythology as well as showing elements of self-intertextuality. Thus, Valentina Visconti and Charles d'Orléans are two important figures amongst the gallery of characters introduced by D'Annunzio as a legitimation of his next French work (in date), *Le Martyre de Saint Sébastien* (in the *Prologue* to the play). Also, quotes from the *Sonnets* can be found in the *Martyre*: for instance, the '*voix d'or et d'airain*' (the voice of gold and bronze) from 'Mélpomène',[61] a poem which was initially dedicated to Sarah Bernhardt, is very close to '*l'or le cristal et l'airain*' (gold, crystal and bronze) from the Zodiac scene in the *Martyre*.[62] Since their publication, the *Sonnets* have not been spared from supercilious criticism. Gullace labels them as being

58 Ibid., p. 444.

59 *Georges Hérelle à Gabriele D'Annunzio*, ed. by Guy Tosi, p. 309.

60 See Coletti, 'Nascita del D'Annunzio francese', p. 91.

61 *Georges Hérelle à Gabriele D'Annunzio*, p. 314.

62 D'Annunzio, *Tragedie, sogni e misteri*, vol. 2, p. 628. Elements of internal intertextuality which are present throughout D'Annunzio's literary production, from the *Consolazione della morte* to the *Libro segreto*, show that the *Martyre* is probably the work he most cherished out of his French production. Quotes from the hagiographical play are in fact often decontextualised and inserted elsewhere, in political texts as well as in love letters. For example, in the 'Aveux de l'ingrat', a series of four articles from 1919 (published in a volume by Bernard Grasset in France, and then included in D'Annunzio's collection *Il sudore del sangue* in 1931), he quotes the following lines from the play: 'Il faut que chacun tue son amour pour qu'il revive sept fois plus ardent.'

characterised by 'a certain strain and affectation in the expression, due to insufficient mastery of the language'.[63] Coletti claims that they have 'evident artistic limits'.[64] Labelling them as a second-rate works prevents us from recognising their role in the establishment of the style, motifs, and canon of reference of D'Annunzio's French writing.

The same remarks can apply to D'Annunzio's self-translations into French. These were motivated on the one hand by the dissatisfaction he often showed as regards his translators, and in particular Hérelle, and on the other by the attempt to disprove the widespread idea that he was 'untranslatable' (see the Editor's note to the first instalment of *Il fuoco* in French, in the 'Revue de Paris', 1 May 1900).[65] D'Annunzio's self-translations from Italian into French began even earlier than his French writing, in June 1894, with three poems from the *Poema paradisiaco* and the *Isottèo* translated into French and sent to Hérelle, which he probably never received, and which were published only in 1938 by Gentili Di Giuseppe.[66] D'Annunzio explained to Hérelle that the main aim of accomplishing this seemingly daring activity was to 'be understandable' to a French readership, not only as a novelist but also as a poet.[67] This is evidence that D'Annunzio himself considered his poetry impossible to translate by someone else, even (or especially) by Hérelle.[68] Their letters also show that, each time Hérelle translated D'Annunzio's poetry or verse plays, tensions between the two ran high. That is why D'Annunzio attempted these translations, which were produced at a time when, in contrast to the *Sonnets*, his mastery of French was probably insufficient to avoid awkwardness. Indeed, these translations are very literal; he did not try to follow a rhyme scheme (one of the stanzas of the 'Ballata delle donne sul fiume' is even translated in prose form); and the French syntactic order is much more regular than that of the Italian version. All of these features of his early self-translations disappear from the *Sonnets*, whose metrics and rhyme scheme on the contrary are regular, and whose syntax is almost as complicated as that of

[63] Gullace, *Gabriele D'Annunzio in France*, p. 210.

[64] Coletti, 'Nascita del D'Annunzio francese', p. 90.

[65] Quoted by Muriel Gallot, 'Gabriele D'Annunzio et Georges Hérelle: érotisme et traduction', in *Traduire avec l'auteur*, ed. by Patrick Hersant (Paris: Sorbonne Université Presses, 2020), pp. 129–46 (p. 134).

[66] Gabriele D'Annunzio, 'Ébauches inédites de poèmes', in *Hommage à Gabriele D'Annunzio*, special issue of *Dante*, 5–6, May–June 1938, pp. 161–2; see also Gullace, 'The French Writings', p. 208 and footnote 3.

[67] *Carteggio D'Annunzio-Hérelle (1891–1931)*, p. 194.

[68] On this see in particular Ducrey, 'Is There Such a Thing as a "Decadent Translator"?'

D'Annunzio's Italian poetry. Nonetheless, these three self-translations deserve mentioning, not only because of their precociousness, but also for the fact that the variants which the manuscripts show, in the form of deleted words and syntagms, were clearly aimed at finding the poet's own 'voice' in French. Moreover, they demonstrate that this was not simply a trifling activity, and that D'Annunzio, as early as 1894, already had a precise idea of what his writing in French should sound like, even if he was seemingly not proficient enough in that language to attain his goal.

D'Annunzio's self-translations into French are quite sporadic, but their characteristics show that, contrary to what Meter affirms,[69] he was perfectly capable of producing a self-translated text in the common meaning of the expression, i.e., an interlingual act of writing based on a source text. According to Meter,[70] *Le Chèvrefeuille/Il ferro* would be the only text which D'Annunzio had written himself in both languages – even if he refuses to call it a 'proper self-translation'. However, several documents[71] show that *Le Chèvrefeuille* has been translated into French from the Italian original *Il ferro* by the marquis de Casa Fuerte.[72] That is why Fabio Regattin speaks more accurately of a '*pseudo-auto-traduction*'.[73]

Apart from the example of the three juvenile poems discussed above, D'Annunzio's self-translations into French are normally inserted into works or collections of writings containing also texts written in Italian, which gives birth to bilingual works or indicates that the writer wants to present himself in the guise of a bilingual literary *persona*.[74] For instance, the late collection *Teneo te Africa* contains different French texts, some of which are self-translations. I am thinking in particular of the already-mentioned 'Pour lealté maintenir', which was partially published in Italian in the newspaper

[69] Meter, 'D'Annunzio und die Dramatik des doppelten Registers', p. 190.

[70] Ibid., p. 178; Helmut Meter, 'Bilinguismo letterario e autotraduzione. Alcune riflessioni su tre scrittori del Novecento (G. D'Annunzio, Y. Goll, S. Beckett)', in *Eteroglossia e plurilinguismo letterario. II: Plurilinguismo e letteratura*, ed. by Furio Brugnolo and Vincenzo Orioles (Roma: Il Calamo, 2002), pp. 351–65.

[71] Discussed in Pierre de Montera and Guy Tosi, *D'Annunzio, Montesquiou, Matilde Serao. Documents inédits* (Roma: Edizioni di Storia e Letteratura, 1972), pp. 66–7.

[72] See also Gullace, *Gabriele D'Annunzio in France*, p. 222, and Andreoli, *D'Annunzio archivista*, p. 135 footnote 52 for bibliography.

[73] Fabio Regattin, 'D'Annunzio, le théâtre, l'auto-traduction. Quelques remarques sur *La città morta/La Ville morte* et *Il ferro/Le Chèvrefeuille*', in *Forum*, 12: 2 (October 2014), pp. 87–106 (p. 88).

[74] See Chapter 3 in this volume.

Il Popolo di Brescia as 'Lealtà passa tutto e con vertà fa frutto' on 8 September 1935. This text was written by D'Annunzio in August 1935 as a commission by Mussolini, who wanted D'Annunzio to send a message to both the French and the Italian people. It is largely inspired by the *Dit*, which he was writing at the time, and by the 1914 French poem 'Ode pour la resurrection latine'. 'Pour lealté maintenir' was first sent through diplomatic channels to the President of the French Republic, Albert Lebrun. Then, still in its French version, the facsimile of the autograph manuscript was sent to Mussolini and to King Vittorio Emanuele III (letter 'Alla Maestà di Vittorio Emanuele terzo Re d'Italia – Gabriele D'Annunzio duca di Ragusa' of 4 November 1935).[75] D'Annunzio finally chose to include both the French and Italian versions in *Teneo te Africa*. The same collection also contains a text entitled 'Guglielmo Oberdan e le sue gesta. Dal messaggio ai latini di Francia', which is, once more, an Italian self-translation of a passage from the *Dit*.

From D'Annunzio's Other Languages to the Triumph of Babel

Much has been said about D'Annunzio's knowledge of other languages apart from French. Unfortunately, researchers lack evidence to claim that he mastered any other language, with the partial exception of ancient Greek and Latin – as his juvenile translations and later projects show.[76] For instance, D'Annunzio wrote to Mussolini on 26 September 1936 that he was working on a Latin translation of the latter's speech at Avellino (30 August 1936), and that, for this purpose, he chose 'the language of Caesar tinted with Sallustian asperities'.[77] D'Annunzio intended his translation to be used as a foreword to Mussolini's collected speeches, but neither did he participate

75 Reproduced in Mario Palmieri, *Gabriele D'Annunzio. Al Re Imperatore e al duce* (Milano: Impresa Editoriale Italiana, 1941), pp. 38–46.

76 See Luciano Anceschi's emphasis on this in Gabriele D'Annunzio, *Versi d'amore e di gloria*, vol. 1, ed. by Annamaria Andreoli and Niva Lorenzini. Introduction by Luciano Anceschi (Milano: Mondadori, 1982), pp. IX–XII. Nonetheless, it is also significant that the translations from ancient Greek and Latin published by D'Annunzio in his first collection of poems, *Primo vere*, composed a section entitled 'Imitations' in the first edition of the book, which became 'Treasons' in the second edition. See also Chapter 1 in this volume.

77 *Carteggio D'Annunzio-Mussolini (1919–1938)*, ed. by Renzo De Felice and Emilio Mariano (Milano: Mondadori, 1971), p. 366.

in the editorial enterprise, nor has any evidence of this translation been found.

What seems even more enigmatic is that D'Annunzio actually published Italian translations from German, or even Russian. I am referring to his supposed translation, or rather adaptation-amplification, of Hofmannsthal's article 'Gabriele D'Annunzio' (published in German in the *Frankfurter Zeitung* in 1893 and in Italian in the *Tavola Rotonda* in the same year). Even if the Vittoriale archives conserve an autograph manuscript of D'Annunzio's translation,[78] one can legitimately doubt that the writer possessed a sufficient knowledge of German to accomplish the task without the assistance of someone else, especially when we remember that he always read even those German authors who were very important for him (Nietzsche, Goethe, Wagner) in French translations, as abundant quotes from D'Annunzio's works show.[79] The same remark can be made for Italian translations of Heine D'Annunzio published in newspapers, which are retranslated from the French versions by Nerval and Gautier.[80] And there is likewise no evidence that the short passage from Shakespeare's *A Midsummer Night's Dream*, which can be found along with one sonnet by Heine in a newspaper article,[81] was produced without the help of an anglophile – one might naturally think of Nencioni.[82] An even stranger case may appear in the instance of the translation from a Russian original of a poem by Pascal Getzel, a Russian living in Naples at the same time as D'Annunzio, and one of his acquaintances, which D'Annunzio published as 'Un sogno' in *La Tavola Rotonda* in January 1892. Once again, it is hardly credible that D'Annunzio's role went beyond that of revising an already Italianised text, even if a manuscript kept at the Vittoriale might lead one to think differently.[83] These, albeit scarce, contrary pieces of evidence may be explained in terms of D'Annunzio's own conception of the activity of translation, and of original writing too (especially in French), up to a certain point, as a collaborative enterprise, which is particularly evident from a reading of his letters to Hérelle and from manuscripts of Hérelle's translations, which systematically contain

[78] Published in Andreoli, *D'Annunzio archivista*, pp. 17–27.

[79] See Guy Tosi, *D'Annunzio e la cultura francese*, ed. by Maddalena Rasera (Lanciano: Carabba, 2013). See also Chapter 9 in this volume.

[80] Gabriele D'Annunzio, *Tutte le novelle*, ed. by Annamaria Andreoli and Marina De Marco (Milano: Mondadori, 1992), pp. 1050–2.

[81] Ibid., pp. 802–3.

[82] See also Chapter 14 in this volume.

[83] See Andreoli, *D'Annunzio archivista*, pp. 31–6.

abundant comments and thorough rewritings in D'Annunzio's hand.[84] Apart from French and Italian, we might then assume that D'Annunzio's translations from other languages were seldom solitary acts. Finally, one has of course to consider the case of D'Annunzio's linguistic competence in the Abruzzese dialect. Abruzzo was his place of birth, the setting of many of his works, a place whose culture and legends were very important even in writings one would not necessarily suspect – the *Martyre de Saint Sébastien* introduces a legend from the ancient Abruzzese population of the Marsi. It was also the territory where he started his political career and where his triumphs as a public speaker began. For him, it was a land whose linguistic imaginary runs parallel to those of Italian and French. Abundant evidence of this can be found in his letters, but also in a scarce poetical production and in translations from Abruzzese into Italian.[85]

Back to Babel: Conclusion

In conclusion, I would like to briefly discuss the *Dit du sourd et muet*, which is probably the most sophisticated amongst D'Annunzio's multiple accomplishments in French. It was written in 1929–30 and was published in 1936.[86] It was meant to be the first part of a trilogy on Brunetto,[87] which shows that, up to the final years of his life, D'Annunzio was still clinging to the Franco-Italian canon he made up from the *Sonnets* onward. This work mostly confirms the assumptions unearthed above, particularly those about the nature of the 'synoptic' dimension of D'Annunzio's allophone writing. The *Dit*, which is a work written in modern French, contains numerous words and expressions borrowed from Old and Middle French, or whose orthograph is voluntarily archaic; for instance: 'fableau' (a dialectal variety of *fabliau*),[88] 'asseurer',[89] 'bouticle' (probably from an ancient form for *boutique*),[90] 'escolier',[91] 'compains',[92] 'escriveins',[93] 'escriptel',

[84] See also Chapter 7 in this volume.
[85] See the section of translations in D'Annunzio, *Tutte le novelle*.
[86] D'Annunzio, *Prose di ricerca*, vol. 2, pp. 2371–451.
[87] Gullace, *Gabriele D'Annunzio in France*, pp. 226–7.
[88] D'Annunzio, *Prose di ricerca*, vol. 2, p. 2373 and *passim*.
[89] Ibid., p. 2373 and *passim*.
[90] Ibid., p. 2374.
[91] Ibid., p. 2376 and *passim*.
[92] Ibid., p. 2379.
[93] Ibid., p. 2396.

probably for *écriteau*,[94] 'enfantosmé', meaning 'bewitched', 'haunted',[95] 'rondet' for *rondeau*,[96] 'partance',[97] 'calangue' for *calanque*,[98] 'arquenciel' for *arc-en-ciel*,[99] 'ménestraudie' (the corporation of minstrels).[100] In the same work we also find daring neologisms – which probably led to Contini's irritation; for instance: 'duriuscule' for 'rather tough',[101] or the two verbs 'nordir', 'to go North', and 'nordester', 'to stay in the North',[102] in which we find the Latin root of the verb 'ire' and the Old French 'ester' for 'stay'. He also permits himself some Italianisms, for example: 'cheval balzan'[103] for a temperamental horse, or 'abstème', 'who does not drink alcohol'.[104]

We likewise find in the *Dit* many references to the abovementioned Franco-Italian canon, both as a literary and a scholarly one, particularly through references to D'Annunzio's self-proclaimed training in Romance Philology under the supervision of Gaston Paris and Ernesto Monaci. Declarations of love for his two languages are often present in the work, for instance he refers to 'la dilection des deux patries' ('the love for the two fatherlands'[105]), even if somehow French prevails upon Italian, which he defines nonetheless as 'the first of my two languages'.[106] This is evident from the main narrative turn in the novel, the miracle that happens in Paris's Sainte-Chapelle with the result of healing the protagonist, who was deaf and dumb. This autobiographical Tuscan character, in fact, starts speaking, singing and composing poetry not in his own mother-tongue, Italian, but in the *langue d'oïl*.[107]

[94] Ibid., p. 2387.
[95] Ibid., p. 2389.
[96] Ibid., p. 2394.
[97] Ibid., p. 2389.
[98] Ibid., p. 2385.
[99] Ibid., p. 2385.
[100] Ibid., p. 2376.
[101] Ibid., p. 2387.
[102] Ibid., p. 2389.
[103] Ibid., p. 2385.
[104] Ibid., p. 2390. We find voluntary Italianisms in every one of D'Annunzio's French works. In the *Martyre*, for example, he uses the word 'castrats', which is drawn from the Italian 'castrati', instead of the French 'châtrés'. D'Annunzio defended his choice for maintaining this word against the advice of Hérelle and other proofreaders of the *Martyre*.
[105] Ibid., p. 2376.
[106] Ibid., p. 2374.
[107] Ibid., pp. 2392–3.

Galderisi[108] has established a link between writing in someone else's language and a natural tendency to the experimental use of forms,[109] which is particularly evident in the *Dit*. The novel, apart from being D'Annunzio's last and principal legacy written in French, should be considered a plurilingual work.[110] Reading the *Dit* as the culminating point of D'Annunzio's overall French production is particularly useful in order to understand the dynamics of his love of, and of his use and abuse of, the several languages of the 'Latin sister', as well as, more generally, the dynamics of his relationship to multilingual writing and his ambition to access a transnational canon.

To sum up, and as the example of the *Dit* shows well, the strong relationship between D'Annunzio and the French language can hardly be defined merely as a form of bilingualism. It is probably closer to a form of diglossia, a socially-oriented dimension of communication, according to which an individual attributes different communicative functions as well as distinct social and performative characteristics to different languages. What is important to underline here is that both in Italian and in French, D'Annunzio displays a deep knowledge of and a paramount interest in the historical dimension of languages, and in literature as a canon and a tradition grounded in a particular use of language. This does not mean that his tendency is to conform to that tradition. On the contrary, the deep knowledge of a literary and linguistic canon is for him the foundation upon which to build his own language and to innovate tradition. D'Annunzio's 'extraterritoriality' thus emerges in a clearer way both from his attitudes toward the French language and from his works in French and his self-translations.

108 Claudio Galderisi, 'Faute contre nature?', p. 63.

109 See in particular Steven G. Kellman, *The Translingual Imagination* (Lincoln: University of Nebraska Press, 2000).

110 Or 'heterolingual', if we consider the deep dialogical dimension of D'Annunzio's texts, as well as his approach to writing in more than one language, which is, as I have shown here, a non-hierarchical one. For the notion of 'heterolingual', see Rainier Grutman, 'Le moment biculturel de la littérature française', in *Paradoxes du plurilinguisme littéraire 1900*, ed. by Britta Benert (Bruxelles, etc.: Peter Lang, 2015), pp. 125–41.

Part II

Translators as Transcultural Negotiators

Chapter 6

Gabriele D'Annunzio and Georges Hérelle: Virility, Machismo and the Homoerotic

Clive Thomson

'Naples me séduit toujours, comme un vice'

(Naples always seduces me, like a vice)
Georges Hérelle (*Notes de voyage en Italie, 1896*, MS 3392, f° 181).

George Hérelle's multi-layered relationship with Gabriele D'Annunzio began in 1891 and continued until the early 1930s. For a period of almost twenty years starting in 1892, Hérelle translated two or three of D'Annunzio's works per year (novels, short stories, poetry, theatre). The novels and short stories usually appeared first in Paris newspapers and periodicals, such as *Le temps*, *La Revue de Paris*, *Revue des deux mondes*, *La Revue européenne* and then later as volumes with Éditions Calmann-Lévy. While some aspects of Hérelle and D'Annunzio's personal and professional interactions have been documented and discussed at considerable length,[1] there are still many questions that remain unanswered. Hérelle claimed insistently that his discovery of D'Annunzio's novels was purely 'an accident'

[1] See: Raffaele Giglio, *Per la storia di un'amicizia: D'Annunzio, Hérelle, Scarfoglio, Serao: documenti inediti* (Naples: Loffredo, 1977); Mario Cimini, ed., *Carteggio D'Annunzio – Hérelle (1891–1931)* (Lanciano, Italy: Casa Rocco Carabba, 2004); Thomas Loué and Blaise Wilfert-Portal, 'D'Annunzio à l'usage des Français: la traduction comme censure informelle (fin du XIXe siècle)', *Ethnologie française*, 36: 1 (2006), pp. 101–10; Daniel Fabre, 'Inversion et dislocation : les vies savantes de Georges Hérelle', *Ce que la science fait à la vie*, ed. by Nicolas Adell and Jérôme Lamy (Paris: Éditions du comité des travaux historiques et scientifiques, 2016), pp. 269–303; Guy Ducrey, 'Is There Such Thing as a 'Decadent Translator'? The Case of Georges Hérelle (1848–1935)', *Volupté*, 3: 2 (2020), pp. 11–27; Muriel Gallot, 'Gabriele D'Annunzio et Georges Hérelle: érotisme et traduction', in *Traduire avec l'auteur*, ed. by Patrick Hersant (Paris: Sorbonne Université Presses, 2020), pp. 129–46.

and that his subsequent interest in the Italian writer was based on his admiration for his style. The 'accident' in question took place in 1891. While on vacation in Naples, Hérelle decided to learn Italian by reading the local press and took a particular liking to *Il Corriere di Napoli*. Back to France, he subscribed to the newspaper, and it is here that he came across D'Annunzio's novel, *L'Innocente*, published in serial form. In *Comment je suis devenu traducteur*, a memoire he wrote in the 1920s, Hérelle reports that without knowing anything about D'Annunzio,[2] just to amuse himself, he began to translate the novel. This memoire contains what we propose to call Hérelle's idealised version of his first encounter with D'Annunzio's writings. Hérelle seeks to present a certain image of himself, that of the scholar whose interests are primarily intellectual. A close examination of his 1895 and 1898 travel diaries reveals, however, another side of the story, one in which he describes quite candidly his ambivalent reactions toward D'Annunzio's personality. His reactions include both a certain admiration and homoerotic tensions. What are we to make of Hérelle's ambivalence and his seemingly simplistic explanation of how he discovered D'Annunzio's novel? My research suggests that there is much more to be said about Hérelle's motivation, attitude and the circumstances surrounding his encounter with D'Annunzio. What, for example, did Hérelle think of D'Annunzio's hyper-masculinity? This chapter seeks to answer these questions.

To do so, the chapter begins with a review of some of the existing scholarship on the Hérelle-D'Annunzio relationship. It then explores two very different threads in Hérelle's telling of the story of how his career in translation began and the reasons for his interest in D'Annunzio. One thread emphasises the role of chance and the intellectual affinities of the two men, the other has to do with matters homoerotic.[3]

[2] Médiathèque Jacques Chirac Troyes Champagne Métropole, Petits mémoires littéraires, t. III, Deuxième partie, 1° *Mes traductions, Comment je suis devenu traducteur*, MS 3170, f°2–3. In *Comment je suis devenu traducteur*, Hérelle first describes the events that triggered his interest in translation and then goes on to outline in great detail the principles that guided him and his advice for those who might be contemplating a career in translation. Note: all manuscripts quoted in our article are held in the Fonds Georges Hérelle at the Médiathèque in Troyes and our transcriptions are an exact representation of the text that appears in the manuscripts. The following website provides detailed information about Georges Hérelle and the Fonds Hérelle at the Troyes Médiathèque: http://www.garae.fr/spip.php?article220 (consulted on 20 March 2022).

[3] We have left aside the question of how Hérelle dealt with language issues relating to gender in his translations of D'Annunzio, or the extent to which his translations

Translation, Phagocytosis and Censorship

Recent scholarship on D'Annunzio and Hérelle includes Mario Cimini's critical edition of their correspondence – the most substantial published source of information about how they worked together to produce translations of D'Annunzio's works. This edition contains a total of 457 letters, 359 written by D'Annunzio and 98 by Hérelle, between 1891 and 1931. Because of the availability of a significantly greater number of letters penned by D'Annunzio, researchers have been able to provide a very detailed and nuanced account of his contribution to the translation process and of his attitude toward his translator. It is also the case that Hérelle's letters tend to be shorter and more concise, whereas D'Annunzio adopts a much more expansive and openly expressive epistolary style. These reasons explain why Guy Tosi, in his seminal 1947 study of Hérelle's translations, described D'Annunzio as playing the leading, and hence, by implication, more interesting role in the relationship.[4] Similarly, Muriel Gallot, in her 2020 study on the subject, devotes more attention to D'Annunzio's role which, according to her, is the dominant one, and argues that Hérelle 'never gets the last word' and 'discovers upon publication a text whose mastery has escaped him'.[5] Gallot concludes her article by summarising D'Annunzio's vision of translation

of D'Annunzio's prose and poetic writings might have been done in a homoerotic key. Such a project would need to be undertaken by a scholar with several areas of specialisation: an expertise in the Italian and French languages; a solid knowledge of D'Annunzio's works and the literature of the Decadent movement; a background in gender and sexuality studies. Using the electronic 'search' function, however, we carried out a very preliminary study to see if Hérelle used any lexical terms related to homosexuality in the six prose texts by D'Annunzio he translated between 1892 and 1900. We found no examples of the following French terms, all of which were current during this period: 'péderaste', 'sodomite', 'uraniste', 'homosexuel', 'inverti' (pederast, sodomite, uranist, homosexual, invert). The reason for this situation is that the equivalents of such terms do not appear in D'Annunzio's texts. Hérelle uses adjectives such as 'effeminé' (effeminate) and 'éphèbe' (ephebe) to translate the Italian terms 'effeminato' and 'efebo', both of which had homosexual connotations when associated with men in 'fin-de-siècle' novels and which D'Annunzio uses infrequently. Hérelle's translations contain multiple uses of the French adjective 'viril', the Italian equivalent of which is consistently used by D'Annunzio to describe, with positive connotations, heterosexual male characters. Some women characters are described as having a combination of 'virile' and 'feminine' qualities.

4 Guy Tosi, *D'Annunzio en Grèce* (Paris: Calmann-Lévy, 1947).

5 Muriel Gallot, 'Gabriele D'Annunzio et Georges Hérelle: érotisme et traduction', p. 135. All translations from French in this chapter are my own.

as a process in which the author and translator merge, and the translator is 'phagocytized' by the author to enable the original language to 'shine through the translated text'.[6] The connotations of Gallot's overarching view, expressed here in stark metaphorical terms, suggest an image of D'Annunzio as a malevolent individual who wished to devour (figuratively) his passive partner and thus make him disappear altogether.

Over a period of several years, the disagreements about the translation process between D'Annunzio and Hérelle became more and more frequent and eventually reached a level of intensity that Hérelle could no longer tolerate. Their collaboration ended in 1912. Although D'Annunzio had a good basic command of spoken and written French, Hérelle felt that his mastery of the subtleties of the language was weak, especially as regards the syntax and semantics of literary French.

In 1897, Hérelle was awarded the prestigious Langlois Prize by the French Academy for his translation of *Le vergini delle rocce*. His reputation as a highly skilled translator remained intact for many years following this recognition, with his translations being regularly reprinted. In 1994, for example, Hérelle's 1891 translation of *L'Innocente* was issued with a preface by Thierry de Vulpilliers, who underlined that the reputation of the book was due 'above all to its translator, Georges Hérelle'.[7] His translation of *Il fuoco* was reissued as recently as the year 2000. In his 2005 article, Hugo Vandal-Siroir refers to Hérelle as a 'somewhat utopian translator'.[8] This point of view, which aligns with that of de Vulpilliers, positions Hérelle as the well-intentioned translator who was doing his best to capture the content and form of D'Annunzio's prose and poetry. It assumes that translation is an apolitical or acultural activity in which the translator's dual responsibility is to capture the essence of the text to be translated while at the same time respecting the spirit of the national language used to carry out the translation. According to the final section of *Comment je suis devenu traducteur*, where Hérelle describes

[6] Ibid., p. 136.

[7] Gabriele D'Annunzio, *L'Innocent* (Paris: La Table Ronde, 1994), p. 13. This 1994 translation is published under the title *L'Innocent*, and not *L'Intrus*, which was the original French title that appeared in 1891.

[8] Hugo Vandal-Siroir, review of, Georges Hérelle, *Petit mémoire d'un traducteur*, ed. by Jean-Marie an der Meerschen (Bruxelles: Les Éditions du Hazard, 2005), *Meta*, 55: 3 (2010), p. 135.

his theory and practice of translation, he can be seen to adhere to such a view.[9]

The recent studies by Guy Ducrey, Thomas Loué and Blaise Wilfert-Portal propose, however, a very different perspective in that they raise serious questions about the nature and limitations of Hérelle's translations. Loué and Wilfert-Portal describe in concrete and convincing detail how D'Annunzio's novels were, to use his terms, 'mutilated' and 'massacred'.[10] The value of this article is that it provides concrete examples of how censorship was carried out at a syntactic, semantic and lexical level and outlines how it functioned. First, it shows that the editors of the newspapers and periodicals in which D'Annunzio's novels appeared did not hesitate to intervene in the translation process. For example, severe cuts were made during the publication of *L'Innocente* in *Le temps* in 1892, of *Il Piacere* in *La Revue de Paris* in 1894, and of *Le Vergine delle rocce* in the *Revue des deux mondes* in 1896. Ferdinand Brunetière, the director of the *Revue des deux mondes*, complained in a letter addressed to Hérelle (17 May 1895) that the passages in which D'Annunzio's fictional characters indulge in philosophical and aesthetic debates were 'too long and analysed with too much subtlety'.[11] A very different kind of censorship was instituted by Hérelle himself, who is referred to as an 'invisible censor'.[12] According to this argument, Hérelle's translations are informed by his rigid adherence to a narrow and old-fashioned view, shared by Brunetière, that French translators had an obligation to defend the 'Frenchness' of the language used in French highbrow publications.[13] Loué et Wilfert-Portal conclude that the impact of Hérelle's form of censorship as an 'invisible translator' was perhaps more significant and detrimental than that of the editors who accepted D'Annunzio's works for publication.[14]

Guy Ducrey's 2020 study begins by presenting some of the main features of the Decadent literary movement in Europe and goes on to outline D'Annunzio's place within that movement. The specific objective of Ducrey's article is to explore the extent to which Hérelle

[9] *Comment je suis devenu traducteur: le labeur de la traduction*, MS 3170, f°s 42–109.

[10] Thomas Loué and Blaise Wilfert-Portal, 'D'Annunzio à l'usage des Français: la traduction comme censure informelle (fin du XIXe siècle)', p. 102.

[11] Quoted in: Thomas Loué and Blaise Wilfert-Portal, 'D'Annunzio à l'usage des Français: la traduction comme censure informelle (fin du XIXe siècle)', p. 104.

[12] Ibid., p. 106.

[13] Ibid., p. 107.

[14] Ibid., p. 107.

understood or appreciated the significance of D'Annunzio's style in the context of the Decadent and Symbolist literary movements of the *fin-de-siècle*. Gathering evidence from Hérelle's comments on Laurent Tailhade's translations of Petronius (a translation that engaged with the precious language cherished by the Decadents) and from the silence he kept regarding the French literary scene, Ducrey concludes that 'if D'Annunzio had [. . .] a deep understanding of Symbolist prose and Decadent language, so Hérelle had not' and argues that his life as a Lycée professor in provincial French towns did not allow him to become familiar with the Decadent movement in France, and that he was also ignorant of the wider European literary context.[15] Ducrey's contention that Hérelle did not have a 'deep understanding' of the poetics of the Decadent literary movement is accurate. Loué and Wilfert-Portal go further and affirm that Hérelle, who was functioning as D'Annunzio's international literary agent and recruiter for Paris editors, was negligent because he made no effort to put D'Annunzio in touch with Symbolist periodicals.[16] It is important, however, to note that Hérelle was very much aware of D'Annunzio's exceptionally original style. Hérelle describes D'Annunzio as the only 'great writer and stylist' he had dealt with.[17] This is extremely high praise, given that Hérelle translated the works of many other important writers of this period (Grazia Deledda, Matilde Serao, Antonio Fogazzero, Guglielmo Ferrero, Ventura Garcia Calderon and Vicente Blasco Ibanez, among others) whose works, in some cases, can be associated thematically and stylistically with those of the Decadent literary movement. Hérelle met in person with some of these writers and corresponded with all of them. It seems reasonable to hypothesise, therefore, that he would not have been completely unaware of the ongoing debates about the poetics of Decadence.

Daniel Fabre, another major recent contributor to the study of the D'Annunzio-Hérelle relationship, starts his 2016 article by referring to Hérelle as a 'compartmentalized polygraph'[18] because his areas of interest not only shifted dramatically over his long life but also because they appear unrelated. Although other researchers have

[15] Guy Ducrey, 'Is There Such Thing as a "Decadent Translator"? The Case of Georges Hérelle (1848–1935)', pp. 25–6.

[16] Thomas Loué and Blaise Wilfert-Portal, 'D'Annunzio à l'usage des Français: la traduction comme censure informelle (fin du XIXe siècle)', p. 106.

[17] *Comment je suis devenu traducteur*, MS 3170, f° 35.

[18] 'Inversion et dislocation: les vies savantes de Georges Hérelle', p. 271.

made this point,[19] Fabre is the first to identify and describe in detail a thread that connects the various phases of Hérelle's multi-faceted career. The thread is not to be found by examining the content of Hérelle's early publications on the history of the Champagne region in France, in his translations, in his research on Basque popular theatre, or even in his works on Greek love. The answer to this 'enigma'[20] surrounding Hérelle's career is intimately related, rather, to his biography. Fabre writes that Hérelle saw the queer man as 'a being necessarily divided, fatally separated from himself',[21] and that he had no choice but to compartmentalise his existence and to hide his homosexuality because of contemporary society's hostility and intolerance. Seen by Fabre in spatial terms, Hérelle's seemingly random areas of investigation have a foundation, 'the base of the pyramid',[22] which is constituted by his research and publications on homosexuality. Fabre then shifts his argument to an unconscious level and proposes persuasively that 'the erotics of Georges Hérelle'[23] is what provides another kind of coherence to his existence, as well as a key to understanding the common element in most of his professional activities. In the following discussion, we revisit what we see as Fabre's brilliant insight and attempt to push it further.

Hérelle chose, as Fabre demonstrates, to keep the public and private spheres of his life separate because of social pressures, but there is perhaps another way to understand this choice, which has to do with the image of himself he wished to promote for posterity. In the 1920s, when Hérelle undertook to organise his massive archival collections and to make donations to libraries, he divided the thousands of letters he received into two categories. One category contains the letters related to his life in the academy, to his translations and to his exchanges with researchers and institutions. In other words, these are the letters, all of which have ended up in public archives, that reflect his public persona. The fact that Hérelle did not eliminate any correspondence of this type is evidence of the importance that he attached to it, as these letters underline his activity as a hard-working, highly productive scholar and translator. The other category, which

[19] Mario Cimini, ed., *Carteggio D'Annunzio – Hérelle (1891–1931)*; Clive Thomson, *Georges Hérelle: archéologue de l'inversion sexuelle 'fin de siècle'* (Paris: Éditions du Félin, 2014).

[20] 'Inversion et dislocation: les vies savantes de Georges Hérelle', p. 272.

[21] Ibid., p. 282.

[22] Ibid., p. 291.

[23] Ibid., p. 291.

includes his correspondence with family members, school friends and his relatively small circle of other close friends and his romantic partners, pertains to his private life. Hérelle preserved his correspondence with his family members, as well as approximately 300 letters and documents written in the late 1860s and 1870s by himself and his school friends (Paul Bourget, Félix Bourget, Adrien Juvigny, Maurice Bouchor).[24] He indicated to the municipal library in Troyes that this correspondence with his school friends should not be made available to the public until after 1950. A note appearing on the general inventory of his correspondences that he prepared toward the end of his life demonstrates that he destroyed most of the letters that his intimate friends and lovers sent to him.[25] This decision underlines the extent to which he exercised control on the material preserved in the archive.

Social pressures did indeed determine Hérelle's decisions on how he organised his personal life, but an equally essential part of the story are his diligent efforts to shape his own image as an intellectual, an archivist and a scholar. In his memoires and travel diaries where Hérelle mentions his relations with D'Annunzio, there are moments when this tendency is foregrounded, as well as other moments that allow a rare glimpse of his personal feelings toward D'Annunzio the man, as well as some insight into his 'erotic' relations with the young man who ignited his desire to learn Italian. The clever strategies that he uses to camouflage or downplay certain episodes in his private life have received little attention. For this reason, they are an important focus in the following discussion.

The 'Intellectual' Translator

As mentioned above, Hérelle begins *Comment je suis devenu traducteur* by outlining in detail his retrospective account of the series of 'coincidences' or 'accidents' in the summer of 1891 that led to his career as translator:

> Comment j'ai été amené à connaître l'*Intrus* et D'Annunzio. Par une combinaison de 3 ou 4 hasards. Premier hasard: que j'ai été passer cette

[24] It is also possible that in eliminating these letters he wished to protect from scrutiny the private lives of his friends. A critical edition of this correspondence is slated to appear in 2024, with Éditions Classiques Garnier, prepared by Michael Rosenfeld, Daniel Ridge and myself.

[25] Médiathèque Jacques Chirac Troyes Champagne Métropole, MS 3807, f°s 88–90.

année-là mes vacances à Naples. 2° hasard: que, parmi les nombreux journaux qu'on crie à Toledo au piazza Municipio, j'aie justement, sans savoir, acheté *le corriere di Napoli*, et que j'y aie pris goût pour les charmantes et pétillantes chroniques de Matilde Serao, 3° qu'au retour, pour me perfectionner dans l'Italien, j'ai justement pris un abonnement au *corriere di Napoli*. 4° que juste à cette époque commençait en feuilleton dans ce journal le roman L'Innocente. Quelques pages traduites par amusement, pour moi et mes amis. Lettre à Gabriel . . . etc. Extraordinaire facilité de publication dans *le Temps*: deux ans de correspondance active et bientôt amicale.[26]

(How I came to know *Intrus* and D'Annunzio. Through a combination of 3 or 4 coincidences. First coincidence: that I went to spend my vacation that year in Naples. Second coincidence: that, among the numerous newspapers that are sold on the street in Toledo at the piazza Municipio, I had just, without thinking, bought the *Corriere di Napoli*, and that I had taken a liking for the charming and titillating chronicles of Matilde Serao, third chance: that, on my return, in order to improve my Italian, I had just taken out a subscription to the *Corriere di Napoli*. 4° that just at that time the novel *L'Innocente* began to be serialized in this newspaper. I translated a few pages just for the fun of it, for me and my friends. Letter to Gabriel . . . etc. It was very easy to get it published in *the Temps*: two years of active and soon friendly correspondence.)

Hérelle's simplistic account of the genesis of his career as translator warrants a detailed commentary. After devoting several pages in *Comment je suis devenu traducteur* to the role of coincidence during his travels, Hérelle recounts succinctly in just a few sentences his 'chance' encounter with a 'certain' Alfredo Rosati and downplays the importance of this event:

[. . .] je fis connaissance, dès le lendemain de mon arrivée, avec un certain Alfredo Rosati, garçon d'environ dix-huit, natif de Gora, qui parlait le bon italien et qui avait une prononciation très nette. Gai, désœuvré et sans le sou, il ne demandait pas mieux que de passer avec moi les journées entières, et nous faisions presque quotidiennement de longues excursions, à Anversa, à Pouzzolles, à Torre del greco, à Pompei, à Capri, à Casamicciola, etc. Ces excursions, grâce à la patience de mon compagnon, se passaient en interminables causeries. [. . .] D'ailleurs Alfredo n'était pas assez instruit pour me donner des leçons d'italien, et, heureusment, il ne savait un mot de français. Je fis avec lui de très rapides progrès [. . .].[27]

[26] Médiathèque Jacques Chirac Troyes Champagne Métropole, *Comment je suis devenu traducteur*, MS 3170, f°1bis.

[27] *Comment je suis devenue traducteur*, MS 3170, f°2–3.

([. . .] the day after my arrival, I met a certain Alfredo Rosati, a young man of about eighteen, a native of Gora, who spoke good Italian and had a very clear pronunciation. Cheerful, at loose ends and penniless, he asked nothing more than to spend the whole day with me, and we made almost daily long excursions to Anversa, Pozzuoli, Torre del Greco, Pompeii, Capri, Casamicciola, etc. These excursions, thanks to the patience of my companion, were spent in interminable conversations. [. . .] Besides, Alfredo was not educated enough to give me Italian lessons, and, fortunately, he did not know a word of French. I made very rapid progress with him [. . .].)

Hérelle reports this episode in his 1890 travel diary, but he adds the following detail: 'Dès le second ou le troisième jour, nous commencions à nous comprendre assez bien; au bout de huit jours, nous bavardions comme des pies, du matin au soir'[28] (From the second or third day, we began to understand each other quite well; after eight days, we were chattering like magpies from morning to night). Adopting a somewhat affectless, hence distancing, tone, we see that Hérelle presents his meeting with Rosati as just one more piece of good luck. He implies as well that it was the young Alfredo who took the initiative that led to their month-long affair while they visited the Naples region together ('he asked nothing more than to spend the whole day with me'). However, his 1890 travel diary, in which there is a much more detailed description of their relations, leaves no doubt as regards the intimate and sexual nature of the relationship. Hérelle narrates at length the scenes of jealousy and rivalry among male prostitutes whom he observed in Naples while in the company of his young guide. On one of these occasions, Alfredo expresses his fears that Hérelle might be tempted to get involved with other young men:

Et, lorsque je lui [à Rosati] demandai la raison de tous ces manèges, il ne manquait pas de me répondre : 'Si vous causiez avec un autre, il voudrait vous prendre. – Me prendre ? Et pourquoi ? – Pour faire l'amour avec vous. – Mais je n'ai pas besoin d'un autre pour faire l'amour. – Qui sait ? – Tu sais bien que je ne suis pas volage. – C'est vrai, j'en ai eu la preuve. Mais ils vous diraient toute sorte de mal de moi, que je ne suis pas un 'buono ragazzo', que vous ne devez pas me fréquenter, qu'eux sont plus honnêtes que moi, et vous finiriez peut-être par les croire'.[29]

(And when I asked him the reason for all these intrigues, he would only tell me: 'If you talked to someone else, he would want to have you. –

[28] MS 3173, t. II., f° 49.
[29] MS 3392, f°s 119–25.

> Have me? And what for? – To make love with you. – But I don't need someone else to make love with. – Who knows? – You know very well that I am not unfaithful. – It's true, I've had proof of that. But they would tell you all sorts of bad things about me, that I am not a 'buono ragazzo' [a good boy], that you should not get involved with me, that they are more honest than I am, and maybe you would end up believing them.)

The intimate, erotic relationship with Rosati is, in my view, the essential link in the chain of events that explains the genesis of Hérelle's passion – first, for the Italian language, and subsequently, for the writings of D'Annunzio. It is tempting to speculate that, had his 'chance' encounter with Rosati not taken place, Hérelle's career as translator might never have materialised.[30]

Following the short account of his adventure with Rosati in *Comment je suis devenu traducteur*, Hérelle, ever the intellectual, goes on to analyse two aspects of D'Annunzio that immediately caught his attention – the novelist's literary talent and his temperament: '[. . .] je fus ébloui [. . .] quand il s'agit de littérature, G. D'A. n'est plus maître de ses nerfs [. . .] le seul grand artiste et grand styliste à qui j'ai eu affaire [. . .]'[31] ([. . .] I was amazed [by the style of *L'Innocente*] [. . .] when it comes to literature, G. D'A. is no longer in control of his nerves [. . .] the only great artist and great stylist I have ever dealt with [. . .]). Although Hérelle made almost no public statements about D'Annunzio during the early years of their collaboration, he included a ten-page preface in 1895 with his translation of *Episcopo et Cie*, a collection of short stories. The preface begins with some details related to D'Annunzio's early career, specifically his successes in the field of poetry: 'Son nom courait sur toutes les bouches, aussi célèbre par les succès mondains que par les succès littéraires; et cette double célébrité ressemblait un peu à un

[30] In *Comment je suis devenu traducteur*, Hérelle notes that a chance encounter with a young man was also the catalyst for his decision to learn Spanish: 'C'est par la même méthode que, quelques années plus tard, j'ai commencé à apprendre l'espagnol. Mon professeur de quelques jours fut alors Elisardo Perseverancio Ramos, apprenti lithographe à Burgos' (It was by the same method that, a few years later, I began to learn Spanish. My teacher for a few days was Elisardo Perseverancio Ramos, an apprentice lithographer in Burgos), MS 3170 f° 4. In yet another encounter of the same kind, Hérelle met, in 1899, Leopold Irigaray, a young man who became his friend and interpreter during their visits to Basque villages over several years. Their objective was to watch and, perhaps more importantly, document popular theatre in which, among other type of scenes, young men occasionally impersonated young women during the performances.

[31] Comment je suis devenu traducteur, MS 3170, f°s 5, 34, 35.

scandale'[32] (His name was on everyone's lips, equally famous for social successes as for literary successes; and this dual fame was a bit like a scandal). Referring to D'Annunzio's adolescent years as a period of 'effervescence tumultueuse de puberté virile et artistique'[33] (chaotic turmoil of [his] virile and artistic pubescent period), Hérelle suggests that D'Annunzio is to be admired for giving up his 'chaotic' lifestyle, a decision that puts him on the path to becoming a serious writer. The juxtaposition of the words 'virile' and 'artistic' in this quotation are significant. It is the moment when Hérelle begins to develop his 'theory' that D'Annunzio's literary genius is intimately linked to his 'nervous' temperament and his hyper-masculinity. Hérelle also points to another aspect of D'Annunzio's novels that he appears to admire – their autobiographical content. In *Comment je suis devenu traducteur*, he writes, with reference to *Trionfo della morte*: '[. . .] l'auteur essaie de faire l'analyse physiologico-psychologique de sa propre activité mentale'[34] (The author attempts a physiologico-psychological analysis of his own mental life). The fact that D'Annunzio possessed a solid knowledge of Classical literatures and languages also helps to explain Hérelle's admiration and fascination.[35]

In the subsequent pages of the preface to *Episcopo et Cie*, Hérelle confirms that it was precisely the combination of D'Annunzio's 'art' and his psychological mindedness, les 'spectacles et les drames plus mystérieux de la vie psychologique' (spectacles and the more mysterious dramas of psychological life) that so impressed him. D'Annunzio is described as 'l'orfèvre et le ciseleur de mots'

32 *Episcopo et Cie* (Paris: Calmann-Lévy, 1895), p. iii.

33 Ibid., p. iii.

34 *Comment je suis devenu traducteur*, f° 25. Mario Cimini emphasises this point as follows, while identifying the many fictional characters who are the author's 'doubles': 'L'innéité psychologique est la seule catégorie pouvant expliquer l'élan vers la surhumanité chez d'Annunzio, et ses incarnations littéraires, tels que Andrea Sperelli, Tullio Hermil, Giorgio Aurispa, Claudio Cantelmo, Stelio Effrena, ne seraient que les doubles de celui qui les a créées' (Psychological innateness is the only category that can explain the impulse toward superhumanity in D'Annunzio's works, and its literary incarnations, such as Andrea Sperelli, Tullio Hermil, Giorgio Aurispa, Claudio Cantelmo, Stelio Effrena, are just the doubles of he who has created them), in Georges Hérelle, *Gabriel D'Annunzio ou Théorie et pratique de la surhumanité*, ed. Mario Cimini (Berne: Peter Lang 2015), p. 9.

35 Ibid., passim. Hérelle, an accomplished scholar and teacher of Classical literature, made a major contribution to the study of Aristotle: *Aristote: Problèmes sur l'amour physique*, ed. and trans., by Agricola Lieberfreund (En Pyrogopolis: 1900). Agricola Lieberfeund is Hérelle's pseudonym.

(the goldsmith and sculptor of words), and 'ce questionneur d'âmes' (this questioner of souls). Hérelle goes further and expresses his opinion that D'Annunzio's novels are highly original because they focus on 'des anomalies morales', des 'perversions', 'des passions criminelles', and 'des égarements imbéciles de superstition idolâtrique'[36] (moral anomalies, perversions, criminal passions, imbecilic deviations of superstitious idolatry). Expressions like 'moral anomalies' and 'perversions' refer, of course, to psychological phenomena in which Hérelle had always been intensely interested. As he writes in his memoires, his fascination with such psychological topics dates back to his days as a student in the 1860s at the Collège Saint-Barbe in Paris:

> Dès le temps où j'étais élève de philosophie, la psychologie était l'objet de ma prédilection, et j'avais pris beaucoup de notes sur moi-même et sur les camarades. J'avais même essayé de composer quelques petits traités, notamment sur l'amour, sans m'apercevoir que tout cela n'était, au fond, que de l'autobiographie déguisée. J'ai conservé longtemps ces cahiers de notes et ces prétendues théories psychologiques ; mais j'ai reconnu enfin que mes griffonnages n'avaient aucun intérêt, même à titre de souvenirs, et j'ai jeté tout au feu.[37]
>
> (From the time when I was a student of philosophy, psychology was the object of my predilection, and I had taken a lot of notes on myself and on my fellow students. I had even tried to compose some small treatises, notably on love, without realizing that all that was, in the end, just autobiography in disguise. For a long time, I kept these notebooks and these so-called psychological theories; but I finally recognized that my scribblings were totally uninteresting, even as memories, and I burned everything.)

Hérelle saw D'Annunzio as a kindred spirit because they shared, perhaps more than anything else, an intellectual curiosity for psychological matters.[38] It is crucial to note as well that the particular

[36] Ibid., p. vii, viii.

[37] *Petits mémoires littéraires, Mes ouvrages*, MS 3170 (1), f° 220.

[38] Here is another example of how Hérelle sees D'Annunzio as a psychological novelist: 'À la différence des grands écrivains réalistes – tel que Balzac – qui conçoivent la littérature en termes d'objectivité et qui donnent vie à des personnages autonomes, D'Annunzio 'vit au contraire en lui-même. Pour lui, ce qui se passe dans le monde extérieur a beaucoup moins d'importance que ce qui se passe dans son propre esprit. Son œuvre est presque entièrement subjective' (Unlike the great realist writers – such as Balzac – who conceive of literature in terms of objectivity and who create autonomous characters, D'Annunzio 'lives within himself. For him, what happens in the outside world is of much less importance

psychological phenomena that interested them were the same – the passions associated with perversion, criminality and madness, all of which are recurrent topics in the literature of the Decadent movement. Although we do not know the exact extent to which Hérelle was aware of or interested in the poetics of Decadent writing, our discussion here does allow us to posit that the conceptual categories represented by some of his particular interests are well reflected in those of writers like Gabriele D'Annunzio.

The Translator and the Homoerotic

Having examined Hérelle's account of how his career in translation began, the alleged role of 'chance' in his discovery of D'Annunzio and the features that drew him to D'Annunzio's writing, it is now time to consider the thread which has to do with matters homoerotic. In the preface to his edition of *Théorie et pratique de la surhumanité* (Hérelle's study of the thematics of D'Annunzio's oeuvre), Mario Cimini sees a paradox in the D'Annunzio-Hérelle relationship. The Italian writer, he notes, 'was very eager to experiment with all the erotic possibilities, and in particular 'extreme' experiences, including incest, with however the exclusion – curious for Hérelle – of homosexual love'.[39] Cimini suggests that, since D'Annunzio's writings focus primarily on an erotics of heterosexuality, it is 'curious' that Hérelle would be interested in such a writer. According to Cimini, there are only five or six explicit references to homosexuality in D'Annunzio's entire oeuvre of novels, theatre and poetry; D'Annunzio's focus is primarily on a heterosexual erotics, and his writings contain little homosexual content.[40]

---

than what happens in his own mind. His work is almost entirely subjective'). Quoted in Mario Cimini's preface, *Gabriel D'Annunzio ou Théorie et pratique de la surhumanité*, p. 7.

[39] *Gabriel D'Annunzio ou Théorie et pratique de la surhumanité*, p. 11. This study, which Hérelle did not publish during his lifetime, appeared for the first time in 2015, edited by Mario Cimini. Hérelle presents the detailed version of his theory that 'virility' is the essential ingredient that explains D'Annunzio's great literary talent.

[40] It is important to add that there is very interesting research that goes beyond Cimini's content-based approach to the question of D'Annunzio's relationship to homosexuality. See, for example, Derek Duncan, *Reading and Writing Italian Homosexuality: A Case of Possible Difference* (Aldershot: Ashgate, 2005);

Over the many years of their acquaintanceship, Hérelle and D'Annunzio met in person on only five or six occasions. In 1895, they spent a month together travelling on a cruise through the Mediterranean Sea that took them to Greece, where they spent their time visiting archaeological sites and museums. In his 1895 travel diary, Hérelle recounts several episodes in which the novelist's hyper-sexuality is foregrounded. The following passage describes the events of the very first evening when D'Annunzio and his travelling companions arrived in Greece and set off in search of a brothel:

> Après dîner, Scarfoglio et D'Annunzio veulent absolument célébrer leur arrivée en Grèce par une soirée d'amour. On s'adresse donc au drogman Bertucci, qui paraît y mettre beaucoup de bonne volonté, mais qui nous avertit qu'en Grèce cela ne se fait point de cette manière, et que nous ne pourrons trouver ainsi, au pied levé, ce que nous désirons. Sur l'insistance de Scarfoglio et D'Annunzio, il se met pourtant en campagne, non sans nous avoir prévenu que nous n'avons chance d'obtenir que ce qu'il y a de plus vil. – Sur quoi, nous rôdons avec lui dans toute la ville ; nous entrons dans de petits cafés qui sont des bouges à soldats et à marins, et nous nous sauvons. Bertucci finit par nous conduire dans une maison écartée, où nous montons par un escalier extérieur, en bois ; nous trouvons en haut une femme toute vêtue de blanc, ni jeune, ni belle, qui dégoûte aussitôt tout le monde, et, après quelques paroles échangées, nous tournons le dos. Alors sort d'une pièce voisine, une très vieille femme, vêtue aussi de blanc, et avec des cheveux blancs, qui nous demande de l'argent. On lui donne quelques drachmes et on se sauve.[41]

> (After dinner, Scarfoglio and D'Annunzio absolutely want to celebrate their arrival in Greece with an evening of love. They therefore turn to Bertucci the translator, who seems to put a lot of good will into it, but who warns us that in Greece it is not done in this way, and that we will not be able to find, at the drop of a hat, what we desire. On the insistence of Scarfoglio and D'Annunzio, he begins nevertheless the search, not without having warned us that we are unlikely to find anything except the most ordinary. – Thereupon, we prowl around the city with him; we enter small cafés which are the haunts of soldiers and sailors, and we take off. Bertucci ends up taking us to a remote house, where we go up

---

Elisa Segnini, *Fragments, Genius and Madness: Masks and Mask-Making in the fin-de-siècle Imagination* (Oxford: Legenda, 2021), pp. 95–120.

[41] *Croisière du yacht Fantasia en Italie méridionale, Grèce, Sicile, avec des notes de Gabriele D'Annunzio et Edoardo Scarfoglio,* MS 3134, f° 23. Hérelle's travel diary is published in: Mario Cimini, ed., *D'Annunzio, Boggiani, Hérelle, Scarfoglio: viaggio in Grecia et Italia meridionale (1895)* (Venise, Marsilio, 2010).

> an external wooden staircase; we find a woman dressed in white, neither young nor beautiful, who immediately disgusts everyone, and, after a few words are exchanged, we turn our backs. Then a very old woman comes out of a nearby room, also dressed in white, with white hair, who asks us for money. They give her a few drachmas and we escape.)

Although Hérelle adopts his typical matter-of-fact style in narrating this scene, there is a certain ambivalence that can be deduced from his use of the pronouns 'nous' (which can only be translated into English as 'we') and 'on' (which can be translated as 'we', 'they' or 'one', depending on the context). At two specific moments in this scene, when D'Annunzio and Scarfoglio ask the translator to help them find a brothel and when the prostitute is given some money, Hérelle could be said to distance himself from the group through his use of 'on' (which in this case can be translated as 'they'). Elsewhere in this passage, his narrative strategy of using the pronoun 'nous' suggests that at those moments Hérelle is identifying with the heterosexual men in the group. We can also detect in this quotation a hint of Hérelle's annoyance or impatience with D'Annunzio and Scarfoglio, who 'absolutely want to celebrate their arrival in Greece by an evening of love'. Hérelle appears to imply here that such behaviour is both excessive and unreasonable, and that his own priority would be to start visiting right away the historical sites of Greece, which he had been studying for so many years. Later on in their journey, he registers his perplexity at D'Annunzio's seeming indifference when the two men are visiting some archaeological sites that Hérelle found exceptionally beautiful.

The following quotation contains another episode in which Hérelle's ambivalence is evident. In this passage, he describes the scene on board the sailboat when D'Annunzio is taking a shower, fully naked, in front of his travelling companions:

> En 1895, j'eus maintes fois l'occasion de voir le poète nu. Comme nous voyagions au mois d'août, il faisait extrêmement chaud et chaque matin G. d'A. se faisait donner sur le pont une douche d'eau de mer. Stefano, le matelot factotum, qui servait aussi de valet de chambre à Scarfoglio, lui jetait deux ou trois seaux d'eau sur la nudité, tandis que nous étions là, sur des fauteuils, à fumer des cigarettes. La nudité sous le grand soleil produisait dans l'organe un commencement de turgescence. Je fus étonné de la grosseur et de la longueur de cet organe, où la verge se terminait par un gland en forme de massue un peu aplati au bout et d'un diamètre beaucoup plus grand que celui de la verge.[42]

[42] Ibid., f° 46.

(In 1895, I had many opportunities to see the poet naked. As we were traveling in August, it was extremely hot and every morning G. d'A. was given a shower of sea water on the deck. Stefano, the handyman sailor, who was also Scarfoglio's valet, threw two or three buckets of water on his naked body, while we were sitting in armchairs, smoking cigarettes. Being nude in the full sun, the organ began to have an erection. I was astonished by the size and length of this organ; on the end of the penis was a club-shaped gland which had a slightly flat shape and a diameter much larger than that of the penis.)

D'Annunzio's lack of inhibition is highlighted in this scene. It's a quality that does not appear to surprise Hérelle, probably because, as he points out, he had many occasions to observe D'Annunzio's daily shower, and he perhaps became aware of this kind of exhibitionistic behaviour the previous year when the two men spent ten days visiting Venice together. The description of D'Annunzio's penis is, however, significant, primarily because Hérelle usually keeps his intimate feelings to himself while recording notes during his travels. Hérelle's reaction to the penis has connotations of the erotic (the beginning of an 'erection') and the grotesque (the 'club-shaped gland').

Our analysis of the scenes involving the trip to the brothel and the penis allows us to place Hérelle's personal relationship with D'Annunzio firmly under the sign of ambivalence, and to argue that D'Annunzio's machismo and hyper-sexuality were a source of homoerotic curiosity, fascination and perhaps even attraction for Hérelle, but these feelings were accompanied by their opposite – frustration, irritation and distaste. Over the next two years and on a broader cultural level, Hérelle would articulate these fluctuating feelings. In his 1896 travel diary, he expresses in erotic terms his attachment to the city of Naples: 'Naples mé séduit toujours, comme un vice'[43] (Naples always seduces me, like a vice). In 1898, however, his attitude was no longer the same:

Arrivé à Naples le 7 juillet. Le premier jour de mon arrivée, je reçois de Naples une impression plutôt fâcheuse. La ville me semble sèche et sale, pleine de poussière, aussi pouilleuse que jamais, et cependant moins pittoresque. D'où vient que je trouve moins de charme aux haillons napolitains ? Est-ce parce que j'ai vu ceux du Maroc ? Certes, une vieille jaquette en lambeaux et une culotte sans fond ont moins de caractère que les sordides et splendides draperies des petits musulmans ? Je soupçonne pourtant qu'il y a encore autre chose : je vieillis'.[44]

[43] 'Naples still seduces me, like a vice', *Notes de voyage en Italie*, MS 3392, f° 181.
[44] *Dicenda, Tacenda, Naples, 1898*, MS 3155, f° 1.

(Arrived in Naples on July 7. On the first day of my arrival, I get a rather unpleasant impression of Naples. The city seems dried out and dirty to me, full of dust, as seedy as ever, and also less picturesque. Why do I find Neapolitan rags less charming? Is it because I have seen those of Morocco? Certainly, a tattered old jacket and breeches full of holes have less character than the sordid yet splendid clothes of the young Muslim boys? I suspect however that there is still something else: I'm getting older.)

Conclusion

Georges Hérelle had two very different ways of telling the story about his relations and adventures with Gabriele D'Annunzio. The story that Hérelle crafted largely in the 1920s in his memoires, well after the period when the two men met in person and during the time when they were no longer writing to each other, is a version in which Hérelle takes great care to present a somewhat sanitised image of himself. The episode involving the young Alfredo Rosati, his travel companion in Naples, is downplayed and minimised by being told briefly and in matter-of-fact terms. In this idealised thread of the story, which appears to be written for public consumption, the translator is characterised as high-minded, highly principled, self-denying and motivated almost exclusively by his intellectual affinities with the novelist. The other version of the story, which is contained in his travel diaries from the 1890s and in which Hérelle gives the impression of being in private dialogue with himself, has a more spontaneous and immediate quality because, in part, it is contemporaneous with the events described. This version allows us to get a glimpse of an intimate, emotional and conflicted Hérelle, and most importantly, of the homoerotic tensions that were clearly an integral part of his feelings toward D'Annunzio. The analysis that we present in this article is certainly not intended to solve completely the 'enigma' (to use Daniel Fabre's word) of Georges Hérelle's life, but we do hope that it provides new insight into his relations with the man whom he described as 'the only great artist and great stylist I have ever dealt with'.[45]

[45] *Comment je suis devenu traducteur*, MS 3170, f° 35.

Chapter 7

After Hérelle: André Doderet, the (In)visible Translator

Annalisa Ciano

Very little has been written on André Doderet (1879–1949), who took up the challenge of translating D'Annunzio's prose, drama and poetry after Georges Hérelle, inspiring renewed interest in D'Annunzio's works after the events of Fiume.[1] Doderet remains an invisible figure. His role as translator nevertheless merits investigation, as it sheds light on the expectations that D'Annunzio had for translators and the role of translation in D'Annunzio's 'later' international reception. Doderet's achievements should not be underestimated: he worked closely with D'Annunzio, obtaining approval of his translations of drama and poetry – something his eminent predecessor, Hérelle, had failed to accomplish. He also strengthened the relationship between D'Annunzio and France. Furthermore, translation was not Doderet's only responsibility: he became a spokesperson for the author, a sort of cultural manager who represented D'Annunzio as a voice of the new Latin Renaissance and encouraged the publication, adaptation and staging of his works.

Drawing on Doderet's posthumous memoir *Vingts ans d'amitié avec Gabriele D'Annunzio* (1956), as well as on articles and reviews published in journals that followed the critical debate on D'Annunzio after Fiume, this chapter explores the relationship between Doderet and D'Annunzio, focusing on their translation method. To do so, it first considers Doderet's attitude toward D'Annunzio and his first

[1] The main contributions on André Doderet are Enea Balmas, 'L'amicizia fra Gabriele D'Annunzio e il suo traduttore André Doderet', *Quaderni dannunziani*, XXII–XXIII (1962), 1112–19; Giovanni Gullace, *Gabriele D'Annunzio in France: A Study in Cultural Relations* (Syracuse: Syracuse University Press, 1966); and Luciano Curreri, 'Lettere, "lavoro comune" e traduzione. Appunti e ipotesi su D'Annunzio e i traduttori francesi', in *Silenzi, Solitudini, Segreti. Altre metamorfosi dannunziane* (Arcireale/Roma: Bonanno Editore, 2011).

translations against the background of the French social and literary context. Secondly, it investigates why Doderet began collaborating with D'Annunzio and followed him to Fiume. Finally, it analyses the strategies Doderet adopted to satisfy D'Annunzio's requests. I argue that Doderet's translations come very close to realising D'Annunzio's ideal translation, providing a literal translation that complies with all the author's requests. Doderet's goal was satisfying D'Annunzio rather than French readers, and this involved complete submission to the author, a type of invisibility different from what Lawrence Venuti describes in his account of translators in North American culture.[2]

Doderet, D'Annunzio, Hérelle

Long before Doderet's intervention, George Hérelle's translation of his novels had paved the path to D'Annunzio's breakthrough beyond the Alps. With their distinctly modern, cultured, elegant and yet perturbing Mediterranean characters, these novels had charmed French readers. Hérelle's adaptations prioritised the target audience, making D'Annunzio's language more accessible in translation than in Italian. Their success was astonishing, and it contributed to D'Annunzio's prestige even during a period of relative setback during his stay in France (1910–1915) when his dramaturgical works met less success. In a letter dated 2 May 1894, D'Annunzio acknowledged his name would forever be associated with his first translator: 'Oramai il vostro nome è legato per sempre al mio; oramai in Francia noi siamo *una sola persona*' (Your name is now tied to mine forever; in France we are now *a single person*).[3]

The aura of prestige surrounding D'Annunzio clarifies the admiration that Doderet had for the Italian poet, whom he considered a living myth. Doderet's posthumous volume *Vingts ans d'amitié avec Gabriele d'Annunzio* recalls their twenty-year-long friendship. In vivid evocations of the past, journal entries, telegrams and letters, admiration borders on devotion, reverence merges with loyalty, and the story of a friendship turns into a passionate encomium. Reading the memoir, one is struck by Doderet's humble pose: he is honoured to be D'Annunzio's translator and remembers each of their exchanges with

[2] Lawrence Venuti, *The Translator's Invisibility: A History of Translation* (London – New York: Routledge, 1995/2008).

[3] Carteggio, *D'Annunzio – Hérelle (1891–1931)*, ed. by Mario Cimini (Lanciano: Rocco Carabba: 2004), p. 177.

pride and gratitude. This submissive attitude is key to understanding his position as a translator and his translation strategies.

Doderet describes and counts himself among a group of D'Annunzio's admirers in awe of his person, achievements and works. In his eyes, D'Annunzio exerts the fascination of a living work of art. He considers interacting with him, accessing his spaces and touching his books and objects to be a great privilege. The memory and presence of his friend is often conjured by the objects that he received from him or that were part of the time they shared, which Doderet handles with the care of a museum curator.[4] Several times, Doderet directly or indirectly compares D'Annunzio to the Great Poet, Dante – whose verses he was to later translate.[5] In Doderet's eyes, D'Annunzio's talent transcends national and linguistic boundaries, and he holds a rightful place in the French literary tradition.[6] Similar awe surrounds his persona: D'Annunzio's occupation of Fiume divided public opinion, yet even his hostile detractors must admire his audacity, which earned him the title '*Commandant*'.[7]

The Italian poet is also a figure of authority in the eyes of his translator. This emerges in a statement printed in *The Excelsior* (6 December 1927), right before the debut of *La torche sous le boisseau* (*La fiaccola sotto il moggio*, 1905) at the Comédie-Française. Doderet first distanced himself from the perspective offered by the abbot Barthélemy Mercier de Saint-Léger, according to whom all literary works translated into French lose their native colour; then, he responded to French critics, prioritising D'Annunzio's judgement over the public's reception:

> Depuis sept ans que je traduis Gabriele d'Annunzio, j'ai connu plus d'un jugement sévère, mais aussi de singulières récompenses [. . .]. Je subis, une fois, une épreuve assez rare. Mme Ida Rubinstein joua sur le théâtre Costanzi, à Rome, ma traduction de la *Phædre* dannunzienne. D'avancé j'étais sûr du succès de la belle interprète ; mais qu'allait-on penser de moi ? [. . .] Que va penser le public français, le public de la Comédie-Française d'une traduction de *La torche sous le boisseau ?* [. . .] Dois-je

[4] André Doderet, *Vingts ans d'amitié avec Gabriele D'Annunzio* (Paris: Éditions du Cerf-volant, 1956), pp. 124–5.

[5] The main works by Doderet on Dante include *La Divine Comédie* (Paris: Union latine d'éditions, 1938), *Dante et son son époque* (Paris: Union latine d'éditions, 1938), and *Dante* (Paris: Éditions de la 'Nouvelle revue critique', 1942).

[6] See the poem Doderet published after D'Annunzio's death, reprinted at the end of *Vingts ans*.

[7] Doderet, *Vingts ans*, pp. 18–19.

m'inquiéter, dois-je craindre, alors que si peu d'heures me séparent de la première ? Mais non. Je sais que mon maître n'est pas trop mécontent de mon travail.[8]

(In the seven years that I have been translating Gabriele D'Annunzio, I have experienced more than one harsh judgement, but I have also received special rewards [. . .]. I was once confronted with a rather exceptional challenge. Mrs Ida Rubinstein performed my translation of D'Annunzio's *Phaedre* at the Costanzi Theatre in Rome. I was always confident of the success of the beautiful performer; but what would people think of me? [. . .] What will the French public, the public of the *Comédie-Française*, think of a translation of *La torche sous le boisseau*? [. . .] Should I be worried, should I be afraid when only a few hours separate me from the premiere? Of course not. I know that my master is not too dissatisfied with my work.)

D'Annunzio is the privileged and ideal target for Dodoret's translations: they must satisfy *him*, not French readers.

In his memoirs, Doderet reflects on when he first heard of D'Annunzio, while still a student at the Lycée Michelet. Another student had just read a novel he was sure Doderet would appreciate: *L'Innocente*, or rather, *L'Intrus* in Herelle's translation. Doderet was so impressed by the elegance of the translation, through which he could sense 'the music of the original', that he decided to start studying Italian.[9] He soon became fond of Italy and began to travel there frequently. Interestingly, Dodoret's book, dedicated to the memory of D'Annunzio, begins with an indirect tribute to Georges Hérelle, whose translation of *L'Innocente* functions as a mediator between D'Annunzio and Doderet. Like Hérelle, Doderet introduces himself first as D'Annunzio's admirer, and only later as his translator. In his *Petit mémoire d'un traducteur*, Hérelle recalls how he decided to translate D'Annunzio after reading *L'Innocente* in Italian and being struck by the author's talent. Doderet follows his footsteps but goes even further, saying his eagerness to read D'Annunzio in the original led him to learn Italian.[10] But while Hérelle imposed his personality, Doderet was a '*timidum animae*', as D'Annunzio defined him to

8 'Une pièce de Gabriele D'Annunzio à la Comédie-Française', *Excelsior,* 6 December 1927, section Les Theatres, p. 5.

9 Doderet, *Vingts ans*, p. 9.

10 Asté d'Esparbès, 'Avant "La Torche sous le boisseau. M. André Doderet nous parle de Gabriele d'Annunzio', *Comœdia*, 5 Decembre 1927, frontpage; Doderet, *Vingts ans*, Avant-propos.

Guido Treves in his letter of 13 December 1921 (now preserved at the Vittoriale). From this perspective, it can be suggested that Hérelle inspired Doderet, but the latter adopted a very different translation strategy. Doderet was impressed by the original musicality he sensed in Hérelle's translation; however, Hérelle is known to have given D'Annunzio's work a distinct French style, often intervening into the text, and D'Annunzio reproached him for being unable to render the Italian rhythm of the original.[11] Doderet's appreciation of the musicality of Hérelle's French is thus a tribute to D'Annunzio's first, more established translator; but it also marks a contradiction, since to satisfy D'Annunzio Doderet's translations had to renounce any aspiration to an 'impeccable' French style.

Further proof of his esteem for Hérelle can be found in his article published in the French edition of *Ariel Casqué* (1933) by Angelo Sodini, translated by Jean Chuzeville. There, Doderet criticised Chuzeville's translations, which included new versions of extracts from *Trionfo della morte* and *Notturno*; he likewise argued that Hérelle's translations should be respected.[12] Literary chronicles of the time referred to him as Hérelle's successor,[13] but Doderet did not directly encourage this narrative until he wrote an article following Hérelle's death. There, he recalls that he and Hérelle met only once but kept in contact – though their correspondence is yet to be found – and says he knew him first as a writer and only later on a personal level. His respect for Hérelle increased when he was called upon to continue translating D'Annunzio; only when confronted with the problems posed by translating the Italian poet did he truly understand the complexity of Hérelle's task:

> Avant que je connusse l'homme, j'avais depuis toujours pour l'écrivain au style aisé, souple et très pur, la plus sympathique admiration. Ce sentiment s'accrut encore, augmenté du plus déférent respect, lorsque Georges Hérelle, fatigué par l'âge, ayant cessé de traduire Gabriele d'Annunzio, je fus appelé, en 1920, à reprendre et poursuivre sa tâche. Mieux que personne, je connais donc ce que furent l'effort, la science et l'art de Georges Hérelle. Les difficultés qu'il rencontra, je les ai à mon tour rencontrées : je souhaiterais de les avoir surmontées comme lui même les surmonta.[14]

[11] Ibid., pp. 40–52.

[12] André Doderet, Section 'Section Essais', *Les Nouvelles Littéraires*, 3 June 1933.

[13] See for example: C. A. – T., 'Ce qui dit le traducteur de Gabriele D'Annunzio', *Comœdia*, 24 August 1924.

[14] Doderet, 'Georges Hérelle (1849–1935)', *Les Nouvelles Littéraires*, 21 December 1935.

(Before I got to know the man, I had always had the most sincere admiration for the writer with his easy, fluent, and very pure style. This feeling grew even stronger, enhanced by the most deferential respect, when Georges Hérelle, fatigued by his age, ceased to translate Gabriele d'Annunzio, and in 1920 I was called upon to take over and continue his task. Therefore, I know better than anyone else, what the efforts, the science, and the art of Georges Hérelle were. I have encountered the same difficulties he encountered, and I wish I had been able to overcome them as he did.)

It is significant that Doderet does not mention the rupture between D'Annunzio and Hérelle, attributing D'Annunzio's choice to change translators merely to Hérelle's advanced age. In his characteristic shyness and modesty, he does not dare to compare himself to the senior translator. However, there were those who did make comparisons in favour of Doderet. Benjamin Cremieux, an established translator from Italian, fully endorsed Doderet's endeavours:

Il est curieux, à ce propos, qu'en dehors des traducteurs, qui sont eux-mêmes des créateurs, [. . .] le seul traducteur de métier qui se soit, comme on dit, fait un nom, ait été M. Hérelle, le traducteur de d'Annunzio. M. Hérelle écrit une langue fluide et agréable, mais il escamote sans cesse les difficultés contenues dans les textes d'annunziens. Pour ma part, je trouve les traductions d'annunziennes de M. André Doderet – il vient, tout récemment, de publier *Contemplation de la mort* – bien supérieures à celles de M. Hérelle.[15]

(It is curious, in this respect, that apart from the translators who are themselves authors, [. . .] the only professional translator who has, as they say, made a name for himself, is Hérelle, D'Annunzio's translator. Hérelle writes in a fluid and pleasant language, but he constantly sidesteps the difficulties of d'Annunzio's texts. Personally, I find André Doderet's translations of D'Annunzio's works – he has just recently published *Contemplation de la mort* – far superior to those of Hérelle.)

Doderet recalls how his first meeting with D'Annunzio took place in 1910 in Paris through a mutual friend, Charles Derennes. The two did not discuss a possible collaboration but became acquainted with each other as writers. Doderet had just published one of his first novels (*Le triomphe d'Armide*, 1910), and he gifted D'Annunzio

[15] Benjamin Cremieux, 'Les Livres. Stefan Zweig: «Tolstoi» -- John dos Passos: «Manhattan Transfer»', *Les Annales politiques et littéraires*, 1 October 1928, p. 306.

a copy.[16] In return, D'Annunzio gave him an autographed print of *Forse che sì forse che no* in Nathalie de Goloubeff's (Donatella Cross) translation.

Given the absence of research on the topic, we know very little about Doderet's activity as a creative writer. Literary chronicles of the time note that his novels often commented critically on contemporary society.[17] In his comments on *Jicky* (1929), Maurice Martin du Gard described Doderet's style as elegant, light and brilliant.[18] This marked a strong contrast to D'Annunzio's work. In his article, du Gard was amazed by Doderet's light tone, given that he had been translating D'Annunzio for years, travelled to Fiume with him, and 'had even begun to resemble him'.[19] In 1932, Doderet was awarded the *Prix de l'Enfance* for *Enfant blessé*, a novel highlighting the impact a troubled childhood has on a person's future.[20] D'Annunzio was amongst those lauding Doderet's works; *Les Nouvelles Littéraires* (20 June 1930) reports a telegram in which D'Annunzio praised *Carnaval* (1925), even saying that for an author of such quality he was ready to renounce his own translator.[21] Luciano Curreri suggests that Doderet's fidelity to D'Annunzio's style and language may reflect the fact that, unlike Hérelle,[22] he had his own creative outlet,

[16] Doderet's works include: *Le Diabolo, simples paroles ou le jouet à la mode. . .* (Paris: Union Littérature et d'Art, 1907); *La fontaine aux acanthes. Étretat, L'Isle-Adam Taormina* (Paris: D. Tassel, 1908); *Le Triomphe d'Armide* (Paris: E. Fasquelle, 1910); *La nuit sans étoiles. Roman venetian* (Paris: E. Fasquelle, 1918); *La flamme au soleil* (Paris: Albin Michel,1922); *Carnaval. Mémoires d'un danseur russe* (Paris: M. Seheur, 1925); *Voyage aux îles de la société* (Paris: Éditions de France, 1927); *Malamoa* (Paris: La Renaissance du Livre 1928); *L'Amour à la mode. Jicky* (Paris: La Renaissance du Livre 1929); *Enfance* (Paris: Ernest Flammarion, 1932); Chansons marines (1933); *Sérénade Sanglante* (Avignon: E. Aubanel, 1943); *À quoi rêvent les vieilles filles* (Avignon: E. Aubanel, 1944).

[17] La Masque de Verre, 'Échos', *Comœdia,* 30 June 1910, p. 1; Francis de Miomandre, 'Le voyage d'André Doderet aux Iles de la Société', *Les Nouvelles Littéraires*, 25 June 1927.

[18] Maurice Martin Du Gard, 'Le roués d'aujourd'hui', *Les Nouvelles Littéraires,* 3 August 1929, frontpage.

[19] Ibid.

[20] 'Le Prix d'Enfance', *Les Nouvelles Littéraires,* 13 February 1932, p. 5.

[21] Section 'La vie des Lettres', *Les Nouvelles Littéraires*, 28 June 1930.

[22] Hérelle remarks that his income as a professor enabled him to translate for pleasure: Hérelle, *Petit mémoire d'un traducteur*, p. 19. Though not an author of fiction, he wrote essays and studies on history, ethnography and the anthropology of homosexuality: Florence Galli-Dupis, 'Un ethnographe, érudit historien et traducteur littéraire: Georges Hérelle (1848–1935) et la pastorale basque', *Garae ethnopole* (2007), http://www.garae.fr/spip.php?article220

making it easier not to impose himself on D'Annunzio's text.[23] Certainly, Doderet's career as an author may have contributed to his profile as a translator by differentiating his creative process from his translating one; however, it is very likely that Doderet's adherence to D'Annunzio's principles depended above all on his submissive attitude and reverence toward the author.[24]

It was several years before Doderet offered his service to D'Annunzio. Although they met on other occasions – such as on the Champs-Êlysées in 1914 – Doderet was too shy to approach him: 'Par suite de quelle hardiesse inattendue osai-je me proposer?' (Out of what sudden audacity did I dare to propose myself?).[25] It was only after the war, through the intercession of Marcel Boulanger, that the possibility finally presented itself. Boulanger arranged for sample translations to be sent to the Italian poet. D'Annunzio wasted no time: after receiving Doderet's translations, he asked for his address.[26]

In June 1920, Doderet travelled to Fiume to ask for D'Annunzio's help in the translation process, assistance the poet was only too happy to provide.[27] D'Annunzio noticed the translator's insecurity, and Doderet recalls that he laughed amicably about it.[28] The close collaboration between the two was made known to the French press, where the approval of the author was taken as a guarantee of the quality and authenticity of Doderet's translations. While we lack sufficient information to establish Doderet's political profile, we know that he became involved in D'Annunzio's cause during the occupation of Fiume. In the 1927 interview by Asté d'Esparbès, Doderet recalls his time in Fiume with nostalgia and notes that, spending time there with D'Annunzio, he grew enthusiastic about the cause of the 'pure Italy'. Likewise he became well integrated and taught French to his 'camarades, legionnaires, arditi et marines' (comrades, legionnaires, *arditi* and marines).[29]

In this phase, D'Annunzio's entourage accused Doderet of what would later be recognised as his merit, namely leading D'Annunzio back to poetry, distracting him from his military and political

[23] Curreri, p. 119.
[24] Balmas, 'L'Amicizia fra Gabriele D'Annunzio e il suo traduttore', p. 1113.
[25] Doderet, *Vignts ans*, p. 17.
[26] Ibid., p. 17.
[27] Gullace, p. 46.
[28] Doderet, *Vignts ans*, p. 17.
[29] Asté d'Esparbès, 'Avant "La Torche sous le boisseau. M. André Doderet nous parle de Gabriele d'Annunzio', *Comœdia*, 5 Decembre 1927, p. 1.

commitment.[30] Nonetheless, it is important to note that Doderet understood the importance that politics held for D'Annunzio.[31] Together with other friends, he enjoyed fantasising about D'Annunzio ruling Rome, uniting right and left. While discussing the 'Commandant's' position in between politics and poetry, Doderet recalls an anecdote: during an evening with his friends, D'Annunzio flipped a coin to decide whether or not he should focus on politics, and three times the coin landed on tails – politics was heads. Doderet remembers that everyone in the room was nervous about this gamble, knowing that it could actually influence the poet, and that D'Annunzio had to force a laugh at the result because he was struck as if he had read from the book of his destiny.[32]

Thus began a close cooperation between D'Annunzio and Doderet. Taking Hérelle's place, Doderet became D'Annunzio's last French translator during his lifetime: among the works he edited and translated are *La fiaccola sotto il moggio* (1905), *La nave* (1907), *Fedra* (1909), *La leda senza cigno. Racconto, seguito da una licenza* (1916), *Contemplazione della morte* (1919), *Ritratto di Luisa Bàccara* (1920), *Notturno* (1921) and *Solus ad solam* (1939).[33] In addition to these, Doderet translated poems and other extracts that were only published in fragments.[34]

As a result of his successful collaboration with D'Annunzio, Doderet was once described as 'l'écho fidèle du grand poète italien' (the faithful echo of the great Italian poet).[35] His activity did not concern literary work only, but also the poet's personal relations. For instance, we know from the telegrams and stories Doderet shares in *Vingts ans* that D'Annunzio used him as a sort of ambassador in France to handle his communications, his contacts with reviews and

[30] Doderet, *Vingts ans*, pp. 37–8.

[31] Ibid., p. 73.

[32] Ibid., pp. 73–4.

[33] *La Léda sans cygne, récit de la lande, suivi d'un Envoi à la France* (Paris: Calmann-Lévy, 1922); *Aspects de l'inconnu. Nocturne* (Paris: Calmann Lévy, 1923); *Phædre*, in *La Revue de Paris*, 5 August, 1 September, 15 September, 1 October 1924, pp. 721–55, 88–124, 299–336, 535–55; *Portrait du Lojse Baccaris* (Paris: Éditions du 'Sagittaire'); *La torche sous le boisseau* (Paris: Impr. de l'Illustration); *Contemplation de la mort* (Paris: Calmann-Lévy, 1928); *La nef* (Radiodiffusion nationale, 19420514, 1942); *Solus ad solam. Journal d'un amour* (Paris: Édition Balzac).

[34] For instance, he translated *Alcyone* (book III), published in *Revue des deux mondes* (1938), pp. 576–81.

[35] G.L.F., 'D'Annunzio viendra-t-il?', *L'Intransigeant*, 6 December 1927, p. 1.

magazines, his publishing agreements and his finances. Moreover, Doderet's role is most evident in the management of the translation and staging of dramatic works: he supervised and intervened on all levels of production, from the translation to the organisation and evaluation of the acting, costumes and scenography. An emblematic example is the French transposition of the opera *Phaedre* (1923), where Doderet played an important role even in the innovation of the musical sections commissioned to Ildebrando Pizzetti.

Doderet, the 'Invisible' Translator

From his correspondence with Hérelle, we know that D'Annunzio had a very precise idea of the ideal translation: he expected a replication of all the formal, rhythmic and stylistic characteristics of the source text. For D'Annunzio, translation involved neither choices nor creative contributions from the translator. Rather, he saw translation as transposing a work from one language into another, with all its qualities and imperfections. The translator should not manifest their presence in the translated work but should rather fully render the voice of the author. The poet's position might lend itself to a critical reading of the translator's invisibility as theorised by Lawrence Venuti,[36] but the comparison between these two ideas of the transparency and invisibility of translators reveals a significant difference. In fact, for Venuti the invisibility of the translator coincides with the fluency of the translated text;[37] consequently, the translator is invisible when he domesticates the source text. In contrast, for D'Annunzio the translator's invisibility is a guarantee of the author's own visibility and their artistic and linguistic specificity. Therefore, D'Annunzio's transparent translation is one in which the foreignness

[36] Venuti, *The Translator's Invisibility*.

[37] Venuti's contribution develops ideas previously advanced by Friedrich Schleiermacher, who identified two strategies: 'Either the translator leaves the writer in peace as much as possible and leads the reader towards them, or the translator leaves the reader in peace as much as possible and leads the writer towards him' (*On the Different Methods of Translating*, 1813/2012, p. 49). Schleiermacher promoted foreignising translations. Interestingly, we find a similar argument in D'Annunzio's letter to Hérelle dated 10 January 1905: 'La buona traduzione moderna non deve avvicinare l'opera al lettore ma sì bene il lettore all'opera, magari *malgré lui*': *Carteggio D'Annunzio – Hérelle (1891–1931)*, p. 588.

of another language can and must emerge and where the figure of the translator is suppressed, therefore invisible.[38]

Word-for-word translation entails a loss of the overall vision of the text by dwelling on individual units. At the same time, one must consider the importance D'Annunzio places on the poetic word. As we can infer, for instance, from a letter sent to Hérelle between 21 and 29 May 1892, the poet gives weight to his own words, conceived as the depository of the poet's essence and the work; in fact, he does not establish a hierarchy between form and content.[39] This relationship between signifier and signified underlies the idea of the untranslatability of the literary work, as expressed, for instance, by Giovanni Gentile and Antoine Berman.[40] These scholars emphasise the impossibility of preserving the relationship between form and content, which extend to all linguistic and structural elements of the text, including punctuation, which is inseparable from the aesthetic value of literary work.[41] D'Annunzio was aware of these critical issues and consequently argued that altering the word balance of a page or verse in any way was to alter the work itself and undermine the author's style.

Questions of style acquire a central position in D'Annunzio's translation theory. In an interview with Ugo Ojetti, D'Annunzio connects style to the uniqueness of the artist and claims that it contains the essence of the poet and his ability to be creative: to violate style, altering or undermining it in any way, is to compromise what makes the artist an artist, namely the ability to generate life.[42] For these reasons, the poet's style is sacred and inviolable like life itself. This idea is not D'Annunzio's invention; he takes up an expression of Ernest Hello (1828–85), who linked the inviolability of style to the manifestation of the divine in art through the artist. Given the significance D'Annunzio attaches to the style, it is evident why translation (and translating poetry, in particular) poses a problem.[43]

[38] Muriel Gallot, 'D'Annunzio et son traducteur: à la recherche d'un alter ego', *Cahiers d'études romanes*, 24 (2011), pp. 81–9.

[39] Guy Tosi, *Gabriele d'Annunzio à Georges Hérelle, correspondance accompagnée de douze sonnets cisalpins* (Paris: Denoël, 1946), pp. 282–3.

[40] Giovanni Gentile, 'Il torto e il diritto delle traduzioni', in *Frammenti di estetica e di letteratura* (Lanciano: Carabba, 1921), p. 369; Antoine Berman, *La traduction et la lettre ou l'auberge du lointain* (Paris: Le Seuil 1999), p. 36.

[41] Eugenio Coseriu, *Linguistica del testo* (Roma: Carocci, 1997).

[42] Ugo Ojetti, *Alla scoperta dei letterati. Colloquii con Carducci, Panzacchi, Fogazzaro. . .* (Milano: Bocca, 1899), p. 311.

[43] This idea was repeatedly expressed in his correspondence with Hérelle.

Doderet was aware of D'Annunzio's expectations: anxious to please him, he submitted everything he translated to his scrutiny and did not accept any intervention from editors without first obtaining D'Annunzio's approval. In this regard, the case of the publication of the French translation *Nocturne* in the *Revue des deux mondes* is significant. After submitting the translation approved by D'Annunzio, Doderet received an amended version from the editor, who had the text revised by 'some insignificant professor of Italian'.[44] Doderet was appalled by the revisions, which he considered both excessive and inadequate. He admits to having read the first publication of *Nocturne* with great apprehension, fearing D'Annunzio's reaction to the corrections and cuts he had not personally authorised. Doderet was not mistaken: as soon as D'Annunzio saw how Doderet's translation had been revised, torn and 'mutilated' without any consultation, he ordered the publication be halted.[45] The translator's embarrassment and the author's indignation reveal how Doderet was at the service of the author, unlike the translator of the *Revue* (and Hérelle, earlier) who acted in the interest of the French reader. Doderet claims not to have encouraged a public controversy on this matter to avoid shifting attention from the author and *Nocturne* onto himself; nonetheless, when rumours about his translation's inaccuracies started to spread, he wrote a letter to *L'intrasigeant* explaining what happened and guaranteeing that he had translated alongside D'Annunzio and received his approval.[46]

D'Annunzio's expectations were an important factor leading to the end of his collaboration with Hérelle, and they formed the basis of Doderet's translation objectives. For instance, D'Annunzio complained that Hérelle failed to use the word that most closely resembled the relevant Italian term not only orthographically but also etymologically and phonically (2 May 1894). He accused the

44 Doderet, *Vingts ans*, p. 84.

45 Doderet quotes a letter from D'Annunzio dated 17 February 1922, 'j'y découvre votre traduction déchirée et mutilés de la manière la plus cruelle' ('I discovered your translation torn and mutilated in the most cruel way'): Doderet, *Vingts ans*, p. 86.

46 '[. . .] si d'Annunzio fit suspendre la publication de son œuvre, c'est que des mutilations sans nombre finissaient par la rendre incompréhensible. Or, vous connaissez mon respect pour d'Annunzio: personne ne songerait à m'accuser d'une telle irrévérence envers lui' (If D'Annunzio had the publication of his work suspended, it was because of the numerous mutilations that made it unintelligible. Now, you know my respect for D'Annunzio: no one would dream of accusing me of such irreverence towards him): *L'Intransigeant*, 25 June 1922, Section *Lettres*, p. 2.

translator of deforming his style, and considered him insufficiently daring in his linguistic choices. In contrast, in the available sources documenting D'Annunzio and Doderet's collaboration, there are no such complaints. In fact, Doderet describes D'Annunzio's reproaches about what happened with *Nocturne* as the first and only 'shadow' throughout their twenty years of friendship,[47] whereas the correspondence between Hérelle and the poet was frequently polemic.[48]

D'Annunzio's request for the translator to *dannunzianeggiare* seems to match a spontaneous approach taken by Doderet. For Doderet, to *dannunzianeggiare* required full identification with the author, experiencing the text coming back to life and revealing itself to him in French:

> Je lui parlais de sa tragédie [. . .] Et la parole du poète redonnait la vie première aux vers momentanément endormis dans le volume, qui ne demandaient que ce réveil, et dont le rude contour, grâce à lui bien plus qu'à moi-même, commençait à se dessiner dans notre langue. En le quittant et rentré dans ma chambre, je me remettais au travail avec l'impression qu'il était encore près de moi pour m'aider à chaque hésitation.[49]

> (I would talk to him about his tragedy [. . .] And the poet's words would give new life to the verses momentarily asleep in the volume, which were simply waiting to be awakened, and whose rough outline, thanks to him much more than to myself, was beginning to take form in our language. Upon leaving him and returning to my room, I would resume my work with the impression that he was still with me to help me with any hesitation.)

This reflection provides interesting insight into D'Annunzio's role in Doderet's translation as well as explaining the translator's perspective. By dwelling on literary conversations with the poet, Doderet welcomes the author in the space of the translated text. As a result, Doderet's intervention develops around D'Annunzio's output, once again rendering the line between author and translator invisible. The consequence of such deep interaction is Doderet's ability to identify with the poet and his style. This might be why once he started working with him, D'Annunzio no longer turned to other translators but

[47] Doderet, *Vingts ans*, p. 87.

[48] Hérelle, *Petit mémoire*, p. 46.

[49] André Doderet, 'Comment j'ai tradui l'œuvre de d'Annunzio', *L'Intransigeant,* 27 November 1927, p. 6.

rather had Doderet work anew on *La nave* and *Fedra*, which had already been translated by Ricciotto Canudo.

The 'Visible' Translator: Doderet's Role as Cultural Mediator

When Doderet began translating D'Annunzio, relations between France and Italy were tense.[50] The Versailles Peace Conference had disregarded the political and territorial aspirations of Italy, refusing the requests of the Italian delegation regarding the concession of Dalmatia and Fiume. The Allies' lack of support led to growing hostility in Italian public opinion, culminating in D'Annunzio's idea of the 'mutilated victory'. D'Annunzio's physical absence from France teased the public's expectations: was D'Annunzio going to address his political and military experiences? Was he distancing himself from France? Had his consideration for France changed? As the articles and interviews that appeared in the periodicals of that time attest, Doderet was expected to know the answers to these questions, and French critics expected him to present them a renewed version of D'Annunzio.[51]

The interplay between these expectations and the identification of Doderet as a new representative of D'Annunzio might help clarify the particular event of the 1932 *Prix de la Latinité*. The 10,000 francs prize was awarded annually to a literary work by an emerging neo-Latin author translated into French. The aim of the competition, funded by the Accademia Latinitatis Excolendae, was to promote contemporary voices and encourage the international exposure of a new Mediterranean literature. Although the rules provided for the evaluation of works that were published and written in prose, in 1942 Doderet won the prize for his translation of *La nave* (originally 1907), *La nef*. Contradictions arose immediately: how could D'Annunzio be considered an emerging voice? What was the purpose of promoting an author who was already famous, and whose peak of success had passed? Why was the prize being given to a translator when it was supposed to be awarded to a literary work? Moreover, *La nef* was in verse and still a manuscript. Despite the protests and the withdrawal of certain members of the jury, Doderet's *Prix de la*

[50] Gullace, 'After the Victory', in *Gabriele D'Annunzio in France*, pp. 173–88.

[51] See for instance the notice in *L'Intransigeant*, 15 May 1921, p. 3, which Doderet discusses in *Vingts ans*, p. 62.

Latinité was confirmed. The final arguments included recognition of the superiority of Doderet's translation skills and evaluation of all his translations carried out with D'Annunzio to that moment. Moreover, the eligibility of *La nef* was explained as an acknowledgement of Doderet's significant contribution to the translation of D'Annunzio's theatre and the fact that he had also overcome the impossibility of translating the poet's lyrics, effectively introducing to France a side of D'Annunzio that had been unknown.[52] The prize can be seen as an official and symbolic recognition of Doderet, who had rekindled interest in the Italian poet for his French readers. Another testimony highlighting the importance of Doderet to this renewed interest in D'Annunzio after Fiume can be found in Lionello Fiumi's article in *La nuova Italia* (3 September 1929). Discussing the French reception of D'Annunzio's works, Fiumi mentions Doderet as the 'exquisite' translator who enabled the circulation of the poet's work in France after the war.[53] Doderet, the 'invisible' translator, became a visible cultural mediator. While his translations themselves direct all attention to the author, his presence and activities were crucial to promoting a renewed cultural relationship between D'Annunzio and France.

Doderet's visibility, we can argue, compensated for D'Annunzio's prolonged absence and allowed for a continuous conversation across national borders. An interesting reading of Doderet's 'diplomatic' role is provided by Paul Lombard, who comments on the production of *Phædre* (1923):

> Que les temps sont changés ! Autrefois, M. Gabriele d'Annunzio communiquait avec son public au moyen du langage français le plus pur. [. . .] Aujourd'hui, M. d'Annunzio, frais émoulu de sa dictature de Fiume, ne veut pas avoir de rapports avec le monde civilisé que par le canal d'un chargé d'affaires. M. André Doderet s'acquitte d'ailleurs à sa merveille de son rôle diplomatique. Sa traduction est fidèle, et il y a fait passer une partie des ardeurs dont s'enflamment les démons familiers qui habitent M. d'Annunzio.[54]

[52] The reconstruction of this debate can be followed through the papers of that time. Among the many articles, see Section 'Notizie Artistiche', *La Nuova Italia*, 21 January 1932; François de Miomandre, 'La fin d'un accident', *Les Nouvelles Littéraires*, 28 May 1932; Section 'Petit courrier littéraire', *Comœdia*, 3 February 1932; Maurice de Waleffe, 'Le métier de juré', *Paris-soir,* 4 June 1932.

[53] Lionello Fiumi, 'Gli Italianisti di Francia. Divulgatori delle lettere e scrittori di politica', *La Nuova Italia*, 3 September 1929, frontpage.

[54] Paul Lombard, 'Les premières', *L'Homme libre*, 17 June 1923, p. 2.

(How times have changed! In the past, Gabriele d'Annunzio communicated with his public through the purest French language. [. . .] Today, D'Annunzio, just out of his dictatorship in Fiume, refuses to interact with the civilised world other than through a representative. André Doderet fulfills his diplomatic role to perfection. His translation is faithful, and in it he has conveyed some of the ardour that inflames the familiar demons that inhabit D'Annunzio.)

D'Annunzio used his collaboration with Doderet to underline his appreciation for France: if he had such a close relationship with his translator, it must mean that his relationship with France was not over. In his memoirs, Doderet recalls an interview with Maurice Prax, writer for the *Petit Parisien*, in which D'Annunzio, annoyed by the number of questions, grabbed Doderet's arm and stated that he was not going to leave Fiume but loved France and was glad to have a French friend by his side.[55] Once the experience of Fiume came to an end, French suspicions about D'Annunzio slowly faded: Doderet's translation of *Envoi à la France* in 1921 was an open declaration of affection for his second homeland, initiating rumours about his potential return to France to make theatre.[56] For this reason, when the French production of *Phaedre* was announced for June 1923 there was a general assumption that D'Annunzio was making his definitive return. In an interview promoting the French adaption of the tragedy, Doderet emphasised D'Annunzio's love for and engagement with France.[57] He had worked closely on the adaptation of the mythical tragedy, acting on the poet's behalf in many decisions;[58] yet, the translator too was expecting the poet to make his appearance and was deeply surprised when D'Annunzio never showed up. D'Annunzio was aware that his absence could be interpreted as disregard; for this reason, he sent a telegram to the director of the Opéra de Paris, saying 'before the war, during the war, after the war, I have always been and always am loyal to my second homeland,

[55] Reported in Doderet, *Vingts ans*, p. 38. The interview resulted in the article by Maurice Praz, 'Avec D'Annunzio son idole et son roi', *Le Petit Parisien*, 20 July 1920, frontpage.

[56] Gullace, p. 180.

[57] André Rigaud, 'La "Phædre" de Gabriele D'Annunzio à l'Opéra', *Comœdia*, 5 June 1923, frontpage.

[58] On the French translation of *Phædre* see Annalisa Ciano, 'Oltre i confini del tempo e dello spazio: un'analisi comparativa sulla traduzione e ricezione della *Phaedre* di D'Annunzio in Francia', *Novecento Transnazionale. Letterature, Arti e Culture*, 5: 2 (2021), pp. 169–88.

in spite of everything and even so'.[59] Apparently, this message was held up in Rome for about a week due to the censorship regime in place, provoking D'Annunzio to protest directly to the Minister of the Interior, Aldo Finzi.[60]

Translating as Self-Identification

During translation sessions, D'Annunzio shared with Doderet details, anecdotes and thoughts about the pieces to be translated. This enabled the translator to experience the moment of the work's composition as its author had, to understand and identify with D'Annunzio's experience and language.[61] This process of self-identification and emotional engagement was particularly significant for the translation of *Nocturne*, on which Doderet commented in a journal article, 'D'Annunzio devant la Mort'.[62] There, Doderet recalls how D'Annunzio's insights into *Notturno* overwhelmed him with emotion and how he was able to imagine and feel exactly what the poet had gone through. Elsewhere, he recalls how reading a passage of the text to D'Annunzio resulted in a recollection of memories and emotions that touched both him and D'Annunzio, who left the room silently, after having written a note of appreciation.[63] Later that year, D'Annunzio gifted him some of the bandages on which he had written during his partial blindness, dedicating them 'to my dear and loyal friend André Doderet who, with his translation, gave a "second life" to this book'.[64]

One of Doderet's great merits is having revitalised D'Annunzio's theatre in France, as well as the completion of a few lyrical translations approved by the poet. D'Annunzio always considered theatre to be particularly difficult to translate, mainly because the foreignising effect he sought in prose would be perceived as distant from the effect of the original in a dramatic text. As mentioned before in

[59] Doderet, *Vingts ans*, pp. 111–12.

[60] Ibid., pp. 111–12.

[61] Doderet noted that the time spent in Fiume in June 1920, for example, enabled him to 'be initiated to the secrets of his style and of his personal language'. Doderet, *Vingts ans*, p. 33.

[62] André Doderet, 'D'Annunzio Devant la Mort', *Les Nouvelles Littéraires*, 9 June 1923, frontpage.

[63] Doderet, *Vingts ans*, pp. 70–1.

[64] Ibid., p. 79.

reference to *Phaedre, La nef* and *La torche sous le boisseau*, Doderet found an equilibrium to present D'Annunzio's theatre in France. As for translating poetry, D'Annunzio's theory of translation made it almost impossible to do this literally. For this reason, French critics regarded the verses translated by Doderet with great surprise and appreciation, as they considered these to be 'faithfully translated'. Such is the case of the famous poem 'La pioggia nel pineto' (1902), which appeared in an issue of *Comœdia* (24 June 1931) with the title 'La Pluie sur la Pinède'. Introducing the verses, the director of the journal underlines that the poem had never been translated because the task was considered impossible. This French translation was also discussed in Italy, where the news of a literal, yet pleasant, translation of D'Annunzio's most appreciated poem appeared in the pages of *La Nuova Italia* (8 September 1932).

In his translation, Doderet had to deal with Latinisms, obsolete terms, neologisms and technical terms.[65] D'Annunzio's syntax was often difficult, full of parentheses that were foreign to the French language. Literary allusions and sonorous cross-references also constituted a challenge. Doderet preserved these features to the best of his abilities and defended D'Annunzio's style against the domesticating demands of French editors.[66] He sought a balance between accessibility and authenticity. In his translations, unlike in Hérelle's, D'Annunzio's style is recognisable. At the same time, the difficulty that a French reader may encounter when confronted with D'Annunzio's language is no greater than that which an Italian reader may find in the original. In a telegram to Doderet, which appeared in *Les Nouvelles Littéraires* on 8 May 1926, on the occasion of the staging of the French adaptation of *Phaedre* at the Teatro Argentina, D'Annunzio congratulated Doderet on having performed a prodigy, namely having made a work translated into French appreciable for the Italian public.[67]

Conclusion

Doderet played a significant and multifaceted role in renewing interest in D'Annunzio's work after the war. He began translating

[65] Ibid., p. 18.

[66] See Thomas Loué and Blaise Wilfert-Portal, 'D'Annunzio in France: Translation as Informal Censorship in the Late Nineteenth Century', *Ethnologie française*, 36: 1 (2006), pp. 101–10.

[67] *Les Nouvelles Littéraires*, 8 May 1926, p. 2.

D'Annunzio out of admiration for his literary works, but the collaboration soon became a journey into the author's self and biography. Although he did not acquire notoriety equal to that of Hérelle, Doderet significantly marked D'Annunzio's literary and personal life. In their twenty-year-long friendship, the two authors established a bond that facilitated the French publication of D'Annunzio's works, nourishing a renewed interest in them in France.

The deep connection that the translator established with the poet and his work allowed for the realisation of author-approved French versions of prose, poetry and theatre that balanced D'Annunzio's requests for literal translation and the preservation of his style, including rhythmic and formal aspects of the texts. Unlike Hérelle, Doderet took the risk of neglecting the taste of the French public, displaying an intentionally Dannunzian style at the expense of sobriety and clarity, both so cherished by the French.[68] This approach made him an 'invisible' translator: by fully submitting to the author, he effaced his presence in the translated texts. His contribution, however, became visible when he acted as a cultural mediator between D'Annunzio and France at a time in which D'Annunzio's absence was mistaken for distance from his second homeland. His tangible presence beyond the Alps enabled an international conversation with the author and symbolically reminded the French of D'Annunzio's affection for and ties with their country. Bringing together D'Annunzio's charisma and his literary talent through his *timida* and (in)visible signature, André Doderet presented D'Annunzio's works under a new light that confirmed and enhanced his position beyond Italy's national and cultural borders.

[68] Doderet, *Vingts ans*, p. 33.

Chapter 8

'An Artist in Translation': D'Annunzio, Arthur Symons and Symbolist Drama

Stefano Evangelista

An essay published in *Cosmopolis* in 1898 greets D'Annunzio's arrival into world literature with a feeling of ambivalence. The English critic Virginia M. Crawford hailed the Italian writer as 'the founder of a new school in the history of Italian literature' and compared him to Maeterlinck as 'the precocious geniuses of the age'.[1] But she also noted the hypersensuality, autobiographical obsession, cynicism and sexism of his novels – bound to cause 'a sense of actual nausea' in many readers.[2] Writing for a multilingual periodical that promoted exchange between European cultures, Crawford gave a detached assessment of D'Annunzio's international success from an English point of view. At the time only two of D'Annunzio's novels had been published in England: *Trionfo della morte* and *Il Piacere* – the latter just that year.[3] Crawford knew the English reception lagged behind the French, spearheaded by Melchior de Vogüé's critical patronage and Georges Hérelle's extensive translation activity. And she was aware the tastes and moral codes of the English public made it necessary that English translations be even more heavily expurgated than the French ones. Yet, for this very reason, she was keen to emphasise the challenging intellectual content of his work: his psychological complexity, stylistic power, engagement with music and musical aesthetics and Symbolism – the latter showing that '[i]n his literary studies d'Annunzio has clearly

[1] Virginia M. Crawford, 'Gabriele D'Annunzio', *Cosmopolis*, 11 (August 1898), 384–98 (pp. 398, 388).

[2] Ibid., p. 385.

[3] Parallel translation activity occurred in America: Arthur Hornblow translated *The Triumph of Death* (New York: G. H. Richmond & Co., 1896) and *The Intruder* (New York: G. H. Richmond & Co., 1898), and A. H. Antona translated *The Maidens of the Rocks* (New York: G. H. Richmond & Co., 1898).

included the Belgian school'.[4] Crawford was caught between the desire to make D'Annunzio known to English-speaking readers in his full complexity and the need to warn them about elements that made his work ethically untranslatable: it is as if his worlding should necessarily be accompanied by acts of censorship and concealment.

In the years following Crawford's article, the poet and critic Arthur Symons produced in quick succession three English translations of D'Annunzio's dramas – *The Dead City* (1900), *La Gioconda* (1901) and *Francesca da Rimini* (1902) – supplemented by numerous critical interventions scattered across books and periodicals. Symons was drawn to the highly literary D'Annunzio that attracted Crawford; but, unlike her and most English critics at the time, he championed an unexpurgated D'Annunzio, refusing the tension between artistic and Decadent elements in his works. Symons was closely associated with Decadence and cosmopolitanism after publishing controversial collections of urban poetry in the early 1890s.[5] He had also established himself as a leading translator and expert on modern French literature.[6] Symons's high profile meant his mediation had considerable impact on D'Annunzio's English reception, even if he focused on dramatic works now considered marginal. This essay charts Symons's double engagement with D'Annunzio as translator and critic. It shows that Symons played an important role promoting D'Annunzio within the English-speaking world, but he also developed an ambivalent relationship with D'Annunzio's dramatic experiments, most evident in the textual and biographical triangulation between Italian writer, English translator and Eleonora Duse.

The Decadent Translator

Symons first became interested in D'Annunzio through French Decadence. In 'The Decadent Movement in Literature' (1893),

[4] Crawford, 'Gabriele D'Annunzio', p. 396.

[5] See Arthur Symons, *Selected Early Poems*, ed. by Jane Desmarais and Chris Baldick (Cambridge: MHRA, 2017).

[6] See especially Bénédicte Coste, 'Arthur Symons the Translator: Translation, Remediation, Recognition', *Parallèles*, 33: 2 (2021), 1–17; and Matthew Creasy, '"The neglected, the unutterable Verlaine": Arthur Symons, the *Saturday Review*, and French Literature in the 1890s', *Victorian Periodicals Review*, 52: 1 (2019), 103–23. The present chapter develops new elements expanding on Stefano Evangelista, 'Symons and D'Annunzio: Decadence in Translation', in *Arthur Symons: Poet, Critic, Vagabond*, ed. by Elisa Bizzotto and Stefano Evangelista (Cambridge: Legenda, 2018), pp. 54–68.

originally published in the transatlantic *Harper's Magazine*, Symons mentioned *Il Piacere*, together – surprisingly enough – with Luigi Capuana's naturalist novel *Giacinta* (1879), as exemplifying literary Decadence, which he otherwise associated with French authors: 'an intense self-consciousness, a restless curiosity in research, an over-subtilizing refinement upon refinement, a spiritual and moral perversity'.[7] Cursory though it was, Symons's gloss of D'Annunzio's novel as 'a triumph of exquisite perversity' was important because it introduced D'Annunzio's name, then largely unknown to English-speaking readers, as part of a transnational network of advanced literature emanating from France, which Symons saw as a sweeping trend of modern European literature.[8] Symons placed D'Annunzio among vernacular versions of French Decadence taking root across Europe, including Ibsen in Norway, Emilia Pardo-Bazán in Spain and Walter Pater and W. E. Henley in Britain. In *The Symbolist Movement in Literature* (1899), a book-length reworking of the essay, he foregrounded references to D'Annunzio in the expansive dedication to W. B. Yeats. Addressing the Irish poet as 'the chief representative' of Symbolism in the English-speaking world, Symons now argued that D'Annunzio, 'the one new force in Italy' (Capuana has been wisely elided), was permeated with the spirit of Symbolism – a literary movement, in Symons's understanding, that shifted emphasis from the perverse to the mystical.[9] More than conveying any real knowledge of the author, these brief references represent a prominent early effort to frame D'Annunzio within the evolving and somewhat blurring genealogy of international Decadence and Symbolism, which Symons traced chiefly in relation to French authors.

The Symbolist Movement was published shortly after Crawford's intervention in *Cosmopolis*, when British and international audiences were quickly becoming more familiar with D'Annunzio. Symons, among the earliest English discoverers of the Italian writer, followed this evolution closely. In an acerbic, detailed review of Georgina Harding's *The Triumph of Death*, he highlighted the translation's many shortcomings, from stylistic failings to expurgations and egregious omissions.[10] In his view, these cheapened the original and,

[7] Arthur Symons, 'The Decadent Movement in Literature', in Symons, *The Symbolist Movement in Literature*, ed. by Matthew Creasy (Manchester: Carcanet, 2014), pp. 169–83 (p. 183).

[8] Ibid., p. 181.

[9] Symons, *The Symbolist Movement in Literature*, p. 3.

[10] Symons, 'D'Annunzio in English', *Saturday Review*, 85 (29 January 1898), 52–3.

paradoxically, made the English version seem more voluptuous and immoral by excising the novel's artistic and philosophical content – a point that anticipated John Woodhouse's criticism of the early translations.[11] Symons tersely described Harding as 'not an artist in translation'. Indeed, the rocky reception of Harding's translation sparked a mini controversy in English periodicals.[12] Everyone seemed upset by her version: progressive commentators complained she had gone too far toning down the text and conservative ones that she had not gone far enough. Many denounced the novel as Decadent using well-known clichés. Critics and readers debated whether it was *possible* to translate D'Annunzio into English given the perceived gulf separating Britain and Italy in terms of public morality. In a country that had recently sent Zola's translator to gaol for obscene libel,[13] at stake was the wider issue of how to regulate the circulation of foreign literatures in English: how English national identity could be protected and managed by the moral censorship of translations.

The ground was now ready for Symons to assert himself as the foremost English critic of D'Annunzio's works. William Heinemann, publisher of *The Triumph of Death*, asked him to contribute an introduction to the translation of *Il Piacere*, also by Harding, which came out later that year. There, Symons took credit for suggesting that *The Child of Pleasure* should follow the title and reworked structure of Hérelle's French version. But he also distanced himself from the English version by claiming, tendentiously perhaps, to have not seen Harding's translation. He therefore limited his 'responsibility', as he put it, to the introduction and verse translations of the sonnets composed by the novel's protagonist, Andrea Sperelli, during his rural interlude at Schifanoja.[14] His introduction provided the blueprint for a critical portrait of D'Annunzio that Symons would revise multiple times and repurpose in various contexts in the following decades. There, he tried to restore the artistic and intellectual content that was

[11] Cf. John Woodhouse, *Gabriele d'Annunzio tra Italia e Inghilterra* (Pescara: Ediars, 2003), pp. 43–4.

[12] A digest of critical reactions is provided by [Anon.], 'Book Reviews Reviewed', *The Academy* (12 February 1898), 184–5.

[13] Henry Vizetelly was prosecuted in 1888 and again in 1889 for his translation of *La Terre* (1887): Anthony Cummins, 'Émile Zola's Cheap English Dress: The Vizetelly Translations, Late-Victorian Print Culture, and the Crisis of Literary Value', *Review of English Studies*, 60 (2009), 108–32.

[14] Arthur Symons, 'Introduction', in Gabriele D'Annunzio, *The Child of Pleasure*, trans. by Georgina Harding and Arthur Symons (London: Heinemann, 1898), pp. v–xii (p. v).

lost in the English translations. He therefore emphatically presented D'Annunzio as an ambitious innovator of the novel, a literary form that, Symons argued, had otherwise traditionally appealed, internationally, to 'an altogether lower audience'.[15] Freeing themselves from conventional realism and becoming instead 'states of mind' and explorations of 'the hidden, inner self', D'Annunzio's novels were in step with a new international trend to aestheticise the novel, 'to consider beauty as its highest aim'.[16] Although Symons did not say so explicitly, efforts to hybridise poetry with prose and to go beyond material reality placed D'Annunzio in the company of the French Decadent and Symbolist authors Symons was busy mediating at this point.

To situate D'Annunzio vis-à-vis a broader map of European culture, Symons relied on a dialectics of cosmopolitan and national traits used by Crawford and numerous foreign critics. D'Annunzio could thus act as a channel for the ideas of Nietzsche, Dostoevsky and Tolstoy while being an ethnic writer; that is, quintessentially Italian and Latin. Symons's characterisation of D'Annunzio's Latin identity came straight from de Vogüé's ideas about the 'Renaissance latine'. The French critic is particularly visible in Symons's argument that D'Annunzio's alleged immorality, far from being a perversion, should be seen as part of his Italian heritage, which prevented him from sharing 'those unconscious reticenses in feeling, which races drawn further from nature by civilization have thought it needful to invent in their relations with nature'.[17] What is original to Symons is his framing D'Annunzio in relation to Walter Pater, the figurehead of the English Aesthetic movement whose writings had a determining influence on Symons's own. This strategy simultaneously aimed to highlight D'Annunzio's formalism and to domesticate him, assimilating the Italian writer to a familiar cultural context for English readers. Even when Symons described D'Annunzio as a belated offshoot of the Italian Renaissance, his vision of the Renaissance as a movement that saw life through the prism of art was filtered through the sensibility of Pater and English Aestheticism.[18] This hybrid of English Aestheticism, French Symbolism and Latin ethnos was to dominate the English image of D'Annunzio as Symons's essay went through various iterations in periodicals and collections.

[15] Ibid., p. ix.

[16] Ibid., pp. viii, ix, x.

[17] Ibid., p. vii; cf. Eugène-Melchior de Vogüé, 'La Renaissance latine: Gabriele D'Annunzio, poèmes et romans', *Revue des deux mondes* (1 January 1895), 187–206.

[18] See Evangelista, 'Symons and D'Annunzio', pp. 58–61.

The Literal Translator

Sharing *The Child of Pleasure* with Harding, about whom he had expressed serious reservations, must have been frustrating for Symons. It seems logical that he should have wanted to try his own hand. The ideal opportunity presented itself that very year with D'Annunzio's breakthrough as a dramatist: on 21 January 1898, the Théâtre de la Renaissance in Paris staged the international première of *La città morta* (*Ville morte*), with Sarah Bernhardt as the blind tragic heroine, Anna. The play originated in D'Annunzio's trip to Greece in 1895, when he visited some of the country's most important classical sites.[19] Inspired by Heinrich Schliemann's archaeological excavations and recovery of the so-called mask of Agamemnon, D'Annunzio set the action in modern Mycenae, when the ancient remains are brought back to life. Together with the precious relics, however, the Italian archaeologist Leonardo resurrects the curse of classical Greek tragedy: trapped in the claustrophobic atmosphere of the titular dead city and plagued by the unrelenting heat of the Greek summer, the four main characters spiral into a plot of adultery, incest and murder that looks back to Greek classical models. Despite its extremely modest public success, *La città morta* represented an important artistic development for D'Annunzio. It launched an ambitious programme for the modernisation of Italian theatre that he undertook in partnership with the Italian actress Eleonora Duse, with whom D'Annunzio started a relationship in the mid-'90s. The play was also D'Annunzio's attempt to embed himself more deeply in France and increase his international profile, emboldened by the positive French reception of his novels.[20] This move was signalled by his controversial choice of Bernhardt over Duse for the opening production.

Translation already inhabits the source text of *La città morta* in multiple forms. On a general level, the play translates ideas and conventions of classical tragedy: for instance, as noted in a review by D'Annunzio's friend, the critic Angelo Conti, the character of Anna recreates the function of the Greek tragic chorus.[21] D'Annunzio made extensive use of translations in drafting the play. These included Jules Girardin's French translation of Schliemann's account of his excavations, which he used to construct the modern setting; Leconte de Lisle's prose translations of Homer and the ancient tragedians;

[19] See Chapters 1 and 6 in this volume.

[20] See Chapters 5, 6 and 7 in this volume.

[21] Angelo Conti, 'La "Città Morta"', *Il Marzocco* (23 January 1898), n.p.

and Gabriel Mourey's French prose translation (1891) of A. C. Swinburne's *Poems and Ballads* (1866), important sources of poetic inspiration.[22] Swinburne's 'Triumph of Time' in particular influenced D'Annunzio's treatment of the key eros/Thanatos dynamics.[23] D'Annunzio's problematic habit of liberally availing himself of other writers is well-known. Ethical questions aside, his close engagement with these and other French translations can be seen as moulding the very aesthetics of the play: *La città morta* opens with one of the characters reading from a translation of Sophocles' *Antigone*; and, just as the Greek tragic urtext haunts the characters' actions in ways they seem unable to control, the ghosts of previous translations (translations being themselves a form of literary afterlife) work as overlapping echoes creating an effect of eclecticism and removal. By incorporating translations of translations, *La città morta* can be read as a poetic meta-commentary on the mechanism of poetic reception, tied to a Decadent vision of history as a narrative of decline and perverse returns.

Close engagement with translations also triggered interesting reflections on the nature of dramatic language. According to what he wrote to Hérelle, D'Annunzio seems to have planned to write the play in French, believing Italian posed an almost unsurmountable difficulty for dramatic dialogue: given the wide gap between spoken and literary language, modern Italian playwrights had to sound either vulgar or affected. By contrast, he found French more natural: 'Writing in Italian, the French phrase very often comes under my pen and seems to me more effective and – how can I say? – more *vocal*.'[24] This striking image represents the Italian source text as itself a translation: the translation of a ghostly French text D'Annunzio fought to repress. Putting aside psychoanalytic readings, D'Annunzio had a practical motive for describing his work in these terms: he wanted Hérelle to translate the play without being credited, with the play

[22] Henry Schliemann, *Mycènes: récit des recherches et découvertes faits à Mycènes et à Tirynthe*, trans. by Jules Girardin (Paris: Hachette, 1879); Homère, *Odyssée*, trans. by Leconte de Lisle (Paris: Alphonse Lamerre, 1893); A. C. Swinburne, *Poèmes et ballades*, trans. by Gabriel Mourey (Paris: Albert Savine, 1891). See Milva Maria Cappellini, 'Introduzione', in Gabriele D'Annunzio, *La Città Morta*, ed. by Milva Maria Cappellini (Milan: Mondadori, 1956), pp. v–xxxiv (pp. xvii, xviii, xxi).

[23] Cappellini, 'Introduzione', p. 166.

[24] D'Annunzio to Hérelle, [before 19 October 1896], in *Carteggio D'Annunzio – Hérelle (1891–1931)*, ed. by Mario Cimini (Lanciano: Rocco Carabba, 2004), p. 419. All translations are my own unless otherwise noted.

advertised and performed as if he had originally written it in French. 'In the theatre this very word – *translation* – seems almost to insert a veil between the drama and the audience. It seems as if the audience, by means of a translation, should not receive a *direct* emotion. Listening to or reading a translation, one instinctively thinks of what the original text might have been. And this causes something like a diminished enjoyment.'[25] Hérelle not only agreed to this manipulative request but he also offered to give up his translator's fee.[26] *La città morta* thus first went on stage as a ghost translation. This blatant attempt to naturalise his work in France was strategic, for it went against the ethnic reading promoted by de Vogüé that dominated the French reception: writing Symbolist drama afforded D'Annunzio an opportunity to present himself as a cosmopolitan writer. In this sense, the linguistic crossings that underlie the composition of *La città morta* directly anticipate D'Annunzio's experiment with the French language in *Le Martyre de Saint Sébastien* (1911).

Rendering *La città morta* into English, Symons opted for a rigorously literal style of translation based on the Italian book version of the play, which was published on the day of the Parisian premiere. This followed the practice he had adopted in rendering Émile Verhaeren's *Les Aubes* (*The Dawn*, 1898), his only previous attempt at dramatic translation.[27] Like *The Dawn*, which alternated prose and verse, the translation of *The Dead City* was very much a work for the page rather than the stage, intended to be received within a written literary culture. Implicitly establishing continuity between the widely esteemed Belgian Symbolist and D'Annunzio, Symons used his cultural capital as a translator/poet to shift the English reception of D'Annunzio: while the novels had landed in a grey zone between highbrow Decadence and cheap sensationalism, D'Annunzio's dramatic work was pitched to the cultural elite. Extreme literalism was thus an antidote to the lowering effects of Harding's bowdlerisations. The reviewer for the prestigious journal *The Academy* had negatively characterised Harding's work as presenting D'Annunzio 'to English eyes through a sheet of smoked glass'.[28] Two years later, the positive review of *The Dead City* in that same journal showed that Symons had hit the mark, with lavish praise for the poetic

[25] Ibid., p. 419.

[26] Hérelle to D'Annunzio [end of October 1896], in ibid., p. 427.

[27] See Clément Dessy, 'Arthur Symons, a Mediator of Belgian Symbolist Writers', in Bizzotto and Evangelista (eds), *Arthur Symons*, pp. 84–102 (pp. 95–8).

[28] [Anon.], 'D'Annunzio in English', *The Academy* (5 February 1898), 141–2 (142).

power of D'Annunzio's writing, finally visible in English thanks to Symons's 'beautiful' translation.[29] Paradoxically, even the problematic theme of moral decay, which this reviewer also identified, and the play's dramatic failings – the speeches were too long and 'almost certainly too subtle for a popular audience' – contributed to lifting it to highbrow literature.[30] Most importantly, though, the reviewer encouraged readers to relate *The Dead City* to Maeterlinck's dramas, Symbolism, Decadence and *fin-de-siècle Nervenkunst* – markers of literary prestige that simultaneously promoted the cosmopolitan interpretation that D'Annunzio desired for his work.

It is worth probing more deeply into the aesthetics of Symons's extreme literalism. Comparing the Italian and English versions, it is striking how little Symons departed from D'Annunzio's Italian. He refused to cut anything and followed D'Annunzio's word order and choice of vocabulary even when more idiomatic choices were possible or expressions that gestured more openly to the many intertextual allusions (for instance, Homer and Swinburne) could be found. D'Annunzio had struggled to find the right register for the Italian dialogue, taking inspiration from French and producing, in this process, an interlinguistic experiment of sorts, where the Italian took shape as the calque of an absent French text. Symons's literal translation, by refusing to bow to the idiomatic and literary conventions of English, captured the linguistic in-betweenness of the original.

At the same time, Symons's literalism can be traced to the ideas on translation of his mentor, Walter Pater, whom Symons associated with D'Annunzio in matters of literary aesthetics. In his influential late essay 'Style', Pater complained that most literary translation into English was too strongly driven by 'idiom or construction'; he instead advocated 'an exact following, with no variation in structure, of word after word, as the pencil follows a drawing under tracing-paper'.[31] This radical method of 'word after word' translation should be seen as a way of stressing affinity, rather than difference and loss, when moving literary content from one language to another. It was simultaneously an appeal to keep English literary culture open to foreign ideas and influences ('Style' is largely about Flaubert) and to reject

29 [Anon.], '"And yet – he is a Master"', *The Academy* (2 June 1900), 464–6 (p. 466).

30 Ibid., p. 465.

31 Walter Pater, 'Style' in *The Library Edition of the Works of Walter Pater*, 10 vols (London: Macmillan, 1910), V: *Appreciations*, pp. 5–38 (pp. 14–15). In 'The Decadent Movement in Literature', Symons named Henley and Pater the two foremost representatives of English Decadence.

moral pressures of self-censorship and bowdlerisation. Always highly receptive to Pater's ideas, Symons made this the hallmark of his literary translations. Indeed, in a much later essay on whether translators should be allowed to 'improve' the originals, Symons argued a related point (in a style loosely resembling Pater's) about the virtue of extreme fidelity in carrying 'rhythm' across languages, referring to translating prose: 'It is rarely realised how perfectly possible it is to render cadence by cadence the rhythm of a foreign language. Good style; style which is not eccentric, makes its cadence out of the natural order of its words, and a translation which follows closely the order of words in the original will generally bring some of the tune as well as most of the sense into another language.'[32] His English version of *La città morta* carried over intact the rhythm and cadences of D'Annunzio's Italian to render a studied poetic effect of defamiliarisation in English, true to Pater's cosmopolitan translational aesthetics of the drawing on tracing-paper.

It would be wrong, therefore, to understand Symons's literal method as either the product of hastiness (Symons did have a reputation for turning round work quickly and in too large quantities) or an attempt to erase himself from the text. Rather, Symons was deliberately exercising the restraint Pater recommended, not only as the best practice of translation but also as a key characteristic of good literary writing. Symons wanted to make the point that D'Annunzio deserved 'an artist in translation' such as himself. In a now classic intervention in translation theory, Lawrence Venuti has argued that Anglo-American literary translation has been dominated by the imperative to domesticate the original, causing the translator's work to become invisible. Foreignising translation practices, by contrast, draw attention to the otherness of the foreign text and, by extension, to the mediating presence of the translator in the target text.[33] Symons's literal method is an extreme example of foreignisation as described by Venuti. This practice was in line with D'Annunzio's wish, expressed repeatedly to Hérelle, to be translated in a way that would preserve the foreign flavour of his idiom, respecting the cosmopolitan and exotic character of his original Italian. But, while D'Annunzio might have thought this a way of reinforcing his own presence and authority in the translated text, the consequence of Symons's literalism was to

[32] Symons, 'Should Translators improve their Authors?', *Bookman's Journal and Print Collector*, 5: 4 (1922), 109–12 (p. 109).

[33] Laurence Venuti, *The Translator's Invisibility: A History of Translation* (London: Routledge, 2008).

draw attention to the act of mediation and the translator's agency.[34] Indeed, that Symons's adoption of a literal, foreignising translation method by no means aimed to make him invisible is evident in his custom of using his translations to stage public dialogues with foreign authors. In his introduction to *The Dawn*, he quoted from a private letter from Verhaeren where the Belgian author emphatically approved of Symons's work, effectively recognising him as a poetic peer.[35] *The Dead City* had no introduction, but Symons took the highly unusual step of dedicating his translation to the author: 'To Gabriele D'Annunzio I dedicate this translation, begun at Arles and finished at Toledo, the two dead cities which I love most in Europe.'[36] By assimilating D'Annunzio's idea of the dead city to his own literary sensibility, Symons staged a performance of poetic kinship with the author, inviting readers to view the translation as a dialogue or artistic collaboration rather than a mere linguistic exercise.

The Translator and the Stage: Symons and Duse

Symons stuck to literalism for the next two translations, *La Gioconda* and *Francesca da Rimini*, even if the latter posed a greater challenge, being written in verse. In his introduction Symons explained his version of *Francesca da Rimini* was 'literal, alike in words and rhythm, but [his] lines do not in every case correspond precisely with the lines of the original. They are intended to reproduce every effect of the original, as that can best be done in English verse, written on the principle of D'Annunzio's Italian verse.'[37] Together with detailed technical explanations of poetic metre in Italian and English, this was a tortuous justification for Symons's poetic licence in rendering D'Annunzio's more elevated and complex language in *Francesca da Rimini*.

Compared to the novels that made D'Annunzio famous in Europe, the early dramas translated by Symons were less favourably received

[34] In Chapter 7 in this volume, Annalisa Ciano notes a similar literal approach by D'Annunzio's second French translator André Doderet, which she relates instead to the translator's readiness to submit to D'Annunzio's authority.

[35] Symons, 'Introduction', in Emile Verhaeren, *The Dawn (Les Aubes)*, trans. by Arthur Symons (London: Duckworth, 1898), pp. 1–8 (p. 8).

[36] Gabriele D'Annunzio, *The Dead City*, trans. by Arthur Symons (London: Heinemann, 1900).

[37] Symons, 'Introduction', in Gabriele D'Annunzio, *Francesca da Rimini*, trans. by Arthur Symons (London: Heinemann, 1902), pp. vii–xiv (p. xi).

by both critics and audiences. Nonetheless, they did bring Italian theatre to the attention of foreign audiences at a time when the international circulation of Italian literature was dominated by *verista* prose fiction. D'Annunzio bemoaned that domestic theatre culture was swamped by bourgeois French imports such as Dumas and Sardou, leaving little room for experimentation. These works were popular with the public but were hardly in step with artistic modernity. With characteristically grand ambition, he sought to revolutionise this scene by producing highly literary play texts inspired, as we have seen, by classical tragedy and Symbolist drama (which D'Annunzio knew through Parisian journals such as the *Revue wagnérienne* and the *Revue blanche*). However, he did not like the avant-garde model represented by Lugné-Poë's Théâtre de l'Oeuvre, with its small following of metropolitan intellectuals. As a dramatist, D'Annunzio saw his role as inspiring the masses: he wanted performances in the biggest established theatres, with lavish stage designs and large audiences.[38] His vision of the theatre was informed by widespread avant-garde ideas of art regenerating society, compounded with a Nietzschean self-myth of the writer as spiritual leader of the people. This theory is embedded in the fictional fabric of *Il fuoco* (1900, translated into English that same year as *The Flame of Life*), where the autobiographical protagonist Stelio Effrena designs a play that is essentially *La città morta*.

D'Annunzio's reforming mission took on a practical dimension. In collaboration with Duse (fictionalised as the actress/romance heroine la Foscarina in *Il fuoco*), he planned to found an open-air theatre at Albano, near Rome, inspired by the recent restoration of the Roman theatre at Orange and by Richard Wagner's experiment at Bayreuth, which by the end of the century had become a huge international success. In contrast with Bayreuth's emphasis on Germanic culture and national identity, the Teatro d'Albano was to provide the stage for a distinctly Italian art theatre: it would reform Italian literary culture at home and promote it internationally within the competitive field of world literature. This theatrical enterprise exemplifies the complex interweaving of cosmopolitanism and nationalism in D'Annunzio's work. More intimately bound with the public sphere than the novel, drama lent itself particularly well to nationalist gestures of the type D'Annunzio increasingly preferred. For instance, after the Parisian premiere of *La città morta*, the Italian periodical

[38] Valentina Valentini, *La Tragedia moderna e mediterranea: Sul Teatro di Gabriele D'Annunzio* (Milan: FrancoAngeli, 1992), pp. 29, 33.

Il Marzocco (operating under D'Annunzio's influence) quickly proclaimed D'Annunzio the most successful foreign dramatist in France, announcing his victory over Maeterlinck and Sudermann.[39] In actual fact, *La città morta*, *La Gioconda* and *Francesca da Rimini* enjoyed very limited success, in Italy as well as internationally. The long and wordy plays translated poorly to the stage. As Hérelle tactfully put it to D'Annunzio, 'such dramas are more pleasant to read because readers have the time to collect themselves, to linger over important words, to interpret the stage directions at their will and realise them in mental images'.[40]

Despite these shortcomings, the self-consciousness and anti-naturalism of D'Annunzio's theatre resonated with Symons's interest in the modern art of the stage – a branch of literary culture that Pater overlooked and that Symons claimed, starting from the 1890s, as an area of specialism. His translations of D'Annunzio therefore need to be read in tandem with his extensive activity as theatre critic. Symons was an omnivorous theatregoer and regularly reviewed music hall and dance for the periodical press. But his interest in theatre was also prominent in the main books from this period: *The Symbolist Movement in Literature* to *Plays, Acting and Music* (1903) and *Studies in Seven Arts* (1906), which Symons saw as part of an overarching project to work out a 'system of aesthetics' operating across all the arts.[41] There Symons provided long explorations of topics that were highly germane to D'Annunzio's dramatic interests, such as Wagner's theatrical innovations, Nietzsche's views on tragedy and Symbolism (*Plays, Acting and Music* was dedicated to Maeterlinck); but strikingly D'Annunzio himself played only a marginal role. Indeed, Symons often used his essayistic voice to perform a critical distance from those works he had translated and to get close to Duse instead, as if encouraging readers to view his translations more in relation to her art than D'Annunzio's.

Duse helped D'Annunzio (as far as he would listen to her) with the great practical knowledge she had gained during her career as actress/manager; and, at the height of her fame, she also acted as his international ambassador. She included both *La città morta* and

[39] [Anon.], 'Il successo della "Ville Morte" a Parigi', *Il Marzocco* (23 January 1898), n.p.

[40] Hérelle to D'Annunzio, quoted in Velentini, *La Tragedia moderna e mediterranea*, p. 50, n. 26.

[41] Symons, *Plays, Acting and Music: A Book of Theory* (London: Constable, 1909), p. vii.

La Gioconda in her repertoire on tour in Europe and America, bringing them, in Italian, to international audiences largely unable to understand the actual words (let alone the subtleties of D'Annunzio's literary language) but who nevertheless enjoyed watching Duse perform her famous tragic roles. At the same time, her close connection with D'Annunzio propelled Duse into the network of world literature, where she was a powerful conduit for D'Annunzio's influence but also an object of literary interest in her own right. She fascinated numerous European writers including Rainer Maria Rilke and the young James Joyce, and became a myth inspiring poets and writers. As Elena Raponi has argued, for instance, Duse's Viennese performances in *La Gioconda* and *Francesca da Rimini* influenced the composition of Hugo von Hofmannsthal's *Elektra* (1903), which Symons also translated into English (1908).[42] The cosmopolitan Danish Decadent writer Laura Marholm, who saw Duse on stage in Berlin, dedicated a chapter to her in her internationally successful *Das Buch der Frauen* (1895), where Duse appeared as the icon of a controversial essentialist model of *fin-de-siècle* feminism: for Marholm, Duse's genius consisted in her refusal to disguise, in life and on stage, a strong essential femininity untapped by male writers and artists.[43] On the level of popular culture, the news of her affair with D'Annunzio filled the columns of gossip magazines.

Symons, whose fascination with Duse bordered on idolatry, was among the most active makers of the Duse myth in English. According to John Stokes, Duse combined an extraordinary personal integrity – the quality Marholm read in a feminist key – with 'renunciation, austerity, [and] desperate ambitions'.[44] Playing up this mix of qualities, Symons often contrasted Duse favourably to Sarah Bernhardt, the most star-like international diva of the turn of the century. As Stokes also notes, Duse fulfilled Symons's ideal of the Decadent artist, to the extent that he even openly identified with her allegedly neurotic traits.[45] Duse's connection with literary Decadence had already been

[42] Elena Raponi, 'L'*Elettra* (1903) di Hugo von Hofmannsthal tra Sofocle e D'Annunzio', *Studia austriaca*, 21 (2013), 131–54.

[43] Marholm's book resonated internationally. It was translated into English by Hermione Ramsden (1896) and published by John Lane's Bodley Head, the leading English publisher of Decadent literature: Stefano Evangelista, *Litereray Cosmopolitanism in the English Fin de Siècle: Citizens of Nowhere* (Oxford and New York: Oxford University Press, 2021), pp. 159–62.

[44] John Stokes, 'The Legend of Duse', in *Decadence and the 1890s*, ed. by Ian Fletcher (London: Edward Arnold: 1979), pp. 151–71 (p. 154).

[45] Ibid., p. 154.

established by the critic Helen Zimmern, an influential mediator between Britain and Italy in this period. Zimmern noted that English was a 'closed book' to Duse because she could not read the language, but she portrayed her as an otherwise wide-ranging and intelligent reader most interested, 'as might be expected, in the Decadents' and in Maeterlinck's plays.[46] These contemporary impressions of Duse as an attentive literary reader have been recently corroborated by Anna De Domenico Sica's research into Duse's library.[47]

Symons's first major essay on Duse came out only one month after Zimmern's and, like hers, drew heavily on a French literary portrait of the actress by Giuseppe Primoli in the *Revue de Paris* (1897).[48] Like Primoli and Zimmern, he stressed her artistic genius, which was, he claimed, only accidentally connected with the stage, as it could easily have found an outlet in any other art form. Symons saw Duse as first and foremost an Aesthete. He described her as 'passionate after beauty', setting her apart from other women; he made her sound like one of the hyper-refined, neurotic male Decadent heroes of D'Annunzio novels, 'devoured by the life of the soul, by the life of the mind, by the life of the body'.[49] In a distinctly voyeuristic turn, he described watching her transported in body and mind as she looked at artworks by Rodin, Whistler and Turner. But of D'Annunzio himself there is no mention. Indeed Symons goes out of his way to communicate Duse's distinctive voice as a theatre theorist and reformer, quoting a series of aphorisms he claims to have jotted down from memory following a private conversation:

> To save the theatre, the theatre must be destroyed, the actors and actresses must all die of the plague. They poison the air, they make art impossible. It is not drama that they play, but pieces for the theatre. We should return to the Greeks, play in the open air; the drama dies of stalls and boxes and evening dress, and people who come to digest their dinner.[50]

[46] Helen Zimmern, 'Eleonora Duse', *Fortnightly Review*, 67 (June 1900), 980–93 (p. 990).

[47] Anna De Domenico Sica, 'Eleonora Duse's Library: The Disclosure of Aesthetic Value in Real Acting', *Nineteenth Century Theatre and Film*, 37: 2 (2010), 66–85.

[48] Joseph Primoli, 'La Duse', *La Revue de Paris* (June 1897), 486–532. The aristocratic Franco-Italian Primoli was a friend of Symons, as well as of D'Annunzio and Duse, who gravitated around his Roman salon. The well-connected Primoli was also an important sponsor of D'Annunzio and Duse's project for a theatre at Albano.

[49] Symons, 'Eleonora Duse', in *Studies in Seven Arts* (London: Constable, 1906), pp. 331–46 (p. 334). The essay was originally published in the *Contemporary Review* in July 1900.

[50] Ibid., p. 336.

With these words, which Edward Gordon Craig would use as an epigram for his landmark essay 'The Actor and the Über-Marionette' (1908), Symons attributed to Duse and to Duse alone the militant critique of commercial bourgeois theatre that marked her artistic partnership with D'Annunzio. That very year, Symons's translation of *The Dead City* was released.

Duse's affinity with avant-garde aesthetics becomes even more prominent in another essay from this period, 'Duse in some of her Parts', collected in *Plays, Acting and Music*. Here Symons compares Duse's acting technique to Whistler's portrait of Carlyle, the very painting he recounted seeing with her in the previous essay: both embodied the art of perfectly expressing and suppressing at the same time, 'so that a kind of negative thing becomes a thing of the highest achievement'.[51] Symons now describes Duse's performances as a form of creative intelligence that deconstructed the dramatist's work, almost competing with it: 'The acting of Duse is a criticism; poor work dissolves away under it, as under a solvent acid.'[52] As an example, he cites *The Second Mrs Tanqueray* (1892) by the popular English playwright Arthur Pinero, which she performed during one of her London tours: Duse improved Pinero's superficial characterisation by adding depths of emotional understanding impossible for ordinary actresses to reach while simultaneously revealing to the audience the shortcomings of Pinero's writing.

It is not surprising to see Symons lambasting the middlebrow Pinero as a representative of the commercial bourgeois theatre he disliked. But, in the same essay, *La Gioconda* also comes under attack as one of those dramatic works that dissolved, to use Symons's metaphor, under the corrosive effect of Duse's performance. While Symons recognises the poetic power of D'Annunzio's play and credits it as giving Duse the opportunity to shine in her tragic talent, he is also absolutely clear about its failings as a work of literature and a dramatic piece, calling it 'horrible with a vulgar material horror' and condemning the ending, where the character of Silvia, played by Duse, suffers the mutilation of both hands in a vain attempt to save one of her husband's sculptures from destruction.[53] Symons did not shrink from exposing the conclusion of the play that he had recently

[51] Symons, 'Duse in some of her Parts', in *Plays, Acting and Music*, pp. 60–76 (p. 63).

[52] Ibid., p. 60.

[53] Ibid., p. 66.

translated as inartistic, gratuitous and grotesque, and from summing up *La Gioconda* as 'bad tragedy'.[54]

The shortcomings of D'Annunzio's dramatic vision came under even heavier criticism in 'The Price of Realism', also in *Plays, Acting and Music*. Here Symons's target was the 1901 opening production in Rome of *Francesca da Rimini*, which, in the introduction to his translation, he had compared to Victor Hugo's verse play *Hernani* (1830) for causing a huge public controversy.[55] As Symons knew, D'Annunzio was heavily involved in planning the lavish production, where Duse again played the main role. Symons criticised as 'costly and inartistic' D'Annunzio's fussy demands of having a fresh pot of basil brought up from Naples every day and of commissioning fine craftsmen to execute the stage decorations in precious metal.[56] Now D'Annunzio was emphatically no longer on the side of artistic modernity, as in the essays on Decadence and Symbolism dating from only a few years earlier: he had become the problem, rather than the solution, of the perceived crisis of the modern stage. Symons exposed D'Annunzio's vision of the theatre as old-fashioned and kitsch, in contrast to the ideas of the English designer Gordon Craig, whose future-looking art of the stage relied on suggestion and Symbolism rather than realistic imitation.

In the early twentieth century Symons retouched and republished his essays on Duse several times, finally collecting them in book form after Duse's death: *Eleonora Duse* (1926) was a collage of critical and biographical writings, including personal letters that Symons used to perform an intimate knowledge of his biographical subject. The book also incorporated a much reworked version of Symons's introductory essay from *The Child of Pleasure*, which he had expanded and reissued. The publication of *Eleonora Duse* was the culmination of a long process of reclaiming her as the superior artist between the two – a process that started immediately after his translations. Symons tried to rescue Duse's individual vision and voice, relegating D'Annunzio to the wings of their dramatic partnership. He now also used Duse's voice to express some cutting criticisms of D'Annunzio as dramatist. For instance, he reported Duse confessing to him in 1900 – that is, in the heyday of their professional involvement – that

[54] Ibid., p. 67.

[55] Symons, 'Introduction' to *Francesca da Rimini*, p. vii.

[56] Symons, 'The Price of Realism', in *Plays, Acting and Music*, pp. 162–6 (p. 164).

D'Annunzio's 'most vital fault' was that he was 'a great lyric poet, but not in the real sense a dramatist'.[57]

Symons himself was ambivalent about seeing the dramas on stage. The first time he saw Duse perform *La città morta* was in Zurich in 1903. Having translated the play into English, he was curious to see what impression it would make in the theatre. Needless to say, he was enchanted by Duse, who brought 'nobility and a kind of intellectual quality' to her role.[58] And he stood firm in his admiration of D'Annunzio's poetic power. But the undistinguished performances of the other actors revealed the technical shortcomings of the dramatist: D'Annunzio, he remarked, 'has transplanted the novel to the stage', and *La città morta* 'is almost more of a poem than a play'.[59] He would have to wait until 1918 to see a production of his English version, when the Stage Society put on *The Dead City* in London's Court Theatre. His unpublished impressions show that Symons was enthralled by the nervous force and androgynous beauty of Robert Farquahrson, who had played Herod in the first English performance (1905) of Wilde's *Salomé* and now was D'Annunzio's Leonardo. He loved how Farquahrson conveyed, undiluted and uncensored, the essence of D'Annunzio's Decadence: 'The passion he has to express, in this drama, is itself an abnormal, an insane thing, and that passion comes to us with all its force and in all its perversity.'[60] The belated stage performance of *The Dead City* in February 1918 was a one-off, taking place in a changed cultural landscape. Now English audiences were less likely to be interested in D'Annunzio's Decadence than, as the reviewer for *The Stage* pointed out, his much publicised war exploits.[61]

While he continued celebrating Duse's genius to ensure her myth would endure undiminished after her death, Symons speculated that D'Annunzio had brought about the suicide of his own genius.[62] In this light, his protracted critical engagement with Duse shows that his translations of D'Annunzio's dramas should also be seen as an attempt to establish an artistic rapport with the actress he passionately believed to be a great creative artist. In this triangular relationship between dramatist, translator and dramatic interpreter,

[57] Symons, *Eleonora Duse* (London: Elkin Mathews, 1926), p. 111.

[58] Ibid., p. 161.

[59] Ibid., p. 161.

[60] Symons, 'The Question of the Dead City', Arthur Symons Papers, Princeton University Library, box 16, folder 3, p. 13.

[61] [Anon.], 'The Stage Society: *The Dead City*', *The Stage* (28 February 1918), p. 16.

[62] Symons, *Eleonora Duse*, p. 126.

Symons's poetic versions of D'Annunzio acted as an equivalent of sorts to Duse's stage performances of the Italian source texts that, if we are to believe Symons's words, they both regarded as artistically flawed. There was also an ulterior motive in all this, for Symons developed the ambition that Duse should one day act in a play of his own. The translator attempted to take on the author's role and substitute himself for D'Annunzio. Knowing about Duse's interest in literature, Symons started to present her with copies of his poems and critical works, including his essays about her.[63] Then, in 1902, as he was translating *Francesca da Rimini*, Symons composed his own Symbolist play, *Tristan and Iseult*, conceived especially for Duse, and which she, according to his account, was 'anxious' to have translated into Italian. After reading a prose version, Duse seems to have promised she would perform Symons's play, and so the text was put into Italian verse by Adolfo de Bosis, a leading exponent of Aestheticism in Italy and translator of P. B. Shelley. According to Symons's account, the play was to have premiered in Italy in 1903 or 1904, with costumes inspired by Robert Engels's illustrations of Joseph Bédiere's edition of *Tristan et Iseult* (1900) and stage scenery by Duilio Cambellotti, who later designed the settings for D'Annunzio's bombastic nationalist play *La nave* (1908).[64] In the end, nothing came of this tantalisingly ambitious plan, and *Tristan and Iseult* was only published, in English, in 1917 with a dedication to Duse – an Italian translation of two of Symons's own verses from the play – channelling a Decadent eroticism with a distinctly Dannunzian flavour:

> Non sentite il sangue delle rose stillare
> Tra le mie dita nelle vostre due mani?[65]

Conclusion

In her essay on Duse, Helen Zimmern was particularly acerbic about D'Annunzio's plays. She tersely noted that Duse 'endeavoured, but with scant success, to make his exquisitely-written, innately-repulsive,

[63] Ibid., p. 86.
[64] Ibid., p. 87.
[65] Arthur Symons, *Tristan and Iseult: A Play in Four Acts* (London: Heinemann, 1917). The English original goes, 'Do you not feel the blood of the roses burn / Between my fingers into both your hands?' (p. 64)

unwholesome and unnatural plays acceptable to the Italian public.'[66] Here was the familiar rhetoric of moral indignation English critics employed regarding D'Annunzio's appeal. But Zimmern drew attention to an ironic circumstance applying specifically to the plays: while even the Neapolitan public (clearly the lowest common denominator of Italian laxness for Zimmern) had received *La Gioconda* with unmitigated indignation, 'Puritan England' greeted the same play with enthusiasm when Duse brought it to the London stage.[67] The blame for this odd anomaly lay with the English audiences' ignorance of the Italian language, which prevented them from balking at the poetic excesses and perverse nuances of the untranslated text.

At the turn of the twentieth century, Symons, like Duse, worked to bring D'Annunzio's 'unnatural plays' to the English. In this process, he took on multiple roles as translator, mediator, critic, poetic peer and at times even competitor. Symons's hyperliteral versions of D'Annunzio's plays helped promote the reception of European Symbolism and Decadence in England, just as they embodied a distinctively Decadent aesthetics of translation based on careful preservation of the foreign literary idiom. It would be impossible to claim that Symons made D'Annunzio into a popular author or even an 'acceptable' one. Nonetheless, his authority and the fact that his translations were produced and received as written literary texts gave them greater freedom, in 'Puritan England', to circulate uncensored among a highly educated minority readership. In the early twentieth century, Symons's attitude toward D'Annunzio's dramatic art became increasingly ambivalent. However, despite his public distancing, he kept following D'Annunzio's evolution with attention and even made versions of *La figlia di Iorio* (1904) and *La fiaccola sotto il moggio* (1905), which have remained unpublished to this day. Pace Zimmern, this may well be the most ironic circumstance in Symons's conflicted engagement with D'Annunzio, given that these two later plays, where Decadent and Symbolist elements have been replaced by a markedly naturalist flavour, were much more successful at the time and later enjoyed a more evenly positive critical reception, at home and internationally.

[66] Zimmern, 'Eleonora Duse', p. 986.
[67] Ibid., p. 986.

Chapter 9

Gabriele D'Annunzio and Karl Gustav Vollmoeller: From Classical Culture to the Attractions of Motor Power

Adriana Vignazia, translated by Stuart Oglethorpe

This chapter considers the German translations undertaken or overseen by Karl Gustav Vollmoeller (1878–1948) and the relationship that developed between him and Gabriele D'Annunzio. Vollmoeller – an archaeologist, poet, dramatist, theatrical innovator, discoverer of new talents and entrepreneur – has received little critical attention, despite his role as screenwriter for *The Blue Angel*, the 1930 film that made Marlene Dietrich famous, and his contribution to the discovery of Josephine Baker.[1] Vollmoeller shared D'Annunzio's interests in theatre, classical culture and motor engines; like the Italian, he embraced the new media, especially cinema. He had a crucial role mediating the reception of D'Annunzio's works in German-speaking countries. By analysing correspondence and publishing contracts conserved in the Vittoriale archive, the Klassik Stiftung in Weimar, the Deutsches Literaturarchiv in Marbach, and the Landesarchiv in Bern, the chapter follows Vollmoeller's career as a translator, highlighting the relationship between his creative writing and translation, his experience of collaborative translation and his efforts to secure work with Max Reinhardt.[2] Finally, it addresses the suspension of authorised translations of D'Annunzio on the eve of the First World War.

[1] For portrayals of Vollmoeller, see Frederik D. Tunnat, *Karl Vollmoeller: Dichter und Kulturmanager. Eine Biographie* (Hamburg: Tredition, 2008); Frederik D. Tunnat, *Karl Vollmoeller: Ein kosmopolitisches Leben im Zeichen des Mirakels* (Hamburg: Tredition, 2008); Klaus Konrad Dillmann, *Dr. Karl Gustav Vollmoeller: Eine Zeitreise durch ein bewegtes Leben* (Heidelberg: Gingko Medien, 2012).

[2] See Adriana Vignazia, *Die deutschen D'Annunzio-Übersetzungen* (Frankfurt a.M.: Peter Lang, 1995).

The Reception of D'Annunzio's Work in German-speaking Countries

D'Annunzio's work was first acclaimed in German-speaking countries some years before Vollmoeller's involvement, thanks to two prominent writers, Hugo von Hofmannsthal (1874–1929) and Stefan George (1868–1933), who lived in the two major centres of Germanic culture – Vienna and Berlin respectively. George had encountered D'Annunzio's writing in Symbolist poetry circles in Paris; in 1891, in Vienna, he discussed him with Hofmannsthal, who in turn introduced him to writers in the 'Jung–Wien' (Young Vienna) group led by Hermann Bahr (1863–1934). More formal recognition came in 1893, when George published translations of three of D'Annunzio's poems in his prestigious review *Blätter für die Kunst* and Hoffmansthal's article 'Gabriele d'Annunzio' appeared in the newspaper *Frankfurter Zeitung* (9 August 1893).[3] Soon after, in December 1894 and January 1895, Bahr published a translation of the short novel *Giovanni Episcopo* in successive numbers of the Viennese review *Die Zeit*, which he founded in 1894.

These first appearances, supplemented by the success of the French translation of *L'Innocente*, interested the Berlin publishing house S. Fischer, which was then opening toward the literatures of southern Europe.[4] The Florentine journalist Ernesto Gagliardi (1854–1933) put Samuel Fischer in touch with D'Annunzio, who then negotiated in French due to his very limited German.[5] Between 1896 and 1902, S. Fischer Verlag published twelve works by D'Annunzio: five novels, a collection of short stories and six plays, which enjoyed great success. In 1901, however, this publishing relationship deteriorated. D'Annunzio was annoyed by the translations, whose quality he considered poor. Moreover, he was not happy with their mid-price editions. Alongside the Pre-Raphaelite artists of the *In arte libertas* movement, and like William Morris and the Kelmscott Press in England, D'Annunzio wanted to rekindle interest in the *liber pictus*

3 Hofmannsthal's article was translated into Italian and then 'corrected' by D'Annunzio himself prior to its publication in the Neapolitan journal *La tavola rotonda*, on 17 December 1893: Roberta Ascarelli, 'Hugo von Hofmannsthals "Gabriele d'Annunzio" in der Übersetzung von Gabriele d'Annunzio', *Hofmannsthal Jahrbuch zur europäischen Moderne*, 3 (1995), 169–213.

4 Peter de Mendelssohn, *S. Fischer und sein Verlag* (Frankfurt a.M.: S. Fischer, 1970), p. 190.

5 See Samuel Fischer and Hedwig Fischer, *Briefwechsel mit Autoren*, ed. by Dierk Rodewald and Corinna Fiedler (Berlin: S. Fischer, 1989), p. 521.

of the Renaissance and saw a book as the sum of its text, paratextual features and publishing format. For the verse tragedy *Francesca da Rimini*, he demanded a verse translation in a deluxe edition, like the Italian one published by Treves. As translators, he suggested that Fischer use poets who had already engaged with his works: George, Paul Heyse (1830–1914) or Hofmannsthal. On 19 February 1902, Fischer wrote to George, offering to send him the drafts of the book.[6] In a letter the following month, however, he advised D'Annunzio both against the choice of George as translator, because his 'pallid verse' would not adapt well to the poet's 'vigorous and powerful' poetry, and against the adoption of an elitist publishing practice that would limit the number of copies to between 300–400 and be prohibitively expensive. As an alternative, Fischer suggested a young and promising poet with a good knowledge of Italian and Dante: Karl Gustav Vollmoeller.[7]

Early Contact between D'Annunzio and Vollmoeller

Born in Stockholm into a large and wealthy Protestant family of clothing manufacturers sensitive to the social problems caused by industrialisation and open to culture, Karl Gustav had a varied and polished education: his father, first a merchant and then a manufacturer, taught him to treat business with exactitude and perseverance; his uncle Karl Vollmoeller, a medievalist, philologist and professor of Romance languages and English, educated him in the Humanities; and his tutor Karl Bauer, a painter and poet, helped foster his artistic inclinations. His family's social network was advantageous, bringing him into contact with prominent figures. Through Bauer he met Stefan George, who welcomed Vollmoeller into his elite circle and in 1897 published five of his poems in *Blätter für die Kunst*; these were subsequently included in Vollmoeller's first poetry collection *Parcival – Die frühen Gärten*.[8] Subsequently, George published other works, including his play *Catherina Gräfin von Armagnac und ihre beiden Liebhaber* (Catherina, Countess of Armagnac, and Her Two Lovers). Hofmannsthal wrote to George praising the subtle and

[6] S. Fischer to S. George, in Fischer and Fischer, *Briefwechsel*, p. 1008.

[7] S. Fischer to D'Annunzio, in Fischer and Fischer, *Briefwechsel*, p. 527.

[8] 'Als ein Prolog', 'Odysseus', 'Parcival', 'Herbstphantasie' and 'Am Ende', *Blätter für die Kunst*, 4th ser., 1–2 (1897), 39–46.

empathic characterisation in Vollmoeller's work.[9] It is not clear when Vollmoeller first met D'Annunzio; it may have been during one of his long stays in Italy for his health, or perhaps in January 1898 in Paris, where D'Annunzio stayed three weeks for the first performance of *La ville morte*. This play made such an impression on Vollmoeller that a few months later he decided to visit Greece with the poet Max Dauthendey (1867–1918). On his return he enrolled in the Faculty of Archaeology and Classical Philology at the University of Berlin and Bonn, took part in the excavations around Thebes and in Turkey overseen by Paul Wolters, and graduated with a thesis entitled 'Griechische Kammergräber mit Totenbetten' (Greek Burial Chambers with Funerary Couches) in 1901. That same year, D'Annunzio invited him to the opening of *Francesca da Rimini* at the Teatro Costanzi in Rome, on 9 December. Despite the play's mixed reception by the public and negative verdicts from the critics, Vollmoeller liked it, seeing parallels with his own verse tragedy *Catherina Gräfin von Armagnac*, set in the Middle Ages. Thus, while negotiations over the choice of a translator were under way, D'Annunzio and Vollmoeller were already establishing a bond of friendship.

In 1902, influenced by D'Annunzio's aesthetic and typographical choices, Vollmoeller presented his poetry collection *Parcival – Die frühen Gärten* with D'Annunzio's publisher Treves, in German and in a deluxe edition; in this and other early works, he opted for Latin lettering rather than the Gothic normally used for German-language authors.[10] More specifically, he adopted the same lettering that had been used for *Francesca da Rimini*, made available to him by Treves, for the printing of *Catherina Gräfin von Armagnac*, *Assues Fitne und Sumurud* and *Der deutsche Graf*, published in 1903, 1904 and 1906 respectively by S. Fischer.[11] The first two of these plays have the same extravagant layout as *Francesca da Rimini*. Dedicated to love, faithfulness and their inevitable tragic consequences, they illustrate D'Annunzio's influence on a thematic level. Even before translating the Italian poet, Vollmoeller had therefore come under his sway both as a person and as a writer.

[9] *Blätter für die Kunst*, 4th ser., 5 (1899), 137–40; 5th ser., 1 (1900–1), 65–92; Hofmannsthal to George, 18 June 1902, in Stefan George, *Briefwechsel zwischen George und Hofmannsthal*, 2nd edn (Munich: Küpper, 1953), p. 157.

[10] In Germany, the print alphabet had acquired national meaning and connotations of protest, with the use of Gothic ('Fraktur') lettering used for German authors and others in Latin ('Antiqua') lettering.

[11] D'Annunzio to Vollmoeller, 19 November 1902. *Francesca da Rimini* uses the 'Venetian Renaissance Antiqua' (or 'Humanist') font.

The First Translation: *Francesca da Rimini*

At the end of March 1903, with negotiations concluded, Vollmoeller started translating *Francesca da Rimini*, which he completed that autumn. His contract with Fischer, signed in mid-May, was unusual in regard to both the high payment and the freedom he was granted to cut the text with a view to future staging. Similar conditions also featured in later translation contracts signed by Vollmoeller, so it is worth pausing to elaborate key facets here. Clause 2 guaranteed remuneration for the translator's work with a down payment of 1,000 marks, deducted from future royalties from book sales at 10 per cent of the cover price. D'Annunzio was also to get 10 per cent, but without any guaranteed sum. Clause 3 set out an equal division between author and translator of the proceeds from performances in which Vollmoeller's translation was used. Clause 4 anticipated that Vollmoeller would prepare a stage version that could also appear in *Neue deutsche Rundschau*, the publisher's journal.[12] For this shorter version, the fee would be 100 marks 'per folio', to be divided between author and translator, 'in the instance that D'Annunzio does not surrender his share to Sig. Vollmoeller'. The phrase suggests that payment for this work might well go to the translator alone, perhaps acknowledging that the cuts would be his decision and confirming his creative independence in recreating the text in the target language and culture.[13]

The elevated cost of translations characterised the relationship between D'Annunzio and Vollmoeller from the start. This provided a marked contrast to the approach of the French translator Georges Hérelle, who in 1892 had accepted a three-way division of revenues, and who had offered his translation of *La ville morte* to D'Annunzio out of friendship.[14]

The correspondence between D'Annunzio and Vollmoeller shows that differences emerged in their conceptions of theatre, illustrated by their discussion of oversize initial lettering. D'Annunzio gave staging and set design the 'rank of an independent aesthetic object', as Katia Lara Angioletti puts it, and therefore saw the stage directions

[12] Gabriele D'Annunzio, 'Francesca da Rimini', trans. by Karl Gustav Vollmoeller, *Neue deutsche Rundschau*, 14 (1903), 1063–101, 1167–212.

[13] Vollmoeller to D'Annunzio, 9 October 1910, in Vignazia, *Übersetzungen*, p. 115. Translations in this chapter from Italian are by Stuart Oglethorpe, those from German sources are by Adriana Vignazia and Stuart Oglethorpe.

[14] See Gabriele D'Annunzio and Georges Hérelle, *Carteggio D'Annunzio – Hérelle*, ed. by Mario Cimini (Lanciano: Carabba, 2004), pp. 103, 426–7.

as crucially important.[15] To highlight them at the beginning of each act, in a letter of 2 June 1902 he asked Vollmoeller to specify the five initial letters so that he could have large dies made. Vollmoeller, who believed that the play's text was more important, advised against this, suggesting as a model his own *Catherina*, which had the stage directions printed in smaller lettering. A final indication of Vollmoeller's freedom is his suggestion to D'Annunzio that George should be asked to translate the opening poem dedicated to Eleonora Duse, ostensibly because of its difficulty; this may have been an attempt to repair his deteriorating relations with George by giving him work that had initially been offered to himself. After George turned this down, the poem was replaced by a wood engraving by Adolfo de Carolis (1874–1928), the illustrator and set designer for *Francesca da Rimini* in 1901, with a dedication to Duse. The book was printed in late 1903.

The translation met with critical acclaim because Vollmoeller had managed to find a sympathetic style in which the sound and structure of the German language adapted well to the original text. The book was not a publishing success, however, as theatres were reluctant to stage the play due to challenges the costly set designs and large cast presented.[16] From a letter from Vollmoeller to D'Annunzio dated 9 July 1910, we know that by then just 786 copies had been sold; *Francesca da Rimini* only appears in the publisher's record of receipts in 1909, showing revenues of 237.70 marks. The first performances in German took place in Freiburg's Stadttheater on 10 and 20 February 1914, enjoying modest success with the audience.

In his translation, Vollmoeller adapted the text to the culture of the target audience by reducing the level of erudition, which had been judged counterproductive by both Italian and German critical opinion.[17] Removing the paratexts – the ode to Eleonora Duse; Dante's sonnet 'A tutti i fedeli d'amore' and D'Annunzio's sonnet in reply, 'Paolo Malatesta A Dante Alighieri'; the concluding *canzone* 'Commiato' (Leave-taking) – deprived the German edition of the game of mirrors between reality and invention that was in the original, uprooting the work from its cultural context and pushing the love story into the spotlight. The largest cuts occurred in the stage

[15] Katia Lara Angioletti, '"Quando io venni in Italia, vinsi perché ero solo": Mario Fumagalli attore, capocomico, innovatore', *ACME. Annali della Facoltà di Lettere e Filosofia dell'Università degli Studi di Milano*, 64: 3 (2011), 117–36 (p. 123).

[16] Fischer to D'Annunzio, 23 January 1904, in Vignazia, *Übersetzungen*, p. 30.

[17] For example: 'Francesca da Rimini' [review], *Neue deutsche Rundschau*, 13 (1902), 555.

version, shortening the duration of the performance, but there were also cuts to the theatrical text. These principally affect scenes peripheral to the central plot, and can be seen, in quantitative terms, in Act I, Scene 1: the original text has 367 lines and half-lines, the full German text 305, and the stage version 76. Jokes among Francesca's women and the court jester were removed, as are vulgar references and the list of historical fables and poetry in fashion in thirteenth-century Italy, while the songs and the girls' dances, a choreographic element sure to be well received, were retained. The translation also adjusted lines whose meaning or purpose might not be clear.

These decisions demonstrate Vollmoeller's awareness of issues related to theatrical performance. He had been persuaded of the need to reform theatre – at the time directed at a narrow bourgeois audience seated well away from the stage – by spending time with D'Annunzio and Duse, who envisioned a theatre of myth and poetry, in the open air, where a large audience would come together to celebrate a ritual and a people's festival. D'Annunzio was not yet prepared to make any concessions to the audience in terms of the comprehensibility of the text, length of the performance, or logic of character development and plot, because he believed that the audience should take responsibility for rising to the level of his poetry.[18] Vollmoeller, by contrast, aimed to make the performance successful by streamlining the text and making it comprehensible. His knowledge of archaeology and classical culture, in which theatre had a cathartic function for its large audiences, prompted him to think about restructuring the theatrical space to draw in a bigger audience, bringing it close to the stage and involving it emotionally with the music, songs and dances. For Vollmoeller, theatre involved a quest for the right actors, who were expected to play a central role, and commercial organisation of all related activity. His concept of theatre thus clashed with the ideas of not only D'Annunzio but also George, for whom theatre was essentially about its spoken lines and liturgical nature: plays should be read before a small audience, not aimed at making money, emphasising comprehension of the text and giving no ground to the performative tradition of actors.[19] In a letter to Hofmannsthal dated

[18] D'Annunzio's approach would change in the 1920s, with the establishment of the Istituto Nazionale per le Rappresentazioni dei Drammi di Gabriele d'Annunzio.

[19] Franziska Merlin, *Stefan Georges moderne Klassik. Die 'Blätter für die Kunst' und die Erneuerung des Dramas* (Wurzburg: Ergon, 2014), pp. 64–5.

22 November 1903, Vollmoeller said that theatre was his priority, while he was only giving intermittent attention to writing verse.[20]

Vollmoeller's vision was shared by Max Reinhardt (1873–1943), with whom he collaborated throughout his life. Reinhardt and his brother Edmund had previously established a company for independent theatre management, without any public subsidy, using advertising, investors and the involvement of newspapers and reviews.[21] In 1905, Reinhardt acquired the Deutsches Theater in Berlin; this gave him the freedom to try out new forms of staging, involving technical innovations such as the revolving stage and novel ways of using light, music, dance and aromas. This theatre appealed to its audiences on many fronts, stirring their imagination and emotions. Thanks to Vollmoeller's persistent efforts to persuade him, Reinhardt agreed to perform Greek tragedies in modern translations and in a new space: the circus, a modern version of the classical theatre, where the involvement of a large number of walk-on actors and audience members allowed for a performance much like a popular festival, with a new relationship between the stage and the public involving the latter more directly. In Vollmoeller's view, D'Annunzio's plays were well suited to Reinhardt's repertoire and creative direction.

The Publisher Insel and Vollmoeller's Collaboration with Rudolf von Binding

The resumption of translation of D'Annunzio's works into German between 1908 and 1912 needs to be seen in relation to the developments in theatre discussed above. The publisher was Insel Verlag of Leipzig, which wanted the books it produced to be a harmonious ensemble of text, typography, illustration and paper, but pursued a somewhat idealistic approach to publishing. Unlike Samuel Fischer, Insel's director Anton Kippenberg (1874–1950) rejected recourse to advertising methods in the belief that a book should establish itself in the market on the basis of its own strengths. It was Vollmoeller

[20] Vollmoeller to Hofmannsthal, 22 November 1903, in Hans Peter Buohler (ed.), 'Briefwechsel zwischen Karl Gustav Vollmoeller und Hugo von Hofmannsthal', *Hofmannsthal Jahrbuch zur europäischen Moderne*, 18 (2010), 105–37 (p. 123).

[21] See Christopher Balme, 'Die Marke Reinhardt. Theater als moderne Wirtschaftsunternehmen', in *Max Reinhardt und das deutsche Theater*, ed. by Roland Koberg, Bernd Stegemann and Henrike Thomsen (Berlin: Henschel, 2005), pp. 41–9.

who conducted negotiations with Insel, and the contract, signed by D'Annunzio on 26 August 1909, has interesting features including assigning the role of impresario to Vollmoeller. It authorised him to represent D'Annunzio's interests in Germany, granting him the right to publish the novel *Forse che sì, forse che no* and the plays *La nave* and *Fedra* in instalments in reviews, either as unabridged texts or as selected episodes; furthermore, it guaranteed Vollmoeller payment of 1,200 marks for each of the three works to be translated and D'Annunzio 4,000 lire for these works on signature of the contract, to be set against proceeds from the performance royalties and the sale of books. The contract provided for the involvement of another translator, if acceptable to the three parties, and the right of the publisher and translator, either together or independently, to exercise options on *La figlia di Iorio*, *La fiaccola sotto il moggio* and *Più che l'amore*, which had all been published in Italy already. Vollmoeller, collaborative by nature, was very different from the stereotypical solitary artist or writer. He was happy to help from behind the scenes; he could recognise the potential of artists who were just starting out and would put them in touch with people who could further their career. He did this with Reinhardt, for instance, contributing to his success by persuading him to adopt new spaces for staging plays, an idea that had come from his own archaeological studies.

This spirit, along with his lack of time for translation in verse, brought Vollmoeller to collaborate with Rudolf von Binding (1867–1938). A lawyer by training, Binding had met D'Annunzio in Italy in 1907, and the poet had entrusted him to translate the lyrical prose piece 'La resurrezione del centauro'.[22] Once back in Germany he published the short piece in June 1909 with Insel, along with his translation of D'Annunzio's poem 'La morte del cervo', and with a novice's enthusiasm he started work on *La nave*, offering this to Insel and to various theatres. Vollmoeller, as D'Annunzio's representative in Germany, had Kippenberg send him a sample of work to establish whether Binding, a literary unknown, had talent and was interested in collaborating.[23] Once their mutual mistrust had been overcome, the two men agreed to work together revising the translation of *La nave*, which Binding thought was 'a strong piece' if suitably staged.[24]

[22] Rudolf G. Binding, *Erlebtes Leben*, in *Gesammeltes Werk*, vol. 2 (Hamburg: Dulk, 1954), pp. 396–7.

[23] Vollmoeller to Kippenberg, 6 April 1909, in Vignazia, *Übersetzungen*, pp. 72–3.

[24] Binding to Vollmoeller, 10 June 1909, ibid., p. 77.

For Binding, who still had little experience and came from outside the worlds of performance and publishing, collaboration with Vollmoeller was undoubtedly a help. Sharing the work and the profits with someone of talent was also convenient for Vollmoeller, who at that point had far too much to do: he was busy translating the *Oresteia*, staging of his own *Catherina*, and with international motor rallies to test and publicise the cars he had improved and was producing at the Italian factory Züst, which he jointly owned. The partnership between Binding and Vollmoeller was therefore presented to D'Annunzio as a product of circumstances.[25] The two of them met in September to work together on the translation of *La nave*, which was sent to the publisher in late October. The return of the proofs was delayed by three months, probably due to the firm's concerns about the play's nationalistic content at a time when Germany was seeking to strengthen its navy, while in Austria voices of alarm were being raised over the literary glorification of Italian expansionism in the Adriatic.[26] The volume went on sale at the beginning of June 1910. In view of the interest shown by the Deutsches Theater, Vollmoeller and Binding decided to pursue the same process with *Fedra*; while Binding thought the play weak, in Vollmoeller's view the potential returns when staged made it interesting, and it sat neatly within the literary trend that saw Greek mythology symbolically pitted against modern society. With D'Annunzio's approval, the translation of *Fedra* began in the autumn of 1909, was revised in April 1910, and then sent to Kippenberg in mid-May.[27] The first proofs were printed in June, and by 5 September the book was ready for sale. In order to support Binding, who was keen to make his name in the literary world, and in recognition of Binding's greater input, Vollmoeller ceded his right to appear as the co-translator of *La nave*, and with *Fedra* played down his own involvement with the formula 'Unter der Mitwirkung von' (with the collaboration of).

[25] Vollmoeller to D'Annunzio, 20 October 1909, in Vignazia, *Übersetzungen*, p. 78.

[26] Piero Violante, 'Il navalismo di Otto Hintze', in Otto Hintze, *Stato e esercito*, ed. by Piero Volante (Palermo: Flaccovio, 1991), pp. 53–92; Leopold Freiherr von Chlumecky, 'Politische Dramen – Dramatische Politik', *Österreichische Rundschau*, 14 (1908), 239–44 (p. 244).

[27] Vollmoeller to D'Annunzio, 20 October 1909, in Vignazia, *Übersetzungen*, p. 78.

Flight and Literary Production: *Forse che sì, forse che no* and *Wieland*

D'Annunzio's novel *Forse che sì forse che no* was something of a literary innovation, in that it incorporated his passion for flight. This was something he shared with Vollmoeller, who had thrown himself into constructing aeroplane prototypes with his brother Hans, had acquired his pilot's licence, and in 1909 had been with D'Annunzio at the air show at Brescia discussed in the novel. The novel's drafting and translation took place in extreme conditions: D'Annunzio started to write it in the autumn of 1909 and wanted it published simultaneously in Italy, France and Germany. Vollmoeller translated each part as soon as he received the author's corrected proofs, the last batch of which was delivered to him at the sanatorium in Davos, and by June 1910 the German proofs were ready. Vollmoeller had promised D'Annunzio, who at the time was besieged by creditors, that he would maximise the financial return, and therefore considered publishing the novel in instalments and in different publications at the same time, the best options being the Viennese *Neue Freie Presse* and the *Berliner Tageblatt*. This plan could not be realised because, firstly, these publications had already planned their content for 1910 and, secondly, Kippenberg wanted to publish the novel that autumn in order to make the most of the Christmas market. Binding also advised against waiting, given that a literary treatment of the theme of flying was something completely new.[28] The novel's protagonist, Paolo Tarsis, was a modern hero who did not dissipate his energies in aesthetic, psychological or philosophical considerations, but channelled them into technology, engines and efficiency, foreshadowing the futurist aesthetic. In consequence, Vollmoeller wrote to D'Annunzio on 20 July listing his attempts with fifteen German and Austrian publications and advising him to accept the compromise the publisher was offering: payment for nine editions of the novel rather than six, as compensation for the loss from not publishing it in instalments. By 13 September, the book was ready.[29] Before leaving again for Davos, Vollmoeller looked for newspapers and periodicals prepared to publish a full review of the novel, identifying the *Berliner Tageblatt* and the *Frankfurter Zeitung*. By November the novel was selling well, although ten thousand copies needed to be purchased if the publisher's expenditure was to be matched.

[28] Binding to Vollmoeller, 17 January 1910, in Vignazia, *Übersetzungen*, p. 89.
[29] Vignazia, *Übersetzungen*, pp. 90–3.

As with *Francesca da Rimini*, Vollmoeller's translation only reduced the elements of erudition; there were no cuts to passages that might have offended people's sense of decency, a frequent fate of D'Annunzio's texts. In the rush to publish, the novel was printed using Gothic lettering, unlike the two plays.

The flying experience and translation of the novel encouraged Vollmoeller to write the poem 'Volare necesse est', a hymn to the technological progress that allows fulfilment of the human dream of flight, and the play *Wieland: Märchen in drei Akten* (Wieland: A Fable in Three Acts), inspired by an unfinished opera by Wagner and based on the epic Germanic tale of the eponymous blacksmith.[30] In this text, started in 1909 and published by Insel in 1911, Vollmoeller unites classical and literary themes with modern ones: the myth of flight and the saga of aircraft construction, the first flight across the English Channel and the unscrupulousness of journalists and editors.

Projects for Max Reinhardt and the First Misunderstandings

In the lulls during translation of *Forse che sì forse che no*, Vollmoeller, while a patient in the Davos sanatorium, wanted to prepare more of D'Annunzio's works to present to Reinhardt for performance. With this in mind, he suggested that Kippenberg publish *La figlia di Iorio*, a play that had been very successful in Italy, and *Più che l'amore*, a modern tragedy from 1906.[31] The publisher reluctantly agreed to take on production of the latter when Vollmoeller decided to exercise his option independently.[32] D'Annunzio was unhappy with the contract drawn up in May 1910 because it failed to respect the norm of parity between author and translator: the net profit was to be split evenly, but set against this were guaranteed sums of 700 marks for the translator and only 350 for D'Annunzio. The contract was only signed in early July, when one of Vollmoeller's brothers went to Paris to meet the poet. To explain his actions, Vollmoeller wrote D'Annunzio two letters, dated 9 July 1910, which are in Vollmoeller's family archive

[30] For 'Volare necesse est', see Karl Vollmoeller, *Gedichte. Eine Auswahl*, ed. by Herbert Steiner (Marbach a.N.: Schiller Nationalmuseum, 1960), pp. 7–11.

[31] Vollmoeller to D'Annunzio, 20 October 1909, in Vignazia, *Übersetzungen*, p. 78.

[32] *Più che l'amore* was not printed in book form and does not appear in the publisher's catalogues.

and may therefore never have been sent.[33] In the first and slightly abrupt letter, Vollmoeller set out his conception of the task of translating and promoting D'Annunzio's works. As the author had already earned money from the original version, any proceeds from translations were a bonus that derived from the work of the translator and publisher; the translator, Vollmoeller argued, ought to have some guaranteed sum for the often complex work undertaken, to be set against his percentage share of the actual profit, which would as always be divided between author and translator. In the second and more conciliatory letter, Vollmoeller explained the twofold nature of the translator's work: first, the full translation, and second, editing and adapting the play for the stage, as earnings would only be generated by its performance. The production of two versions justified doubling the guaranteed payment for the translator. Leaving the decision about withdrawal from the contract to D'Annunzio, he regretted that he could not talk to him in person as he was confined to his bed. These two letters are crucial to understanding their subsequent disagreements about the translation of *Le Martyre de Saint Sébastien*.

Le Martyre de Saint Sébastien: Collaboration with Gustav Schneeli

Le Martyre de Saint Sébastien, D'Annunzio's mystery play in French verse with incidental music by Debussy, opened on 21 May 1911 in Paris, at the Théâtre du Châtelet; the ballerina Ida Rubinstein (1885–1960) appeared as the saint in her first ever pure acting role. The evening was a success, but according to Kippenberg, who attended the performance, this was thanks to the staging, cast, music and interest drummed up by the press. To him, the play itself seemed boring, and he therefore declined to publish it.[34] Vollmoeller, by contrast, was convinced that if Reinhardt had staged it in a circus, with large crowds in attendance, its enduring merits would have been clear; his positive experience with his translation of the *Oresteia*, performed this way some three years earlier, supported this belief. At the time, Vollmoeller was also working on *Das Mirakel*, a sort of religious mime show, which was first performed in London on 23 December 1911; in this multi-faceted performance, music by Engelbert Humperdinck enhanced the spectators' experience, helping

[33] Vignazia, *Übersetzungen*, pp. 115 and 309.
[34] Kippenberg to Vollmoeller, 15 June 1911, ibid., p. 120.

them understand the action on stage by fleshing out the locations, characters and events.[35] The great success enjoyed by this show, whose lack of spoken dialogue meant that it could easily be put on in different European cities and across the Atlantic, encouraged Vollmoeller to repeat the experience with D'Annunzio's piece. *Das Mirakel* and *Le Martyre* had much in common: both works had a medieval setting, they appealed to the audience's Christian sentiments, and the involvement of many walk-on parts and music presented a collective cultural experience much like that of the theatres of the ancient world.

Vollmoeller contacted Fischer, and on 30 June 1911 they both signed a contract; as usual, this only specified a down payment for the translator, to be set against the royalties from the performance, which would be divided equally between him and the author.[36] The following July, Gustav Schneeli (1872–1944), a painter, art historian and diplomat, contacted Vollmoeller offering to translate *Le Martyre*. Very busy with his own work, Vollmoeller hoped to match his experience with Binding. In late August 1911, once Schneeli's skills in verse translation had been confirmed, the two men worked together on revision of the text he had produced so far. Their correspondence generated discussion of some problems of translation and led to Schneeli's request that Vollmoeller introduce him to the publishing and theatrical worlds. That October, publication of a catalogue celebrating the twenty-fifth anniversary of the foundation of S. Fischer Verlag, which included a scene from *Le Martyre*, provided an opportunity to inform D'Annunzio of the work's translation. On 13 December 1911, Vollmoeller wrote to the poet from London, stating that this had already been completed by Schneeli and was now with Fischer; he apologised for his recent limited contact, due to his heavy workload and the recent death of his father, which had forced him to take on greater responsibilities with the family firm's board of directors.[37] Praising Schneeli's work, and reminding D'Annunzio of his previous attempts to introduce the poet to Reinhardt, he invited him to London to see the latter at work and to attend rehearsals. The personal contact and discussion, Vollmoeller hoped, would

[35] Julien Segol, '*Das Mirakel*: une cathédrale pour la modernité', in *Max Reinhardt. L'Art et la technique à la conquête de l'espace* (Bern: Peter Lang, 2017), pp. 85–103.

[36] The contract of 30 June, signed by Samuel Fischer and Vollmoeller, is in the Vittoriale archive; the same contract, with D'Annunzio's signature added on August 1912, is in the Deutsches Literaturarchiv. See D: Vollmoeller, Karl Gustav (Mappe 32).

[37] Tunnat, *Biographie*, pp. 200–1.

move matters forward. The letter seems to contain a veiled reproach over the scant interest that D'Annunzio had shown toward developments in contemporary theatre – according to Guy Tosi, D'Annunzio showed little interest in work by most other artists unless it was relevant to his current plans.[38] Meanwhile, the draft translation had not been prepared because the contract still lacked D'Annunzio's signature, something that made Schneeli nervous. It was only the personal involvement of Count Harry Kessler (1868–1937), a writer, patron of the arts and diplomat who attended the opening night of *Le Martyre*, which seems to have helped resolve the impasse. At the end of May 1912, he and Vollmoeller managed to bring D'Annunzio and Reinhardt together; he then introduced the poet to Schneeli, who in turn set up a meeting between D'Annunzio, Reinhardt and Alexander Moissi, the actor likely to play the saint in the German version. In June, Schneeli and Vollmoeller worked on stage versions of both *Le Martyre* and *Fedra*.

However, there was a problem with the contract that led to tensions and ultimately caused Reinhardt to lose interest in collaboration. Reconstruction of the actual sequence of events presents difficulties, because the letters and telegrams that survive offer contradictory information. One issue was certainly the guaranteed payment that Vollmoeller requested for the translator (or translators) alone. At any rate, in August 1912, D'Annunzio signed the contract.[39] However, from a letter that he wrote to D'Annunzio, dated 2 September, it would seem that some sort of dispute developed between Vollmoeller and Fischer, and from a subsequent letter, of 4 October, it appears that Vollmoeller had advised Schneeli to withdraw his translation and instead approach Erich Reiss, a close friend of Reinhardt and director of a publishing house in Berlin. Schneeli signed a contract with Reiss that provided for a guaranteed payment of 900 marks, to be divided between the author (50 per cent), Vollmoeller and himself (25 per cent each); however, writing to D'Annunzio, he accused Vollmoeller of trying to exploit the poet's work.[40] D'Annunzio confirmed his approval by telegram. Vollmoeller had no way of terminating the previous contract with Fischer; no justification for the new one was offered by D'Annunzio; nor was it possible to meet him in Paris.

[38] Guy Tosi, 'Les relations de D'Annunzio dans le monde du théâtre en France', *Quaderni dannunziani*, 6–7 (1957), 36–59 (pp. 36–7).

[39] D'Annunzio to Vollmoeller, undated but after 11 August 1912. See Vignazia, *Übersetzungen*, pp. 109–10, 128.

[40] Schneeli to D'Annunzio, 13 October 1912, ibid., pp. 130–1.

So Vollmoeller returned to London at the end of October to continue working on other projects, including the production of *Das Mirakel* (Vienna, 1912), the film *The Miracle* (London, 1912) and the play *A Venetian Night* (London 1912).[41] D'Annunzio's decision, although understandable in light of Vollmoeller's sometimes inconsistent behaviour and the high cost of his work, demonstrates that D'Annunzio and Schneeli did not fully understand Vollmoeller's role in the complex organisation of performances by Reinhardt's company. Furthermore, it had fateful consequences: when Count Kessler visited Vollmoeller in London in November, hoping to discuss the funding and staging of *Fedra* and *Le Martyre*, he learned to his surprise that Reinhardt was no longer interested.

The situation became even more complicated. In November, with Reiss's support, Schneeli resorted to the German courts; Vollmoeller, hoping that D'Annunzio would entrust him with the next novel, backed down, accepting responsibility for 'financial and moral' damages.[42] S. Fischer, which had a signed contract, would not give way. The case was resolved in February 1913; the translation of *Le Martyre de Saint Sébastien* was published by Reiss at the end of that year, but it never reached the stage in Germany. From the surviving correspondence, there is no evidence that Schneeli engaged in seeking reviews or a performance, leaving these matters in the publisher's hands.[43] Perhaps because of his lack of experience, he also passed up a proposal from Georg Müller, in Munich, that he become D'Annunzio's exclusive publisher in Germany when the current contracts expired.[44]

The Final Translations and Contact between D'Annunzio and Vollmoeller after the Great War

Contact between Vollmoeller and D'Annunzio became less frequent but did not cease. The novel that D'Annunzio was intending to write, *L'uomo che rubò la 'Gioconda'* (The Man who Stole the Mona Lisa), took the Louvre theft of 1911 as its inspiration. Hoping for more promotional success than with *Forse che sì forse che no*, Vollmoeller

[41] Telegrams from Vollmoeller to D'Annunzio, 22 and 27 October 1912, *Übersetzungen*, p. 130.

[42] See the draft telegram from Vollmoeller to D'Annunzio, dated 6 February 1913, in Vignazia, *Übersetzungen*, pp. 133–4.

[43] Schneeli to D'Annunzio, 14 December 1913, ibid., p. 134.

[44] Ibid., p. 145.

started to involve reviews and publishing houses in this project, opening up the possibility that the novel would be printed in instalments in three different languages at the same time, in the *Corriere della Sera*, *Revue de Paris* and *Berliner Illustrierte Zeitung*. The German translation was to be issued in book form by the Berlin publisher Ullstein.[45] Wisely, however, the drafting of any contract was set aside until delivery of the initial chapters. And indeed, the novel was never written; all that emerged was a film script, which was first published in 1920 as a supplement in the Parisian newspaper *Excelsior*.[46]

Vollmoeller's final translation dealt with the captions for *Cabiria*, an epic silent film set in Carthage in the third century BC, directed by Giovanni Pastrone and produced by the Turin company Itala Film.[47] D'Annunzio played a limited part: he suggested the film's title, gave the name 'Maciste' to the male hero and wrote the captions, which were published in their own booklet and given to the audience on arrival. In a letter dated 7 February 1914, he approached Vollmoeller about a translation into German. Both the Italian and German versions of the booklets were published in Milan by Bertieri & Vanzetti, a company known for its meticulous typographical design. They thus display the same features: wood engravings on the cover and at the start of each section, initial letters in red, the same layout and capital letters throughout. The translator's name does not appear. The film premiered at the end of April and was a great success, both in Italy and worldwide; but in Germany and Austria it was blocked by the censors and then banned when Italy entered the war. The German premiere only took place in 1920, in Berlin, when it did well both critically and at the box office.[48]

The outbreak of the war put a stop to publishing relationships. D'Annunzio's interventionism was condemned by both S. Fischer Verlag and Kippenberg, who for several years refused to issue his works.[49] Vollmoeller, whose cultural education rendered him averse to nationalism and conflict, took an 'anti-war' position, countering official rhetoric with soberly realistic articles from the front in Flanders. He then began working on secret missions, including efforts to convince Italy and the United States not to enter the war

45 See the telegram from Vollmoeller to D'Annunzio, dated 6 February 1913.

46 Paolo Alatri, *D'Annunzio* (Turin: UTET, 1983), p. 342.

47 No contracts or other correspondence about this translation survive.

48 Margot Berthold (ed.), *Cabiria. Ein Film von Giovanni Pastrone. Entstehung Geschichte Wirkung Materialien* (Munich: Münchener Filmzentrum, 1979).

49 Vignazia, *Übersetzungen*, pp. 31–2, 61.

against Germany, and to counteract the savage anti-German propaganda appearing in their press and cinema. His idealistic and consensus-based political thinking prompted him to establish Deutsche Gesellschaft 1914, a society joined by figures from the worlds of culture and politics, whose purpose was to preserve internal unity and social peace during the war and to encourage debate and the inclusion of all citizens and elites in the life of each German state. This explains his decision in 1924 to join the Pan-Europa movement promoted by Count Richard von Coudenhove-Kalergi, the precursor of today's European Union.

When the war concluded, Vollmoeller was able to return to Italy, and he established one of his residences in Venice, at the Palazzo Vendramin; he transformed this into a meeting place for international artists, frequented by his friends and open to anyone who needed help with emigration to the United States or Palestine. His contact with D'Annunzio resumed and they were frequently in touch whenever Vollmoeller was in Italy. Since they generally communicated by telegraph, there are not many letters. One of these is dated 22 July 1924: D'Annunzio wrote to Vollmoeller asking him if he might want to translate 'as has been suggested to me, my recent book'. The letter does not specify the book in question, but it was probably *Le Faville del maglio*, the first part of which was published in July 1924. The reply from Vollmoeller, who was busy staging *The Miracle* with Reinhardt in the United States and working on screenplays, has not survived, but the correspondence between him and Rudolf Kommer, one of Reinhardt's associates, shows that he wanted to involve D'Annunzio in another project. Vollmoeller wrote to Kemmer 'I will do all I can to convince D'Annunzio' and reassured him 'we are in touch every day'.[50] The project was probably the staging of *Le Chèvrefeuille*, which Reinhardt had requested a second time in March 1924.[51] After the war, however, D'Annunzio seems to have had little interest in translations into German, because after his involvement with Vollmoeller lapsed he did not look for other translators, nor did he accept any translation requests from Austria or Germany, not even one in 1928 from S. Fischer, which wanted to publish *Il compagno dagli occhi senza cigli*. The translations of the post-war period, for example one of *Notturno* published in Vienna in 1922, were not authorised.

[50] Österreichische Nationalbibliothek: Autograph 522/20–12, letter to Kommer dated 1 August 1924, p. 3.

[51] Vignazia, *Übersetzungen*, p. 167.

Conclusions

The relationship between Gabriele D'Annunzio and Karl Gustav Vollmoeller appears to have been one of equality between two sophisticated and modern writers and poets, who were classical enthusiasts but also open to innovations in technique, and who expected to earn a living from their activity. While initially it was D'Annunzio who inspired Vollmoeller in some of his life choices and aesthetic decisions, only a few years later Vollmoeller had taken on the role of a modern-day cultural entrepreneur in dealings with D'Annunzio, involving himself in promoting his friend's work. As D'Annunzio had little German, he could not follow the translation step by step; this allowed Vollmoeller, and subsequently Binding and Schneeli, to take liberties not permitted to their French counterparts. On the one hand, the adaptation of D'Annunzio's texts for the German context can be seen as the 'domestication' of his works; on the other, Vollmoeller should be recognised for his efforts to pursue their success in German theatres, and for wanting to bring D'Annunzio and Max Reinhardt together.

The reasons for D'Annunzio's apparent loss of interest in translations into German after the war can only be guessed at. He may have been influenced by the initial hostility of the German-speaking world, indicated by the harsh criticism of Hofmannsthal and Thomas Mann.[52] His decision to align himself with 'the Latin race' against Austria and Germany likely also played a role. Moreover, he withdrew to the Vittoriale after his wartime political adventures had concluded; there, his energies were focused on editing his own oeuvre for publication as his 'Collected Works', and on new stagings directed by Giovacchino Forzano. Mussolini's generous funding had eliminated his financial worries, leaving him even less inclined to surrender to the distraction of new projects. Reinhardt and Vollmoeller, by contrast, were launching themselves on intercontinental journeys in the heady pursuit of new cultural stimuli. Whatever the reasons, the post-war period marked a significant shift from the rapid, fecund and complex interactions with his German translators and publishers that helped diffuse D'Annunzio's works in the first decades of the twentieth century.

[52] Thomas Mann, *Reflections of a Nonpolitical Man*, trans. by Walter D. Morris (New York: Ungar, 1983), p. 396. For Hofmannsthal's view, see 'Antwort auf die neunte Canzone Gabriele d'Annunzios' (Reply to Gabriele D'Annunzio's Ninth Song), *Neue Freie Presse*, 2 February 1912, p. 1.

Part III

D'Annunzio's Global *Fin-de-siècle* Reception

Chapter 10

Fin-de-Meiji as *Fin-de-siècle*: D'Annunzio and Japanese Literature

Noriko Hiraishi

Japanese literature followed a distinctive path of development where 'the new did not replace the old, but was added to it'.[1] In the late nineteenth century, after the Meiji Restoration in 1868, Japan was opened to the 'world' after 200 years of isolationist foreign policy and began to integrate into what was termed 'modern civilisation'. The literature of the West had a great influence on Japanese writers in this process: Japanese intellectuals set out to create a literature that would develop modern ideas and shape a new image of themselves.

This chapter explores how Gabriele D'Annunzio's works introduced new images of 'modern' men and women into Japanese literature at that time: a *femme fatale* who reigned over men, and a new male figure with 'keen senses' who replaced the old ideal of the Japanese man. D'Annunzio's works thus functioned as a catalyst for the transformation of the values of Japanese youth.

The first part of the chapter explores D'Annunzio's reception in *fin-de-siècle* Japan. The first work to introduce the image of the *femme fatale* in Japan was Bin Ueda's (1874–1916) abridged translation of *Trionfo della morte*; and intellectuals of the time saw the influence of his novels in the 1905 attempted double suicide of Sōhei Morita (1881–1949) and Haruko Hiratsuka (1886–1971), as well as in Morita's novel based on the incident, *Baien* (*Sooty Smoke*, 1909). The second section introduces a comparison between D'Annunzio's works and Morita's *Sooty Smoke*, demonstrating the extent to which D'Annunzio influenced the new qualities of men and women in Japanese literature. The last section examines how Sōseki Natsume (1867–1916), a prominent writer inspired to read

1 Shuichi Kato, *A History of Japanese Literature: From the Man'yōshū to Modern Times*, trans. and ed. by Don Sanderson (Surrey: Curzon, 1997), p. 2.

D'Annunzio by Morita's scandal, interpreted them to construct an image of a 'new man' with acute sensibilities.[2] This chapter thus explores a complex network of influences across various literary works to argue that the *fin-de-siècle* image of modern people emerged in Japanese literature precisely under the influence of D'Annunzio.[3]

Trionfo della morte as a Starting Point

Gabriele D'Annunzio was introduced to the Japanese literary world at the end of the nineteenth century through French magazines. French translations began appearing in *Le temps*, *Revue de Paris* and *Revue des deux mondes* from 1893.[4] The September 1896 issue of *Taiyō* (The Sun), Japan's first magazine focused on introducing foreign cultures, translated an article from *La revue des revues*, titled 'Shijin to shikisai tono kankei (The Relationship between Poets and Colour)'. The article concluded with a reference to D'Annunzio: 'Finally, let us mention the great Italian poet D'Annunzio. He often uses the colour red in his works, as if in the good old days.'[5]

The first author to draw on this new interest in D'Annunzio's work was Bin Ueda. He referred to 'D'Annunzio, a writer of youth' in the August 1897 issue of *Teikoku Bungaku* (Imperial Literature). The following year he wrote in the same magazine, 'We look forward to seeing what the future holds for D'Annunzio. [. . .] We are counting on the genius of Gabriele D'Annunzio.'[6] These expressions were, in fact, borrowed from European critics like Melchior de Vogüé, who in 1895 had published an article in *Revue des deux mondes* praising D'Annunzio as the new champion of the Latin Renaissance. Ueda came into contact with D'Annunzio's work through French and English translations, and he began to publish his own Japanese translations in 1900. This first moment of D'Annunzio's reception in Japanese literature was thus mediated through French sources and

2 Translations from Japanese are the author's unless otherwise stated.

3 A detailed chronology and discussion of D'Annunzio's reception is in Jōji Hirayama, *D'Annunzio to nihon kindai bungaku* (D'Annunzio and Modern Japanese Literature) (Tokyo: Shironsha, 2011).

4 Giovanni Gullace, *Gabriele D'Annunzio in France: A Study in Cultural Relations* (New York: Syracuse University Press, 1966), pp. 8–10.

5 *Taiyō*, 2–19 (September 1896), 159. Although the Japanese article clearly stated that it was a translation of an article in *Revue des Revues*, we have thus far been unable to find the original article.

6 *Teikoku Bungaku*, 4–6 (June 1898), 100.

French critical perspectives. Since at the time most foreign literature was published in Japan in English translation, D'Annunzio's case could be called an exception.

In December 1901, Ueda published the collection *Miwotsukushi* (*Channel Marks*), which included three translations of D'Annunzio: 'Enjo monogatari' (The Story of a Glamorous Lady) and 'Gakusei' (Musical Voice), both abridged translations of *Trionfo della morte*, and 'Shōrō' (The Bell Tower), a translation of 'Campane' from *Terra vergine* (1882). About the abridged translations from *Trionfo della morte*, Ueda noted:

> The two excerpts from *Trionfo della morte* are known to have been greatly inspired by Nietzsche and Wagner. [. . .] I have translated a chapter, which shows the bitterness, agony, and weariness of lust, with all its seriousness, under the title of 'The Story of a Glamorous Lady', and I named my translation of the part of Wagner's exegesis of Tristan and Isolde 'The Musical Voice'.[7]

These translations had a great impact on Japanese readers, especially young ones. Kinji Shimada criticised *Channel Marks* as 'a pretentious book with an uncut French-style binding, that rushes to be ahead of the rest',[8] but Tōson Shimazaki (1872–1943), in a letter to Bin Ueda dated 27 December 1901, described the three D'Annunzio translations as excellent.[9] In his article 'Miwotsukushi wo yomite (Reading *Channel Marks*)', in the February 1902 issue of *Myōjō* (Rising Star), Tokuboku Hirata (1873–1943) praised both D'Annunzio and the translator as, addressing Ueda, he wrote: 'Loti and D'Annunzio deserve to be translated by your warm, soft and dense pen.'[10] This translation led to further interest in D'Annunzio's *Romanzi della Rosa – Il Piacere* (1889), *L'Innocente* (1892) and *Trionfo della morte* (1894) – which were widely read through English, French and German translations and left their mark on Japanese literature around 1910.

[7] Bin Ueda, *Teihon Ueda Bin zenshū* (The Complete Works of Bin Ueda), vol. 1 (Tokushima: Kyōiku Shuppan Center, 1978), p. 34.

[8] Kinji Shimada, '*Miwokutsukushi* kaidai (Commentary on *Channel Marks*)' in *Teihon Ueda Bin zenshū* (The Complete Works of Bin Ueda), vol. 2 (Tokushima: Kyōiku Shuppan Center, 1979), p. 615.

[9] Tōson Shimazaki, *Shimazaki Tōson zenshū* (The Complete Works of Tōson Shimazaki), vol. 17 (Tokyo: Chikuma Shobō, 1968), p. 61.

[10] Bin Ueda, *Teihon Ueda Bin zenshū* (The Complete Works of Bin Ueda), vol. 4 (Tokushima: Kyōiku Shuppan Center, 1979), p. 6.

It is worth noting that Ueda chose the fifth and sixth parts of *Trionfo della morte* to translate, where frequent references to Nietzsche and Wagner produce a *fin-de-siècle* atmosphere. The heroine, Ippolita Sanzio, was vividly depicted as a *femme fatale* in 'The Story of a Glamorous Lady', published in *Imperial Literature* in October 1900. Interestingly enough, the episode translated by Ueda was deleted when the French translation of *Trionfo della morte* was serialised in the *Revue des deux mondes* in 1895: the sensuality of D'Annunzio's works caused problems in Italy and France at the time, and despite D'Annunzio's wishes, 'more than one hundred pages were amputated from the text'.[11] Ueda wanted to introduce the episode that had been censored by the French magazine, which came to light only when the work was published in book form.

'The Musical Voice', originally published in June 1901, was a complete translation of the first chapter of Part 6, 'L'invincibile', which could be called D'Annunzio's theory of Wagner's opera *Tristan und Isolde*. It is not surprising that Ueda, deeply interested in Western music, took up this part; what is notable is that Isolde, in D'Annunzio's work, is an incarnation of the *femme fatale*. It was, in fact, through the translation of D'Annunzio's work that the archetype of the woman who seduces, charms and leads men to their doom was first introduced to Japan. Rapid modernisation and the influx of Western literature and culture meant that Japanese intellectuals were simultaneously exposed to a large array of European works, from Shakespeare to late-nineteenth-century writers. As a result, archetypes could be established in ways that ignored their historical development. With regard to the *femme fatale*, D'Annunzio's representations were introduced to Japan before those of the Romantics who influenced D'Annunzio.

In *Trionfo della morte*, Giorgio Aurispa, a typical *fin-de-siècle* hero with special sensitivities and nervous irritability, finds Ippolita full of seductive charms. However, over their two-year relationship, the woman begins to outshine the man at every turn. In Giorgio's eyes, Ippolita gives off a 'frightful and almost Gorgonian image',[12] but he cannot escape her sexual attraction. In the fifth part of the story, translated by Ueda as 'The Story of a Glamorous Lady', the protagonist realises that this woman will ruin him. At the beach,

[11] Gullace, p. 17.

[12] Gabriele D'Annunzio, trans. by Arthur Hornblow, *The Triumph of Death* (New York: George H. Richmond & Co., 1897), p. 301.

Giorgio witnesses her lasciviously fastening her garters and perceives in her powerful gesture and gaze a triumphant declaration:

> 'I am always the unconquered. [. . .] I am stronger than your thought. I know the secret of my transfigurations in your soul. I know the gestures and the words that have the virtue of metamorphosing me in your eyes. The odor of my skin has the power to dissolve a world in you.'[13]

As Mario Praz has noted, 'The Fatal Woman as imagined by Swinburne became grafted on to D'Annunzio's own intuition and completed it.'[14] Through Ueda's translations, modern Japan also discovered this Dannunzian feminine archetype.

The Shiobara Affair and the Impact of *Sooty Smoke*

A strange incident, known as 'the Shiobara Affair', imprinted D'Annunzio's name in Japanese society in March 1908. The case began with the disappearance of Haruko Hiratsuka, a young woman who had just graduated from Japan Women's University – she would later become a leading figure of Japanese feminism. Her disappearance was reported in the newspapers and developed into a scandal branded as a '20th century-style elopement' involving Sōhei Morita, an elite bachelor from Tokyo Imperial University. The scandal was initially called the 'Zen School Lady Affair' because Hiratsuka was a Zen practitioner; it later became known as the '*Triumph of Death* case' when it was discovered that D'Annunzio's novel inspired the double suicide attempt. Hiratsuka was taken into custody at the Shiobara Mountain Pass four days after her disappearance.

Morita was a disciple of Sōseki Natsume, one of the most highly regarded writers at the time. After the incident, Natsume hid Morita in his house, writing an account of what happened to serialise in the *Tokyo Asahi Shinbun* (Tokyo Asahi Newspaper), where he was the chief writer of the literary section. This resulted in *Baien* (*Sooty Smoke*), a fictionalised version of Morita's affair written by Morita himself.

The 'discovery' that the affair was inspired by D'Annunzio brought the Italian writer to the public's attention. In the May 1908

13 D'Annunzio, p. 309.

14 Mario Praz, trans. by Angus Davidson, *The Romantic Agony* (London: Oxford University Press, 1954), p. 259.

issue of *Jogaku Sekai* (Women's Education World), Roan Uchida (1868–1929) wrote an article titled 'A Strange Phenomenon in the Spiritual World', stating: 'It is said that this bachelor [Morita] had read D'Annunzio's *Trionfo della morte* and intended to play it for real. If that's true, it was an absurd farce. [. . .] This bachelor is really a Don Quixote of today's New Thought'.[15] The *Yorozu Chōhō* newspaper reported that Morita was moved by the last part of *Trionfo della morte*, interpreting the ending of the novel in this way: 'The man and the woman struggled with each other's ego, and finally the man led the woman into the mountain and kicked her down from the precipice. The woman, entangled in the ivy, cried out, "Help me", and the man, hearing this, laughed at his victory and jumped into the valley to his death' (29 March 1908).

In the West, there was a name for the phenomenon of literary works influencing real life: the 'Werther effect', derived from Goethe's novel. Competing with the first generation of the Meiji era, the young people of the second generation immersed themselves in Western literature and the 'new thoughts and ideas' depicted in it; but in their infatuation, the boundary between the literary world and the real world blurred. Even an experienced writer like Sōseki Natsume was not immune from the fascination with D'Annunzio. On 29 November 1908, Natsume wrote to Toyotaka Komiya (1884–1966), his other disciple: 'If you find any work by D'Annunzio, please buy it for me.'[16]

Morita was familiar with D'Annunzio's works from early on. In his own handwritten chronicle from 1904 he wrote: 'Prof. Ryūson [Bin's pseudonym] Ueda, together with Baba, published the magazine *Geien* [Garden of Arts], and I joined the coterie with Chōkō Ikuta and others. I read D'Annunzio's *Triumph of Death* for the first time under his guidance.'[17] Morita was immediately hooked on the book and identified with D'Annunzio's characters. From an anonymous article published in 1907, titled 'Chōkō Ikuta, Fuyō Oguri, and

[15] Roan Uchida, 'Ryōnin no koui ni taisuru shoka no ronpyō Higeki? Kigeki? (Various Commentaries on their Actions: A Tragedy? A Comedy?)', *Uchida Roan zenshū* (The Complete Works of Roan Uchida), vol. 6 (Tokyo: Yumani Shobō, 1984) pp. 19–20.

[16] Sōseki Natsume, *Sōseki zenshū* (The Complete Works of Sōseki Natsume) vol. 5 (Tokyo: Iwanami Shoten, 1994) p. 231.

[17] Sōhei Morita, 'Jihitsu nenpu (Self-written Chronology)', in *Gendai nihon bungaku zenshū* (The Complete Anthology of Modern Japanese Literature), vol. 42 (Tokyo: Kaizōsha, 1930), p. 572.

Bin Ueda have been working on a joint translation of D'Annunzio's work, having already completed a draft of *The Sacrifice of Love*' (*Yomiuri newspaper*, 30 August 1907), it looked like more translations of D'Annunzio were on their way. The work referred to here as *Sacrifice of Love* was *L'Innocente*, of which only the introduction had been translated by Tokuboku Hirata in 1902.[18] The January issue of *Shumi* (Hobby), Vol. 3 (January 1908), announced that '*Trionfo della morte*, translated by Fūyō Oguri and Chōkō Ikuta, was almost ready last December. It will be published in the near future.'[19] However, these translations were never published, and it was not until 1913 that Chōkō Ikuta's translation of *Trionfo della morte* appeared. Instead, it was Sōhei Morita who made D'Annunzio famous in Japan.

Morita's *Sooty Smoke* was serialised in the *Tokyo Asahi Newspaper* from 1 January to 16 May 1909. The first half discusses the dark background of the main character, and the second half his encounter with a woman in Tokyo. In July 1909, Toyotaka Komiya wrote an article titled 'D'Annunzio's *Triumph of Death* and Sōhei Morita's *Sooty Smoke*' in the literary magazine *Hototogisu* (Lesser Cuckoo), in which he compared the two works:

> When *Sooty Smoke* first appeared in the *Asahi Newspaper*, I told Sōhei that I was going to write a review of it when it was finished, and he wrote me a note asking me to read *Triumph of Death* by D'Annunzio, *Crime and Punishment* by Dostoyevsky, and *Anna Karenina* by Tolstoy. [. . .] When I asked him if I could read only *Triumph of Death*, he replied that since he was most influenced by that book, it would be enough if I read that. When I read it, I found that it was very similar to Sōhei's work. They were not merely alike in part, but alike as a whole. Very similar in tone, in tendency, and in characters.[20]

Komiya underlines that D'Annunzio and Morita's novels share a 'most striking' sense of 'strong and intense stimulation', that both feature a protagonist who is an 'extreme egoist' and that the novels 'do not have climax'.

[18] Tokuboku Hirata, 'D'Annunzio ga L'INNOCCETE [sic.] no jo', *Myōjō* (Rising Star), 3rd period, 1 (June 1902), 32.

[19] 'Ihō bungeikai shōsoku (Report: Trends in the literary world)' in *Shumi* (Hobby), 3–1 (January 1908), 3.

[20] Toyotaka Komiya, 'D'Annunzio no *Shi no shōri* to Morita Sōhei no *Baien* (D'Annunzio's *Triumph of Death* and Sōhei Morita's *Sooty Smoke*)', *Hototogisu* (Lesser Cuckoo), 12–10 (July 1909), 2.

The two novels are also semi-autobiographical. *Sooty Smoke* was based on the previous year's Shiobara Affair. *Trionfo della morte* could be read by replacing Giorgio with D'Annunzio and Ippolita with Barbara Leoni, his lover since 1887. Most of the letters that Morita received from Haruko Hiratsuka were included in *Sooty Smoke* without any modification, just as in *Trionfo della morte* the letters D'Annunzio exchanged with Barbara are reflected in the words and actions of the novel's protagonists.[21] The dark shadow of the protagonist Yōkichi Kojima's upbringing, developed in the first half of *Sooty Smoke*, is a projection of the author's own troubles. Similarly, Giorgio's dislike of his father in *Trionfo della morte* is a reflection of the conflict between D'Annunzio and his father.

Another interesting point is the cascade of influences. Since 'influence' in Morita was close to 'imitation', the most striking feature of *Sooty Smoke* was the theatricality that pervaded the entire story. This is most apparent in the relationship between the hero and the heroine, Tomoko Manabe, which deviates from traditional literary representations of love. Japanese literature tended to avoid direct expressions of affection. For instance, traditional *waka* poetry spoke of love in a formulaic and euphemistic way.[22] Men whispering sweet nothings to women was considered 'unmanly' and rarely described in detail in pre-modern literature. The text of *Sooty Smoke*, however, contains a variety of pick-up lines and expressions of affection. In fact, *Sooty Smoke* borrows some of these passages from D'Annunzio's works. In Chapter 14, when the protagonists are alone for the first time, Yōkichi asks Tomoko what she thinks of love, proceeding to then muse: 'Is it true love to fall madly in love with a woman, as if you were blowing hard on the mouth of a flute? Or is it true love to move quickly from one woman's lips to another, like running one's fingers over the keys of a piano, and to find the harmony between them?'[23] In Chapter 17, which features the characters' first date, passionate words appear one after another. Lending D'Annunzio's *Trionfo della morte* to Tomoko, Yōkichi says: 'If there are any passages you like,

21 Annamaria Andreoli, 'Note', in Gabriele D'Annunzio. *Prose di Romanzi vol. 1* (Milano: Mondadori, 1988) pp. 1304–1334.

22 On D'Annunzio's interest in and emulation of Japanese *waka* poetry, see Chapter 2 in this volume.

23 Sōhei Morita, *Baien* (Sooty Smoke) in Hideaki Sasaki (ed.), *Shōchū Baien* (Detailed Notes on *Sooty Smoke*) (Kyoto: International Research Center for Japanese Studies, 1999), p. 140.

please leave them underlined. Use your fingernails, red ink is not good, make scars so deep that they show through to the back.'[24] Then, when they part, he asks her, 'Please give me one of your gloves, so that I can at least have something that looks like your hand.'[25]

These lines, which diverge from traditional Japanese representations of love, were taken verbatim, or adapted, from the English translation of D'Annunzio's novels – Morita, in fact, did not read French. The discussion of true love in *Sooty Smoke* is inspired by the scene in *Il Piacere* where the protagonist, Andrea, meets Elena and asks her:

> Which do you consider the truest, noblest way of love--- to imagine you have discovered every aspect of the eternal Feminine combined in one woman, or to run rapidly over the lips of women as you run your fingers over the keys of a piano, till, at last, you find the sublime chord of harmony?[26]

And the chain of influence does not stop there, for D'Annunzio had borrowed these lines from Joséphin Péladan's *L'Initiation sentimentale* (1887), who in turn was parodying Hamlet's monologue.

Because no information about D'Annunzio's lover, nor the 'borrowing' in these lines, nor indeed of Péladin's work had been introduced to Japan during this period, we can conclude that while Morita's imitation of D'Annunzio's words was deliberate, he also coincidentally ended up imitating D'Annunzio's habit of taking his cues from various works and often plagiarising them overtly. At any rate, Morita's borrowing initiated a new image of women in this novel and in Japanese literature.

The *Femme Fatale* and the *New Man*

After learning of the Shiobara Affair, Morita's mentor, the writer Sōseki Natsume, recommended he write a novel about the events. But Morita was too shaken to start immediately, and meanwhile Natsume himself wrote the novel *Sanshiro*, inspired by the story he

[24] Morita, *Sooty Smoke*, p. 180.

[25] Ibid., p. 191.

[26] Gabriele D'Annunzio, trans. by Georgina Harding, *The Child of Pleasure* (Boston: The Page Company. 1898), p. 15.

had heard from his student. It was serialised in the *Asahi Newspaper* (September to December 1908); then from January 1909, Morita's *Sooty Smoke* began appearing in the same newspaper.

Natsume shaped the heroine of *Sanshiro*, Mineko Satomi, after Haruko Hiratsuka, the girl Morita had attempted to commit suicide with. In Natsume's work, the heroine was portrayed as an 'unconscious hypocrite'. Morita, however, saw things differently. As a result, Tomoko, the heroine of Morita's *Sooty Smoke*, offered a contrast to the image of Mineko in *Sanshiro*. *Sooty Smoke*'s protagonist, Yōkichi, expresses his discomfort with Mineko by portraying Tomoko's self-awareness:

> I could see in Tomoko's gesture that she was forcing herself to act in some way. At the very least, everything she does seems to be done consciously by herself. I don't mind that. It is better to be conscious of what she is doing than to be unconscious.[27]

And comments: 'First of all, to see this woman as a coquette, or simply as a half-wit intellectual with a taste for modern literature, doesn't seem to match the expression on her face'.[28] In *Sooty Smoke*, Tomoko is not just an Ibsen-obsessed woman as in *Sanshiro* but a 'consciously performative' *femme fatale* who manipulates men and leads them to their doom.

The physical type of the *femme fatale* is central in *Sooty Smoke*, aligning with D'Annunzio and European traditions. Talking with his friend, Yōkichi contrasts 'fair' and 'dark' women, referring to the trend in European art to distinguish the blonde, fair-haired, innocent maiden from the dark-haired woman who destroys men with her bewitching charm. Tomoko Manabe, who has 'a face that you see once and never forget', is portrayed as having a 'dark face', 'as if she had a brand of the underworld stamped on her face'.[29] Yōkichi's friendship with Tomoko was rooted in his critique of Tomoko's work *Matsujitsu* (*The Last Day*), which stated: 'According to legend, Sapho was a dark-skinned woman'.[30] In fact, while Hiratsuka, the model for Tomoko, was apparently not pale, Tomoko was a sallow-faced 'dark lady' who reigned over men. In *Trionfo della morte*

[27] Morita, *Sooty Smoke*, p. 192.
[28] Ibid., p. 211.
[29] Morita, *Sooty Smoke*, p. 114.
[30] Ibid., p. 148.

Ippolita, too, is a dark-faced woman. *Sooty Smoke* directly identifies Ippolita with Tomoko:

> 'I thought you had the symptoms of an epileptic. I may have thought that on my own, but I want you to be like that at all costs'. Tomoko took five steps forward in silence, then ten again. After a long time, she looked up and said: 'The woman in *Triumph of Death* seems to have had epilepsy'. It had been so long since I read it that I hadn't noticed it, Yōkichi thought, perhaps unknowingly I was seeking a parallel among women.[31]

In Yōkichi's imagination, Tomoko is also represented as a dead woman, pale as wax, and as a sadistic woman who sticks a needle into the head of a canary, prompting further identification with D'Annunzio's heroine.

The male counterpart to this Japanese version of the *femme fatale* is a 'new' man. Yōkichi is dependent on Tomoko and 'feels as if the spirit of his own life is being taken away when the woman's smile disappears'.[32] For him, Tomoko is invincible, and he is aware that 'in both wit and skill, he has clearly been defeated'.[33] He is at the mercy of a woman he describes as 'unapproachable like a demon king, a symbol of wounded arrogance'.[34] Moreover, Yōkichi feels the pleasure of being toyed with by Tomoko: 'It was annoying that she seemed to assume that a man would always do what she wanted him to do. But on the other hand, it was also interesting to play right and left at the will of a woman. There was a kind of Decadent pleasure in being at the mercy of a woman, in becoming her slave and controlling her.'[35] Japanese men of the time were taught that they must not show weakness in front of women. Male chauvinism was taken for granted, and being ridiculed by a woman was seen as shameful. Yet in *Sooty Smoke*, for the first time in modern Japanese literature, Morita portrays Yōkichi's weaknesses, describing his subservience to the point that he felt like 'kneeling there if [he] were not seen'.[36] This changed relationship to women constitutes the 'newness' of the modern man for Japanese literature.

Furthermore, Yōkichi is a man of tears. When he sees his old mother in Gifu, he is choked up and tries his best not to cry. He often

31 Ibid., p. 339.
32 Ibid., p. 247.
33 Ibid., p. 207.
34 Ibid., p. 346.
35 Ibid., p. 243.
36 Ibid., p. 157.

bursts into tears in his relationship with women. When Tomoko is resolute, Yōkichi becomes weepy, or tries to win her sympathy by crying: 'When I think that I must finally give up all hope of ever coming near her, my heart feels as if it were held by a great stone, and I want only to fall down there and cry like a child'.[37] In reality too, the author, Sōhei Morita, seems to have been a 'man who cries'. When he and Hiratsuka were taken back to Tokyo from Shiobara, it was not the woman but Sōhei who cried out during this humiliating act.[38]

What I would like to point out here is that Yōkichi, as well as the author Morita, broke away from the Japanese tradition of 'being a man'. The influence of D'Annunzio can also be seen in the fact that this Meiji intellectual was able to openly display his own weakness. The heroes in D'Annunzio's works are also 'men who cry'. Giorgio, in *Trionfo della morte*, feels 'an unconquerable repugnance' at the thought that 'he must face his father, that he must accomplish an act of vigour, and of his own will'.[39] However, he feels compassion and affection for his mother, who is being tormented by his father, and he 'pressed her in his arms, sobbing, wetting her with burning tears'.[40] Tullio in *L'Innocente* uses tears in a more calculated way. He knows well 'the prodigious effect on woman of the tears of a man whom she loves'.[41] His own tears of self-pity attract the sympathy of his wife, Giuliana, and move her.[42] Morita's tearful male character may be referring to these descriptions in D'Annunzio's works. Thus, Morita, through his reception of D'Annunzio's literature, proposed the image of a Japanese 'new man'.

Sōseki Natsume's Decadence at the End of an Era: Daisuke in *And Then*

In *Il Piacere* and *Trionfo della morte*, the protagonists' aesthetic sense and their theory of art are discussed in great detail. In this we see the influence of Joris-Karl Huysmans and others: aesthetic

[37] Ibid., p. 283.

[38] Raichō Hiratsuka, *Genshi, josei wa taiyō de atta* (*In the Beginning, Women Were the Sun*), vol. 1 (Tokyo: Ōtsuki Shoten, 1971), p. 118.

[39] D'Annunzio, *The Triumph of Death*, p. 86.

[40] Ibid., p. 88.

[41] D'Annunzio, *The Intruder*, trans. by Arthur Hornblow (New York: George H. Richmond & Co. 1898), p. 22.

[42] Ibid., p. 23.

contemplation was considered essential for the *fin-de-siècle* gentleman with heightened sensitivity. These aspects of D'Annunzio's heroes left little impact on Morita's *Sooty Smoke*. For Morita, D'Annunzio was a teacher of the intricacies of romantic love; he had no need for metaphysical speculations on art or the ideas of *fin-de-siècle* intellectuals. It was Morita's mentor, Sōseki Natsume, who focused on the ideas and aesthetics of the protagonists of D'Annunzio's works.

As mentioned, Morita was dissatisfied with *Sanshiro*, and *Sooty Smoke* expressed his rebellion against it. For his part, Natsume was very critical of his disciple's novel. On the cover of his copy of Oscar Wilde's *The Picture of Dorian Gray* (1890),[43] Natsume noted that Yōkichi of *Sooty Smoke*, along with Dorian and Giorgio Aurispa, are 'in short, madmen'.[44] Although Natsume had studied in London for two years starting in 1900 on a Japanese scholarship and had an understanding of European literary trends and sympathy for *fin-de-siècle* aesthetics, he observed the feudal morality of the Old Tokugawa Shogunate, according to which a man should be silent, not show his emotions, and let his actions speak for themselves. This moral outlook, typical of the first generation of the Meiji era, was incompatible with the behaviour of *fin-de-siècle* heroes. He thus could not sympathise with Wilde's and D'Annunzio's protagonists.

When Natsume heard the details of the Shiobara Affair from Morita, he was initially interested in the woman involved, but when he read *Sooty Smoke*, he was surprised by the image of the man depicted in it. In his next novel *Sorekara* (*And Then*), which was serialised in the same *Asahi Newspaper* from 27 June 1909, after *Sooty Smoke* had finished in May, Natsume depicted a scene in which Daisuke, the protagonist, criticises *Sooty Smoke*:

> Daisuke had always regarded himself as an original. But he was forced to recognize that Yōkichi was far ahead of him in this respect. He had started reading [*Sooty*] *Smoke* out of curiosity, but lately, since he had begun to feel too great a distance between himself and Yōkichi, he had let many days go without even scanning the day's instalment.[45]

[43] Natsume owned an English copy in the series *Collection of British Authors*, published by Bernhard Tauchnitz in Leipzig in 1908.

[44] Sōseki Natsume, *Sōseki zenshū* (The Complete Works of Sōseki Natsume), vol. 27 (Tokyo: Iwanami Shoten, 1997), p. 399.

[45] Sōseki Natsume, *And Then*, trans. by Norma Moore Field (Tokyo: Tuttle Publishing. 2011), p. 56. e-book.

Natsume himself must have felt that there was too much of a gap between himself and Yōkichi. He had read a series of D'Annunzio's works, including *Trionfo della morte*. His values were incompatible with D'Annunzio's; nonetheless, as Takehiko Kenmochi has pointed out,[46] there was also something in D'Annunzio's works that Natsume was strongly attracted to: the depiction of acute sensation.

Natsume had always been very sensitive to colour, and he took pride in that sensitivity.[47] For instance, Sanshiro, the eponymous protagonist of his novel, is portrayed as a 'country bumpkin' who is therefore insensitive to colour. From the middle of the nineteenth century onward, European interest in synaesthesia and a keen sense of colour was introduced to Japan, and D'Annunzio was noticed for his use of colour, as already discussed in regard to the article from the *Revue des revues* translated for *The Sun* in 1896.

The colours in D'Annunzio's works were mainly red and blue. Red is the colour of excitement, the colour of fire. Blue, in contrast, is the colour of calming nerves, the colour of peace. When Andrea first visits Elena in *Il Piacere*, he notices the crimson wallpaper and bedspread. This 'red' makes the man talk about his love for the woman. *Francesca da Rimini* (1901) – a work known in Japan early on – features the recurrent images of red roses and red flames. Blue is the colour of the sea.

The idea of colours affecting the human body was proposed in the late nineteenth century in the United States.[48] In 1877, Doctor Seth Pancoast, who used red and blue light irradiation to treat the nervous system, published *Blue and Red Light: or, Light and its Rays as Medicine*, while Edwin D. Babbit published *The Principles of Light and Color* in 1878. Babbit's book was so well received that it was soon translated in Europe, so it is possible that D'Annunzio could have used it as a reference. As far as Natsume is concerned, he owned *Gabriele D'Annunzio* (1905), a biography written by the German poet Alberta von Puttkamer, which described how, in real

[46] Takehiko Kenmochi, 'Natsume Sōseki *Sorekara* to D'Annunzio *Shi no shōri* (Sōseki Natsume's *And Then* and D'Annunzio's *The Triumph of Death*') in Toshiaki Tsukamoto (ed.), *Hikaku bungaku kenkyū Natsume Sōseki* (Comparative Literature Studies on Sōseki Natsume) (Tokyo: Asahi Press, 1978).

[47] See Hideaki Sasaki, *Natsume Sōseki to josei – aisareru riyū* (Tokyo: Shintensha, 1990), Toshio Ōkuma, *Shikisai bungaku-ron – Shikisai hyōgen kara minaosu kindai bungaku* (The Theory of Colour Literature: Modern Literature Reviewed from the Perspective of Colour Expression) (Tokyo: Gogatsu Shobō, 1995).

[48] Frank H. Mahnke, *Color, Environment and Human Response* (New York: John Wiley & Sons, 1996), p. 33.

life, D'Annunzio used different colours to suit the mood of a room. In his note *Fragments*, from 1908, Natsume wrote:

> Going out. I go out, my heart is taken away by blue, and I return. The family suddenly talks about red.
> 1. Standing in the blue world and pitying those in the red world.
> 2. Struggle to move from the blue world to the red world.
> 3. Anxiety and regret when moving from the blue world to the red world, etc.[49]

Natsume thus had in mind the contrast between red and blue while plotting *And Then*. In the novel, the male protagonist, Daisuke Nagai, reflects on D'Annunzio's use of colours:

> Then, suddenly, he remembered a story about a man named D'Annunzio, who had furnished part of his house in blue and part in red. D'Annunzio's reasoning seemed to be that these two colours expressed the two principal moods of existence. Accordingly, rooms where excitement was called for, such as the study or the music room, should be painted in red as much as possible. Bedrooms and the like, were to be done in bluish tones. Thus the poet seemed to have satisfied his curiosity by applying a psychologist's theory.[50]

In June 1909, just before the serialisation of *And Then* began, Natsume wrote a letter to Kyoshi Takahama (1874–1959), in which he stressed: 'Colour has a great influence on me.'[51]

The protagonist of *And Then*, Daisuke, is characterised as a *fin-de-siècle* intellectual set apart from previous characters both in Natsume's work and in *Sooty Smoke*. Sensitivity to colour brings him closer to European models of the modern intellectual:

> Daisuke was puzzled that a man so readily aroused as D'Annunzio should have required the presence of the colour red, which could reasonably be deemed a potent excitant. Daisuke himself was not pleasantly affected by the brightly painted gates at shrines. Had it been possible, he would gladly have set his head adrift by itself to sleep peacefully in the deep green sea.[52]

49 Sōseki Natsume, *Sōseki zenshū* (The Complete Works of Sōseki Natsume), vol. 19 (Tokyo: Iwanami Shoten, 1995), p. 382.
50 Natsume, *And Then*, pp. 43–4.
51 Sōseki Natsume, *Sōseki zenshū*, vol. 23 (Tokyo: Iwanami Shoten, 1996), p. 191.
52 Natsume, *And Then*, p. 43.

Yōkichi from *Sooty Smoke* did not share this sensitivity to colour. Moreover, contrary to the protagonist of *Sooty Smoke*, Daisuke is also rich.[53] This is also a contrast to the protagonist of Natsume's previous novel, Sanshiro, who was a young man fresh from the countryside, 'not yet [. . .] exposed to the artificial atmosphere to the extent that he is happy', and so not 'the face of fin-de-siècle'.[54] Unlike Sanshiro, Daisuke is a dashing *fin-de-siècle* intellectual. And while Yōkichi's innovation lay in his rejection of traditional Japanese male masculinity, Daisuke's novelty comes from his keen sense of colour, something that previous heroes in Japanese literature had not possessed. What Natsume learned from D'Annunzio was to give his hero this keen sense, as proof that he was a modern intellectual.

'Nerve' as a Privilege

A man of keen senses, Daisuke is not only concerned about colours; he is also attentive to the sound of his own heart, and he often uses the scent of flowers to induce slumber when outrageously painful stimuli from the outside world assail him. He has come to regard being 'nervous' as a privilege:

> Daisuke, in turn, regarded his own nerves as the tax he had to pay for his uniquely keen speculative powers and acute sensibilities. It was the anguish that echoed from the achievement of a lofty education; it was the unwritten punishment dealt with natural aristocrats, those designated by heaven.[55]

The privileging of 'nerve' in *And Then* is discussed by Hirotaka Ichiyanagi.[56] Here, I would like to draw attention to the fact that this privileged 'nerve' is reserved for aristocrats, something which resonates with Charles Baudelaire's concept of dandyism. For a dandy, the taste for material elegance is merely a symbol of 'his aristocratic superiority of mind' and part of 'the burning need to create for

[53] Natsume writes that 'D'Annunzio's heroes were men without money worries, so it was not unreasonable that their excesses should lead to folly; when it came to the hero of Sooty Smoke, there was no such leeway': Natsume, *And Then*, p. 55.

[54] Sōseki Natsume, *Sōseki zenshū*, vol. 5 (Tokyo: Iwanami Shoten, 1994), p. 345.

[55] Natsume, *And Then*, p. 7.

[56] See Hirotaka Ichiyanagi, 'Tokkenka sareru "Shinkei" – *Sorekara* ichimen (Privileged "Nerves": one aspect of *And Then*', *Sōseki kenkyū* (Sōseki Studies), 10 (1998), 34–44.

oneself a personal originality'.[57] Thus the privileging of nerve in *And Then*, from 1909, also reflects the extent to which Japanese intellectuals of the period drew on European literature.

In 1905, Masao (Koson) Katayama published an article entitled 'Shinkeishitsu no bungaku' (The Literature of Nervousness) in *Teikoku Bungaku* (Imperial Literature), discussing the 'literature of the Décadents at the Fin de siècle' in Germany. Katayama wrote: 'Nervousness is indeed a disease of the late nineteenth century, the *fin-de-siècle*'.[58] He cites Hermann Bahr as a leading figure in the German 'literature of nervousness' and introduces Bahr's chapter 'Decadence' in *Studien zur Kritik der Moderne* (Studies on the Critique of Modernity, 1894). In this work, Bahr defines Decadents as 'romantics of nerves'[59] and then identifies Baudelaire and others as Decadents. According to Bahr, European Decadents, including Baudelaire, considered innovation to be the expression and transmission of what was founded on their nerves.

Daisuke's keen 'nerve' was a new weapon against old values. Being a 'man of sense' completely separated him from the old times. Daisuke's father is portrayed as a strict first-generation man of the Meiji era, educated in 'Bushido', the ethical and moral code of the Samurai, and being 'enormously proud of having gone to war'.[60] Daisuke negates the old era of his father without hesitation. He can only think that '[p]eople like his father were either primitives with undeveloped nervous systems or fools who persisted in deceiving themselves'.[61] He admits to being a coward but 'he could feel no shame in this',[62] as he believes that 'many qualities incompatible with courage were to be valued far above it'.[63] He himself does not have courage because he has *more* than that: instead of courage and boldness, he has acquired the weapons of 'uniquely keen speculative powers and acute sensibilities'.

The 'privileging of nerves', as in the case of Daisuke, became a literary trend in the late Meiji period. Here again, D'Annunzio

57 Charles Baudelaire, *The Painter of Modern Life and Other Essays*, trans. and ed. by Jonathan Mayne (London and New York: Phaidon Press, 1964), p. 27.

58 Koson Katayama, 'Shinkeishitsu no bungaku', *Teikoku bungaku*, 11–8 (August 1905), 31.

59 Hermann Bahr, *Studien zur Kritik der Moderne* (Weimar: VDG Weimar 2006), p. 25.

60 Natsume, *And Then*, p. 22.

61 Ibid., p. 23.

62 Ibid., p. 22.

63 Ibid., p. 22.

played a key role. The importance of depicting the senses, including the sense of colour, which flourished in various areas of Europe after Baudelaire until the end of the century, was introduced to the Japanese literati by Katayama:

> The way forward for them (the nervous literati) was the sense of colour. Red, green, blue, purple, black, white, etc., all became symbols of serious sorrow, and thought, emotion, smell, and taste were all created from colours, resulting in green songs, blue sensations, blood-red thoughts, echoing colours, and ringing emotions. The concepts and senses are all jumbled together.[64]

However, the Japanese literary world had not yet been introduced to many works that focused on this kind of sensory description. In this context, D'Annunzio's depictions of the senses, helped by the popularity of Natsume's *And Then*, inspired many Japanese literary figures. An example is the first collection of poems by Hakushū Kitahara (1885–1942), *Jashūmon* (*Heretics*), published in March 1909 and enthusiastically received by the youth of the time. As Hirayama pointed out, Kitahara and his poet colleagues had read D'Annunzio's works.[65] In *Heretics*, Kitahara repeats the image of the colour red as dripping blood, the setting sun or the dark and heavy air, and explores his own world of 'red', aesthetics and Decadence. Hitoshi Manzōji (1886–1957), another young poet and a friend of Kitahara, published a traditional poem in the February 1910 issue of *Subaru* (The Pleiades), a literary magazine noted for publishing talented poets, incorporating D'Annunzio's name: 'You weep gorgeously / D'Annunzio would call it red sorrow'.[66]

Daisuke, shaped by Natsume in the same year, was an intelligent man who shared much with these new literary youths. Rich, fashionable, sensitive and intelligent – the refined and confident appearance of this new hero made the young people of the time yearn for Daisuke. Ryūnosuke Akutagawa (1892–1927), who was just seventeen when *And Then* was published, recalled later:

> It seems that many people around our age were moved by Master Sōseki's *And Then*. Of those who were moved by the novel, I would like to write

[64] Katayama, p. 31.

[65] See Hirayama, Chapter 7, 'Kitahara Hakushū, Manzōji Hitoshi, Kinoshita Mokutarō to D'Annunzio (Hakushū Kitahara, Hitoshi Manzōji, Mokutarō Kinoshita and D'Annunzio)' pp. 173–84.

[66] *Subaru*, 2–2 (February 1910), 97.

> here about those who fell in love with the character of its hero, Daisuke Nagai. Not only did many of them fall in love with him, but many of them even took him for their own personal assistant. But the hero is the kind of man we seldom see around us. [. . .] This is true not only of *And Then*, but also of Werther and René. They are all personalities who have upset a generation.[67]

This image of the 'new man' who uses his keen senses and sensitivity to overturn the values of the first generation of the Meiji era was also developed by Bin Ueda and Kafū Nagai (1879–1959), another talented young writer of the day, after the publication of *And Then*. The protagonists of *Uzumaki* (*Whirlpool*, 1910) by Ueda and *Shin Kichōsha no Nikki* (*Diary of a New Returnee*, 1910) by Nagai were both 'new men' who had rejected traditional Japanese 'masculinity' and tried to live an artistic life, turning their backs on success. For them, the end of the Meiji era was the end of the century, and they rejected the traditional values of the time, fortifying themselves with a new nervous sensitivity. Daisuke, inspired by D'Annunzio, was thus a young man ahead of his time.

Conclusion

In this way, D'Annunzio's works brought new elements to Japanese literature in the beginning of the twentieth century. Through D'Annunzio, Japan was introduced to the *fin-de-siècle* aesthetics of the troubled protagonist, to the *femme-fatale* heroine, and to the effective use of floral scents and music in love scenes. This model also created a new kind of hero – a man free from traditional masculinity who openly declares himself timid and who can cry in front of women. The image of a man who does not deny his weaknesses had been the object of scorn and ridicule as 'effeminate' in traditional Japanese society. The portrayal of the protagonist of *Sooty Smoke* as a 'dull middle-aged man' who cried in front of a woman was something new, but was not regarded as 'cool'. In contrast, Daisuke, the protagonist of Natsume's *And Then*, is an upper-class young man who, having acquired knowledge of modern Western society, rejects old-fashioned masculinity as 'pre-modern' and uses his keen nerves

[67] Ryūnosuke Akutagawa, 'Nagai Daisuke', *Akutagawa Ryūnosuke zenshū* (The Complete Works of Ryūnosuke Akutagawa), vol. 7 (Tokyo: Iwanami Shoten, 1996), pp. 255–6.

as a new weapon of modern manhood. Daisuke's image as a 'modern civilised man' – indebted to D'Annunzio – was admired by Japanese youth. The fact that young writers such as Morita, as well as veteran writers such as Natsume and Ōgai Mori (1862–1922), drew themes and concepts from D'Annunzio's works and projected them into their own says something about D'Annunzio's extensive influence.

As a concluding thought, we may also wonder whether the enthusiasm for D'Annunzio among Meiji-era literary figures means that Japanese readers were comfortable with the *Japonisme* sprinkled throughout *Il Piacere* and other early works. In D'Annunzio's first novel, the description of flowers as snow, a topos in Japanese literature, goes beyond mere exoticism. Such images may have resonated with D'Annunzio's popularity in Japan – but this complex topic requires further research.

Chapter 11

D'Annunzio's Feminine Archetypes, Nationalist Ideology and Catalan Modernism

Assumpta Camps, translated by Alessia Zinnari

'The lilies and languors of virtue
For the raptures and roses of vice'

Swinburne

The *fin-de-siècle* literary and artistic scene is characterised by the opposition of two well-defined female types that recur in multiple versions and recreations: the angelic woman and the *femme fatale*. This dichotomy was recovered by romanticism, consolidated by Théophile Gautier in the mid-nineteenth century, and continued to structure the representation of women in the works of artists associated with Decadence and Symbolism. The recurrence of this archetype in different national literatures underlines the extent to which texts circulated across cultural and linguistic boundaries during the European *fin-de-siècle*. It also offers an example of how D'Annunzio's vision of the feminine, a central element of his poetics which is inscribed in cosmopolitan literary exchange, in turn influenced the reception of his work in other literary contexts. This study will focus on the Catalan reception of D'Annunzio's female archetypes and on the political connotation that this motif assumes in the works of Catalan writers.

The artists writing at the end of the nineteenth century were attracted by a type of sensuality leading, on the one hand, to the abyss and, on the other, to an ideal of purity that brings comfort and redemption. Their writings feature a tension between the *donna angelicata*, of immaculate purity, and the cruel and perverse beauty of the *femme fatale*; between the *femme fragile* and the *belle dame sans merci*. In short, *fin-de-siècle* artists stand between Beatrice and Lilith.

Gabriele D'Annunzio reproduced this dichotomy of the feminine in his own writing, thereby introducing it to the Italian literary tradition. He did so at the beginning of the 1890s, during his time as a chronicler writing for *Il mattino*, *Tribuna* and *Cronaca bizantina*, and later developed these themes in his poetry, prose and theatre. One feature distinguishes D'Annunzio's *femme fatales* from other *fin-de-siècle* literary representations of women from which they derive or with which they have literary affiliations. D'Annunzio's women use seduction to attract men, dominate them and offer them power, connecting in this way two fundamental characteristics of his poetics: an aggressive voluptuousness and a will to dominate. As Mario Praz noted, 'With D'Annunzio lust is closely connected with the desire for power [. . .] woman represents the active principle not only in the giving of pleasure, but also in the ruling of the world. The female is aggressive, the male vacillating.'[1] This distinctive element links D'Annunzio to Maurice Barrès's *Le Culte du Moi* (1888–91), and it is crucial for the circulation of D'Annunzio's texts in Catalan Modernism. Moreover, in D'Annunzio, the dichotomy of the *femme fatale* and the *femme fragile* resolves in a *coincidentia oppositorum*, as the synthesis of the two types gives rise to the ideal lover. This happens, for example, in *Il Piacere*, where the author conflates the two protagonists, Elena and Maria,[2] in a way that implies the alternation of the masculine position in respect to female alterity.

Exploring the theme of the Dannunzian *femme fatale* and its circulation in Catalan Modernism enables us to trace the literary sources of a good part of Catalan Modernist production, and to measure the influence that D'Annunzio – a writer who was truly in fashion between approximately 1898 and 1914 – had among Catalan artists. As this chapter demonstrates, D'Annunzio's influence goes beyond the strictly literary and enters the political in the configuration of a nationalist ideology of a messianic character, especially in the late-nineteenth and early-twentieth centuries.

The Dannunzian Feminine Prism in Catalan Modernism

D'Annunzio's works had several channels of circulation in Catalonia. Theatre played an important role. The premieres of D'Annunzio's plays in Italy and Paris were regularly reviewed in Catalan media, and many of his works were performed in Barcelona, almost exclusively in Italian and Catalan. Another medium of dissemination was translation, in Castilian (especially of narrative prose) or in

1 Mario Praz, *The Romantic Agony*, 2nd edn, trans. by Angus Davidson (Oxford: Oxford University Press, 1951), p. 264.

2 Hans Hinterhäuser, *Fin de siglo: Figuras y mitos* (Madrid: Taurus, 1980), pp. 91–103.

Catalan (mainly of poetry), which thrived between the late nineteenth and early twentieth century. Finally, there were plenty of imitations. These included all those literary works, written in Catalan, that reproduced features of D'Annunzio's writing. Invested in renewing and modernising Catalan literary language, imitators not only recreated D'Annunzio's style, but also incorporated topics and literary motifs present in his work, especially female archetypes. Through D'Annunzio, a whole turn-of-the-century literary repertoire was imported into Catalan literature and contributed to its modernisation.

Five authors stand out when it comes to the reception of D'Annunzio in Catalan Modernism, and all of them engage with female archetypes, often attributing to them political connotations. These writers are Jeroni Zanné, Ramon Vinyes, Alexandre Plana, Josep Tharrats, and Ambrosi Carrión. In most cases – with the exception of Tharrats – it is *la belle dame sans merci* who arouses interest among these authors. Among its many recreations, a Dannunzian figure stands out: that of Basiliola, the protagonist of D'Annunzio's tragedy *La nave* (1908). This is one of D'Annunzio's most linguistically complex plays as it features archaisms, technical terms, lines in Mediaeval Latin and complex rhythmic effects. To understand the references that Catalan authors make to this play, it is useful to briefly summarise its plot. Set in 552 CE, *La nave* celebrates the founding of an autonomous and imperial Venice, and it indirectly addresses D'Annunzio's colonial ambitions for Italy. Basiliola, who is equated to Jezebel, Circe, Hecate and other historical pre-figurations of the vindicative *femme fatale*, seeks vengeance for her brothers and father, who were mutilated by the faction of Marco Gratico, the male imperialist hero. She first seduces Marco and then begins a relationship with Marco's brother, the bishop Sergio. After instigating the two brothers to a fight in which Sergio is killed, she sacrifices herself on the altar, where she burns, crowned by her long red hair in flames, in a symbolic act of purification that enables Venice's imperialist mission. Basiliola finds several new embodiments in Catalan writing. These works, as we will see, often elaborate on the political scope of *La nave* and adapt it to the Catalan context.

Jeroni Zanné is one of the most representative writers of the group that, at the beginning of the twentieth century, gathered around the newspaper *El Poble Català*.[3] He was a sonnetist, his style was greatly

[3] For more information about this author, see, among other sources: Llorenç Soldevila, 'Introducció a l'obra de Jeroni Zanné i Rodríguez' (Thesis, supervised by Dr J. Molas, Universidad Autónoma de Barcelona, 1975); Jeroni Zanné, *Una*

influenced by D'Annunzio and he translated D'Annunzio on several occasions. In Zanné's unpublished novel *El fill pròdig* (The Prodigal Son), the title echoes D'Annunzio's use of parables. Widely disseminated in Catalan Modernism at the end of the nineteenth century through several notable translations, these parables were interpreted by Catalan artists as an evocation of the resurgence of the Latin spirit and as a change of direction in *fin-de-siècle* literature. Combining elements from across the whole arc of D'Annunzio's novels, of which Zanné aspired to create a compendium, *El fill pròdig* blurs and interweaves echoes of D'Annunzio's various male protagonists, including Andrea Sperelli, Giorgio Aurispa, Claudio Cantelmo and Stellio Èffrena. Zanné resorts to the feminine archetype typical of D'Annunzio's fiction in order to show the spiritual evolution of the male hero, from an epicurean Aestheticism, as in *Il Piacere*, to the profession of Nietzscheanism, as in *Il fuoco*.

Ramon Vinyes, the 'Catalan wise man' mentioned by García Márquez,[4] was a keen admirer of D'Annunzio in the years prior to his self-exile in Colombia. The poetic prose collected in *L'ardenta cavalcada* (The Ardent Cavalcade) (1909), like most of his production, features archaic, baroque, sometimes profanatory language which, by disrupting linguistic norms, also aims to subvert socially established conventions. The motto by D'Annunzio that opens the collection 'L'aspro vin di giovinezza brilla ed arde / ne le arterie umane' (The sour wine of youth shines and burns / in the human arteries)[5] is a hymn to the fullness of life and the sensual force of youth. However, the author does not delve into vitalist motifs, but rather follows the example of D'Annunzio in the appropriation and

---

Cleo i altres narracions, ed. by Llorenç Soldevila (Barcelona: Edicions 62, 1978); Josep-Luis Marfany, '"JOVENTUT", Revista Modernista', *Serra d'Or*, 12: 135 (1970), 53–6; Joaquim Molas, 'El Modernisme i les seves tensions', *Serra d'Or*, 12: 135 (1970), 45–52.

4 For more information about this author, see, among other sources: Jaume Huch i Camprubí, 'Ramon Vinyes, jove: Contribució a l'estudi de la 1ª etapa catalana (1904–12)' (Bachelor's Degree Thesis, supervised by Dr J. Molas, Universidad de Barcelona, 1986); Molas, 'El Modernisme i les seves tensions'; P. Elies i Busqueta, *Ramon Vinyes i Cluet: Un literat de gran volada, vida i obra d'un berguedà exemplar* (Barcelona: Dalmau, 1972); M. J. McCarthy, 'Catalan "Modernisme", Messianism and Nationalist Myths', *Bulletin of Hispanic Studies*, 52: 4 (1975), 379–95.

5 Gabriele D'Annunzio, *Versi d'amore e di gloria*, vol. 2 (Milan: Mondadori, 1982), I, p. 159. This line corresponds to the 4th composition of the 'Canto dell'Ospite', published in *Canto Novo* (1881). This was a popular publication among Catalan Modernists.

recreation of Decadent clichés, as well as in the preciousness of his style, aimed at renewing and dignifying the Catalan language.

Vinyes's move toward theatrical production took place around 1910 with *Al florir dels pomers (Apunt d'ambient)* (*When the appletrees blossom (Atmosphere note)*), and was also inspired by D'Annunzio.[6] The play premiered on 13 May at the Teatro Romea, in Barcelona, produced by the Borràs Theater Company. Two scenic poems in three acts, *L'arca i la serp* and *Llegenda de boires*, modelled after D'Annunzio's poetic theatre, also feature Dannunzian themes.

In *L'arca i la serp*, a play with a Byzantine setting and a biblical tone, the character of Cozbi is an incarnation of Basiliola. Cozbi appears wrapped in veils and adorned with jewels and perfumes; at times she is described as a vampire, others as a snake, and she can kill simply with her gaze, which burns like a flame. In this piece, the confrontation between Cozbi and Moses over the leadership of the people of Israel becomes a dialectical and symbolic struggle between lust and virtue, instinct and reason. Moses is forced to make a pact with Cozbi, for her rhetorical skills are much more persuasive to the masses to lead the people to the promised land. On a symbolic level, this work proposes a synthesis between instinct and reason in the search for a persuasive political discourse. There are plenty of images charged with sadism; a reddish sunset described as a 'sky of fratricide' (evocative of the fratricide that occurs in *La nave*) confers a spectacular framework to the play, while the sexual encounter between Cozbi and Zimri, the androgynous prince, before the altar evokes Basiliola's profanatory relationship with Marco's brother, the bishop Sergio Gratico. Finally, the play reworks the idea of purification through fire. Moses defeats the serpent and leads his people to their destiny, but at the price of having to fight and kill; therefore, like Marco Gratico, he ceases to be pure and immaculate. The ultimate aim of this work is to recreate and articulate, through theatre, a messianic message at the service of the political ideals that Vinyes introduced to Catalan Modernism.

The *Llegenda de boires* features several connections to D'Annunzio's *La figlia di Iorio*. We rediscover the dialectic of purity versus lust represented through the opposition between Bernardeta and the 'Home Roig' (the Red Man); or, perhaps more accurately, the polarity between idealistic love (between Bernardeta and Jan) and carnal passion (between the 'Home Roig' and Bernardeta). We also

[6] Ramon Vinyes, *Al florir els pomers (Apunt d'ambient)* (Barcelona: Biblioteca Teatràlia, 1910).

find the theme of the 'desecrated' (raped) virgin redeemed through motherhood. Bernardeta is portrayed as a saint with Madonna-like qualities: she is pure, her marriage to Jan is chaste, she dreams of having a child conceived just like Jesus. Her son is, however, conceived not through the Holy Spirit at the time of the Angelus, but through the evil 'Home Roig' – that is, the Devil himself – as the result of a violation that took place on Saturday, in clear allusion to the Sabbath. The sadistic configuration of the 'Home Roig' is evident, and deeply imbued with Dannunzian and Byronian echoes. He is a fallen angel with eyes of fire, looks like a snake, is restless, adventurous and eternally dissatisfied. But he is also the prodigal son who returns home after a long absence. And, finally, he is the wolf who dies defenestrated, in a very explicit evocation of the theatre of another great Catalan playwright of the time, Àngel Guimerà. As in D'Annunzio's tragedy, the erotic relationship is seen as either desecration (on the male part) or sacrifice (on the female part). The work of the Italian writer is likewise echoed in the pervasive mixing of the erotic and the sacred, found, for example, in the description of Bernardeta's room as a kind of desecrated sanctuary, and in the liturgical elements in the third act. The evangelical message is subverted as the holy mystery of the immaculate conception becomes a grotesque joke, and the iconic image of the pure Virgin stepping on the serpent falls from the pedestal. The use of roses as a symbol of pleasure and sensuality is a recurring element in Vinyes that unfailingly refers to D'Annunzio: Bernardeta – the naïve woman – is opposed, in Vinyes's work, to Rosa – the woman with experience, whose name is not accidental, as it evokes the polarity between Maria and Elena, the two female protagonists of *Il Piacere*.

Alexandre Plana is a literary figure who joined Modernism in Barcelona around 1909.[7] Historical and mythical themes, as well as the exploration of typical motifs of end-of-the-century Byzantinism, constitute the core of Plana's literary practice in the early years of the twentieth century. At this point in his career, he was strongly influenced by Ramon Vinyes and, through him, he absorbed D'Annunzio's style. When, years later, he dissociated from Modernism, he also openly distanced himself from the influence of D'Annunzio.

[7] For more information about this author, see, among other sources: Iolanda Pelegrí, 'Alexandre Plana, crític literari' (Thesis, supervised by Dr J. Molas, Universidad Autónoma de Barcelona, 1974) and Alexandre Plana, *Teoria i crítica del teatre* (Barcelona: Edicions 62, 1976), as well as McCarthy 1975.

There are two moments in which Plana refers explicitly to D'Annunzio in his production. In the first instance, he does so with the motto that opens the poem 'Cleopatra i l'ibis' (Cleopatra and the Ibi): 'Sembrami che ne l'aria s'effonda / quel lento odor che lentamente uccide' (It seems as if it's spreading, into the air, / that slow smell that slowly kills).[8] The quote from D'Annunzio introduces the *fin-de-siècle* theme of voluptuous death, embodied in the exotic figure of Cleopatra. A few months after winning the 'Natural Flower' award at the 1908 Olot Floral Games with this poem, Plana authored a series of three sonnets entitled 'El darrer triomf de Basiliola' (The Last Triumph of Basiliola), published in the Barcelona-based newspaper *El poble Català*.[9] Each sonnet was preceded by a brief introduction in prose, which worked as a summary of its contents, and opened with a quote from *La nave*. Although D'Annunzio's tragedy is never explicitly mentioned, Plana's title referred to its protagonist, and the three poetic compositions followed the tragedy's plot. In these sonnets, Plana aims to recreate the sacrifice of Basiliola and the expedition of the tragedy's imperialist hero, Marcus Gratico. These are two moments that Plana sees as peaks in the founding of the future city, Venice, which in D'Annunzio's play is a synecdoche for Italy. In D'Annunzio's play, Basiliola ultimately wins, because her sacrifice purifies the Venetians and grants success to their imperial mission. What Plana takes from D'Annunzio is, on the one hand, the value of the personal and collective regeneration arising from immolation and sacrifice; and, on the other hand, a certain conception of theatre (and of art in general) capable of inciting the action of a people in the midst of a phase of nationalist expansion. In Plana's interpretation, *La nave* shows the apotheosis of Latin strength in its expansive imperial-nationalist force. He therefore places at the beginning of the third sonnet, as a motto, the words that the chorus insistently repeats in the epilogue of D'Annunzio's play: 'La patria è su la Nave' (our homeland is on the Ship). In this way, Plana endorsed the reclaiming of Latinity that, at the time, was strongly associated with D'Annunzio in the Catalan literary sphere. In Plana's case, as well

[8] Alexandre Plana, 'Cleopatra i l'ibis', *El Poble Català*, 14 September 1908, p. 2. The quote corresponds to the beginning of the second quartet of the sonnet 'Crepuscolo', included in the series 'Verso l'antica gioia', published in *Intermezzo* (D'Annunzio, *Versi d'amore e di gloria*, p. 305).

[9] Alexandre Plana, 'El darrer triomf de Basiliola (I–II–III)', *El Poble Català*, 22 February 1901, p. 3.

as in that of many Catalan Modernists, this revindication was at the service of a messianic ideology that defended the project of national reconstruction – that is, of the 'creation of the Future City' through Modernism. The revindication of Latinity would become a crucial theme during the Great War, as one learns from the articles published in the magazines *Iberia*, of which Plana was the editor, and *Cultura*, with which Plana collaborated, as he was a close friend of its editor, Josep Tharrats.

Among Catalan writers, Josep Tharrats was the one who was most influenced by D'Annunzio. His first volume of lyrical prose, published in Girona in 1909, entitled *Orles*, was dedicated to the 'maestro Gabriele D'Annunzio'.[10] Tharrats wrote nearly 5,000 sonnets throughout his life and, by 1924, he had collected an important part of his production in the volume *Les ofrenes espirituals*. The collection opened with a sonnet entitled 'Gabriele D'Annunzio', and it included another sonnet titled 'Paràfrasi', inspired by a female character from D'Annunzio's *Gioconda*, Silvia Settala.[11] The volume exudes Dannunzian resonances, and it presents a particular vision of Mediterraneanism that involves the exaltation of the Latin race and of a pagan spirit at the service of the ideal of the Future City. It is a literary transposition of D'Annunzio's vision, as elaborated in *La nave*, onto the political aspirations of Catalan Modernism. Direct references to D'Annunzio are also prominent in Tharrats's unpublished literary production, now held in his family archive. This is the case of three sonnets significantly titled 'Sonetti d'una sera paradisiaca' (Sonnets of a Heavenly Night), written in Italian, most likely written at the beginning of the twentieth century. Like Tharrats's translations, they constitute poetic exercises that aimed to forge,

[10] For more information about Tharrats, see, among other sources: Maria Àngels Cerdà i Surroca, *Els pre-rafaelites a Catalunya (Una literatura i uns símbols)* (Barcelona: Curial Edicions, 1981); Dolors Fulcarà, *El Modernisme a Girona* (Girona: I. E. G., 1976); Joaquim Molas, 'Notes sobre la prehistòria poètica de Carles Riba', *Els Marges*, 1 (1974), 9–23; J. F. Ràfols, *Modernisme i modernistes* (Barcelona: Destino, 1982).

[11] Sonnet XXV presents an elegy to the hands of the protagonist of *La Gioconda*, Silvia Settala. This sonnet appeared one year later (in 1914) in the Girona magazine directed by Tharrats, *Cultura*, with the title 'Oració a les mans de Silvia Settala (en un ejemplar de *La Gioconda* de G. D'Annunzio)'. The sonnet was part of the collection 'Gemmes votives', clearly inspired by D'Annunzio. Tharrats here makes reference to *La Gioconda*, although avoiding, both in 'Paràfrasi' and in 'Oració a les mans . . . ' the most sadistic and sensationalist aspects of D'Annunzio.

through the assimilation of D'Annunzio, a sophisticated, refined, musical language. Tharrats's writing involved an investigation of literary themes, images and motifs typical of D'Annunzio's work put in the service of his Modernist poetic and cultural agenda. However, in Tharrats's case, sensualism is freed from its subversive scope, and is more formal than ethical, circumscribed to an experimental plane. This distinguishes Tharrats from the other Catalan writers who were steeped in Dannunzianism, such as Vinyes.

The protagonist of the poetic prose *La dansatriu de la cabellera d'ombra* (The Dancer of the Shadow Hair), a composition also held at the family archive, is another incarnation of Basiliola. Like her, she is enveloped in fire, described as having burning hair, and turns into pure rhythm as she dances naked before the crowd. However, Tharrats distances himself from D'Annunzio, as he rejects the most libidinous aspects of the dance by describing the dancer as an incarnation of beauty that can elevate the spirits. He draws on a Dannunzian theme but alters its meaning and transforms it into a decorative vision. His poetic prose is rich in musical and plastic suggestions, features a variety of registers and is characterised by an intense and exotic sensuality.

Another prose poem – incomplete and undated – insists on the theme of the 'chaste' dancer. The author shows that aesthetic contemplation reaches a higher degree of complexity through dance, due to the combination of music, rhythm, movement and plasticity. By performing an ethical and aesthetic purification of the dance of Basiliola, Tharrats responds to a willingness to manipulate, or, as he says, 'mediterranear' (make Mediterranean) Decadent motifs in order to reduce their subversive and provocative content. The Decadent themes that the author recreates are charged with a deep idealism and freed from connotations considered 'impure' or 'immoral'. Tharrats presents aesthetic contemplation in its most Apollonian aspect: it is a contemplation that purifies, elevates the spirit and is a source of creative inspiration – never an incitement to follow primordial, low human instincts. D'Annunzio influenced Tharrats for a very long time, something that cannot be said for the other Catalan Modernists. This influence can even be observed in the work he produced during the Great War, which took on connotations linked to the racial discourse of the time, and lasted until the publication of *Les ofrenes espirituals* in 1924. At that point the vision of D'Annunzio as an exemplary character had declined almost completely on the Catalan scene.

Critics of the time frequently noted D'Annunzio's influence on Ambrosi Carrión, an author of tragedies and a poet.[12] In his case, the affinity between the two authors goes beyond the recreation of well-known clichés – such as, for example, an exacerbated sensuality highlighted by mysticism or sublimated into heroism – and must be sought, instead, in a theatrical experimentation that aims to recover the tragic sense of Greek antiquity. This leads, into both Carrión and D'Annunzio, to a return to the Greek classics and their revision in a modern key. They present us with a world of unleashed passions and vague fatalities that weigh on the individual, recreated on the basis of Greek tragedies. Carrión was already approaching this theatrical concept around 1909 with his *Tribut al mar (Tragèdia en un acte)* (Tribute to the Sea (Tragedy in One Act)), a work written in verse and an example of the impact of the Latinist current on Catalan Modernism.[13] Like D'Annunzio, Carrión explores from a modern perspective the recovery of the classical theme. The messianic vocation of this dramatic work recalls *La città morta* and *La figlia di Iorio*, but is inspired first and foremost by the D'Annunzio of *La nave*, and has similar nationalist and imperialist resonances. The protagonist, Nike, is named after the Greek goddess but a direct transposition of D'Annunzio's Basiliola, and is at the service of the imperialist will of the male protagonist. This character features all the characteristics of the *belle dame sans merci*: jewellery, perfumes, long hair, sensuality, seduction, lasciviousness . . . Carrión insists on the theme of morbid, contaminated beauty and focuses on the moral perversion of the protagonist. The parallelism of this work with *La nave* becomes evident when Nike heroically sacrifices herself, an action that will redeem her, and consequently, her people. The only difference is that, here, the sacrifice is not consummated with self-immolation in the fire, but with her leap off a cliff. The Dannunzian influence, recognised

[12] For more information about this author, see, among other sources: Carles Batlle, 'El teatre d'Ambrosi Carrión' (Thesis, supervised by J. Castellanos, Universidad Autónoma de Barcelona, 1988); Xavier Fàbregas, *Aproximació a la Història del teatre català modern* (Barcelona: Curial Edicions, 1972); Fàbregas, 'El Modernisme i la seva iconografia teatral', *Serra d'or*, 12: 135 (1970), 72–7; Carrión Ambrosi, *Comte Arnau (Tragèdia, dues parts)* (Barcelona: Publicacions de l'Abadia de Montserrat, 1972) and McCarthy 1975.

[13] Carrión wrote *Tribut al mar* in 1909, but the play was premiered in theatres only in 1911 (Estampa de Manuel Tasis, de Barcelona). The premiere took place on the 19th of May 1911 in the 'Teatre Català Romea' in Barcelona. It received very good reviews in the *Almanaque del 'Diario de Barcelona' para el año bisiesto 1912* (Barcelona 1911, p. 107).

by the author, inspires Carrión to create a national poetic theatre in Catalan, a theatre that is at once messianic and political and has clear nationalist intent. *La nave* offered a greater degree of exemplarity for Carrión if compared to other more popular Dannunzian tragedies. In this light, *Tribut al mar* can be seen as the direct result of the impact that D'Annunzio's neo-tragic vision had on Modernist Catalonia at the beginning of the twentieth century.

Conclusion

D'Annunzio thus constitutes an important, unavoidable cultural reference not only for Catalan Modernism but also for a good part of contemporary Catalan literature. His influence is even present in authors operating in the second half of the twentieth century. In almost all cases, beyond the obvious direct references to his work, we can observe typical Dannunzian dichotomies in female archetypes. Most evident of all, however, is the messianic meaning that these motifs acquire in the articulation of a nationalist discourse that is constructed against the background of Decadent motifs.

Chapter 12

Gabriele D'Annunzio and the Austrian Reception after Italy's Entry into the War

Arturo Larcati, translated by Peter Bruckner

'Dir aber wehe,
Stampfende Zeit!
Wehe dem scheußlichen Gewitter
der eitlen Rede!'

(Franz Werfel, Der Krieg)
[4 August 1914]

When Italy declared war on Austria-Hungary, this ended what the historian Manfried Rauchensteiner has described as a story of 'misjudgement and confusion, unfriendly neighbours, "deceitfulness and treachery" and "sacred selfishness"'.[1] With this assessment Rauchensteiner addressed the wavering attitude that the Austrian government took towards Italian neutrality after the outbreak of the First World War in August 1914. Instead of entering serious diplomatic negotiations to outdo the Entente powers' territorial offers and thus prevent Italy's entry into the war, the Austrian government underestimated the seriousness of the 'Italian crisis' and postponed decisions. The deadline was 25 May 1915: Italy justified entering the war in the name of 'sacred selfishness' and the fulfilment of national unity. The declaration of war by the 'unfriendly neighbour' was followed by a wave of indignation in Austria. Public opinion and the press projected negative images onto Italians, of which the accusation of 'deceitfulness and treachery' was not even the worst.

[1] Manfried Rauchensteiner, 'Kriegserklärung an Österreich. Das sterbende Kamel', *Die Presse* (22 May 2015); see Manfried Rauchensteiner and Josef Broukal, *Der Erste Weltkrieg und das Ende der Habsburgermonarchie 1914–1918. In aller Kürze* (Vienna: Böhlau, 2015).

During these political developments, a so-called 'intellectual war' (Krieg der Geist)[2] broke out among writers, intellectuals and scientists from both nations. The undeniable Italian protagonist of this conflict was Gabriele D'Annunzio, who was the most internationally renowned poet of Italian Symbolism/Decadence and had distinguished himself as the prototype of the *poeta vates*, the national poet. In this role, he campaigned early on for a stronger Italy with his *Odi navali* (1906) and the drama *La nave* (1908). At the same time, he denigrated the Austrians as 'barbarians'.[3] In 1912, he had supported Italy's imperialist ambitions in Africa with the *Canzone dei Dardanelli*, directed against Turkey and partly censored for mocking Austria-Hungary and its emperor. After the outbreak of the Great War, D'Annunzio advocated Italy's entry on the side of the Entente. The central parts of his pro-war propaganda were two speeches in May 1915: the first, in Liguria, for the inauguration of a monument to Garibaldi, and the second, shortly thereafter, in the Chamber of Deputies in Rome. In the secret London Treaty of 26 April 1915, Italy had promised the Entente military alliance to join the war within thirty days, which it did just on time on 25 May. Therefore, D'Annunzio's speeches had no direct political impact. Nevertheless, they contributed to the aura of legend around him and strengthened his role as 'the nation's poet' both in Italy and Austria-Hungary.[4] D'Annunzio became the most important polemical target for the reactions of Austrian writers. Among these were numerous authors who had previously supported and admired D'Annunzio:[5] Hugo von Hofmannsthal had called him 'the most original artist in contemporary Italy';[6] Hermann Bahr, who held Eleonora Duse in high regard,

[2] Uwe Schneider and Andreas Schumann, eds, *Krieg der Geister. Erster Weltkrieg und literarische Moderne* (Würzburg: Königshausen & Neumann, 2000).

[3] Lea Ritter-Santini, 'Pari e Impari. Gabriele D'Annunzio e i barbari', in *Italia viva. Studien zur Sprache und Literatur Italiens. Festschrift für Hans Ludwig Scheel*, ed. by Willi Hirdt and Reinhard Klesczewski (Tübingen: Narr, 1983), pp. 335–51.

[4] Renate Lunzer, '»O poésie, voilà le fruit de tes accouplements avec la politique. . .« D'Annunzio all'avanguardia contro l'Austria', in *Felix Austria – Italia infelix? Tre secoli di relazioni culturali italo-austriache*, ed. by Nicoletta Dacrema (Rome: Aracne, 2004), pp. 104–24.

[5] Anne Kupka, *Der ungeliebte D'Annunzio. D'Annunzio in der zeitgenössischen und der gegenwärtigen deutschsprachigen Literatur* (Frankfurt/M., Bern: Lang, 1992).

[6] Hugo von Hofmannsthal, 'D'Annunzio', in *Gesammelte Werke in zehn Einzelbänden. Reden und Aufsätze I*, ed. by Bernd Schoeller (Frankfurt/M.: S. Fischer, 1979), pp. 174–85 (p. 176); see also Elena Raponi, *Hofmannsthal e l'Italia. Fonti italiane nell'opera poetica e teatrale di Hugo von Hofmannsthal* (Milan: Vita e Pensiero Università, 2002).

had favourably reviewed performances of D'Annunzio's plays in Austria.[7] The situation changed abruptly when Austrian writers, with few exceptions, began to fulfil their patriotic duty in the 'intellectual war'.

In the following discussion of the debate around D'Annunzio in Austria, I first focus on Stefan Zweig. While it is known that Hofmannsthal retracted his affection for D'Annunzio when the Italian poet became involved in politics, Zweig's reaction has not yet been examined. Zweig's view on D'Annunzio also changed after Italy entered the war, even though Zweig, despite harsh criticism of D'Annunzio's political interference, tried again and again – unlike Hofmannsthal – not to lose sight of D'Annunzio's importance as a poet. The second and third parts of the chapter examine the aforementioned 'intellectual war' in its complexity, showing the consequences that these debates had on the reception of D'Annunzio in the twentieth century.

D'Annunzio and Stefan Zweig

Although Zweig responded to D'Annunzio before the beginning of the First World War and also much later, the war gave rise to his secret D'Annunzio studies. Zweig's relationship with D'Annunzio was characterised by an unresolved contradiction: his love for the unique poet was opposed to his consistent dislike of the *poeta vates*. In 1903, Zweig compared D'Annunzio's lyrical talent to that of Stefan George, admiring his poetic virtuosity and ability to evoke the world of dreams.[8] He regarded the author of the *Laudi* as a lyrical innovator who introduced a new rhythm into poetry. In 1912, working with the German writer Ernst Lissauer on an international anthology of poets using free rhythms, he planned to include D'Annunzio.[9] The First World War did not dampen his admiration for the Italian poet.

7 Elsbeth Dangel-Pelloquin, '»Mondaine Stimmungsakrobaten«. Bahrs und Hofmannsthals Kreation der Moderne am Beispiel von Eleonora Duse und Isadora Duncan', in Hermann Bahr, *Österreichischer Kritiker europäischer Avantgarden*, ed. by Martin Anton Müller, Claus Pias and Gottfried Schnödl (Bern: Lang, 2014), pp. 51–81.

8 Stefan Zweig, 'Die um Stefan George', *Das literarische Echo* 6: 3 (1 November 1903), pp. 169–72 (p. 169).

9 See Stefan Zweig's letter to Benno Geiger, 24 May 1912, cited in Marco Meli and Elsa Ariè Geiger, eds, *Benno Geiger e la cultura europea* (Florence: Leo Olschki, 2010), p. 5.

Zweig recommended examples from his prose work for publication by the publisher Insel-Verlag. He admired Italian editions of D'Annunzio for their bibliophilic character and the illustrations by De Carolis, and he held D'Annunzio in high regard as a refined interpreter of Dante. Nevertheless, admiration for D'Annunzio was from the outset mixed with criticism. In a 1904 review of the German translation of D'Annunzio's *Elegie romane* (1892), published in German, Zweig expressed doubts about the poet's status as a modern classic and his implicit ambition to be seen as a successor of Goethe[10] – a view that he soon needed to revise, considering the international recognition D'Annunzio achieved with novels such as *Il Piacere* (1889), *L'Innocente* (1892) and *Trionfo della morte* (1894). This criticism was an expression of uneasiness about D'Annunzio's growing commitment to irredentism and pan-Italianism. Further objections to D'Annunzio as a national poet can be found in the review of *Das Schiff* (La nave), published in the same year as the play, in 1908. According to Zweig, D'Annunzio's play justified Italy's imperialist ambitions, shortly afterwards enacted by Italy's invasion of Libya (1911). Zweig argued that D'Annunzio was trying to persuade his people to re-establish hegemony in the Adriatic, as in the time of the Venetian Republic in the late Middle Ages and early Renaissance. He found these claims preposterous and considered D'Annunzio a nationalist who came 'too late', who misjudged the real needs of Italians.[11] In his reviews of Italian works published around the turn of the century, Zweig continued to criticise D'Annunzio's nationalistic tone. Instead, he praised novels by Sibilla Aleramo and Giovanni Cena, *Una donna* (1906) and *Gli ammonitori* (1903), seeing them as examples of contemporary literature with 'European breath'. Zweig's disapproval of D'Annunzio reached its climax after the outbreak of war, in mid-1914. His diaries from the years 1914 and 1915 document his concern over the discussions about Italy's possible entry into the conflict. His tone is surprising: the cosmopolitan writer, and future pacifist, frequently uses xenophobic stereotypes and does not refrain from chauvinistic statements. For example, he writes of D'Annunzio's May 1915 speech in Quarto: 'D'Annunzio's speech becomes a state danger for us, the [Italian] newspapers were so insolent as to consider it "presumptuous" that we ran a French warship

[10] Stefan Zweig, 'Römische Elegien. Von Gabriele D'Annunzio', *Das literarische Echo* 5: 18 (15 July 1904).

[11] Stefan Zweig, 'Venedigs glückhaftes Schiff. Gabriele d'Annunzios »La Nave«', *Neue Freie Presse* (31 January 1908), pp. 1–3.

aground in the Adriatic Sea.'[12] The usually reserved writer angrily scolds Italians, whom he believes guilty of treason against the former allies of the Triple Alliance:

> Dennoch vermöchte ich niemals einem Italiener mehr frei ins Gesicht zu blicken. Sie haben uns zu sehr gequält mit ihrer Perfidie, mit ihrer Verlogenheit, die diesem Raub noch edle Motive unterschiebt. Gegen sie wird sich Deutschlands Haß noch nach Jahrhunderten wenden: es ist eigentlich Wahnsinn, den sie begehen.[13]

> (I never wish to look an Italian in the face freely again. They have tormented us too much with their perfidy, with their mendacity, and have attributed noble reasons to this robbery. Germany's hatred against them will still be felt for centuries to come: what they are doing is almost madness.)

When D'Annunzio delivered his second famous speech to the Italian Parliament on 20 May, a few days before the declaration of war, Zweig commented with sarcasm: 'Boundless jubilation for D'Annunzio. He has reached it, *l'alta cima*, higher than Victor Hugo, he has risen in the state as a modern man. It cost 100,000 lives.'[14] Zweig recognised D'Annunzio's success as an event of great symbolic importance. In his eyes, the recognition and honour he was receiving in Italy exceeded even Victor Hugo's standing in France. In his review of *La nave*, Zweig compared D'Annunzio to that French writer, who he depicted as the prototype of the national poet who understands the demands of the people and represents them. In contrast, he saw D'Annunzio's causes as neither timely nor real priorities for Italians. After D'Annunzio's pro-war speeches, Zweig revised his opinion and presented the Italian poet as having achieved higher status than his French competitor. However, the price of this success was the many lives of soldiers and civilians lost in the war.

After Italy's declaration of war, official propaganda in Austria began a powerful press campaign against Italy as an alliance-breaker and against D'Annunzio as a warmonger. At this point, based on his previous opinions, one would expect Zweig to engage in, or even increase, his attacks. Instead, the diary entries of this period show that he stepped apart from the chorus of anti-Italian voices

[12] Stefan Zweig, *Tagebücher*, ed. by Kurt Beck, Frankfurt/M.: S. Fischer, 1984 (6 May 1915), p. 167.

[13] Ibid., p. 167.

[14] Ibid., p. 173.

and defended D'Annunzio. He denounced accusations of cowardice against Italians as misplaced and sharply polemicised against journalists who decried D'Annunzio while lacking even a shred of his poetic talent.[15] He made no comment on D'Annunzio's famous flight over Vienna on 8 August 1918.

D'Annunzio as the Target of Austrian Writers, 1915–1916

The critical reactions of Austrian writers against D'Annunzio can be divided into two major phases. Immediately after the declaration of war there were indignant statements portraying D'Annunzio as the quintessence of negative features attributed to Italians – a presumed penchant for treason, lust for fame and cowardice. This was followed by a second phase in which persiflage became central. It is striking how almost everyone involved in Austrian art and culture took part in criticising D'Annunzio. In the first year of the war, Arthur Schnitzler's diaries do not contain any detailed comments on political developments in Italy. However, in a letter of 22 May 1915 to the publisher Samuel Fischer, he used sharp words:

> Wenn dieser Brief in Ihre Hände kommt, haben die Feindseligkeiten mit Italien wohl schon in aller Form ihren Anfang genommen. Wie ich eben versuche mehr dazu zu sagen, fühle ich zugleich, daß ich darauf verzichten muß, da der deutsche Sprachgeist das Wort noch nicht gefunden hat, in dem die Begriffe Verrat, Erpressung, Tücke, Verlogenheit und d'Annunzio sich vereinigt ausdrucken ließen.[16]

> (When this letter comes into your hands, the hostilities with Italy will already be started in all forms. While I'm just trying to say more, I feel at the same time that I cannot say more, since the spirit of the German language has not yet found a word to express altogether the terms betrayal, blackmail, malice, mendacity and d'Annunzio.)

The letter had serious consequences for D'Annunzio's reception in German-speaking countries, as Fischer removed his books from its publishing program.

[15] Zweig, *Tagebücher* (28 May 1915), p. 175.

[16] Arthur Schnitzler, *Briefe 1913–1931*, Bd. II, ed. by Peter Michael Braunwarth, Richard Miklin, Susanne Peterlik and Heinrich Schnitzler (Frankfurt/M.: Fischer, 1984), p. 88.

The Austrian critic and writer Alfred Polgar also reacted to Italy's entry into the war with an attack on D'Annunzio. Five days after the declaration of war, on 30 May, he wrote an essay entitled 'D'Annunzio'. He portrayed the Italian poet as a great seducer and demagogue who tricked Italians into exchanging 'desires with realities'[17] – suggesting that winning the war against Austria-Hungary was an illusion. D'Annunzio, he continues, exercised this seductive power despite his ornamental and artificially overloaded language, which he describes as 'a lavish gush that [makes] his [D'Annunzio's] books unbearable'.[18] On the other hand, he cannot help but acknowledge the public impact of D'Annunzio's rhetoric. Despite all criticism, he admits the modernity of D'Annunzio's rhetorical strategies and staging techniques, as well as his ability to seduce the masses. Most people realised that D'Annunzio was a master of mass manipulation only after the events of Fiume in 1919;[19] but Polgar recognised this as early as 1915. He was particularly interested in why an Aesthete like D'Annunzio suddenly wanted to leave his ivory tower to win the favour of the *profanum vulgus*, which he had despised up to that point. Polgar believed this was motivated by dissatisfaction with purely aesthetic existence and the desire to bring art into life. But he also wanted to expose D'Annunzio as a liar, so he argued that his speeches lacked any real passion, that he charmed people at the expense of the truth. He pitied Italians, and he believed they would soon realise what a mistake they had made in following D'Annunzio – a prophecy about the country's future that resembled Zweig's. Polgar then posed the fundamental question of whether it is legitimate for 'a poet, a civilized human being, an aristocrat by spirit'[20] to preach war. He condemned D'Annunzio as a 'pied piper, who fills the grave with the childlike and the trusting and the curious', and described the war as a great catastrophe for mankind. Despite the general atmosphere of extreme aggressiveness, Polgar's language is free of any form of chauvinism. The way in which he talks about

[17] Alfred Polgar, 'd'Annunzio', in *Kleine Schriften*, Vol. I, ed. by Marcel Reich-Ranicki (Reinbek bei Hamburg: Rowohlt, 1982), pp. 6–10 (p. 6).

[18] Ibid., p. 6.

[19] Hans Richard Brittnacher, '»Der Rhythmus hat immer recht.« D'Annunzio verhängt den Ausnahmezustand in Fiume', in *Europa neu denken II. Mentalitätsgeschichte der Adria – Neugierde und Konflikt als Betriebsgeheimnis*, ed. by Michael Fischer and Johannes Hahn (Salzburg: Verlag Anton Pustet, 2015), pp. 47–58; Hans Ulrich Gumbrecht, Friedrich Kittler and Bernhard Siegert, eds., *Der Dichter als Kommandant. D'Annunzio erobert Fiume* (Munich: Fink, 1996).

[20] Polgar, 'd'Annunzio', p. 8.

Italians, despite animosity against D'Annunzio, differs from the diary entries by Schnitzler and Zweig. Polgar portrays Italians as uncritical victims of a clever demagogue, defining them primarily as 'trusting' and 'curious'. In contrast to Zweig and Schnitzler, he regrets their tragic fate and imagines their disillusionment: 'When [the people] will reach for the golden words of their poet in days of sorrow and need, only straw and chaff will remain in their hands'.[21]

The attacks reach a climax in the 1915 essay *Von Dante zu d'Annunzio* by Egon Friedell, the prominent Austrian historian, actor, playwright and critic. Friedell pursued the goal of discrediting Italians by comparing them to other 'civilized peoples' and postulated that Italians have produced fewer 'achievements of European renown' than neighbouring peoples. He provocatively asks: 'Why does Italy only send swindlers and flatheads across its borders?' to then answer: 'because it has nothing else'.[22] As evidence for this he cites the presumed superiority of Theodor Mommsen's portrayal of Julius Caesar over that of Guglielmo Ferrero.[23] The inferiority of Italians, he believed, was also evident from the state of Italian theatre,[24] where actors such as Ermete Zacconi and Ermete Novelli offered weak performances relative to other European actors. In the scientific field Italians similarly underperformed. Cesare Lombroso's *Genio e follia* (1872, translated into German in 1887), from Friedell's point of view, demonstrated only one thing: 'The God of Italy is nonsense'.[25] In the central part of his essay, Friedell argues that Italy's path from Dante to D'Annunzio was one of catastrophic and irreversible decay, questioning D'Annunzio's view of himself as Dante's successor, especially since the author of the *Commedia*, in Friedell's view, is only partially Italian: 'This great Lombard [sic!] has stood over Italy for six hundred years as a burning warning sign, a sign of what Italian genius could have become while it has become the very opposite.'[26] While Hofmannsthal had sharply differentiated between D'Annunzio's 'false' Italy and the authentic Italy of great

[21] Ibid., p. 8.

[22] Egon Friedell, *Von Dante zu d'Annunzio* (Vienna and Leipzig: Rosner) 1915, p. 55.

[23] Polgar refers to Theodor Mommsen's *Römische Geschichte* Volumes 1–3, (Weidmann: Leipzig, 1854–56) and to Guglielmo Ferrero's *Größe und Niedergang Roms* (Stuttgart, Julius Hoffman, 1908).

[24] Friedell, *Von Dante zu d'Annunzio*, p. 56.

[25] Ibid., p. 58.

[26] Ibid., p. 58.

art (Mantegna) and great politics (Mazzini),[27] Friedell distinguishes between Dante's Italy and that of D'Annunzio. For Friedell, even Eleonora Duse's 'great and pure art' was 'certainly not Italian':[28] it arose from her femininity and was therefore something 'quite international'.[29] In this essay, D'Annunzio becomes representative of the 'Italian Soul' in the most negative sense, even referring to him as a 'Renaissance man' to accentuate the negative characteristics associated with this topos: 'Has D'Annunzio forgotten who is struck by the most terrible curse in the Inferno? Traitors! The utmost distance from God is their punishment. They are stuck in the eternal ice, where even tears freeze.'[30] At the end of his remarks, he compares D'Annunzio to 'a depraved hairdresser's assistant, for whom the German word '*Laffe*' [fop] seems to have been invented, and who now, cheered on by appropriate tips, handles his rancid pots of pomade with dexterity.'[31] Friedell refers here to the stereotypes of the Italian barber or Figaro, thus denigrating D'Annunzio's pose as an Aesthete, as well.

After the first phase of rants, D'Annunzio gradually became the target of a campaign of wartime propaganda that culminated in 1916. In this context, it is revealing to consider the book *Die Front im Tirol* (The Front in Tyrol) by Franz Karl Ginzkey, a good friend of Stefan Zweig who had helped his better-known colleague obtain a position in the war press archives. Ginzkey and Zweig both wrote newspaper articles and books praising the heroism of Austrian soldiers, until Zweig gradually found his way to pacifism and emigrated to Switzerland in 1917. In *Die Front im Tirol*, Ginzkey builds a sharp contrast between a Tyrolean singer who has become a soldier and the Italian *poeta vates*, to the benefit of the former:

> Das klare, erdgetreue Wesen dieses stolzbescheidenen Sängers, der seinem Volke todesmutig auch zur Tat voraneilt, sticht wunderbar bezeichnend gegen seinen ungleich berühmteren Kollegen im feindlichen Lager und dessen bombastisch in sich selbst erhitzte Phrasen ab. Sitzt auch Herr Gabriele d'Annunzio bereits bei seinen Alpini droben auf irgendeinem umschossenen Felsengrat? So zwischen zwei- und dreitausend

[27] Hugo von Hofmannsthal, 'Antwort auf die »neunte Canzone« Gabriele D'Annunzios', in *Gesammelte Werke in Einzelausgaben. Prosa III*, ed. by Herbert Steiner (Frankfurt/M.: Fischer, 1984), pp. 81–6.

[28] Friedell, *Von Dante zu d'Annunzio*, p. 56.

[29] Ibid., p. 57.

[30] Ibid., p. 60.

[31] Ibid., p. 60.

> Meter, zur Rechten den Gletscher –, zur Linken den Kugeltod? Er könnte dort mithelfen, die Suppe auslöffeln, die er seinem verirrten Volke eingebrockt. Aber die Macht seiner wohlgedrechselten Rede hatte dort droben im Angesicht der schweigenden Hohen wenig Gewalt. Seine Leute würden ihm sagen: Mann, gib uns die Tat und entschäle den Kern deines Denkens. Das Spiel der Begriffe verliert hier jeglichen Wert.[32]
>
> (The clear, down-to-earth nature of this unassuming singer, who undaunted by death hurries on ahead of his people to action, stands out significantly compared to that of his incomparably more famous colleague in the enemy camp and his bombastic, self-heated phrases. Is Gabriele D'Annunzio also already sitting up there with his *Alpini* on some all-round fired-at ridge of rock? Between two and three thousand meters, on the right the glacier – on the left death by bullet? He could have helped out there, spooning out the soup that he brought to his lost people. But the power of his well-crafted speech had little impact up there, as they faced the silent mountain heights. His people would say to him: man, give us action, unravel your thinking and get to the point. The game of rhetoric loses all value here.)

While the Tyrolean soldier sings a war song to encourage his people to action, the Italian poet is portrayed as a perfidious seducer, who uses his oratory to persuade Italians, 'lost people', to undertake a disastrous enterprise. D'Annunzio's oratory proves useless in combat: only the heartfelt courage of the Austrian soldier counts. Ginzkey assumes that D'Annunzio would abandon his *Alpini* in the decisive moment, something that D'Annunzio's combat missions, from the so-called 'Beffa di Buccari' to the to the flight over Vienna, do not substantiate.

The topos of D'Annunzio as a seducer of the masses was also reworked in the aphorisms by the Austrian writer and poet Peter Altenberg, who invoked the duty of the authentic writer to bear moral responsibility for guiding his 'immature' audience, avoiding agitation. Someone like D'Annunzio, in his view, is a 'cowardly rascal, not a poet!'[33] Altenberg accentuates the accusation of cowardice against D'Annunzio already voiced by many writers, denying him the rank of poet because he assumes that a poet should stay away from politics, not instigate people to war. None of his fellow writers had come to this radical conclusion before.

32 Franz Karl Ginzkey, *Die Front im Tirol* (Berlin: Fischer, 1996), p. 14.
33 Peter Altenberg, *Nachfechsung* (Berlin: Samuel Fischer Verlag, 1916), p. 20.

In polemics against D'Annunzio, bantering and caricature form a genre of their own, not only in Austria but also in Italy and France.[34] The most important contribution to this particular genre in Austrian literature is that of the writer Franz Blei, who in his *Bestiary of Modern Literature* (1920) compares D'Annunzio to a Pegasus – a reference to the Italian poet's great passion for flying,[35] and possibly also to his spectacular flight over Vienna in August 1918:

> Der Pegasus d'Annunzio schlug mit seinen eleganten Hufen die herrlichsten, herrlichsten Takte der letzten drei Jahrzehnte [. . .]. Später dann verlangte die Zeit Probe aufs große Wort, und der Pegasus gab sie. Er ließ sich die Hufe mit Eisen beschlagen, wirbelte damit die Trommel und wieherte Fanfaren. Die an tönenden Worten reichste Zeit, die des Krieges und seines Après, machte aus dem Pegasus nicht den Tyrtaios, aber das lauthinwiehernde Schlachtpferd gab den hellen italienischen Trompeten Brust, Luft und Schwung. Ein römischer Kaiser hat sein Leibpferd zum Konsul gemacht – der Pegasus d'Annunzio konnte es für möglich halten, daß ihn sein Volk zum Kaiser der Adria erhebe.[36]

> (With his elegant hooves, Pegasus-d'Annunzio beat the most magnificent, most magnificent strokes of the last three decades [. . .]. Later, time demanded proof of his grand words, and Pegasus gave this proof. He had his hooves shod with irons, twirled the drum with them, and neighed fanfares. The time richest in resounding words, that of the war and its aftermath, did not turn Pegasus into Tyrtaeus, but the loudly neighing battle-horse gave the bright Italian trumpets breast, breath, and momentum. A Roman emperor made his personal horse a consul. Pegasus-d'Annunzio thought it possible that his people would make him emperor of the Adriatic.)

Blei mocks D'Annunzio's self-stylisation as Italy's national bard and his propaganda, without, however, disputing the European rank he has achieved as a poet. The question of the legitimacy of a poet's involvement in politics, already raised by Hofmannsthal and Zweig, as well as by others, would continue to influence the debate about D'Annunzio for the next two decades.

34 Gec (Enrico Gianeri), *D'Annunzio nella caricatura mondiale* (Milan: Garzanti, 1941).

35 Peter Demetz, *Die Flugschau von Brescia. Kafka, d'Annunzio und die Männer, die vom Himmel fielen* (Vienna: Zsolnay, 2002).

36 Franz Blei, *Das große Bestiarium der modernen Literatur*, ed. by Rolf-Peter Baacke (Hamburg: Europäische Verlagsanstalt, 1995), p. 21.

Conclusions

As evidenced in these examples, Austrian writers reacted to Italy's entry into the war by deploying negative stereotypes and applying nationalistic slogans to ridicule the enemy and its bard, inciting hatred against them. Only in some cases does irony counterbalance the sharpness of these attacks.

In *Die letzten Tage der Menschheit*, Karl Kraus questioned the basic premises of the widespread polemic against D'Annunzio. In this work, two Austrian officers fighting on the Isonzo Front, called *Fallota* and *Beinsteller* – names built around 'fall' and 'tripping' – are ridiculed for their chauvinism. A song sung by both officers (Act III, Scene 3) summarises anti-Italian propaganda stereotypes:

Wir haben sie guat getroff 'n
Die andern do san gloff 'n.
Tschiff, tscheff, tauch, der Wallisch liegt am Bauch.

Könnan nimma Katzl mach'n,
Es tuat halt gar zviel krach'n.
Tschiff –

Den Annunzio und Sonnino
Den machma a no hino.
Tschiff – [. . .][37]

(We've scored a direct hit on them,
the others have run away,
Tschiff, tscheff, the Italian lies on its belly.

They can't produce any more children[38]
because there are too many explosions,
Tschiff –

D'Annunzio and Sonnino,
We'll soon kill them too.
Tschiff – [. . .])

[37] Karl Kraus, *Die letzten Tage der Menschheit. Tragödie in fünf Akten mit Vorspiel und Epilog* (Frankfurt/M.: Suhrkamp, 1986), p. 329.

[38] The verse 'Könnan nimma Katzl mach'n' literally means 'they can't make any more kittens'. In Austria, the Italians are still called 'Katzlmacher' (cat makers). This has nothing to do with cats but is supposedly derived from famous bowls that the Italians made. The poet is thus playing a phonetic word game which the translation elides.

By openly pillorying a mainstay of the monarchy such as the officer caste and ridiculing its representatives, Kraus launched an attack on the monarchy as a whole. At the same time, his drama depicts the brutalisation of man at war. In other episodes dealing with Italy, Kraus shows the striking difference between the behaviour of the same man in times of war and peace – for example, when the Fregattenleutnant (Frigate Lieutenant) reports having bombed the same Venice that he had loved as a tourist in peacetime (Act II, Scene 30). In some cases, Kraus attacked his fellow writers directly. In the run-up to the war, for example, he exposed the weaknesses of Hofmannsthal's reaction to D'Annunzio's ninth *Canzone*. He made fun of Hofmannsthal's claim that he felt Italian and of his desire to be part of the 'authentic Italy' to which D'Annunzio, after his political engagement, no longer belonged: 'But M. d'Annunzio is not Italian. At least Herr Hofmannsthal knows what Italian is. Maybe he is even Italian [. . .]. Perhaps Herr Hofmannsthal is d'Annunzio and d'Annunzio is just a Hofmannsthal.'[39]

Curiously, some of the writers who had attacked D'Annunzio supported Kraus when it came to taking up arms against the press. Zweig referred to journalists as a 'mob',[40] while Polgar called them 'Brüder im Ungeiste von D'Annunzio' (Brothers in D'Annunzio's mischief), with a play of words that turned the saying 'Brüder im Geiste' (Brothers in spirit), denoting brotherly similarity in attitude and mentality, into its very opposite.[41] In Polgar's view, journalists, with an un-brotherly attitude, multiplied the echo of D'Annunzio's demagogic speeches.

In the 1920s, debate over D'Annunzio intensified because of his support for Mussolini. Twelve years after he first spoke against D'Annunzio, Alfred Polgar, for example, wrote again about him in an essay entitled *Paderewski D'Annunzio*, published in 1927. By then war had ended, the Fiume enterprise had taken place, and D'Annunzio was celebrated alongside Mussolini. Whereas in 1915 Polgar had described D'Annunzio as an absolute novelty in cultural history, he now considered him together with another nationalist artist, the Pole Paderewski. Polgar comments on both: 'They were artists and became "statesmen". They belonged to themselves and now belong to the general public. They traded fame for popularity.

39 Karl Kraus, 'Es wird ernst', *Die Fackel* XIII, 343/344 (29 February 1912), pp. 44f (p. 45).

40 Zweig, *Tagebücher* (28 May 1915), p. 175.

41 Polgar, *d'Annunzio*, p. 9.

They give the strangely parodic spectacle of a regression from freedom to servitude.'[42] Like Zweig, Polgar criticised the intellectuals who chose to take part in politics. In his eyes, this involvement only leads to loss: D'Annunzio lost his freedom and standing as an artist; in return, Polgar adds sarcastically, he gained a uniform. Even more important for the Austrian critic was the fact that D'Annunzio could no longer be seen as an individual case: he became a European problem.

Julien Benda's *La Trahison des Clercs* (*The Betrayal by the Intellectuals*) was also published in 1927. In this book, the French philosopher cited D'Annunzio as an example of the betrayal of the values of the Enlightenment, which an intellectual should defend regardless of ethnicity or nationality. Like Zweig, Benda mentioned the drama *Das Schiff* (La nave) as evidence of his nationalist ideology. Like Polgar's book, Benda's viewed the betrayal by intellectuals not as a national problem but a European problem.[43] In contrast to these opinions, Stefan Zweig, after the war, returned to his earlier admiration for D'Annunzio, renouncing the ideological suspicion of his former role model. In a survey of the Italian magazine *Leonardo* in 1925, he described D'Annunzio as a 'passionate word-maker, an ardent artist intoxicated with himself and with all forms of beauty'.[44] In 1925 he published a book in which he theorised a 'poetics of the demonic' based on the examples of Hölderlin, Kleist and Nietzsche, an irrational poetics based on the fateful determination of existence.[45] At the centre of this concept of art are creativity, fanaticism, heroism and also tragedy. One has to ask oneself whether the designation of D'Annunzio as a *daimon* artist – in the Greek sense – applied to the Italian poet or not. What is certain is that Zweig here revised his demand for a fusion of literature and morality, which he had made in 1914 following his criticism of D'Annunzio and Verhaeren.[46] At that time, he believed literature that used beautiful words to represent

[42] Alfred Polgar, 'Paderewski. D'Annunzio', in *Kleine Schriften*, Vol. I (Reinbek bei Hamburg: Rowohlt, 1982), pp. 389–91 (p. 389).

[43] Renate Lunzer, 'Zum Thema »trahison des clercs«. Fallbeispiel Gabriele D'Annunzio', in *Wenn Ränder Mitte werden. Festschrift für Fritz Peter Kirsch*, ed. by Chantal Adobati (Vienna: WUV, 2001), pp. 617–26.

[44] Schweig, *Leonardo* 11 (1925).

[45] Stefan Zweig, *Der Kampf mit dem Dämon. Hölderlin, Kleist, Nietzsche* (Frankfurt/M.: Fischer, 2007); see also Matjaž Birk and Thomas Eicher, eds, *Stefan Zweig und das Dämonische* (Würzburg: Königshausen & Neumann, 2008).

[46] Romain Rolland and Stefan Zweig, *Briefwechsel 1910–1940*, Vol. I (Berlin: Rütten & Leoning, 1987), p. 124.

morally questionable content was unsuitable in times of political tensions.[47] Ten years later, he changed his stance. While Zweig criticised D'Annunzio's ideology, labelling him a chauvinist poet or precursor of Fascism, he nevertheless distinguished his poetic achievements from his politics and appreciated the former despite the latter.

Involvement in the debate over D'Annunzio was commensurate with his importance as a literary role model for each writer. Among the most important authors involved, along with Polgar and Hofmannsthal, was Robert Musil, for whom *Il Piacere* had been 'one of the first books through which I became acquainted with "modernity", 40 years ago, and one of the first to have an impact on me. I would give anything to know what impact. Probably a general immorality and also a general Aestheticism.'[48] Looking back on his early interest in D'Annunzio on the occasion of the poet's death (2 March 1938), shortly before the annexation of Austria into Nazi Germany, Musil noted: 'He was a good patriot as far as he was a good poet. But turn it around: he was a good poet because he was a good patriot.'[49] On the same day, Franz Werfel wrote a diary entry in which he recalled D'Annunzio's time as a *poeta vates* during the First World War. Here, D'Annunzio's poetic achievement disappears in the shadow of his disproportionate ego and hunger for fame:

> Alle seine Masken verschwimmen in die letzte, die Totenmaske. Er war ein großer Dichter, doch hat er das Dichtertum nicht erhöht. Er unterordnete den Dichter im Range dem politischen, dem militärischen Führer, ja dem nationalen Filibustier. Das geschah, weil sein Ehrgeiz so ungeheuerlich [war], daß ihm kein Ruhm genügte, nicht die stille, echte, beständige Ehre, die einzig und allein das geistige Sein und Schaffen zu vergeben hat. Er betete die Macht an und den grellen Erfolg sehr kühner Abenteuer, die er mit großem Mute unternahm, teils aus wirklichem Fanatismus, teils um sich dadurch zum nationalen Heros heraufzunumerieren.[50]

(All his masks blur into the last one, the death mask. He was a great poet, but he did not exalt poetry. He subordinated the poet in rank to the political, the military leader, even the national filibuster. This happened because his ambition [was] so outrageous that no fame was enough for

[47] Ibid., p. 124.

[48] Robert Musil, 'Tagebücher, Aphorismen, Essays und Reden', in *Gesammelte Werke in Einzelausgaben*, Heft 30, ed. by Adolf Frisé (Reinbek bei Hamburg: Rowohlt, 1955), p. 470.

[49] Ibid., p. 142.

[50] Franz Werfel, *Zwischen Oben und Unten. Prosa, Tagebücher, Aphorismen, literarische Nachträge* (Munich: Langen-Müller, 1975), p. 455.

him, certainly not the quiet, genuine, constant honour that only spiritual existence and creativity can bestow. He worshipped the power and glaring success of daring adventures, which he undertook with great courage, partly out of real fanaticism, partly to elevate himself to national hero.)

Yet other authors believed that, despite his unacceptable political stance, D'Annunzio's contribution to modernity could be saved. We have seen that this was the position of Stefan Zweig, who strongly condemned D'Annunzio's relationship with Mussolini yet took D'Annunzio's poems with him into exile in 1934. Walter Benjamin's and Bertolt Brecht's attitudes toward D'Annunzio were similar. After Benjamin read the *Laudi* and *Merope* during his stay on Capri in 1916, he was happy to translate D'Annunzio's poem to Eleonora Duse for the journal *Der Querschnitt*,[51] yet twenty years later he condemned the 'aestheticisation of politics' in his essay on 'The Work of Art in the Age of Mechanical Reproduction'. Brecht, similarly, could not deny his fascination with D'Annunzio's language and translated his most famous poem, 'La pioggia nel pineto'.[52] He wrote in private about D'Annunzio: 'He was a charlatan, but that charlatan wrote pastoral poetry that will never be forgotten.'[53] Despite ideological differences, he attributes to artistic personalities such as D'Annunzio, George, Kipling and Ezra Pound 'a certain feudal dignity'.[54] Like Polgar and Benda, Brecht argued for understanding the 'D'Annunzio phenomenon' in a European context. Unlike them, he thought the Italian poet and his 'colleagues' deserved respect because of their work: they were, after all, part of a literary tradition that could be continued productively.[55]

[51] Gabriele D'Annunzio, 'Die göttliche Eleonora Duse', in Walter Benjamin, *Gesammelte Schriften. Supplement I. Kleinere Übersetzungen*, ed. by Rolf Tiedemann (Frankfurt/M.: Suhrkamp, 1999), pp. 12–15.

[52] Bertolt Brecht, 'Regen in Pinienhain', in *Gedichte aus dem Nachlass. Gesammelte Werke in 8 Bänden*, ed. by Herta Ramthun (Frankfurt/M.: Suhrkamp, 1982), p. 449f.; see also Alberto Destro, 'Die Faszination des Unpolitischen. Brecht übersetzt D'Annunzio', in *Wo bleibt das »Konzept«? Dov' e il »concetto«? Festschrift für/Studi in onore di Enrico De Angelis*, ed. by Carlo Carmassi, Giovanna Cermelli, Marina Foschi Albert and Marianne Hepp (Munich: Iudicium-Verlag, 2009), pp. 247–55.

[53] Bertolt Brecht, *Arbeitsjourna I*, vol. I: 1928–1942, ed. by Werner Hecht (Frankfurt/M.: Suhrkamp, 1973), p. 495.

[54] Bertolt Brecht, *Arbeitsjournal II*, vol. II: 1942–1955, ed. by Werner Hecht (Frankfurt/M.: Suhrkamp, 1973), p. 764.

[55] Jan Knopf, *Brecht-Handbuch. Lyrik, Prosa, Schriften* (Stuttgart: Metzler, 1984), p. 382.

D'Annunzio's anti-Austrian position, speeches inciting Italy's entry into the war, and eventual collaboration with Mussolini, all earned him a reputation in the German-speaking world as the 'unbeloved poet' (Anna Kupka) or the 'John the Baptist of Fascism'[56] – a reputation that lingers today. Despite these reservations, the recognition of his poetic talent by such diverse artistic figures as Zweig, Benjamin and Brecht shows that D'Annunzio stands for a modernity that cannot simply be discredited with the accusation of proto-Fascism. This contradictory modernity represents a challenge – like that of Filippo Tommaso Marinetti, Gottfried Benn, Ernst Jünger, Ezra Pound or Louis-Ferdinand Céline. A challenge that, today, we must consider without prejudice.

[56] Stefan Andres, 'Die Tode eines Ungeliebten. Eine Annäherung an Gabriele D'Annunzio, den Johannes der Täufer des Faschismus', *Kritische Ausgabe*, 2 (2004), 19–23.

Part IV

Complex Legacies

Chapter 13

D'Annunzio and Argentina: From Elitism to Mass Nationalism

Sandro Abate, translated by Alessia Zinnari and Sophie Maddison

This chapter examines the complex relationship between Gabriele D'Annunzio and Argentina. It explores references to Argentina in D'Annunzio's writing, his relationship to the Italo-Argentinian community, and offers a critical journey through key moments in the reception of D'Annunzio's work in a country with one of the largest Italian communities in the world. Italian migration to Argentina, as I shall show, played a marginal role as a subject for D'Annunzio's work, but a pivotal role for the poet's access to the Spanish-speaking world. Among the strange characters that stand out as intermediaries between D'Annunzio and Argentina are Guido Boggiani, who inspired one of the first representations of the Italian emigrant as a literary topos, and Giovanni del Guzzo, a real life immigrant who organised a trip to Argentina for D'Annunzio that was, however, never realised.

Three phases of D'Annunzio's reception in Argentina can be outlined within a period of fifty years, between 1894 and 1944. These do not correspond to the evolution of D'Annunzio's work and thought, but rather indicate three different stages in the intellectual and literary landscape in Argentina. In the first phase, which spanned the last decade of the nineteenth century, D'Annunzio's aesthetics spoke to elites and became a point of reference for the modern artistic innovation that Rubén Dario promoted in the Hispanic world. In the second phase, which coincided with the Argentina Centennial in 1910, D'Annunzio's work was read in connection to the discourse of *latinidad*, the idea of a cultural heritage shared by the Latin people, and celebrated by the ruling classes of the national bourgeoisie. During the third phase, which took place after the author's death in 1938, D'Annunzio became the most widely circulated Italian author in Argentina. His work was read extensively by the middle classes, the proletariat and suburban audiences alike; this increase of the author's popularity fits within nationalist and populist discourses that would later lead to Peronism.

Neither a strictly comparative lens nor an approach grounded in reception studies appear sufficiently apt to approach the complexity of D'Annunzio's reception in Argentina. Any such research necessitates significant methodological overlaps, accounting for instances of cultural and discursive mediation. For this reason, I have adopted a broad approach inspired by literary sociology and cultural history. On the one hand, Argentina belongs to one of the largest linguistic communities in the world, the Spanish-speaking world. The translation and reception of a European author like D'Annunzio is therefore heavily affected by echoes, appropriations and resonances of an international and intercontinental nature. On the other hand, it is essential to consider that already by the last decades of the nineteenth century and carrying into the present, Argentinian society has included a strong Italian component due to mass immigration. This means that cultural formations and structures in Argentina have come to differ from those of any other Spanish-speaking nation, offering notable resonances with things originating in the Italian peninsula. Finally, the reception of literary works is always strongly affected by variations within the target literary system. D'Annunzio's works have been interpreted, and often acquired different meanings, through the social and political discourses that accompanied the transformations of Argentinian society.

Argentina in D'Annunzio's Work: D'Annunzio and Guido Boggiani

Curiously, the only time that Argentina is mentioned in all of D'Annunzio's extensive literary work is in his poetic production, where he refers to the painter and photographer Guido Boggiani (1861–1902) in the epic poem 'Laus vitae', included in *Maia* (1903). Originally from Novara, Boggiani was a close friend of D'Annunzio. Together with Edoardo Scarforglio, Georges Hérelle and Pasquale Masciantonio, in 1895 he shared with D'Annunzio the experience of sailing through the Aegean Sea on board Scarfoglio's boat, *Fantasia*. Inspired by Nietzsche's writings, the group embarked on a traditional trip to the main archaeological sites of ancient Greece.[1] A few years

[1] On this boat voyage to Greece, see Chapters 1 and 7 in this volume.

later, Boggiani travelled to the subtropical jungle of Chaco in northern Argentina and Paraguay, where he spent his last days as a settler explorer, engaged in studying local indigenous tribes, before meeting his death, besieged by the aborigines whom he had photographed with ethnographic zeal.

In the fifteenth section of the first book of the *Laudi*, D'Annunzio elevates Boggiani to the status of a mythical hero by comparing him to none other than the protagonist of the *Odyssey*. D'Annunzio's Ulysses draws on the representation of the 'modern' man found in Dante's *Divine Comedy*. In D'Annunzio's extensive poem, Ulysses and Boggiani share physical and moral attributes that emphasise their belonging to a hegemonic space built in open hostility to the periphery. The dominant model is that of the European white man, an ethnic type that is reflected on a textual level through the accentuation of characteristics semantically related to lightness. Boggiani is 'il piu pallido' (the palest)[2] with 'occhi chiarissimi' (extremely clear eyes),[3] 'biondi capelli' (blond hair)[4] and a 'capo d'oro' (golden head).[5] His propensity for travel fits the imperial heroic model of the colonialist explorer: his heart is 'ebro e folle d'immensità' (intoxicated and full of immensity),[6] he is characterised by his 'piede veloce' (quick feet),[7] walks at a 'passo spedito' (brisk stride)[8] and is 'certo e leggero' (sure and swift).[9] He is, as the text remarks on at least five occasions, a '*Ulisside*', a worthy substitute for Ulysses, from whom he has inherited a seafaring instinct as well as the desire to navigate, grow and expand. Boggiani is also presented as the 'eletto' (chosen one)[10] and 'sempre operoso' (always hardworking).[11] His 'pronto vigore latino' (eager Latin vigor)[12] destines him to perish in adventurous circumstances, with his 'sangue ottimo' (excellent blood)[13] spilling out over

[2] Gabriele D'Annunzio, 'Laus Vitae', XV, in *Maia*, ed. by Cristina Montagnani (Gardone Riviera: Il Vittoriale degli italiani, 2006), v. 317.

[3] Ibid., v. 315.

[4] Ibid., v. 319.

[5] Ibid., v. 412.

[6] Ibid., v. 388.

[7] Ibid., vv. 456–7.

[8] Ibid., vv. 407–8.

[9] Ibid., v. 437.

[10] Ibid., v. 304.

[11] Ibid., v. 393.

[12] Ibid., v. 460.

[13] Ibid., vv. 432–3.

the distant land which, thanks to him, has been explored and is now known to Europeans.

For D'Annunzio, the territory explored by Boggiani brings together a range of geographical and cultural paradigms relating to ideologies about America as well as to traditional colonialist ideologies and to travel chronicles of that time. D'Annunzio underlines the supernatural aspects of what he calls 'new world', the 'uncivilised' dimension of its inhabitants and the competencies needed to dominate them. When referring to the Gran Chaco jungle in northern Argentina, great emphasis is placed on conditions linked to darkness, ignorance, the wild, the unknown, the primitive and unindustrialised, the dangerous and lethal. This perception of the other is particularly evident when D'Annunzio recounts the days that Boggiani spent 'tra fosche, incognite stirpi' (among sinister, unknown races),[14] 'nell'inviluppo terrestre' (in covered land),[15] among the 'smisurata fronda opulenta' (vast leafy branches),[16] before finally falling 'sotto la clava del selvaggio predone' (under the club of the savage marauder).[17] As I have argued elsewhere, D'Annunzio uses the comparison to Ulysses to present a new archetype of the hero: the explorer and coloniser of distant lands, the European white man who, through great art and skill, is able to gain control of a wide range of subordinate cultures.[18]

With his *Cuore* (1886), and particularly in the chapter 'Dagli Appennini alle Ande', Edmondo De Amicis had already brought Argentina into the Italian literary imaginary of the late-nineteenth century. But it is D'Annunzio who, in 'Laus vitae', formulated ideas and stereotypes that would be taken up by those writers most sensitive to what was a central issue in Italian life at that time.[19] The perspective that D'Annunzio provides on Boggiani's adventures reflects the ways in which Italy dealt with the dramatic phenomenon of the diaspora between the last decades of the nineteenth century and

[14] Ibid., v. 343.

[15] Ibid., 345.

[16] Ibid., vv. 375–6.

[17] Ibid., vv. 442–3.

[18] Sandro Abate, 'Poesia y colonialismo: *Maia* de Gabriele d'Annunzio', *Cuadernos de Filología Italiana*, 16 (2009), 187–200 (p. 187).

[19] Pirandello, Pascoli, Campana and Corradini are among the authors who focus on this theme of migration, as noted in recent investigations. See Marco Nifantani, *Los lugares del otro: Las imágenes culturales de lo ajeno identitario en la narrativa argentina e italiana del siglo XX* (Bahia Blanca: Editorial de la Universidad Nacional del Sur, 2008) and Fernanda Bravo Herrera, *Huellas y recorridos de una utopía: La emigración italiana en la Argentina* (Buenos Aires: Teseo, 2015).

the Second World War. Far from being considered in terms of loss or absence, emigration was presented in these years by the government and popular media as an epic missionary programme. During Fascism, it was associated with representations of a coloniser flying the flag of Latin civilisation. D'Annunzio uses Boggiani to construct a representational prototype of the Italian emigrant that had widespread repercussions in cultural, political and literary terms.

Early Reception and Translations

Ever since the last decades of the nineteenth century, Argentina has had the largest community of Italian immigrants in the world. Between 1881 and 1914, more than two million Italians arrived in the country, seeking to escape from poverty after the great crisis of the Italian agrarian model.[20] In Buenos Aires and the other main Argentinian cities, the significant presence of Italians generated a profound cultural transformation and a rich enthusiasm for Italian customs. This was evident not only in the activities of various organisations, but also in the consumption and distribution of Italian art and literature. It was also encouraged by the Argentinian ruling class, whose political and economic interests were receptive to European trends.

The initial reception of D'Annunzio in Argentina took place in the late nineteenth and early twentieth centuries. Originally known only in literary circles, between the 1920s and the 1930s D'Annunzio became increasingly popular due to the publication and consumption of his principal works in translation. By the 1940s, his work circulated widely, coinciding with the emergence of nationalist discourses directly linked to Peronism. As indicated by Fernando Murga,[21] Franco Meregalli,[22] Alma Novella Marani[23] and

20 Fernando Devoto, *Historia de la immigración en la Argentina* (Buenos Aires: Sudamericana, 2004).

21 Fernando Murga, 'Gabriele d'Annunzio e il mondo di lingua spagnola', in *Gabriele d'Annunzio nel primo centenario della nascita*, (Rome: Centro di vita italiana, 1963), pp. 143–60.

22 Franco Meregalli, 'D'Annunzio in Spagna', in *L'arte di Gabriele d'Annunzio: Atti del convegno internazionale di studio Venezia-Gardone Riviera-Pescara, 7–13 ottobre 1963* (Milan: Mondadori, 1968), pp. 481–503.

23 Alma Novella Marani, 'D'Annunzio en la Argentina', in *D'Annunzio in America Latina: Ciclo di convegni su D'Annunzio e le letterature moderne, nel 500 anniversario, 1938–1988* (Pescara: Universitá degli Studi Gabriele d'Annunzio, 1990), pp. 99–111.

Gabrielle Morelli,[24] the first accounts of D'Annunzio's reception in Argentina and throughout the Spanish-speaking world are found in material written by Rubén Darío and published in the *Revista de América*, which Dario co-directed in Buenos Aires. During the publication's brief existence (three issues) in 1894, it included reviews and commentaries relating to D'Annunzio's work. In the article 'Un esteta italiano' (An Italian Aesthete), Darío, who had read *Trionfo della morte* earlier that year, identified D'Annunzio as a poet participating in the latest European poetic trends and praised the book as 'the ideal of modern prose; artistic prose, prose that has roots in France and that has just begun to appear in England, Scandinavia and Germany'.[25]

Darío was interested in promoting authors who represented ideals of 'modernity', beyond the slightly rhetorical and largely naturalistic forms that Spanish literature provided at the time. In its preference for 'strange', 'marginal' writers, the *Revista de América* included French, English and Italian authors. A few years later, such writers' work appeared in *Los Raros* (1896), the book with which Darío opened the door to a new aesthetics in poetry written in the Spanish language. During the years he spent in Buenos Aires, Darío read D'Annunzio's work in Italian. At the time, D'Annunzio had only produced and published a small portion of his work: a collection of short stories, two novels from the trilogy *I romanzi della Rosa* and six lyrical collections that were later grouped in *Versi d'amore*. Darío's discovery of the Italian author was undoubtedly an early one, and he was also one of the first to recognise and admire D'Annunzio outside Italy. Furthermore, he was the main catalyst not only for the diffusion of D'Annunzio's work in the Spanish-speaking world, but also of his intercontinental reputation. Praising, above all, his 'poetic prose', he introduced the author to audiences in Latin America as well as in Spain. Likewise, it is worth noting that the first translations of D'Annunzio's work into Spanish were published in Buenos Aires: *Traducciones* (Translations) (1897) by Leopoldo Díaz contains several texts by the Italian writer, while Carlos Ortiz published his translation of the first act of *La ciudad muerta* (*La città morta*)

[24] Gabrielle Morelli, 'D'Annunzio in Spagna', in *Itinerari dannunziani: Atti della giornata di studio organizzata dal Cenacolo orobico di poesia, Bergamo, 24 ottobre 1998* (Bergamo: Edizioni dell'Ateneo, 1999), pp. 95–102.

[25] Rubén Darío, 'Un esteta italiano (Gabriel d'Annunzio)', *Revista de América*, 1 (1894), 1–2.

in the *El Mercurio de América* magazine in 1898. The first complete Spanish translation of *La ciudad muerta* was produced by Adriano Malusardi, who was Argentinian, and published in Buenos Aires by *La Revista National* in 1901.

The publicity created by Rubén Darío also led to the first significant translations of D'Annunzio's work in Spain, where he was still practically unknown. In 1898, the Nicaraguan poet arrived in Madrid, sent by the Buenos Aires newspaper *La Nación* to report on the aftermath of the Spanish defeat in Cuba. From 1900 onwards, versions of D'Annunzio's texts were translated and published in Spain, and his principal works began to be disseminated. There was already a considerable consumer market for novels among the middle and lower-middle classes, and the affordable editions of the Barcelona publisher Maucci launched a series of Dannunzian novels translated into Spanish. *El inocente* (*L'Innocente*) translated by Augusto Riera and *El fuego* (*Il fuoco*) by Tomás Orts-Ramos both appeared in 1900. In the same year, they were followed by *El Placer* (*Il Piacere*) translated by Emilio Reverter Delmos and *El Triunfo de la muerte* (*Trionfo della morte*) by Orts-Ramos.

As far as theatrical productions are concerned, in 1909 the nineteen-year-old Ricardo Baeza, one of the main translators of D'Annunzio into Spanish, released his first version of *La ciudad muerta* and *Sueño de una mañana de primavera* (*Sogno d'un mattino di primavera*). Years later, almost all of D'Annunzio's plays were released one after the other. *La Gioconda* and *Sueño de un atardecer de otoño* (*Sogno d'un tramonto d'autunno*) were the first to be published in Madrid where, in 1929, Baeza set out to publish D'Annunzio's entire theatrical output in the context of an editorial project by *Mundo Latino*. After the Spanish Civil War, Baeza settled in Buenos Aires and continued his work. His translations enabled the Argentinian public to access D'Annunzio's theatrical works. Several of these were reissued, particularly those that had been published in Spain during the 1910s. *La hija de Iorio* (*La figlia di Iorio*) (Losada, 1938), *La antorcha escondida* (*La fiaccola sotto il moggio*) (Hachette, 1943), *La Gioconda, Sueño de las estaciones* (*I sogni delle stagioni*) (Shapire, 1943) and *La ciudad muerta* (Hachette, 1945) were some of the titles reprinted by major Buenos Aires publishing houses. In many cases, especially from the 1940s onwards, these publishing runs produced several thousand copies. Baeza was also the first literary critic to address D'Annunzio's work in the Spanish-speaking world, with an article about *La figlia di Iorio* that included pertinent observations regarding the connections between

Dannunzian tragedy and Nietzschean thought.[26] The three-volume edition of D'Annunzio's complete works, translated by Julio Gómez de la Serna and published in Mexico by Aguilar in 1960, remains the most ambitious version of the author's output in Spanish.

The Argentina Centennial

On the centenary of the May Revolution in 1910, a national Argentinian project based on oligarchic principles was established. Its objective was to integrate communities of European immigrants into public life and build a reputation as a nation aligned with the main European powers. From this point of view, there was a notable promotion of Old-World intellectuals, artists and writers – by the state and within the main circles of high culture. The International Centennial Exhibition, organised in Buenos Aires in 1910, attracted well-known figures such as Enrico Ferri, Guglielmo Ferrero, Pietro Gori and even Edmondo De Amicis.

Even though D'Annunzio's work had not been widely read at this time, everyone in Argentinian literary circles knew who he was. Thanks to the author's interventions in the press and in public life, they were especially familiar with his self-constructed reputation as a Decadent and elitist writer. Though it is true, as Borgoño points out, that 'D'Annunzio was not a writer who enjoyed instant popularity in [Argentina] in the same way that Edmondo De Amicis did',[27] newspaper articles testify to his notoriety around the time of the Centennial.

In the autumn of 1907, the Argentinian journalist Juan José Soiza Reilly managed to interview D'Annunzio in his home in Settignano (Florence). On this occasion, they discussed the author's imminent visit to Buenos Aires, where he was due to attend the performances of the actress Eleonora Duse, his partner at the time, and give a series of lectures. In the end, the trip did not take place, though Duse did cross the Atlantic to perform at the Odeón Theater in Buenos Aires – a forum for the most prestigious Centennial events. It was Duse's second visit to Buenos Aires, as she had toured there for the first time in 1885. Nevertheless, D'Annunzio approved the report and the article, entitled 'La vida artística de Gabriel D'Annunzio' (The Artistic

[26] Ricardo Baeza, 'Gabriel d'Annunzio y *La hija de Iorio*', *Cervantes*, 4 (1916), 7–14 (p. 8).

[27] Ariela Borgoño, 'Revista *Idea latina*: una mirada a la traducción cultural en los espacios de la diversidad', *Transfer*, 2 (2010), 47–61 (p. 51).

Life of Gabriele D'Annunzio), was published in the prominent magazine *Caras y caretas* on 7 December 1907. During its most successful period, between 1898 and 1939, *Caras y caretas* covered current affairs, culture and entertainment involving people with national and international profiles. It was a relatively informative magazine distributed in several American and European countries. Although the report was intended, perhaps, as an advertising strategy, the only three comments made by D'Annunzio that were included in the article ended up being extremely offensive to Argentina and to America in general, severely damaging his public image in the country. The author of the article points out, among other things, that:

> He [D'Annunzio] greeted me with a papal gesture. I had previously written to him asking for an interview. He had replied, refusing: 'I am not a ballerina . . . ' But when he understood that he could use a large American newspaper to advertise his next trip to Buenos Aires, he welcomed me in the manner of an amiable pope. And then I saw the reality of the legends that we have been led to believe, back in America. And speaking with him, observing him, so small, so tired, trembling so much inside his feminine corset made of iron, seeing him so human, I thought painfully about the dangers of coming close to stars in real life . . . D'Annunzio will soon go to Buenos Aires. He told me that he 'wants to do us the honour of his presence'. As I smiled at him with astonishment, he added: 'I'm going to America to visit my possessions . . . I have slaves there too . . . ' I couldn't smile. But I asked him if he had already arranged the contract for the two hundred thousand lire they would pay him in Buenos Aires, for five lectures at the Opera . . . he understood. And turning around, he showed me a bust of Dante. A Dante who seemed to be crying on the table . . . When I left, I asked the maestro for a signed greeting to the people of the Argentinian Republic. At this point, he replied with a questioning gesture: 'What for? I don't know if they deserve it yet'.[28]

In addition to such statements, the article conveys a tone of mocking irony on the part of Soiza Reilly, especially when read alongside the photographs showing D'Annunzio in his summer home, the vulgarity of which contrasts with the artist's proverbial prima-donna temperament. Two years later, in 1909, the article was included with other reports by Soiza Reilly in *Cien hombres célebres* (One Hundred Famous Men), a volume that sold more than 20,000 copies in Argentina. In *Escritores iberoamericanos de 1900* (Ibero-American

[28] Juan José Soiza Reilly, 'La vida artistica de Gabriel d'Annunzio', *Caras y caretas*, 10: 479 (1907), 29–32 (p. 32).

Writers of 1900) (1943),[29] Manuel Hugarte notes that this put Soiza Reilly out of favour with D'Annunzio forever.

In March 1910, the Buenos Aires-based periodical *Ideas y figuras* published an edition dedicated to D'Annunzio. The main article bears the signature of Filippo T. Marinetti, a prominent poet linked to the emerging Futurist movement, and is made up of comments (some of which are quite entertaining) relating to the more obscure elements of D'Annunzio's artistic life: from picturesque descriptions of his native Pescara to the duels of his youth, love affairs and anecdotes about the dressing rooms of theatres where his works were performed. The publication is complete with the reproduction of the Spanish version of the third act of *La nave*, in a translation by Andrés Demarchi. An important example of D'Annunzio's nationalism, *La nave* was translated for the first time into Spanish by Demarchi and published in 1909 by *La Revista Artística de Buenos Aires* – just one year after its original appearance in Italian. The early translation into Spanish and its publication during the Argentina Centennial constitutes a strong sign of the nationalist interpretation of D'Annunzio that would develop further in the 1920s and 1930s.

The content of *Ideas y figuras*, a monthly cultural journal that appeared between 1909 and 1914, reflects the particularities of D'Annunzio's reception in Argentina during this period. Such interest in the writer is underlined by other key figures of the time, including the writer Roberto Giusti, who in his memoir *Visto y vivido* (1965) recalls the passion with which a young generation of Argentinian writers discovered D'Annunzio's work in the early twentieth century.[30]

D'Annunzio and Giovanni Del Guzzo, 'Tenacious Latin Settler'

In the context of this 'D'Annunzio fever', Giovanni Del Guzzo, a businessman who had emigrated from Abruzzo and made his fortune in Argentina, contacted the author in March 1910 to try and finalise his visit to Buenos Aires during the Centennial celebrations. Together, they were involved in one of the most curious but least discussed episodes of D'Annunzio's life. The varied and unusual

[29] Manuel Hugarte, *Escritores iberoamericanos de 1900* (Santiago de Chile: Ediciones 'Orbe', 1943), p. 167.

[30] Roberto F. Giusti, *Visto y vivido: Amécdotas, semblanzas, confesiones y batallas* (Buenos Aires: Losada, 1965), p. 96.

circumstances surrounding the bond between D'Annunzio and Del Guzzo are documented by the latter, in a book entitled *Pignus ac Monumentum Amoris di Gabriele d'Annunzio al 'tenace colono latino' Giovanni Del Guzzo* (*Pignus ac Monumentum Amoris* by Gabriele D'Annunzio to the 'tenacious Latin settler' Giovanni del Guzzo) published by Unione Arti Grafiche in L'Aquila (1911).[31] Del Guzzo's book recounts in detail the series of meetings and exchanges he had with D'Annunzio between 1910 and 1911. In almost 250 pages he reproduces letters, commercial documents, testimonies, photographs, telegraphic exchanges and even extracts of judicial summaries that bear witness to the bond between the two and the lawsuit that followed. The details of the relationship exceed the scope of this chapter, but it is clear that the wealthy businessman suggested that he would take charge of all the poet's debts in exchange for a visit to Argentina, during which the author would participate in conferences and offer public readings. Not only did D'Annunzio accept and collect important advances on the agreed stipends, but he also promised to write an ode to Argentina, adhering to the celebration of the Centennial of the May Revolution.

Del Guzzo was a sincere and generous admirer of D'Annunzio, though not an expert in literature. The great expectation that the meeting aroused in the indebted poet is documented in the autographed note that he gave to Del Guzzo the same day he met him: 'Al Messia invocato e soppraggiunto, a Giovanni Del Guzzo con osanna GD., Bologna 10 marzo 1910' (To the Messiah who has been invoked and has arrived, to Giovanni Del Guzzo with a hosanna GD, Bologna 10 March 1910).

Two weeks after this initial meeting, when conversations about the project were at an advanced stage, D'Annunzio wrote a letter to the Argentinian President, José Figueroa Alcorta. In this letter, he mentioned the meeting with the 'daring Latin settler' Del Guzzo and voiced his desire to visit the 'young nation' of 'magnificent strength' where his work had been so well received. However, he expressed some hesitation toward a forthcoming trip. As a homage, he sent a copy of *Forse che sì. Forse che no*, which had just been published, with a dedication inside to the President of the Argentine Republic,

[31] The title refers to verse 572 of canto V of *The Aeneid* ('ese sui dederat monumentum et pignus amoris'), alluding to the horse that Dido had given to Iulo 'as a testimony and pledge of his affection'. D'Annunzio quotes the verse alluding to the delivery he made to Del Guzzo, on 18 March 1910, of seventeen of his manuscripts.

who he recognised as the head of a young government destined for greatness.[32]

Del Guzzo accompanied D'Annunzio in his activities, even in his talks, over the course of a few weeks during March 1910, and the negotiations about the poet's trip to Argentina led to a commercial contract, entitled 'Patto d'alleanza' (alliance pact), that was handwritten by D'Annunzio himself on 23 March. In this 'pact', which consisted of eleven articles, D'Annunzio agreed to travel to Argentina before 25 May that year, deliver six lectures and some twenty public readings, and write an ode to celebrate the Centennial. Del Guzzo, on the other hand, committed to finalising the contract with the theatres where the events would take place and – in agreement with the lawyer Francesco Coselchi – liquidating the painful financial situation in which D'Annunzio found himself before the trip. He agreed to send the poet the sum of 15,000 lire in order to settle his debts and prepare for the trip. The contract ensured that the proceeds of the operation would not be less than 200,000 lire and that D'Annunzio would receive eighty per cent of the profits. D'Annunzio assured Del Guzzo that he would undertake his transoceanic journey after a short trip to France for dental treatment. Far from sticking to his word, he stayed in France for several years, dishonouring not only the commitment he had made to Del Guzzo (and for which he had already received significant amounts of money), but also the claims of many other creditors.

Considering that he led a very active life that involved writing, talks, conferences and even military campaigns and incursions, D'Annunzio travelled very little outside Italy. At the time, the proposed trip to Argentina, which meant crossing the Atlantic and spending entire weeks at sea, constituted a real adventure. So far, his travels had been limited to France, a very brief stay in London and a trip to Greece, where he had also suffered the consequences of seasickness. It is therefore very likely that he never took the contract with Del Guzzo seriously and only agreed to it because of the arduous financial difficulties he was going through.

The news of D'Annunzio's visit had been well received in the Argentinian capital at the time, as testified by newspapers of the period – particularly those that were distributed among the large Italian community, which knew of the poet and were eager for him

32 Giovanni Del Guzzo, *Pignus ac Monumentum Amoris, di Gabriele d'Annunzio al 'tenace colono latino' Giovanni Del Guzzo* (L'Aquila: Unione Arte Grafiche, 1911), p. 64.

to visit. Del Guzzo himself even promoted a press campaign aimed at raising awareness ahead of D'Annunzio's arrival, reintroducing him and bolstering his public image as a writer, which had been damaged after the provocative statements published in *Caras y caretas*. For this reason, when saying goodbye to Del Guzzo in the port of Genoa, D'Annunzio sent a second copy of his recent novel as a gift to the director of the Buenos Aires newspaper *Patria degli italiani*, with the following dedication: 'A Basilio Cittadini, che custodisce i penati dello spirito latino nella terra d'oltremare, questo libro è offerto coralmente, Genova, marzo 1910' (To Basilio Cittadini, who ushers the penates of the Latin spirit to the land across the sea, this book is warmly offered, Genoa, March 1910).

Del Guzzo, whose naivety earned him the nickname 'lo zio dell'America' (the uncle of America) among Italian journalists at the time, never managed to recover the money that was invested in paying off D'Annunzio's debts, and his own financial situation was seriously damaged as a result. In Argentina, the unfortunate episode did not become well known as it was overshadowed by the glamour of the Centennial celebrations.

Toward a Nationalist Reading

During the first decades of the twentieth century, a new movement began to emerge among Argentinian intellectual circles that questioned the nation-building project imposed by the liberal model of the so-called 'Generation of 80'. This movement resisted embracing cosmopolitanism and openness to flows of migration, arguing that they endangered the country's moral and cultural traditions. Under the influence of foreign capital and as a result of sociopolitical heterogeneity, the discourse of *latinidad* began to gain sway as a way of neutralising the contradictions of the liberal system, coming closer and closer to nationalist currents. As Carlos Paz argues, these ideas reflected the views of European intellectuals whose nations were latecomers to the process of colonisation.[33] In this context, D'Annunzio and his works were re-evaluated. The poet's vindication of the Latin spirit and his clear defence of nationalism represented a break with the emerging anarchism that threatened bourgeois power structures. Given these factors, it is possible to identify the origin of a second

[33] Carlos Paz, 'Roberto Arlt: Narrativa y crisis en la Argentina de los años 30', *Margen*, 4 (1993), 1–9 (p. 1).

reading and a newfound appreciation of D'Annunzio in Argentina. New interpretations were neither aesthetic nor merely artistic, as was the one instigated and promoted by Rubén Darío in 1894, but decidedly political. Nor were they focused on the journalistic curiosity that his image as a writer and his propaganda had previously generated. In this context, there was a renewed interest in the D'Annunzio of *La città morta* and *La nave*, as these works (particularly the former) are centred around the desire to recover the model of Ancient Greek tragedy and imbued in pre-Fascist imperialist nationalism. Both tragedies were performed with great success on the main stages of the Buenos Aires theatre circuit in the 1910s.

Examining this phase of D'Annunzio's reception, the magazine *Nosotros* deserves particular attention, as it marked a long and significant period in Argentinian intellectual history. Born in Lucca (Italy), Roberto Giusti arrived in Buenos Aires in 1895 and, together with Alfredo Bianchi, directed the publication during its various stages between 1907 and 1943. In the pages of *Nosotros*, D'Annunzio acquired a special visibility, becoming a 'popular and persistent cult'.[34] Several pieces were dedicated to him, including translations and reviews, some of which were authored by the Argentinian poet Alfredo Bufano. Following the poet's death, the twenty-fourth edition of the magazine, published in March 1938, included an extensive essay by the Italian intellectual Nella Passini about his entire oeuvre. Although marked by the critical subjectivism of this historical moment, the essay is quite comprehensive. It concludes with a paragraph that once again brings up the discourse of *latinidad*:

> On the Vittoriale tomb, the evergreen laurels of Rome are the symbol of the *latinidad* that the poet glorified with his language forged not exclusively in his mother tongue, but also in the sweet language of France, and to which, in addition to his imperishable work of art, he made an offering of human heroism.[35]

The ideological reception experienced by the Italian author in Argentina during the 1920s and 1930s is essential to understanding the positive re-evaluation that occurred after his death in 1938. This coincided with the emergence of Peronism and was the period of greatest visibility for D'Annunzio in the country. It constitutes a third phase in the history of his reception in Argentina: one that is

[34] Novella Marani, p. 102.

[35] Nella Passini, 'Gabriel d'Annunzio', *Nosotros*, 3: 24 (1938), 223–63 (p. 263).

characterised by the popularisation of D'Annunzio as a figure and the mass dissemination of his work not only in the high society of Buenos Aires, but also among middle-class, proletarian and suburban audiences. It is important in this regard to bear in mind that in 1940s Argentina, there was already a publishing industry that had developed out of a substantial consumer market, catering to readers of books, magazines and newspapers. This industry developed through processes of modernisation during previous decades. The 1940s and 1950s are considered the golden age of Argentinian books, not only in terms of the domestic market but also concerning exports in Latin America, thanks to openings left by the Spanish Civil War.

In this context, D'Annunzio became one of the most widely read foreign authors, even from the point of view of popular culture, and was undoubtedly the Italian author who enjoyed the greatest circulation in Argentina during the mid-twentieth century. Both his novels and his dramatic works, which had been translated in previous decades, were reissued in affordable editions that ran to several thousand copies. Recent work in the field of translation studies has highlighted the way in which D'Annunzio's work was marketed to respond to political contingency, while at the same time promoting the cult of the classic hero among the emergent middle classes.[36] From this moment onwards, D'Annunzio's reception in the Río de la Plata was restricted to the dissemination of novellas and short stories adapted for magazines and for a mass readership. Emblematic in this regard is *Leoplán*, the magazine run by the Sopena Argentina publishing house in Buenos Aires between 1934 and 1965. This was a fortnightly, and subsequently a monthly, publication that included texts by prominent authors from Europe and America. It was aimed at providing cultural and educational content for a population which, by this stage, was outgrowing Buenos Aires – a city that had become a metropolis thanks to intense industrialisation and high population growth. Self-defined as the 'popular Argentinian magazine', *Leoplán* was a key source of entertainment but also of education, for large parts of the middle-class and suburban communities.

In the period between 1942 and 1944, several short stories and novellas by D'Annunzio appeared in *Leoplán*, especially those most closely linked to the tones of macabre naturalism from his first collections, *Terra vergine* and *Le novelle della Pescara*. In most cases, published translations did not state the author's name. In multiple

[36] Andrea Pagni et al., *Traductores y traducciones en la historia cultural de América Latina* (Mexico City: UNAM, 2011), pp. 8–9.

issues of the magazine the following titles appeared, translating D'Annunzio's Italian into Spanish: 'Epíscopo y Cía', 'La cuñada', 'San Pantaleón', 'Las campanas', 'El heroe' and 'La siesta'. But in other cases, the titles of translations did not correspond to the original title in Italian, for example: 'El arca' (La mandia), 'Monedas de oro' (I marenghi) and 'El mártir' (Il ceruscio di mare). From the outset of its commercial activities in the country, Sopena Argentina intervened in the transformation occurring within the publishing industry during the 1940s and, along with other companies belonging to the Argentinian Book Chamber, was involved in a process whereby the state aimed to broaden the bases of citizen participation and outline a new structure capable of bringing together mass organisations.

Conclusion

D'Annunzio's reception in Argentina predated an awareness of his work in many European countries. This was due on the one hand to a high volume of Italian emigration to the country, which resulted in an interest in the author. On the other hand, it points to a cultural scene that was particularly receptive to the late-nineteenth-century trends and aesthetics that D'Annunzio represented. Argentina was not only a country where D'Annunzio was read, but also a place where he was introduced to the Spanish-speaking world. Each of the phases of reception outlined above – the aesthetic phase at the end of the nineteenth century; the political one at the beginning of the twentieth century; and the popular reproduction of his works in the mid-1900s – reflects how the poet's reception was conditioned by different Argentinian cultural policies that illuminated different facets of the writer. After the Second World War, D'Annunzio disappeared from the Argentinian literary scene for a long time. The centenary of his birth in the 1960s hardly sparked any interest in academic circles. New trends and changing literary tastes meant that he was no longer the most widely read Italian author outside Italy, nor the most admired foreign writer in Argentina.

Chapter 14

Gabriele D'Annunzio in the United States: Politics and Stereotypes

Guylian Nemegeer and Mara Santi

In 1922, Carlo Bertelli, the Hearst Corporation's Chief of the editorial staff for France and Southern Europe, asked Gabriele D'Annunzio to write a column on Italian Fascism. The request reached D'Annunzio a few days after the March on Rome (27–9 October 1922), Benito Mussolini's National Fascist Party act to seize power. The Corporation – a leading US media empire founded in 1887 by William Randolph Hearst – sought an authoritative voice to explain this political movement to the US public, which he claimed did not fully understand Fascism, as indicated by publications comparing it to the Ku Klux Klan that 'terrorises the American population by arrogating itself executive power'.[1] Hence, Bertelli wrote, D'Annunzio's article should counterbalance the news on Fascist violence that reached the USA and endorse the rise of Fascism by explaining its ideals and values. Bertelli contacted D'Annunzio because he was a well-known leader of the Italian right-wing and an established columnist in Hearst's news network. He thus supposed that D'Annunzio's political stance would align with Hearst's pro-Fascist political line. Although D'Annunzio was offered a considerable sum for the article, he refused to praise Fascism in the US press (just as he never praised it in Italy).

This little-known episode illustrates two aspects of D'Annunzio's reception in the USA. On the one hand, it shows D'Annunzio's authority among the US public, which derived from his reputation as

[1] Carlo F. Bertelli, 5 November 1922, Fondazione il Vittoriale degli Italiani, Archives, Gardone Riviera XLII, 1, 5. Translations from the Italian are our own. Bertelli probably refers to an article published in the *Boston Evening Transcript* on 26 October 1922 that suggested the analogy and underlined the excesses of Fascism. On this article see Gian Giacomo Migone, *The United States and Fascist Italy: The Rise of American Finance in Europe* (New York: Cambridge University Press, 2015), p. 37.

an opinionist in US newspapers from the late 1890s and from his role in both the First World War and the Fiume crisis.[2] In this chapter, we assess this aspect by examining D'Annunzio's correspondence with US editors and representatives of the US government, as well as his articles published in the US press.[3]

On the other hand, this episode is an early indication of the critical misconceptions regarding D'Annunzio's relationship to Italian Fascism, a misconception that 'became automatic from the 1920s–1930s and would remain as such in the post-war period'.[4] From the 1970s onwards, authoritative scholars have pointed out that Mussolini celebrated D'Annunzio as the precursor of Fascism and appropriated his political style, but also that D'Annunzio was in disagreement with major political decisions of the regime, such as the Lateran Pacts of 1929 and the imminent alliance with Hitler.[5] Moreover, as Maurizio Serra noted, 'the seventeen years of the Vittoriale were interwoven with attempts to distance himself [from Fascism]', attempts that contrast with 'the conformism of most of the Italian intelligentsia during the twenty years of Fascism'.[6] In other words, D'Annunzio was an exponent of the Italian right-wing, and while he was not anti-Fascist, he was nonetheless disillusioned by the evolution of Fascism.

Despite this academic revisionism, US popular reception throughout the 1980s and the 1990s continued to promote D'Annunzio's blind adherence to Fascism. For example, in the seventh episode of the seventh season of the police series *Cagney & Lacey* (first aired 16 November 1987), a TV show quiz master asks who wrote poems

[2] D'Annunzio supported Italian intervention and fought as a volunteer in the First World War. He became so recognised as a political and military leader that he led the military occupation of the city of Fiume (now Rijeka) on 12 September 1919. The occupation, which reacted to the Treaty of Versailles (1919), aimed for the annexation of the city to the Italian kingdom, but it failed on 27 December 1920. See Dominique Kirchner Reill, *The Fiume Crisis: Life in the Wake of the Habsburg Empire* (Cambridge: Harvard University Press, 2020).

[3] D'Annunzio wrote these articles in Italian, as he never sufficiently mastered the English language. He had no long-term collaboration with a fixed translator, and the exact translator of each text is not always documented. However, from 1914 onwards, the translation of his articles for Hearst's network was supervised by Carlo Bertelli.

[4] Maurizio Serra, 'D'Annunzio oggi all'estero', *Rassegna Dannunziana*, 72 (2018), 7–10 (p. 9).

[5] Renzo De Felice, *D'Annunzio politico, 1918–1938* (Bari: Laterza, 1978); *L'Italia e la «Grande Vigilia»: Gabriele D'Annunzio nella politica italiana prima del fascismo*, ed. by Romain H. Rainero and Stefano B. Galli (Milan: Franco Angeli, 2007).

[6] Serra, p. 9.

and was one of Italy's first Fascists. The 'correct' (yet wrong) answer given in the show is: Gabriele D'Annunzio. A second example shows how the association of D'Annunzio with Fascism remained frequently unquestioned, even in leading newspapers such as *The New York Times* (henceforth *NYT*), where an article by the journalist Barbara Jepson, published on 30 March 1997, presents D'Annunzio as 'a Mussolini supporter during World War II'.[7] The historical blunder was rectified with irony by a reader, Harvey Fried, who wrote that 'he must have been a silent defender, because D'Annunzio died in 1938'.[8]

We address this misconception in the last parts of this chapter and show that, from the 1930s onward, propaganda against D'Annunzio as a Fascist combined two elements to which the US public was already attuned: a negative myth about the Italians' character in general and a tradition of superficial gossip about D'Annunzio's life. Moreover, our analysis reveals that this framework still pervades D'Annunzio's contemporary popular reception in the USA, as moral anecdotes and sensationalist accounts continue to hinder the dissemination to the wider public of the critical reconsideration that originated from the 1970s onwards in Italy and from the mid-1980s in US academia.[9] Our contribution is embedded in the reassessment of D'Annunzio's works, which in the US academic debate was advocated most strongly by Paolo Valesio, who in 1992 promoted 'revisionism' as a keyword in his reaction against the mainstream attitude toward D'Annunzio's works and legacy.[10] We maintain that the over-generalised associations present in the American reception of D'Annunzio's works should be better understood so as to allow for a more nuanced approach to this seminal Italian writer.

1898–1911: D'Annunzio's Presence in the USA

The first known article by D'Annunzio published in the USA dates back to 22 May 1898, when the *New York Journal* printed the article

[7] Barbara Jepson, 'The Music Befits a Saintly Legend', *NYT*, 30 March 1997, p. 32.

[8] Harvey Fried, 'D'Annunzio's Politics', *NYT*, 13 April 1997, p. 14.

[9] In the USA, the fiftieth anniversary of D'Annunzio's death in 1988 prompted the publication of a special issue of *Annali d'Italianistica* devoted to D'Annunzio (1987), Charles Klopp's *Gabriele D'Annunzio* and the conference *D'Annunzio a Yale* (both in 1988).

[10] Paolo Valesio, *Gabriele D'Annunzio: The Dark Flame* (New Haven: Yale University Press, 1992). See also Lara Gochin Raffaelli and Michael Subialka, 'Introduction: D'Annunzio's Beauty, Reawakened', *Forum Italicum*, 2 (2017), 311–34.

'Gabriel [sic] D'Annunzio describes Italian riots for the *Journal*: everywhere in the grime and smoke of battle, starved mothers forced the fighting unterrified by death'.[11] D'Annunzio comments on the popular riots against the Italian government in Florence during May of 1898 and underlines three topics to appeal to the US public: women's participation in the riots, the damage caused to Cellini's Perseus and the popular insurrection.[12] Indeed, the riots' female protagonists attracted the attention of a female readership, which was typically larger for Sunday issues. Moreover, the reference to Cellini spoke to US readers' fondness for the Italian Renaissance. Finally, popular riots were a burning issue in US newspapers following the support given by the USA to the Cuban popular insurrection against the Spanish government during the Spanish-American war (1898).[13]

A second relevant article is 'The Third Life of Italy', published in the November 1900 issue of the *North American Review*, a prominent periodical of the period offering political, economic and cultural commentaries written by both US and European opinionists.[14] The title of the article refers to an expression used at the time in Italy to indicate the third rebirth of the nation after the glorious periods of ancient Rome and the Renaissance.[15] The article, therefore, refers to Italians' ambitions for a new surge in the domestic and international growth of the nation; it likewise presents an exposition, for its foreign audience, of D'Annunzio's political stance. D'Annunzio states that the post-1861 Italian governments have betrayed the Risorgimento ideals of a great Italy and that the nation should rediscover the industriousness of the Italian men of the past to claim her position among imperialist powers such as Japan, Germany and Great Britain.

D'Annunzio's presence as a political opinionist is also documented by an article published on 9 October 1911 in the *New York American*, which replaced the *New York Journal* while continuing its editorial line. The article is devoted to the Italo-Turkish War (29 September 1911–18 October 1912) and to the Italian colonial occupation of the North-African territories of Tripolitania

[11] Gabriele D'Annunzio, 'Gabriel D'Annunzio Describes Italian Riots for the *Journal*: Everywhere in the Grime and Smoke of Battle, Starved Mothers Forced the Fighting Unterrified by Death', *New York Journal*, 22 May 1898, p. 3.

[12] Shirley Smith, 'D'Annunzio Journalist in America', *Yearbook of Italian Studies*, 9 (1991), 147–58 (p. 150).

[13] Ibid., p. 150.

[14] Gabriele D'Annunzio, 'The Third Life of Italy', *North American Review*, 528 (1900), 627–52.

[15] The article summarises D'Annunzio's speeches of the electoral campaign in 1900.

and Cyrenaica. As a supporter of the colonial enterprise, D'Annunzio sought support from the US public via Hearst's network, which saw an opportunity for the USA in the Italian enterprise.[16] Indeed, Hearst's editorial stance represented that part of US public opinion and politics advocating free international trade routes against British naval supremacy. It welcomed Italy's imperial ambitions, for these would counterbalance French-British control of the traffic in North Africa and facilitate the access of other nations to the Suez Canal, which, since opening in 1869, had brought the Mediterranean back to the centre of global economic interests.

These three articles foreground the keywords that, for D'Annunzio, should guide the rising Italian nationalist movement and that the Italian right-wing shared with the USA: militarism, liberalism, naval power and expansionism against the dominant imperialistic powers. Although D'Annunzio's presence in the US political debate was rather limited between 1898 and 1911, it is still remarkable given the pronounced lack of interest on the part of the American public and political leaders in European and Italian politics at the time.[17]

1914–1918: D'Annunzio and the USA

During the First World War, the US press closely followed the European situation and its protagonists and proposed multiple articles on D'Annunzio's political involvement and war actions. For example, on 5 June 1915 the *NYT* exposed the German attempt to discredit the poet via a racist accusation. The article, 'Says D'Annunzio is a Pole. *Frankfurter Zeitung* denies the poet's Italian parentage', reports that the *Frankfurter Zeitung* published a Budapest newspaper's insinuation that D'Annunzio's father was a Polish-Jewish lawyer. According to the *NYT*, this news ruined D'Annunzio's popularity in Germany since the latter perceived the Poles as an inferior people and, therefore, the connection between D'Annunzio and Poland also entailed the author's inferiority.[18]

16 Gabriele D'Annunzio, *Lettere ai Treves*, ed. by Gianni Oliva (Milan: Garzanti, 1999), p. 409.

17 Daniela Rossini, *L'America riscopre l'Italia: l'Inquiry di Wilson e le origini della questione adriatica, 1917–1919* (Rome: Edizioni Associate, 1992); Federico Robbe, *'Vigor di Vita'. Il nazionalismo italiano e gli Stati Uniti (1898–1923)* (Rome: Viella, 2018).

18 'Says D'Annunzio is a Pole. Frankfurter Zeitung denies the poet's Italian parentage', *NYT*, 5 June 1915, p. 4.

Upon entering the First World War in April 1917, US military involvement on the Italo-Austrian front was limited (they sent only one Infantry Regiment, the 332nd), but the USA nevertheless ran a mass propaganda campaign in the territory via the American Red Cross, the YMCA and the Committee on Public Information (CPI), the propaganda office created by President Wilson in 1917 to exercise war censorship and foster both American domestic popular support for the intervention and US self-promotion in the allied territories.[19] Wilson's mass propaganda aimed at presenting the USA as a *super partes* nation defending freedom and peace throughout the world and as saviours of other countries' national integrity against aggressive colonialist powers.

In this context, D'Annunzio became a figure of reference in American institutional war propaganda. In June 1918, Harvey Carroll – the US Consul in Venice and regional director of the US Red Cross – informed D'Annunzio that Captain Charles Merriam – the CPI's High Commissioner in Italy – would personally come to Venice to commission D'Annunzio on behalf of the US government to write an ode celebrating the US intervention.[20] The 'Ode to America in Arms', meant to be published in both Italy and the USA on 4 July, appeared in the *Corriere della Sera* on 4 July 1918 and the following day in *Tribuna*. Yet, although Carroll himself immediately provided a translation of the 'Ode', excerpts were published in the USA only in August when John R. Slater partially translated the poem for *The Outlook*.[21]

The text did not have a great impact on the US public, but it is relevant since it indicates how D'Annunzio used his literary production for political aims. Indeed, D'Annunzio stressed similarities and common values between the two nations, and he adapted the historical and cultural references that always enrich his texts to make them legible to a foreign public. More specifically, D'Annunzio wrote on 27 June 1918 to Giulio Zorzanello, the director of the Venetian Marciana Library, asking him to send the French translation of Walt Whitman's *Leaves of Grass*.[22] D'Annunzio referenced the American

[19] Rossini, *L'America*, p. 26.

[20] Harvey B. Carroll, June 1918, Vittoriale Archives, XL, 4.

[21] Harvey B. Carroll, July 1918, Vittoriale Archives, 4, 2. See also Carl A. Swanson, 'D'Annunzio's Ode all'America in armi (IV luglio MCMXVIII)', *Italica*, 3 (1953), 135–43 (p. 140).

[22] Maria Rosa Giacon, 'Presenze e letture marciane di D'Annunzio', in *Libri e librerie di Gabriele D'Annunzio*, ed. by Edoardo Tiboni (Pescara: Centro Nazionale di Studi Dannunziani, 2006), pp. 49–86 (p. 53).

poet in his texts for the US public, starting with the articles of 1900 and 1911 discussed above, aiming to establish analogies between himself and Whitman as poets of the homeland and the national spirit. D'Annunzio's effort to appeal to the American public was appreciated by both Merriam and Carroll. The latter, expressing his gratitude, asked D'Annunzio to gift the USA with the manuscript of his *Ode to America in Arms*, which he wanted to be archived in the 'Library of Congress in Washington'.[23] Unfortunately, Carroll lost the manuscript when he moved from Venice to Naples.[24]

1921: The Washington Conference

During the peace negotiations and the Fiume exploit (see below), D'Annunzio continued to attract the attention of the American public to the extent that Bertelli, on Hearst's mandate, asked him to participate in the Washington Conference on naval disarmament (1921–1922) as a reporter for Hearst's network. The conference gathered the largest naval powers after the First World War and aimed to relieve the growing tensions in East Asia and to prevent a conflict between First World War allies via a mutual control agreement on naval armaments. The discussions were led by the USA, the UK and Japan, the nations with the largest fleets and the most significant interests in the Pacific area.[25]

D'Annunzio agreed to comment on this political meeting because the conference discussed topics that occupied his political thought during and after the Fiume occupation: the military balance between the world's great powers and the dominant states' areas of economic and political interference. Indeed, during the Fiume crisis, D'Annunzio planned to found a League of Fiume (January 1920), which would be an alliance of smaller countries oppressed by the imperialist powers and in opposition to Wilson's League of Nations. In the same vein, D'Annunzio addressed the American public during the Washington Conference and advocated an anti-imperialist alliance between Italy and the USA.[26] He envisioned an alliance in

[23] Harvey B. Carroll, 2 July 1918, Vittoriale Archives, 4.

[24] Swanson, p. 140.

[25] Brian R. Sullivan, 'Italian naval power and the Washington disarmament conference of 1921–22', *Diplomacy & Statecraft*, 4:3 (1993), 220–48.

[26] Emilio Mariano, *Il San Francesco di Gabriele D'Annunzio* (= Quaderni del Vittoriale, 12 (1978)).

which the USA would revolt 'against the treaty of Versailles' signed by 'the already trembling and convulsed Woodrow Wilson',[27] oppose European colonialism represented by the UK (and France) and defend Italy, as well as other smaller countries and nationalities.[28] Indeed, in D'Annunzio's eyes, the USA could still amend the injustice they had done to Italy at the Paris Peace Conference.

D'Annunzio commented on the Washington Conference from Italy since he was not willing to travel abroad. Bertelli, who probably also provided the English translation of D'Annunzio's articles,[29] sent him telegrams with the necessary information to give his take on the debates. Bertelli's telegrams focus mainly on American foreign policy. During the interwar period, with the end of Wilson's second mandate in 1921, the USA reverted to an isolationist policy toward Europe. Besides their traditional control of the American continent, the USA turned to China and Japan, where they pursued an Open Door Policy (which implied equal privileges among countries trading with China and the US protection of China's territorial integrity and autonomy). Under the leadership of Warren G. Harding, the USA opted not to join the League of Nations, and the US Senate did not ratify the Treaty of Versailles even though Wilson and his delegates played a major role in the Paris Peace Conference. Despite the new isolationist trend, smaller European countries still 'thought that only the United States could provide the impartiality in politics in face of the traditional European power games'.[30] This vision derived in part from the USA's self-representation in the First World War as the champion of liberty, while proclaiming its moral superiority on an international scale. Likewise, US interest in counterbalancing British colonialist power and their lack of interest in European internal policies could benefit other European countries.

In sum, D'Annunzio's political thought in 1921–1922 was rooted in the diplomatic post-war events and in the political issues arising from the Fiume crisis, which resulted from the Pact of London (1915) being discarded thanks to Wilson's decisive support and Italy failing

[27] Gabriele D'Annunzio, 'Easter Treaty only Portends more Trouble', *Washington Times*, 30 April 1922, p. 3.

[28] Gabriele D'Annunzio, 'World is Beginning Herculean Drama of Races, says D'Annunzio', *Washington Times*, 11 December 1921, p. 3.

[29] D'Annunzio, *Lettere ai Treves*, p. 682.

[30] Zoltán Peterecz, 'American Foreign Policy and American Financial Controllers in Europe in the 1920s', *Hungarian Journal of English and American Studies*, 1/2 (2012), 457–85 (p. 458).

to obtain the territories promised by the Triple Entente.[31] To fully grasp this issue it is necessary to take a step back in time, looking to the events of 1919.

1919: The Peace Conference and the Fiume Crisis

At the negotiating table, despite his propagandistic claims of impartiality and his overt hostility to European colonialism, Wilson was forced to compromise with the strongest allies (the UK, France and Japan). Therefore, he pursued an intransigent policy toward the territorial claims of weaker countries, including Italy. Wilson had little expertise on the Italian situation and the Inquiry, i.e. the commission of experts he gathered since 1917 to prepare American policy for the post-war period, counted not a single expert on Italy.[32] Wilson's plans for Italy discarded the nation's claims – except for Trento and Trieste – and in Paris, Italy felt betrayed by her allies. This also happened because the Inquiry extensively relied on information received by the British Foreign Office, which was hostile to Italy because the expansion of the Italian area of influence, as stipulated in the Pact of London, implied a reduction of the British one: as of 1917, British policy makers began to openly invoke a reduction of Italian territorial claims, and this policy was received positively by the US government.[33] To reject the Italian claims, the USA put forward the principle of nationality as a basis for determining borders. Yet, the same principle motivated the wave of protest aroused by the peace negotiations, leading D'Annunzio (and a part of the Italian army and public opinion) to claim Fiume as a legitimate extension of the country's national territory. Indeed, the delusion of Italy's expectations at the peace conference informed D'Annunzio's harsh attacks against Wilson, in which he fashioned Fiume as 'a martyr city' and the Fiumians 'as sacrificial victims battling the forces of international diplomacy' to overturn Italy's mutilated victory.[34]

[31] The pact stipulated that upon entering the war alongside the Triple Entente, Italy would receive Trentino, South Tirol, Venezia-Giulia, part of Istria (except for Fiume), part of Dalmatia, a protectorate over Albania, a naval base in Valona, the Dodecanese and territories from the division of Asiatic Turkey and the African colonies.

[32] Daniela Rossini, *Woodrow Wilson and the American Myth in Italy: Culture, Diplomacy, and War Propaganda* (Cambridge: Harvard University Press, 2008).

[33] Rossini, *L'America*, p. 76.

[34] Kirchner Reill, p. 5.

Fiume became topical after the First World War and a burning question in the American press, not only for the strategic relevance of the town in itself, but as a matter of principle in an internal ideological debate. American observers and public opinion debated not only whom Fiume should belong to, but also whether or not the USA should take a stance on the matter and meddle in other nations' internal disputes. Whitney Warren, one of the strongest voices in favour of the Italian reclamation, insisted on these issues in his addresses to the US public. A renowned American architect, Warren had supported D'Annunzio since 1915, and he promoted the annexation of Fiume to Italy as the Fiume government's representative to the US government. Indeed, Warren stated that the responsibility for the crisis fell on the US, President Wilson, and their foreign policy after Paris because people cannot be treated 'as if they were merchandise or cattle' as in Fiume, he says, where the US 'are playing the policeman' which is 'a dangerous and detestable game'.[35]

In this debate, D'Annunzio became the hero denouncing American injustice and defending the principle of nationality against imperialist nations, which is one of the principles that theoretically inspired US foreign policy, as Bertelli reminds us in his abovementioned telegram to D'Annunzio. According to D'Annunzio, the US, under Wilson's leadership, betrayed American values as well as its weaker allies. The articles on the Washington Conference show that after the end of Wilson's mandate, D'Annunzio once again endorsed an alliance between Italy and the US as nations carrying the banner of freedom against enslavement to foreign powers. Yet, his last political messages to the US turned out to address a public opinion that progressively lost interest in his political thought. This loss of interest derived from several factors. First, there was the American focus on the rise of the Fascist movement. As mentioned at the beginning of this chapter, D'Annunzio was invited by Bertelli (on behalf of Hearst) to take a public stance on this topic, but he declined the invitation, which had the consequence of not allowing the US public to properly assess the distance between himself and Mussolini. Second, over the years, the Fascist regime exerted rigorous control on D'Annunzio, limiting his freedom of movement and expression.[36] This prevented

[35] Whitney Warren, October 1919, Vittoriale Archives, VI, 5, 6.

[36] Roberto Festorazzi, *D'Annunzio e la piovra fascista. Spionaggi al Vittoriale nella testimonianza del federale di Brescia* (Rome: Il minotauro, 2005); Raffaella Canovi, *D'Annunzio e il fascismo. Eutanasia di un'icona* (Rome: Bibliotheka Edizioni, 2019).

him from taking an active role in the public debate, and, at the same time, the regime exploited D'Annunzio's popularity and appropriated him as its national poet. Consequently, D'Annunzio was overshadowed by Fascism in the American popular mind. After a first period of friendly political relations, the US began to question Mussolini and to condemn Fascism on both political-ideological and moral grounds. As we will show in the remainder of this chapter, this re-invigorated negative stereotypes that had long been present in the American representation of Italians; at the same time, the close association assumed to exist between D'Annunzio and Fascism also entailed D'Annunzio's denigration: his reputation was soon stained by the moral condemnation of Fascism and therefore gossip about his persona and sentimental life began to take centre stage. This played off the fact that, besides the political framework sketched above, D'Annunzio had always been popular largely for much more trivial reasons, which overlapped with a series of widespread US stereotypes about Italians. In what follows, we highlight these stereotypes and show how anti-Fascist propaganda fused them with an anecdotal-sensationalist approach to D'Annunzio's life to ridicule his persona. This critical framework proved so enduring that it can still be detected in American criticism today.

Italian Stereotypes and D'Annunzio's Mainstream US Reception

The American representation of Italy was historically characterised by the highbrow reception of US grand-tour travels, the lowbrow mass reception of Italian immigrants and a substantial lack of interest in academic and political circles regarding the Italian situation. On every level, the reception of Italy was biased by stereotypes and prejudices deriving from the European (mainly British) reception.[37] At first, the Americans' vision of Italy between the nineteenth and twentieth centuries was derived from tourism. Writings on Italy proliferated and produced an ambivalent discourse in which picturesque and idealised images of Italy coexisted with nativist representations

[37] *The Fatal Gift of Beauty: The Italies of British Travellers*, ed. by Manfred Pfister (Amsterdam: Rodopi, 1996); Silvana Patriarca, *Italian Vices: Nation and Character from the Risorgimento to the Republic* (Cambridge: Cambridge University Press, 2013).

of the Italians as a vicious people.[38] Italy was a country where the past was seen to persist in the present and where sensualism, beauty and *otium* provided an alternative to America's puritanism, materialism and pragmatism. Yet, darker elements and vices were latent in this idyllic place, since beauty was contaminated by poverty and decay and, moreover, sensualism and *otium* implied indolence, dedication to sensual pleasures and lack of moral boundaries. This sublime decadence 'evoked Machiavellian-Caglostrian-Casanovan characters that were tricky, shrewd, seductive and even, dangerous, but none-the-less alluring'.[39]

This negative stereotype of the vicious Italian was reinforced by the wave of xenophobia arising from the mass immigration from Italy and the social issues this entailed. Indeed, between 1880 and 1921, over 4.5 million Italian immigrants arrived in the US, around eighty per cent of them illiterate peasants from the South.[40] Consequently, the US tended to look at Italy either as a destination of exotic cultural tourism or else as the homeland of a mass of immigrants whose problematic integration generated significant issues for the existing social order.

Later on, a lack of interest in Italy's participation in the First World War was evident in US political debates, as the Italo-Austrian front was perceived as being rather peripheral. Only when the Austro-German army conducted a successful offensive campaign in 1917 did the Italian situation become a matter of concern. The US feared that mutinies in the Italian army, provoked by the dramatic situation of the soldiers, could inspire a socialist revolution as in Russia. Yet, even when the attention toward Italy peaked, US access to information about Italy remained limited or filtered through the perspectives of other nations, especially Great Britain.[41]

In line with the British filter and the touristic view of Italy, in the US D'Annunzio was often interpreted as a 'morbid' poet. This term expresses the moral prejudice Anglo-Saxons maintained toward

[38] John P. Diggins, *Mussolini and Fascism: The View from America* (Princeton: Princeton University Press, 1972); Joseph P. Cosco, *Imagining Italians: The Clash of Romance and Race in American Perception, 1880–1910* (Albany: State University of New York Press, 2003).

[39] Carla Anne Simonini, 'Constructing America by Writing about Italy: How Nineteenth-Century Travel Writing Informed Ethnic Identity Construction in Italian-American Literature', *Italian Americana*, 2 (2015), 136–56 (p. 148).

[40] Donna R. Gabaccia, *Italy's Many Diasporas* (Seattle: University of Washington Press, 2000).

[41] Rossini, *Woodrow Wilson*, p. 20.

the 'Latin peoples' and derives from a perception of Decadence, the 'mixture of religion, politics, art and sex' framing the 'reception of Italian production in the Anglo-Saxon world from Chaucer onwards'.[42] For instance, in the *NYT* of Saturday 30 January 1904, the US writer Gertrude Atherton fashioned D'Annunzio's novels the epitome of Italy's Decadence as the author's 'repulsive works of art' reflect Italy's 'rottenness, degradation, disease'.[43]

This prejudice also permeated the translation of D'Annunzio's novels. Its pervasiveness is evident in *The Child of Pleasure*, Georgina Harding's 1898 translation of *Il Piacere* and *The Triumph of Death* (*Trionfo della morte*), translated by Arthur Hornblow in 1896, both of which were heavily bowdlerised.[44] Both Harding and Hornblow omitted sexually-oriented passages that could offend Victorian morality and American puritanism. This censorship was needed because of UK and US obscenity laws. In the USA, the Comstock laws of 1873 (named after the anti-vice activist Anthony Comstock) made it possible to 'seize publications and devices [. . .] considered immoral and to prosecute their senders'.[45] Comstock himself sued the publishers of Hornblow's translation, George H. Richmond and his son, in 1897.[46] Although the defendants were found not guilty, and such anecdotes may seem something of the past, today's English-language reader is still confronted with their legacy, as *Trionfo della morte* still awaits an unabridged translation while *Il Piacere* received a full translation only as recently as 2013 (translated as *Pleasure* by Lara Gochin Raffaelli).[47] As a consequence, while scholarship has been reassessing D'Annunzio's poetics and legacy, the broader

42 Luca Scarlini, *D'Annunzio a Little Italy. Le avventure del Vate nel mondo dell'emigrazione* (Rome: Donzelli, 2008), p. 27.

43 Gertrude Atherton, 'Mrs. Atherton on D'Annunzio. The Bookman', *NYT*, 30 January 1904, p. 79.

44 Gabriele D'Annunzio, *The Triumph of Death*, trans. by Arthur Hornblow (New York: George H. Richmond & CO, 1896) and *The Child of Pleasure*, trans. by Georgia Harding (New York: George H. Richmond & Son, 1898). See also John Woodhouse, 'Trionfo della Morte: traduzioni, reazioni e interpretazioni anglosassoni', in *Il trionfo della morte: Atti del III convegno Internazionale di studi dannunziani*, ed. by Edoardo Tiboni and Luigia Abrugiati (Pescara: Centro Nazionale di Studi Dannunziani, 1981), pp. 239–60.

45 Marjorie Heins, *Not in Front of the Children: Indecency, Censorship and the Innocence of Youth* (New Brunswick: Rutgers University Press, 2007), p. 32.

46 'Triumph of Death Trial. Justices of Special Sessions Exclude Expert Testimony Concerning D'Annunzio's Book', *NYT*, 26 March 1897, p. 12.

47 Gabriele D'Annunzio, *Pleasure*, trans. by Lara Gochin Raffaelli (New York: Penguin Books, 2013).

English-language public's access to D'Annunzio's texts is still limited and largely biased by earlier phases of reception and translation.[48]

Moreover, mainstream accounts of D'Annunzio's persona still need to come to terms with similar moral biases. A crucial stereotype that negatively shaped D'Annunzio's reception in the US was that of the seducer, inaugurated by local tabloids' passionate interest in D'Annunzio's love affair with the famous actress Eleonora Duse, who toured the USA in 1893, 1896, 1902 and 1923–1924. Among many examples, we find an article by Towse J. Ranken, published in *Critics*, entitled 'Duse and the Degenerate D'Annunzio' (1904) and, as early as 1899, a headline that says: 'Broken-hearted in Paris. Famous actress, scorned by Gabriele D'Annunzio, Italian author and poet, finds real tragedy in her own life.'[49] In the article, D'Annunzio is represented as a 'selfish egotist' who has trampled Duse's 'splendid intellect' and 'passionate nature' under foot.[50]

This attention paid to the D'Annunzio-Duse love affair initiated a persistent critical tendency where an extensive focus on anecdotes and gossip provides the American public with an image of D'Annunzio as a degenerate, sex-obsessed poet. This makes him the exemplary incarnation of the stereotyped image in American culture of the Italian as a Machiavellian-Casanovan character.

[48] Further examples of these persistent biases can also be detected in recent translations. For example, Lara Gochin Raffaelli translates 'ebro', which means drunkard, as 'Jew', which is 'ebreo' in Italian: 'E la volontà, disutile come una spada di cattiva tempra, pendeva al fianco di un ebro o di un inerte' ('And his will, as useless as a badly tempered sword, dangled as at the side of a drunkard or a paralyzed man') Gabriele D'Annunzio, *Il Piacere*, in *Prose di Romanzi*, ed. by Annamaria Andreoli e Niva Lorenzini (Milano: Mondadori, 2005), p. 143. Raffaelli misreads *ebro* for *ebreo*, yet the antisemitic insult is not justified by the text, Italian politics of the late nineteenth century or D'Annunzio's stance. On the topic of D'Annunzio's stance on the Jewish community see Michael A. Ledeen, *The First Duce: D'Annunzio at Fiume* (Baltimore: The John Hopkins University Press, 1977), pp. 110–13.

[49] Article mentioned in Felicia Londré, 'Eleonora Duse: an Italian Actress on the American Stage', *Studies in Popular Culture*, 2 (1985), 60–70 (p. 65).

[50] Londré, p. 65. This image is also spread by: Bertita Harding, *Age Cannot Wither: The Story of Duse and D'Annunzio* (Philadelphia: J.B. Lippincott Co., 1947); Frances Winwar, *Wingless Victory: A Biography of Gabriele D'Annunzio and Eleonora Duse* (New York: Harper, 1956). See also Paolo Fasoli, 'Le ali della vittoria: note sulla fortuna di D'Annunzio nell'America del Nord', *Rassegna Dannunziana*, 72 (2018), 42–51. For an alternative reading, see Annamaria Andreoli, *Più che l'amore. Eleonora Duse e Gabriele D'Annunzio* (Venice: Marsilio, 2017).

The Influence of the UK

D'Annunzio's reception as a shameless seducer conflicts with the political credit he gained throughout the years. The image of the shameless libertine has a long-lasting appeal to the mass public, while the figure of the political leader dominated the US press mainly between the First World War and the first half of the 1920s. An analysis of the articles published in the *NYT* between 1914 and 1938 shows that gossip was almost absent until the second half of the 1920s. From 1925 onwards and during the 1930s, all political news about D'Annunzio was related to his proximity to Benito Mussolini, since D'Annunzio was progressively pushed to the margins of the national and international political scene. Only a few, yet authoritative, voices – such as the *NYT* – correctly reported that the bond between the two was anything but friendly. For instance, on 26 May 1926 the journal stressed D'Annunzio's suspicion toward Fascism and mentioned that 'his anti-Fascist attitude [. . .] was so pronounced that he at one time was considered almost the head of opposition against Mussolini'.[51]

When in the 1930s Fascism became a concern in the USA, the complex political relations between D'Annunzio and Mussolini were no longer addressed and anti-Fascist propaganda explicitly used an anecdotal-sensationalist account of D'Annunzio as a Machiavellian-Casanovan character to denigrate him. In this regard, the US reception was biased by the British one, which included Gerald Griffin's *Gabriele D'Annunzio: The Warrior Bard* (1935). Griffin focuses on the war period and explicitly ridicules D'Annunzio's persona. In the first chapter, for example, he presents the author as 'a cynical exploiter of the love of women' for whom 'the purpose of life was mating' and as 'the man prepared [. . .] to exploit anything or anybody ruthlessly for his own ends'.[52] It thus seems that the American reception incorporated stances, such as Griffin's, that were embedded in British propaganda against the Fascist regime and that single D'Annunzio out as a preferred target from 1925 onwards.[53] Indeed, Griffin's anecdotal account of the Fiume exploit revolves around

[51] 'Premier visits D'Annunzio. Mussolini will take over Villa, Il Vittoriale, for the Nation', *NYT*, 26 May 1925, p. 6.

[52] Gerald Griffin, *Gabriele D'Annunzio: The Warrior Bard* (Port Washington: Kennikat Press, 1970), pp. 14–5.

[53] John Woodhouse, 'Gabriele D'Annunzio's reputation and critical fortune in Britain', *Annali d'Italianistica*, 5 (1987), 245–58 (p. 245).

D'Annunzio's presumed connivance with Italian Fascism. He fashions D'Annunzio as the trailblazer for Mussolini and the precursor of Hitler, which makes Griffin 'almost wish that D'Annunzio had never been born'.[54] Additionally, Griffin insists on the 'sterling friendship' between D'Annunzio and Mussolini after Fiume, while adding that the author 'firmly believed that Mussolini alone could save the country'.[55]

Thus, the moral and political denigration directed against D'Annunzio's persona as the embodiment of the Italians' supposedly despicable nature, the old stereotypes about Italians and the gossip about D'Annunzio all merged to form an image of the degenerate seducer and Fascist. This reception created a mainstream image of D'Annunzio in the US consolidating the anecdotal and sensationalist approaches to D'Annunzio's life as a popular critical matrix. Indeed the framework is so popular that it overshadowed the (more historically correct) post-1970 readings of D'Annunzio's complex relations with Fascism. This limits the dissemination of critics' political-revisionist operation among the general public, as concrete historical and political claims are outweighed by the sensationalist elements that the US public has been historically well-disposed to receive.[56]

A case in point is Michael A. Ledeen's study of the Fiume exploit and its connections with Fascism (1977). Ledeen correctly argues that these connections must be understood in terms of a stylistic resonance between D'Annunzio and Fascism: as a way of doing mass politics.[57] As for their ideology, Ledeen stresses the differences between the two political phenomena that emerge in the Constitution of Fiume (Carta del Carnaro) and from D'Annunzio's commitment to organising the

[54] Griffin, p. 6.

[55] Ibid., pp. 257–8.

[56] Another factor that determines the unsuccessful attempts to divulge revisionist readings to the general public is the often-contradictory account of the D'Annunzio-Fascism association. A good example is Anthony Rhodes, who states that Fascism capitalised on 'the supposed D'Annunzio-Mussolini friendship' and endorsed the idea of D'Annunzio as 'a kind of John the Baptist to Mussolini'. Rhodes seems to dismiss such a stance. Yet, a few pages later, he affirms that D'Annunzio was in his life 'Mussolini's forerunner' and that for that reason the expression '*John the Baptist of Fascism*, is not unjust'. Anthony Rhodes, *D'Annunzio: The Poet as Superman* (New York: McDowell Obolensky Inc, 1960), p. 244, p. 264 and p. 288.

[57] Ledeen, p. vii. Becker, a critic of this view, fashions D'Annunzio as the architect of Fascist ideology for, in Fiume, he enacts a nationalist socialism that would form the basis for Fascism: Jared M. Becker, *Nationalism and Culture. Gabriele D'Annunzio and Italy after the Risorgimento* (New York: Peter Lang, 1994), p. 3.

League of Fiume. Therefore, Ledeen rejects the supposition of 'an important ideological continuity between Dannunzian Fiume and Mussolini's Italy'.[58] Yet, Ledeen's argument about the complex relationship between D'Annunzio and Fascism does not find resonance among the general public because his narration of the Fiume exploit relies mainly on an anecdotal approach that upholds 'the stereotype of a theatrical, salon-dwelling D'Annunzio'.[59] Hence, what remains impressed in the American public's memory is precisely D'Annunzio's profile emerging from the title: he is *The First Duce*, the precursor of Fascism and Mussolini, which is the dominant view during the 1980s and 1990s, as exemplified by the examples of *Cagney & Lacey* and Barbara Jepson discussed in the introduction.

D'Annunzio's Reception Today

As we have shown, between 1898 and 1911, D'Annunzio was known as a literary author, a political opinionist of the Italian right-wing and a womaniser. The war endowed D'Annunzio with greater political clout, which then disappeared from the 1930s onwards when the association of D'Annunzio with Fascism and the moral stigma that the association involved worked together to favour the re-emergence of old prejudices against Italians as a primary lens for the author's reception. This consolidated a popular image of D'Annunzio as a pervert, seducer and Fascist – an image that relied primarily on anecdotes and sensationalism. This focus prevented an unbiased popularisation of D'Annunzio's cultural and political engagement.[60]

D'Annunzio's reception in the US is exemplary of this dynamic even today. As there is no reference biography on the author in the US, its market relies, just as the rest of the world (except for Italy and France), on British books. These accounts are not always totally trustworthy. This is testified by the difference between the last two UK biographies of international resonance: John Woodhouse's *Gabriele D'Annunzio: Defiant Archangel* (1998) and Lucy Hughes-Hallett's *The Pike: Gabriele D'Annunzio, Poet, Seducer and Preacher*

[58] Ledeen, p. 201.

[59] Letizia Argenteri, 'La presenza di D'Annunzio in America', in *L'Italia e la «Grande Vigilia»*, pp. 293–302 (p. 293).

[60] Guylian Nemegeer and Mara Santi, 'Gabriele D'Annunzio's *Notturno*, the Book of the Italian War: Political Commitment, National Regeneration and its Ideological Roots', *Forum Italicum*, 3 (2021), 710–40.

of War (2013). Woodhouse's biography accurately pays attention to but does not capitalise on the sensational aspects of D'Annunzio's life.[61] By contrast, Hughes-Hallett presents *The Pike* as a political biography that aims to divulge the complexity of the D'Annunzio-Fascism association to the wider public, yet in the end her historical account proves to be less trustworthy.

In the introduction, Hughes-Hallett stresses not only Mussolini's appropriation of D'Annunzio's political style, but also D'Annunzio's disdain toward Mussolini and Hitler. However, throughout her book, there is little real talk of politics, and the book reveals itself to be the culmination of a whole tradition of anecdotal approaches and gossip. Hughes-Hallett relies on a sensationalist-anecdotal narration of D'Annunzio's eventful life. The historical claims about D'Annunzio and Fascism are once again largely overshadowed by the moralistic bias against D'Annunzio's persona, that, as we have shown, is a concrete legacy of the prejudices that from the 1930s onwards associated him directly with Italian Fascism. In the end, the biography fails to diffuse a profile of D'Annunzio as an exponent of the right-wing who was critical of Mussolini. Instead, it primarily repeats the stereotyped image of D'Annunzio as a vicious eroticist, which is far from unprejudiced: he is 'a Don Giovanni who seduced and deserted his women without a qualm', an 'incorrigible spendthrift' and even affected by 'mental abnormality'.[62] This biography won awards and is present in libraries worldwide, having been translated into Italian, Spanish, Slovenian, Japanese and Korean. The book's significant international success proves how the market worldwide still rewards sensationalist-anecdotical accounts, hindering the popularisation of more nuanced views proposed by the ongoing academic reassessment of D'Annunzio beyond political and moral censorship.

[61] John Woodhouse, *Gabriele D'Annunzio: Defiant Archangel* (Oxford: Clarendon Press, 1998), p. 6.

[62] Lucy Hughes-Hallett, *The Pike: Gabriele D'Annunzio, Poet, Seducer and Preacher of War* (New York: Alfred A. Knopf, 2013), p. 55, 115 and 292.

Chapter 15

The Myth of Gabriele D'Annunzio in Russian Culture, 1890–2010: From 'Songs of the Native Land' to the 'Winged Cyclops'

Elda Garetto and Sofia Lurie,[1]
translated by Stuart Oglethorpe

The myth of Gabriele D'Annunzio in Russian culture, which goes back almost 130 years, can be seen as falling into three distinct phases: the period of his greatest fame, covering the first quarter of the twentieth century; his almost total disappearance during the Soviet era; and, from the 1990s to the present, a resurgence in interest. In the early twentieth century, at the peak of D'Annunzio's 'translatability' (to use Walter Benjamin's term), perceptions of him as an 'artist of his own life' meant his personality aroused the same interest as his works. Studies on the Russian enthusiasm for D'Annunzio during this period are greatly indebted to Cesare G. De Michelis, who demonstrated that at the beginning of the century D'Annunzio stood alongside Ibsen, Hamsun and Maeterlinck, the European writers most translated, discussed and represented on the stages of Imperial Russia; knowledge of his work had become common in learned circles of the period.[2] Between 1918 and 1989, in a political climate that was increasingly hostile to bourgeois culture and D'Annunzio's ideologies, the image of the soldier-poet resurfaced occasionally, but in a more peripheral way and mainly in satire.

[1] Sofia Lurie worked on documents in Russian libraries and archives and Elda Garetto on documents in the Vittoriale archive and on material on Russian emigration.

[2] Cesare G. De Michelis: 'D'Annunzio nella cultura russa', in *D'Annunzio nelle culture dei paesi slavi*, ed. by Giuseppe Dell'Agata, Cesare G. De Michelis and Pietro Marchesani (Venice: Marsilio, 1979), pp. 13–39; 'D'Annunzio, la Russia, l'Unione sovietica', *Quaderni dannunziani*, n.s., 1–2 (1987), 311–17; 'D'Annunzio, la Russia, i paesi slavi', in *D'Annunzio europeo. Atti del convegno internazionale, Gardone Riviera–Perugia 8–13 maggio 1989*, ed. by Pietro Gibellini (Rome: Lucarini, 1991), pp. 317–27.

The interest in D'Annunzio that Russian culture had sustained in the early twentieth century had a rather muted but still significant echo in some circles within the Russian diaspora in Italy in the 1920s and 1930s. In the 1990s, D'Annunzio once again attracted attention as a political figure and a European forebearer of radical activism. Interest in D'Annunzio the writer was also rekindled: with new research in Russia into the country's 'Silver Age', there was a revival of studies on his work and his contacts with the Russian world.[3] These two strands of interest have been fuelled by the republication of not only D'Annunzio's literary works, sometimes in new translations, but also his political oratory from the Great War period.[4] This new phase culminated in the first Russian biography of the poet, *Krylatyi tziklop* (The Winged Cyclops), by the St Petersburg poet Elena Shvarts.[5]

This chapter has two main aims. First, it intends to deepen understanding of the first phase of D'Annunzio's success, which has recently aroused fresh interest from scholars thanks to the publication of new archival material including diaries and letters from key figures. Second, it aims to shed light on the period since the

[3] L. M. Koval, 'Gabriele d'Annunzio v Rossii', *Kniga. Issledovaniia i materialy*, 76 (1999), 165–71; Pavel Dmitriev, '"Son v osennii vecher" G. D'Annunzio v perevode M. A. Kuzmina', in *Russko-Ital'ianskii arkhiv*, 2 vols, ed. by Daniela Rizzi and Andrey Shishkin (Salerno: Poligrafica Ruggiero, 2002), vol. 2, pp. 89–93; K. A. Chekalov, 'D'Annunzio na russkoi stsene: rubezh dvukh stoletii', *Novye rossiiskie gumanitarnye issledovaniia*, 3 (2008): http://www.nrgumis.ru/articles/archives/full_art.php?aid=76&binn_rubrik_pl_articles=277 (accessed 30 October 2021); Sofia Lurie, 'Un'impronta russa nell'opera di d'Annunzio: "La Leda senza cigno" e *l'affare dei russi*', in *Percorsi russi al Vittoriale: archivi, testimonianze, prospettive di studio*, ed. by Maria Pia Pagani (Cinisello Balsamo: Silvana, 2012), pp. 25–30; Tatiana Bystrova, 'Gabriele d'Annunzio v russkoi kul'ture', in *Dialog kul'tur. Kul'tura dialoga*, ed. by Elena Tareva and Larisa Vokulova (Moscow: Jazyki narodov mira, 2016), pp. 83–7; Aleksandr Aleksandrov, 'K istorii podgotovki perevoda tragedii "Francesca da Rimini" Gabriele d'Annunzio Viach. Ivanovym i V. Briusovym', *Filologicheskie nauki*, 6 (2016), 53–60.

[4] Gabriele D'Annunzio, 'Rech, proiznesennaia s balkona Kapitoliia 17 maia 1915 goda' (Speech from the Campidoglio balcony, 17 May 1915), trans. by Il'ya Kormiltsev *Inostrannaia literatura*, 11 (1999). New editions of literary works include *Leda bez lebedia*, trans. by Nikolay Bronshtein et al. (Moscow: Bestseller, 1995); *Noktiurn*, trans. by Sofia Gerie, *Inostrannaia literatura*, 11 (1999); *Sobranie sochinenii v shesti tomakh,* trans. by Jurgis Baltrušaitis et al. (Moscow: Knigovek, 2010); *Naslazhdenie,* trans. by Jurgis Baltrušaitis (St Petersburg: Azbuka, 2011); and *Nevinnyi*, trans. by Olga Khimona (St Petersburg: Azbuka, 2012).

[5] Elena Shvarts, *Krylatyi tziklop* (St Petersburg: Vita Nova, 2010).

Russian Revolution, which until now has been the subject of very little research.

Scandalous Imitator or Triumphant Innovator: D'Annunzio's Image in the Early Twentieth Century

Despite the substantial presence of D'Annunzio's output and image in Russia, his reception within Modernism presents a somewhat mixed picture. While his poetry was nearly absent in Russian translation, his plays conquered the stages of both state and independent theatres, which were focusing on a new, avant-garde repertoire. In 1907, after his break with the Kommissarzhevskaya theatre, Vsevolod Meyerhold planned to include D'Annunzio's work among the plays staged by his anti-naturalistic 'theatre of fantasy'.[6] Meanwhile, the Kommissarzhevskaya's production of *Francesca da Rimini*, directed by Nikolay Evreinov, met with success.[7] Performances of *Le Martyre de Saint Sébastien* and, especially, *La Pisanelle*, an innovative and much-discussed Russian, Italian and French collaboration, represent the most significant encounter between D'Annunzio and Russian culture. The poet's French period coincided with the Parisian success of Russian painting and ballet, stimulated by the constant innovation emerging from the city's cultural melting pot. The response to these plays, which were covered by the press and discussed by figures including Meyerhold and Leon Bakst, helped confirm D'Annunzio's position as a cosmopolitan cultural figure and innovator in international theatre.

D'Annunzio's translators and reviewers included major Symbolist poets such as Baltrušaitis, Briusov, Ivanov and Blok, as well as the 'clarist' Kuzmin. His theatrical themes attracted Russian writers and artists not least because of their interest in ancient Greece, a dominant current in contemporary culture. D'Annunzio also established himself in Russia as the most prominent representative of a 'Mediterranean' variant of Modernism. In 'Pesni zemli' (Songs of the Native Land) – an introduction to D'Annunzio's collected works in Russian by Zinaida Vengerova, a key figure of intercultural exchange – he was portrayed as a showman experimenting with every cultural era, conveying each 'with Mediterranean passion and an artist's refinement'

6 Vsevolod Meyerhold, *Perepiska: 1896–1939* (Moscow: Iskusstvo, 1976), p. 48.

7 Chekalov, 'D'Annunzio na russkoi stsene'.

in a pantheistic and vibrant 'passion for his native land'.[8] As a result, his works could also be a lens for looking at Italy, the favoured goal of the 'pilgrimage of the soul' for figures of Russia's Silver Age.[9]

As time passed, early admiration for D'Annunzio's literary achievements and persona gave way to more reserved and even adverse assessments. Valery Briusov, for example, respected D'Annunzio's poetry and translated 'Isolda' (1900) and 'Argentea' (1914), but by 1897 he described D'Annunzio as 'a great, great poet, but the most disgraceful of men'.[10] In 1907, having been persuaded by Vera Kommissarzhevskaya to work with Ivanov on translating *Francesca da Rimini*, he described the work as 'a piece of limited worth, almost a lyrical play, which even a state theatre could perform without effort'.[11] In 1908, Aleksandr Blok praised *La nave* to his wife as 'a very intelligent play'; in 1913, reflecting on similarities between his own drama *The Rose and the Cross* and *Francesca da Rimini*, his verdict was that 'D'Annunzio is infinitely more superficial and high-flown'.[12] Jurgis Baltrušaitis translated six of D'Annunzio's plays and contributed to the journal *Skorpion*, a focal point of nascent Russian Symbolism, helping introduce D'Annunzio to a Russian audience in the 1890s; but by about 1910, even he expressed reservations about the poet's personality, having had more direct contact with Italian cultural circles.[13] D'Annunzio's persona, which attracted as much attention in Russia as his literary output, generated substantial reservations. The reactions of Russians who met him in person, taken as a whole, give the impression of an egotistical and eccentric philanderer who craved success. The publisher Aleksei Suvorin, referring to the response of a woman friend in Rome, wrote that 'she had

[8] Zinaida Vengerova, 'Pesni zemli (Gabriele D'Annunzio)', in *Sobranie sochinenii Gabriele D'Annunzio v dvenadcati tomakh* (St Petersburg: Shipovnik, 1910), I, pp. 9–38 (p. 11).

[9] N. P. Komolova, *Italiia v russkoi kulture Serebrianogo veka: vremena i sudby* (Moscow: Nauka, 2005), p. 20.

[10] S. I. Gindin, 'Kommentarii', in Valery Briusov, *Zarubezhnaia poeziia v perevodakh Valeriia Briusova* (Moscow: Raduga, 1994), p. 817.

[11] Aleksandrov, p. 58.

[12] Aleksandr Blok, *Sobranie sochinenii v vos'mi tomakh*, vol. 8, *Pisma*, ed. by Vladimir Orlov and others (Moscow–Leningrad: Gosudarstvennoe izdatel'stvo khudozhestvennoi literatury, 1963), p. 244; *Dnevnik Al. Bloka: 1880–1921*, ed. by Pavel Medvedev (Leningrad: Izdatel'stvo pisatelei v Leningrade, 1928), pp. 180–1.

[13] Michele Colucci, 'Baltrušajtis e D'Annunzio', in *D'Annunzio nelle culture dei paesi slavi*, ed. by Giuseppe Dell'Agata, Cesare G. De Michelis and Pietro Marchesani (Venice: Marsilio, 1979), pp. 40–50 (p. 43).

many interesting things to say about D'Annunzio, whom she had met. He has enormous self-regard, to the point of ridiculousness'.[14] The painter and art critic Alexandre Benois, writing from Paris, provided a satirical description of Bakst, D'Annunzio and the latter's women: '[Bakst] is crazy about Mme Golubeva, who currently lives with D'Annunzio but is already jealous of Ida Rubinstein.'[15]

D'Annunzio's reception reflects a complex picture of Russian Modernism as particularly influenced by French avant-garde circles, which the Italian poet also drew on freely. It was during D'Annunzio's French period, when he had increasing personal contact with Russian cultural circles, that a plan to organise a series of events for him in St Petersburg and Moscow emerged. The diary of the scholar Fedor Fidler reveals that in 1911 Grigorii Kirdetsov, who had conceived of this tour, intended to pay for D'Annunzio's first-class travel and a modest fee of 1000 lire, which he thought would suffice to attract him. Kirdetsov, who said he knew D'Annunzio personally, referred to him as a gigolo maintained by his lovers, 'including E. Duse, whom he mercilessly defamed in the novel *Il fuoco*'.[16]

These reactions from representatives of various literary generations convey distaste toward a man of letters who was nakedly ambitious and used questionable conduct to draw attention to himself. This kind of image was to be adopted by the Futurist Vladimir Mayakovsky and the Ego-Futurist Igor Severianin, but it was at odds with the dignified vision of the poet held in Symbolist circles. Oddly, D'Annunzio's version of '*zhiznetvorchestvo*' (life as a work of art), a concept that was also very important to the Russian Decadent and Symbolist school, disconcerted not just those favouring social commitment, like Aleksei Suvorin, but also advocates of new forms of expression who had been early promoters of D'Annunzio in Russia.

The huge range of sources from which the Italian poet drew inspiration elicited varying responses from different Russian writers, including the 'clarist' Mikhail Kuzmin, the Acmeist Nikolay Gumilev and Marina Tsvetaeva, who does not really belong to any specific poetic movement. For the young Kuzmin, who visited Italy in 1897 and soon after set off on a pilgrimage to remote Russian monasteries,

[14] Aleksei Suvorin, *Dnevnik A. S. Suvorina*, ed. by Mikhail Krichevskii (Moscow: L. D. Frenkel, 1923), p. 148.

[15] Alexandr Benois, *Dnevnik: 1918–1924*, ed. by Ivan Vydrin (Moscow: Zakharov, 2016), p. 70.

[16] Fedor Fidler, *Iz mira literatorov: kharaktery i suzhdeniia*, ed. by Konstantin Azadovskii (Moscow: Novoe literaturnoe obozrenie, 2008), p. 575.

fascination with D'Annunzio was one of the extremes in his spiritual quest: 'sometimes I wanted nothing but religiousness, the simplest of lives and the ways of the people, and I rejected all culture and modernity; but then I would rave over Gabriele D'Annunzio, the "new culture" and sensuality'.[17] In 1898, Kuzmin translated 'Sogno d'un tramonto d'autunno' in a notebook, and he returned to the Italian poet several times in his diary and later writings. In 1907, he wrote that 'items in the press about works by D'Annunzio in preparation have brought back all my old love for this passionate maestro'.[18] After seeing *Le Chèvrefeuille* performed at the Michailovsky Theatre in 1914, he observed that 'it is truly wonderful how D'Annunzio has managed to create something so touching, with genuine feeling, from a second-rate, stolen and implausible plot'.[19] According to Pavel Dmitriev, who published the translation of 'Sogno' when it was discovered in the archives, Kuzmin was drawn not so much by the literary quality of D'Annunzio's writing as by the wealth of creative invention yet to be developed: 'the aesthetics of unrealised ideas'.[20] That Kuzmin was not one of D'Annunzio's blind admirers is indicated by his criticism of works by Sergey Gorodecky and Fiodor Sologub, where he identified the same weaknesses that characterised the prose and plays of the Italian writer.[21] His opinion is even more explicit reviewing the staging of *La figlia di Iorio*: D'Annunzio, he says, had some sense of the theatrical effect he wanted but failed to realise it, filling the dialogue with cumbersome rhetoric and stylistic devices that were 'inauthentic, false, and a little artificial'.[22] In 1934, reflecting on the sources for his own *Alexandrian Songs*, he confirmed both D'Annunzio's influence and the Italian's secondary ranking in his aesthetic hierarchy, placed after Ebers.[23]

The young Tsvetaeva who read *Il Piacere*, *Il fuoco* and *Le vergini delle rocce* found in them the tension that she felt was a necessary condition for creativity and existence: themes of transgression, love

[17] Quoted in Nikolay Bogomolov, *Mikhail Kuzmin: stat i materialy* (Moscow: Novoe literaturnoe obozrenie, 1995), p. 19.

[18] Mikhail Kuzmin, *Dnevnik 1905–1907*, ed. by Nikolay Bogomolov and Sergei Shumikhin (St Petersburg: Izdatelstvo Ivana Limbakha, 2000), p. 387.

[19] Mikhail Kuzmin, *Dnevnik 1908–1915*, ed. by Nikolay Bogomolov and Sergei Shumikhin (St Petersburg: Izdatelstvo Ivana Limbakha, 2005), p. 428.

[20] Dmitriev, p. 87.

[21] Ibid., p. 91.

[22] Mikhail Kuzmin, 'Doch Iorio', *Zhizn iskusstva*, 8 May 1919, p. 49.

[23] Nikolay Bogomolov and John Malmstad, *Mikhail Kuzmin: iskusstvo, zhizn, epokha* (St Petersburg: Vita Nova, 2007), p. 165.

of danger and nostalgia for the greatness and vigour of previous eras. In 1907, after the failure of the First Russian Revolution, she rejected the idea of a revolution based on mundanely pragmatic aspirations in words that could almost have come from D'Annunzio: 'one can only fight inspired by books read, or by one's own ideas (no mere economic or Marxist ideal can inspire one); one can only fight inspired by a *dream*, the dream of an extraordinary beauty, and of an unachievable, *unachievable*, liberty'.[24]

Among the Russian writers of the period, the only one whose respect for D'Annunzio's artistry and image did not change over time seems to have been Nikolay Gumilev, whose work combined Aesthetic sensibilities with patriotic spirit and the idea of poetry as action. Although he was particularly interested in D'Annunzio as soldier and politician, the Italian's influence was apparent as early as 1911, when Gumilev wrote that 'Wilde showed us art as a playful game, and D'Annunzio shows us an art that emerges from the depths where the differences between races originate.'[25] The idea of Latinness and dominion of the great civilisations over the barbarians, celebrated in *Il fuoco* and *La nave*, matched Gumilev's Kiplingesque colonialism, linked in his poetry to adventure and conquest. In 1912 Gumilev and his young bride Anna Akhmatova toured Italy, and on their return he composed a series of poems constituting a sort of travel diary. Echoes of D'Annunzio are especially noticeable in the poems 'Rome' and 'Villa Borghese'. However, while D'Annunzio's characters call for the return of a glorious past, for Gumilev the past is already present in the modern era.[26] His 'Rome' is the city 'of the marvellous Caesars, of saints and popes', protected by 'the she-wolf and her gory mouth', which also serves as a symbol for Italy's colonial aspirations.[27] In the sombre and spectral imagery of the sonnet 'Villa Borghese', by contrast, the spirit of *Trionfo della morte* is in the air with themes of melancholy lovers, suicide and moonlight.[28]

24 Marina Tsvetaeva, *Sobranie sochinenii v semi tomakh*, 7 vols (Moscow: Ellis Lak, 1995), VII, p. 730 (emphasis in the original).

25 Nikolay Gumilev, *Polnoe sobranie sochinenii*, 10 vols, ed. by Jury V. Zobnin (Moscow: Voskresenie, 2006), VII, p. 105.

26 A. S. Roslyj, 'Dante v estetike i poezii akmeizma: sistema kontzeptov (na materiale tvorchestva A. Akhmatovoi, N. Gumileva, O. Mandelshtama)' (unpublished doctoral thesis, Rostov State University, 2005), p. 32.

27 Gumilev, II, pp. 115–16.

28 Gumilev, II, p. 138.

In 1915, D'Annunzio's speech at Quarto inspired his 'Ode to D'Annunzio', in which Gumilev expressed enthusiasm for the poet and orator of 'the beautiful War, the envy of Alexander and Agamemnon'. The exaltation of D'Annunzio, 'to whose delicate hands the people entrusts its fate', clearly also refers to Gumilev, who had enlisted at the beginning of the war. To honour the poet-hero, Gumilev places him alongside other Italian poets such as Virgil, Dante and Tasso; he also scatters the piece with elements from D'Annunzio's *Laudi*, including the Roman she-wolf, the sea and mountains, and patriotic pride.[29] From January to April 1918 Gumilev was in London, where he had the opportunity to meet G. K. Chesterton and present his utopian project of rule by poets, the only people worthy to govern. Jokingly, he allotted the British throne to Chesterton, gave France to Anatole France and Italy to D'Annunzio.[30] Gumilev's vision of government by poets was realised by D'Annunzio about a year later, prompting a strong reaction from the Russian, who in 1921 put the Fiume venture on the stage, taking the role of Commandant.[31] Gumilev pursued the same transition from poet to soldier and then defender of his political ideals, which in 1921, during the Red Terror, led to the tragic outcome of his shooting.

1919–1923: Akim Volynsky and the Brothers Grigoriy and Mikhail Lozinsky

After the Bolshevik revolution, the political aspects of D'Annunzio's image came to the fore in Russia. The poet's contacts with the Soviet regime are documented: in 1921, he offered a donation for famine victims in the Volga region; and in May 1922, while the Genoa Conference was under way, he received Russia's People's Commissar for Foreign Affairs Georgy Chicherin, an admirer of his talents, at the Vittoriale.[32]

Between 1919 and 1923, new editions of D'Annunzio's works appeared in Russian. These testify to a climate of conflict between the Modernist line, still holding sway, and the formation of a new canon, within which D'Annunzio's 'Realist' period and short stories

[29] Gumilev, III, pp. 78–9.

[30] Elaine Rusinko, 'Gumilev in London: An Unknown Interview', *Russian Literature Triquarterly*, 16 (1979), 73–85.

[31] Irina Odoevtseva, *Na beregakh Nevy* (Moscow: AST, 2010), p. 366.

[32] De Michelis, 'D'Annunzio nella cultura russa', p. 30.

were favoured. The 'populist' line is represented by the republication of *Le novelle della Pescara* in 1919 (originally 1901), as well as the appearance of *La Pisanelle* (1922 [originally 1913]), a new translation of *Forse che sì, forse che no* (1923 [1910]), and the more recent *Notturno* (1924 [1916]).

In the introduction to *Le novelle della Pescara*, issued by the prestigious publisher Vsemirnaia literatura (World Literatures), the Marxist critic Rafail Grigoriev presented the stories as authentic and honest, free of Decadent tendencies: a 'monument to [D'Annunzio's] provincial homeland', portraying the soul of the people as 'simple and obscure, wise and complex'.[33] Curiously, in order to confirm D'Annunzio's 'modest' origins, Grigoriev reproduced the romantic myth of his birth on board a ship in the Adriatic, which D'Annunzio had offered to Georges Hérelle, his French translator, to aid the reception of his works in France. Not long after this attempt to adapt D'Annunzio to new ideological requirements, a plan emerged for the same publishing house to produce an edition of his selected works. This was to be edited by Akim Volynsky, an art critic and theorist of literary Modernism and Decadence among the most respected writers for the review *Severnyi vestnik* (Northern Messenger), which had published the first translations of D'Annunzio into Russian: *L'Innocente* in 1893; *Trionfo della morte* (1894 [1894]); *Giovanni Episcopo* (1894 [1892]); and *Sogno d'un mattino di primavera* (1897 [1897]). There were parallels between the journalistic and cultural energy of the early D'Annunzio and the activities of Volynsky, an eclectic intellectual who treated a wide range of topics, from Leskov and Dostoyevsky to the Italian Renaissance and from dance theory to Symbolist theatre. Like the author of the novel *Le vergini delle rocce*, Volynsky had read Walter Pater and studied the Italian Renaissance, making Leonardo a central figure with his book *Leonardo da Vinci* in 1900. In 1910, he founded his own small publishing house, Grjadušy den (The Day to Come), which printed Russian and European Modernists including Richard Wagner and Remy de Gourmont, as well as art criticism, paying special attention to the aesthetics of book production. In 1911, the publisher contacted D'Annunzio through Angelo Flavio Guidi, a correspondent for *Il Giornale d'Italia*, to ask if he could write a preface for the editions of his selected poetry

[33] Rafail Grigoriev, 'Predislovie', in Gabriele D'Annunzio, *Peskarskie rasskazy* (Peterburg: Vsemirnaia literatura, 1919), pp. 5–11 (p. 11).

and prose.[34] This would have been the first authorised edition of D'Annunzio's poetry in Russia, but unfortunately it never came to fruition. In 1919, however, under the auspices of *Vsemirnaia literatura*, Volynsky returned to his plan to publish D'Annunzio. The preparatory material for translations of *La città morta* and *La Gioconda* shows he intended to restore the original style: *La città morta*'s epigraphs and ending formulas in Greek are brought back, names are Italianised, the author's characteristic use of emphatic repetition is resurrected and his elevated literary style is reproduced.[35] However, these translations never emerged; the only published volume was the new Russian translation of *Forse che sì forse che no*, printed in Berlin in 1923 with the addition of a preface by the translator Grigory Lozinsky and a bibliography of D'Annunzio's works. An enthusiastic letter from Lozinsky to Volynsky shows that the translation had already been completed in 1919, before Lozinsky left Russia.[36]

Lozinsky's introduction to *Forse che sì forse che no* is of particular interest as the only known writing on D'Annunzio by one of his Russian translators. Rather than listing the 'isms' that influenced D'Annunzio's ideology, Lozinsky explored how his prose was constructed. He noted the repeated use of particular phrases, described as 'authorial formulas' serving to organise the narrative much like refrains within poetry or song.[37] By analysing numerous comparisons, explicit or implicit, he also explored the feature of D'Annunzio's poetics that Luciano Anceschi later called its 'system of analogy'.[38] Furthermore, he commented on the difficulties of conveying the wordsmith's affected style. Issues were sometimes resolved by recourse to translation through description when there was no equivalent Russian word for a particular term, and sometimes by inventing words such as '*parusolet*': this was a literal translation of D'Annunzio's famous neologism '*velivolo*' (aeroplane), which he had

[34] Gardone Riviera, Fondazione 'Il Vittoriale degli Italiani', Archivio Generale, Palchetto XLIX, Cassetta 2, Letter from A. F. Guidi dated 21 October 1911.

[35] Moscow, Rossijsky Gosudarstvenny arkhiv literatury i iskusstva (hereinafter RGALI), f. 692, op. 1, ed. 751, 752.

[36] RGALI, f. 95, op. 1, ed. 610, letter from G. L. Lozinsky to A. L. Volynsky dated 25 August 1919.

[37] Grigory Lozinsky, 'Predislovie', in Gabriele D'Annunzio, *Mozhet byt da, mozhet byt net* (Berlin: Vsemirnaia literatura, 1923), pp. 7–17 (p. 14).

[38] Luciano Anceschi, 'D'Annunzio e il sistema della analogia', in *D'Annunzio e il simbolismo europeo. Atti del convegno di studio, Gardone Riviera, 14–15–16 settembre 1973*, ed. by Emilio Mariano (Milan: Il saggiatore, 1976), pp. 63–110 (p. 65).

introduced in his recent novel to bestow aircraft with a name 'of golden Latinness' and which was subsequently assimilated by technical and newspaper language.

In 1922, a year before the publication of Grigory Lozinsky's translation, his brother Mikhail's Russian version of *La Pisanelle*[39] appeared. This drama was not previously translated, which is curious considering that D'Annunzio's theatrical output was very successful in Russia before 1917. This omission was probably due to cultural constraints: the Parisian works, interpreted by the uninhibited Ida Rubinstein, would have encountered numerous obstacles with the imperial censor. Moreover, the play was written in an archaic French full of erudite historical and literary allusions and Mediaeval terms; D'Annunzio himself described the 'tone' adopted by some of the characters as 'almost untranslatable'.[40] Furthermore, the Russian critics who had seen the performance at the Châtelet theatre did not receive it well.

Why, then, did Mikhail Lozinsky translate this work? It may have been a side project he took due to financial difficulties.[41] *La Pisanelle* was exotic and sensual, sometimes genuinely funny and might have proved successful with readers looking for historical and adventure novels to escape the brutal reality of 'war communism'. On the other hand, it could be presented as compatible with the new ideology thanks to its satire of the clergy in the first and second acts. The translator brothers' interest in D'Annunzio was probably encouraged by their bond with Gumilev, Mikhail Lozinsky's close friend. It is significant that the translation of *La Pisanelle* was issued by Mysl, a cooperative that was then the largest private publisher in Petrograd, producing both popular literature and work by poets who were starting to clash with the new authorities. Personal contacts with the publishing house, which in 1922 issued both the only poetry collection by Mikhail Lozinsky and the posthumous edition of the works of Gumilev, may have prompted the decision to translate a work with the potential to attract a mass readership.

With his customary attention to poetic form, Mikhail Lozinsky retained the original text's number of lines, observing their strophic and rhythmic pattern. Where lines rhymed in the original he created

[39] Gabriele D'Annunzio, *Pisanelle, ili Blagoukhannaya smert'*, trans. Mikhail Lozinskij (Petrograd: Mysl, 1922).

[40] D'Annunzio to Luigi Albertini (19 March 1913), quoted in Franco Di Tizio, *D'Annunzio e Albertini. Vent'anni di sodalizio* (Altino: Ianieri, 2003), p. 177.

[41] See RGALI, f. 95, op. 1, ed. 611, letter from M. L. Lozinsky to A. L. Volynsky dated 25 January 1921.

Russian rhymes, and he used alternating iambic pentameters and iambic trimeters to recreate the rhythm of the metrical form that D'Annunzio borrowed from Honoré d'Urfé's *La Sylvanire ou la Morte-vive*.[42] In his choice of vocabulary, by contrast, Lozinsky toned down the exotic and mediaevalizing colour: he sometimes replaced feudal concepts with terms belonging to serfdom and the Russian peasant world or that were more general, and modified expressions he felt too explicit, such as '*pute*', '*gros coïon*' and '*coïonner*' (roughly: 'whore', 'arsehole' and 'to arse about'). Enhancing the cultural refinement of the text made it more attractive for Russian readers, who had no visual mediation since the play was never staged and thus relied entirely on the work's literary qualities.

The Soviet Period: Rejection and Satire

The second phase of Russian interest in D'Annunzio drew to a close with the translations discussed above. Toward the end of the 1920s, the figure of the Italian poet seems to have disappeared from Russia's cultural world. As the Marxist critic Vladimir Frice put it in D'Annunzio's entry in the Russian literary encyclopaedia of 1930, 'today he has no relevance at all for our literature'.[43] For the generation taking up literature in the 1920s, he represented only 'what we are not'. The playwright Evgeny Shvarts, recalling his education and youthful reading, stimulated by issues of *Satiricon* and *Shipovnik*, listed Gabriele D'Annunzio, Heinrich Mann and Stanislaw Przybyszewski among the few authors that he could not endure, contrasting 'the wholesome and straightforward Jack London' with the complicated social and cultural diatribes of the pre-revolutionary period.[44]

This new attitude toward the Italian poet was encapsulated in the lines of Vladimir Maiakovsky's 'Sovetskaia azbuka' (Soviet ABC), written in 1919 to promote Bolshevist ideas in the trenches: 'handsome pheasant, feather brain, D'Annunzio took Fiume on a drunken whim'.[45]

[42] Annamaria Andreoli, 'Notizia sul testo e note di commento', in Gabriele D'Annunzio, *La Pisanelle* (Milan: Mondadori, 2014), 4984. Ebook.

[43] Vladimir Frice, 'Gabriele d'Annunzio', in *Literaturnaia enciklopediia*, 11 vols (Moscow: Izdatelstvo Kommunisticheskoi Akademii, 1930), I, pp. 167–9.

[44] Evgeny Shvarts, *Zhivu bespokoino: iz dnevnikov,* ed. by Ksenia Kirilenko (Leningrad: Sovetsky pisatel', 1990), pp. 165–6.

[45] Vladimir Maiakovsky, 'Sovetskaia azbuka', in *Sochinenia v dvukh tomakh*, 2 vols, ed. by Al. A. Michailov (Moscow: Pravda: Khudozhestvennaia literatura, 1987), I, p. 113.

The Italian poet appeared as a comedic figure in the satirical novel *The Little Golden Calf* by Il'ya Ilf and Evgeny Petrov, published in 1931, which is full of references to current affairs. When one of the characters, the aviator Sevryugov, disappears on an expedition to the North Pole, a fictional version of D'Annunzio promptly informs the press of his readiness to rescue 'the courageous Russian'.[46] There is something of D'Annunzio in the novel's protagonist Ostap Bender, an adventurer, impostor and Soviet dandy called 'Commander' by his followers, whose rhetorical skills allow him to instil respect in the timorous Soviet citizens. The satirical perspective continued into 1986, with the biographical film *Chicherin*, directed by Aleksandr Zarkhi. When the People's Commissar for Foreign Affairs visits the Vittoriale, D'Annunzio, played by Rolan Bykov, shows off his residence, crammed with objects d'art of debatable quality. He also scorns sentimental humanism and toasts his friend Mussolini and the future leader of Germany 'who will unite the cry of Roman legionaries with the sound of Teutonic swords'. The Soviet diplomat naturally refuses to raise his glass. At this point in the development of the Soviet collective imaginary, D'Annunzio was firmly established as an Aesthete, dilettante and supporter of not only the Fascist Party, with which he actually had a complex relationship, but also Nazism and Hitler, toward whom he harboured a profound and unconcealed aversion.

D'Annunzio and the Russian Diaspora

While D'Annunzio was ostracised by Bolshevik Russia, his fame was kept alive in the vast archipelago of the Russian diaspora. For the Russian refugees who settled in Italy, the country represented a spiritual fatherland that they had long yearned for, and D'Annunzio was a magnetic point of reference. This is evident from the poet's personal correspondence conserved in the Vittoriale archives: Russians writing to him included representatives of the artistic and cultural world who requested meetings and help, or simply conveyed

[46] Il'ya Ilf and Evgeny Petrov, *The Little Golden Calf*, trans. by Anne O. Fisher (Montpelier, VT: Russian Life Books, 2009; first published as *Zolotoj telenok* in the journal *30 Dney*, 1931), p. 179.

personal admiration.[47] For example, the established actress Tatiana Pavlova, subsequently a well-known director, wrote expressing her desire – never realised – to perform his works; the young Rinaldo Küfferle described his tragic experience as a refugee and subjected D'Annunzio to his early experiments in poetry.[48]

For many educated Russians in exile, D'Annunzio was not only Italy's greatest living writer, but also a courageous warrior who could help relieve the suffering of the Russian people. This was the hope of the cellist Aleksandr Barianskii, who first met D'Annunzio in Paris and then, in August 1921, after moving to Italy, urged him to find 'sublime and prophetic words' to help Russia raise funds for famine victims.[49] Enlisting the hero of Fiume in the struggle to defeat Bolshevism was the hope of more than one opponent of the new regime, but this soon proved illusory, especially after formal international recognition of the Soviet state. Nevertheless, D'Annunzio continued to attract the admiration of many Russians: for example, in 1933, the young and already established composer Daniele Amfiteatrov presented him with some 'funeral fanfares' dedicated to the dead of the Fiume legions, to be performed at dawn on Christmas Day among the trees of the Vittoriale.[50] Some correspondence relates to D'Annunzio's time in Paris, including letters from Leon Bakst, who had been responsible for set designs for *La Pisanelle*, *Le Martyre de Saint Sébastien* and *Fedra*. After a long gap, communication resumed in 1922, with news of the new staging of *Le Martyre*, and continued in 1923, with an emotional letter thanking D'Annunzio for sending him *Notturno*. Bakst too had suffered temporary blindness, and he read *Notturno* with a thorough understanding of the difficulties of emerging from a heightened inner vision.[51]

Perhaps the most fascinating aspect of the enduring interest expressed by Russians in Italy is the phenomenon of the literati, sometimes barely known, who either translated his verses into Russian – like Lidia Lebedeva, a relative of Konstantin Balmont and

47 Elda Garetto, ed., 'Lettere di corrispondenti russi a Gabriele d'Annunzio', in *Percorsi russi al Vittoriale: archivi, testimonianze, prospettive di studio*, ed. by Maria Pia Pagani (Cinisello Balsamo: Silvana, 2012), pp. 105–9.

48 See Vittoriale, Archivio Generale, LVII, 4 (for Pavlova); XXVIII, 1 (for Küfferle). See also Maria Pia Pagani, 'Rinaldo Küfferle e il mito di d'Annunzio', *ENTHYMEMA*, 10 (2014), 168–88: https://doi.org/10.13130/2037-2426/3943

49 Vittoriale degli Italiani, Archivio Fiumano, AF Corr.

50 Vittoriale, Archivio Generale, XXIX, 5.

51 Vittoriale, Archivio Generale, IX/4.

amateur poet who enclosed two translations from *Canto novo* – or modelled their own work on D'Annunzio's – like the versatile Mikhail Sukennikov, who left Russia for Berlin and sent the poet part of his verse novel *Fedor Volgin*, with its explicit references to *Il fuoco*.[52] One of the most well-known émigré writers was Dmitrii Merezhkovsky, whose translated work *La naissance des dieux* is conserved by the Vittoriale: its dedication, in French, reads 'To my great brother in spirit Gabriele D'Annunzio, I offer my fervent admiration. D. Merejkovsky [*sic.*] 1926, Paris.'[53] Among the archived correspondence from Russians are also ample examples of the female infatuation that characterised D'Annunzio's entire life; this is illustrated by letters from the Futurist writer and translator Eva Kühn Amendola, displaying pronounced fervour for the poet, hero and conqueror.[54] Requests for assistance include one from Dostoievsky's daughter, asking D'Annunzio to recommend her biography of her father to an Italian publisher.[55] The biography was published in 1922 by Treves, and it is entirely possible, although not documented, that D'Annunzio intervened in some way.[56]

Among the Russian émigrés who performed a mediating role between the two cultures, some sought new styles that did not take D'Annunzio as a model. These included Aleksandr Amfiteatrov, a prose writer influenced by positivism, who enthused over the novels of Giuseppe Borgese – one of the first to attack the mythology around D'Annunzio. Amfiteatrov thought that 'Russians absolutely must get to know him [Borgese]; they cannot just revolve around D'Annunzio!'[57] For the Russian diaspora in Italy, however, D'Annunzio was unavoidable. In the Russian libraries established in Italian cities, works by D'Annunzio, emblematically, stood next to those of Dante. In 1936, Russian writers helping to form an Italian committee to celebrate the centenary of Pushkin's death put D'Annunzio forward as the honorary president, although their Italian counterparts favoured Pirandello. The sentiments of some Russian émigrés are illustrated by

[52] See Vittoriale, Archivio Generale, XLIX–2 (for Lebedeva); XXVII/5 (for Sukennikov).

[53] The dedication is on the title page of the French edition, Merejkowsky, Dmitri, *La naissance des dieux. Toutankhamon en Crète* (Paris: Calmann-Lévy, 1924): Biblioteca del Vittoriale.

[54] Vittoriale, Archivio Generale, XVI/6.

[55] Vittoriale, Archivio Generale, XV/3.

[56] See Aimée Dostoevskaja [*sic.*], *Dostoevskij nei ricordi di sua figlia* (Milan: Treves, 1922).

[57] From a letter to Rinaldo Küfferle dated 11 September 1926 (Bloomington, Indiana University, Lilly Library, Amfiteatrov mss.).

a passage from a letter of 1936 from the painter Elena Grigorovich, a friend of Balmont and Viacheslav Ivanov, to Olga Signorelli, friend and biographer of Eleonora Duse:

> I do not think that even the 'D'Annunzians' have grasped the fundamental value of D'Annunzio. Moreover, perhaps the 'D'Annunzians' have long been the ones who have obscured and distorted the *real* figure of D'Annunzio, by imitating the features of 'Decadent' literature that he employs [. . .] without them having the power of *his* words and the height of *his* passion. [. . .] I think that D'Annunzio has been not only a diviner and prophet, but the creator of this spirit of heroism and sacrifice to which we have been witnesses.[58]

Aspects of this vision, including acknowledgement of the many facets of D'Annunzio's persona, can be linked back to that held by some Russians during the Silver Age.

Revival for the New Millennium: From Political to Poetical Interpretation

After an extended absence, interest in D'Annunzio made a return to Russia in the 1990s with studies of the Fiume venture and his autobiographical writing, including *Le Faville del maglio* and *Il libro segreto*.

D'Annunzio's partial 'rehabilitation' was signalled by the first Russian translations, in 1995, of *La Leda senza cigno*, 'Tre parabole del bellissimo nemico' and 'La pioggia nel pineto'.[59] The introduction to this collection, edited by the Italianist Zlata Potapova, restates the typical Soviet-era verdict condemning D'Annunzio's espousal of 'superman' ideals, but also acknowledges the enduring merits of some of his work: his poetry; his short stories, which maintained 'the noble Italian tradition'; *La figlia di Iorio*, which 'renders the people's lives as poetry'; and his lyric prose.[60]

58 Quoted in Elda Garetto, 'Una russa a Milano: Elena Grigorovič, pittrice, antroposofa, ex-terrorista', in *Territoria russkogo slova*, ed. by Rosanna Casari, Ugo Persi and Maria Chiara Pesenti (Salerno: Vereja, 2012), pp. 123–42 (p. 136) (emphasis in original).

59 D'Annunzio, Leda bez lebedia.

60 Zlata Potapova, 'Mnogolikii Gabriele D'Annunzio', in D'Annunzio, *Leda bez lebedia*, pp. 2–22 (p. 22).

This renewed interest in D'Annunzio was subsequently confirmed by the republication of individual prose works and translation of some of his best-known poems.[61] In 2010, this culminated in the six-volume collected works, which brought together prose and plays, including some new translations (not always entirely faithful to the original) alongside the old.[62] This project, undertaken by the publisher of the literary supplement to the weekly magazine *Ogonek*, is reminiscent of earlier Russian editions, hurriedly produced for a mass readership. The introduction to the collection places D'Annunzio relative to European, especially French, Modernism and emphasises links with early twentieth-century Russian culture.[63]

In modern Russia, D'Annunzio has also become a point of reference or comparison for warrior and guerrilla writers with nationalistic inclinations who see themselves as spiritual heirs of Gumilev. These have included Eduard Limonov, who devoted a few respectful lines to him in his book *Sviashchennye monstry* (Sacred Monsters), and, more recently, Zakhar Prilepin, a battalion commander in the People's Republic of Donetsk. Il'ya Kormiltsev, a poet and publisher in the countercultural mould who produced the books by Limonov, made his own contribution to this perspective. In 1995, for the journal *Inostrannaia literatura*, he translated D'Annunzio's Campidoglio speech of 17 May 1915 and wrote a biographical essay, comparing the poet's trajectory through the three phases of his life – writer, military commander and literary patriarch – with that of Maxim Gorky. For Kormiltsev, D'Annunzio's characters, 'born in the delirium of a Decadent opium den', are now part of literary history, whereas the poet's 'inimitable life' might still be instructive on both a personal and political level, because it shows that 'governing the people is a skill neither more nor less easy than entertaining the public'.[64]

The new millennium also witnessed the posthumous publication of *Krylatyi tziklop* (The Winged Cyclops) by Elena Shvarts, a metaphysical poet who remained a solitary figure in Leningrad's unofficial 'second culture' and whose abstruse, polyphonic world seems remote

[61] See Evgenii Solonovich, *Italianskaia poeziia v perevodakh Evgeniia Solonovicha* (Moscow: Raduga, 2000), p. 252.

[62] D'Annunzio, *Sobranie sochinenii v shesti tomakh*.

[63] Anna Sabashnikova, 'V chas khimery', in D'Annunzio, *Sobranie sochinenii v shesti tomakh*, I, pp. 5–30.

[64] Il'ya Kormiltsev, 'Tri zhizni Gabriele D'Annunzio', *Inostrannaia literatura*, 11 (1999): https://magazines.gorky.media/inostran/1999/11/tri-zhizni-gabriele-d-annunzio.html (accessed 20 November 2021).

from D'Annunzio's multiloquence. This project, the only biography of D'Annunzio written in Russian, consumed the final phase of her life and generated the longest book of her corpus. Shvarts transcends the customary criteria of biography: underlying her epistemological journey is the idea that she and D'Annunzio are both members of the order of poets, sharing the vocation that leads them to put themselves to the test. In this regard, her 'guide to the life of the poet' is different from other recent biographies undertaken by women authors, who either maintain a detached position as they reveal the strategies their subject pursued to establish literary success or emphasise their disapproval of his lifestyle.[65] Shvarts was determined not to transform her biography into a moral verdict. In the meantime, the figure of the aviator and angel, and that of the ambivalent and one-eyed old man who surveys the world he has himself created, became part of her own poetic cosmogony.

While Shvarts's biography is attentive to the facts, it is free from the usual academic constraints and includes elements of novelisation: the account of D'Annunzio's life and its key moments 'in which his human essence is expressed to the maximum' is intercut with authorial digressions, including the juxtaposition of D'Annunzio with figures from Russian culture ranging from Velimir Khlebnikov, David Burliuk and Konstantin Leont'ev to Pushkin and the Khlysty sect.[66] The author also reconstructs D'Annunzio's background and the 'entrances' in the theatre of his life: relatives, literary intermediaries like Treves and Hérelle, companions in arms, enemies and false friends such as Mussolini, and, naturally, the women, especially Eleonora Duse, whose humanity and suffering provide the contrasting complement to D'Annunzio's implacable vital energy.

The narrative takes its cue from *Il libro segreto*, uncovering the mythological substratum in episodes of the poet's life: he is constantly led toward metamorphosis by a series of encounters and experiences with classical overtones. The book's title brings together references to the man-eating Cyclops – frequently emphasising that D'Annunzio was essentially a monster who brought pain to those who loved him by shattering every internal and external boundary – and Daedalus, the skilful builder of the labyrinth who was also able to conquer the skies. Shvarts continues D'Annunzio's inventive

65 For the first approach, see Annamaria Andreoli, *Il vivere inimitabile. Vita di Gabriele D'Annunzio* (Milan: Mondadori, 2000); for the second, Lucy Hughes-Hallett, *The Pike: Gabriele d'Annunzio, Poet, Seducer and Preacher of War* (London: Fourth Estate, 2013).

66 For the description of the key moments, see Shvarts, *Krylatyi tziklop*, p. 8.

play, developing his metaphor of the poet as a messenger who flies between the two worlds, shuttling from the material to the sublime.[67]

What are the points of contact between the author and D'Annunzio? The first is the romantic idea of poets as chosen ones and visionaries who sacrifice their lives on the altar of the Muses. D'Annunzio was one of the last of his era to take the poet's sacral role seriously, and for Shvarts 'the true poet is an independent luminary, a solitary being' who must suffer in order to find their unique voice.[68] Shvarts was inspired by the idea of art as an act of courage and by the radical gesture: she asserted that had she been born in a different era, she would have joined the Narodnaia Volia, the revolutionary organisation responsible for the assassination of Alexander II. Another affinity lies in the theatre. Her mother worked with the renowned director Georgii Tovstonogov, so Shvarts was connected to the theatre from her childhood. In her biography, she devotes particular attention to D'Annunzio's theatre projects and to his collaboration with Eleonora Duse. Moreover, she sees his life in terms of staging a tragedy, as 'the bizarre carnival of a great life, which ends with Lent'.[69] In her view, D'Annunzio's constant changes of role and persona are an existential quest for the real self, although after the trial and rejection of various masks this remains fundamentally incomprehensible.

A theme running through Shvarts's account is death and what waits beyond, not only for the hero but also for his biographer. Shvarts relates D'Annunzio's eroticism to his quest for spiritual transcendence; there are similarities not only with Buddhist philosophy, but also with Russian sects, as according to a well-known saying used by Rasputin amongst others, 'you cannot repent if you have not sinned'.[70] The many quotations translated into Russian by the author include one from *Il libro segreto*:

> I have no certainty. And I have no limits. I am without limits, with the result that at some moments I even lose the limits of my flesh. Pleasure makes my flesh infinite. In the excesses of pleasure I find my greatest spirituality.[71]

[67] Tatiana Alekseeva, 'Poet i smert'. O knige Eleny Shvarts "Krylatyi tsiklop"', *Russkaia kultura*, 12 May 2018.

[68] Elena Shvarts, 'Poetika zhivogo. Beseda s Antonom Nesterovym', *Kontekst* 9, 5 (2000), 314–34 (p. 315).

[69] Shvarts, *Krylatyi tziklop*, p. 490.

[70] Edvard Radzinsky, *Rasputin: zhizn' i smert'* (Moscow: Vagrius 2000), p. 294.

[71] Gabriele D'Annunzio, *Cento e cento e cento e cento pagine del libro segreto di Gabriele D'Annunzio tentato di morire* (Milan: Istituto nazionale per la edizione di tutte le opere di Gabriele D'Annunzio, 1935), p. 309. Ebook (2011).

The final part of Shvarts's book, headed 'The Labyrinth of Daedalus', recounts the elderly poet's final months as he awaits his death, bidding farewell to the people and things dear to him one by one. As these are also the final passages produced by the author, her writing takes on autobiographical tones. The lines by D'Annunzio that she chose as an epigraph become a sort of valediction addressed to the world: 'No longer can I live on this enslaved, measured and thoroughly exploited earth'.[72]

In the end, the figure of D'Annunzio is absorbed into his biographer's poetic world, and seemingly materialises in particular poems; the poet and critic Andrei Anpilov suggests that these thus become an interpretative key for her book, and vice versa. In Shvarts's collection *Vino sed'mogo goda* (Wine of the Seventh Year), in the poems 'Noch teatra' (Night of Theatre), 'Kosmicheskoe prichastie' (Cosmic Communion) and the cycle 'Selvy pozdnego leta' (Woods of Late Summer) a phantasmal and ambiguous character emerges, exhibiting different features on each appearance: blind in one eye, an onlooker, a childlike old man, angelic but also satanic, a being who is 'cosmic, airy, chthonic'.[73] In one poem from the 'Woods of Late Summer' series, the image of two military aeroplanes from the Great War era recalls her descriptions of D'Annunzio's flights, detailed extensively in her biography. According to Shvarts's close friend Kirill Kozyrev, Shvarts went as far as purchasing a videogame simulating the flight of early aeroplanes to better identify with D'Annunzio.[74]

Shvarts's book signals the renewed possibility of a moment of 'translatability' for D'Annunzio 100 years after the period of his greatest success in Russia. His biographer, who possessed extensive knowledge and great sensitivity, takes a stance that allows her to represent the voice of poets, and to resist the influence of the dozens of previous interpretations.

[72] D'Annunzio, *Il libro segreto*, p. 96.

[73] See Anpilov, 'Grozovaia zvezda'. For the poems in question, see Elena Shvarts, *Vino sed'mogo goda* (St Petersburg: Pushkinsky fond, 2007), pp. 50–2, 55.

[74] Interview with Kozyrev by Sofia Lurie, 24 August 2021.

Chapter 16

From 'Great Italian Poet' to 'Fascist Writer': D'Annunzio and Arabic Culture

Hussein Mahmoud and Christine Samir Girgis

D'Annunzio's library at the Vittoriale features numerous books dedicated to Islam, among with several fine editions of the Koran, which testify to his interest in Arabic culture. The fascination with Egypt, to which he travelled in 1899 with Eleonora Duse and Matilde Serao, resurfaces in *Notturno*. This openness toward the 'other' only apparently contrasts with his colonialist stance. It is known that, like his friend Edoardo Scarfoglio, he was a convinced supporter of the occupation of Libya, to which he paid tribute in *Merope. Canti della guerra d'oltremare* (1912), and that he went as far as praising Italian aerial bombings that violated the Aja Convention.[1] Given D'Annunzio's involvement in colonial history, and his association with Fascism, it is not surprising that the reception of his work in the Arab world should be a complex matter. This chapter explores the image that the media, cultural magazines and the academic establishment shaped of D'Annunzio from the 1930s to today. Drawing on articles issued in the Arabic press by renowned intellectuals like Jorji Zaydan and Derrini Khashaba in the first half of the twentieth century, as well as articles published recently in the Arab media, it investigates what aspects of D'Annunzio attracted Arab intellectuals during the time in which modern Italian literature was beginning to be translated into Arabic. It also examines the dramatic changes that this reception has undergone in the last few decades.

[1] On D'Annunzio's interest in Arab culture, and on the poems published in support of the invasion of Libya, see Elvira Diana, 'Gabriele D'Annunzio e il mondo Arabo', *Rassegna Dannunziana* (2018), pp. 61–5.

D'Annunzio and Cultural Journalism in Egypt between 1876 and 1935

As Isabella Camara D'Afflitto notes, Arabic intellectuals, between 1876 and 1935, had a cosmopolitan outlook. In these years, they commented on, reviewed and translated a great deal of literary works published in Europe. Italian literature remained marginal in this project, and Italian authors were often translated from French, English or Russian editions.[2] Maria Avino notes that three cultural magazines played a crucial role in divulgation of the Occidental cultural production: *al-Hilāl*; *al Muqtaṭaf*, the publication of which lasted several decades; and *al-Ǧāmi'ah*.[3] These magazines acquired a great authority in literary matters, and it is to these publications that we refer to research the image of D'Annunzio that emerges in the Arab world during these years.

In the period in which D'Annunzio was an active player on the international cultural scene, Egyptian cultural magazines were following social and political developments with great interest. Since 1882, Egypt had been under British domain, but the population had begun to rebel, a situation that would reach a climax in the 1919 revolution.[4] At the same time, Egypt was home to several communities of foreign immigrants, called *Mutamasserin*, that is the 'Egyptianised', with a heavy presence of Italians, who were aligned against Britain. As Andrew Heiss notes, by 1907 the number of Italians in Egypt had risen to 35,000, which made the Italian community the second largest foreign community in Egypt, after the Greeks.[5] Italy was preparing to conquer Libya and considered Egypt as an entry point for its colonisation project. Italians realised that the flourishing Egyptian

[2] Elvira Diana, 'Gabriele D'Annunzio e il mondo arabo', p. 61.

[3] Maria Avino, *L'Occidente nella cultura araba* (Milan: Jouvence, 2002), p. 12.

[4] Kathryn Louise James describes the 1919 events as follows: 'The British responded by exiling four of the leaders to Malta in March 1919. This unleashed the pent-up emotions of the Egyptian people. Demonstrations turned into riots. Peasant and worker, women and men took to the streets against the perceived abuse of rights of citizens. Student demonstrations in Cairo from law and religious schools, women's demonstrations spoke strongly of their autonomy and assertion of rights. Strikes and violence against British outposts in the country showed a nation on the move': Kathryn Louise James, *Creating a Nation in Adversity: Advent of Egyptian Nationalism in British Occupation* (UNLV Theses, Dissertations, Professional Papers, and Capstones, 2012), p. 48.

[5] Andrew Heiss, *Manufacturing Consent: Italy, The Mutamassirun, Egypt, And the Invasion of Libya* (Master of Art in Middle East Studies, Middle East Studies Center, 2010), p. 46.

press could be used to their advantage, and used Egyptian media instrumentally to maintain Italian cultural and political prestige, as well as to forge consensus for the invasion of Libya among both the Egyptian and expatriate Italian communities.[6] The ties between the Italians and the Egyptians were so powerful, that one of the greatest Egyptian poets of all times, Ahmed Shawqui, wrote a poem that recalled the glories of ancient Rome[7] at the same time as the Italian writer and poet, Filippo Tommaso Marinetti, wrote a book titled *Il fascino dell'Egitto*.[8] With the advent of Egyptian nationalism and the onset of the war in Libya, the relationship between the two communities deteriorated. Many Egyptian newspapers became hostile to Italy during the war: *Al-Mahrousa*, for example, regularly published pro-Islamic articles that sought to incite anti-Italian sentiments and swell the numbers of the volunteer mujahideen force in Libya. On 4 October 1911, only a week after the official start of the war, *Al-Mahrousa* reported that Muslims as far away as India had pledged their full support, and some even their services as volunteers, to support the Ottoman provinces against Italy.[9]

D'Annunzio was introduced to Arab readers for the first time in 1919 by the influential Jorji Zaydan, a polyhedric intellectual who was a respected Islamist, linguist, fiction writer and literary scholar. Zaydan wrote an article about D'Annunzio in *Al Hilal*, a magazine he had funded and that could count on readerships within and beyond the Arab world.[10] The title of the article, 'The Bizarre Poet and Soldier', already reveals something of the angle through which D'Annunzio was introduced to the educated readers of *Al Hilal*.[11] Zaydan presented D'Annunzio as an extraordinary individual and stressed first and foremost his military enterprises. The focus of the article was on the seizing of Fiume and the consequences of this military adventure, which the author viewed as a provocation of the Italian government, the Allies, President Wilson, the Paris Peace Conference, the Supreme Council and the League of Nations.

6 Andrew Heiss, *Manufacturing Consent*, p. 61.

7 Ahmed Shawqui, *Kan fy al-Rome al 'azim*, in *Al-Shawkyat*, vol. 4 (Al-Maktaba Al-Togareya Al-kobra, Al-Kahera, 1951).

8 Filippo Tommaso Marinetti, *Il Fascino Dell'egitto*, Milano: Mondadori, 1933.

9 ' 'Kalkūta fī al-thani min oktūbir', *Al-Maḥrūsa*, 4 October 1911, p. 25.

10 On the magazine *Al Hilal*, see Maria Avino, *L'Occidente nella cultura araba*, pp. 39–40.

11 See Jorji Zaydan, December 1919, pp. 196–200. Translations from Arabic are our own.

D'Annunzio's presentation as a world hero must be considered against the background of Egypt's enmity with Great Britain. In fact, during the 1919 peace negotiations in Paris, D'Annunzio had attempted to meet with Egyptian intellectuals to organise a league of 'oppressed nations' against the British, who were the main enemy of Egypt at that time.[12] Zaydan attributed D'Annunzio's fame in Italy to his enthusiastic, eloquent speeches, which backed the government's decision to wage a war against Libya and called for Rome to restore its old glory. For Zaydan, D'Annunzio was a skilled pilot, a fighter whose life was full of unique incidents and intense emotions. He admired D'Annunzio's ability to write while engaging in all these activities, and he conveyed his admiration to the public.

Zaydan included in the article a dialogue between the military governor of Fiume – General Pittaluga – and D'Annunzio, a dialogue that did not take more than a few minutes but was central to the invasion of Fiume. It concluded with all parties, conquerors and defenders shouting 'Long Live Fiume! Long live Italy!' The dialogue provided the opportunity to emphasise D'Annunzio's charisma and his ability to conquer sympathy. Here is an extract of the dialogue, as presented by Zaydan:

> Military Governor: Can I know your intentions?
>
> D'Annunzio: Not a shot will be fired if we are given unmolested passage.
>
> Military Governor: I must execute my orders, [. . .].
>
> D'Annunzio interrupts: I understand. General, rather than opening fire on soldiers who are your brothers, I prefer that you shoot me first.
>
> And saying so he uncovers his breast, decorated with the gold medal awarded to the wounded. Then he resumes: — Here I am!
>
> And the general, subjugated by the sacristy offered and D'Annunzio's passionate tone, approaches him, shakes his hand, and in a less frank voice exclaims: — [. . .]. I am delighted and honored to meet you, as a great poet, a courageous fighter. I hope that your dream will be fulfilled, and with you I cry: 'Long live Italian Fiume!'[13]

[12] Adriano Scianca, 'La rivolta dei popoli giovani. Gabriele D'annunzio e la "lega dei popoli oppressi"', *Il Cannocchiale* (September 2006): http://coc.ilcannocchiale.it/?id_blogdoc=1161666

[13] There are no major differences between Zaydan's rendering of this episode in Arabic and the Italian original.

For Zaydan, D'Annunzio represented the hero able to rely on intelligence when facing a military general who can count on his armed soldiers. The article continues by praising D'Annunzio's public speaking, and the Italian poet is figured as the most eloquent man in Europe. Zaydan then praises his deep knowledge of Greek and Latin literature. Even D'Annunzio's expensive lifestyle before the war, and consequent debts, are recalled in a tone fit for hailing a hero. Only after all these details does Zaydan comment on D'Annunzio's literary production. He notes that D'Annunzio debuted in poetry, but that it was his novels that made him one of the finest artists in Europe, an international writer translated into numerous languages. Among D'Annunzio's novels, he praises in particular his best-selling *Trionfo della morte*. He then quotes from the entry on D'Annunzio in the Encyclopaedia Britannica, which underlines that D'Annunzio's work was heavily influenced by French, Russian, Scandinavian and German sources, and therefore hardly original, but stresses the 'faultlessness of his style' and 'wealth of his language'.[14] Zaydan's article was so influential that, after its publication, *Al Hilal* and other cultural magazines, like *Al-Resalah*, directed by one of the most popular Arabic translators in the contemporary age,[15] started publishing short stories by D'Annunzio in Arabic.[16]

In 1937, the Egyptian writer/translator Derrini Khashaba, in 'D'Annunzio in the Royal Academy of Italy's presidency' commented on the appointment of D'Annunzio as President of the Royal Academy of Italy (Accademia dei Lincei). By 1937, Khashaba could write with the assumption that D'Annunzio was internationally known, a familiar name among Arab readers. He referred to him as the 'most famous Italian writer and poet', and the 'greatest Italian writer of modern times'. Despite this, the author explains D'Annunzio's appointment mainly through his role as 'a great patriot and soldier'. A great deal of the article is devoted to explaining D'Annunzio's relationship to Mussolini:

> Mussolini notes [. . .] that this choice is not only due to the literary value of the poet, but also to his national past; D'Annunzio was not only a great poet and writer, but also a great patriot and soldier [. . .].

[14] Hugh Chisholm, ed., 'Annunzio, Gabriele D''. *Encyclopedia Britannica*, 2. Eleventh Edition (Cambridge: Cambridge University Press, 1911).

[15] In *Al-Resalah* magazine, interest in D'Annunzio's works began in the 1930s, but it was only in the 1960s that the complete translations of some of D'Annunzio's works were published.

[16] As an example, see the short story *Cincinnato*, published in *Al-Resala* with the title: 'That Mad Man'.

> During the Great War, D'Annunzio was in France, and in his books and poems he called for Italy to join the Allies. When Italy entered the war, D'Annunzio joined the army as an artillery officer and lost one eye in the aviation service. At the end of the war, there was a dispute between Italy and Yugoslavia over the ownership of the port of Fiume, and the dispute ended with Italy agreeing to leave it for Yugoslavia, but D'Annunzio did not accept this solution and marched on Fiume at the head of 1,000 volunteers, forcibly occupied the city, and announced its annexation to Italy. There, Mussolini visited him, being a journalist at the time, and admired him and his high national and military qualities. When the Fascist regime had won and Mussolini held power and authority, there was a sort of coldness between the two men at first, but it was soon warmed; Mussolini, then, surrounded the great poet with all honors, and [D'Annunzio] was awarded the title of principality in 1925, and he now holds the presidency of the Italian Academy and behind it the glorious past full of poetry, literature, patriotism, and war.[17]

Khashaba is engaged in denying the voices that suggested bad relations between D'Annunzio and Mussolini and in confirming the close friendship between the two men. This involvement in Italian affairs can be explained by the large numbers of Italians in Egypt. The following publication, in *Al-Resala* magazine, was written in 1934 and confirms that D'Annunzio's association with Fascism, in these years, did not constitute a problem for the Egyptians. On the contrary, the friendship with Mussolini here is mentioned to confirm D'Annunzio's status as a great poet:

> The Signor Mussolini recently visited his friend, the great poet D'Annunzio in the Vittoriale Palace, in a special visit, but without any kind of formality, and was received by D'Annunzio with joy and enthusiasm, the two men hugged at the meeting, and D'Annunzio shouted at his friend, 'Here you are, you finally came'. The last time Mussolini visited his friend was two years ago when he visited Turin and Milan celebrating the anniversary of the Fascist Revolution. Mussolini came to the poet at sunset and had dinner with him and continued with him until midnight.[18]

As these publications demonstrate, the Fascist revolution, Mussolini and D'Annunzio were elements of the Italian reality received by the Arabic cultural magazines with great ease.

[17] Derrini Khashaba, *Al-Resala*, November 1937, p. 1837.
[18] 'Al- Bareed Al-adby', *Al-Resala*, October 1934, p. 1795.

The Decadent movement was looked at disparagingly by Arabic intellectuals, as references to sexuality in the writings of many French and European writers associated with the movement were too explicit to be appreciated by Arabic readers. This was, curiously, never an issue with D'Annunzio's writings. In the comments published by the Arabic writers and poets on his death, we find only respect. It is astonishing that Ahmed Rafiq al-Mahdawi (1898–1961), a Libyan poet who was against the Italian occupation of Libya and who used his poetic talent as an arm in the political struggle against the Italian occupiers, should express profound sadness for the death of D'Annunzio, who had so ardently backed the invasion of his country. Despite their opposing political stances, Rafiq admired D'Annunzio, to whom he dedicated essays and verses.[19] This is testified by the elegy that Rafiq wrote in 1938 after the announcement of D'Annunzio's death, in which he addresses D'Annunzio's soul:

أصبحت طليقــة في خيال الشعــر،
كم حومت، تبغين الحقيقة
كنت في سجـن، من الجسم الترابي،
أسيــرة تستشفين حجاب الغيب، من نــور البصيرة
كان ذاك الجســم يخفي،
نزوة الروح الكبيرة فانجلى،
الآن، حجاب الشك، عن شمس الحقيقة
! فامــرحي، في عالم الأرواح،
أصبحت طليقة.

Fly, in the spirit world,
you have become free in the imagination of poetry,
as far as you have had wings, looking for the truth.
You were in prison, of the body made from mud,
you were trying to reveal the invisible,
from the light of the vision, that that body secreted
the whim of the great soul,
now the veil of doubt is lightened,
from the sun of truth!
Cheer, in the spirit world, you are now free.[20]

Among the intellectuals who wrote elegies for D'Annunzio, we also find Khashaba. The fact that Khashaba's elegy was written only one

[19] Elvira Diana, *L'immagine degli italiani nella letteratura libica dall'epoca coloniale alla caduta di Gheddafi* (Rome: IPOCAN, 2011), pp. 40–4.
[20] The translation is our own.

day after D'Annunzio's death, and published four days later, testifies to the promptness with which the Arabic press was following the news. In the elegy, Khashaba compares D'Annunzio to the Italian poet Carducci, a Nobel Prize winner. By describing D'Annunzio's production as 'an amazing mix of Greek, Latin, French, and English influences',[21] he underlines D'Annunzio's cosmopolitanism; and by stressing that each literature 'left a great mark on his literary production' but that he 'went beyond their literatures in a rich manner, because he had a strong independent personality', he stresses D'Annunzio's originality, something that had been contested by Zaydan. Khashaba had many reasons to consider D'Annunzio a great Italian poet and writer, and presented him as such. He confirmed D'Annunzio's place in Arabic culture by referring to recent translations, citing, as an example, the short story 'The Letter', published in Arabic translation the week before.[22] He was so invested in presenting D'Annunzio to his readers that prior to the elegy, he published an Arabic version of the short story 'Cincinnato' (first published in Italy in *Il Fanfulla della domenica*, 12 December 1880). The latter was accompanied by a commentary, in which he described the typical style of D'Annunzio's early writings.[23]

The Reception of D'Annunzio in the Arab World Today

The reception of D'Annunzio in the Arab world is very different today. The new profile of D'Annunzio can be inferred by what has been written about him recently in the Arabic press. When Lucy Hughes-Hallett's *The Pike: Gabriele D'Annunzio, Poet, Seducer and Preacher of War* was awarded the 2013 Samuel Johnson prize for non-fiction, an anonymous book review appeared on the Arabic 24-hour rolling news channel, Sky News Arabia. The review's title was 'A British Prize for a Book about a Fascist Poet'. In this text, the author, quoting a comment by the jury, referred to D'Annunzio as 'the debauched artist who became a national hero'.[24] This article shows that D'Annunzio's personal conduct, hailed in the first half of the twentieth century, has become an issue in the twenty-first

[21] Derrini Khashaba, *Al-Resala* (March 1938), p. 391.
[22] Ibid., p. 391.
[23] Derrini Khashaba, 'Sensanatos', *Al-Resala* (February 1938), p. 350.
[24] 'A British Prize for a Book about a Fascist Poet', Sky News Arabia (November 2013): https://www.skynewsarabia.com/varieties/463705

century. The conquest of Fiume, once so admired by the Arab press, is described as a 'failed attempt to create a fascist State in Italy'.[25] This publication demonstrates that D'Annunzio's fame in Egypt, as is the case in many other countries, has been overshadowed by his association with Fascism. In an article published in 2019 in the Arabic newspaper *El Sabah*, Mousa El Khamisi, an Arabic-language correspondent in Italy, reported on the celebration of the anniversary of the foundation of the Fiume Republic by its 'fascist' poet D'Annunzio.[26] Mousa describes D'Annunzio as a controversial character, a 'hateful, arrogant individual who soon gained literary fame and became a national hero'.[27] He also criticises D'Annunzio for supporting the occupation of Libya and for denigrating those who resisted the Italian occupation of the Arab country.[28] D'Annunzio, the former world-hero, is now presented to the Arab public as an enemy. His 'immorality in literature' – a trait previously ignored by the Arabic press – is conflated with his 'immorality in personal life', as shown by this excerpt:

> [. . .] He was overly selfish, totally surrendering to the seduction of privileged circumstances and the insatiable pleasure in which he drowned all his life with a continuing curiosity without limits. Many left-wing intellectuals described him during the fascist period as oppressive and inhuman. [. . .] He was much preoccupied about his excessive elegance, loved to show off himself: loved titles and the Aesthetic life, searching for rare and exciting feelings that cannot stand the social and conventional environment of that period [. . .].[29]

The year 2013 marked the 150th anniversary of D'Annunzio's birth. The events organised to celebrate the anniversary attracted some of the big names among contemporary Arab poets, such as Ahmed Abdel Moeti Hijazi and Hassan Teleb. In this occasion, D'Annunzio was compared by Dante Marianacci to Ahmed Shawqui (1868–1932), known as 'The Prince of Poets',[30] who pioneered the modern Egyptian

25 Ibid.

26 Mousa El Khamisi, 'Italy Celebrates the Centenary of Fiume City, Founded by the Fascist Poet D'Annunzio', *Al-sabah al-jadeed* (April 2019).

27 Ibid.

28 Ibid.

29 Ibid.

30 D. Marianacci, 'D'Annunzio, la guerra e gli altri', in *L'anno iniquo. 1914: Guerra e letteratura europea. Atti del Congresso di Venezia, 24–26 Novembre 2014*, ed. by Alessandro Scarsella and Giovanni Capecchie Matteo Giancotti (Rome: Adi Editore, 2017), p. 6.

literary movement by introducing the genre of poetic epics to the Arabic literary tradition. Marianacci, who at this time was the director of the Italian Institute in Cairo, hosted a series of conferences and events dedicated to D'Annunzio, which were covered by the major Egyptian newspapers. Amongst this series, he held a photographic and documentary exhibition on the Vittoriale at the Italian Institute in El Cairo. During the inauguration by Vittoria Sgarbi, some texts by D'Annunzio, translated into Arabic, were read by local poets. This event demonstrated that many Egyptian poets, such as Ahmed Abdel Moeti Hijazi, were familiar with D'Annunzio's works, even if not in the original language. With the collaboration of the Italian Institute, Hussein Mahmoud invited researchers and Italian literature critics to participate in an event held at Misr University of Sciences and Technology ('Must') in Cairo, where he was working at that time. He faced some reluctance: many researchers did not want to participate because they believed that D'Annunzio was one of the writers who were loyal to Mussolini and his Fascist regime, and they feared that by celebrating the poet, they would be associated with Fascism. Despite this, the event was a success and saw a significantly high number of attendees.

The renewed interest in D'Annunzio's writing is also testified by the translations that have appeared in recent decades, such as Naglaa Waly's 2001 translation of three stories taken from *Novelle della Pescara*.[31] In 2013, Waly read the Arabic version of 'La pioggia nel pineto', also translated by her, at the Italian Institute in Cairo. Four years later, the rest of the short stories were translated by Mahmoud and Waly.[32] In addition, there are also translations by Issa Anna'ouri and Taha Fawzi, respectively of 'Il tesoro dei poveri' and *L'Innocente*.

What we have explored up to this point provides material enabling us to look at the reception of D'Annunzio in the Arab world with a critical eye. In the first decades of the twentieth century, D'Annunzio was seen by Arabic intellectuals as the best public speaker in Europe, a world hero, a charismatic leader and soldier, a friend of Mussolini, a patriot and a best-selling novelist with a unique style of life. On

[31] Elvira Diana, *L'immagine degli italiani nella letteratura libica dall'epoca coloniale alla caduta di Gheddafi*, p. 62.

[32] For more details on the translation of D'Annunzio's works into Arabic see Hussein Mahmoud, 'Geocultura: prospettive, strumenti, strategie per un mondo in italiano', *Società Dante Alighieri,* Rome, 2016: https://pure.ulster.ac.uk/ws/portalfiles/portal/76038397/DanteCorPub.pdf

the other hand, there was uncertainty about the literary value of his works, and he was criticised for his support of the intervention in Libya. The years following D'Annunzio's death saw increased interest in his literary works, which began to be translated into Arabic through the mediation of other European languages. More recently, the uncovering of the atrocities committed by the Fascists worked against D'Annunzio's popularity. D'Annunzio is described in the media, and perceived by the general public, as a 'Fascist writer' – a label that prevents serious engagement with his work. Despite this, this complex, controversial figure and his writing continue to stir the interest of Arab intellectuals and contemporary translators to the present day.

Chapter 17

Morlach's Blood in Fiume's *Mensa*: D'Annunzio and the Intimate Adriatic

Russell Scott Valentino

> 'The Atlantic and Pacific are seas of distance, the Mediterranean a sea of propinquity, the Adriatic a sea of intimacy.'
>
> Predrag Matvejević
> *Mediterranean: A Cultural Landscape*[1]

Gabriele D'Annunzio's Fiume escapade of 1919 has sometimes been incorporated into the story of nineteenth-century Italian irredentism described by Angelo Vivante in his 1914 *Irredentismo Adriatico*, where it serves as something of a coda to the Italo-Austrian conflict that ended with the First World War. It was also, however, a transitional episode, setting the stage for Italy's long and troubled relationship with the independent territories that would become Yugoslavia and, subsequently, its successor states. In this context, a number of figures, objects of art, culture and political life would change locations, crossing from one shore to the other, sometimes in forced migrations. Their stories became a staple of Italian and Yugoslav life for some three generations.

This chapter explores a single, somewhat unlikely example, in the form of the 'maraschino' cherry brandy for which the city of Zara, today's Zadar of Croatia, was once renowned. Specifically, it follows the life trajectory of the Luxardo brand begun by the entrepreneur Girolamo Luxardo in 1821, which bears a name worth exploring in the context of D'Annunzio's worldwide notoriety. This name is announced on the bottle itself, where, just beneath 'Cherry Brandy', one finds the words *Sangue Morlacco*, below which appears this explanatory phrase: 'Il liquore cupo che alla mensa di Fiume chiamavo "Sangue Morlacco"', (the dark liqueur that I called 'Morlach's blood' at the Fiume mess hall), which is followed by D'Annunzio's flowing

[1] See Predrag Matvejević, *Mediterranean: A Cultural Landscape*, trans. by Michael Henry Heim (Berkley and Los Angeles: UC Press, 1999), p. 14.

signature. The history of this coinage, which is associated with the Luxardo family, their company and the long afterlife of D'Annunzio's Fiume adventure, provides an opportunity for exploring D'Annunzio's perceived cultural authority, especially for Italians displaced from Istria and Dalmatia following the Second World War, as well as the stereotypes and cultural assumptions of Italians vis-a-vis their eastern neighbours. As Noel Malcolm has shown in his *Agents of Empire*, trading families often served as the primary conduits for crossings of commerce, culture and politics over centuries of Adriatic life.[2] This was no less true of the D'Annunzios and the Luxardos.

The Luxardos of Zara

The Marchesa Maria Canevari settled in Zara with her husband Girolamo Luxardo in 1821, having moved from her home region of Liguria to accompany him in his business ventures. Beginning in approximately 1823, such ventures included his appointment as Sardinian vice-consul to the Kingdom of Dalmatia. Thoroughly occupied with setting up her household, seeing to her five children – the oldest, Bartolomeo, was ten at the time of the move, the youngest, Michelangelo Nicolò, had just turned two – she nevertheless found time to begin exploring the local culinary traditions, including the making of the cherry brandy for which the region was even then famous. First to establish an industrial distillery for the 'rosolio maraschino', which had been made from the local marasca cherry since the Middle Ages, was the Venetian Francesco Drioli, who had moved to Zara from his native Isola d'Istria in the late 1750s. Like many locally made liqueurs around the world, the production process for Drioli's maraschino was a strict secret, though the original recipe he used is thought to have been initially developed by the Venetian Giuseppe Carceniga.[3]

By the time of the Luxardo family's arrival, the repute of Drioli's maraschino had grown considerably, with lines of distribution firmly established through Trieste and Fiume into Central and Eastern Europe, on the one hand, and westward to Great Britain and the United States

[2] See Noel Malcom, *Agents of Empire: Knights, Corsairs, Jesuits, and Spies in the Sixteenth-Century Mediterranean World* (Oxford: Oxford University Press, 2019).

[3] R. Tolomeo, 'Drioli, Francesco', *Dizionario bibliografico degli italiani*, vol. 41 (Roma: Società Grafica Romana S. p. A., 1992), p. 700. See also Antonio Teja, *La fabbrica di maraschino Francesco Drioli all'epoca del suo fondatore: la sua importanza nel quadro dell'Industria zaratina dei rosoli* (Genova: S.A.I.G.A. già Barabino e Graeve, 1938), p. 6.

on the other. Drioli's product had been widely recognised, granted privileged status by the Habsburg Emperor (in 1804) and been the frequent object of counterfeiting, forcing its producer to take legal action on more than one occasion.[4] Drioli had, in effect, created a vast distribution and advertising network for Zara's most important export, a foundation whose benefits would be enjoyed by its three most important producers: the Fabbrica di Maraschino Francesco Drioli (1759–1980), the Distilleria Romano Vlahov (1861–ca. 1950), and the Excelsior Girolamo Luxardo (1821–present).

The Luxardo household, in the meantime, continued to grow, with the birth of another daughter, Maria Francesca, within a year of their arrival, and six more children over the next fourteen years – the last, Eugenio Bernardo, in 1832, when Maria was some six months shy of her forty-third birthday. In all, by the time of her death on 7 May 1846, Maria Canevari Luxardo had given birth to fifteen children, nine of whom remained to mourn her passing. In his memoir of the family and its famous brand, *I Luxardo del Maraschino*, Nicolò Luxardo De Franchi describes his maternal ancestor as 'wise, modest, and indefatigable', the 'silent and irreplaceable collaborator of Girolamo in the creation and development of the maraschino industry, an enterprise to which she contributed with all her good feminine sense and the perspicacity of the Ligurian race'.[5] The historical record is somewhat murky on the details of their collaboration. Some sources claim that the motivation for perfecting the liqueur, as well as the recipe itself, were Maria's,[6] but Luxardo De Franchi tells a somewhat different story:

> Si tratta, in un primo momento, di dedicarsi alla sperimentazione strettamente tecnica condotta con criteri rigorosi, affinchè il risultato finale possa soddisfare i requisiti di un prodotto di valore. *In questa fase gli fornisce un prezioso aiuto la consorte Maria.* (Emphasis added)[7]

[4] Litigation cases regarding falsified 'Drioli' labels are on record in England from the middle of the nineteenth century: https://discovery.nationalarchives.gov.uk/details/r/C79335970. Nicolò Tommaseo remarks in passing on the counterfeiting of maraschino in a pamphlet entitled *Via facti*, first published in Trieste in 1861: *Via facti. La Croazia e la Fraternità. Di nuovo ai Dalmati*, originally 1861 (Sacramento: Wentworth Press, 2019, p. 16); the remnants of legal actions associated with the brand can be found up to 2015 in a commentary by Luca Guidobaldi on a recent Tribunale di Roma decision: 'Commento', *Il Diritto Industriale*, 1 (2015), pp. 43–54.

[5] Nicolò Luxardo de Franchi, *I Luxardo del Maraschino* (Gorizia: Libreria Editrice Goriziana, 2004), p. 50.

[6] See for instance: https://www.webfoodculture.com/maraschino-liqueur-history-info-interesting-facts/

[7] Luxardo De Franchi, p. 26.

> (At this first moment, it was a matter of dedication to strictly technical experimentation conducted according to rigorous criteria, leading to a result that could satisfy the requirements for a worthwhile product. *In this phase, his wife Maria provided him with valuable assistance.* (Emphasis added))

Regardless of the exact division of labour, once the recipe had been perfected, the entrepreneurial spirit for industrialising the liqueur's production and distribution was clearly provided by her husband, who was consistently ambitious in seeking out new business opportunities. Indeed, as noted above, the very vice-consulship that is often cited, erroneously, as the reason for the family's relocation to Zara, is better understood as an extension of Luxardo's entrepreneurial endeavours, which frequently, in the spirit of the age, combined politics and trade in a manner that would become remarkably consistent in the more than 200-year history of the family's most famous legacy.

Girolamo appears to have been attracted to the vice-consulship, for which he made a formal application in Trieste in 1822, by the expansive trade policy of King Charles Felix of Sardinia in the southern and eastern Mediterranean.[8] Acquiring the post, moreover, took effort and skill, as did ensuring that it provided him with adequate leeway and authority:

> [P]er Girolamo sarebbe iniziata una lunga battaglia diplomatica, condotta sul triangolo Zara-Vienna-Torino tra mille cavilli giuridici, per il conseguimento dell'*exequatur* imperiale al vice-consolato e non solo delle autorità locali ad 'Agente consolare', come volevano le autorità austriache.[9]

> (For Girolamo there ensued a long diplomatic battle conducted at the intersection of Zara, Vienna, and Torino, amid a thousand legal cavils, to obtain the imperial exequatur as vice consul and not just with the authority of 'consular agent', as the Austrian authorities wanted.)

In this period Luxardo was constantly travelling, and it was in the midst of shuttling between the centres of regional political power and his trade connections, during a brief stay in Venice in January of 1823, that he met a well-to-do young tradesman from Abruzzo by the name of Antonio D'Annunzio, great uncle of Gabriele and the source of the family name.[10]

[8] Ibid., p. 27.

[9] Ibid., pp. 27–8.

[10] Ibid., p. 28; see also Joseph Guerin Fucilla, *D'Annunzio Abroad: A Bibliographical Essay* (New York: Columbia University Press, 1935), p. 29.

Two Views of Adriatic Nationalism

While Vivante's focus in his early twentieth-century treatise was on Trieste and, to a lesser extent, Gorizia and the western portions of Istria – he has little to say about Fiume/Rijeka or Dalmatia, with the exception of a short segment in Chapter Three on Italo-Slavic relations in somewhat broader terms[11] – D'Annunzio's attention was directed at the Adriatic as a whole, including Dalmatia, a focus of Italian national aspirations since at least 1908. As Egidio Ivetic has noted, D'Annunzio's *La nave*, which premiered in January of that year with the king and queen of Italy in attendance at Rome's Teatro Argentina, made such aspirations apparent: 'A tutti era chiaro che la nave era l'Italia. L'Italia sarebbe dovuta salpare alla conquista del suo mare, che era quello di Venezia, l'Adriatico' (It was clear to everyone that the ship was Italy. Italy was to set sail on the conquest of its sea, which had been that of Venice, the Adriatic).[12]

At this moment, with the crumbling of the multi-national Habsburg empire, one Adriatic conflict was in effect merging with and transforming into another, and in its unfolding, the cultural crossings would come to be imagined and narrated in stories that became a staple of Italian and Yugoslav life. Indeed, this cultural industry of 'exile' and 'return', of the *partiti* and the *rimasti*, continues to this day, with Trieste serving as a major hub of books, articles, memoirs and other testaments to the long heritage of what Pamela Ballinger has referred to as 'history in exile'.[13] Its best known exemplars include Italian novelists such as Fulvio Tomizza, whose Istrian trilogy (*Materada*, *La ragazza di Petrovia* and *Il bosco di acacie*) document the departure and resettlement of ethnic Italians in the 1940s and 50s, and Enzo Bettiza, whose 1958 *Il fantasma di Trieste* powerfully evokes the clandestine irredentism of the city at the phenomenon's heart; the journalist Anna Maria Mori, whose collaborative memoir with Nelida Milani, *Bora* (1999), sets the *partiti* and the *rimasti* in sharp relief; the Croatian author Slobodan Novak, whose 1968 *Mirisi, zlato i tamjan* recounts the story of the remnants of Dalmatia's Italian nobility; and the celebrity

[11] Angelo Vivante, 'L'Irredentismo adriatico: contributo alla discussione sui rapporti austro-italiani (1912)', in *Irredentisimo adriatico. Dal covo dei 'traditori'* (Genova: Graphos, 1997), pp. 119–33.

[12] Egidio Ivetic, *Storia dell'Adriatico: Un mare e la sua civiltà* (Bologna: Il Mulino, 2019), p. 259.

[13] Pamela Ballinger, *History in Exile: Memory and Identity at the Borders of the Balkans* (Princeton: Princeton University Press, 2003).

chef and restaurateur Lidia Bastianich, whose marketing formulas generally claim her as 'northern Italian' but whose heritage is rooted in the mixed Slavic and Italian culture of Istria.[14] Zara's historic maraschino industry played a representative role in these Adriatic crossings: while its roots were firmly planted in the hills of Dalmatia, it owed its prominence to a combination of Dalmatian-Venetian maritime trade and Habsburg imperial sponsorship. Its branches, moreover, reached out through the ports of Trieste and Fiume, inflected, at various moments in the late-nineteenth and early-twentieth centuries, by the region's national aspirations, as well as Fascism, state socialism and the post-Second World War 'exodus' of ethnic Italians and anti-Communists from Tito's Yugoslavia. The story of the Luxardo brand, in particular, furnishes the details for a rich micro history of the northern Adriatic, not to mention a gripping narrative.

Until the Fiume adventure of 1919, the role of the D'Annunzio family in this story was largely in the background, through the commercial rapport established by Girolamo and Antonio, which included trade in Luxardo products between Zara and Pescara and bills of exchange provided by the D'Annunzios.[15] With D'Annunzio's para-military operation came an intensification of the family ties, as Pietro Luxardo (1892–1944), second son of the then Luxardo company owner Michelangelo (1857–1934), joined D'Annunzio as a legionnaire in Fiume's occupation. It was Michelangelo who had significantly expanded the business operation in Zara in the early twentieth century, with the construction of new facilities, including the largest and most modern distillery in the Habsburg Empire, and new products, including the deep red cherry brandy that would, thanks to D'Annunzio, acquire the curious name *Sangue morlacco*.

In a letter penned during the winter of 1921–22 at the Vittoriale degli italiani, destined for the Luxardo family on the eastern shore of the Adriatic, he wrote:

> Ecco la malinconia di Zara, chiusa in una bottiglia di Maraschino ed il liquor cupo che alla mensa di Fiume chiamavo 'Sangue Morlacco.'[16]

[14] On Bastianich's Istrian heritage, see in particular Lidia Bastianich and Jay Jacobs, *La Cucina di Lidia: Distinctive Regional Cuisine from the North of Italy* (New York: Doubleday, 1990); and *My American Dream: A Life of Love, Family, and Food* (New York: Knopf, 2018). These works do not acknowledge her continued connections to the region of her birth and the fact that, in addition to her native Italian, she also speaks fluent Croatian.

[15] Luxardo de Franchi, p. 28.

[16] Qtd. in Ibid., p. 110.

> (Here is the melancholy of Zara, enclosed in a bottle of Maraschino and the dark liqueur that, in Fiume's mess hall, I used to call 'Morlach's Blood.')

The air of nostalgia here is unmistakable, and it is easy to imagine D'Annunzio waxing lyrical in his new abode far from the centres of power and glamour to which he was accustomed, harkening back to a moment of past 'glory' and sharing these sentiments with his old friends, the Luxardos. It is also not difficult to understand why they, in turn, might take these words as a sobriquet for the 'dark liqueur' in question, and even tell part of its story on the bottle's label, quoting D'Annunzio's words and displaying his distinctive signature just below them. But the exotic-sounding name provides more than a mere nostalgic prompt and marketing tool: it fits squarely within the unique historical mixture of cultures at the source of the drink itself. I shall return to this below.

Some members of the Luxardo family at this point in time clearly sided with the Italian irredentists. Pietro and his brother Nicolò, in particular, believed that Dalmatia's fate should fall to Italy. Nicolò would eventually support the Fascists and, in 1939, be elected to the Chamber of Fasces and Corporations.[17] The question of Fiume/Rijeka, Istria and Dalmatia occupied Pietro no less, as his support for D'Annunzio's 'liberatory' movement attests. It would be an oversimplification, however, to label the Luxardos as mere Italian patriots, let alone single-minded nationalists: the conditions on the ground in the late Habsburg Empire were not that simple. For one thing, the family was large, well-educated, successful and had various branches, such that some Luxardo descendants would end up fighting on different sides during World War I.[18] The family as a whole, moreover, were Habsburg subjects, beneficiaries of Habsburg patronage and infrastructure. Like the multi-national empire in which their business had blossomed, theirs was a cosmopolitan world that reached far to the east, with important trade connections in the Russian Empire, and to the west, across the Atlantic to North America. Their very products were part of that cosmopolitan world view; indeed, among the company's various online marketing materials today is a note that the Luxardo maraschino was found on board the Titanic. The Luxardo brand, moreover, while expressive of the family's Italian roots (for instance, in the colour scheme of the Murano-manufactured green bottles, white labels and red caps, suggesting the

[17] M. Barbot, 'Luxardo, Giorgio', *Dizionario bibliografico degli italiani*, vol. 66 (Rome: Società Grafica Romana S. p. A., 2006), p. 695.

[18] Luxardo De Franchi, pp. 98–100.

Italian flag), was also marketed with an exotic flair, capitalising on the imagined 'Eastern' quality of Dalmatia. The Luxardos and their famous beverage were clearly products of the multi-national Adriatic.[19]

Pietro, as a Habsburg subject, had been called up to an armed Austrian cavalry unit in 1914, the Reitende Dalmatiner Schützen, or Dalmatian Mounted Riflemen, then stationed in the Bosnian town of Banja Luka. His younger brother Giorgio would also be attached to this unit in 1915. There, during manoeuvres to safeguard the Vrbas River, Pietro contracted a life-threatening case of pleurisy that left lasting traces in his lungs. He was saved by the quick action of his Serbian commander, who transferred him to a hospital in Split in time. Pietro's lingering weakness did not, however, prevent him from enthusiastically supporting D'Annunzio's cause, including with the family fortune,[20] in recognition of which the Commandante would award him a special commendation in 1920, in the name of the Reggenza Italiana del Carnaro, Commando dell'Esercito Liberatore. This much is emphasised in the stories of the Luxardo brand that one can find in online sources, including those provided by the company itself.

Like their father Michelangelo, who conducted his business correspondence in Italian, German and French, and was named 'vice consul honoraire' of Argentina in 1913, Pietro and his brothers attended schools in Vienna, were well-travelled and multilingual. They had also lived most of their lives in a majority Croatian region, where their business interests would have regularly sent them into the countryside and interior, including to the marasca cherry growing region of Ravni kotari, just east of present-day Zadar, in the heart of what the Venetians had called 'Morlacchia'. In this they were quite different from D'Annunzio and his main supporters in Italy, who might have theoretically understood notions of national plurality but had never lived them in quite this way. The historical sources are unclear on this point, but I find it difficult to imagine that the Luxardos of the day were not to some degree ambivalent about the rise of exclusionary nationalism in the early-twentieth century, especially about the possibility that their multilingual, pluralistic reality, which was the reality of the Eastern Adriatic until just after the Second World War, could be forced into a singular national narrative; or, as Dominique Kirchner Reill has put it, about the question of what would happen 'if their political, economic, and social realities were

[19] On Adriatic multi-nationalism, see Dominique Kirchner Reill, *Nationalists Who Feared the Nation: Adriatic Multinationalism in Habsburg Dalmatia, Trieste, and Venice* (Stanford: Stanford University Press, 2012).

[20] Luxardo De Franchi, p. 109.

made to cohere to the confines of one "nation"'.[21] This, of course, is exactly what would happen.

Sangue Morlacco

D'Annunzio's use of the term *morlacco*, and his explicit mention of its melancholic associations, can be fit into a narrative initiated by the Paduan Alberto Fortis, whose *Viaggio in Dalmazia*, published in Venice in 1774, saw an expanded translation published in London as *Travels into Dalmatia* in 1778, along with other editions in French and German. In his account, the *morlacchi* are approached as a distinct people. Fortis describes their customs, songs, beliefs, language, food and dress in ethnographic detail, referring to them as a *nazione*, indeed occasionally hinting at himself during his stay as something like the insider-outsider of twentieth-century anthropology.[22] Fortis's explicit rationale for undertaking his study was to temper the accepted European stereotype of the *morlacchi* as 'a race of men, fierce, unreasonable, void of humanity, and capable of any crime',[23] a picture very likely developed in the years of Venice's self-appointed 'civilising' mission in Dalmatia,[24] which was widespread enough by the late eighteenth-century for Voltaire to routinely refer to them among the various 'savages' on the peripheries of Europe where civilisation and colonisation might be possible.[25] One of the effects of his treatise, however, was to give birth to a small industry of observations of these *morlacchi* and cultural appropriations and adaptations of their image in multiple languages, which would include scholarly and ethnographic works, plays and operas extending into the mid-nineteenth century and travellers' accounts into the early-twentieth.[26]

[21] Reill, pp. 1–2. Reill's excellent treatment does not, unfortunately, include reference to the Luxardo family.

[22] Alberto Fortis, 'De' Costumi de' Morlacchi', in *Viaggio in Dalmazia* (1774), vol. 2 (Munich and Sarajevo: Verlag Otto Sagner, Izdavačko preduzeće 'Veselin Maslesa', 1974), pp. 67–126; the first (unattributed) English translation is found in 'Of the Manners of the Morlacchi', in *Travels into Dalmatia* (1778) (New York: Arno Press & The New York Times, 1971), pp. 43–89.

[23] Fortis, p. 44.

[24] Larry Wolff, *Venice and the Slavs: The Discovery of Dalmatia in the Age of Enlightenment* (Stanford: Stanford University Press, 2001), 131–47.

[25] Ibid., pp. 156–7.

[26] Of particular relevance is the history provided in Larry Wolff, 'The Rise and Fall of *Morlacchismo*: South Slavic Identity in the Mountains of Dalmatia', in Norman

The term *morlacco* is rare in contemporary Italian usage today, whether as a geographical or ethnic designation. Some Italian maps, for instance, still use the place name Canale della Morlacca for the Velebit Channel along the Dalmatian coast, but *morlacco* as applied to a type of person has virtually disappeared. Its English versions, which, according to the 1910 *Encyclopaedia Britannica*, included Morlach, Morlak and Morlack,[27] sound distinctly fantastical to contemporary ears, a bit like something one might find in a Mediaeval-based fantasy or science fiction novel. Indeed, Larry Wolff has suggested that H. G. Wells adapted the term for use in his 1895 *The Time Machine* to designate the beastly, subterranean Morlocks, who feed on the angelic (and bovine) Eloi during the night, a form of human regression away from civilisation that, Wells seemed to suggest, could be the future of a fractious *Homo sapiens*. To my knowledge, Wells scholars have not picked up this thread of inquiry, but the claim is not outlandish, given the phenomenon of *morlacchismo* that Fortis's account inaugurated. While the term *morlacchi* appears to have initially been largely devoid of ethnic associations,[28] Fortis, by using it in a proto-anthropological manner and focusing attention on the group's distinctive way of life, in effect reinforced the word and the people it designated as an ethnonym to be wielded by travellers, readers of travel narratives and a wide audience of eighteenth- to twentieth-century theatre and opera goers. As Wolff has carefully shown, the term, and the concept of a distinct, picturesque, semi-savage people known by it, continued to be found in travellers' accounts into the early twentieth century, when, he explains, it began to fade and be replaced by something else.

M. Naimark and Holly Case, eds, *Yugoslavia and its Historians: Understanding the Balkan Wars of the 1990s* (Stanford: Stanford University Press, 2003).

27 'The name of *Morlachs, Morlaks, or Morlacks* commonly bestowed by English writers on the Dalmatian Slavs, though sometimes restricted to the peasantry of the hills, is an abbreviate form of *Mavrovlachi*, meaning either "Black Vlachs" or, "Sea Vlachs."' K. G. J. 'Dalmatia', *Encyclopedia Britannica*, 11th ed., vol. 7 (1910), p. 773.

28 See, for instance, Wayne Vucinich, *A Study in Social Survival: Katun in the Bileća Rudine* (Denver: University of Denver Press, 1975), pp 13–18; Wayne Vucinich, 'Serbian Military Tradition', in Bela Kiraly and Gunther Rothenberg, eds, *War and Society in East Central Europe*, vol. 1 (New York: Brooklyn College Press and Columbia University Press, 1979), p. 290; and C. W. Bracewell, 'Uskoks in Venetian Dalmatia before the Venetian-Ottoman War of 1714–1718', in Gunther Rothenberg et al., eds, *East Central European Society and War in the Pre-Revolutionary Eighteenth Century* (Boulder and New York: Social Science Monographs and Columbia University Press, 1982), pp. 431–2.

> Maria Todorova, in *Imagining the Balkans*, has described the emergence of 'balkanism,' a discourse of disparagement in which the name 'Balkan became a synonym for a reversion to the tribal, the backward, the primitive, the barbarian.' [. . .] The term *Morlacchi* in the eighteenth and nineteenth centuries similarly designated the tribal, the backward, the primitive, the barbarian, and in a notable coincidence of chronology the Morlacchi vanished from history right around the time of the Balkan wars and World War I.[29]

In other words, at this point in its history, the old Dalmatian-Venetian coinage appears to have faded in use, becoming something of a marker for a bygone age, until it was replaced by another term covering much the same semantic territory, even if not as an explicit ethnic designation. In this, *morlacco* resembles another famous Venetian lexical gift to the world, *ghetto*, which by the end of the nineteenth century had begun to take on similarly nostalgic and touristic connotations, whose overtones are palpable in the late-nineteenth-century fiction of Israel Zangwill's *Children of the Ghetto*. Rather than be replaced by another term, however, *ghetto* would be appropriated for new uses and transferred elsewhere, first to Nazi Germany and then to the United States.[30]

The nostalgic or melancholic associations of *morlacco*, then, for D'Annunzio were likely two-dimensional. The first was turned toward the national past, Venice's lost territories in the Eastern Adriatic and a bygone era in which La Serenissima's civilising mission pictured a barbaric and ferocious Other in the form of an untamed *Morlacchia* in the country's interior. As noted above, this discourse was tied up with the late Venetian Enlightenment project in Dalmatia explored by Larry Wolff in his *Venice and the Slavs*. The second faced D'Annunzio's own recent triumphs and failures, celebrated and mourned, in Fiume's *mensa* no less, with the famous drink in hand.

But there is a third and more immediate potential source for D'Annunzio's Morlach, beyond the tradition of travel narratives from that of Fortis to those of late-nineteenth- and early-twentieth-century German, English and American tourists in search of a Slav

[29] Wolff, 'The Rise. . .', pp. 49–50; Maria Todorova, *Imagining the Balkans* (Oxford: Oxford University Press, 1997), pp. 3, 19.

[30] On the term's appropriation by the Nazis and its subsequent transfer across the Atlantic, see Daniel B. Schwartz, *Ghetto: The History of a Word* (Cambridge, MA: Harvard University Press, 2019); on its late-nineteenth-century nostalgic connotations, see Russell Scott Valentino, 'Taking the Traghetto to the Ghetto: or, Performing Jewish Culture in Venice': https://www.academia.edu/50306096/Taking_the_Traghetto_to_the_Ghetto_or_Performing_Jewish_Culture_in_Venice (accessed September 2021).

'noble savage': Luxardo's own marketing materials frequently featured a stylised depiction of a Morlach in colourful dress, wearing a hat resembling a Turkish fez, pointed shoes and a wide belt with a dagger, short sword or both tucked in. His moustachioed face appears to be smiling slightly, one hand extended forward to indicate, and perhaps offer, the bottle, the other hanging casually by a thumb from his waistband. This figure appears on the Luxardo advertisements, postcards and placards that had been displayed across Europe from as early as 1828, just seven years after the company's creation, and continues to be found in such publicity materials through the early-twentieth century. The answer to why the Luxardos would have chosen, way back at the origins of their company, to associate their maraschino with the old Venetian image of the Morlach, becomes clear when one recalls the popular imagination of Dalmatia that Fortis's account inaugurated. The ethnic designation was immediately taken up through German proto-Romantic notions of the nation. As Wolff points out, in the form it would be given by figures such as Goethe and Herder in the 1770s, 'Morlackisch' became 'a cultural category alongside "Deutsch" or "Spanisch," or "Englisch".'[31] Following the publication of Giustiniana Wynne's widely popular, and widely imitated, *Les Morlaques* in 1788 and Camillo Federici's 1793 dramatic comedy *Gli Antichi Slavi*, dressing *à la morlaque* could be not only recognised but fashionable.[32] Thanks, therefore, to the Luxardo branding savvy in attaching itself to this Dalmatian-inspired but internationally recognised type, the stylised figure of the Morlach was ready-made if not ubiquitous in association with the drink with which D'Annunzio and his compatriots were well-provisioned by Girolamo's great-grandson Pietro. By coining his phrase, D'Annunzio in essence took the pictured Morlach from the company's marketing materials and translated him to the bottle itself, where he remains to this day. I cannot help noting a degree of irony in the imagined manly, heroic drink that D'Annunzio had named, given its perceived sophistication, the careful experimentation that went into its creation, and the fact that it would likely not have ever been consumed by the *Morlacchi* announced and, in a sense, celebrated in its name.

[31] Wolff, *Venice and the Slavs*, p. 190.

[32] *Les Morlaques* includes a scene in which a statue of Catherine the Great is described as being dressed *à la morlaque*. J. Wynne, Comtesse des Ursins & Rosenberg, *Les Morlaques* (Venice, 1788), pp. 118–20.

Conclusions: Dannunzian Marketing

There is a somewhat easy analogy to D'Annunzio's literary oeuvre to be found in his naming of the drink, a crystallisation in effect of what might be seen as his artistic approach in general. He routinely drew upon sources associated with the past glories of the Italian peninsula, mining them, as it were, for characteristics and characters as sources of inspiration and hope for the future of the Italy of his day. In this case, he took up the colourful, semi-savage, but also sub-altern Morlach of Venice's past glory, which just also happened to be associated with an object of commerce and consumption produced by an Italian family with irredentist leanings. To this figure, he lent his characteristic flair and flamboyance, what contemporaries described as a 'faultlessness of style' and, in fact, 'a language, neither pompous nor vulgar [. . .] suited to the requirements of modern thought' – in other words, perfect advertising copy.[33] In this, like a handful of other prominent Modernists of his day, D'Annunzio, with his inclination to turn life into spectacle and deploy language as an instrument in that cause, was at the forefront of the emerging era of mass-market advertising.[34] The entire package was then wrapped with the poet's perceived cultural authority, an authority that was especially powerful in the case of the Luxardos and others like them who had been displaced from Istria and Dalmatia following the Second World War.

Indeed, it was the brothers Pietro, Nicolò and Giorgio who would furnish the dramatic final chapter of Luxardo maraschino in Habsburg Zara and its first chapter on the other shore of the Adriatic. Pietro and Nicolò, both staunch advocates for the Italian annexation of Dalmatia, had remained in Zara during the fighting, the Allied bombing that reduced the family business to rubble, and what were in effect the first steps of the post-Second World War nationalisation of the maraschino industry by Yugoslavia. Nicolò and his wife would be drowned off the coast of the city as they tried to escape in 1944. Pietro, the one-time legionnaire in D'Annunzio's

[33] The description of D'Annunzio's stylistic genius comes from the 1911 Encyclopedia Britannica entry on his work available at: https://en.wikisource.org/wiki/1911_Encyclop%C3%A6dia_Britannica/Annunzio,_Gabriele_D%27

[34] Sergei 'Serge' Dhiagilev was a contemporary with a similar flair. For other takes on the connection between Modernism and incipient marketing of the early-twentieth century, see Luke Parker, 'The Shop Window Quality of Things: 1920s Weimar Surface Culture in Nabokov's *Korol', dama, valet*', *Slavic Review*, 77: 2 (July 2018), 390–416; and Sianne Ngai, *Our Aesthetic Categories: Zany, Cute, Interesting* (Cambridge, MA: Harvard University Press, 2015).

Fiume adventure, would be arrested, deported and never heard from again. Giorgio, however, who had opted from the start for a less overt political stance, would re-establish the company on entirely new foundations on the Adriatic's western shore. In a detail fit for a family saga, he would be aided in this endeavour by Alessandro Morettini, Professor of Botany at the University of Florence, who for some years preceding the Second World War had been studying Dalmatia's marasca cherry, a number of specimens of which he had transported to Italy for cultivation in the university's greenhouses. It would be Morettini who, on the basis of his research, would identify the Eugenean Hills to the southwest of Padova as the most suitable location for the new groves that would eventually supply the company the cherries it required for use in its new facilities.

There is, thus, a double nostalgia in the continued use of *sangue morlacco* to designate a drink that no longer has any physical connection to the territories that gave it birth. Once the nostalgia of D'Annunzio and his like-minded brethren, who had dreamed of a greater Italy and the 'unredeemed' lands across the sea, now it suggests the losses of a family and, for those familiar with this history, the lost multi-national, pluralist heritage of the Eastern Adriatic. Those familiar with the history, which I have tried to elucidate in this essay, will likely find it difficult to avoid the ethnocentric and even racist connotations that 'Morlach's blood' must evoke, the blood of the 'semi-savage Slavs' of the opposite shore. In fact, at a time when the image of the Morlach, and the use of the term, was fading, D'Annunzio's designation of the drink helped to give it new life, even if only in the intimate association of this particular liqueur. The name, thus, remains despite the clear stereotypes and derogatory cultural assumptions of the Venetians – and Europeans in general – of an earlier age vis-a-vis their eastern neighbours. Today it conjures but vaguely, and I cannot help but think that it remains possible because the people it once was used to designate have largely been forgotten. It is also worth recalling D'Annunzio's belief in the spilling of blood for the nation. Here too the drink's perceived sophistication, its actual sugary taste, clashes with the apparent claims embedded in the name, and here too D'Annunzio's particular genius, his ability to craft words that move us, shift our perceptions, even alter the way we experience something so basic as a liquid on our tongue, testify to his lasting legacy.

Chapter 18

Infatuated with *Il Vate*: Mishima's Transnational Mimesis of D'Annunzio as Decadent Poet, Patriot and Celebrity

Ikuho Amano

Mishima Yukio (1925–1970) was one of the most vocal and controversial literati of post-Second World War Japan. Notwithstanding the five decades of diachronic gap between the lives of D'Annunzio and Mishima, the personality and aesthetic credos of the Japanese writer attest to undeniable synergies with his Italian Modernist predecessor, who was the paragon of *fin-de-siècle* Decadence and a zealous patriot for his home nation. Parallel socio-political conditions in Italy and Japan – countries that achieved their respective unifications in the 1860s and only at this time began to pave the roads to modern nationhood – surely fuelled the Japanese empathy for the Italian poet, but Mishima's admiration for D'Annunzio exceeded a simple matter of artistic emulation. For nearly three decades, Mishima tacitly restaged D'Annunzio's life through writing, public image and patriotic resolution, even though the historical gap between them made his attempt anachronistic. In order to analyse the untimely transcultural impact of D'Annunzio on Mishima, this chapter builds on the concept of 'transmesis', which I borrow from Thomas O. Beebee, a mode of translation that crosses diachronic, spatial and cultural gaps by means of imitation. While the notion of 'mimesis' involves mimicry, identification and verisimilitude, transmesis accommodates extra-linguistic dimensions of translation that go beyond a simple linguistic equation, encompassing cultural, historical and socio-political negotiations.[1] I venture to suggest that Mishima's life and persona embody a translated Japanese rendition of D'Annunzio,

[1] Thomas O. Beebee, *Transmesis: Inside Translation's Black Box* (New York: Palgrave Macmillan, 2012), p. 3.

which was made possible by virtue of various trans-mimetic attempts. The Japanese writer's act of transmesis shaped itself through literary adaptation, conversion, imitation, pastiche and the theatrical display of all these elements in his writing and actual life. Concretely, the following discussion focuses on three aspects of transmesis: Mishima's Modernist Aesthetic sensibility; his exaltation of the male body inspired by D'Annunzio's *Martyre de St Sebastien*; and, finally, his re-actualisation of D'Annunzio's public persona as patriotic poet and militant man.

D'Annunzio and the Japanese reception

Socio-political parallels between modern Italy and Japan played a key role in the Japanese reception of D'Annunzio. Both countries underwent a radical reformation to build a modern national polity and experienced transitions from a feudalistic *ancien regime* in the mid- through late-nineteenth century. With the nomenclature of the Risorgimento (the Resurgence) and the Meiji Restoration respectively in the 1860s, Italy and Japan achieved unification and established the structures of constitutional monarchies. Being latecomers to Western modernity, these countries strived to develop their social infrastructure, economies and industry. In this climate of nation building, most literati in Italy and Japan embraced literary naturalism, which endorsed scientific positivism and the realistic depiction of human behaviour from sociological and psychological viewpoints. From the 1890s through the Great War, D'Annunzio represented Italy's input to *fin-de-siècle* Decadence, a movement against rational approaches to literary discourses. Closely related to Symbolism and Aestheticism, Decadent aesthetics extolled the anti-naturalistic spirit of art for art's sake. This European literary and cultural trend reached Japan about two decades later and influenced its literary modernity in the first decade of the twentieth century. As had happened in Europe, Japanese literary circles previously dominated by naturalism branched out to cultivate a local offshoot of Aestheticism and Decadence. The shift occurred after Japan's victory in the Russo-Japanese War of 1904–5, which was seen as a significant accomplishment congenial with the Meiji Restoration's slogans, *fukoku kyōhei* (rich country, strong army) and *shokusan kōgyō* (promotion and development of new industry). After the war, the Aestheticist circle, *Pan no kai* (the Circle of Pan), attracted a wide range of talents that represented Japanese variants of anti-naturalism and romantic literary movements around 1908–13.

Polyglots who had lived in Europe, such as Ueda Bin and Nagai Kafū, introduced D'Annunzio and *fin-de-siècle* literature to Japanese literary circles through their own translation of fiction, poetry and literary essays.[2]

D'Annunzio held an unparalleled position in Japan's literary modernity. For the writers of Japanese Aestheticist circles, including Mori Ōgai's *Kanchōrō utakai* (the Poets' Circle of Tower Overlooking Tides) and the Circle of Pan, D'Annunzio's creative charisma became a significant conduit through which they accessed European Modernist themes and literary language. Deeply resonant with the philosophy of Henri Bergson's élan vital and Friedrich Nietzsche's Übermensch, D'Annunzio's oeuvre, popularised in Japan through Ueda Bin's translations, significantly contributed to innovate a literary style perceived as obsolete, galvanising both form and content.[3] Dannunzian sensibility, underpinned by musicality and lavish poetics, was literally a wakeup call for Japan's literary Modernism. Marked by the insatiable desire to cultivate the self, D'Annunzio's persona was an object of fascination and admiration in Japan for all those associated with Aestheticism and literary Decadence. Despite his immeasurable influence, in the post-Second World War decades, the memory of D'Annunzio faded in Japan as the new geopolitical conditions and social ambience demanded shaking off the national memory of militant Fascism. Yet, precisely because of his legendary heroism and encyclopaedic erudition, along with an image of Italy as part of the former Axis alliance, a cult of D'Annunzio never completely ceased among a limited group of Japanese writers, readers and critics. His reputation as a maverick who aimed for a '*vivere inimitablile*',[4] a life impossible to imitate, stirred Japanese *han'mon seinen* (youth agonising for modern selfhood). His multi-dimensional profile as poet, novelist, playwright, journalist, politician, patriot, militant, aviator and flamboyant celebrity exemplified the notion of Decadent 'excess'. In Japan, a country where social conformism overrides individual values and ideals, the egocentric overachiever had a magical, beguiling effect as a notable galvaniser.

[2] On D'Annunzio's relation to Japanese Decadence and Modernism, see Chapters 2 and 10 of this volume, as well.

[3] Ueda Bin, 'Shisō mondai' (Problems on Thoughts), *Teihon Ueda Bin zenshū* (The Final Collection of Ueda Bin's Works, vol. 5 (Tokyo: Kyōiku Shuppan, 1985), pp. 136–139.

[4] Laura D'Angelo, 'Music and Soul: Gabriele D'Annunzion and his Abruzzo Homeland', *Bridge Across Cultures* (2017), p. 60.

Dannunzian Echoes in Mishima's Works

Mishima read several of D'Annunzio's works, including the novel *Trionfo della morte* and the plays *Francesca da Rimini* and *La Gioconda* from the 1930s to the 1940s.[5] He had no knowledge of Italian and relied on translations available through major publishers such as Shinchō and Kawade.

Mishima's interest in D'Annunzio throughout his career has been noted by Tsutsui Yasutaka in the essay 'Danuntsuio ni muchū' ('Hooked on D'Annunzio', 1989) published nearly twenty years after Mishima's suicide. Mishima's major novels, *Forbidden Colours* (1951), *Spring Snow* (1969) and *The Decay of the Angel* (1971, published posthumously) echo *fin-de-siècle* Decadent sensibilities, ennui and scepticism; they are marked by Dannunzian 'immorality' and embellished language, and likewise engage with melody and rhythm.[6] Mishima's protagonists conspicuously inherit the contempt for mass vulgarity and neurotic obsession with sensual beauty typical of D'Annunzio's heroes and, like them, are fatalistic Aesthetes unable to become a Nietzschean Übermensch. However, in Mishima's works the radical pursuit of Aesthetic ideals collides with an impasse rooted in modern pragmatism.

According to Tsutsui, in his formative years Mishima borrowed D'Annunzio's narrative motifs and settings, in particular those of double suicide and the sea. The novella *Yūkoku* (Patriotism, 1960), like *Trionfo della morte*, revolves around an intended double suicide, and it is not a coincidence that the film version (1966) adopts Richard Wagner's opera *Tristan und Isolde* as the sole audio element. This pairing of deterministic death and the intensity of love thus binds D'Annunzio, Wagner and Mishima. Echoes of *Trionfo della morte* are also prominent in the novella *Misaki nite no monogatari* (A Story at the Cape, 1946), where the young protagonist witnesses a couple's double suicide from a cliff.[7] Like D'Annunzio, Mishima utilised the setting and motif of the sea in numerous works, including *Gogo no eikō* (a.k.a. *The Sailor Who Fell from Grace with the Sea*, 1963) and the tetralogy *Hōjō no umi* (The Sea of Fertility, 1964–70). His adoration for the sea was also fostered by D'Annunzio's poems, which he read in Ueda's versions.

It is not clear when Mishima learned about D'Annunzio's mystic play *Le Martyre de Saint Sébastien* (1911) composed by D'Annunzio

[5] Tsutsui, *Danuntsuio ni muchū* (Hooked on D'Annunzio) (Tokyo: Chūōkōron, 1989), p. 13.

[6] Ibid., p. 18.

[7] Ibid., p. 16.

in French. Tsutsui surmises that it was long before he wrote *A Story at the Cape* as a twenty-year old.[8] In 1966, Mishima co-translated the play with Ikeda Kōtarō. Despite his limited knowledge of French, he wrestled with the original text out of his zealous interest in the martyr, ambitiously retaining in Japanese D'Annunzio's opulent linguistic nuances. Mishima believed that all artistic creations are fundamentally recreations of an archetype in search of their 'mould'.[9] D'Annunzio's exuberant theatricality was a lifelong inspiration for the Japanese writer, who lived in the age of socio-cultural lassitude under the influence of post-war American democracy.

Mishima, D'Annunzio, St Sebastian

Mishima's fascination with D'Annunzio is not a manifest case of literary reception, transmission and imitation that foregrounds a cultural hierarchy between Western Europe and East Asia. His infatuation is far more personal and relies on his admiration for the patriotic Italian hero and his Decadent artistry. D'Annunzio functioned for Mishima as an 'ego ideal' – to borrow Freud's term. In Freud's theory, one's 'ego ideal' provides a substitute for the lost narcissism of childhood.[10] It contributes to the formation of the child's ego, but also functions as 'the most powerful factor favoring repression', moving through inner conflict to awaken a new motivation and orient them toward a goal.[11] An ego ideal thus serves as a guiding model and fuels the individual's desire to emulate the achievements of that ideal self.

Mishima envisioned D'Annunzio as his ideal self. In his childhood, he spent most of his time with his grandmother who doted on him. Her crotchety affection and the pride of having grown up in an imperial household suffocated him, causing his symptom of autotoxemia.[12] Mishima returned to his parents' home when he was twelve years old.[13] His new life required rigid discipline: his austere father did not accept the child's artistic fancy, and he destroyed one of his

[8] Ibid., p. 13.

[9] Mishima, 'Hanjidai teki na geijutsu ka' (The Anti-Epochal Artist), *Mishima Yukio zenshū*, vol. 27 (Tokyo: Shinchō, 2003), p. 86.

[10] Sigmund Freud, 'On Narcissism: An Introduction', *Essential Papers on Narcissism*, ed. by Andrew P. Morrison (New York: New York University Press, 1986), p. 36.

[11] Ibid., p. 37.

[12] Muramatsu Takeshi, *Mishima Yukio no sekai* (The World of Mishima Yukio) (Tokyo: Shinchō, 1990), p. 53.

[13] Ibid., p. 93.

first manuscripts.[14] One day, Mishima flipped through some volumes of art reproductions from his father's bookshelf. Here, he came upon a reproduction of Guido Reni's *St. Sebastian* at the Palazzo Rosso in Genoa. In the Christian saint, the young Mishima perceived the 'strong flavor of paganism', 'the springtime of youth, only light and beauty and pleasure'.[15] Sebastian's sensual physique provoked in him a sudden, intense sensation of ardour. This encounter led to 'a secret, radiant something [that rose] swift-footed to the attack from inside'.[16] In the well-known scene of his first ejaculation in *Kamen no kokuhaku* (Confessions of a Mask, 1949), the narrator, purportedly Mishima himself, links his somatic excitement and the Christian saint through heretic imaginings that made him tremble with 'pagan joy.'[17] He then inserts an unfinished piece of prose to conjure his sensual rapture. It is too long to quote in its entirety, but an excerpt reads as follows:

> *[D]uring the time following his enthronement when Diocletian was dreaming of power as limitless as the unobstructed soaring of a bird, there was a young captain of the Praetorian Guard who was seized and charged with the crime of serving a forbidden god. He was a young captain endowed both with a lithe body reminding one of the famous Oriental slave beloved by the Emperor Hadrian and with the eyes of a conspirator, as emotionless as the sea. He was charmingly arrogant. On his helmet he wore a white lily, presented to him each morning by maidens of the town. Drooping downward gracefully along the flow of his manly hair as he rested from fierce tourneying, the lily looked exactly like the nape of a swan's neck.*
>
> [. . .]
>
> *This was Sebastian, young captain in the Praetorian Guard. And was not such beauty as his a thing destined for death? Did not the robust women of Rome, their senses nurtured on the taste of good wine that shook the bones and on the savor of meat dripping red with blood, quickly scent his ill-starred fate, yet unknown to him, and love him for that reason? His blood was coursing with an even fiercer pace than usual within his white flesh, watching for an opening from which to spurt forth when that flesh would soon be torn asunder. How could the women have failed to hear the tempestuous desires of such blood as this?*[18]

[14] Ibid., pp. 91–2.

[15] Mishima Yukio, *Confessions of a Mask*, trans. Meredith Weatherby (New York: New Directions, 1958), 39.

[16] Ibid., p. 40.

[17] Ibid., p. 40.

[18] Ibid., pp. 44–5. The original text is in italics.

When he authored *Confessions of a Mask*, Mishima was most likely unaware of D'Annunzio's *Le Martyre de Saint Sébastien*. Curiously, the unfinished prose above nevertheless condenses features of St Sebastian that are strikingly akin to the image rendered in D'Annunzio's play. Both texts mystify the provenance of Sebastian, removing him from the geographical framework of Christendom. Instead, both D'Annunzio and Mishima identify paganism as St Sebastian's quintessential attribute and emphasise the saint's sensual beauty incommensurate with Christian austerity. In both texts, St Sebastian is likened to the slave loved by the Roman Emperor Hadrian, Antinous, a *fin-de-siècle* icon of homosexuality. Fourteen years before he translated *Le Martyre de Saint Sébastien*, in 1952, Mishima had visited the Vatican Museums. His travelogue, 'Apollo's Cup' (1952), records his impressions of the statue and underlines the conflation of subtle homosexual desire with Decadence:

> Antinous condenses the beauty of Greece that remained unaffected by Christianity. He is the final holdover of Greekness that foresees the day when the Roman Empire is headed for the decadent phase.[19]

According to John Woodhouse, D'Annunzio's fixation on St Sebastian was 'sensual, sado-masochistic' in nature.[20] He identified with the saint, equating his mistress Olga Ossani's love-bites on his body to the wounds left by the arrows piercing the body of the martyr.[21] With the far more outright imagery, Mishima also identified with the saint. In 1968, Mishima posed as St Sebastian in Shinoyama Kishin's photographs and physically realised the climactic scene where Sebastian, pierced by arrows, faces the agony of death.

Both D'Annunzio and Mishima's fixations thus took place at the level of psychosomatic desire. As his ego ideal, D'Annunzio guided Mishima's artistic vision. And yet, while he acknowledged the influence of Oscar Wilde and Thomas Mann, the Japanese writer was never explicit about his aesthetic indebtedness to D'Annunzio. Even in the postscript to his translation of *Le Martyre de Saint Sébastien*, he remains silent about his long-term infatuation.[22] Tsutsui speculates that Mishima's reasons for doing so lie in D'Annunzio's status as

[19] Ibid., p. 637. My translation.

[20] John Woodhouse, *Gabriele D'Annunzio: Defiant Archangel* (Oxford: Clarendon, 1998), pp. 56–7.

[21] Ibid., pp. 56–7.

[22] Tsutsui, p. 26.

'the patriotic national hero'.[23] Out of fear that the mass media might disparage his hidden ambition to become a national hero, which after the Second World War seemed oddly anachronistic, he camouflaged his passion for D'Annunzio with adulation for Radiguet, a French writer who died at age twenty.[24]

D'Annunzio's Influence on Mishima's Public Persona: Life as Imitation

The Japanese writer had a deterministic vision of life which assumed that one's life is an imitation of an already existing reality.[25] Without asserting his admiration, Mishima idolised and followed D'Annunzio's multifarious profile as poet, writer, artist, political activist, patriot militant and socialite. The Italian poet's audacious life provided Mishima with a role model that helped determine the trajectory of his career as a writer and public persona. Tsutsui underscores that Mishima 'clearly identified himself' with D'Annunzio in terms of both artistic creativity and lifestyle.[26] In fact, we do not know to what extent Mishima learned about the Italian poet's upbringing and life. Nevertheless, as Tsutsui has noted, there are indeed parallels with the life of the Japanese artist.[27] Both D'Annunzio and Mishima were born into affluent families, a business owner and the mayor of Pescara, and an elite bureaucrat of the Ministry of Agriculture, Forestry and Fisheries, respectively. Both displayed precocious talent: when he was seventeen years old, D'Annunzio was inspired by Giosuè Carducci's *Odi barbare* and published his first poetry collection, *Primo vere* (1879). Two years later, he made a debut in Italian literary circles with *Canto novo* (1882). In turn, Mishima at the age of fifteen contributed haiku and poetry to a literary magazine called *Kuchinashi* (Gardenia). When he was sixteen, he serialised his first novella, *Hanazakari no mori* (Forest with Blooming Flowers, 1941), in *Bungei bunka* (Literary Artistry and Culture), and three years later he published his first collection of short stories with the same title. Their debut in their late teens led to further parallels in their twenties: at twenty-four, D'Annunzio established his fame with *Il Piacere* (1889), the first novel of the *Romanzi della*

[23] Ibid., p. 26.
[24] Ibid., p. 26.
[25] Ibid., p. 23.
[26] Ibid., pp. 23–4.
[27] Ibid., pp. 18–19.

Rosa trilogy. Mishima's *Confessions of a Mask* (1949) likewise gained substantial attention from Japan's post-war literary circles while the author was in his late twenties.

There are also uncanny parallels between D'Annunzio's and Mishima's physical dispositions and personalities. Unlike his virile protagonists, the Italian poet was rather short and effeminate. Similarly, Mishima was also of small build and weak from his chronic illness of autointoxication. Furthermore, while D'Annunzio intentionally dodged military service, Mishima was classified as physically frail and not even qualified for service during the Second World War. When he was thirty-three years old, Mishima chose a conservative arranged marriage. Unlike D'Annunzio, who was seen as a womaniser, Mishima evasively acted like a homosexual socialite in the urban cultural circles he associated with.[28] Even so, the Japanese writer, not unlike D'Annunzio, utilised his sexuality as part of his artistry to enhance his public image as an Aesthete.[29] Alongside such efforts at self-branding, his desire to follow D'Annunzio's steps extended to a material level. Mishima most likely knew about the Vittoriale degli Italiani, D'Annunzio's villa and, later, mausoleum in Gardone on Lake Garda. In the city centre of Tokyo, possessing a massive amount of land on the scale of the Vittoriale was inconceivable. Compromising this ambition, Mishima built a single-family residence reminiscent of the Victorian-Colonial style. Its front yard was adorned with a replica Apollo statue that might remind the viewer of the Veranda dell'Apollino.[30] While the house is ivory white, it stylistically echoes the Vittoriale's Villa Mirabella, which is painted in Maria Theresa yellow.[31]

Belated Patriotism

D'Annunzio was undeniably a patriotic hero, thanks to his poetic artistry and his staunch nationalist actions during the Great War and thereafter. Furthermore, he was considered an 'astonishingly skillful manipulator of the mass audience'.[32] He campaigned for Italy

[28] Muramatsu, p. 194.

[29] Tsutsui, p. 32.

[30] Annamaria Andreoli (ed.), *The Vittoriale degli Italiani* (Milan: Skira, 2004), p. 77.

[31] Ibid., p. 53.

[32] Jared M. Becker, *Nationalism and Culture: Gabriele D'Annunzio and Italy after the Risorgimento* (New York: Peter Lang, 1994), p. 10.

to join the Allies, and he volunteered for military service to fight on the battlefield. His proactive military operations, such as the Bakar Mockery (La Beffa di Buccari) in 1911 and the campaign over the skies of Vienna, marked his status as poet-soldier. Even if the effects of those operations were limited, his charismatic aura had a significant impact on the Italian people's enthusiastic support for him. D'Annunzio was keenly aware that advertising was the rising mode of communication for reaching out to the mass audience. Flying over Trieste, as Hughes-Hallett puts it, 'he was flyering', combining the military notion of a campaign with an advertising campaign to win his compatriots' sympathy.[33] When D'Annunzio flew over Vienna, instead of bombs he dropped 50,000 copies of a text, printed on Italian-tricolor paper, which urged the Viennese people to 'plead for peace' to their government.[34] The culmination of his heroic military operations was the occupation of Fiume (today's Rijeka in Croatia) in 1919, which was backed by the city's Italian-dominated National Council as well as Benito Mussolini. D'Annunzio's entry into Fiume was highly dramatised, with the spectacle of a motorcade; he called himself 'Il Duce' and referred to his arrival in the city as '*Sacra Entrata*' (sacred entry).[35] The occasion provoked Dionysiac enthusiasm among the crowds, which excited the poet and drove him to declare: 'Here I am . . . Here is the man . . . *Ecce Homo*.'[36] In reality, D'Annunzio governed Fiume in a quite disorganised fashion, without exercising the necessary leadership to achieve the annexation of the city into Italy. His occupation of Fiume was a spectacular pageant to begin with, but in the end catered mostly to his personal pleasure.[37]

In Mishima's eyes, D'Annunzio's impact as a literatus and his heroic deeds were a sort of oracle, a prescribed fate he was bound to repeat. Nonetheless, despite his strong desire to emulate the Italian poet, Mishima could not wipe away the sense of being belated, as a writer and as a public leader in history.[38] There was a significant gap between the historical conditions of 1910–20s Italy and post-Second World War Japan. The post-war socio-political milieus in Japan were not amenable to the heroic vitalism exhibited by D'Annunzio during

[33] Lucy Hughes-Hallett, *The Pike: Gabriele D'Annunzio, Poet, Seducer and Preacher of War* (London: Fourth Estate, 2013), p. 324–45.

[34] Ibid., p. 376.

[35] Ibid., p. 413.

[36] Ibid., p. 415.

[37] Ibid., p. 427.

[38] Tsutsui, p. 26.

the Great War. In the age of post-war growth during the 1950s and 60s, Japan shifted gears, moving its focus from wartime ideology to fierce economic and industrial re-development. In the realm of geo-politics, post-war Japan's national security was under the tutelage of the United States, formed by the occupation period (1945–52) and the domestic turmoil stirred by the controversy over the Treaty of Mutual Cooperation and Security ratified in 1960. While public antagonism against the US remained, Japan was saturated with political ideologies aligned with American-style democracy. In this context, there was no space where a symbolic poet laureate could invent, to borrow George Mosse's words on D'Annunzio, a 'national liturgy'.[39] Such an ambition, however, gradually surged in Mishima in the 1960s, when his fictional writing noticeably bore nationalistic ethos extolling Japan's cultural legacies. The public and leftist critics received such novellas like *Eirei no koe* (The Voices of the Heroic Dead, 1966), *Yūkoku* (Patriotism, 1966) and essays such as *Bunka bōei ron* (On Defense of the Culture, 1969), as dangerously anachronistic and anti-democratic. In their eyes, these works would potentially re-instigate wartime totalitarianism and militaristic Fascism. Given his keen sensibility, Mishima was well-aware of being a *persona non grata* in his epoch.[40]

The Coup, a Fabricated Tabloid Play

In Mishima's view, the defeat in the Second World War had driven Japan to forget its cultural heritage, awe of the emperor and national pride. Whereas the high post-war growth created the second largest economy on the globe, the spiritual state of Japanese citizens, ensconced in lassitude, was castrated by US military protection, wiping away any possibility of restaging D'Annunzio's heroic vitalism. With the constitution drafted by US officials, which stipulates the eternal renunciation of warfare, Japan compromised itself into a semi-colonialised status in geopolitics. Against this backdrop of yielding to the American Other, Mishima stood out of the crowd in the 1960s. In 1968, while completing the tetralogy *The Sea of Fertility*, he built

[39] George Mosse, 'The Poet and the Exercise of Political Power', in *Masses and Man: Nationalist and Fascist Perceptions of Reality* (New York: Fertig, 1980), p. 89.

[40] Hashimoto Osamu, '*Mishima Yukio' towa nanimono dattanoka* (Who was 'Mishima Yukio?') (Tokyo: Shinchō, 2005), p. 418.

Tate no kai (Shield Society), a private army designed to defend Japan's traditional cultural values and the emperor as the supreme institution of the nation. While making this move, he was conscious of D'Annunzio's army and of his occupation of Fiume.

The root of the sensational coup d'état in 1970 was once again his fervent desire to be faithful to his ego ideal. On 25 November 1970, he visited the office of the superintendent general at the Ground Self-Defense Force in Ichigaya, Tokyo, together with four members of Shield Society. Suddenly, they took the superintendent general hostage, and Mishima demanded that all the officials of the Self-Defense Force come out in the front yard. Borrowing from D'Annunzio's method, Mishima then threw his manifesto flyers into the audience. In his statement, he claimed that this coup was inevitable because the Self-Defense Force had been the locus where 'an intense patriotic spirit' still lived in 'lukewarm contemporary Japan'.[41] He continued the manifesto, deploring the decay of 'the national spirit and the collective oblivion of the national cause'.[42] He argued that Japan had degenerated, and hoped that the Self-Defense Force could preserve 'genuine Japan, genuine Japanese people, and [the] genuine spirit of militants.'[43] In the meantime, when about 800 officers gathered there, Mishima began to deliver a speech. However, his voice was undermined by the noises of helicopters roaming over the scene, along with the officers' loud booing.

In reality, the raison d'être of the Self-Defense Force was at stake because the entity had existed in a constitutional paradox ever since 1954, when it was established shortly after the end of the occupation period. Article 9 of the Japanese constitution outlawed not only the nation's participation in warfare but also possession of military forces. Mishima confronted this issue with his audience, arguing that, by accepting these conditions, Self-Defense Forces had disgraced themselves.[44] His sense of urgency offered harsh criticism of the zeitgeist of post-war Japan, which lacked solid agency and the ability to legally defend its own national polity.

At the climax, the coup restaged D'Annunzio's actions in Fiume. Just as D'Annunzio had invoked the splendour of the national past, and likened his compatriots to heroes, martyrs and the staunch

[41] Mishima Yukio, 'Geki' (The Manifesto), *Mishima Yukio zenshū*, vol. 36 (Tokyo: Shinchō, 2000), p. 402.

[42] Ibid., p. 402.

[43] Ibid., pp. 402–3.

[44] Ibid., p. 405.

legions of Ancient Rome,[45] Mishima's speech escaladed to remind his audience of the gallant demeanour of *bushi*, militant men in the pre-Meiji period, invoking dignity and self-respect as qualities of foremost importance – fatally absent in the Self-Defense Forces.[46] Alongside the oral speech, the manifesto also underlined that militant mentality, cultivated with vigorous sense of ethics and extreme dedication to one's lord, was crucial national spirit. As rendered in both oral speech and manifesto, the ultimate objective of the coup was to articulate the autonomy of the militant forces that should guard the national polity, as well as Japan's history, culture and tradition.[47] Outwardly, both D'Annunzio and Mishima demonstrated their ideological commitments by acting on behalf of their respective nations as resolute patriots. Nonetheless, compared with D'Annunzio's dramatic spectacle, zealously supported by Fiuman-Italians and Italians, in the eyes of the Self-Defense Forces and the public, Mishima's coup was a fabricated tabloid play, sheer nonsense.

Playing the role of both impresario and actor, Mishima spent more than three years setting up the props for this staging, beginning with his trial enrolment in the Self-Defense Forces in 1967, which led to the foundation of Shield Society. Simultaneously, Mishima intensified his practice of bodybuilding to prepare his vigorous physique for dying beautifully, especially by developing his muscular abdomen. Despite all the efforts for restating D'Annunzio's legendary presence and oratory in Fiume, the final stage of the attempted coup turned out to be a failure – Mishima's speech without microphone only proved his poor vocal technique and invited increasingly agitated hecklers.[48] Unable to receive the audience's approbation, Mishima quickly moved to take responsibility for the public commotion. He retired to the room inside, and without delay, initiated a ritual of *seppuku* – radical suicide by disembowelment – in the presence of his military apprentices, who responded by enacting the practice of *kaishaku* (beheading to end the man's excruciating pain). On the surface, his suicide was part of the prescribed plot that had to be implemented due to the absence of emphatic responses to his speech. At a subtextual level, his act of dying, or more precisely, an annihilation of his

[45] Hughes-Hallett, p. 328.

[46] Mishima discusses the same idea extensively in 'Hagakure nyūmon' ('An Introduction to Hagakure'), in *Mishima Yukio zenshū*, vol. 34 (Tokyo: Shinchō, 2003), p. 477.

[47] Mishima, 'Geki', p. 403.

[48] Tsutsui, p. 42–6.

body at forty-five years old, was the only remaining possibility to overcome his ego ideal. Unlike D'Annunzio, who deplored his aged body, calling it a '*mostro*' (monster and show – as in freak show) in the last ten years of his life before dying at the age of seventy-four due to a brain haemorrhage,[49] Mishima constantly dreamed of ending his life while his body enjoyed the remnants of youth. For this aestheticised death, his ardent bodybuilding in the late 1960s was imperative.[50]

Conclusions

In 1954, Mishima wrote that 'all creations entail a mould [. . .], and the mould annihilates [the artist] at the moment of achieving a coalescence'.[51] This aphoristic line predicted his own fate, his death immediately following the failed coup. It was D'Annunzio himself whom Mishima considered the exemplar of artistry, the mold he desired to fit.

Mishima's emulation of D'Annunzio involved socio-cultural translations that resisted diachronic differences, as well as downright anachronism. And it resonates with Emily Apter's proposition that 'everything is translatable', and that translation can occur beyond the limits of text-based linguistic equivalencies. Apter has suggested that what lies behind translation is the aspiration to salvage 'the dismembered subject of historical trauma and repressed memory'.[52] This effort to recuperate loss held significant relevance for Mishima, who felt that the Second World War trampled upon Japan's dignity and cultural tradition. For him, translating both D'Annunzio's literary aesthetics and persona were a lifelong project that, to borrow Apter's words, meant recuperating 'the post historical subject' through negotiation 'between the lost origin and foreclosed teleologies'.[53] Such mediation was made possible by the commensurate social, cultural and historical conditions in modern Italy and Japan.

49 Hughes-Hallett, pp. 529, 542.

50 Mishima, 'Narusisizumu ron' (On Narcissism), in *Mishima Yukio zenshū*, vol. 34 (Tokyo: Shinchō, 2000), pp. 145–6.

51 Mishima, 'Hanjidai teki na geijutsu ka' (The Anti-Epochal Artist), in *Mishima Yukio zenshū*, vol. 27 (Tokyo: Shinchō, 2003), p. 86.

52 Emily Apter, *The Translation Zone: A New Comparative Literature* (Princeton: Princeton University Press, 2011), p. 226.

53 Ibid., p. 226.

Mishima's transmesis, restaging D'Annunzio's legacies, ended in public bewilderment and dismay over his shocking spectacle. Despite his attempt to conceal the imitation of D'Annunzio, Mishima was perceived as no more than a historical latecomer. In the eyes of most Japanese individuals, including literary critic Hashimoto Osamu, Mishima was merely an epigone of European culture, a pastiche of the unattainable ideal, symbolically comparable to the copy of Apollo's statue he placed in his residence.[54] A statue, it bears reiterating, inspired by those D'Annunzio collected at his Vittoriale degli Italiani.

[54] Hashimoto, pp. 14–15.

D'Annunzio in the Twenty-First Century

Elisa Segnini and Michael Subialka

Throughout this volume, we have paid particular attention to the role of translators as agents mediating D'Annunzio's place in world literature. As a conclusion, we return to the role of translators, this time to consider our contemporary context. To this end, we contacted and interviewed a number of translators, working in different languages, who engaged with D'Annunzio's texts from the late 1970s to today. The questions we asked concerned a range of issues, including the translators' backgrounds (whether they were familiar with D'Annunzio scholarship, and/or with translation theory), the context of their translation (whether they were commissioned the translation, or else their motivation for choosing this piece/author), their approach to D'Annunzio's style, their goals and who they had in mind as a reader. We also asked them to comment on their stance on aspects of D'Annunzio that were – at least in some contexts – controversial, such as his treatment/portrayal of women, his ideology and his relation to Fascism. We concluded with a question that concerned the value of translating D'Annunzio today, and what aspects of his writing may still speak to contemporary readers.

Establishing contact with translators was not always easy. D'Annunzio, despite the increasing interest in his persona testified by recent biographies, is far from being a popular author in our contemporary moment, and recent translations are thus relatively limited. Moreover, not all translators accepted our invitation. Others answered questions on background and approach but declined to comment on questions of gender and politics.

Even with these limitations, a look at the responses we did receive allows for interesting comparisons to emerge. We have paired the responses from these interviews with comments emerging from other venues, as well, to fill out the 'story' of D'Annunzio's place in contemporary translation. These other sources include a blog on translating D'Annunzio by Susan Bassnett (2020) and a recent conference panel at the MLA International Symposium held in Glasgow (2–4 June 2022). What follows is thus a reconstruction that draws on translators' direct responses, which we quote or summarise as indicated (all quotes come from translators' responses to our questionnaire unless otherwise noted), seeking not to exhaustively catalogue the responses but rather to ensure a fair representation while also putting translators' thoughts and experiences into dialogue with one another. We were particularly interested in translators' opinions about the status of women in D'Annunzio's work, and what it means to translate him from a feminist perspective or a perspective attuned to contemporary gender theories, and those responses have often been highlighted in the 'dialogue' that follows.

A Dialogue with Translators

In 1991, Susan Bassnett translated *Il fuoco* (1900) into English as *The Flame* for Quartet books, making the text accessible again as it had previously been available only in the 1900 translation by Vivaria Kassandra. Drawing on this experience, and on her body of work as a translation studies expert, Bassnett wrote a blog post on 'Translating D'Annunzio for the 21st century' (2020) at the invitation of the Decadence and Translation Network.[1] In this piece, she describes D'Annunzio's style as 'overblown' and 'convoluted', hard to follow because of the varying pace from 'breathless to absurdly descriptive'. She also remarks that allusions and historical references woven into the novel 'probably mean nothing to English readers'. In translating the novel, her impulse was to 'simplify the language to cut down the long drawn-out sentences, to excise the number of adjectives', but she adds that she resisted doing so to remain true to D'Annunzio's style, which is the product of an aesthetics very different from our own. In her summary of D'Annunzio's biography, she notes two recurring factors: 'firstly, that despite being extremely ugly, he seems throughout his life to have been very attractive to women of all ages, nationalities and professions and secondly, that he treated them all appallingly'. For Bassnett, this is reflected in D'Annunzio's

[1] Susan Bassnett, 'Translating D'Annunzio for the 21st century', https://dandtnetwork.glasgow.ac.uk/translating-gabriele-dannunzio-for-the-twenty-first-century-reader/ All following quotations from Bassnett refer to the same blog entry.

novels, in which the male protagonist causes women's suffering and 'women are objectified, either as emblems of idealised perfection of destructive figures of obscure desires'.

Bassnett's approach to D'Annunzio was mediated by the research she had undertaken on actor Eleonora Duse, D'Annunzio's muse and lover, disguised in *Il fuoco* as the actress Foscarina. Given her sympathy for Duse, Bassnett acknowledges that her translation was 'not unbiased'. As a feminist, she was tempted to modify the text, but she resisted this urge: 'with all translations, there is a responsibility to the author to try and give the second language readers a sense of what the original author was doing'. For Bassnett, D'Annunzio's 'abhorrent' ideology is today more dangerous than ever. 'D'Annunzio's cult of the superman', she writes, 'can no longer be considered history and needs to be watched with care.'

Lara Raffelli, who in 2013 translated *Il Piacere* (1889) into English as *Pleasure*, had a different experience with D'Annunzio. Her interest in the Italian author was also mediated by her research on a female artist, Maria Messina, who in turn was influenced by D'Annunzio. But her translation of *Il Piacere* was the result of an accident: she was lecturing on 'Aspects of Eros from Sappho to Cyber' at the University of Cape Town and had decided to include this text. As she was preparing the lectures, she discovered that Georgina Harding's 1898 translation was heavily bowdlerised, and that vast tracts of the text – especially those having to do with erotic scenes – were missing. She therefore set about translating the gaps from the original Italian into English, and subsequently took the decision to translate the entire original book from scratch.

Unlike Bassnett, Raffaelli found D'Annunzio's writing to be 'of incomparable beauty'. To render the tone of the original, she made an effort to use rarefied terms and a high register. Seeking inspiration for her text to 'flow and be beautiful,' and mindful of the importance of musical prose in Decadent writing, she listened to music as she translated. The complex network of references embedded in D'Annunzio's work, for Raffaelli, is a strength: 'D'Annunzio had a wide knowledge of many aspects of life and culture. Reading *Il Piacere* is like reading an encyclopaedia of art, music, literature, culture and human behaviour. I don't believe that there are many authors alive today with just such an array of knowledge and ability to transmit it so eloquently.'

Raffaelli was struck by our question about whether, in her view, translation could mitigate problematic portrayals of women – something quote common in *fin-de-siècle* literature – and this led her to contact the eminent translation studies scholar Lawrence Venuti to discuss the matter. She reports that in their conversation he advised her to revise her 2013 translation from today's standpoint, accounting for the surge in new translation theory in recent years. When she shared this exchange in a presentation for a panel that we organised at the MLA 2022 symposium in Glasgow, the anecdote gave rise to a lively debate.[2] While acknowledging that feminist approaches have redefined translation in crucial ways, most panellists felt that D'Annunzio's texts provided historical evidence of the context in which they were produced. A related discussion arose considering how to contend with D'Annunzio's ideology. As noted in this volume's introduction, D'Annunzio's *Il Piacere* engaged (though briefly, compared to others of his texts) with the question of Italy's colonial expansion in Abyssinia (present-day Ethiopia). Raffaelli commented that she translated these elements and sought to transmit the meaning and feeling that D'Annunzio put in the original without amending or softening Sperelli's views: 'The anti-democratic views of Andrea Sperelli speak to the heart of Decadent literature – a refusal of the commonplace, the mass-produced. I didn't wish to rewrite the past.' The question that ensued was whether a translation could ever be 'neutral'. Responding to this, Raffaelli acknowledged that when she came across a rather unsympathetic reference to a 'Jew', as a Jewish person she tried to handle it with as much discretion as possible. Since translation, as Venuti emphasises, is fundamentally an interpretation,[3] mitigating processes of various sorts, whether we are aware of it or not, are always at play.

For Raffaelli's translation, the publisher, Penguin Classics, had in mind a mainstream audience, as suggested by the cover featuring a graphic depiction of a woman's corseted back – over which Raffaelli had no influence. However, Raffaelli noted that the audience was rather limited to the academic sphere. She also commented that, surprisingly, there have been some Italian readers of her translation; the book can be challenging in the original, and the English

[2] The panel, 'D'Annunzio as World Literature', was organised as part of a network on 'D'Annunzio and World Literature' with the aim of fostering a global dialogue on D'Annunzio: https://www.hastac.org/groups/dannunzio-and-world-literature-multilingualism-translation-reception This network and the associated panel were important steps toward the publication of the present volume.

[3] Lawrence Venuti, 'World Literature and Translation Studies', in *The Routledge Companion to World Literature*, ed. by Theo D'haen, David Damrosch and Djelal Kadir (London and New York: Routledge, 2012): 180–93 (p. 180).

translation unveils some of its mysteries. It is worth noting that this was something boasted also by D'Annunzio's first French translator – Georges Hérelle – which suggests that resorting to translation to read D'Annunzio was an established practice already during the *fin-de-siècle*. Raffaelli concludes that D'Annunzio's work matters 'in an historical sense as it captures an epoch, and it because it is, quite simply, written so very beautifully. Each line of a novel is poetic verse. It is luminous and rich in sensory description that is never trite.'

While historical translations into English are considered dated and bowdlerised, and the need to re-translate these texts is discussed by Raffaelli and others, in the French context, Hérelle's status is such that his translations are read as texts in their own right, classics of *fin-de-siècle* literature, an exception to the overall rule that translations are bound to age. For example, the altered 1895 edition of *L'Enfant de volupté* has not been retranslated, but rather complemented with the addition of missing bits by scholar Pierre de Montera in 1971.[4] Thus, new translations are limited to texts that have remained untranslated/unpublished. Among these, Muriel Gallot translated *Le novelle della Pescara* (*Les nouvelles de la Pescara*, Gallimard 1998), *Versi d'amore e di gloria* (*Poèmes d'amour et de gloire*, Institut culturel italien de Paris, 2008); poems from *Alcyone* and other collections (*De l'Alcyone et autres poèmes*, Orphée 2013); and, recently, *Le Faville del maglio* (*Les Étincelles de l'enclume*, Les Hotel de Galliffet, 2020). For Gallot, D'Annunzio's archaic, sophisticated language is not a problem, as contemporary translators can resort to footnotes. She notes that the sensual aspect of D'Annunzio's novels, which in the past had been censored by both Harding and Hérelle, is no longer controversial. D'Annunzio, she writes, is today better known in France thanks to the recent biography by Maurizio Serra (2018) and to the work of the Italian Cultural Institute in Paris. His novels are out of fashion, but his theatre and the opera librettos are considered classics: *Le Martyre de Saint Sébastien*, put into music by Debussy, and *Francesca da Rimini*, fruit of a collaboration with Zandonia, are still represented today.

Gallot notes that D'Annunzio was considered scandalous and immoral at the time in which he was writing, but at the same time he was also admired: the image of the poet soldier appealed to people. His writing, she argues in line with Raffaelli, must be seen in the

[4] Gabriele D'Annunzio, *L'Enfant de volupté*, trans. by Georges Hérelle, completed and rearranged in the original order by Pierre de Montera (Paris, Calmann-Lévy, 1971).

context of the time in which it was written, but, she stresses, 'he's never been a misogynist' and his love for women is manifested through 'real heroines such as Duse', to whom *Le Faville del Maglio* is dedicated. She mentions that D'Annunzio insisted that Ida Rubinstein, a woman and a Jew, take up the role of the saint in *Le Martyre de Saint Sébastien*. In Gallot's view, the fact that the opera, after its première in France, was forbidden by the archbishop of Paris shows that D'Annunzio was in fact ahead of his time with respect to the configurations of new gender identities. In line with what Guylian Nemegger and Mara Santi have argued in this volume, she contends that D'Annunzio's reputation as a Fascist writer is the result of a prejudice. The Italian poet, she writes, never adopted what our question had phrased as an 'anti-democratic stance': 'he was a nationalist, just like Ukrainians today, and this is not to be condemned. It is love for Italy that pushed him to occupy Fiume.' This is, of course, itself a controversially Dannunzian statement, for the opposite could also be said to be true (that, like Russia today, he occupied a territory outside of Italy using the excuse of an Italian ethnic majority). The elderly D'Annunzio, Gallot continues, weakened by the outcome of the Fiume enterprise, found refuge in building his Vittoriale degli Italiani and the art collection there, and he accepted having his work published in luxury editions by the Fascist regime. However, she insists, just as there are neither objects nor symbols of Fascism at the Vittoriale, 'there are no texts that exalt fascism. The poet hated the Nazism that influenced Mussolini. And he has never been an antisemite.' She concludes that D'Annunzio 'has as much value as other so-called "Decadent" artists. Today, we highlight the originality of his poetry, and of his late writings. Many are not yet translated. He certainly deserves inclusion among the classics of the European literary heritage.'

In contrast to the French case, where translation and diffusion of his texts has long been centred in a single national context, D'Annunzio's presence in Spanish-speaking countries is more complex. Sandro Abate, Professor of Modern European Literature at the Universidad Nacional del Sur (Bahía Blanca, Argentina), who also contributed a chapter in this volume, highlights the need to distinguish between peninsular and Latin American translations. Abate edited and translated two volumes of D'Annunzio: *El último humanista. Antología bilingüe 1882–1893* (2008), which gathers poems from the cycle *Versi d'amore* (1882–1893); and *Los jardines del Vate* (2011), a selection of poems from the *Laudi* (1903–1933). His interest in D'Annunzio is part of his family legacy. His parents, of

Abruzzese origin, were formed by a school system characterised by a devotion to D'Annunzio, which they in turn transmitted to their children. In his translations, Abate aimed to produce editions suitable for global Spanish readers interested in D'Annunzio's lyrical work. D'Annunzio, he notes, is one of the least-translated poets into Spanish among the great European authors of the late-nineteenth century. While Baudelaire, Rimbaud or Wilde are available in current editions, versions of D'Annunzio's poetry are extremely rare. Only the translation by Julio Gómez de la Serna, published by the Aguilar publishing house in 1967, can in Abate's view be considered 'a global project', but it is rarely found on the market.

As a translator, Abate tried to remain as close as possible to the Italian original. He had in mind an academic reader, and this allowed him to forego simplification and to focus on respecting the semantics of the text, as shaped by the cultural and aesthetic contexts in which it was composed. His is at once a global project and a very local one, relying on the Spanish spoken in Argentina and, more specifically, around the Río de la Plata basin. He opted for the second person singular, the form of 'tu', which preserves a lyrical tone, and avoided 'vos', which would have conveyed a colloquial tone alien to the original. In spite of this, whenever possible, he suppressed the form 'vosotros' for the second person plural, practically in disuse in the Spanish spoken in Río de la Plata, and replaced it with the more frequent 'ustedes', because he felt it did not alter the tone of the original. To render sophisticated literary terms, he made use of two instruments: the Latin dictionary, which enabled him to reconstruct in Spanish the etymological meanings conjured by D'Annunzio's terms, and the poetry of the Modernist poet Rubén Darío, which, by virtue of philological closeness and Darío's cultural relationship with the Italian poet, offered precise words in Spanish to connote a similar expressive and poetic atmosphere. The outcome of these efforts has been the incorporation of his translations into Italian literature programmes at universities in Argentina, which previously did not include D'Annunzio.

Abate chose not to comment on D'Annunzio's treatment/portrayal of women, and he notes that the poems he translated do not speak to D'Annunzio's compromise with Fascism, although there is evidence of his affiliation to nationalist discourses in the texts. His stance is that even the most controversial forms of speech should be translated as accurately as possible and placed, with the help of a critical apparatus, into the context in which they were written. D'Annunzio's values, he notes, are likely to feel far-removed from the preferences of contemporary readers. However, he maintains that 'he was one of the exponents of the values and aesthetic categories prevailing at the time, together with authors like Arthur Rimbaud, Paul Verlaine, Oscar Wilde, Max Beerbohm', and his poetry, loaded with powerful and very current expressive resources, remains of the greatest relevance: 'In short, the world that D'Annunzio speaks of is no longer the current one. But his way of saying it, his sensitivity can continue to be very attractive for contemporary readers.'

Translations into Russian, as Natalia Stavrovskaia notes, are yet another complex case. Up until the 1990s, D'Annunzio's works were available in Russian primarily in a historical 12-volume series issued by Shipovnik (Saint Petersburg, 1909–1910) and in another 12-volume series by V. M. Sablin (Moscow, 1910–1912). In the 1990s, publishers hurried to put new translations on the market, especially of books which for ideological reasons had been inaccessible to readers during the Soviet period. These new publications aimed to fill gaps in the market without targeting a precise readership, and were frequently put together in haste. In 1994, Vadim Polev, a scholar of Italian literature, attempted to edit a more carefully assembled edition of D'Annunzio's works for Progress-Bestseller, but failed to come to an agreement with the publisher. Stavrovskaia was thus asked to complete this task. The only text she had previously translated by D'Annunzio was the novella *La Leda senza cigno* (1916), published in the journal *Inostrannaia Literatura* in 1994. However, the publisher knew of her from her translations of Leonardo Sciascia and trusted her. The collection *La Leda senza cigno* that she edited for Progress-Bestseller (1995) included: a revised version of the 1912 translation of *L'Innocente* by Nikolaï Bronstein – chosen because Stavrovskaia thought it would resonate with readers familiar with the film adaptation by Luchino Visconti; her own translation of *La Leda*; *Tre parabole del bellissimo nemico*; seven stories from *Le novelle della Pescara*, which she assigned to Irina Zaslavskaia and Elena Molochkovskaia; and *La pioggia nel pineto* in a recent translation by Andreï Yevdokimov.

In her own translation of *La Leda senza cigno*, Stavrovskaia used footnotes for erudite references and did her best to reproduce D'Annunzio's erudite style. In her answers to our questions, she comments that she found the work challenging 'above all because D'Annunzio's identity in many senses was quite the opposite of mine' and because 'it is always hard to swallow lauds of the immoralism of an unfettered individual, an overman'. However, she adds that the text she had chosen to translate didn't pose ideological problems.

Today, she writes, D'Annunzio's work continues to be issued in Russia in dated translations. In 2010, for instance, the publisher Knizhny Klub – Knigovek issued a six-volume set that reproduced unedited versions of early-twentieth-century translations. In Stavrovskaia's view, D'Annunzio is 'more lively, emphatic, vital' than other European Decadent writers, but she also notes that his status remains niche. Not unlike Raffaelli, she comments that 'in times of globalization, with the world turning faster and faster, D'Annunzio's best works, with their melodiousness, verbal niceties, their modulations of sentiments and senses, their exotic preciousness, may act as shocking therapy'.

A dialogue with Assumpta Camps, professor of Italian philology at the University of Barcelona, and like Abate, a contributor to this volume, enabled us to consider the case of translation into Catalan. During Franco's dictatorship (1939–1975), Catalan was forbidden in schools, and Catalan institutions were repressed. Only in 1978 did Catalan become an official language of the State. In the same year, Camps was invited by the publisher of Edicions 62 to translate *Il Piacere* and write a preface to the text. Hers was the first translation into Catalan of a novel that, as her chapter in this volume shows, had been incredibly influential in Catalonia, but that had always been read in Italian or in Castilian. It was published in a collection of classics, and, in Camps's words, was 'a real hit'. As Itamar Even-Zohar has argued, translations play a crucial role when a work of literature is at an important point in its development;[5] the translation of a text considered a European 'classic', in such cases, makes a language capable of engaging in cosmopolitan debates.[6] In this light, the translation of *Il Piacere*, which had inspired linguistic innovations and a burgeoning sense on nationalism in Catalan Modernists, continued to have an important political function in the late 1970s. Despite this, Camps notes that, in today's Catalonia, D'Annunzio is read only in intellectual and academic circles. His association with Fascism was a major factor in D'Annunzio's loss of status after the First World War, and it continues to influence the way his writings are received in Catalonia now. As for D'Annunzio's portrayal of women, she notes that this aspect was not raised with the publisher at the time in which

[5] Itamar Even-Zohar, 'The Position of Translated Literature within the Literary Polysystem', *Poetics Today* 11: 1 (1990): 45–51 (p. 47).

[6] On this subject, see Elisa Segnini, 'Global Masterpieces and Italian Dialects: Shakespeare in Neapolitan and Vicentino', *Journal of World Literature* 2 (2017): 236–54.

she worked on the translation. 'I believe', Camps writes, 'that to alter this characteristic, which D'Annunzio shares with many *fin-de-siècle* authors, would have been detrimental to his introduction in the Catalan context.'

Conversations with other translators offered the opportunity to consider the dynamics of translating D'Annunzio beyond European languages. Naglaa Waly, currently Professor of Arabic at the University of Turin, translated the *Novelle della Pescara* in 2000, and two famous poems from *Alcyone*, 'La pioggia nel pineto' and 'I pastori' in 2020. To render D'Annunzio's precious language and sophisticated style, she used classical Arabic, and, like Raffaelli and Stavrovskaia, she made use of footnotes to explain erudite references. D'Annunzio, Waly comments, is little-known today in the Arabic world, familiar only to readers interested in European classics. Her translations, by adding to the material available in Arabic, have thus paved the way for his introduction in courses on *fin-de-siècle* literature. In contrast with what Hussein Mahmoud and Christine Samir Girgis argue in their chapter, Waly does not think that D'Annunzio is a particularly controversial author today among readers of Arabic. That said, she did specify that she would not be willing to translate writing that celebrates Italy's expansionist politics. In her opinion, women characters in D'Annunzio's works reflect the Decadents' conception of woman as volitional and sensual, but this is not misogynistic per se: 'Although he depicts women as creatures in whom the senses prevail, he confirms their right to sexual pleasure.' Waly believes that D'Annunzio can still speak to a general reader today, as his writing deals with themes such as love, revenge, betrayal, murder and hatred, which are universal.

The Japanese reception, interestingly, offers some parallels with the context of reception in Catalonia. In Japan, too, D'Annunzio was extremely popular until the 1930s, disappeared from sight after the Second World War and became a controversial object of study in the 1970s. Mariko Muramatsu, a professor at the University of Tokyo and a contributor to this volume, translated several poems for the small anthology *D'Annunzio ni muchū datta koro* (*Studies on Gabriele D'Annunzio Today*, Tokyo, 2015).[7] This translation complemented an exhibition on D'Annunzio's works and life (Tokyo–Kyoto 2013–2014), which included objects on loan from the Vittoriale alongside D'Annunzio's texts. Her aim was to enable

[7] cfr. https://www.u-tokyo.ac.jp/biblioplaza/en/B_00166.html

visitors of the exhibition to read these works in Japanese. As the essays in this volume have shown, there was significant enthusiasm for D'Annunzio in Japan during the period leading up to the Second World War, when, in Muramatsu's words, D'Annunzio was 'widely read and translated, almost more than Dante himself'. This can be at least partially attributed to the notoriety of the literary figures who translated him: Ikuta Choko's 1913 translation of *Trionfo della morte*, for example, became a bestseller. However, after the war, discussing D'Annunzio became fraught or taboo, and scholars from the post-war era have often shied away from his texts for fear of being associated with Fascism or the far right. Today, D'Annunzio is not widely read by right-wing militants or Fascists in Japan, and so that association no longer holds. Tellingly, the whole series of D'Annunzio's early novels, the *Romanzi della Rosa*, have found renewed circulation in the twenty-first century, translated by Isao Waki and published by Shoreisha in Kyoto: *Il Piacere* (2007), *L'Innocente* (2008) and *Trionfo della morte* (2010). A translation of *L'Innocente* by Waki had been previously published in 1979, to coincide with the release of Luchino Visconti's film adaptation of the story. Visconti is very well-liked in Japan, and as in the Russian context, his film became an ambassador for the novel that inspired it.

In response to our query about issues of gender and politics in his writing, Muramatsu stated that neither problematic portraits of women nor nationalist elements of D'Annunzio's work should be altered in translation. Accurate contextualisation, she suggests, should be provided by a critical apparatus, but 'his verse should be free'. For Muramatsu, D'Annunzio's writings are not inferior to those of Verlaine, Huysmans, Wilde or other more widely known poets writing in English or French, and the value of studying D'Annunzio today is to be found in his eloquence in relation to media and society. His ability as a translator, she adds, is also increasingly coming to the fore.

While we reached out to Emei Shen, whose translation of *L'Innocente* in Chinese was published in 2004 (无辜者, Nanjing: Yilin Press) and recently reissued in 2020 (Shanghai: Shanghai Translation Publishing House), we have unfortunately been unable to include an interview with her, as she was very ill as we were working on this volume. No doubt there is a story to be told about the reception of D'Annunzio in China and what it means to translate his work in a Communist country, and into one of the largest languages in the world, but that will be a story for future research. Likewise, there are many languages that we have not been able to include here.

Nevertheless, the comments we were able to gather indicate that approaches to translating D'Annunzio are diverse, shaped by individual circumstances – Bassnett's formation as a feminist, Abate's family heritage – but also by what Bourdieu calls 'habitus', the 'subjective but not individual system of internalised structures, schemes of perception, concentration, and action common to all members of the same group'.[8] Naturally, the reception history of D'Annunzio in specific contexts, and the status of the language into which translators are working, play an important role. Overall, the views shared by the translators we quoted do not offer a coherent, unifying narrative. While some see D'Annunzio's florid and sometimes overbearing prose style as a problem to confront, others consider it a source of great beauty that makes his writing desirable to translate in the first place. D'Annunzio's encyclopaedic knowledge is seen both as an impediment to translation – something that, in Bassnett's words, means 'nothing to contemporary readers' – and as a valuable form of slow reading, an antidote to the rapid reading demanded by social media and digital texts – an outlook shared by Raffelli and Stavrovskaia. Some translators, like Bassnett and Raffaelli, associate D'Annunzio's nationalism with Fascism, but others, like Abate and Camps, see nationalism as a feature shared by many Decadent authors, and still others, like Gallot, suggest that it is not necessarily negative to be a nationalist. Finally, while some, like Bassnett, are vehement in their condemnation of D'Annunzio's misogyny, others, like Gallot, insist that he was in fact not a misogynist at all. It is interesting to see how varied and complex the picture of D'Annunzio is even among those who have, arguably, devoted some of the most intense and careful attention to his work – after all, there is no closer reading of a text than that required to produce a translation.

There are, of course, many open questions left to consider. That of whether feminist translation theory could inform strategies for translating D'Annunzio seems to us of particular relevance. Several of the translators who engaged with our questions share feminist views but expressed concern that a highly interventionist translation would lead to a misunderstanding of the text and lessen its value documenting the outlook of an artistic movement, and, more broadly, of an epoch. Prefaces have improved the status of translators (especially women translators) by making their agency visible, and footnotes –

[8] Pierre Bourdieu, *Outline of a Theory of Practice*, vol 16. (Cambridge: Cambridge University Press, 1977), p. 86.

a practice despised by D'Annunzio himself – have given them an opportunity to supplement the text. Several of the translators we interviewed admitted to 'mitigating' aspects that made them feel uncomfortable (whether this concerned the portrayal of women or Jews, for instance), but overall, the translators' preoccupation with historical accuracy prevailed. A reinterpretation of D'Annunzio's texts from a feminist perspective, which made a productive use of all the strategies that Luise Von Flotow lists as strengthening women's subjectivity (supplementing, prefacing, footnotes and hijacking, that is, correcting the sexist language of the source text),[9] is, to our knowledge, yet to be produced. Endeavours like these would lead to yet new ways of reading D'Annunzio. But this is a question for the future, and one that may open up new avenues for research as the global reception of D'Annunzio continues to unfold with new translations, adaptations and responses.

[9] Luise Von Flotow, 'Feminist Translation: Contexts, Practices and Theories', *TTR*, 4: 2 (1991): 69–84. http://search.proquest.com/docview/85564252/

Bibliography

Editors' Note: In this Bibliography, the entries for works by D'Annunzio follow special formatting to make it easier to locate multiple versions or translations of D'Annunzio's texts. Subsequent versions of a text are indented following the entry for the original version, allowing readers to quickly see the multiple editions of a text to which reference is made in the volume. All other entries follow standard formatting practices.

Abate, Sandro, 'Poesia y colonialismo: *Maia* de Gabriele D'Annunzio', *Cuadernos de Filología Italiana*, 16 (2009), 187–200.

Akutagawa, Ryūnosuke, 'Nagai Daisuke', in *Akutagawa Ryūnosuke zenshū* (The Complete Works of Ryūnosuke Akutagawa), vol. 7 (Tokyo: Iwanami Shoten, 1996), pp. 255–6.

Alatri, Paolo, *D'Annunzio* (Turin: UTET, 1983).

Aleksandrov, Aleksandr, 'K istorii podgotovki perevoda tragedii "Francesca da Rimini" Gabriele D'Annunzio Viach. Ivanovym i V. Briusovym', *Filologicheskie nauki*, 6 (2016), 53–60.

Alekseeva, Tatiana, 'Poet i smert'. O knige Eleny Shvarts "Krylatyi tsiklop"', *Russkaia kul'tura*, 12 May 2018.

Altenberg, Peter, *Nachfechsung* (Berlin: Samuel Fischer Verlag, 1916).

Ambrosi, Carrión, *Comte Arnau: Tragèdia en dues parts*, 2 vols (Barcelona: Publicacions de l'Abadia de Montserrat, 1972).

—— *Tribut al mar: Tragèdia: un acte* (Barcelona: Estampa de Manel Tasis, 1911).

Anceschi, Luciano, 'D'Annunzio e il sistema della analogia', in *D'Annunzio e il simbolismo europeo. Atti del convegno di studio, Gardone Riviera, 14–15–16 settembre 1973*, ed. by Emilio Mariano (Milan: Il saggiatore, 1976), pp. 63–110.

Andreoli, Annamaria, *D'Annunzio archivista. Le filologie di uno scrittore* (Florence: Olschki, 1996).

—— *Il vivere inimitabile. Vita di Gabriele D'Annunzio* (Milan: Mondadori, 2000).

—— ed., *The Vittoriale degli Italiani* (Milan: Skira, 2004).

—— 'Notizia sul testo e note di commento', in Gabriele D'Annunzio, *La Pisanelle* (Milan: Mondadori, 2014), Format PUB2 con Adobe DRM <https://www.amazon.it/Pisanelle-Meridiani-Mondadori-Gabriele-dAnnunzio-ebook/dp/B00IGJJQNO> [accessed 21 November 2022].

—— *Più che l'amore: Eleonora Duse e Gabriele D'Annunzio* (Venice: Marsilio, 2017).

Andres, Stefan, 'Die Tode eines Ungeliebten. Eine Annäherung an Gabriele D'Annunzio, den Johannes der Täufer des Faschismus', *Kritische Ausgabe*, 2 (2004), 19–23.

Angioletti, Katia Lara, '"Quando io venni in Italia, vinsi perché ero solo": Mario Fumagalli attore, capocomico, innovatore', *ACME. Annali della Facoltà di Lettere e Filosofia dell'Università degli Studi di Milano*, 64: 3 (2011), 117–36.

[Anon.], '"And yet – he is a Master"', *The Academy* (2 June 1900), 464–6.

[Anon.], 'Book Reviews Reviewed', *The Academy* (12 February 1898), 184–5.

[Anon.], 'D'Annunzio in English', *The Academy* (5 February 1898), 141–2.

[Anon.], 'The Stage Society: *The Dead City*', *The Stage* (28 February 1918).

[Anon.], 'Il successo della "Ville Morte" a Parigi', *Il Marzocco* (23 January 1898).

Anpilov, Andrei, 'Grozovaia zvezda. Na poliakh knigi Eleny Shvarts "Krylatyi tsiklop"', *Novaia Kamera Khraneniia*, 15 July 2010 <http://www.newkamera.de/ostihah/anpilov_07.html> [accessed 21 November 2022].

'Appendice alla memoria nella causa per "Il figlio di Iorio" contro Eduardo Scarpetta', submitted 24 April 1908, State Archive of Naples.

Apter, Emily, *The Translation Zone: A New Comparative Literature* (Princeton, NJ: Princeton University Press, 2011).

Argenteri, Letizia, 'La presenza di D'Annunzio in America', in *L'Italia e la 'Grande Vigilia': Gabriele D'Annunzio nella politica italiana prima del fascismo*, ed. by Romain H. Rainero and Stefano B. Galli (Milan: Franco Angeli, 2007), pp. 293–302.

Ascarelli, Roberta, 'Hugo von Hofmannsthals "Gabriele D'Annunzio" in der Übersetzung von Gabriele D'Annunzio', *Hofmansthals Jahrbuch zur Europäischen Moderne*, 3 (1995), 169–213.

Atherton, Gertrude, 'Mrs. Atherton on D'Annunzio. The Bookman', *NYT*, 30 January 1904.

Avino, Maria, *L'Occidente nella cultura araba*, vol. 18 (Milan: Jouvence, 2002).

Babbit, Edwin D., *The Principles of Light and Color* (New York: Babbit & Co., 1878).

Bärtås, Magnus and Fredrik Ekman, *Bebådaren: Gabriele D'Annunzio och fascismens födelse* (Stockholm: Albert Bonniers, 2017).

Baeza, Ricardo, 'Gabriel D'Annunzio y *La hija de Iorio*', *Cervantes*, 4 (1916), 7–14.

Bahr, Hermann, *Studien zur Kritik der Moderne* (Weimar: VDG Weimar, 2006).

Ballinger, Pamela, *History in Exile: Memory and Identity at the Borders of the Balkans* (Princeton, NJ: Princeton University Press, 2003).

Balmas, Enea, 'L'amicizia fra Gabriele D'Annunzio e il suo traduttore André Doderet', *Quaderni dannunziani,* XXII–XXIII (1962), 1112–19.

Balme, Christopher, 'Die Marke Reinhardt: Theater als moderne Wirtschaftsunternehmen', in *Max Reinhardt und das deutsche Theater*, ed. by Roland Koberg, Bernd Stegemann and Henrike Thomsen (Berlin: Henschel, 2005), pp. 41–9.

Barberi Squarotti, Giorgio, 'Il Parato di Carta', in *Il Piacere: atti del XII Convegno: Pescara-Francavilla al Mare, 4–5 maggio 1989*, ed. by Edoardo Tiboni and Umberto Russo (Pescara: Centro nazionale di studi dannunziani, 1989), 15–36.

Barbot, Michela, 'Luxardo, Giorgio', *Dizionario bibliografico degli italiani*, vol. 66 (Rome: Società Grafica Romana, 2006), p. 695.

Barrès, Maurice, *Le Culte du Moi*, trilogy of novels 1888–91 (Paris: Plon, 1904).

Bassnett, Susan, 'Translating Gabriele D'Annunzio for the Twenty-first Century Reader', 6 March 2020, on *Decadence and Translation Network* <https://dandtnetwork.glasgow.ac.uk/translating-gabriele-dannunzio-for-the-twenty-first-century-reader/> [accessed 21 November 2022].

Bastianich, Lidia and Jay Jacobs, *La Cucina di Lidia: Distinctive Regional Cuisine from the North of Italy* (New York: Doubleday, 1990).

—— *My American Dream: A Life of Love, Family, and Food* (New York: Knopf, 2018).

Batlle, Carles, 'El teatre d'Ambrosi Carrión' (Thesis, supervised by J. Castellanos, Universidad Autónoma de Barcelona, 1988).

Baudelaire, Charles, *The Painter of Modern Life and Other Essays*, trans. and ed. by Jonathan Mayne (London: Phaidon, 1964).

Becker, Jared M., *Nationalism and Culture: Gabriele D'Annunzio and Italy after the Risorgimento* (New York: Peter Lang, 1994).

Beebee, Thomas O., *Transmesis: Inside Translation's Black Box* (New York: Palgrave Macmillan, 2012).

Benda, Julien, *La Trahison des Clercs* (*The Betrayal by the Intellectuals*), trans. by Richard Aldington (Boston, MA: Beacon Press, 1955).

Benjamin, Walter, *Gesammelte Schriften: Supplement I. Kleinere Übersetzungen*, ed. by Rolf Tiedemann (Frankfurt am Main: Suhrkamp, 1999).

—— 'The Work of Art in the Age of Its Technological Reproducibility. Second Version', in *The Work of Art in the Age of Its Technological*

Reproducibility, and Other Writings on Media, ed. by Michael W. Jennings, Brigid Doherty and Thomas Y. Levin, trans. by. Edmund Jephcott, Rodney Livingstone and Howard Eiland (Cambridge, MA: Harvard University Press, 2008), pp. 19–55.

Benois, Alexandr, *Dnevnik: 1918–1924*, ed. by Ivan Vydrin (Moscow: Zakharov, 2016).

Berman, Antoine, *La traduction et la lettre ou l'auberge du lointain* (Paris: Le Seuil, 1999).

Bertelli, Carlo F., 5 November 1922, Fondazione Vittoriale, Archives, Gardone Riviera XLII, 1, 5.

Berthold, Margot, ed., *Cabiria. Ein Film von Giovanni Pastrone. Entstehung Geschichte Wirkung Materialien* (Munich: Münchener Filmzentrum, 1979).

Bettiza, Enzo, *Il fantasma di Trieste* (Milan: Longanesi, 1958).

Bielsa, Esperança, 'Cosmopolitanism as Translation', *Cultural Sociology*, 8: 4 (2014), 392– 406.

Binding, Rudolf G., *Erlebtes Leben*, in *Gesammeltes Werk*, vol. 2 (Hamburg: Dulk, 1954), pp. 396–7.

Birk, Matjaž and Thomas Eicher, eds, *Stefan Zweig und das Dämonische* (Würzburg: Königshausen & Neumann, 2008).

Bizzotto, Elisa and Stefano Evangelista, eds, *Arthur Symons: Poet, Critic, Vagabond* (Cambridge, UK: Legenda, 2018).

Blei, Franz, *Das große Bestiarium der modernen Literatur*, ed. by Rolf-Peter Baacke (Hamburg: Europäische Verlagsanstalt, 1995).

Blok, Aleksandr, *Sobranie sochinenii v vos'mi tomakh*, vol. 8, *Pis'ma*, ed. by Vladimir Orlov and others (Moscow–Leningrad: Gosudarstvennoe izdatel'stvo Khudozhestvennoi literatury, 1963).

—— *Dnevnik Al. Bloka: 1880–1921*, ed. by Pavel Medvedev (Leningrad: Izdstel'stvo pisatelei v Leningrade, 1928).

Blum, Léon, '*Le Martyre de Saint Sébastien*', in *Au théâtre, réflexions critiques*, vol. 4 (Paris: Ollendorff, 1911), pp. 247–57.

Bogomolov, Nikolai, *Mikhail Kuzmin: stat i materialy* (Moscow: Novoe literaturnoe obozrenie, 1995).

Bogomolov, Nikolai and John Malmstad, *Mikhail Kuzmin: iskusstvo, zhizn, epokha* (St Petersburg: Vita Nova, 2007).

Borgese, Giuseppe Antonio, 'Grasso allo zenit', *Corriere della Sera*, 19 October 1930; republished in Alfredo Barbina, *La mantellina di Santuzza. Teatro siciliano tra Ottocento e Novecento* (Rome: Bulzoni, 1983), pp. 129–30.

—— 'Con D'Annunzio a quei tempi', in Giuseppe Antonio Borgese, *Da Dante a Thomas Mann*, ed. by Giulio Vallese (Verona: Mondadori, 1958), pp. 282–9.

Borgoño, Ariela, 'Revista *Idea latina*: una mirada a la traducción cultural en los espacios de la diversidad', *Transfer*, 2 (2010), 47–61.

Bourdieu, Pierre, *Outline of a Theory of Practice*, vol. 16. (Cambridge, UK: Cambridge University Press, 1977).

Braccesi, Lorenzo, *L'antichità aggredita: Memoria del passato e poesia del nazionalismo* (Rome: L'Erma di Bretschneider, 1989).

Bracewell, Catherine W., 'Uskoks in Venetian Dalmatia before the Venetian-Ottoman War of 1714–1718', in *East-Central European Society and War in the Pre-Revolutionary Eighteenth Century*, ed. by Gunther Rothenberg, Béla Kiraly and Peter F. Sugar (Boulder, CO, and New York: Social Science Monographs and Columbia University Press, 1982), pp. 431–47.

Brecht, Bertolt, *Arbeitsjourna I*, vol. I: 1928–1942, ed. by Werner Hecht (Frankfurt am Main: Suhrkamp, 1973).

—— *Arbeitsjournal II*, vol. II: 1942–1955, ed. by Werner Hecht (Frankfurt am Main: Suhrkamp, 1973).

—— 'Regen in Pinienhain', in *Gedichte aus dem Nachlass. Gesammelte Werke in 8 Bänden*, ed. by Herta Ramthun (Frankfurt am Main: Suhrkamp, 1982).

—— 'Regen im Pinienhain', in *Gesammelte Werke in 20 Bänden, Gedichte aus den Nachlaß 2, Supplementband IV* (Frankfurt am Main: Suhrkamp, 1982).

—— 'Journale 2', in *Werke: große kommentierte Berliner und Frankfurter Ausgabe*, vol. 27 (Berlin: Aufbau Verlag, 1995).

Brittnacher, Hans Richard, '"Der Rhythmus hat immer recht": D'Annunzio verhängt den Ausnahmezustand in Fiume', in *Europa neu denken II. Mentalitätsgeschichte der Adria – Neugierde und Konflikt als Betriebsgeheimnis*, ed. by Michael Fischer and Johannes Hahn (Salzburg: Verlag Anton Pustet, 2015), pp. 47–58.

Buohler, Hans Peter, ed., 'Briefwechsel zwischen Karl Gustav Vollmoeller und Hugo von Hofmannsthal', *Hofmannsthal Jahrbuch zur europäischen Moderne*, 18 (2010), 105–37.

Bystrova, Tatiana, 'Gabriele D'Annunzio v russkoi kul'ture', in *Dialog kul'tur. Kul'tura dialoga*, ed. by Elena Tareva and Larisa Vokulova (Moscow: Yazyki narodov mira, 2016), pp. 83–7.

Caliaro, Ilvano, *D'Annunzio lettore-scrittore* (Florence: Olschki, 1991).

Canovi, Raffaella, *D'Annunzio e il fascismo. Eutanasia di un'icona* (Rome: Bibliotheka Edizioni, 2019).

Cappellini, Milva Maria, 'Introduzione', in Gabriele D'Annunzio, *La Città Morta*, ed. by Milva Maria Cappellini (Milan: Mondadori, 1956), pp. V–xxxiv.

Carducci, Giosuè, *Odi barbare* (Bologna: Zanichelli, 1877).

Caronia, Sabino, 'Gabriele D'Annunzio: "Torna con me nell'Ellade scolpita"', in *Il mito nella letteratura italiana*, III: *Dal neoclassicismo al decadentismo*, ed. by Raffaella Bertazzoli (Brescia: Morcelliana, 2003), pp. 293–332.

Carroll, Harvey B., June 1918, Vittoriale Archives, XL, 4.

—— July 1918, Vittoriale Archives, 4, 2. See also Carl A. Swanson, 'D'Annunzio's Ode all'America in armi (IV luglio MCMXVIII)', *Italica*, 3 (1953), 135–-43 (p. 140).

—— 2 July 1918, Vittoriale Archives, 4.

Casanova, Pascale, *The World Republic of Letters*, trans. by M. B. DeBevoise (Cambridge, MA: Harvard University Press, 2004).

—— *La République mondiale des Lettres* (Paris: Le Seuil, 2008).

Catullo, *Le poesie*, ed. by Guido Ceronetti (Turin: Einaudi, 1969).

Chekalov, K. A., 'D'Annunzio na russkoi stsene: rubezh dvukh stoletii', *Novye rossiiskie gumanitarnye issledovaniia*, 3 (2008): <http://www.nrgumis.ru/articles/archives/full_art.php?aid=76&binn_rubrik_pl_articles=277> [accessed 30 October 2021].

Chisholm, Hugh, ed., 'Annunzio, Gabriele D''. *Encyclopaedia Britannica*. 2. Eleventh Edition (Cambridge, UK: Cambridge University Press, 1910–11).

Chomel, Luisetta Elia, *D'Annunzio: un teatro al femminile* (Ravenna: Longo, 1997).

Ciano, Annalisa, 'Oltre i confini del tempo e dello spazio: un'analisi comparativa sulla traduzione e ricezione della *Phaedre* di D'Annunzio in Francia', *Novecento Transnazionale. Letterature, Arti e Culture*, 5: 2 (2021), 169–88.

Cimini, Mario, ed., *Carteggio D'Annunzio-Hérelle (1891–1931)* (Lanciano: Rocco Carabba, 2004).

—— ed., *D'Annunzio, Boggiani, Hérelle, Scarfoglio: viaggio in Grecia et Italia meridionale (1895)* (Venice: Marsilio, 2010).

Coletti, Fernando, 'Nascita del D'Annunzio francese I: *Sonnets cisalpins*', in *Annali della Facoltà di Lingue e Letterature Straniere di Ca' Foscari*, vol. 3 (Milan: U Mursia & Co., 1964), pp. 81–95.

Colucci, Michele, 'Baltrušajtis e D'Annunzio', in *D'Annunzio nelle culture dei paesi slavi*, ed. by Giuseppe Dell'Agata, Cesare G. De Michelis and Pietro Marchesani (Venice: Marsilio, 1979), pp. 40–50.

Conti, Angelo, 'La Città Morta', in *Il Marzocco* (Florence, 23 January 1898).

Contini, Gianfranco, 'Vita macaronica del francese dannunziano' [1937], in *Esercizi di lettura* (Turin: Einaudi, 1974), pp. 274–85.

Corradini, Enrico, 'Marginalia: "La figlia di Iorio" in siciliano', in *Il Marzocco* (Florence, 9 October 1904).

Coseriu, Eugenio, *Linguistica del testo* (Rome: Carocci, 1997).

Coste, Bénédicte, 'Arthur Symons the Translator: Translation, Remediation, Recognition', *Parallèles*, 33: 2 (2021), 1–17.

Crawford, Virginia M., 'Gabriele D'Annunzio', *Cosmopolis*, 11 (August 1898), 384–98.

Creasy, Matthew, '"The Neglected, the Unutterable Verlaine": Arthur Symons, the *Saturday Review*, and French Literature in the 1890s', *Victorian Periodicals Review*, 52: 1 (2019), 103–23.

Crémieux, Benjamin, 'Les Livres. Stefan Zweig: «Tolstoi» — John dos Passos: «Manhattan Transfer»', *Les Annales politiques et littéraires*, 1 October 1928, pp. 305–6.

Cummins, Anthony, 'Émile Zola's Cheap English Dress: The Vizetelly Translations, Late-Victorian Print Culture, and the Crisis of Literary Value', *Review of English Studies*, 60 (2009), 108–32.

Curreri, Luciano, ed., *D'Annunzio come personaggio nell'immaginario italiano ed europeo (1938–2008): una mappa* (Peter Lang, 2008).

Curreri, Luciano, 'Lettere, "lavoro comune" e traduzione. Appunti e ipotesi su D'Annunzio e i traduttori francesi', in *Silenzi, Solitudini, Segreti. Altre metamorfosi dannunziane* (Arcireale, Rome: Bonanno Editore, 2011).

D'Ambra, Lucio, 'Le Théâtre. À propos de la nouvelle édition de "La figlia di Iorio"', *L'Italie* (Rome), 16 September 1904.

'Dalmatia', *Encyclopedia Britannica*, 11th ed., vol. 7 (1910).

Damrosch, David, *What is World Literature?* (Princeton, NJ: Princeton University Press, 2003).

—— 'Frames for World Literature', in *Tensions in World Literature: Between the Local and the Universal*, ed. by Weigui Fang (Singapore: Springer, 2018), pp. 93–102.

D'Angelo, Laura, 'Music and Soul: Gabriele D'Annunzio and his Abruzzo Homeland', Bridge Across Cultures Proceedings, Vasto, 11–13 June, 2017.

Dangel-Pelloquin, Elsbeth, '"Mondaine Stimmungsakrobaten": Bahrs und Hofmannsthals Kreation der Moderne am Beispiel von Eleonora Duse und Isadora Duncan', in *Hermann Bahr: Österreichischer Kritiker europäischer Avantgarden*, ed. by Martin Anton Müller, Claus Pias and Gottfried Schnödl, Jahrbuch für Internationale Germanistik 118 (Frankfurt am Main: Peter Lang, 2014), pp. 55–82.

D'Annunzio, Gabriele, *Primo vere* [1879] (Chieti: Tipografia G. Ricci, 1879).

—— *Primo vere; Canto novo; Intermezzo*, ed. by Enzo Palmieri (Bologna: Zanichelli, 1953).

—— *Il Piacere* (Milan: Fratelli Treves, 1889).

—— *Child of Pleasure* [Il Piacere], trans. by Georgina Harding and verse trans. by Arthur Symons (London: Heinemann, 1898).

—— *El Placer* [Il Piacere], trans.by Emilio Reverter Delmos (Barcelona: Maucci, 1900).

—— *L'Enfant de volupté* [Il Piacere], trans. by Georges Hérelle, completed and rearranged in the original order by Pierre de Montera (Paris, Calmann-Lévy, 1971).

—— *Il Piacere*, critical edition with an introduction by Ivanos Ciani (Milan: Il Saggiatore, 1976).

—— *Il Piacere*, in *Prose di Romanzi*, ed. by Annamaria Andreoli and Ezio Raimondi (Milan: Mondadori, 1988), pp. 1105–49.

—— *Il Piacere*, ed. by Giansiro Ferrata (Milan: Mondadori, 1989).

—— *Il Piacere*, in *Prose di Romanzi*, ed. by Annamaria Andreoli and Niva Lorenzini (Milan: Mondadori, 2005).
—— *Kairaku* [Il Piacere], trans. by Isao Waki (Kyoto: Shōraisha, 2007).
—— *Naslazhdenie* [Il Piacere], trans. by Jurgis Baltrušaitis (St Petersburg: Azbuka, 2011).
—— *Pleasure* [Il Piacere], trans. by Lara Gochin Raffaelli (New York: Penguin Books, 2013).
—— *L'Isottèo, Chimera* (Milan: Treves, 1890).
—— *Elegie romane (1887–91)* (Bologna: Zanichelli, 1892).
—— *L'Innocente* (Naples: Bideri, 1892).
—— *L'intrus* [L'Innocente], trans. by Georges Hérelles (Paris: Calmann Lévy, 1893).
—— *The Intruder* [L'Innocente], trans. by Arthur Hornblow (New York: G. H. Richmond & Co., 1898).
—— *El inocente* [L'Innocente], trans. by Augusto Riera (Barcelona: Maucci, 1900).
—— *L'innocent* [L'Innocente], trans. by Georges Hérelles (Paris: La Table Ronde, 1994).
—— 无辜者 [L'Innocente], trans. by Emei Shen (Nanjing: Yilin Press, 2004).
—— *Tsumi naki mono* [L'Innocente], trans. by Isao Waki (Kyoto: Shōraisha, 2008).
—— *Nevinnyi* [L'Innocente], trans. By Olga Khimona (St Petersburg: Azbuka, 2012).
—— *Trionfo della morte* (Milan: Treves, 1894).
—— *The Triumph of Death* [Trionfo della morte], trans. by Arthur Hornblow (New York: George H. Richmond & Co., 1897).
—— *El Triunfo de la muerte* [Trionfo della morte], trans. by Tomás Orts-Ramos (Barcelona: Maucci, 1900).
—— *Shi no shōri* [Trionfo della morte], trans. by Isao Waki (Kyoto: Shōraisha, 2010).
—— *Episcopo et Cie* [Giovanni Episcopo, 1892], trans. by Georges Hérelles (Paris: Calmann-Lévy, 1895).
—— *Le vergini delle rocce* (Milan: Treves, 1896).
—— *The Maidens of the Rocks* [Le vergini delle rocce], trans. by Annetta Halliday-Antona (New York: G. H. Richmond & Co., 1898).
—— *La città morta* (Milan: Treves, 1898).
—— *The Dead City* [La città morta], trans. by Arthur Symons (London: Heinemann, 1900).
—— *Poema paradisiaco – Odi navali, 1891–3* (Milan: Treves, 1899).
—— *Il fuoco* (Milan: Treves, 1900).
—— *El fuego* [Il fuoco], trans. by Tomás Orts-Ramos (Barcelona: Maucci, 1900).

—— *The Flame of Life* [Il fuoco], trans. by Vivaria Kassadra [pseudonym of Magda Sinici] (London: Heinemann; Boston: H. Fertig; New York: L. C. Page, 1900).

—— *The Flame* [Il fuoco], trans. by Susan Basnett (London: Quartet, 1991).

—— 'The Third Life of Italy', *North American Review*, 528 (1900), 627–52.

—— *La Gioconda* [1899], trans. by Arthur Symons (London: Heinemann, 1901).

—— *Francesca da Rimini* [1901], trans. by Arthur Symons (New York: Frederick A. Stokes Company, 1902).

—— 'Francesca da Rimini' [1901], trans. by Karl Gustav Vollmoeller, *Neue deutsche Rundschau*, 14 (1903), 1063–101.

—— *La figlia di Iorio: tragedia pastorale* (Milan: Treves, 1903).

—— *La figlia di Iorio, con a fronte la traduzione in dialetto abruzzese di Cesare de Titta*, ed. by Vittore Verratti (Pescara: Centro Nazionale di Studi Dannunziani, 1988).

—— *Laudi del cielo, del mare, della terra e degli eroi*, vol. 1 (*Maia* [1903], *Elettra* [1903], *Alcyone* [1899–1903]), (Milan: Treves, 1903–4).

—— *Alcyone* (*Laudi* Book III), trans by André Doderet, published in *Revue des deux mondes* (1938), pp. 576–81.

—— 'Laus Vitae', XV, in *Maia*, ed. by Cristina Montagnani (Gardone Riviera: Il Vittoriale degli italiani, 2006).

—— *Alcyone*, ed. by Pietro Gibellini, with commentary by Giulia Belletti, Sara Campardo and Enrica Gambin (Venice: Marsilio, 2018).

—— *La fiaccola sotto il moggio: Tragedia* (Milan: Treves, 1905).

—— *La torche sous le boisseau* [La fiaccola sotto il moggio], trans. by André Doderet (Paris: Calmann Lévy, 1928).

—— *Più che l'amore: Tragedia Moderna* (Milan: Treves, 1906)— *La nave: Tragedia* (Milan: Treves, 1908).

—— [La nave], trans. by Andrés Demarchi (Beunos Aires: *La Revista Artística de Buenos Aires*, 1909).

—— *La nef* [La nave], trans. by *André* Doderet (Radiodiffusion nationale, 19420514, 1942).

—— *Fedra: Tragedia* (Milan : Treves, 1909).

—— *Phædre* [Fedra] trans. by André *Doderet*, in *La Revue de Paris*, 5 August, 1 September, 15 September, 1 October 1924, pp. 721–55, 88–124, 299–336, 535–55.

—— *Fedra*, ed. by Pietro Gibellini, with notes by Tiziana Piras (Milan: Mondadori, 2001).

—— *Forse che sì forse che no* (Milan: Treves, 1910).

—— *La Pisanelle, ou La Mort Parfumée* (Paris: La Revue de Paris, 1911).

—— *La Pisanella* (Milan: Treves, 1914).

—— *Pisanella, ili Blagoukhannaya smert'*, trans. by Mikhail Lozinsky (Petrograd: Mysl, 1922).

—— *Le Martyre de Saint Sébastien*, with music by Claude Debussy (Paris: Calmann Lévy, 1911).
—— *Pignus ac Monumentum Amoris di Gabriele D'Annunzio al 'tenace colono latino' Giovanni Del Guzzo* [Pignus ac Monumentum Amoris by Gabriele D'Annunzio to the 'tenacious Latin settler' Giovanni del Guzzo] (L'Aquila: Unione Arti Grafiche 1911).
—— *Contemplazione della morte* (Milan: Treves, 1912).
—— *Contemplation de la mort* [Contemplazione della morte], trans. by Andre Doderet (Paris: Calmann Lévy, 1928).
—— *Laudi del cielo, del mare, della terra e degli eroi*, vol. 4 *Merope. Canzoni della gesta d'oltremare* (Milan: Treves, 1912).
—— *L'armata d'Italia* (Venice: Zanetti, 1915).
—— *La Leda senza cigno. Racconto seguito da una Licenza* (Milan: Treves, 1916).
—— *La Léda sans cygnet: récit de la lande, suivi d'un envoi à la France* [La Leda senza cigno], trans. by André Doderet (Paris: Calmann Lévy, 1921).
—— [La Leda senza cigno, 1916], trans. by Natalia Stavrovskaia, *Inostrannaia Literatura*, 1994.
—— *Leda bez lebedia* [La Leda senza cigno], trans. by Nikolai Bronshtein et al. (Moscow: Bestseller, 1995).
—— *Notturno* (Milan: Treves, 1921).
—— *Nocturne: Aspects de l'inconnu* [Notturno], trans. by André Doderet (Paris: Calmann Lévy, 1923).
—— *Noktiurn* [Notturno], trans. by Sofia Gerie, *Inostrannaia literatura*, 11 (1999).
—— 'World is Beginning Herculean Drama of Races, says D'Annunzio', *Washington Times*, 11 December 1921.
—— 'Easter Treaty Only Portends more Trouble', *Washington Times*, 30 April 1922, p. 3.
—— *Le Faville del maglio*, 2 vols. (Milan: Treves, 1924–28).
—— *Portrait du Lojse Baccaris* [Ritratto di Luisa Bàccara, 1920], trans. by André Doderet (Paris: Éditions du Sagittaire, 1925).
—— *Cento e cento e cento e cento pagine del libro segreto di Gabriele D'Annunzio tentato di morire* (Milan: Istituto nazionale per la edizione di tutte le opere di Gabriele D'Annunzio, 1935).
—— *Teneo te Africa* (Milan: Officina del Vittoriale, 1936).
—— *Le Dit du sourd et muet qui fut miraculé en l'an de grâce 1266* (Rome: Il Vittoriale degli Italiani, 1936).
—— *Solus ad solam: Journal d'un amour*, trans. by André Doderet (Paris: Édition Balzac, 1944).
—— *Asterope: Canti della guerra Latina* [1914–1918] (Bologna: Zanichelli, 1948).
—— *Obras Completas*, 3 vols., trans. by Julio Gómez de la Serna (Mexico: Aguilar 1959–1960).

—— *Carteggio D'Annunzio-Mussolini (1919–1938)*, ed. by Renzo De Felice and Emilio Mariano (Milan: Mondadori, 1971).
—— *Versi d'amore e di gloria*, 2 vols, ed. by Annamaria Andreoli and Niva Lorenzini. Introduction by Luciano Anceschi (Milan: Mondadori, 1982).
—— 'Lungo l'Africo. Nella sera di giugno dopo la pioggia', in *Versi d'amore e di gloria*, II, ed. by Annamaria Andreoli and Niva Lorenzoni (Milan: Mondadori, 2006).
—— 'Outa occidentale,' in *Versi di amore e di gloria*, I, ed. by Annamaria Andreoli and Niva Lorenzoni (Milan: Mondadori, 2006).
—— *Tutte le novelle*, ed. by Annamaria Andreoli and Marina De Marco (Milan: Mondadori, 1992).
—— *Scritti giornalistici, 1882–1888*, vol. 1, ed. by Annamaria Andreoli (Milan: Mondadori, 1996).
—— *Lettere ai Treves*, ed. by Gianni Oliva, Katia Berardi and Barbara Di Serio (Milan: Garzanti, 1999).
—— 'Die göttliche Eleonora Duse', in Walter Benjamin, *Gesammelte Schriften. Supplement I. Kleinere Übersetzungen*, ed. by Rolf Tiedemann (Frankfurt am Main: Suhrkamp, 1999), pp. 12–15.
—— 'Rech, proiznesennaia s balkona Kapitoliia 17 maia 1915 goda' (Speech from the Campidoglio balcony, 17 May 1915), trans. by Il'ya Kormiltsev, *Inostrannaia literatura*, 11 (1999).
—— 'Del cinematografo considerato come strumento di liberazione e come arte di trasfigurazione' [1914], in *D'Annunzio, Scritti giornalistici, II: 1889–1938*, ed. by Annamaria Andreoli and Giorgio Zanetti (Milan: Mondadori, 2003), pp. 668–74.
—— *Prose di ricerca*, vol. 2, ed. by Annamaria Andreoli and Giorgio Zanetti (Milan: Mondadori, 2005).
—— *Il libro segreto* [1935], ed. by Pietro Gibellini (Milan: Rizzoli, 2010).
—— *Sobranie sochinenii v shesti tomakh,* trans. by Jurgis Baltrušaitis et al. (Moscow: Knigovek, 2010).
—— *Tragedie, sogni e misteri*, vol. 2, ed. by Annamaria Andreoli and Giorgio Zanetti (Milan: Mondadori, 2013).
—— *Le Chèvrefeuille/Il ferro* [1913], ed. by Annamaria Andreoli (e-Meridiani Mondadori, 2014).
'D'Annunzio viendra-t-il?', *L'Intransigeant*, 6 December 1927, p. 1.
Darío, Rubén, *Los Raros* (Buenos Aires: Tipográfica La Vasconia, 1896).
—— 'Un esteta italiano: Gabriel D'Annunzio (no. 1)', *Revista de América*, 1 (1894).
De Amicis, Edmondo, *Cuore* (Milan: Treves, 1886).
De Felice, Renzo, *D'Annunzio politico, 1918–1938* (Bari: Laterza, 1978).
De Franchi, Nicolò Luxardo, *I Luxardo del Maraschino* (Gorizia: Libreria Editrice Goriziana, 2004).
De' Medici, Giuliano [pseudonym of Vincenzo Moretti], *Bibliografia di Gabriele D'Annunzio*, (Rome: Edizioni del centauro, 1928).

De Mendelssohn, Peter, *S. Fischer und sein Verlag* (Frankfurt am Main: S. Fischer, 1970).

De Michelis, Cesare G., 'D'Annunzio nella cultura russa', in *D'Annunzio nelle culture dei paesi slavi*, ed. by Giuseppe Dell'Agata, Cesare G. De Michelis and Pietro Marchesani (Venice: Marsilio, 1979), pp. 13–39.

—— 'D'Annunzio, la Russia, l'Unione sovietica', *Quaderni dannunziani*, 1–2 (1987), 311–17.

—— 'D'Annunzio, la Russia, i paesi slavi', in *D'Annunzio europeo: Atti del convegno internazionale, Gardone Riviera–Perugia 8–13 maggio 1989*, ed. by Pietro Gibellini (Rome: Lucarini, 1991), pp. 317–27.

De Michelis, Eurialo, *Guida a D'Annunzio* (Turin: Meynier, 1988).

de Miomandre, Francis, 'Le voyage d'André Doderet aux Iles de la Société', *Les Nouvelles Littéraires*, 25 June 1927, pp. 1–2.

—— 'La fin d'un accident', *Les Nouvelles Littéraires*, 28 May 1932.

de Montera, Pierre, 'L'accueil de D'Annunzio en France de 1910 à 1915', in *D'Annunzio in Francia. Atti del Colloquio italo-francese (Rome, Accademia Nazionale dei Lincei, 9–10 maggio 1974)* (Rome: Accademia Nazionale dei Lincei, 1975), pp. 23–58.

de Montera, Pierre and Guy Tosi, *D'Annunzio, Montesquiou, Matilde Serao: Documents inédits* (Rome: Edizioni di Storia e Letteratura, 1972).

de Titta, Filippo, 'Un capolavoro di G. D'Annunzio', *La Fiaccola* (Ortona), 25 December 1914.

de Vogüé, Eugène-Melchior 'La Renaissance Latine : Gabriele D'Annunzio, Poèmes et romans', *Revue des deux mondes* (1 January 1895), 187–206.

de Waleffe, Maurice, 'Le métier de juré', *Paris-soir*, 4 June 1932.

Del Guzzo, Giovanni, *Pignus ac Monumentum Amoris, di Gabriele D'Annunzio al 'tenace colono latino' Giovanni Del Guzzo* (L'Aquila: Unione Arte Grafiche, 1911).

Demetz, Peter, *Die Flugschau von Brescia. Kafka, D'Annunzio und die Männer, die vom Himmel fielen* (Vienna: Zsolnay, 2002).

d'Esparbès, Asté, 'Avant "La Torche sous le boisseau": M. André Doderet nous parle de Gabriele D'Annunzio', *Comœdia*, 5 December 1927, p. 1 (frontpage).

Dessy, Clément, 'Arthur Symons, a Mediator of Belgian Symbolist Writers', in *Arthur Symons: Poet, Critic, Vagabond*, ed. by Elisa Bizzotto and Stefano Evangelista (Cambridge: Legenda, 2018), pp. 84–102.

Destro, Alberto, 'Die Faszination des Unpolitischen. Brecht übersetzt D'Annunzio', in *Wo bleibt das »Konzept«? Dov' e il »concetto«? Festschrift für/Studi in onore di Enrico De Angelis*, ed. by Carlo Carmassi, Giovanna Cermelli, Marina Foschi Albert and Marianne Hepp (Munich: Iudicium-Verlag, 2009), pp. 247–55.

Devoto, Fernando, *Historia de la inmigración en la Argentina* (Buenos Aires: Sudamericana, 2004).

Di Tizio, Franco, *D'Annunzio e Albertini: Vent'anni di sodalizio*, 2 vols. (Altino: Ianieri, 2003).

Diana, Elvira, *L'immagine degli italiani nella letteratura libica dall' epoca coloniale alla caduta di Gheddafi* (Rome: IPOCAN, 2011), pp. 40–4.

—— 'Gabriele D'Annunzio e il mondo Arabo', *Rassegna Dannunziana*, 72 (2018), pp. 61–5.

Diano, Carlo, 'D'Annunzio e l'Ellade', in *L'arte di Gabriele D'Annunzio*, ed. by Emilio Mariano (Milan: Mondadori, 1968), pp. 51–67.

Díaz, Leopoldo, *Traducciones* (Buenos Aries: Pablo E. Coni, 1897).

Dillmann, Klaus Konrad, *Dr. Karl Gustav Vollmoeller: Eine Zeitreise durch ein bewegtes Leben* (Heidelberg: Gingko Medien, 2012).

Dmitriev, Pavel, '"Son v osennii vecher" G. D'Annunzio v perevode M. A. Kuzmina', in *Russko-Ital'ianskii arkhiv*, 2 vols, ed. by Daniela Rizzi and Andrey Shishkin, Vol. 2 (Salerno: Poligrafica Ruggiero, 2002), pp. 89–93.

Doderet, André, 'D'Annunzio Devant la Mort', *Les Nouvelles Littéraires*, 9 June 1923.

—— 'Comment j'ai tradui l'œuvre de D'Annunzio', *L'Intransigeant*, 27 November 1927, p. 6.

—— 'Une pièce de Gabriele D'Annunzio à la Comédie-Française', *Excelsior*, 6 December 1927, section *Les Theatres*, p. 5.

—— Section 'La vie des Lettres', *Les Nouvelles Littéraires*, 28 June 1930.

—— 'Le Prix d'Enfance', *Les Nouvelles Littéraires*, 13 February 1932, p. 5.

—— Section 'Section Essais', *Les Nouvelles Littéraires*, 3 June 1933.

—— 'Georges Hérelle (1849–1935)', *Les Nouvelles Litteraires*, 21 December 1935.

—— *Vingts ans d'amitié avec Gabriele D'Annunzio* (Paris: Éditions du Cerf-volant, 1956).

Dostoevskaja [*sic.*], Aimée, *Dostoevskij nei ricordi di sua figlia* (Milan: Treves, 1922).

Du Gard, Maurice Martin, 'Le roués d'aujourd'hui', *Les Nouvelles Littéraires*, 3 August 1929.

Ducrey, Guy, 'Is There Such a Thing as 'Decadent Translator?': The Case of Georges Hérelle (1848–1935)', *Volupté* 3: 2 (2020), 11–27.

Duncan, Derek, *Reading and Writing Italian Homosexuality: A Case of Possible Difference* (Aldershot, UK: Ashgate, 2005).

Elies, Pere i Busqueta, Pere *Ramon Vinyes i Cluet: Un literat de gran volada, vida i obra d'un berguedà exemplar* (Barcelona: Dalmau, 1972).

Emmerson, Charles, *Crucible: The Long End of the Great War and the Birth of a New World, 1917–1924* (London: The Bodley Head, 2019).

Evangelista, Stefano, 'The Remaking of Rome: Cosmopolitanism and Literary Modernity in Gabriele D'Annunzio's *The Child of Pleasure*', *Forum for Modern Language Studies*, 53: 3 (2017), 314–24.

—— 'Aestheticism in Italy: A New Sense of Place', in *The Edinburgh Companion to Fin de Siècle Literature, Culture and the Arts*, ed. by Josephine M. Guy (Edinburgh: Edinburgh University Press, 2018), pp. 263–80.

—— 'Symons and D'Annunzio: Decadence in Translation', in *Arthur Symons: Poet, Critic, Vagabond*, ed. by Elisa Bizzotto and Stefano Evangelista (Cambridge: Legenda, 2018), pp. 54–68.

—— 'Transnational Decadence', in *Decadence and Literature*, ed. by Jane Desmarais and David Weir (Cambridge, UK: Cambridge University Press, 2019), 316–31.

—— *Literary Cosmopolitanism in the English Fin de Siècle: Citizens of Nowhere* (Oxford: Oxford University Press, 2021).

Even-Zohar, Itamar, 'The Position of Translated Literature within the Literary Polysystem', *Poetics Today* 11: 1 (1990): 45–51.

Fabre, Daniel, 'Inversion et dislocation: Les vies savantes de Georges Hérelle', in *Ce que la science fait à la vie*, ed. by Nicolas Adell and Jérôme Lamy (Paris: Éditions du comité des travaux historiques et scientifiques, 2016), pp. 269–303.

Fàbregas, Xavier, 'El Modernisme i la seva iconografia teatral', *Serra d'or*, 12: 135 (1970), 72–7.

—— *Aproximació a la Història del teatre català modern* (Barcelona: Curial Edicions, 1972).

Falcone, Aniello, '"Il figlio di Iorio" di Eduardo Scarpetta. Scarpetta a . . . Canossa! – La pace con D'Annunzio', *Tribuna*, 15 September 1904.

—— 'La catastrofe del "Figlio di Iorio"', *L'Illustrazione Italiana*, 5 December 1904.

Fasoli, Paolo, 'Le ali della vittoria: note sulla fortuna di D'Annunzio nell' America del Nord', *Rassegna Dannunziana*, 72 (2018), 42–51.

Ferrata, Giansiro, 'Introduzione', *Il Piacere* (Milan: Mondadori, 1951), pp. 33–5.

Festorazzi, Roberto, *D'Annunzio e la piovra fascista. Spionaggi al Vittoriale nella testimonianza del federale di Brescia* (Rome: Il minotauro, 2005).

Fidler, Fedor, *Iz mira literatorov: kharaktery i suzhdeniia*, ed. by Konstantin Azadovskii (Moscow: Novoe literaturnoe obozrenie, 2008).

Fischer, Samuel and Hedwig Fischer, *Briefwechsel mit Autoren*, ed. by Dierk Rodewald and Corinna Fiedler (Berlin: S. Fischer, 1989).

Fiumi, Lionello, 'Gli Italianisti di Francia. Divulgatori delle lettere e scrittori di politica', *La Nuova Italia*, 3 September 1929.

Fogu, Claudio, *The Fishing Net and the Spider Web: Mediterranean Imaginaries and the Making of Italians* (London: Palgrave, 2021).

Folena, Ugo, '"La figlia di Iorio" in Siciliano', *Il Tirso* (Rome), 18 September 1904.

Fortis, Alberto, 'De' Costumi de' Morlacchi', in *Viaggio in Dalmazia (1774)*, vol. 2 (Munich and Sarajevo: Verlag Otto Sagner, Izdavačko preduzeće 'Veselin Maslesa', 1974), pp. 67–126.

—— 'Of the Manners of the Morlacchi', in *Travels into Dalmatia* (1778) (New York: Arno Press, 1971), pp. 43–89.

'Francesca da Rimini' [review], *Neue deutsche Rundschau*, 13 (1902), 555.

Frau, Sergio, 'D'Annunzio Scarpetta: Miseria e nobiltà', *La Repubblica*, 17 December 1996.
Freud, Sigmund, 'On Narcissism: An Introduction', *Essential Papers on Narcissism*, ed. by Andrew P. Morrison (New York: New York University Press, 1986).
Frice, Vladimir, 'Gabriele D'Annunzio', in *Literaturnaia enciklopediia*, 11 vols (Moscow: Izdstel'stvo Kommunisticheskoi Akademii, 1930), I, pp. 167–9.
Fried, Harvey, 'D'Annunzio's Politics', *New York Times*, 13 April 1997, p. 14.
Friedell, Egon, *Von Dante zu D'Annunzio* (Vienna and Leipzig: Rosner, 1915).
Friedman, Susan Stanford, *Planetary Modernisms: Provocations on Modernity across Time* (New York: Columbia University Press, 2018).
Fucilla, Joseph G. and Joseph M. Carrière, *D'Annunzio Abroad: A Bibliographical Essay*, 2 Vols (New York: Columbia University Press, 1935–1937).
Fulcarà, Dolors, *El Modernisme a Girona* (Girona, Spain: Instituto de Estudios Gerundenses, 1976).
Gabaccia, Donna R., *Italy's Many Diasporas* (Seattle: University of Washington Press, 2000).
Gabriele D'Annunzio nelle culture dei paesi slavi, *Quaderni del Vittoriale*, 7 (Gardone Riviera: Fondazione del Vittoriale degli Italiani, 1978).
Gagnier, Regenia, *Individualism, Decadence and Globalization: On the Relationship of Part to Whole, 1859–1920* (London: Palgrave, 2010).
—— 'The Global Circulation of the Literatures of Decadence', *Literature Compass* 10: 1 (2013), 70–81.
Galderisi, Claudio, 'Faute contre nature? D'une langue à l'autre ou Gabriele D'Annunzio le collectionneur', in *Écrire dans la langue de l'autre*, ed. by Anna Maria Babbi (Verona: Fiorini, 2011), pp. 57–74.
Galli-Dupis, Florence, 'Un ethnographe, érudit historien et traducteur littéraire: Georges Hérelle (1848–1935) et la pastorale basque', *Garae ethnopole* (2007), http://www.garae.fr/spip.php?article220 [accessed 18 October 2022].
Gallot, Muriel, 'D'Annunzio et son traducteur: à la recherche d'un alter ego', *Cahiers d'études romanes*, 24 (2011), 81–9.
—— 'Gabriele D'Annunzio et Georges Hérelle: érotisme et traduction', in *Traduire avec l'auteur*, ed. by Patrick Hersant (Paris: Sorbonne Université Presses, 2020), pp. 129–46.
Garetto, Elda, ed., 'Lettere di corrispondenti russi a Gabriele D'Annunzio', in *Percorsi russi al Vittoriale: archivi, testimonianze, prospettive di studio*, ed. by Maria Pia Pagani (Cinisello Balsamo: Silvana, 2012), pp. 105–9.
—— 'Una russa a Milano: Elena Grigorovič, pittrice, antroposofa, ex-terrorista', in *Territoria russkogo slova*, ed. by Rosanna Casari, Ugo Persi and Maria Chiara Pesenti (Salerno: Vereja, 2012), pp. 123–42.

Gautier, Judith, *Poémes de la libellule*, trans. by Judith Gautier and M. Saionzi (Paris: Gillot, 1885).

Gauvin, Lise, ed., '"Besos para golpes": l'ambiguïté d'un titre hugolien', in *Les langues du roman: Du plurilinguisme comme stratégie textuelle*, ed. by Lise Gauvin (Montreal: Presses de l'Université de Montréal), pp. 37–51.

Gentile, Giovanni, 'Il torto e il diritto delle traduzioni', in Giovanni Gentile, *Frammenti di estetica e di letteratura* (Lanciano: Carabba, 1921).

George, Stefan, *Briefwechsel zwischen George und Hofmannsthal*, 2nd edn (Munich: Küpper, 1953).

Giacon, Maria Rosa, 'Presenze e letture marciane di D'Annunzio', in *Libri e librerie di Gabriele D'Annunzio*, ed. by Edoardo Tiboni (Pescara: Centro Nazionale di Studi Dannunziani, 2006), pp. 49–86.

Giammattei, Emma, '«Il figlio di Iorio», D'Annunzio, Scarpetta e Croce', in *'La figlia di Iorio'. Atti del VII Convegno internazionale di studi dannunziani, Pescara, 24–6 October 1985*, ed. by Edoardo Tiboni (Pescara: Centro nazionale di studi dannunziani in Pescara, 1986), pp. 255–62.

Gianeri, Enrico, *D'Annunzio nella caricatura mondiale* (Milan: Garzanti, 1941).

Gibellini, Pietro, 'Per la cronologia di "Alcione"', *Studi di filologia italiana*, 33 (1975), 393–424.

—— 'L'archeologia linguistica della "Città morta"', *Italianistica*, 5: 1 (1976), 88–92.

—— *Logos e mythos: Studi su Gabriele D'Annunzio* (Florence: Olschki, 1985).

—— 'La storia di "Alcyone"', in Pietro Gibellini, *Logos e mythos* (Florence: Olschki, 1985), pp. 31–84.

—— ed., *D'Annunzio europeo: atti del convegno internazionale, Gardone Riviera-Perugia 8–13 maggio 1989* (Rome: Lucarini, 1991).

Giglio, Raffaele, *Per la storia du un'amicizia: D'Annunzio, Hérelle, Scarfoglio, Serao: documenti inediti* (Naples: Loffredo, 1977).

Gindin, S. I., 'Kommentarii', in Valery Briusov, *Zarubezhnaia poeziia v perevodakh Valeriia Briusova* (Moscow: Raduga, 1994).

Ginzkey, Franz Karl, *Die Front im Tirol* (Berlin: Fischer, 1996).

Giusti, Roberto F., *Visto y vivido: Amécdotas, semblanzas, confesiones y batallas* (Buenos Aires: Losada, 1965).

Gordon Craig, Edward, 'The Actor and the Über-Marionette', *The Mask: Journal of the Art of the Theatre* 1: 2 (1908), 3–15.

Griffin, Gerald, *Gabriele D'Annunzio: The Warrior Bard* [1935], (Port Washington: Kennikat Press, 1970).

Grigoriev, Rafail, 'Predislovie', in Gabriele D'Annunzio, *Peskarskie rasskazy*, trans. by Zinaida Vengerova (Petersburg: Vsemirnaja literatura, 1919).

Grutman, Rainier, 'Le bilinguisme littéraire comme relation intersystémique', *Canadian Review of Comparative Literature/Revue Canadienne de Littérature Comparée*, 17 : 3/4 (1990), 198–212.

—— 'Refraction and Recognition: Literary Multilingualism in Translation', *Target*, 18: 1 (2006), 17–47.

—— 'Le moment biculturel de la littérature française', in *Paradoxes du plurilinguisme littéraire 1900*, ed. by Britta Benert (Bruxelles: Peter Lang, 2015), pp. 125–41.

Guerri, Giordano Bruno, ed., *Da Ovidio a D'Annunzio: Miti di metamorfosi e metamorfosi dei miti: Atti del convegno di studi, Gardone Riviera, 12 ottobre 2018* (Cinisello Balsamo, Milan: Silvana, 2019).

Guidi, Angelo Flavio, letter to publisher *Grjadušy den* (Gardone Riviera: Fondazione 'Il Vittoriale degli Italiani', General Archive, Palchetto XLIX, Cassetta 2, 21 October 1911).

Guidobaldi, Luca, 'Commento', *Il Diritto Industriale*, 1 (2015): 43–54.

Gullace, Giovanni, 'Les débuts de D'Annunzio en France et la question de la "renaissance latine"', in *Symposium*, 7: 2 (1953), 232–49.

—— 'The French Writings of Gabriele D'Annunzio', in *Comparative Literature*, 12: 3 (1960), pp. 207–28.

—— *Gabriele D'Annunzio in France: A Study in Cultural Relations* (Syracuse, NY: Syracuse University Press, 1966).

Gumbrecht, Hans Ulrich, Friedrich Kittler and Bernhard Siegert, eds, *Der Dichter als Kommandant: D'Annunzio erobert Fiume* (Munich: Fink, 1996).

Gumilev, Nikolai, *Polnoe sobranie sochinenii*, 10 vols, ed. by Jurij V. Zobnin (Moscow: Voskresenie, 2006).

Hägg, Göran, *D'Annunzio: dekadent diktare, krigare och diktator* (Stockholm: Norstedts, 2015).

Harding, Bertita, *Age Cannot Wither: The Story of Duse and D'Annunzio* (Philadelphia: J. B. Lippincott Co., 1947).

Hartley, Julia, Wanrug Suwanwattana and Jennifer Yee, eds, *French Decadence in a Global Context: Colonialism and Exoticism* (Liverpool: Liverpool University Press, 2022).

Hashimoto, Osamu, '*Mishima Yukio*' *towa nanimono dattanoka* [Who was Yukio Mishima?] (Tokyo: Shinchō, 2005).

Hayot, Eric and Rebecca L. Walkowitz, eds, *A New Vocabulary for Global Modernism* (New York: Columbia University Press, 2016).

Heins, Marjorie, *Not in Front of the Children: Indecency, Censorship and the Innocence of Youth* (New Brunswick, NJ: Rutgers University Press, 2007).

Heiss, Andrew, *Manufacturing Consent: Italy, The Mutamassirun, Egypt, and the Invasion of Libya*. Master of Art in Middle East Studies, Middle East Studies Center, 2010.

Hérelle, Georges, trans., *Problemes sur l'amour physique*, by Aristotle (En Pyrogopolis, 1900) [pseudonym: Agricola Lieberfeund].

—— *Notolette dannunziane*, ed. and trans. by Ivanos Ciani (Pescara: Centro Nazionale di Studi Dannunziani, 1984).

—— *Pétit mémoire d'un traducteur* (Brussels: Les Éditions du Hazard, 2005).

—— *Gabriel D'Annunzio ou Théorie et pratique de la surhumanité*, ed. by Mario Cimini (Berne: Peter Lang 2015).

Herrera, Fernanda Bravo, *Huellas y recorridos de una utopía: La emigración italiana en la Argentina* (Buenos Aires: Teseo, 2015).

Hiddleston, Jane, 'Un Nouvel Internationalisme Littéraire? Dreams and Delusions of "World Literature" in Khatibi, Djaout, and Adimi', *Publications of the Modern Language Association of America*, 137: 2 (2022), 389–95.

Hinterhäuser, Hans, *Fin de siglo: Figuras y mitos* (Madrid: Taurus, 1980).

Hirata, Tokuboku, 'D'Annunzio ga L'INNOCCETE [sic.] no jo', *Myōjō* (Rising Star), 3rd period, 1 (June 1902), 32.

Hiratsuka Haruko (Raichō), *Genshi, Josei wa Taiyō de atta* [In the Beginning, Women Were the Sun], vol. 1, 3 vols. (Tokyo: Ōtsuki Shoten, 1971–1973).

Hirayama, Jōji, *D'Annunzio to nihon kindai bungaku* [D'Annunzio and Modern Japanese Literature] (Tokyo: Shironsha, 2011).

Homère, *Odyssée*, trans. by Leconte de Lisle (Paris: Alphonse Lamerre, 1893).

Horowitz, Jason, 'New Statue Unsettles Italian City: Is It Celebrating a Poet or a Nationalist?', *The New York Times*, 16 November 2019 <https://www.nytimes.com/2019/11/16/world/europe/trieste-statue-dannunzio-fascism.html?smid=url-share> [accessed 18 October 2022].

Huch i Camprubí, Jaume, 'Ramon Vinyes, jove: Contribució a l'estudi de la 1ª etapa catalana (1904–1912)' (Bachelor's Degree Thesis, supervised by Dr J. Molas, Universidad de Barcelona, 1986).

Hugarte, Manuel, *Escritores iberoamericanos de 1900* (Santiago de Chile: Ediciones 'Orbe', 1943).

Hughes-Hallett, Lucy, *The Pike: Gabriele D'Annunzio, Poet, Seducer and Preacher of War* (London: 4th Estate, 2013).

—— *Gabriele D'Annunzio: L'uomo, Il Poeta, Il Sogno Di Una Vita Come Opera D'arte*, trans. by Roberta Zuppet (Milan: Rizzoli, 2021).

Ichiyanagi, Hirotaka, 'Tokkenka sareru "Shinkei" *Sorekara* ichimen [Privileged "Nerves": one aspect of *And Then*'], *Sōseki kenkyū* [Sōseki Studies], 10 (1998), 34–44.

'Ihō bungeikai shōsoku [Report: Trends in the Literary World]' in *Shumi* [Hobby], 3–1 (January 1908), 3.

Ilf, Il'ya and Evgeny Petrov, *The Little Golden Calf* [Zolotoj telenok 1931], trans. by Anne O. Fisher (Montpelier, VT: Russian Life Books, 2009).

Ivetic, Egidio, *Storia dell'Adriatico: Un mare e la sua civiltà* (Bologna: Il Mulino, 2019).

Jaillant, Lise and Alison E. Martin, eds, 'Introduction: Global Modernism', *Modernist Cultures* (special issue) 13: 1 (2018), 1–13.

James, Kathryn Louise, 'Creating a Nation in Adversity: Advent of Egyptian Nationalism in British Occupation' (University of Nevada, Las Vegas, Theses, Dissertations, Professional Papers and Capstones, 2012).

Jepson, Barbara, 'The Music Befits a Saintly Legend', *New York Times*, 30 March 1997, p. 32.

Kadir, Djelal, 'To World, to Globalize: World Literature's Crossroads', *Comparative Literature Studies* 41: 1 (2004), 1–9.

Kalliney, Peter, *Modernism in a Global Context* (London: Bloomsbury, 2016).

Katayama, Koson, 'Shinkeishitsu no bungaku', *Teikoku bungaku* 11: 8 (August 1905).

Kato, Shuichi, *A History of Japanese Literature: From the Man'yōshū to Modern Times*, trans. and ed. by Don Sanderson (Richmond, Surrey, UK: Curzon, 1997).

Kellman, Steven G., *The Translingual Imagination* (Lincoln, NE.: University of Nebraska Press, 2000).

Kenmochi, Takehiko, 'Natsume Sōseki *Sorekara* to D'Annunzio *Shi no shōri* [Sōseki Natsume's *And Then* and D'Annunzio's *The Triumph of Death*]', in *Hikaku bungaku kenkyū Natsume Sōseki*, ed. by Toshiaki Tsukamoto, Comparative Literature Studies on Sōseki Natsume (Tokyo: Asahi Press, 1978).

Khamisi, Mousa El, 'Italy Celebrates the Centenary of Fiume City, Founded by the Fascist Poet D'Annunzio', *Al-sabah al-jadeed* (April 2019).

Khashaba, Derrini, 'D'Annunzio in the Royal Academy of Italy's presidency', *Al-Resala* (November 1937), p. 1837.

—— Elegy 379, *Al-Resala* (March 1938), p. 391.

—— 'Al- Bareed Al-adby', *Al-Resala* (October 1934), p. 1795.

Kitahara, Hakushū (pseudonym of Kitahara Ryūkichi), *Jashumon* [Heretics], *Subaru* (1909).

Klopp, Charles, *Gabriele D'Annunzio* (Boston, MA: Twayne Press, 1988).

Knopf, Jan, *Brecht-Handbuch. Lyrik, Prosa, Schriften* (Stuttgart: Metzler, 1984).

Komiya, Toyotaka, 'D'Annunzio no *Shi no shōri* to Morita Sōhei no *Baien* [D'Annunzio's *Triumph of Death* and Sōhei Morita's *Sooty Smoke*]', *Hototogisu* [Lesser Cuckoo], 12.10 (1909).

Komolova, N. P., *Italiia v russkoi kul'ture Serebrianogo veka: vremena i sudby* (Moscow: Nauka, 2005).

Kormiltsev, Il'ya, 'Tri zhizni Gabriele D'Annunzio', *Inostrannaia literatura*, 11 (1999), https://magazines.gorky.media/inostran/1999/11/tri-zhizni-gabriele-d-annunczio.html [accessed 20 November 2021].

Koval, L. M., 'Gabriele D'Annunzio v Rossii', *Kniga. Issledovaniia i materialy*, 76 (1999), 165–71.

Kraus, Karl, 'Es wird ernst', *Die Fackel* XIII: 343/344 (29 February 1912).

—— *Die letzten Tage der Menschheit. Tragödie in fünf Akten mit Vorspiel und Epilog* (Frankfurt al Main: Suhrkamp, 1986).

Kupka, Anne, *Der ungeliebte D'Annunzio. D'Annunzio in der zeitgenössischen und der gegenwärtigen deutschsprachigen Literatur* (Frankfurt am Main: Lang, 1992).
Kuzmin, Mikhail, 'Doch Iorio', *Zhizn iskusstva*, 8 May 1919.
—— *Dnevnik 1905–1907*, ed. by Nikolai Bogomolov and Sergei Shumikhin (St Petersburg: izdstel'stvo Ivana Limbakha, 2000).
—— *Dnevnik 1908–1915*, ed. by Nikolai Bogomolov and Sergei Shumikhin (St Petersburg: izdstel'stvo Ivana Limbakha, 2005).
'"La figlia di Iorio" in siciliano', *L'arte drammatica* (Milan), 19 November 1904.
'"La figlia di Iorio" in siciliano', *Il Marzocco* (Florence), 29 January 1905.
'"La figlia di Iorio" tradotta in siciliano da G. A. Borgese', *Corriere della Sera*, 21 December 1904.
Leandro [Giustino Lorenzo Ferri], 'Sul carro di Tespi. Autunno teatrale', *Capitan Fracassa* (Rome), 12 September 1904.
Ledeen, Michael A., *The First Duce: D'Annunzio at Fiume* (Baltimore, MD: The John Hopkins University Press, 1977).
Lennon, Brian, *In Babel's Shadow: Multilingual Literatures, Monolingual States* (Minneapolis, MN: University of Minnesota Press, 2010).
Leopardi, Giacomo, *Zibaldone*, ed. by Michel Caesar and Franco D'Intino (New York: Farrar Straus Giroux, 2013).
Leporello (pseudonym), 'Rivista teatrale. "La figlia di Iorio" in dialetto siciliano', *L'Illustrazione Italiana*, 25 December 1904.
Limonov, Eduard, *Sviashchennye monstry* [Sacred Monsters] (Moscow: Ad Marginem, 2003).
Lombard, Paul, 'Les premières', *L'Homme libre*, 17 June 1923.
Londré, Felicia, 'Eleonora Duse: an Italian actress on the American stage', *Studies in Popular Culture* 2 (1985), 60–70.
Lonsdale, Laura, *Multilingualism and Modernity: Barbarism in Spanish and American Literature* (London: Palgrave, 2018).
Loué, Thomas and Blaise Wilfert-Portal, 'D'Annunzio à l'usage des Français: la traduction comme censure informelle (fin du XIXe siècle)', *Ethnologie française*, 36: 1 (2006), 101–10.
Lozinsky, Grigory, 'Predislovie', in Gabriele D'Annunzio, *Mozhet byt da, mozhet byt net* [*Forse che sì forse che no*], trans. by Grigory Lozinsky (Berlin: Gosudarstvennoe izdatel'stvo, 1923), pp. 7–17.
Lunzer, Renate, 'Zum Thema "trahison des clercs": Fallbeispiel Gabriele D'Annunzio', in *Wenn Ränder Mitte warden: Festschrift für Fritz Peter Kirsch*, ed. by Chantal Adobati (Vienna: WUV, 2001), pp. 617–26.
—— '"O poésie, voilà le fruit de tes accouplements avec la politique . . . " D'Annunzio all'avanguardia contro l'Austria', in *Felix Austria – Italia infelix? Tre secoli di relazioni culturali italo-austriache*, ed. by Nicoletta Dacrema (Rome: Aracne, 2004), pp. 104–24.
Lurie, Sofia, 'Un'impronta russa nell'opera di D'Annunzio: "La Leda senza cigno" e *l'affare dei russi*', in *Percorsi russi al Vittoriale: archivi,*

testimonianze, prospettive di studio, ed. by Maria Pia Pagani (Cinisello Balsamo: Silvana, 2012), pp. 25–30.

Mahmoud, Hussein, 'L'italiano, una lingua privilegiata nel mondo arabo', in *Geocultura: prospettive, strumenti, strategie per un mondo in italiano*, ed. by Valeria Noli (Rome: Società Dante Alighieri, 2016), 170–9, <https://pure.ulster.ac.uk/ws/portalfiles/portal/76038397/Dante CorPub.pdf> [accessed 19 October 2022].

Mahnke, Frank H., *Color, Environment and Human Response* (New York: John Wiley & Sons, 1996).

Maiakovsky, Vladimir, 'Sovetskaia azbuka', in *Sochinenia v dvukh tomakh*, 2 vols, ed. by A. M. Ushakov (Moscow: Pravda: Khudozhestvennaia literatura, 1987).

Malcolm, Noel, *Agents of Empire: Knights, Corsairs, Jesuits, and Spies in the Sixteenth-Century Mediterranean World* (Oxford: Oxford University Press, 2019).

Mandalari, Filippo, 'D'Annunzio in siciliano', *La Sicilia* (Catania), 29–30 September 1904.

—— '"La figlia di Iorio" al Biondo', *L'Ora* (Palermo), 13 May 1905.

Mann, Thomas, *Reflections of a Nonpolitical Man*, trans. by Walter D. Morris (New York: Ungar, 1983).

Mao, Douglas and Rebecca L. Walkowitz, 'The New Modernist Studies', *PMLA* 123: 3 (2008), 737–48.

Marani, Alma Novella, 'D'Annunzio en la Argentina', in *D'Annunzio in America Latina: Ciclo di convegni su D'Annunzio e le letterature moderne, nel 500 anniversario, 1938–1988* (Pescara: Universitá degli Studi Gabriele D'Annunzio, 1990), pp. 99–111.

Marfany, Josep-Luis, '"Joventut", Revista Modernista', *Serra d'Or*, 12: 135 (1970), 53–6.

Marholm, Laura, *Das Buch der Frauen* (Leipzig: Langen, 1895).

—— *Modern Women: An English Rendering of Laura Marholm Hansson's 'Das Buch Der Frauen'*, trans. by Hermione Ramsden (London: Bodley Head, 1896).

Marianacci, Dante, 'D'Annunzio, la guerra e gli altri', in *L'anno iniquo, 1914: Guerra e letteratura europea. Atti del Congresso di Venezia, 24–26 November 2014*, ed. by Alessandro Scarsella and Giovanni Capecchie Matteo Giancotti (Rome: Adi Editore, 2017).

Mariano, Emilio, ed. *D'Annunzio e il classicismo*, Quaderni del Vittoriale 23, (Gardone Riviera, Fondazione del Vittoriale degli Italiani, 1980).

—— ed., *D'Annunzio e il simbolismo europeo. Atti del convegno di studio, Gardone Riviera, 14–15–16 settembre, 1973* (Milan: Il Saggiatore, 1976).

—— 'Il San Francesco di Gabriele D'Annunzio', *Quaderni del Vittoriale*, 12 (1978).

—— 'D'Annunzio e la Grecia', *Il Verri*, 7/8 (1985), 48–76.

Marinetti, Filippo Tommaso, *Il fascino dell'Egitto* (Milan: Mondadori, 1933).

Matvejević, Predrag, *Mediterranean: A Cultural Landscape*, trans. by Michael Henry Heim (Berkeley, CA: University of California Press, 1999).

McCarthy, M. J., 'Catalan *Modernisme*, Messianism and Nationalist Myths', *Bulletin of Hispanic Studies*, 52: 4 (1975), 379–95.

Meli, Marco and Elsa Ariè Geiger, eds, *Benno Geiger e la cultura europea* (Florence: Leo Olschki, 2010).

Mengozzi, Chiara, 'De l'utilité et de l'inconvénient du concept de *World Literature*', *Revue de littérature compare* 3 (2016), 335–49.

Meregalli, Franco, 'D'Annunzio in Spagna', in *L'arte di Gabriele D'Annunzio: Atti del convegno internazionale di studio Venezia-Gardone Riviera-Pescara, 7–13 ottobre 1963* (Milan: Mondadori, 1968), pp. 481–503.

Merejkowsky, Dmitri [*sic.*], *La naissance des dieux: Toutankhamon en Crète* (Paris: Calmann-Lévy, 1924).

Merlin, Franziska, *Stefan Georges moderne Klassik: Die 'Blätter für die Kunst' und die Erneuerung des Dramas* (Wurzburg: Ergon, 2014).

Meter, Helmut, 'D'Annunzio und die Dramatik des doppelten Registers: Die Tragödie *Le Chèvrefeuille* und ihre italienische Fassung *Il ferro*', in *Literarische Polyphonie: Übersetzung und Mehrsprachigkeit in der Literatur*, ed. by Johann Strutz and Peter V. Zima (Tübingen: Gunter Narr, 1996), pp. 175–91.

Meter, Helmut, 'Bilinguismo letterario e autotraduzione. Alcune riflessioni su tre scrittori del Novecento (G. D'Annunzio, Y. Goll, S. Beckett)', in *Eteroglossia e plurilinguismo letterario. II: Plurilinguismo e letteratura*, ed. by Furio Brugnolo and Vincenzo Orioles (Rome: Il Calamo, 2002), pp. 351–65.

Meyerhold, Vsevolod, *Perepiska: 1896–1939* (Moscow: Iskusstvo, 1976).

Michelstaedter, Carlo, *Epistolario*, ed. by Sergio Campailla (Milan: Adelphi, 1983).

Migone, Gian Giacomo, *The United States and Fascist Italy: The Rise of American Finance in Europe* (New York: Cambridge University Press, 2015).

Mishima, Yukio, *Misaki nite no monogatari* [A Story at the Cape] (Tokyo: Sakurai Shoten, 1947).

—— *Kamen no kokuhaku* [Confessions of a Mask] (Tokyo: Kawade Shobō, 1949).

—— *Confessions of a Mask*, trans. by Meredith Weatherby (New York: New Directions, 1958).

—— *Kinjiki* [Forbidden Colours] (Tokyo: Shinchō, 1951).

—— *Yūkoku* [Patriotism] (Chūōkōron-Shinsha, 1960).

—— *Gogo no eikō* [*The Sailor Who Fell from Grace with the Sea*] (Tokyo: Kodansha, 1963).

—— *Hōjō no umi* [The Sea of Fertility] tetralogy (Tokyo: Shinchō, 1965–71).
—— *Eirei no koe* [The Voices of the Heroic Dead] (Tokyo: Kawade Shobō, 1966).
—— 'Haru no yuki' [Spring Snow], *Mishima Yukio zenshū* vol.13, ed. Tanaka Miyoko (Tokyo: Shinchō, 2003) pp. 7–395.
—— *Bunka bōei ron* [On Defence of the Culture] (Tokyo: Shinchō, 1969).
—— *Tennin Gosui* [The Decay of the Angel] (Tokyo: Shinchō, 1971).
—— 'Narusisizumu ron' [On Narcissism], in *Mishima Yukio zenshū*, vol. 34 (Tokyo: Shinchō, 2000).
—— 'Hanjidai teki na geijutsu ka' [The Anti-Epochal Artist], in *Mishima Yukio zenshū*, vol. 27 (Tokyo: Shinchō, 2003).
—— *Mishima Yukio zenshū*, vol. 34 (Tokyo: Shinchō, 2003).
—— 'Geki' [The Manifesto], in *Mishima Yukio zenshū*, vol. 36 (Tokyo: Shinchō, 2000).
Molas, Joaquim, 'El Modernisme i les seves tensions', *Serra d'Or*, 12: 135 (1970), 45–52.
—— 'Notes sobre la prehistòria poètica de Carles Riba', *Els Marges* 1 (1974), 9–23.
Morelli, Gabrielle, 'D'Annunzio in Spagna', in *Itinerari dannunziani: Atti della giornata di studio organizzata dal Cenacolo orobico di poesia, Bergamo, 24 ottobre 1998* (Bergamo: Edizioni dell'Ateneo, 1999), pp. 95–102.
Morita, Sōhei, 'Jihitsu nenpu' [Self-Written Chronology], in *Gendai nihon bungaku zenshū* [The Complete Anthology of Modern Japanese Literature], vol. 42 (Tokyo: Kaizōsha, 1930).
—— *Baien* [Sooty Smoke, 1909] in *Shōchū Baien* [Detailed Notes on *Sooty Smoke*], ed. by Hideaki Sasaki (Kyoto: International Research Center for Japanese Studies, 1999).
Mosse, George, 'The Poet and the Exercise of Political Power: Gabriele D'Annunzio', *Yearbook of Comparative and General Literature*, 22 (1973): 32–41.
Müller, Martin Anton, Claus Pias and Gottfried Schnödl, eds, *Hermann Bahr: Österreichischer Kritiker europäischer Avantgarden*, *Jahrbuch für Internationale Germanistik*, 118 (Bern: Lang, 2014).
Muramatsu, Mariko, *Il buon suddito del Mikado* (Milan: Archinto Editore, 1997).
—— 'La fortuna dannunziana nel Giappone del primo Novecento. Studi dei documenti giapponesi nell'Archivio del Vittoriale degli Italiani', in *Segni e voci dalla letteratura italiana. Da Dante a D'Annunzio* (Tokyo: UTCP, 2012), pp. 95–120.
—— *Segni e voci dalla letteratura italiana. Da Dante a D'Annunzio* (Tokyo: UTCP, 2012).
—— 'D'Annunzio in Giappone', in *Gabriele D'Annunzio 150 'Vivo, scrivo'. Atti del convengno internazionale di studi. Pescara, Aurum, 12–13 marzo 2013* (Milan: Silvana Editoriale, 2014), pp. 183–91.

—— *D'Annunzio ni muchū datta koro* [Studies on Gabriele D'Annunzio Today – Exhibitions and Symposia, Kyoto 2013–14], (Tokyo: University of Tokyo College of Arts and Sciences Italian/Mediterranean Studies, 2015).

Muramatsu, Takeshi, *Mishima Yukio no sekai* [The World of Mishima Yukio] (Tokyo: Shinchō, 1990).

Murga, Fernando, 'Gabriele D'Annunzio e il mondo di lingua spagnola', in *Gabriele D'Annunzio nel primo centenario della nascita* (Rome: Centro di vita italiana, 1963), pp. 143–60.

Musil, Robert, 'Tagebücher, Aphorismen, Essays und Reden', in *Gesammelte Werke in Einzelausgaben*, Heft 30, ed. by Adolf Frisé (Reinbek bei Hamburg: Rowohlt, 1955).

Nagai, Kafū, *Shin Kichōsha no Nikki* [Diary of a New Returnee] (1910).

Natsume, Sōseki, *Sōseki zenshū* vol. 5 [The Complete Works of Sōseki Natsume] (Tokyo: Iwanami Shoten, 1994).

—— *Sōseki zenshū*, vol. 19 (Tokyo: Iwanami Shoten, 1995).

—— *Sōseki zenshū*, vol. 23 (Tokyo: Iwanami Shoten, 1996).

—— *Sōseki zenshū*, vol. 27 (Tokyo: Iwanami Shoten, 1997).

—— *And Then* [Sorekara, 1909], trans. by Norma Moore Field (Tokyo: Tuttle Publishing. 2011).

Nemegeer, Guylian and Mara Santi, 'Gabriele D'Annunzio's *Notturno*, the Book of the Italian War: Political Commitment, National Regeneration and its Ideological Roots', *Forum Italicum*, 3 (2021), 710–40.

Ngai, Sianne, *Our Aesthetic Categories: Zany, Cute, Interesting* (Cambridge, MA: Harvard University Press, 2015).

Nietzsche, Friedrich, *The Birth of Tragedy* [1872], trans. and ed. by Douglas Smith (Oxford: Oxford University Press, 2000).

Nifantani, Marco, *Los lugares del otro: Las imágenes culturales de lo ajeno identitario en la narrativa argentina e italiana del siglo XX* (Bahia Blanca: Editorial de la Universidad Nacional del Sur, 2008).

'Notizie Artistiche', *La Nuova Italia*, 21 January 1932.

'Notizie teatrali ed artistiche. Teatro Carignano', *Gazzetta del Popolo*, 16 March 1905.

Odoevtseva, Irina, *Na beregakh Nevy* (Moscow: AST, 2010).

Ojetti, Ugo, *Alla scoperta dei letterati: Colloquii con Carducci, Panzacchi, Fogazzaro. . .* (Milan: Bocca, 1899).

Oliva, Domenico, 'Intorno alla nuova "Figlia di Iorio" tradotta in dialetto siciliano da G. A. Borgese al Teatro Costanzi', *Il Giornale d'Italia*, 18 September 1904.

Pagani, Maria Pia, ed., *Percorsi russi al Vittoriale: archivi, testimonianze, prospettive di studio. Atti del convegno internazionale di studi, Gardone Riviera-Gargano sul Garda, 14–15 ottobre 2011* (Milan: Silvana Editoriale, 2012).

—— 'Rinaldo Küfferle e il mito di D'Annunzio', *Enthymema* 10 (2014), 168–88.

Pagni, Andrea, Gertrudis Payas and Patricia Wilson, eds, *Traductores y traducciones en la historia cultural de América Latina* (Mexico City: Literatura UNAM, 2011).

Palmerio, Benigno, *Con D'Annunzio alla Capponcina (1898–1910)* (Florence: Vallecchi, 1938).

Palmieri, Mario, *Gabriele D'Annunzio. Al Re Imperatore e al duce* (Milan: Impresa Editoriale Italiana, 1941).

Pancoast, Seth, *Blue and Red Light: or, Light and its Rays as Medicine* (Philadelphia: J. M. Stoddart & Co., 1877).

Paratore, Ettore, ed, *D'Annunzio e la cultura germanica, atti del VI convegno internazionale di studi dannunziani, Pescara, 3–5 maggio 1984* (Pescara: Centro studi dannunziani, 1985).

—— *D'Annunzio a cinquant'anni dalla morte* (Pescara: Centro nazionale di studi dannunziani, 1989).

Parker, Luke, 'The Shop Window Quality of Things: 1920s Weimar Surface Culture in Nabokov's *Korol, dama, valet*', *Slavic Review*, 77: 2 (2018), 390–416.

Passini, Nella, 'Gabriel D'Annunzio', *Nosotros*, 3: 24 (1938), 223–63.

Pater, Walter, 'Appreciations: With an Essay on Style', in vol. 5 of *The Library Edition of the Works of Walter Pater*, 10 vols (London: Macmillan, 1910), pp. 5–38.

Paz, Carlos, 'Roberto Arlt: Narrativa y crisis en la Argentina de los años 30', *Margen* 4 (1993), 1–9.

Péladan, Joséphin, *La Décadence Latine, Ethopée III: L'Initiation sentimentale* (Paris: Edinger, 1887).

Pelegrí, Iolanda, 'Alexandre Plana, crític literari' (Thesis, supervised by Dr J. Molas, Universidad Autónoma de Barcelona, 1974).

Peterecz, Zoltán, 'American Foreign Policy and American Financial Controllers in Europe in the 1920s', *Hungarian Journal of English and American Studies*, 1/2 (2012), 457–85.

'Petit courrier littéraire', *Comœdia*, 3 February 1932.

Pieri, Giuliana, 'Gabriele D'Annunzio and the Self-fashioning of a National Icon', *Modern Italy* 21 : 4: 329–43.

Plana, Alexandre, 'El darrer triomf de Basiliola (I–II–III)', *El Poble Català*, 22 February 1901.

—— 'Cleopatra i l'ibis', *El Poble Català*, 14 September 1908.

—— *Teoria i crítica del teatre* (Barcelona: Edicions 62, 1976).

Polgar, Alfred, 'D'Annunzio', in *Kleine Schriften*, Bd. I, ed. by Marcel Reich-Ranicki (Reinbek bei Hamburg: Rowohlt, 1982), pp. 6–10.

—— 'Paderewski D'Annunzio', [1927], in *Kleine Schriften*, Vol. I, ed. Marcel Reich-Ranicki (Reinbek bei Hamburg: Rowohlt, 1982), pp. 389–91.

Potapova, Zlata Michailovna, 'Mnogolikii Gabriele D'Annunzio', in D'Annunzio, *Leda bez lebedia* (Moscow: Bestseller, 1995), pp. 2–22.

Potolsky, Matthew, *The Decadent Republic of Letters: Taste, Politics, and Cosmopolitan Community from Baudelaire to Beardsley* (Philadelphia: University of Pennsylvania Press, 2013).

Praz, Mario, *La carne, la morte e il diavolo nella letteratura romantica* (Florence: Sansoni, 1948).

—— *The Romantic Agony* [La carne, la morte e il diavolo nella letteratura romantica], trans. by Angus Davidson, 2nd edn (Oxford: Oxford University Press, 1951).

—— 'D'Annunzio nella cultura europea', *Lettere Italiane* 15: 4 (1963), 434–45.

Praz, Maurice, 'Avec D'Annunzio son idole et son roi', *Le Petit Parisien*, 20 July 1920.

'Premier visits D'Annunzio. Mussolini will take over villa, Il Vittoriale, for the nation', *NYT*, 26 May 1925.

Primoli, Giuseppe, 'La Duse', *La Revue de Paris* (June 1897), 486–532.

Racine, Jean, *Phèdre*, ed. by Boris Donné (Paris: Flammarion, 2019).

Radzinsky, Edvard, *Rasputin: zhizn' i smert'* (Moscow: Vagrius, 2000).

Raffaelli, Lara Gochin and Michael Subialka, 'Introduction: D'Annunzio's Beauty, Reawakened', *Forum Italicum*, 51: 2 (2017), 311–34.

—— eds, 'Reawakening Beauty: Gabriele D'Annunzio's Seduction of the Senses', Special Issue of *Forum Italicum*, 51: 2 (August 2017).

Ràfols, José F., *Modernisme i modernistes* (Barcelona: Destino, 1982).

Raimondi, Ezio, '*Gabriele D'Annunzio*', in *Storia della letteratura italiana. Il Novecento*, ed. by Nataliano Sapegno (Milan: Garzanti, 1987).

Rainero, Romain H. and Stefano B. Galli, eds, *L'Italia e la «Grande Vigilia»: Gabriele D'Annunzio nella politica italiana prima del fascismo* (Milan: Franco Angeli, 2007).

Ramaioli, Federico Lorenzo, *Quis Contra Nos? Storia della reggenza del Carnaro da D'Annunzio alla costituzione di Fiume* (Rome: Historia edizioni, 2018).

Ranken, Towse J., 'Duse and the Degenerate D'Annunzio', *The Critic*, 41 (1904), 574–5.

Raponi, Elena, *Hofmannsthal e l'Italia. Fonti italiane nell'opera poetica e teatrale di Hugo von Hofmannsthal* (Milan: Vita e Pensiero Università, 2002).

—— 'L'"Elettra" (1903) di Hugo von Hofmannsthal tra Sofocle e D'Annunzio', *Studia austriaca*, 21 (2013), 131–54.

Rasera, Maddalena, ed., *D'Annunzio e la cultura francese* (Lanciano: Carabba, 2013).

Rassegna dannunziana, Special Issue: 'D'Annunzio in Italia e nel mondo a ottant'anni dalla morte, 45esimo convegno internazionale di studi', *Rassegna dannunziana* 72 (2018).

Rauchensteiner, Manfried, 'Kriegserklärung an Österreich. Das sterbende Kamel', *Die Presse* (22 May 2015).

Rauchensteiner, Manfried and Josef Broukal, *Der Erste Weltkrieg und das Ende der Habsburgermonarchie 1914–1918. In aller Kürze* (Vienna: Böhlau, 2015).
Regattin, Fabio, 'D'Annunzio, le théâtre, l'auto-traduction. Quelques remarques sur La città morta/La Ville morte et Il ferro/Le Chèvrefeuille', *Forum* 12 : 2 (2014), 87–106.
Reill, Dominique Kirchner, *Nationalists Who Feared the Nation: Adriatic Multinationalism in Habsburg Dalmatia, Trieste, and Venice* (Stanford: Stanford University Press, 2012).
—— *The Fiume Crisis: Life in the Wake of the Habsburg Empire* (Cambridge, MA: Harvard University Press, 2020).
Rhodes, Anthony, *D'Annunzio: The Poet as Superman* (New York: McDowell, Obolensky, 1960).
Riccareo, Vice (pseudonym), '"La figlia di Iorio" al Costanzi', *L'arte drammatica* (Milan), 24 September 1904.
Rigaud, André, 'La "Phædre" de Gabriele D'Annunzio à l'Opéra', *Comœdia*, 5 June 1923.
Ritter-Santini, Lea, 'Pari e Impari. Gabriele D'Annunzio e i barbari', in *Italia viva. Studien zur Sprache und Literatur Italiens. Festschrift für Hans Ludwig Scheel*, ed. by Willi Hirdt and Reinhard Klesczewski (Tübingen: Narr, 1983), pp. 335–51.
Robbe, Federico, *'Vigor di Vita'. Il nazionalismo italiano e gli Stati Uniti (1898–1923)* (Rome: Viella, 2018).
Rolland, Romain and Stefan Zweig, *Briefwechsel 1910–1940*, Bd. I (Berlin: Rütten & Leoning, 1987).
Roslyj, A. S., 'Dante v estetike i poezii akmeizma: sistema kontzeptov (na materiale tvorchestva A. Akhmatovoi, N. Gumileva, O. Mandelshtama)', unpublished doctoral thesis (Rostov State University, 2005).
Ross, Stephen and Allana C. Lindgren, eds, *The Modernist World* (New York: Routledge, 2015).
Rossini, Daniela, *L'America riscopre l'Italia. L'Inquiry di Wilson e le origini della questione adriatica, 1917–1919* (Rome: Edizioni Associate, 1992).
—— *Woodrow Wilson and the American Myth in Italy: Culture, Diplomacy, and War Propaganda* (Cambridge: Harvard University Press, 2008).
Rusinko, Elaine, 'Gumilev in London: An Unknown Interview', *Russian Literature Triquarterly*, 16 (1979), 73–85.
Russo, Umberto, 'La traduzione in abruzzese della "Figlia di Iorio"', in *'La figlia di Iorio': Atti del VII Convegno internazionale di studi dannunziani, Pescara, 24–6 October 1985*, ed. by Edoardo Tiboni (Pescara: Centro nazionale di studi dannunziani in Pescara, 1986), pp. 267–74.
Sabashnikova, Anna, 'V chas khimery', in D'Annunzio, *Sobranie sochinenii v shesti tomakh*, I.
Saler, Michael, *The Fin-De-Siecle World* (New York: Routledge, 2015).
Sappho, *Frammenti*, trans. and ed. by Antonio Aloni (Florence: Giunti, 1997).

Sappho, *Stung with Love: Poems and Fragments*, ed. and trans. by Aaron Poochigian (London: Penguin, 2009).

Sasaki, Hideaki, Toshio Ōkuma, *Shikisai bungaku-ron--- Shikisai hyōgen kara minaosu kindai bungaku* [The Theory of Colour Literature: Modern Literature Reviewed from the Perspective of Colour Expression] (Tokyo: Gogatsu Shobō, 1995).

'Says D'Annunzio is a Pole. Frankfurter Zeitung Denies the Poet's Italian Parentage', *NYT*, 5 June 1915.

Scarlini, Luca, *D'Annunzio a Little Italy: Le avventure del Vate nel mondo dell'emigrazione* (Rome: Donzelli editore, 2008).

Scarpetta, Eduardo, *Cinquant'anni di palcoscenico* (Naples: Gennarelli, 1922).

Scego, Igiaba, *Roma negata* (Rome: Ediesse, 2020).

Schleiermacher, Friedrich, *On the Different Methods of Translating* [Über die verschiedenen Methoden des Übersetzens, 1813], trans. by Susan Bernofsky, in *The Translation Studies Reader*, ed. by Lawrence Venuti (London: Routledge, 2012), pp. 43–62.

Schliemann, Henry, *Mycènes: récit des recherches et découvertes faits à Mycènes et à Tirynthe*, trans. by Jules Girardin (Paris: Hachette, 1879).

Schneider, Uwe and Andreas Schumann, eds, *Krieg der Geister. Erster Weltkrieg und literarische Moderne* (Würzburg: Königshausen & Neumann, 2000).

Schnitzler, Arthur, *Briefe 1913–1931*, vol. II, ed. by Peter Michael Braunwarth, Richard Miklin, Susanne Peterlik and Heinrich Schnitzler (Frankfurt al Main: Fischer, 1984).

Schwartz, William Leonard, *The Imaginative Interpretation of the Far East in Modern French Literature 1860–1925* (Paris: Librairie Ancienne Honoré Champion, 1927).

Scianca, Adriano, 'La rivolta dei popoli giovani. Gabriele D'Annunzio e la "lega dei popoli oppressi"', *Il Cannocchiale* (September 2006).

Segnini, Elisa, 'Global Masterpieces and Italian Dialects: Shakespeare in Neapolitan and Vicentino', *Journal of World Literature* 2 (2017), 236–54.

—— *Fragments, Genius and Madness: Masks and Mask-Making in the Fin-de-siècle Imagination* (Cambridge: Legenda, 2021).

—— 'Ethnicity, Gender and the Making of a Transnational Decadent Canon: Georges Hérelle's translations of Matilde Serao and Grazia Deledda', *Modern Philology* (Forthcoming, 2023).

Segol, Julien, '*Das Mirakel*: une cathédrale pour la modernité: Du spectacle populaire à l'art des foules', in *Max Reinhardt. L'Art et la technique à la conquête de l'espace* [Kunst und Technik zur Eroberung des Raums], *Jahrbuch für Internationale Germanistik*, vol. 119, ed. by Marielle Silhouette and Jean-Louis Besson (Bern: Peter Lang, 2017), pp. 85–103.

Serra, Maurizio *D'Annunzio Le Magnifique* (Paris: Grasset, 2018).

—— *L'Imaginifico: Vita Di Gabriele D'Annunzio*, trans. by Alberto Folin (Vicenza: Neri Pozza, 2018).

—— 'D'Annunzio oggi all'estero', *Rassegna Dannunziana*, 72 (2018), 7–10.

Shawqui, Ahmed, *Kan fy al-Rome al 'azim*, in *Al-Shawkyat*, vol. 4 (Al-Maktaba Al-Togareya Al-kobra, Al-Kahera, 1951).

Shimada, Kinji, '*Miwokutsukushi* kaidai' [Commentary on *Channel Marks*], in *Teihon Ueda Bin zenshū* [The Complete Works of Bin Ueda], vol. 2 (Tokushima: Kyōiku Shuppan Center, 1979).

Shimazaki, Tōson, *Shimazaki Tōson zenshū* [The Complete Works of Tōson Shimazaki], vol. 17 (Tokyo: Chikuma Shobō, 1968).

Shvarts, Daniel B., *Ghetto: The History of a Word* (Cambridge, MA: Harvard University Press, 2019).

Shvarts, Elena, 'Poetika zhivogo. Beseda s Antonom Nesterovym', *Kontekst-9*, 8 (2000), 314–26.

—— *Krylatyi tziklop* [The Winged Cyclops] (St Petersburg: Vita Nova, 2010).

—— *Vino sed'mogo goda* (St Petersburg: Pushkinskii fond, 2007).

Shvarts, Evgeny, *Zhivu bespokoino: iz dnevnikov,* ed. by Ksenia Kirilenko (Leningrad: Sovetsky pisatel, 1990).

Sica, Anna De Domenico, 'Eleonora Duse's Library: The Disclosure of Aesthetic Value in Real Acting', *Nineteenth Century Theatre and Film*, 37: 2 (2010), 66–85.

Sillani, Tomaso, *Francesco Paolo Michetti* (Rome: Treves, 1932).

Simeoni, Luigi, *'La figlia di Iorio'. Per Gabriele D'Annunzio e la Società italiana degli Autori. Riduzione stampata. Recita abusiva. Parodia. Nel giudizio contro Eduardo Scarpetta per 'Il figlio di Iorio'* (Naples: Giannini, 1907).

Simoni, Renato, 'L'origine e il significato della "Fedra" dannunziana. Una conversazione col Poeta' [Interview with Gabriele D'Annunzio], *Corriere della Sera*, 9 April 1909.

Simonini, Carla Anne, 'Constructing America by Writing About Italy: How Nineteenth-Century Travel Writing Informed Ethnic Identity Construction in Italian-American Literature', *Italian Americana*, 2 (2015), 136–56.

Smith, Shirley, 'D'Annunzio Journalist in America', *Yearbook of Italian Studies* 9 (1991), 147–58.

Soiza Reilly, Juan José, 'La vida artistica de Gabriel D'Annunzio', *Caras y caretas*, 10: 479 (1907), 29–32.

—— *Cien hombres célebres (confesiones literarias)* [One Hundred Famous Men] (Barcelona: Casa Editorial Maucci, 1909).

Soldevila, Llorenç, 'Introducció a l'obra de Jeroni Zanné i Rodríguez', Thesis, supervised by Dr J. Molas (Barcelona: Universidad Autónoma de Barcelona, 1975).

Solmi, Sergio, 'L'"Alcyone" e noi', *Letteratura*, 3 (1939), 3–12.

Solonovich, Evgenii, *Italianskaia poeziia v perevodakh Evgeniia Solonovicha* (Moscow: Raduga, 2000).

Sorge, Paola, 'D'Annunzio e il mondo germanico', *Rassegna dannunziana* 72 (2018): 75–82.

Spackman, Barbara, *Decadent Genealogies: The Rhetoric of Sickness from Baudelaire to D'Annunzio* (Ithaca: Cornell University Press, 1989).

Spaventa, Il Capitan [pseudonym], 'L'amante onorario. La famiglia di Iorio', *Il Tirso* (Rome), 3 December 1905.

—— 'I teatri di Roma. "La figlia di Iorio" al Costanzi', *Il Tirso* (Rome), 25 September 1904.

Steiner, George, *Extraterritorial: Papers on Literature and the Language Revolution* (London: Faber & Faber, 1972).

Stokes, John, 'The Legend of Duse', in *Decadence and the 1890s*, ed. by Ian Fletcher (London: Edward Arnold: 1979), pp. 151–71.

Subialka, Michael, *Modernist Idealism: Ambivalent Legacies of German Philosophy in Italian Literature* (Toronto: University of Toronto Press, 2021).

'Sul carro di Tespi. A Livorno', *Il Tirso* (Rome), 12 February 1905.

Sullivan, Brian R., 'Italian Naval Power and the Washington Disarmament Conference of 1921–22', *Diplomacy & Statecraft* 4: 3 (1993), 220–48.

Surico, Filippo, *Ora luminosa. Le mie conversazioni letterarie con Gabriele D'Annunzio nell'ospitalità di Villa Cargnacco a Gardone Riviera* (Rome: Urbs, 1939).

Surroca, Mª Àngels Cerdà, *Els pre-rafaelites a Catalunya (Una literatura i uns símbols)* (Barcelona: Curial Edicions, 1981).

Suvorin, Aleksei, *Dnevnik A. S. Suvorina*, ed. by Mikhail Krichevskii (Moscow: L. D. Frenkel, 1923).

Swanson, Carl A., 'D'Annunzio's Ode all'America in armi', *Italica*, 3 (1953), 135–43.

Swinburne, Algernon Charles, *Poèmes et ballades*, trans. by Gabriel Mourey (Paris: Albert Savine, 1891).

Symons, Arthur, 'The Decadent Movement in Literature', first published in *Harpers New Monthly Magazine* 87 (November 1893), 858–67, in *The Symbolist Movement in Literature*, ed. by Matthew Creasy (Manchester: Carcanet, 2014), pp. 169–83.

—— 'The Question of the Dead City', unpublished essay, in *Arthur Symons Papers 1883–1945*, Princeton University Library, Department of Rare Books and Special Collections, box 16, folder 3, p. 13.

—— 'D'Annunzio in English', *Saturday Review*, 85 (29 January 1898), 52–3.

—— 'Introduction', in Emile Verhaeren, *The Dawn (Les Aubes)*, trans. by Arthur Symons (London: Duckworth, 1898), pp. 1–8.

—— 'Introduction', in Gabriele D'Annunzio, *The Child of Pleasure*, trans. by Georgina Harding (London: Heinemann, 1898), pp. v–xii.

—— 'Introduction', in Gabriele D'Annunzio, *Francesca da Rimini*, trans. by Arthur Symons (London: Heinemann, 1902), pp. vii–xiv.

—— 'Eleonora Duse', in *Studies in Seven Arts* (London: Constable, 1906), pp. 331–46.

—— *Plays, Acting and Music: A Book of Theory* (London: Constable, 1909).

—— 'Duse in some of her Parts', in *Plays, Acting and Music: A Book of Theory* (London: Constable, 1909), pp. 60–76.

—— *Tristan and Iseult: A Play in Four Acts* (London: Heinemann, 1917).

—— 'Should Translators Improve their Authors?', *Bookman's Journal and Print Collector*, 5: 4 (1922), 109–12.

—— *Eleonora Duse* (London: Elkin Mathews, 1926).

—— *Selected Early Poems*, ed. by Jane Desmarais and Chris Baldick (Cambridge: MHRA, 2017).

—— *The Symbolist Movement in Literature*, ed. by Matthew Creasy (Manchester: Carcanet, 2014).

Takashina, Erika, *Ikai no umi: Hōsui Seiki Tenshin ni okeru seiyō* (Chiba: Miyoshi Kikaku, 2000).

Taylor-Batty, Juliette, *Multilingualism in Modernist Fiction* (London: Palgrave Macmillan, 2013).

Teja, Antonio, *La fabbrica di maraschino Francesco Drioli all'epoca del suo fondatore: la sua importanza nel quadro dell'Industria zaratina dei rosoli* (Genova: S.A.I.G.A. già Barabino e Graeve, 1938).

Tharrats, Josep, *Orles* (Girona: Imprenta Dalmau Carles & Companyia, 1909).

—— *Les ofrenes espirituals* (Girona: s.n., 1924).

Thomson, Clive, *Georges Hérelle: archéologue de l'inversion sexuelle 'fin de siècle'* (Paris: Éditions du Félin, 2014).

Thovez, Enrico, 'L'arte del comporre del Signor Gabriele D'Annunzio', *Gazzetta letteraria,* 20:1 (1896), reprinted in Enrico Thovez, *Il Pastore, il Gregge e la Zampogna* (Naples: Ricciardi, 1921), pp. 32–47.

Todorova, Maria, *Imagining the Balkans* (Oxford: Oxford University Press, 1997).

Tolomeo, Rita, 'Drioli, Francesco', *Dizionario bibliografico degli italiani*, vol. 41 (Rome: Società Grafica Romana S. p. A., 1992).

Tomizza, Fulvio, *Trilogia Istriani: Materada*; *La ragazza di Petrovia*; *Il bosco di acacie* (Milan: Mondadori, 1967).

Tommaseo, Nicolò, *Via facti. La Croazia e la Fraternità. Di nuovo ai Dalmati*, pamphlet first published in Trieste in 1861 (Sacramento: Wentworth Press, 2019), p. 16.

Tosi, Guy, ed., *Gabriele D'Annunzio à Georges Hérelle. Correspondance, accompagnée de douze sonnets cisalpins* (Paris: Denoël 1946).

—— *D'Annunzio en Grèce. Laus Vitae et la croisière de 1895* (Paris: Calmann-Lévy, 1947).

—— 'Les relations de D'Annunzio dans le monde du théâtre en France', *Quaderni dannunziani* 6/7 (1957), 36–59.

—— 'D'Annunzio découvre Nietzsche (1892–1894)', *Italianistica*, 2: 3 (1973), 481–513.

—— *D'Annunzio e la cultura francese: Saggi e studi (1942–1987)*, 2 vols, ed. by Maddalena Rasera (Lanciano: Carabba, 2013).

—— 'D'Annunzio parnassiano, 'bizantino' e simbolista: alle fonti di una poetica complessa (1886–1894)', in *D'Annunzio e la cultura francese*, vol. 2 (Lancino: Rocco Carabba, 2013).

—— 'Le fonti francesi dell'estetismo di Andrea Sperelli' [1978], in Guy Tosi, *D'Annunzio e la cultura francese*, vol. 2 (Lancino: Rocco Carabba, 2013), pp. 689–728.

Tosi, Jeanne-Marie, 'La fortune française de *L'Enfant de volupté*', in *D'Annunzio europeo*, ed. by Pietro Gibellini (Rome: Lucarini, 1991), pp. 61–78.

'Triumph of Death Trial. Justices of Special Sessions Exclude Expert Testimony Concerning D'Annunzio's Book', *NYT*, 26 March 1897.

Tsutsui Yasutaka,'Danuntsuio ni muchū' [Hooked on D'Annunzio], (Tokyo: Chūōkōron, 1989).

Tsvetaeva, Marina, *Sobranie sochinenii v semi tomakh,* 7 vols (Moscow: Ellis Lak, 1995).

Tunnat, Frederik D., *Karl Vollmoeller. Dichter und Kul'turmanager. Eine Biographie* (Hamburg: Tredition, 2008).

—— *Karl Vollmoeller: Ein kosmopolitisches Leben im Zeichen des Mirakels* (Hamburg: Tredition, 2008).

Uchida Roan, 'Ryōnin no koui ni taisuru shoka no ronpyō Higeki? Kigeki?' [Various Commentaries on their Actions: A Tragedy? A Comedy?], *Uchida Roan zenshū* [The Complete Works of Roan Uchida], vol. 6 (Tokyo: Yumani Shobō, 1984) pp. 19–20.

Ueda Bin, *Kaichōon* [The Sounds of the Sea], partially trans. by Ueda Bin (1905), in *Ueda Bin Zen Yakushishū* [Complete Works of Poetry Translation by Ueda Bin], ed. by Yamauchi Yoshio and Yano Mineto (Tokyo: Iwanami Shoten, 1962).

—— *Uzumaki* [Whirlpool], (Tokyo: Okura-Shoten, 1910).

—— *Teihon Ueda Bin zenshū* [The Complete Works of Bin Ueda], vol. 1 (Tokushima: Kyōiku shuppan sentā, 1978).

—— *Teihon Ueda Bin zenshū* [The Complete Works of Bin Ueda], vol. 4 (Tokushima: Kyōiku shuppan sentā, 1979).

—— 'Shisō mondai' [Problems on Thoughts], *Teihon Ueda Bin zenshū* [The Final Collection of Ueda Bin's Works], vol. 5 (Tokyo: Kyōiku shuppan sentā, 1985).

Valentini, Valentina, *La Tragedia moderna e mediterranea: Sul Teatro di Gabriele D'Annunzio* (Milan: FrancoAngeli, 1992).

Valentino, Russell Scott, 'Taking the Traghetto to the Ghetto: or, Performing Jewish Culture in Venice', Paper delivered at Conference on Venice, the Jews, and Italian Culture (Venice, 2006), <https://doi.org/10.17077/conf.005163>

Valeri, Diego, 'L'"Alcyone" o le nuove metamorfosi', in *L'arte di Gabriele D'Annunzio*, ed. by Emilio Mariano (Milan: Mondadori, 1968), pp. 173–9.

Valesio, Paolo, *Gabriele D'Annunzio: The Dark Flame* (New Haven: Yale University Press, 1992).

Vandal-Sirois, Hugo, review of Georges Hérelle, *Petit mémoire d'un traducteur*, ed. by Jean-Marie van der Meerschen, *Meta*, 55: 3 (2010), 604–6.

Varaldo, Alessandro, '"La figlia di Iorio" al Politeama Regina Margherita', *Il Corriere di Genova*, 3 February 1905.

Vengerova, Zinaida, 'Pesni zemli (Gabriele D'Annunzio)', in *Sobranie sochinenii Gabriele D'Annunzio v dvenadcati tomakh* I (St Petersburg: Shipovnik, 1910), pp. 9–38.

Venuti, Laurence, *The Translator's Invisibility: A History of Translation* (London: Routledge, 2008).

—— 'World Literature and Translation Studies', in *The Routledge Companion to World Literature*, ed. by Theo D'haen, David Damrosch and Djelal Kadir (London: Routledge, 2012), pp. 180–93.

Verratti, Vittore, editorial introduction in D'Annunzio, *'La figlia di Iorio' con a fronte la traduzione in dialetto abruzzese* (Pescara: Centro nazionale di studi dannunziani, 1988), p. 7.

Verre, La Masque de [pseudonym], 'Échos', *Comœdia,* 30 June 1910.

Vignazia, Adriana, *Die deutschen D'Annunzio-Übersetzungen* (Frankfurt am Main: Peter Lang, 1995).

Vinyes, Ramon, *L'ardenta cavalcada* [The Ardent Cavalcade] (Barcelona: Tipografia L'Avenç, 1909).

—— *Al florir els pomers* (Barcelona: Biblioteca Teatràlia, 1910).

—— *L'arca i la serp* (Barcelona: 1910).

—— *Llegenda de boires* (Barcelona: 1926).

Violante, Piero, 'Il navalismo di Otto Hintze', in Otto Hintze, *Stato e esercito*, ed. by Piero Volante (Palermo: Flaccovio, 1991), pp. 53–92.

Vivante, Angelo, 'L'Irredentismo adriatico: contributo alla discussione sui rapporti austro-italiani' (1912), in *Irredentisimo adriatico. Dal covo dei "traditori"* (Genova: Graphos, 1997), pp. 119–33.

Vollmoeller, Karl Gustav, *Gedichte. Eine Auswahl*, ed. by Herbert Steiner (Marbach am Neckar: Schiller Nationalmuseum, 1960), pp. 7–11.

von Chlumecky, Leopold Freiherr, 'Politische Dramen – Dramatische Politik', *Österreichische Rundschau*, 14 (1908), 239–44.

Von Flotow, Luise, 'Feminist Translation: Contexts, Practices and Theories', *Traduction, terminologie, rédaction* 4: 2 (1991), 69–84.

von Hofmannsthal, Hugo, 'Antwort auf die neunte Canzone Gabriele D'Annunzios' [Reply to Gabriele D'Annunzio's Ninth Song], *Neue Freie Presse*, 2 February 1912.

—— 'D'Annunzio', in *Gesammelte Werke in zehn Einzelbänden. Reden und Aufsätze I*, ed. by Bernd Schoeller (Frankfurt am Main: S. Fischer, 1979), pp. 174–85.

—— 'Antwort auf die "neunte Canzone" Gabriele D'Annunzios', in *Gesammelte Werke in Einzelausgaben. Prosa III*, ed. by Herbert Steiner (Frankfurt am Main: Fischer, 1984), pp. 81–6.

von Puttkamer, Alberta, *Gabriele D'Annunzio* (Berlin: Schuster und Loeffler, 1904).

Vucinich, Wayne, *A Study in Social Survival: Katun in the Bileća Rudine* (Denver: University of Denver Press, 1975).

—— 'Serbian Military Tradition', in Bela Kiraly and Gunther Rothenberg, eds, *War and Society in East Central Europe*, vol. 1 (New York: Brooklyn College Press and Columbia University Press, 1979).

Warren, Whitney, October 1919, Vittoriale Foundation, VI, 5, 6.

Weir, David, *Decadence and the Making of Modernism* (Amherst: University of Massachusetts Press, 1995).

—— *Decadence: A Very Short Introduction* (Oxford: Oxford University Press, 2018).

Werfel, Franz, *Zwischen Oben und Unten. Prosa, Tagebücher, Aphorismen, literarische Nachträge* (Munich: Langen-Müller, 1975).

Wilfert-Portal, Blaise, 'Cosmopolis et l'homme invisible', *Actes de la recherche en sciences sociales*, 144 (2002), 33–46.

Winwar, Frances, *Wingless Victory: A Biography of Gabriele D'Annunzio and Eleonora Duse* (New York: Harper, 1956).

Witt, Mary Ann Frese, *The Search for Modern Tragedy: Aesthetic Fascism in Italy and France* (Ithaca: Cornell University Press, 2001).

Wolff, Larry, *Venice and the Slavs: The Discovery of Dalmatia in the Age of Enlightenment* (Stanford, CA: Stanford University Press, 2001).

—— 'The Rise and Fall of *Morlacchismo*: South Slavic Identity in the Mountains of Dalmatia', *Yugoslavia and its Historians: Understanding the Balkan Wars of the 1990s*, ed. by Norman M. Naimark and Holly Case (Stanford, CA: Stanford University Press, 2003).

Wollaeger, Mark and Matt Eatough, eds, *The Oxford Handbook of Global Modernisms* (Oxford: Oxford University Press, 2012).

Woodhouse, John, 'Trionfo della Morte: traduzioni, e interpretazioni anglosassoni', in *Il trionfo della morte: Atti del III convegno Internazionale di studi dannunziani*, ed. by Edoardo Tiboni and Luigia Abrugiati (Pescara: Centro di Studi Dannunziani, 1981), pp. 239–60.

—— 'Curioser and Spurioser: Two English Influences on Gabriele D'Annunzio', *Italian Studies*, 42 (1987), 69–80.

—— 'Gabriele D'Annunzio's Reputation and Critical Fortune in Britain', *Annali d'Italianistica*, 5 (1987), 245–58.

—— *Gabriele D'Annunzio: Defiant Archangel* (Oxford: Clarendon Press, 1998).

—— *D'Annunzio tra Italia e Inghilterra* (Pescara: Ediars, 2003).

Wynne, Giustiniana, Countess of Rosenberg-Orsini, *Les Morlaques* (Venice, 1788).

Young, Robert, 'That Which is Causally Called a Language', *PMLA*, 131: 5 (2016), 1207–21.

Yukiko, Ozaki, 'Poèmes de la libellule e D'Annunzio: nuovi documenti di *Outa occidentale*', *Rassegna Dannunziana*, 59: 60 (2011), 3–10.

Zanné, Jeroni, *Una Cleo i altres narracions*, ed. by Llorenç Soldevila (Barcelona: Edicions 62, 1978).

Zappulla Muscarà, Sarah and Enzo Zappulla, *Giovanni Grasso. 'Il più grande attore tragico del mondo'* (Catania: La Cantinella, 1995).

—— *Gabriele D'Annunzio. 'La figlia di Iorio' tra lingua e dialetti* (Catania: la Cantinella, 1998).

Zaydan, Jorji, 'The Bizarre Poet and Soldier', *Al Hilal* (December 1919), pp. 196–200.

Zimmern, Helen, 'Eleonora Duse', *Fortnightly Review*, 67 (1900), 980–93.

Zweig, Stefan, 'Die um Stefan George', *Das literarische Echo*, 6: 3 (1 November 1903), pp. 169–72.

—— 'Römische Elegien: Von Gabriele D'Annunzio', *Das literarische Echo*, 5: 18 (15 July 1904).

—— 'Venedigs glückhaftes Schiff: Gabriele D'Annunzios "La Nave"', *Neue Freie Presse* (31 January 1908), pp. 1–3.

—— *Tagebücher* [1915], ed. by Kurt Beck (Frankfurt am Main: S. Fischer, 1984).

—— *Der Kampf mit dem Dämon. Hölderlin, Kleist, Nietzsche* (Frankfurt am Main: Fischer, 2007).

Index

EU representative:
Easy Access System Europe
Mustamäe tee 50, 10621 Tallinn, Estonia
Gpsr.requests@easproject.com

www.ingramcontent.com/pod-product-compliance
Lightning Source LLC
Chambersburg PA
CBHW060612100726
47907CB00006B/1595

* 9 7 8 1 3 9 9 5 0 6 8 6 1 *